www.wadsworth.com

www.wadsworth.com is the World Wide Web site for Thomson Wadsworth and is your direct source to dozens of online resources.

At *www.wadsworth.com* you can find out about supplements, demonstration software, and student resources. You can also send email to many of our authors and preview new publications and exciting new technologies.

www.wadsworth.com
Changing the way the world learns®

FROM THE **WADSWORTH SERIES** IN COMMUNICATION STUDIES

Adler/Proctor/Towne	*Looking Out/Looking In, Eleventh Edition*
Backlund/Williams	*Readings in Gender Communication*
Baxter/Babbie	*The Basics of Communication Research*
Benjamin	*Principles, Elements, and Types of Persuasion*
Bettinghaus/Cody	*Persuasive Communication, Fifth Edition*
Borchers	*Rhetorical Theory: An Introduction*
Braithwaite/Wood	*Case Studies in Interpersonal Communication: Processes and Problems*
Brummett	*Reading Rhetorical Theory*
Campbell/Huxman	*The Rhetorical Act, Third Edition*
Campbell/Burkholder	*Critiques of Contemporary Rhetoric, Second Edition*
Conrad/Poole	*Strategic Organizational Communication, Sixth Edition*
Cragan/Wright/Kasch	*Communication in Small Groups: Theory, Process, Skills, Sixth Edition*
Crannell	*Voice and Articulation, Third Edition*
Dwyer	*Conquer Your Speech Anxiety, Second Edition*
Freeley/Steinberg	*Argumentation and Debate: Critical Thinking for Reasoned Decision Making, Eleventh Edition*
Geist-Martin/Ray/Sharf	*Communicating Health: Personal, Cultural and Political Complexities*
Goodall/Goodall	*Communicating in Professional Contexts: Skills, Ethics, and Technologies, Second Edition*
Govier	*A Practical Study of Argument, Fifth Edition*
Griffin	*Invitation to Public Speaking*
Hall	*Among Cultures: The Challenge of Communication, Second Edition*
Hamilton	*Essentials of Public Speaking, Third Edition*
Hamilton	*Communicating for Results: A Guide for Business and the Professions, Seventh Edition*
Hoover	*Effective Small Group and Team Communication, Second Edition*
Huglen/Clark	*Argument Strategies from Aristotle's Rhetoric*
Isaacson/Saperstein	*Service Learning in Communication Studies: A Handbook, Second Edition*
Jaffe	*Performing Literary Texts: Concepts and Skills*
Jaffe	*Public Speaking: Concepts and Skills for a Diverse Society, Fourth Edition*
Kahane/Cavender	*Logic and Contemporary Rhetoric: The Use of Reason in Everyday Life, Ninth Edition*
Knapp/Hall	*Nonverbal Communication in Human Interaction, Sixth Edition*
Larson	*Persuasion: Reception and Responsibility, Tenth Edition*
Littlejohn/Foss	*Theories of Human Communication, Eighth Edition*
Lumsden/Lumsden	*Communicating in Groups and Teams: Sharing Leadership, Fourth Edition*
Lumsden/Lumsden	*Communicating with Credibility and Confidence: Diverse People, Diverse Settings, Third Edition*
Merrigan/Huston	*Communication Research Methods*
Metcalfe	*Building a Speech, Fifth Edition*
Miller	*Organizational Communication: Approaches and Processes, Fourth Edition*
Morreale/Spitzberg/Barge	*Human Communication: Motivation, Knowledge, and Skills*
Natalle/Bodenheimer	*The Woman's Public Speaking Handbook*
Orbe/Harris	*Interracial Communication: Theory Into Practice*
Rothwell	*In Mixed Company: Communicating in Small Groups and Teams, Fifth Edition*
Rubin/Rubin/Piele	*Communication Research: Strategies and Sources, Sixth Edition*
Samovar/Porter	*Communication Between Cultures, Fifth Edition*
Samovar/Porter	*Intercultural Communication: A Reader, Eleventh Edition*
Sellnow	*Confident Public Speaking, Second Edition*
Sprague/Stuart	*The Speaker's Compact Handbook*
Sprague/Stuart	*The Speaker's Handbook, Seventh Edition*
Verderber/Verderber	*The Challenge of Effective Speaking, Thirteenth Edition*
Verderber/Verderber	*Communicate!, Eleventh Edition*
VerLinden	*Critical Thinking and Everyday Argument*
West/Turner	*Understanding Interpersonal Communication: Making Choices in Changing Times*
Williams/Monge	*Reasoning with Statistics: How to Read Quantitative Research*
Wood	*Communication in Our Lives, Fourth Edition*
Wood	*Communication Mosaics: An Introduction to the Field of Communication, Fourth Edition*
Wood	*Communication Theories in Action: An Introduction, Third Edition*
Wood	*Gendered Lives: Communication, Gender, and Culture, Sixth Edition*
Wood	*Interpersonal Communication: Everyday Encounters, Fourth Edition*
Wood	*Relational Communication: Continuity and Change in Personal Relationships, Second Edition*
Wood/Duck	*Composing Relationships: Communication in Everyday Life*

Understanding Interpersonal Communication

MAKING CHOICES IN CHANGING TIMES

RICHARD WEST
UNIVERSITY OF SOUTHERN MAINE

LYNN H. TURNER
MARQUETTE UNIVERSITY

THOMSON
WADSWORTH

Australia • Canada • Mexico • Singapore • Spain
United Kingdom • United States

THOMSON

WADSWORTH

Understanding Interpersonal Communication:
Making Choices in Changing Times
Richard West and Lynn H. Turner

Communication Editor: Annie Mitchell
Publisher: Holly J. Allen
Senior Development Editor: Greer Lleuad
Assistant Editor: Aarti Jayaraman
Editorial Assistant: Trina Enriquez
Senior Technology Project Manager: Jeanette Wiseman
Senior Marketing Manager: Kimberly Russell
Marketing Assistant: Andrew Keay
Advertising Project Manager: Shemika Britt
Project Manager, Editorial Production: Jennifer Klos
Executive Art Director: Maria Epes
Print Buyer: Becky Cross

Permissions Editor: Sarah Harkrader
Production Service: Professional Publishing Services
Text Designer: rosa+wesley
Photo Researcher: Sue Howard
Copy Editor: Meredith Brittain
Illustrator: G&S Typesetters, Inc.
Cover Designer: rosa+wesley
Cover Image: Ferruccio Sardella/Marlena Agency
Cover Printer: CTPS
Compositor: G&S Typesetters, Inc.
Printer: CTPS

Printed in China
3 4 5 6 7 09 08 07

For more information about our products, contact us at:
Thomson Learning Academic Resource Center
1-800-423-0563
For permission to use material from this text or product,
submit a request online at http://www.thomsonrights.com.
Any additional questions about permissions can be submitted by email to **thomsonrights@thomson.com.**

Library of Congress Control Number: 2004115483

Student Edition: ISBN-13: 978-0-534-60588-9
                 ISBN-10: 0-534-60588-5

Instructor's Edition: ISBN-13: 978-0-495-00210-9
                      ISBN-10: 0-495-00210-0

Thomson Higher Education
10 Davis Drive
Belmont, CA 94002-3098
USA

Asia (including India)
Thomson Learning
5 Shenton Way
#01-01 UIC Building
Singapore 068808

Australia/New Zealand
Thomson Learning Australia
102 Dodds Street
Southbank, Victoria 3006
Australia

Canada
Thomson Nelson
1120 Birchmount Road
Toronto, Ontario M1K 5G4
Canada

UK/Europe/Middle East/Africa
Thomson Learning
High Holborn House
50–51 Bedford Road
London WC1R 4LR
United Kingdom

Latin America
Thomson Learning
Seneca, 53
Colonia Polanco
11560 Mexico
D.F. Mexico

Spain (including Portugal)
Thomson Paraninfo
Calle Magallanes, 25
28015 Madrid, Spain

We dedicate this book to the thousands of students

who teach us what interpersonal communication means

and to those others — our family and friends —

whose interactions with us make these lessons come to life.

Brief *Contents*

Contents

2 Communication, Perception, and the Self 32

3 Communication, Culture, and Identity 62

4 Communication and Emotion   90

5 Effective Listening 124

6 Communicating Verbally   150

7 Communicating Nonverbally 182

8 Sharing Personal Information 210

9 Communicating Power and Conflict 246

10 Communicating in Close Relationships 276

Preface

We wrote this text because we believe students should have the knowledge, skills, and motivation to communicate in multiple circumstances with a variety of different people. Today, more than ever, students are confronted with choices in communication. For instance, emerging technologies continually expand their options and choices—in addition to choosing to speak with others in person, they can choose to communicate via email, over videophone, with a text messenger, or via a blog. To be able to navigate this increasingly complex communication environment effectively, they need a well-developed knowledge base for making informed choices and improving their skills. We contend that when students enter their interpersonal communication classrooms, they bring with them many habits and beliefs about effective communication that they have acquired from their own experiences observing friends, families, and coworkers, and from being consumers of popular culture. However, students lack an understanding of the theory and research that animate and clarify these practices and beliefs. In other words, students simply rely too much on what they have seen and heard, with little understanding of theoretical explanations for communication processes and outcomes. Consequently, students frequently make communication choices with an insufficient knowledge base. Such decisions limit their potential, leaving them frustrated and dissatisfied.

It is our belief that one fundamental approach to learning about an interpersonal communication skill is to ground it in adequate theory and current knowledge about the skill. Although knowledge cannot completely guarantee that students are going to be happy with the outcome of every communication transaction, it does provide them with necessary and important analytical skills. In sum, we believe that theory informs skills and skills refine theory. As such, in *Understanding Interpersonal Communication* we intentionally integrate a theory-skill framework throughout each chapter. In this text, we move toward eliminating the false dichotomy between theory and skills. Additionally, we strive to demystify and clarify the intersection of theory and practice. In doing so, we hope to break down misguided and preconceived negative images of theory. Using a conversational tone, our text integrates research and theory in an inviting and engaging manner.

In addition, our approach to skill development provides a discussion of interpersonal skills and the behavioral choices students can make in order to become more effective communicators. We avoid "telling" students how to apply interpersonal skills to various situations. Rather, we provide a list of skills pertaining to the theory students read about in the chapter so students will be able to draw upon a sort of toolbox, or set of skills, that are specific and workable.

And finally, we understand that students come to the interpersonal communication course from a variety of life experiences. We worked, therefore, to make our writing accessible, avoiding clichés and using technical terms only when necessary to make a point, explaining their meanings as needed. We also made a conscious effort to use examples that reflect the diversity of interpersonal encounters. Thus, we include examples of interpersonal communication between teacher-student, physician-patient, painter-client, landlord-renter, politician-voter, clergy-layperson, retail clerk-customer, husband-wife, and friend-friend, among others.

Understanding Interpersonal Communication appeals to a diverse student population, presents scholarship and skills in a readable manner, and contains pedagog-

ical features that will not only sustain interest, but also make a difference in students' lives. The result of our efforts—this text—reflects our commitment to ensuring that students understand the importance of interpersonal communication in their own lives and in the lives of others.

Features of the Book

Our experience teaching this course over many years has prompted us to offer the following pedagogical approach and features. These features are intended first to appeal to students, then to help them better understand the concepts in each chapter and apply them in their own lives.

A Bridge between Theory and Skills

With a clear, accessible presentation of the intersection of theory and practice, *Understanding Interpersonal Communication* will empower your students with the knowledge they need to be skillful communicators in today's society.

In addition to **chapter goals** that provide students with a basic roadmap of the theory and skills that will be discussed in the chapter, each chapter begins with a **Case in Point** case study pertaining to an issue or topic in interpersonal communication discussed in the chapter. These cases are drawn from real-life situations identified by students in past interpersonal communication courses we have taught. For example, in Chapter 3, "Communication, Culture, and Identity," we begin with an example of a U.S. student who learns more about Mexican culture. In Chapter 5, "Effective Listening," we present a director of volunteers for a local political campaign whose listening skills are called into question by a supervisor. These case studies include people of diverse ages, backgrounds, and educational levels. Videotaped versions of many of these case studies and accompanying critical thinking questions are featured on the book's companion CD-ROM. Additionally, **Case in Point Revisited** review questions appear throughout each chapter, tying the Case in Point case study to the concepts discussed in that chapter.

Although each chapter discusses a variety of skills, a particular skill is highlighted and further discussed in the **Skill Spotlight** boxed feature. For example, in Chapter 7, "Communicating Nonverbally," we detail the skill of asking others to give us feedback about the clarity of our nonverbal communication. These spotlights are provided to help students explain at least one skill in sufficient detail and then practice it in their relationships with others. Each Skill Spotlight box also features a **Skills at Work** section that takes a quick look at how the skill can be applied to the workplace.

So that students can assess their own communication behaviors and attitudes, each chapter features a **Communication Assessment Test (CAT)** inventory. This feature provides students with communication instruments, such as a measure of communication apprehension or a quiz that will help students sharpen their vocabulary. For example, in Chapter 2, "Communication, Perception, and the Self," we include a "self-monitoring scale" quiz that asks students to consider the extent to which they actively think about and control their public behaviors and actions. These types of assessments allow students to evaluate their communication skills and take personal responsibility for skill development. We have found that students are also able to create their own assessments once they have read and understood material. The CATs, then, can be used as an effective way for students to become empowered in their classes.

Each chapter ends with **Questions for Understanding,** review and discussion questions that allow students to check their understanding of the chapter material. At least one question per chapter pertains to the chapter-opening Case in Point feature. This question allows students to reconsider how the concepts in the case study can be approached after learning the material in the chapter. Students can answer these questions by working in small groups or on their own.

A Wealth of Choices

Once students have a strong base in theory and skills, they are then able to make informed choices in their interpersonal communication. Many of the features of this book highlight the types of choices available to students in today's changing and technologically advanced world.

To encourage students to think about the material in a personal way, each chapter includes a **Your Turn** journal activity. With this feature, each student is asked to think about a particular topic and write about it in a journal. For example, in Chapter 1, "Introduction to Interpersonal Communication," we ask students to write about the primary influences shaping their interpersonal communication. Our experiences show that journals are excellent outlets for students to share their perceptions and reactions in a way that is personal, reflective, and informative. The Your Turn activities are also featured in the book's student companion workbook.

The **Ethics & Choice** boxed feature appears in each chapter, raising ethical questions and allowing students to consider ethical implications of the key topics or concepts in each chapter. These boxes include examples of ethical dilemmas and critical-thinking questions that challenge students to apply the ethical systems explained in Chapter 1. For instance, in Chapter 11, "Technology and Interpersonal Communication," students are asked to think about the ethical issues associated with knowing that one of their best friends plagiarized a paper from the Internet. The Ethics & Choice feature asks students to delve into how their ethical systems have been formed, influenced, and how they relate to communication choices. Online interactive activities about these ethical dilemmas are featured on the book's companion website. These activities allow students to choose possible responses to the dilemma, and then reflect on the consequences their choice brings about.

As appropriate to the content, select chapters feature discussions of the **dark and bright sides of interpersonal communication.** These discussions touch on topics such as domestic abuse, empathy, and forgiveness. For example, Chapter 4, "Communication and Emotions," discusses the notion of *schadenfreude,* or taking pleasure in another's misfortune. These discussions enable students to see that interpersonal communication can be both helpful and harmful.

At the conclusion of each chapter, the **Choices** boxed feature provides a list of specific and workable skills pertaining to the theory students read about in the chapter. Additionally, each chapter features a section that discusses interpersonal skills and the behavior choices students can make in order to become more effective communicators.

An Approach that Advocates the Wise Use of Technology

Technology has increased our options and choices in communication. Technology such as email and videoconferencing affects who we speak to and how we speak to them in ways that are continually evolving. *Understanding Interpersonal Communication* shows students how they are influenced by technology and how they can use it to become more effective communicators.

This book includes a full chapter on technology's impact on interpersonal communication, **Chapter 11, "Technology and Interpersonal Communication."** We live in a time of unprecedented technological change. One new technology quickly replaces another, affecting our interactions with others. For example, online conversations are now commonplace among people of various races, ages, and cultures. Chapter 11 addresses this relatively new area of interpersonal communication. The chapter identifies and explains characteristics of communication technology, discusses the presentation of the self online and elements of electronic dialogues, explains how relationships function online, and discusses skills that help improve electronic discussions and relationships.

Included in each chapter, the **Facing Change** boxed feature addresses how social and technological changes affect our communication with one another. For instance, in The Facing Change feature for Chapter 2, "Communication, Perception, and the Self," we ask students to think about social changes and write about the perception and self-concept of a new immigrant. In other chapters this feature focuses on technological changes, such as how email, handheld organizers, pagers, and cell phones function in maintaining relationships with friends, family members, and co-workers. For example, in Chapter 9, "Communicating Power and Conflict," we ask students to write about how beepers, cell phones, email and other instant messaging devices might affect the process of an interpersonal conflict. Many Facing Change boxes also feature an accompanying CNN & Change video clip that further highlights the concept discussed in the Facing Change box. These video clips and accompanying critical thinking questions are featured on the book's companion CD-ROM.

In addition to emphasizing technology in the text, we also provide **thorough technology integration** and support for users of the text. **InfoTrac® College Edition exercises** found throughout the book make use of the InfoTrac College Edition database, a virtual library that can be accessed from student computers (see Resources for Students, below, for more information). Web-based **Interactive Activities** that enrich and reinforce chapter content are integrated into every chapter, taking learning beyond the printed page. These brief exercises and activities, highlighted by icons, are easily accessed on the book companion website via the CD-ROM.

Resources for Students

Understanding Interpersonal Communication features an outstanding array of supplements to assist in making this course as meaningful and effective as possible.

- **Understanding Interpersonal Communication CD-ROM** Designed to meet the demands of today's visual, multimedia learners, this CD-ROM is rich with powerful learning resources that will broaden and test your students' critical understanding of each chapter's material. Automatically packaged with every new copy of this text, this CD-ROM provides one-stop access to all of the text's multimedia resources. All students need to do to integrate their text and technology learning resources is load their CD-ROM—they will not have to fumble with long URLs and various passwords. With one simple click, students have access to video clips of the chapter-opening Case in Point scenarios, the CNN & Choice video clips, a direct link to InfoTrac College Edition, and a direct link to the text-specific book companion website.

—*Case in Point* scenarios, taken from the text, are brought to life on the CD-ROM. These scenarios include an interactive critical thinking and analysis section that students can complete and email to their instructors. Students can also compare their responses to the suggested responses of the authors.

—*CNN & Change* videos, featured in select *Facing Change* boxes throughout the text, are included on the CD-ROM and further highlight the role technology plays in interpersonal communication. These videos are accompanied by critical thinking and analysis questions that students can complete and email to their instructors. Students can also compare their responses to the suggested responses of the authors.

Icons throughout the book encourage students to watch the videos, complete the accompanying activities, and access the book's other technology resources.

- **Understanding Interpersonal Communication Book Companion Website** Students can link to the Understanding Interpersonal Communication book companion website through the text's companion CD-ROM for access to premium chapter-by-chapter content. Resources include practice chapter quizzes and a final exam; self-scoring Communication Assessment Test inventories; an interactive glossary that features games and flashcards; interactive Ethics & Choice activities; InfoTrac College Edition and Internet activities that enrich and reinforce chapter content; a comprehensive list of films, television programs, and songs relevant to each chapter; a Web bibliography featuring a full list of references for each chapter that students can access for further reading or as an aid in research; and personal contact information for the authors.

- **InfoTrac College Edition** Every new copy of the text is accompanied by four months of access to InfoTrac College Edition, the online library. This dynamic database allows students to further their research on interpersonal communication and find a wealth of articles of interest. InfoTrac College Edition puts cutting edge research and the latest headlines at your students' fingertips, offering more than 10 million articles from nearly 5,000 diverse sources, such as academic journals, newsletters, and up-to-the minute periodicals. The diverse range of content includes *The New York Times, Newsweek, Time, USA Today, Advertising Age, PR Week, Variety,* and thousands more. Plus, students now also gain instant access to critical-thinking and paperwriting tools through InfoWrite. InfoTrac College Edition exercises that help students explore critical topics and issues in interpersonal communication are integrated throughout the book and can be accessed at the book companion website.

- **Student Companion Workbook** This workbook provides numerous practical, hands-on activities that apply the concepts presented within the

text. The workbook contains the *Your Turn* journal activities featured in each chapter, as well as chapter outlines and goals, activities, and self-tests.

Resources for Instructors

Understanding Interpersonal Communication also features a full suite of resources for instructors. To evaluate any of these instructor or student resources, please contact your local Thomson Wadsworth representative for an examination copy.

- **Instructor's Resource Manual** This helpful manual includes syllabi and course outlines, chapter overviews, class-tested activities and exercises, transparency masters, and test items. The test items are also available electronically via ExamView® (see below).

- **Multimedia Manager for Understanding Interpersonal Communication** Invigorate your lectures with predesigned Microsoft® PowerPoint® presentations containing numerous images and text. Easily customized, you can modify the slides or add your own content in minutes to get a powerful, personalized presentation.

- **ExamView® Computerized Testing** Create, deliver, and customize tests and study guides (both print and online) in minutes with this easy-to-use assessment and tutorial system. ExamView offers both a *Quick Test Wizard* and an *Online Test Wizard* that guide you step by step through the process of creating tests, while its unique interface allows you to see the test you are creating on the screen exactly as it will print or display online. You can build tests of up to 250 questions using up to 12 question types. Using ExamView's complete word processing capabilities, you can enter an unlimited number of new questions or edit existing questions. For users in both Windows and Macintosh formats.

- **WebTutor™ ToolBox for WebCT and Blackboard** Preloaded with content and available free via access code when packaged with this text, WebTutor ToolBox pairs all the content of this text 's rich book companion website with the sophisticated course management functionality of a WebCT or Blackboard product. You can assign materials (including online quizzes) and have the results flow automatically to your gradebook. ToolBox is ready to use as soon as you log on—or, you can customize its preloaded content by uploading images and other resources, adding web links, or creating your own practice materials. Students only have access to student resources on the website. Instructors can enter an access code for password-protected instructor resources. Contact your Thomson Wadsworth representative for ordering information.

- **InfoTrac College Edition Student Activities Workbook for Interpersonal Communication** *by Lori Halverson-Wente.* This workbook features extensive individual and groups activities, focusing on specific course topics that make use of InfoTrac College Edition. Also included are guidelines for instructors and students that describe how to maximize the use of this resource. This workbook can be bundled with this text.

- **Communication Scenarios for Critique and Analysis Videos** Communication concepts previously presented in the abstract come to life in these videos. Each offers a variety of situations that allow students to watch, listen to, and critique model communication scenarios. Video policy is based on adoption size; contact your Thomson Wadsworth representative for more information.

Acknowledgments

The impetus for writing this book rests primarily with our students. We begin our acknowledgements, therefore, by thanking the thousands of students we have taught over a combined 40-plus years of teaching interpersonal communication. The insights, themes, and examples we've included in this book reflect those students who have provided us inspiration throughout our careers.

We also gratefully acknowledge our team at Thomson Wadsworth, whose skills and thoughtfulness are unmatched. We never realized that writing a book with such a large company would result in lasting friendships. We first thank Holly Allen, our publisher, for "turning us on" to textbook writing in 1996. Holly's faith in us has been unwavering, and we will always value that lasting friendship. Annie Mitchell, our acquisitions editor, provided those all-important "nudges" throughout the writing of the book. As anyone who has written a text of this nature understands, support becomes instrumental. Annie's continuing encouragement—and gracious friendship—will always be valued. Greer Lleuad, our developmental editor, is the very *definition* of a perfect developmental editor. Greer's guidance and unwavering good judgment contributed to a book that is more appealing and thought-provoking than we could have created without her. In addition, her sense of humor helped relieve our stress throughout each stage of this book. We also thank Kim Russell, marketing manager, for her expertise, enthusiasm, and ability to understand our ideas and words. Kim's wonderful sense of collegiality has greatly enhanced the final product. We'd also like to acknowledge the following for all their help in producing a quality text: Aarti Jayaraman, assistant editor; Trina Enriquez, editorial assistant; Jeanette Wiseman, senior technology project manager; Maria Epes, executive art director; Edward Wade, editorial production manager; Jennifer Klos, production project manager; Robin C. Hood, production service; and Sarah Harkrader, permissions editor. And, lastly, we're also indebted to Susan Badger, CEO of Thomson Higher Education, for giving us the opportunity to share our ideas with students and teachers. Her original support of our project was important to us as we refined our thoughts and ideas.

Although each of these people contributed to the book you have before you, this text could not have existed without the generous time and talents afforded to us by the reviewers and those who class-tested chapters for us. They numbered many, and their thoughts, examples, and critical observations prompted us to write a book that reflects their voices and the voices of their students.

We are also grateful to Sally Vogl-Bauer for her excellent work and unfailing good humor in preparing the Instructor's Manual. She was able to take our text and provide superior teaching aids to supplement it, making it a more useful tool for classroom teachers. We appreciate her hard work. And many thanks to Bill Price, who wrote the excellent InfoTrac College Edition exercises, Interactive Activities, and Ethics & Choice online activities for the book; Dan Cavanaugh, who prepared the Multimedia Manager; and Leslie Maggard, who wrote activities for the *Understanding Interpersonal Communication* book companion website.

In addition to all those just mentioned, we would like to personally thank the people who've helped us along and supported us through this project. First, Rich thanks his co-author and close friend, Lynn, who, after working with him for more than 20 years, remains one of the most thoughtful and important people in his life. In addition, Stephanie Cushman, Rich's teaching assistant and close friend, was a calm port during some very stormy hours; her kindness is deeply appreciated. Rich

would also like to thank his mother, Beverly, for her ongoing presence in his life. Her genuineness, care, and sense of ethics are instrumental influences on Rich's life. Finally, Rich would like to thank an establishment in which many of his ideas, conversations, and relationships have been cultivated: Starbucks. The team on Exchange Street in Portland, Maine, was pivotal in providing moral support, sharing examples, and refilling dark roast as necessary!

In return, Lynn thanks Rich. His insights, enthusiasm, and enduring friendship are what make writing a joy for her. Lynn also thanks Marquette University, especially Dean Elliott of the College of Communication, who provided enormous support during the writing of this book as well as at other times. Finally, Lynn thanks her husband, Ted, for being with her through thick and thin, cooking dinners, bringing coffee, and telling her to shut off the computer every once and a while!

About the Authors

Richard West is Professor and Chairperson of the Department of Communication and Media Studies at the University of Southern Maine. Rich received his B.A. from Illinois State University in Speech Communication Education and his M.A from ISU in Communication Studies. His Ph.D. is from Ohio University in Interpersonal Communication. Rich's research interests span several areas, including family communication, classroom communication, and culture. Rich is the recipient of the Outstanding Teacher-Scholar award at USM and the Faculty Senate Award for Research in the Social Sciences. He has also been recognized with Outstanding Alumni Awards in Communication from both ISU and OU. Rich is co-author of several books, book chapters, and articles with Lynn Turner. He is President-Elect of the Eastern Communication Association (ECA), Director of the Educational Policies Board of the National Communication (NCA), and past Chair of the Instructional Communication Divisions for both ECA and NCA. Although Rich's passion remains in the classroom, he enjoys gardening, updating his 100-year-old bungalow, and camping in northern Maine during the summer.

Lynn H. Turner is Professor in Communication Studies at Marquette University. Lynn received her B.A from University of Illinois, her M.A. from University of Iowa, and her Ph.D. from Northwestern University. At Marquette she currently teaches interpersonal communication at both the undergraduate and graduate levels, among other courses. Her research areas of emphasis include gender and communication, interpersonal and family communication. She is the co-author or co-editor of over ten books, as well as several articles and book chapters. Her articles have appeared in many journals, including *Management Communication Quarterly, Journal of Applied Communication Research, Women and Language,* and *Western Journal of Communication.* Her books include *From the Margins to the Center: Contemporary Women and Political Communication* (co-authored with Patricia Sullivan; Praeger, 1996; recipient of the 1997 Best Book Award from the Organization for the Study of Communication, Language and Gender [OSCLG]), *Gender in Applied Communication Contexts* (co-edited with Patrice Buzzanell and Helen Sterk; Sage, 2004), *Introducing Communication Theory* (2003) and *Perspectives on Family Communication* (2002) (both co-authored with Richard West). She was the recipient of the College of Communication outstanding research award in 1999. She has served as Director of Graduate Studies for the College of Communication at Marquette University, President of OSCLG, President of Central States Communication Association (CSCA), and Chairperson of the Family Communication Division for the National Communication Association.

1

Introduction to Interpersonal Communication

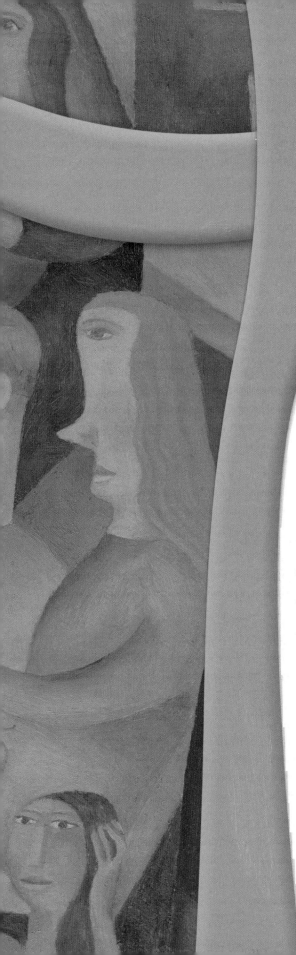

CASE IN POINT: JACKIE ELLIS AND PHIL PERONA

As Jackie Ellis stood in her driveway shoveling snow, she heard her neighbor, Phil Perona, yell across the yard, "Hey, can't get any hired help for that?!" Jackie yelled back, "Sure—show me the money, buddy!" They both laughed. As Phil approached Jackie's driveway, her cat was rolling around on the ground. They began a casual conversation about the weather, but then the topic turned more sobering: Jackie's sister's death. Jackie told Phil that it was exactly a year ago that her sister had died of skin cancer. "I can't believe how fast time goes by, Phil," Jackie said, sighing. "Wow," Phil said. "Incredible that it's been that long. It seems like we were just telling each other that everything would be fine." As the two started to talk about Jackie's sister, tears welled up in Phil's eyes. He told her that if she ever needed to talk, just to let him know. Jackie smiled ruefully and said, "But, hey, we got by that one, and we're still here talking about it. And if we can survive that *and* this stupid winter, we'll make it through anything. Right?" The two laughed awkwardly, but both knew that the topic had to change quickly. They began to talk about Phil's daughters and their holiday concert.

As the minutes ticked by, they found themselves talking about everything from foreign policy to reality television shows, and then Phil went back to his house. Jackie finished shoveling her sidewalk and went back inside. As she sat in her kitchen thumbing through catalogs, she once again thought about her sister. One year, she thought—it couldn't be possible. She felt lucky to have such a good and caring neighbor as Phil. ▪

Each day, we perform one of the most ancient of all behaviors: interpersonal communication. We head off to work and greet people on the bus, in the office, in the carpool, or on the street. We talk to our roommates and discuss last night's party over breakfast. Or we wake up and soon find ourselves in the middle of a heated exchange with a family member about dirty dishes. Although each of these situations differs, they all underscore the pervasiveness of interpersonal communication in our lives.

This chapter's Case in Point scenario between Jackie and Phil represents one of these interpersonal encounters. We rarely think about the fact that we are easily able to carry out conversations like these. In this scenario, Phil established verbal contact with Jackie. In turn, Jackie moved the conversation from the weather to her sister's death. The entire dialogue lasted only a few minutes, but it carried enormous importance. Phil and Jackie not only initiated a conversation—their conversation also showed just how close they are to each other. As you can tell from their conversation, they are more than just neighbors; they are also good friends. The content of their brief conversation gives us an idea that they have more than a superficial relationship with each other.

These dialogues take place all the time without us giving them a second thought. And we often feel content about the way we communicate with others. A national poll commissioned by the National Communication Association (n.d.) reports that nearly two-thirds of U.S. citizens feel very comfortable communicating with others. Women are more likely than men to feel comfortable, and older respondents (55 years and older) are more comfortable than any other age group. This comfort level pertains to informal settings such as talking to a friend, family member, or partner.

Yet, not everyone is comfortable talking to others. In fact, some people are quite anxious and nervous about communicating. The extent to which people exhibit anxiety about speaking to others is called **communication apprehension.** Communication apprehension is a legitimate life experience that researchers contend usually negatively affects our communication with others (Richmond & McCroskey, 1998). People can be fearful and go to great lengths to avoid communication situations. When such people find themselves in uncomfortable circumstances, they are usually shy, embarrassed, and tense.

There are many times when we have difficulty getting our message across to others because of our unique communication circumstances. We may feel unprepared to argue with a supervisor for a raise, to let our apartment manager know that the hot water is not hot enough, or to tell our partner, "I love you." At times throughout the day, we may struggle with what to say, how to say something, or when to say something. We also may struggle with listening to certain messages because of their content or the manner in which they are presented. In addition, communication may seem difficult when others don't respond as we'd wish or when others don't even seem to pay attention to us.

This book is about improving your ability to interact with other people. Improving your interpersonal communication skills will assist you in becoming more effective in your relationships with a variety of people, including those with whom you are close (e.g., family members, friends, coworkers) and those with whom you interact less frequently (e.g., health care providers, contractors, babysitters).

Communication Assessment Test

Personal Report of Communication Apprehension (PRCA)

Directions: This instrument is composed of twenty-four statements concerning feelings about communicating with other people. Please indicate the degree to which each statement applies to you using the following five-point scale:

strongly agree = 1   agree = 2   undecided = 3
disagree = 4   strongly disagree = 5

There are no right or wrong answers. Please mark your first impression and answer quickly. You can also take this test online under Student Resources for Chapter 1 at the *Understanding Interpersonal Communication* website.

_____ 1. I dislike participating in group discussions.
_____ 2. Generally, I am comfortable while participating in group discussions.
_____ 3. I am tense and nervous while participating in group discussions.
_____ 4. I like to get involved in group discussions.
_____ 5. Engaging in a group discussion with new people makes me tense and nervous.
_____ 6. I am calm and relaxed while participating in group discussions.
_____ 7. Generally, I am nervous when I have to participate in a meeting.
_____ 8. Usually, I am calm and relaxed while participating in a meeting.
_____ 9. I am calm and relaxed when I am called upon to express an opinion at a meeting.
_____ 10. I am afraid to express myself at meetings.
_____ 11. Communicating at meetings usually makes me feel uncomfortable.
_____ 12. I am relaxed when answering questions at a meeting.
_____ 13. While participating in a conversation with a new acquaintance, I feel very nervous.
_____ 14. I have no fear of speaking up in conversations.
_____ 15. Ordinarily, I am very tense and nervous in conversations.
_____ 16. Ordinarily, I am very calm and relaxed in conversations.
_____ 17. While conversing with a new acquaintance, I feel very relaxed.
_____ 18. I'm afraid to speak up in conversations.
_____ 19. I have no fear of giving a speech.
_____ 20. Certain parts of my body feel tense and rigid while giving a speech.
_____ 21. I feel relaxed while giving a speech.
_____ 22. My thoughts become confused and jumbled when I am giving a speech.
_____ 23. I face the prospect of giving a speech with confidence.
_____ 24. While giving a speech, I get so nervous I forget facts I really know.

Scoring

There are four categories for scoring: **group discussions, meetings, interpersonal conversations, and public speaking.** To compute your scores, add or subtract the numbers you marked for each item as indicated below:

1. Group discussions
   18 + (plus) scores for items
   2, 4, and 6 − (minus) scores
   for items 1, 3, and 5   = Subtotal _____
2. Meetings
   18 + (plus) scores for items
   8, 9, and 12 − (minus) scores
   for items 7, 10, and 11   = Subtotal _____
3. Interpersonal conversations
   18 + (plus) scores for items
   14, 16, and 17 − (minus) scores
   for items 13, 15, and 18   = Subtotal _____
4. Public speaking
   18 + (plus) scores for items
   19, 21, and 23 − (minus) scores
   for items 20, 22, and 24   = Subtotal _____

To obtain your score, add your four subscores together. Your score should range between 24 and 120. If your score is below 24 or above 120, you have made a mistake in computation. Scores can range, in each context, from a low of 6 to a high of 30. Any score above 18 indicates some degree of communication apprehension.

From www.jamescmccroskey.com. Used by permission.

Throughout this course, you will see how research and theory associated with interpersonal communication can inform your everyday encounters. You will also be introduced to a number of important skills to improve your interpersonal effectiveness with others. Our first task is to map out a definition of interpersonal communication.

Understanding Interpersonal Communication

Even though we engage in interpersonal communication daily, it is a complex process that is not always easy to define. Something that is so integral to our human experience is often difficult to disentangle from everything else we do, and that is the case with interpersonal communication. To make the definition of interpersonal communication more understandable, it helps to distinguish it from other types of communication. Scholars have identified the following kinds of situations in which human communication exists: intrapersonal, interpersonal, small group, organizational, mass, and public. As you review this list, you may notice that the communication department at your school is organized around some or all of these communication types. Many schools use these categories as an effective way to organize their curriculum and course offerings.

Note that, in some ways, these communication types build on each other because they represent increasing numbers of people included in the process. In addition, keep in mind that these communication types aren't mutually exclusive. For example, you may engage in both intrapersonal and interpersonal communication in a single encounter, or interpersonal communication may take place in an organizational context. With these caveats in mind, let's take a closer look at the six types of communication.

- *Intrapersonal communication:* Communication with ourselves. We may find ourselves daydreaming or engaging in internal dialogues even in the presence of another person. These are intrapersonal processes. Intrapersonal communication includes imagining, perceiving, or solving problems in your head. For instance, intrapersonal communication takes place when you debate with yourself, mentally listing the pros and cons of a decision before taking action.
- *Interpersonal communication:* The process of message transaction between people (usually two) who work toward creating and sustaining shared meaning. We will discuss this definition in more detail later in this chapter.

- *Small group communication:* Communication between and among members of a team who meet for a common purpose or goal. Small group communication occurs in classrooms, the workplace, and in more social environments (for example, sports teams or book clubs).
- *Organizational communication:* Communication with and among large, extended groups. Organizational communication may involve other communication types, such as interpersonal communication (for example, supervisor-subordinate relationships), small group communication (for example, a task group preparing a report), and intrapersonal communication (for example, daydreaming at work).
- *Mass communication:* Communication to a large audience via some mediated channel, such as television, radio, the Internet, or newspapers. At times, people seek out others using personal ads either on the Internet or in newspapers or magazines. This is an example of the intersection of mass communication and interpersonal communication.
- *Public communication:* Communication in which one person gives a speech to a large audience in person. Public communication is also often called public speaking. Public speakers have predetermined goals in mind, such as informing, persuading, or entertaining.

Although there is some overlap among these types, are you beginning to get an understanding of interpersonal communication by seeing how it differs from the other types of communication? This classification of communication continues to evolve as communication technology advances. Years ago, interpersonal communication was limited to sending letters or talking to someone personally. However, today the options seem infinite; cell phones, email, pagers, digital personal assistants, and video phones, to name just a few, affect our communication with others. It's safe to say that no one can predict all future communication types. The communication process has been redefined in the twenty-first century with the advent of technology. In Chapter 11, we investigate technology's impact on interpersonal communication specifically.

Models of Communication

To further understand the interpersonal communication process, we draw upon what theorists call models of communication (McQuail & Windahl, 1993). **Communication models** are visual, simplified representations of complex relationships in the communication process. They will help you see how the communication field has evolved over the years and will provide you with a foundation to return to throughout the book. The three prevailing models we discuss will give you insight into how we will frame our definition of interpersonal communication. Let's start with the oldest model.

Mechanistic Thinking and the Linear Model

More than fifty years ago, Claude E. Shannon, a Bell Telephone scientist, and Warren Weaver, a Sloan Cancer Research Foundation consultant, set out to understand radio and telephone technology by looking at how information passed through various channels (Shannon & Weaver, 1949). They viewed information transmission as a linear process, and their research resulted in the creation of the **linear model of communication.**

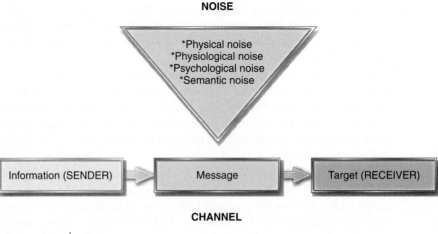

Figure 1.1 | **Linear model of communication**

This approach frames communication as a one-way process that transmits a message to a destination. You may have seen the commercial for a cell phone in which a man travels to a series of places, at each stop yelling into the phone, "Can you hear me now?" When a message is sent and received, communication takes place. Someone can hear you. That is the essence of the linear model.

Several components comprise the linear model of communication (see Figure 1.1). The **sender** is the source of the **message,** which may be spoken, written, or unspoken. The sender passes the message to the **receiver,** the intended target of the message. The receiver, in turn, assigns meaning to the message. All of this communication takes place in a **channel,** which is a pathway to communication. Typically, channels represent our senses (visual/sight, tactile/touch, olfactory/smell, and auditory/hearing). You use the tactile channel to hug a parent, and you use the auditory channel to listen to your roommate complain about a midterm exam.

In the linear model, communication also involves **noise,** which is anything that interferes with the message. Four types of noise can interrupt a message:

- **Physical noise** (also called *external noise*) involves any stimuli outside of the receiver that makes the message difficult to hear. For example, it would be difficult to hear a message from your professor if someone were mowing the lawn outside the classroom. Physical noise can also take the form of something a person is wearing, such as "loud jewelry" or sunglasses, that may cause a receiver to focus on the object rather than the message.

- **Physiological noise** refers to biological influences on message reception. Examples of this type of noise are articulation problems, hearing or visual impairments, and the physical well-being of a speaker (that is, whether he or she is able to deliver a message).

- **Psychological noise** (or *internal noise*) refers to a communicator's biases, prejudices, and feelings toward a person or a message. For example, you may have heard another person use language that is offensive and derogatory while speaking about a certain cultural group. If you were bothered by this language, you were experiencing psychological noise.

- **Semantic noise** occurs when senders and receivers apply different meanings to the same message. Semantic noise may take the form of jargon, technical

"O.K. What part of 'malignant regression and pathogenic reintrojection as a defense against psychic decompensation' don't you understand?"

language, and other words and phrases that are familiar to the sender but that are not understood by the receiver. For example, consider Jim, a 40-year-old Franco American living in Maine. Jim's primary language is French, so he frequently uses the English language in ways that are a bit nonsensical. For instance, when asking to look at something, he says "hand me, see me" instead of "may I see that?" Or, at times, he will say "it will go that" in lieu of the phrase "this is the story." These sorts of phrases and their use could be considered conversational semantic noise.

The linear view suggests that communication takes place in a **context,** or the environment in which a message is sent. Context is multidimensional and can be physical, cultural, psychological, or historical. The **physical context** is the tangible environment in which communication occurs. Examples of physical contexts are the hotel van on the way to the airport, the dinner table, the apartment, and the church hall. Environmental conditions such as temperature, lighting, and the size of the surroundings are also part of the physical context. For example, consider trying to listen to your best friend talk about her financial problems in a crowded coffee shop. The environment does not seem conducive to receiving her message clearly and accurately.

The **cultural context** refers to the rules, roles, norms, and patterns of communication that are unique to particular cultures. Culture always influences the communication taking place between and among people. We discuss culture and interpersonal communication in detail in Chapter 3.

The **social-emotional context** is associated with the nature of the relationship that affects a communication encounter. For example, are the communicators in a particular interaction friendly or unfriendly, supportive or unsupportive? Or do they fall somewhere in between? These factors help explain why, for instance, you might feel completely anxious in one employment interview but very comfortable in another. At times, you and an interviewer may hit it off, and at other times you may feel intimidated or awkward. The social-emotional context helps explain the nature of the interaction taking place.

In the **historical context,** messages are understood in relationship to previously sent messages. Thus, when Billy tells Tina that he missed her while they were separated over Spring Break, Tina hears that as a turning point in their relationship. Billy has never said that before and, in fact, he has often mentioned that he rarely misses anyone when he is apart from them. Therefore, his comment is colored by their history together. If Billy regularly told Tina he missed her, she would interpret the message differently.

We will return to the notion of context throughout this book. Keep in mind that context has a significant influence on our relationships with others. If we don't consider context in our interactions with others, we have no way to judge our interpersonal effectiveness.

Although the linear model was highly regarded when it was first conceptualized, the linear approach has been criticized because it presumes that communication has a definable beginning and ending (Anderson & Ross, 2002). In fact, Shannon and Weaver (1999) later emphasized this aspect of their model by claiming people receive information in organized and discrete ways. Yet, we know that communication can be messy. We have all interrupted someone or had someone interrupt us. The linear model also presumes that the listeners are passive and that communication is done only by the speakers. But we know that often listeners affect speakers and are not simply passive receivers of a speaker's message. With these criticisms in mind, researchers developed another way to represent the human communication process: the interactional model.

Feedback and the Interactional Model

To emphasize the two-way nature of communication between people, Wilbur Schramm (1954) conceptualized the **interactional model of communication.** Schramm's model shows that communication goes in two directions: from sender to receiver and from receiver to sender. This circular, or interactional, process suggests that communication is ongoing rather than linear. In the interactional model, individuals in a conversation can be both sender and receiver, but not both simultaneously (see Figure 1.2).

The interactional approach is characterized primarily by **feedback,** which can be defined as responses to people, their messages, or both. Feedback may be verbal (meaning we respond in words) or nonverbal (meaning we respond in facial expressions, body posture, and so forth). Feedback may also be internal or external. **Internal feedback** occurs when you assess your own communication (for example, by thinking "I never should have said that"). **External feedback** is the feedback you receive from other people (for example, "Why did you say that? That was dumb!").

A person can provide external feedback that results in important internal feedback for himself or herself. For example, let's say that Alexandra gives Dan the following advice about dealing with the death of his partner: "You feel sad as long as you need to. Don't worry about what other people think. I'm sick of people telling others how they should feel about something. These are your feelings." While giving Dan this external feedback, Alexandra may realize that her advice can also be applied to her own recent breakup. Although she may intend to send Dan a comforting message, she may also be providing herself internal feedback as she deals with her relational circumstances.

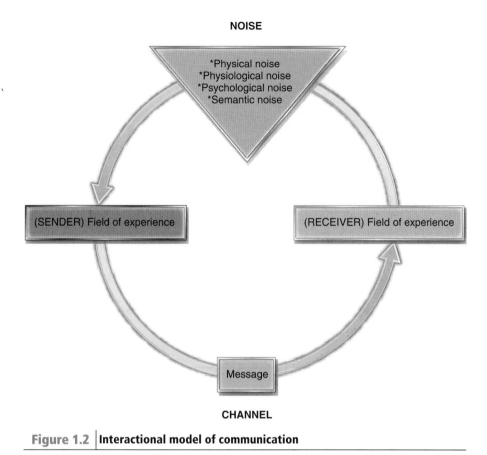

NOISE

*Physical noise
*Physiological noise
*Psychological noise
*Semantic noise

(SENDER) Field of experience

(RECEIVER) Field of experience

Message

CHANNEL

Figure 1.2 | **Interactional model of communication**

Like the linear model, the interactional model has been criticized primarily for its view of senders and receivers—that is, one person sends a message to another person. In addition, neither model takes into consideration what happens when nonverbal messages are sent at the same time as verbal messages. For example, when a father disciplines his child and finds the child either looking the other way or staring directly into his eyes, the father will "read" the meaning of the child's nonverbal communication as inattentive or disobedient. What happens if the child doesn't say anything during the reprimand? The father will still make some meaning out of the child's silence. The interactional view acknowledges that human communication involves both speaking and listening, but it asserts that speaking and listening are separate events and thus does not address the effect of nonverbal communication as the message is sent. It was this criticism that led to the development of a third model of communication, the transactional model.

Shared Meaning and the Transactional Model

Whereas the linear model of communication assumes that communication is an action that moves from sender to receiver, and the interactional model suggests that the presence of feedback makes communication an interaction between people, the **transactional model of communication** (Barnlund, 1970; Watzlawick, Beavin, & Jackson, 1967) underscores the fact that giving and receiving messages is reciprocal. In fact, the word *transactional* indicates that the communication process is cooper-

REVISITING CASE IN POINT

1. How does the conversation between Jackie and Phil depict a transactional process?

2. One feature of the transactional model is that messages build on each other. Apply this feature to Jackie and Phil's interaction.

You can answer these questions online under Student Resources for Chapter 1 at the Understanding Interpersonal Communication website.

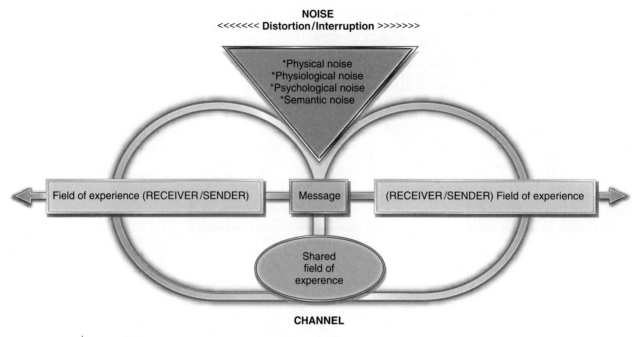

NOISE
<<<<<<< Distortion/Interruption >>>>>>>

*Physical noise
*Physiological noise
*Psychological noise
*Semantic noise

Field of experience (RECEIVER/SENDER)　　Message　　(RECEIVER/SENDER) Field of experience

Shared
field of
experience

CHANNEL

Figure 1.3 | **Transactional model of communication**

ative. In other words, communicators (senders and receivers) are both responsible for the effect and effectiveness of communication. In a transactional encounter, people do not simply send meaning from one to the other and then back again; rather, they build shared meaning.

A unique feature of the transactional model is its recognition that messages build upon each other. Further, both verbal and nonverbal behaviors are necessarily part of the transactional process. For example, consider Alan's conversation with his coworker Pauline. During a break, Pauline asks Alan about his family in Los Angeles. He begins to tell Pauline that his three siblings all live in Los Angeles and that he has no idea when they will be able to "escape the prison" there. When he mentions "prison," Pauline looks confused. Seeing Pauline's puzzled facial expression, Alan clarifies that he hates Los Angeles because it is so hot, people live too close to each other, and he felt that he was being watched all the time. In sum, he felt like he was in a prison. This example shows how much both Alan and Pauline are actively involved in this communication interaction. Pauline's nonverbal response to Alan prompted him to clarify his original message. As this interaction shows, the nonverbal message works in conjunction with the verbal message, and the transactional process requires ongoing negotiation of meaning.

Note that the transactional model in Figure 1.3 is characterized by a common field of experience between communicator A and communicator B. The **field of experience** refers to a person's culture, past experiences, personal history, and heredity, and how these elements influence the communication process.

People's fields of experience overlap at times, meaning that people share things in common. Where two people's fields of experience overlap, they can communicate effectively. And as they communicate, they create more overlap in their experiences. This process explains why initial encounters often consist of questions and answers between communicators, such as "Where are you from?", "What's your major?",

"Do you ski?" The answers to these questions help establish the overlap in the communicators' experiences: "Oh, I was in Chicago over the holidays last year," "Really, that's my major, too," "Yeah, I don't ski either." Further, fields of experience may change over time.

For instance, in class, Rhonda and Marcy have little in common and have little overlap in their fields of experience. They just met this term, have never taken a course together before, and Rhonda is eighteen years older than Marcy. It would appear, then, that their fields of experience would be limited to being women enrolled in the same course together. However, consider the difference if we discover that both Rhonda and Marcy are single parents, have difficulty finding quality child care, and have both received academic scholarships. The overlap in their fields of experience would be significantly greater. In addition, as the two continue in the class together, they will develop new common experiences, which, in turn, will increase the overlap in their fields of experience. This fact may affect their interactions with each other in the future.

Interpersonal communication scholars have embraced the transactional process in their research. For example, Julia Wood (1998) believes that human communication "is always tied to what came before and always anticipates what may come later" (p. 6). Wood believes that many misunderstandings occur in relationships because people are either unaware of or don't attend to the transactional communication process. Consider her words:

> The dynamic quality of communication keeps it open to revision. If someone misunderstands our words or nonverbal behavior, we can say or do something to clarify our meaning. If we don't understand another person's communication, we can look puzzled to show our confusion or ask questions to discover what the other person meant. (p. 6)

In summary, earlier communication models showed that communication is linear and that senders and receivers have separate roles and functions. The interactional approach expanded that thinking and suggested less linearity and more involvement of feedback between communicators. The transactional model refined our understanding by noting the importance of a communicator's background and also by demonstrating the simultaneous sending and receiving of messages. To check out interactive versions of these models, use your Understanding Interpersonal Communication CD-ROM to access Interactive Activity 1.1: Interactive Models of Communication.

Before we move on to the next discussion, consider that our notion of communication models is continually evolving. For example, the transactional model may soon become a bit outdated as technology shapes how we view the communication process. As we develop new ways to communicate technologically, communication scholars may reconsider the communication model to take into account email, keyboard symbols that indicate emotions, and geographically dispersed people. In addition, we recognize that the communication roles described by the models are not absolute and can vary depending on the situation. To check out a website that highlights communication roles in a particular setting, use your Understanding Interpersonal Communication CD-ROM to access Interactive Activity 1.2: Communication in Emergency Situations.

With this foundation, let's now discuss the nature of interpersonal communication.

The Nature of Interpersonal Communication

By now, you may be starting to realize that the interpersonal communication process is a complex undertaking. Although it shares some overlap with other types of communication, it also differs from them in important ways. It is marked by two people who simultaneously send and receive messages, attempting to create meaning. We explained interpersonal communication by elaborating on three models that describe its components. Another way to understand interpersonal communication is by examining its nature through the interpersonal communication continuum.

The Interpersonal Communication Continuum

Gerald Miller and Mark Steinberg (1975) proposed looking at communication along a continuum. Like many interpersonal communication researchers, Miller and Steinberg believed that not all human communication is interpersonal. Our interactions with others can be placed on a continuum from impersonal to interpersonal (see Figure 1.4).

Think about the various interactions you have that could be considered impersonal. You tell a receptionist that you've arrived for a job interview. You tell a man hawking tickets to a sold-out concert that you're not interested. You tell the woman sitting next to you at a wedding that you're a friend of the groom. Typically, these episodes remain on the impersonal end of the continuum because the conversations remain superficial.

Now, consider the many times you talk to people on a much deeper level. You share confidences with a close friend with whom you have tea. You laugh with your grandfather about a treasured family story. You commiserate with a classmate who is disappointed about a grade. In all these cases, your communication is not superficial. You share yourself and respond to the other person as a unique individual.

These two ends of the continuum—impersonal and interpersonal—are the extremes. Most of our conversations fall in between or along various points on the con-

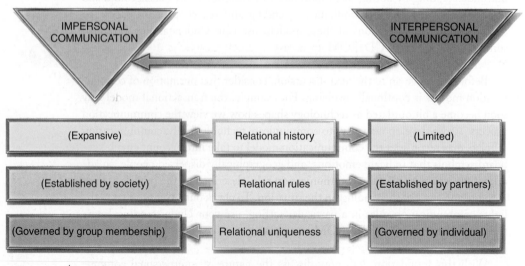

Figure 1.4 **The continuum of interpersonal communication**

tinuum. Your talks with a physician, professor, coworker, or car mechanic are examples of the types of encounters that, although not particularly emotionally fulfilling, have a personal dimension to them. You have to share your health status with your doctor. Your professor sometimes delicately asks what personal problems might have caused a failing grade on an exam. A coworker may share family stories. And a car mechanic may ask if you have enough money for a new transmission. Each of these interactions entails some degree of closeness but not a lot of emotional depth.

What will determine the extent to which an encounter is impersonal, interpersonal, or in between? Three issues seem most important: relational history, relational rules, and relational uniqueness.

First, **relational history** pertains to the prior relationship experiences two people share. For example, Rolanda and Maria have worked as servers in a restaurant for several years. Their relational history is apparent when you consider the amount of time they have spent together. This history may include working the same hours, sharing with each other their personal feelings about their boss, or having social times with each other's friends. Their relational history, then, spans both their professional and personal lives. This rich history enables their conversations to be interpersonal rather than impersonal.

When two people have relational rules, they themselves set guidelines for their behavior in their conversations. Rules help relational partners negotiate how information is managed and stored (Petronio, 2002). Most of the time, these rules (which can be either verbalized or tacitly understood) are not formally noted but are nonetheless important. **Relational rules** indicate what the people in the relationship expect and allow when they talk to each other. Relational rules differ from social rules in that the two relational partners negotiate them as opposed to having them set by an outside source. For example, one relational rule that Rolanda and Maria may have agreed upon is that all restaurant gossip should remain private. Another of their rules may communicate the need to be professional while on the job and to avoid "inside" jokes. If the restaurant manager had set these rules, then when Rolanda and Maria followed them, their communication would be more impersonal.

A final influence on the relationship continuum is **relational uniqueness,** which pertains to how communicators frame their relationship and compare it to others. In other words, how is their relationship unique from others? In the relationship between Rolanda and Maria, they know and treat each other as unique individuals, not as generic coworkers. Thus, Rolanda asks Maria for help in making a financial decision because she knows that Maria has a good head for business. And Maria refrains from teasing Rolanda when she drops a tray (even though many other servers do engage in that kind of banter) because she knows Rolanda is sensitive about being clumsy. Their relational history and rules help develop their sense of relational uniqueness.

Although most of us interact with people all day, the nature of our relationships is what determines whether our interactions are interpersonal.

© Gabe Palmer/Corbis

Again, much of our communication isn't purely impersonal or interpersonal; rather, it falls somewhere between the two ends of the continuum. Further, the relationship you have with someone doesn't always indicate whether your communication is personal or not. At times, personal communication occurs in our impersonal relationships. For example, consider telling a tailor about your divorce or confiding to a fellow passenger that you are deathly afraid of flying. At other times, we may have some impersonal communication in our close relationships. For instance, a couple with five children may be too exhausted to worry about being sensitive, loving, and compassionate with each other. Feeding the kids, bathing them, preparing their lunches, and getting them to the bus present enough challenges. In fact, for the sake of communication efficiency, many couples have developed abbreviated communication systems (Pearson, 1992) that fit the description of impersonal encounters.

Looking at the interpersonal communication continuum provides one avenue to understanding interpersonal communication. However, it may pose overly restrictive limits on our definition by demanding that interpersonal communication always be relationally oriented. We now turn our attention to defining exactly what we mean by interpersonal communication in this text.

Defining Interpersonal Communication

We define **interpersonal communication** as the process of message transaction between people to create and sustain shared meaning. There are three critical components embedded in this definition: process, message transaction, and shared meaning. Let's look at each in turn.

When we state that interpersonal communication is a **process,** we mean that it is an ongoing, unending vibrant activity that is always changing. When we enter into an interpersonal communication exchange, we are entering into an event with no definable beginning or ending, and one that is irreversible. Our focus on process suggests that not only do individuals change, but the cultures in which they live also change. For instance, modern U.S. society is very different than it was in the 1950s. The climate of the United States in the 1950s can be characterized as a time of postwar euphoria, colored by a concern about communism. The feminist movement of the 1970s had yet to occur, and for many white middle-class families, sex roles were traditional. Women's roles were more rigidly defined as nurturers and primary caretakers for children, whereas men's roles were relegated to emotionless financial providers. These roles influenced decision making in various families (Turner & West, 2006).

However, nowadays roles are less rigid. Many dads stay at home to care for children, and many women work outside the home. And more than ever, women and men make all kinds of decisions about the family together. Further, the Cold War has ended, and the threat of communism has been replaced by fears about terrorism. This new type of concern forms a context for conversations between people, if for no other reason than it is a topic of our time. Although it might be very common for people to talk about terrorism today, it is unlikely that they'll spend much time worrying about an invasion by Russia.

The second element of our definition highlights **message exchange,** by which we mean the transaction of verbal and nonverbal messages being sent simultaneously between two people. Messages, both verbal and nonverbal, are the vehicles we use to interact with others. But messages are not enough to establish interpersonal communication. For example, consider an English speaker stating the message, "I need to find the post office. Can you direct me there?" to a Spanish speaker. Although the message was clearly stated in English, no shared meaning results if the Spanish speaker is not bilingual.

Meaning is central to our definition of interpersonal communication because **meaning** is what people extract from a message. As you will learn in Chapter 6, words alone have no meaning; people attribute meaning to words. We create the meaning of a message even as the message unfolds. Perhaps our relational history helps us interpret the message. Perhaps a message is unclear to us and we ask questions for clarity. Or maybe the message has personal meaning to us, and no one else understands the personal expressions used. Make no mistake: Meaning directly affects our relational life. As Steve Duck and Julia Wood (1995) state: "we suspect that 'good' and 'bad' relational experiences are sometimes a matter of personal definition and personal meaning, but always intertwined, sometimes seamlessly, in the broader human enterprise of making sense of experience" (p. 3). In other words, achieving meaning is achieving sense-making in your relationships.

When we say that people work toward creating and sustaining meaning, we are suggesting that there must be some shared meaning for interpersonal communication to take place. Judith Martin and Tom Nakayama (2000) illustrate the problem of assuming that our meaning will automatically be clear to others and result in shared meaning. They point out that meaning is affected by culture in more ways than language differences. For example, in the United States, many people tend to dislike Monday, the first day of the work week, and enjoy Friday, which is the end of the workweek. However, many Muslims dislike Saturday, which is the first day of the week for Muslims after Friday, the holy day. The researchers conclude that cultural expressions such as TGIF (thank goodness it's Friday) may not communicate the same meaning to all individuals, even when accurately translated. Do not assume that others will understand words and phrases you may use on a daily basis. To read an article that examines the complexity associated with the term *message*, read the article "Where Is the 'Message' in Communication Models?" available through InfoTrac College Edition. Use your Understanding Interpersonal Communication CD-ROM to access **InfoTrac College Edition Exercise 1.1: Received as Meant to Be Sent?**

Now that you are getting a clearer picture of what interpersonal communication is, let's turn to a discussion of the value of interpersonal communication in our lives.

The Value of Interpersonal Communication

The National Association of Colleges and Employers (2002) reports that interpersonal skills top the list of skills employers look for in new hires in virtually all professions. In his book *10 Things Employers Want You to Learn in College,* William Coplin (2004) writes that communication skills are paramount. Without solid communication skills, Coplin writes, employees will not be productive. Clearly, without some knowledge and skill in interpersonal communication, you may have a difficult time finding a job in today's marketplace. To read an interesting article about the importance of interpersonal communication at work, use your Understanding Interpersonal Communication CD-ROM to access **Interactive Activity 1.3: Technical versus Interpersonal Skills.** And to take a look at the communication model applied to today's business environment, read the article "Avoiding Breakdowns in the Communication Process," available through InfoTrac College Edition. Use your Understanding Interpersonal Communication CD-ROM to access **InfoTrac College Edition Exercise 1.2: The Communication Model at Work.**

However, jobs are not the only reason to learn about interpersonal communication. Most of us desire long-term, satisfying relationships, and effective interpersonal communication with others can help us establish such relationships. Learning about interpersonal communication can literally improve our lives—physically, emotionally, and psychologically—and it can improve our relationships with others. A number of recent conclusions by both the academic and medical communities (for example, Fleishman, Sherbourne, & Crystal, 2000; American Cancer Society, 2001; Support4Hope, 2004) show the value of communication and relationships:

- Older people with the ability to communicate in extended interpersonal networks improve their physical and emotional well-being.
- The American Cancer Society encourages cancer patients to establish an interpersonal relationship with their physicians. This relationship involves taking the time to ask questions, making concerns known, sharing information, and making choices.
- A chat room for those with depression indicates that limited or no interpersonal contact may lead to permanent changes in brain function that increase one's chances to be clinically depressed.
- Patients have a preference for physicians who show a "patient-centered" approach that includes quality communication skills and a desire to establish a partnership between patient and physician.

To read an article that offers an interesting look at how our interactions with others affect our health, read "Nuances of Interpersonal Relationships Influence Blood Pressure," available through InfoTrac College Edition. Use your Understanding Interpersonal Communication CD-ROM to access **InfoTrac College Edition Exercise 1.3: Interpersonal Communication and Health.**

Another benefit of studying interpersonal communication is that it can improve relationships with family and friends. Communicating in close relationships can be tough. Yet, think about the advantages, for instance, of (1) working toward improving your listening skills with a roommate, (2) committing yourself to using more sensitive language with a sibling, (3) employing nondefensive reactions in your conflicts with parents, and (4) accepting responsibility for your feelings in all interactions. These are a few areas that you will explore in this book.

Another value associated with learning about interpersonal communication pertains to the classroom. Specifically, research has shown that using your communication skills in the classroom may improve your academic performance. For instance, students who are considered to have high degrees of interaction involvement in class are more likely to increase their learning, motivation, and satisfaction with the course (Myers & Bryant, 2002). Learning to listen, to participate, and to involve yourself in class, then, has lasting positive effects on your learning and grades.

A final way that learning about interpersonal communication can improve your life is that it can help you gain information about yourself. Psychologist Abraham Maslow (1954/1970) calls this the process of **self-actualization.** When we are self-actualized, we become the best person we can be. We are tapping our full potential in terms of our creativity, our spontaneity, and our talents. When we self-actualize, we try to cultivate our strengths and eliminate our shortcomings. At times, others help us to self-actualize. For instance, in the movie *As Good As It Gets,* Jack Nicholson's character, Melvin, suffers from an obsessive-compulsive disorder. His date, Carol, portrayed by Helen Hunt, has her own family problems but tries to help Melvin overcome some of his idiosyncrasies. In a poignant exchange that occurs during their first date, Carol becomes distressed and tells Melvin that she will leave the restaurant unless he gives her a compliment. Carol pleads: "Pay me a compliment, Melvin. I need one quick." Melvin responds by saying, "You make me want to be a better man." Although Melvin clearly frames the compliment from his vantage point, he still, nonetheless, manages to help Carol see her value through his eyes.

Overall, then, we can reap a number of benefits from practicing effective interpersonal skills. Aside from the fact that it allows us to function every day, becoming adept at interpersonal communication helps us become more healthy, helps us in the workplace, and aids us in our relationships with family and friends. We have now set the stage for examining some principles and misconceptions about interpersonal communication.

Effective interpersonal communication can help us feel better physically, psychologically, and emotionally. Think of how good it feels to have someone take the time to talk with you when you're feeling lonely, sick, or depressed.

Principles of Interpersonal Communication

To better understand interpersonal communication, let's explore some major principles that shape it. Interpersonal communication is unavoidable, is irreversible, involves symbol exchange, is rule-governed, is learned, and has both content and relationship information.

Interpersonal Communication Is Unavoidable

Researchers have stated that you cannot *not* communicate (Watzlawick, Beavin, & Jackson, 1967). This means that as hard as we try, we cannot prevent someone else from making meaning out of our behavior—it is inevitable and unavoidable. No matter what poker face we try to establish, we are still sending a message to others. Even our silence and avoidance of eye contact are communicative. It is this quality that makes interpersonal communication transactional. For instance, imagine that Maresha and her partner, Chloe, are talking about the balance in their checking account. In this scenario, the two engage in a rather heated discussion because Maresha has discovered that $300 cannot be accounted for in the account balance. As Maresha speaks, Chloe simply sits and listens to her. Yet, Maresha can't help but notice that Chloe is unable to look her in the eye. Maresha begins to think that Chloe's shifting eyes and constant throat clearing must signify something deceptive. Clearly, although Chloe hasn't spoken a word, she is communicating. Her nonverbal communication is being perceived as highly communicative. We return to the impact that nonverbal communication has on creating meaning in Chapter 7.

Interpersonal Communication Is Irreversible

There are times when we wish that we hadn't said something. Wouldn't it be great if we could take back a comment and pretend that it hadn't been spoken? Think about the times you told a parent, a partner, a roommate, or your child something that you later felt was a terrible thing to say. Or what about the times you told a good friend that you couldn't stand his new hair color ("It's too bleached out. You look like an idiot") or her new car ("For *that* you paid how much? You got ripped off!"). Although we might later wish to eat our words, the principle of **irreversibility** means that what we say to others cannot be reversed.

In fact, the principle of irreversibility affects even mediated interpersonal communication such as email. Think about sending an email that was written in haste. It may have been filled with personal attacks against someone because you were upset and were venting. Now imagine that email getting into the hands of the person you were slamming. An apology may help, but saying you're sorry does nothing to erase the original message. The irreversibility of your message becomes apparent.

Interpersonal Communication Involves Symbol Exchange

One important reason interpersonal communication occurs is because symbols are mutually agreed upon by the participants in the process. Yet, **symbols** are arbitrary labels or representations for feelings, concepts, objects, or events. Words are symbols. For instance, the word *table* represents something we sit at. Similarly, the word *love* represents the idea of love, which means feelings for someone or something.

Words like *love* suggest that symbols may be somewhat abstract, and with this abstraction comes the potential for miscommunication. For instance, consider how hard it would be for someone who has never attended college to understand the following:

> I have no idea what the prereqs are. I know that the midterm is pretty much objective. And the prof doesn't like to follow the syllabus too much. I wish that stuff was in the undergrad catalog. I'm sure I'd rather do an independent study than take that class.

Because the verbal symbols used in this message are not understood by everyone, the message would be lost to someone who had never encountered "prereqs" and an "independent study." This example underscores the importance of developing a transactional viewpoint because communication requires mutual understanding. In Chapter 6, we look in more detail at the importance of language in interpersonal relationships.

Interpersonal Communication Is Rule-Governed

Consider the following examples of communication rules:

- As long as you live under my roof, you'll do what I say.
- Always tell the truth.
- Don't talk back.
- Always say "thank you" when someone gives you a present.
- Don't interrupt while anyone is talking.

You probably heard at least one of these while growing up. We noted earlier that rules are important ingredients in our relationships. They help guide and structure our interpersonal communication. Rules essentially say that individuals in a relationship agree that there are appropriate ways to interact in their relationship. Like the rules in our childhood, most of the rules in our relationships today basically tell us what we can or can't do. Susan Shimanoff (1980) has defined a rule as "a followable prescription that indicates what behavior is obligated, preferred, or prohibited in certain contexts" (p. 57). In other words, Shimanoff, like many other communication researchers, thinks that we can choose whether or not we wish to follow a rule. Ultimately, we must decide whether the rule must be adhered to or can be ignored in our interpersonal exchanges.

To understand this principle, consider the Chandler family, a family of three that finds itself homeless. The Chandlers live day to day in homeless shelters in a large city in the South. Still, the family members agree on a communication rule explicitly stating that they will not discuss their economic situation in public. This rule requires all family members to refrain from talking about what led to their homelessness. Each member of the family is obligated to keep this information private, an intrafamily secret of sorts. Whether or not people outside the Chandler family agree on the usefulness of such a rule is not important. Yet, one important test of the rule's effectiveness is whether or not family members can refrain from discussing their circumstances with others. Further, if the rule is not followed, what will the consequences be? Rules, therefore, imply choice, and participants in a relationship may choose to ignore a particular rule.

Interpersonal Communication Is Learned

People obviously believe that interpersonal communication is a learned process. Otherwise, why would we be writing this book, and why would you be taking this course? Yet, as we mentioned at the beginning of this chapter, we often take for

From birth, we are taught how to communicate interpersonally, most significantly by our family. As we grow older, we refine our skills as we interact with a wider and wider group of people, such as our teachers, friends, coworkers, and partners.

© Jose Carillo/PhotoEdit

granted our ability to communicate. Still, we all need to refine and cultivate our skills to communicate with a wide assortment of people. As our book's theme underscores, you must be able to make informed communication choices in changing times.

You're in this course to learn more about interpersonal communication. But you've also been acquiring this information throughout your life. We learn how to communicate with one another from television, our peer group, and our partners. Early in our lives, most of us learn from our family. Consider this dialogue between Laura Reid and her 7-year-old son, Tucker:

TUCKER: Mom, I saw Holly's dad driving a motorcycle today.
LAURA: Really? That must've been cool to see. Holly's dad's name is Mr. Willows.
TUCKER: What's his name?
LAURA: Mr. Willows.
TUCKER: No, Mom—what's his real name?
LAURA: Honey, I told you. Mr. Willows.
TUCKER: Doesn't he have a name like I do?
LAURA: Little kids call him Mr. Willows. Grownups call him Kenny.
TUCKER: Why can't I call him Kenny?
LAURA: Because you're not a grownup and because he is older than you, you should call him Mr. Willows.

Clearly, Laura Reid is teaching her child a communication rule she believes leads to interpersonal effectiveness. She tells her son that he should use titles for adults. Implied in this teaching is that kids do not have the same conversational privileges as adults. Interestingly, this learned interpersonal skill evolves with age. For example, at age 24, what do you think Tucker will call Kenny Willows? This awkwardness about names is frequently felt by newlyweds as they become members of their spouse's family. Does a husband call his wife's mother "Mom," or does he call her by her first name? Of course, his mother-in-law may ask to be called "Mom," and yet her son-in-law may be uncomfortable with accommodating her request, especially if his own biological mother is still alive.

Interpersonal Communication Has Both Content and Relationship Information

Each message that you communicate to another contains information on two levels. **Content information** refers to the information contained in the message. The words you speak to another person and how you say those words constitute the content of the message. Content, then, includes both verbal and nonverbal components. A message also contains **relationship information,** which can be defined as how you want the receiver of a message to interpret your message. The relational dimension of a message gives us some idea how the speaker and the listener feel about each other. Content and relationship information work simultaneously in a message, and it is difficult to think about sending a message that doesn't, in some way, comment on the relationship between the sender and receiver (Knapp & Vangelisti, 2005). In other words, we can't really separate the two. We always express an idea or thought (content), but that thought is always presented within a relational framework. Consider the following example.

Father Paul is a Catholic priest who is the pastor of a large parish in the Rocky Mountains. Corrine Murphy is the parish administrative assistant. Both have been at the parish for more than ten years and have been good friends throughout that time. One of the most stressful times in the church is during the Christmas season. The pastor is busy visiting homebound parishioners, while Corrine is busy overseeing the annual holiday pageant. With this stress comes a lot of shouting between the two. On one occasion, several parishioners hear him yell, "Corrine, you forgot to tell me about the Lopez family! When do they need me to visit? Where is your mind these days?" Corrine shoots back: "I've got it under control. Just quit your nagging!" Those listening to the two couldn't believe their ears. They were a bit taken aback by the way the two yelled at each other.

In this example, the parishioners who heard the conversation were simply attuned to the content dimension and failed to understand that the ten-year relationship between Father Paul and Corrine was unique to the two of them. Such direct interpersonal exchanges during stressful times were not out of the ordinary. Father Paul and Corrine frequently raised their voices to each other, and neither gave it a second thought. In a case like this, the content should be understood with the relationship in mind.

In this chapter so far, we have explored the definition of interpersonal communication in some detail and have described several principles associated with interpersonal communication. Now that you know what interpersonal communication is, let's focus on some of the misconceptions about interpersonal communication, or what it is not.

REVISITING CASE IN POINT

1. Apply Jackie and Phil's conversation to any of the principles of interpersonal communication.
2. Indicate the content and relational dimensions associated with Jackie and Phil's interaction.

You can answer these questions online under Student Resources for Chapter 1 at the Understanding Interpersonal Communication website.

Myths about Interpersonal Communication

Maybe it's the media. Maybe it's Hollywood. Maybe it's Oprah! Whatever the source, for one reason or another, people operate under several misconceptions about interpersonal communication. These myths impede our understanding and enactment of effective interpersonal communication.

Interpersonal Communication Solves All Problems

We cannot stress enough that simply being skilled in interpersonal communication does not mean that you are prepared to work out all of your relational problems. When you learn to communicate well, you may clearly communicate about a problem but not necessarily be able to solve it. Also, keep in mind that communication involves both talking and listening. Many students have told us during their advising appointments that sometimes when they try to "talk out a problem," they achieve no satisfaction. It seems, then, that with the emphasis the media places on talking, many students forget about the role of listening. We hope you leave this course with an understanding of how to communicate effectively with others in a variety of relationships. We also hope you realize that simply because you are talking does not mean that you will solve all of your relationship problems.

Interpersonal Communication Is Always a Good Thing

National best-selling self-help books and famous self-improvement gurus have made millions of dollars selling the idea that communication is the magic potion for all of life's ailments. Most often, communication is a good thing. Yet, there are times when communication results in less-than-satisfying relationship experiences. A relatively new area of research in interpersonal communication is called "the dark side" (Cupach & Spitzberg, 1994, 2004; Spitzberg & Cupach, 1998). The **dark side of interpersonal communication** generally refers to negative communication exchanged between people.

People may be manipulative, deceitful, exploitive, homophobic, racist, and emotionally abusive (Cupach & Spitzberg, 1994). In other words, we need to be aware that communication can be downright nasty at times and that interpersonal communication is not always satisfying and rewarding. Throughout this book, we refer to the dark (and bright) side of communication as we talk about interpersonal relationships. Although most people approach interpersonal communication with an open and thoughtful mind, others are less sincere.

Interpersonal Communication Is Common Sense

Consider the following question: If interpersonal communication is just a matter of common sense, why do we have so many problems communicating with others? We need to abandon the thinking that communication is simply common sense. To put it bluntly, we all can benefit from help in this area.

It is true that we should be sure to use whatever common sense we have in our personal interactions, but this strategy will get us only so far. In some cases, a skilled interpersonal communicator may effectively rely on his or her common sense, but we usually also need to make use of an extensive repertoire of skills to make informed choices in our relationships. One problem with believing that interpersonal communication is common sense relates to the diversity of our population. As we discuss in Chapter 3, cultural variation continues to characterize U.S. society. Making the assumption that all people intuitively know how to communicate with everyone undermines the rich tapestry of groups in the United States. Even males and females tend to look at the same event differently (Wood, 2005). To rid ourselves of the myth of common sense, we simply need to take culture and gender into consideration.

Interpersonal Communication Is Synonymous with Interpersonal Relationships

We don't automatically have an interpersonal relationship with someone merely because we are exchanging interpersonal communication with him or her. Interpersonal communication can *lead to* interpersonal relationships, but an accumulation of interpersonal messages does not automatically result in an interpersonal relationship. Sharing a pleasant conversation about your family with a stranger riding on the bus with you doesn't mean you have a relationship with that person.

Relationships do not just appear. William Wilmot (1995) remarked that relationships "emerge from recurring episodic enactments" (p. 25). That is, for an interaction between you and another person to be considered an interpersonal relationship, a pattern of intimate exchanges over time must take place. Relationships usually will not happen unless two people demonstrate a sense of caring and respect, and have significant periods of time to work on their relational issues.

Interpersonal Communication Is Always Face to Face

Throughout this chapter, most of our discussion has centered on face-to-face encounters between people. Indeed, this is the primary way that people meet and cultivate their interpersonal skills with each other. It is also the focus of most of the research in interpersonal communication. Yet, large numbers of people are beginning to utilize the Internet in their communication with others. This mediated interpersonal communication requires us to expand our discussion of interpersonal communication beyond personal encounters. To establish a relationship, two people

Your *Turn*

There are similarities and differences in the way we communicate with our neighbors, family, friends, and coworkers. Write about these and use examples of the types of conversations you have with each. What conclusions can you draw about how interpersonal communication varies based on particular sets of people with whom you interact? If you'd like, you can use your student workbook to complete this activity.

must eventually meet one another. However, we realize that some people may disagree with this statement. In the spirit of inclusiveness, then, we include technological relations in our interpretation of interpersonal communication and devote Chapter 11 to this issue.

Thus far, this chapter has given you a fundamental framework for examining interpersonal communication. We close the chapter by examining a feature of the interpersonal communication process that is not easily taught and that is often difficult to comprehend: ethics.

Interpersonal Communication Ethics

Communication ethicist Richard Johanneson (2000) concluded that "ethical issues may arise in human behavior whenever that behavior could have significant impact on other persons, when the behavior involves conscious choice of means and ends, and when the behavior can be judged by standards of right and wrong" (p. 1). In other words, ethics is the cornerstone of interpersonal communication.

Ethics is the perceived rightness or wrongness of an action or behavior. Researchers have identified ethics as a type of moral decision making, determined in large part by society (Pfeiffer & Forsberg, 2005). A primary goal of ethics is to "establish appropriate constraints on ourselves" (Englehardt, 2001, p. 1). Ethical decisions involve value judgments, and not everyone will agree with those values. For instance, do you tell racist jokes in front of others and think that they are harmless ways to make people laugh? What sort of value judgment is part of the decision to tell or not to tell a joke? Acting ethically is critical in interpersonal communication. As Raymond Pfeiffer and Ralph Forsberg (2005) concluded, "To act ethically is, at the very least, to strive to act in ways that do not hurt other people, that respect their dignity, individuality, and unique moral value, and that treat others as equally important to oneself" (p. 7). The authors maintain that if we're not prepared to act in this way, one can conclude that we do not consider ethics important.

Five Ethical Systems of Communication

There are many ways to make value judgments in interpersonal communication. Researchers have discussed a number of different ethical systems of communication relevant to our interpersonal encounters (e.g., Andersen, 1996; Englehardt, 2001; Jensen, 1997). We will discuss five of them here. As we briefly overview each system, keep in mind that these systems attempt to let us know what it means to act morally.

Categorical Imperative

The first ethical system, named the **categorical imperative,** is based on the work of philosopher Immanuel Kant (Kuehn, 2001). Kant's categorical imperative refers to individuals fol-

Facing *Change*

We are living in times where we are redefining what it means to have a conversation. For instance, people are using the Internet to meet others and have interpersonal exchanges. What is your impression of looking at interpersonal communication within this technological frame? Do you believe if people are communicating using the Internet that they are engaged in interpersonal communication? Why or why not?

 Use your Understanding Interpersonal Communication CD-ROM to watch the CNN video clip "Gulf War Forces Use of Email," which shows how soldiers in the first Gulf War used email to communicate with their friends and family back home. Click on the "CNN & Change" icon in the menu at left, then click on "Video Menu" in the menu bar at the top of the screen. Select "Gulf War Email" to watch the video (it takes a minute for the video to load). As you watch the video, consider your own use of email. In what ways has email affected your communication with others? You can respond to this and other analysis questions by clicking on "Analysis" in the menu bar at the top of the screen. When you've answered all the questions, click on "Done" to compare your answers to those provided by the authors.

"Miss Dugan, will you send someone in here who can distinguish right from wrong?"

lowing moral absolutes. This ethical system suggests that we should act as though we are an example to others. According to this system, the key question when making a moral decision is: What would happen if everyone did this? Thus, you should not do something that you wouldn't feel is fine for everyone to do all the time. Further, Kant believed that the consequences of actions are not important; what matters is the ethical principle behind those actions.

For example, let's say that Mark confides to Karla, a coworker, that he has leukemia. Karla tells no one else because Mark fears his health insurance will be threatened if management finds out. Elizabeth, the supervisor, asks Karla if she knows what's happening with Mark because he misses work and is always tired. The categorical imperative dictates that Karla tell her boss the truth, despite the fact that telling the truth may affect Mark's job, his future with the company, and his relationship with Karla. The categorical imperative requires us to tell the truth because Kant believed that enforcing the principle of truth telling is more important than worrying about the short-term consequences of telling the truth.

Utilitarianism

The second ethical system, **utilitarianism,** was developed by John Stuart Mill (Capaldi, 2004). According to this system, what is ethical is what will bring the greatest good for the greatest number of people. Unlike Kant, Mill believed the consequences of moral actions were important. Maximizing satisfaction and happiness is essential. For example, suppose you're over at a friend's house and her baby sister is crying incessantly. You notice your friend grabbing her sister, shaking her, and yelling for her to be quiet. Afterward, you observe red marks on the child's arms. Do you report your friend to the authorities? Do you remain quiet? Do you talk to your friend?

Making a decision based on utilitarianism or what is best for the greater good means that you will speak out or take some action. Although it would be easier on you and your friend if you remain silent, doing so will not serve the greater good. According to utilitarianism, you should either talk to your friend or report your friend's actions to an appropriate individual.

The Golden Mean

The **golden mean,** a third ethical system, proposes that we should aim for harmony and balance in our lives. This principle, articulated more than 2,500 years ago by Aristotle (Metzger, 1995), suggests that a person's moral virtue stands between two vices, with the middle, or the mean, being the foundation for a rational society.

Let's say that Cora, Jackie, and Lester are three employees who work for a large insurance company. During a break one afternoon, someone asks what kind of childhood each had. Cora goes into specific detail, talking about her abusive father: "He really let me have it, and it all started when I was 5," she begins before launching into a long description. On the other hand, Jackie tells the group only, "My childhood was okay." Lester tells the group that his was a pretty rough childhood: "It was tough financially. We didn't have a lot of money. But we really all got along well." In this example, Cora was on one extreme, revealing too much information. Jackie was at the other extreme, revealing very little, if anything. Lester's decision to reveal a reasonable amount of information about his childhood was an ethical one; he practiced the golden mean by providing a sufficient amount of information but not too much. In other words, he presented a rational and balanced perspective.

Ethic of Care

Developing an **ethic of care,** the fourth ethical system, means being concerned with connection. Carol Gilligan first conceptualized an ethic of care by looking at women's ways of moral decision making. She felt that because men have been the dominant voices in society, women's commitment toward connection has gone unnoticed. Gilligan (1982) initially felt that an ethic of care was a result of how women were raised. Although her ethical principles pertain primarily to women, Gilligan's research applies to men as well. Some men adopt the ethic, and some women do not adopt the ethic. In contrast to the categorical imperative, for instance, the ethic of care is concerned with consequences of decisions.

For instance, suppose that Ben and Paul are having a conversation about whether it's right to go behind a person's back and disclose that he or she is gay (called *outing* a person). Ben makes an argument that it's a shame that people won't own up to being gay; they are who they are. If someone hides his or her sexuality, Ben believes that it's fine to "out" that person. Paul, expressing an ethic of care, tells his friend that no one should reveal another person's sexual identity. That information should remain private unless an individual wishes to reveal it. Paul explains that outing someone would have serious negative repercussions for the relationships of the person being outed and thus shouldn't be done. In this example, Paul exemplifies a symbolic connection to those who don't want to discuss their sexual identity with others.

Significant Choice

The fifth ethical system, **significant choice,** is an ethical orientation conceptualized by Thomas Nilsen (Nilsen, 1966). Nilsen argued that communication is ethical to the extent that it maximizes people's ability to exercise free choice. Information should be given to others in a noncoercive way so that people can make free and informed decisions. For example, when personal ads are placed on the Internet, if you fail to disclose that you are married, you are not ethical in your communication with others. However, if you give information regarding your relationship status and other details, you are practicing the ethical system of significant choice.

Understanding Ethics and Our Own Values

Ethics permeates interpersonal communication. We make ongoing ethical decisions in all our interpersonal encounters. Should someone's sexual past be completely revealed to a partner? How do you treat an ex-friend or ex-partner in future encounters? Is it ever okay to lie to protect your friend? These kinds of questions challenge millions of interpersonal relationships.

Raymond Pfeiffer and Ralph Forsberg (2005) conclude that when we are confronted with ethical decisions, "we should not ignore our society's cultural, religious, literary, and moral traditions. Our values have emerged from and are deeply enmeshed in these traditions. They often teach important lessons concerning the difficult decisions we face in life" (p. 8).

The five ethical systems, which are summarized in Table 1.1, can give you strategies for making ethical decisions. However, making sense of the world and of our interpersonal relationships

"On the Internet, nobody knows you're a dog."

Table 1.1 | **Ethical Systems of Interpersonal Communication**

Ethical System	Responsibility	Action
Categorical imperative	To adhere to a moral absolute	Tell the truth
Utilitarianism	To ensure the greatest good for the greatest number of people	Produce favorable consequences
Ethic of care	To establish connection	Establish caring relationships
Golden mean	To achieve rationality and balance	Create harmony and balance for the community and the individual
Significant choice	To enable free choice	Maximize individual choice

Adapted from Englehardt, 2001.

requires us to understand our own values. We also need to understand how those values influence our ethical decisions. Today more than ever, ethics should guide us on a daily basis. Being aware of and sensitive to your decisions and their consequences will help you make the right choices in these changing times.

Choices for Changing Times

We close Chapter 1 by reiterating two themes that guide this book: choice and changing times. Throughout this text, you will explore many topics associated with interpersonal communication. We encourage you to consider the importance of choice and change as you read the material.

First, we believe that you have an abundance of choices available to you in your communication with others. Simply stated, we hope you choose to become a more effective communicator. At the core of this effectiveness is **communication competency,** or the ability to communicate with knowledge, skills, and thoughtfulness. As you read the following chapters, you will acquire a lot of knowledge about interpersonal communication. You will also be asked to apply much of that knowledge as you consider several interpersonal skills. Developing a large repertoire of skills and applying them appropriately is a hallmark of a competent communicator.

Second, as we often remind you in this book, we live in changing times. Over the course of our lives, many of us have discovered that what were communication skills that were once effective may have to be revisited. Adapting to the culture and individuals around us is paramount in the twenty-first century. As you learned earlier in this chapter, interacting with others is often challenging because of their various fields of experience. Varying backgrounds can affect how a message is sent and received.

Throughout the rest of this text, we continue to reiterate how interpersonal communication functions in our lives. These are changing times, and with change comes

Ethics & Choice

Lenora Watkins was clearly in a bind. She had dated Luke for about a month. She really didn't have any serious complaints about him but felt that Luke was sending her mixed messages. One day, he'd come over to her dorm room, and they'd sit together studying on the bed. The next time they were together, Luke would act distant, not wanting to even hold her hand. This back-and-forth intimacy was driving Lenora nuts, and she was quite frustrated over the situation.

Lenora thought nothing could be much worse than her current experiences with Luke, so she let her friend Carmen set her up with a coworker. On a coffee date, Lenora met Rodney, a professional who had divorced about three months ago. Lenora and Rodney got along great, and she felt less frustration with him than with Luke. They started dating regularly, and Lenora enjoyed his company a lot.

Lenora wasn't sure what she should do in this situation. Although neither Luke nor Rodney had said they expected an exclusive relationship with her, she knew they probably assumed she wasn't dating anyone else. Plus, she just felt funny trying to juggle the two relationships. She felt her silence to each of the guys about the other was a lie of omission, but she wasn't sure what would happen if she told them the truth.

Lenora is facing an ethical dilemma. Discuss the ethical problems pertaining to her relationships with Luke and Rodney. How should she handle the question of whether to tell them about each other? Justify your answers by using one or more of the ethical systems of communication (categorical imperative, utilitarianism, golden mean, ethic of care, or significant choice).

Use your Understanding Interpersonal Communication CD-ROM to access an interactive version of this scenario on the Understanding Interpersonal Communication website. Look under Student Resources for Chapter 1 and click on the "Ethics & Choice" menu at left. The interactive version of this scenario allows you to choose an appropriate response to this dilemma and then see what consequences your choice brings about. You can also compare your answers to the questions at the end of the scenario to those provided by the authors and, if requested, email your response to your instructor.

challenge. One such challenge is to communicate interpersonally in a diverse culture. As a start, assess your current communication skills by using your Understanding Interpersonal Communication CD-ROM to access **Interactive Activity 1.4: Communication Skills Test**. In addition, see whether you are (mostly) an intuitive, thinking, feeling, or sensing communicator by reading the article "What Type of Communicator Are You?" available through InfoTrac College Edition. Use your Understanding Interpersonal Communication CD-ROM to access **InfoTrac College Edition Exercise 1.4: What Type of Communicator Are You?**

Summary

We often take our ability to communicate for granted, and the majority of people living in the United States believe they communicate well. However, some people experience communication apprehension in uncomfortable situations, and all of us can improve our interpersonal communication skills in some way.

Interpersonal communication is a complex process that is unique from other forms of communication, such as intrapersonal, small group, organizational, mass, and public. The definition of interpersonal communication has evolved over the years as several models of communication have been advanced. The earliest, the linear model, says that communication is a one-way process in which a sender transmits a message to a receiver. In this model, several types of noise—physiological, physical, psychological, or semantic—can interfere with a message while it's being transmitted. The linear view also specifies that context—be it physical, cultural, or social-emotional—affects communication. The drawback of this model is that it fails to account for the receiver as an active participant in conversations.

According to the interactional model, communication goes from sender to receiver and from receiver to sender. This approach focuses on feedback, which can consist of words (verbal) or body language (nonverbal). Feedback can also be internal, meaning you assess your own communication, or external, meaning you receive feedback from others. The drawback of this model is that it assumes that nonverbal and verbal messages cannot be sent concurrently.

The transactional model views communication as a cooperative process in which the sender and receiver are both responsible for the effectiveness of communication. In this model, messages build upon each other as people negotiate shared meaning. This model also takes into account people's fields of experience, which are their culture, heredity, and personal history. The more people's fields of experience overlap, the more they have in common, which can lead to more and deeper personal communication. The transactional model may soon become a bit outdated because technological communication, such as email, may affect scholars' view of the communication process.

Another way to understand the nature of interpersonal communication is to look at the interpersonal communication continuum. Interactions come in all degrees of closeness, not just the extremes of impersonal and interpersonal, which are at either end of the continuum. Where an interaction falls on the continuum depends on the relational history, relational rules, and relational uniqueness of the people involved.

After you understand the definition, evolution, and nature of interpersonal communication, you can appreciate its value. Employers look for this quality in their employees, and good communication skills can reap you personal benefits as well. To make the most of interpersonal communication, you need to understand

that it is unavoidable, is irreversible, involves symbol exchange, is rule-governed, is learned, and involves both content and relationship dimensions. Also, you need to avoid the common myths of interpersonal communication, such as that it will solve all your problems, it's always a good thing, it's common sense, it's synonymous with interpersonal relationships, and it's always face to face. Finally, you have to understand the ethics—that is, the perceived rightness or wrongness of an action or behavior—involved in interpersonal communication. Five systems—categorical imperative, utilitarianism, ethic of care, golden mean, and significant choice—can guide you, but ultimately you need to understand your own values as well as the consequences of your actions. This book is geared to improve your communication competency in the changing times in which we live.

Understanding Interpersonal Communication Online

Now that you've read Chapter 1, use your Understanding Interpersonal Communication CD-ROM for quick access to the electronic study resources that accompany this text. Your CD-ROM gives you access to the video of Jackie and Phil's interaction on pages 3–4, the Communication Assessment Test on page 5, the CNN video clip "Gulf War Forces Use of Email" on page 25, the Ethics & Choice interactive activity on page 28, InfoTrac College Edition, and the Understanding Interpersonal Communication website. When you get to the Understanding Interpersonal Communication home page, click on "Student Book Companion Site" in the Resource box at right to access the online study aids for this chapter, including a digital glossary, review quizzes, and the chapter activities. ■

Terms for Review

categorical imperative 25
channel 8
communication apprehension 4
communication competency 28
communication models 7
content information 22
context 9
cultural context 9
dark side of interpersonal
   communication 23
ethic of care 27
ethics 25
external feedback 10
feedback 10
field of experience 12
golden mean 26

historical context 10
interactional model of
   communication 10
internal feedback 10
interpersonal
   communication 16
irreversibility 20
linear model of
   communication 7
meaning 17
message 8
message exchange 16
noise 8
physical context 9
physical noise 8
physiological noise 8

process 16
psychological noise 8
receiver 8
relational history 15
relational rules 15
relational uniqueness 15
relationship information 22
self-actualization 18
semantic noise 8
sender 8
significant choice 27
social-emotional context 9
symbols 20
transactional model of
   communication 11
utilitarianism 26

Questions for Understanding

Comprehension Focus

1. Distinguish between interpersonal communication and the other types of human communication.
2. Compare and contrast the primary models of communication.

3. Identify several principles associated with interpersonal communication.
4. Explain the myths pertaining to interpersonal communication.
5. Why should we consider ethical

systems of communication while relating to others?

Application Focus

1. **CASE IN POINT**

    Our chapter opening story represents the sort of interpersonal exchanges we all often experience. Do you believe that Phil and Jackie's dialogue is realistic? Discuss the various types of conversations that start out quite simply and then proceed to a more complex level.

2. Discuss how you developed your interpersonal communication skills before enrolling in this course. What strategies did you undertake—if any—to make sure that

meaning was achieved in your exchanges? Include examples in your response.

3. Indicate times when physiological, physical, psychological, or semantic noise affected how you received a message. Recount the specifics of the situation and explain how you managed the noise.

4. What do you hope to gain from enrolling in this course? What practical results do you expect to gain from studying interpersonal communication?

5. Discuss your career choice and how you think interpersonal communication skills will be needed in your future occupation.

Interactive Activities and InfoTrac College Edition Exercises

Complete the Interactive Activities and InfoTrac College Edition Exercises for Chapter 1 online at the Understanding Interpersonal Communication website. Select the chapter resources for Chapter 1, then click on "Activities" or "InfoTrac College Edition." If requested, you can submit your answers to your instructor.

Interactive Activities

1.1 Interactive Models of Communication 13
1.2 Communication in Emergency Situations 13
1.3 Technical versus Interpersonal Skills 17
1.4 Communication Skills Test 29

InfoTrac College Edition Exercises

1.1 Received as Meant to Be Sent? 17
1.2 The Communication Model at Work 18
1.3 Interpersonal Communication and Health 18
1.4 What Type of Communicator Are You? 29

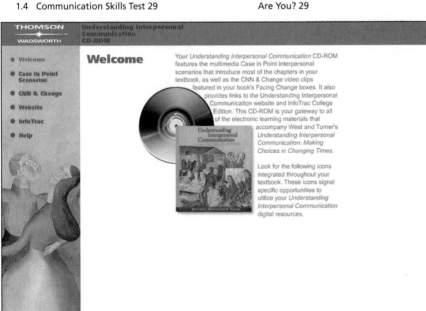

2

Communication, Perception, and the Self

CHAPTER GOALS

Explain the influences on the perception process

Discuss the dimensions of self-concept

Identify the relationship between identity management and facework

Describe the strategies for identity management

Select skills for perception checking

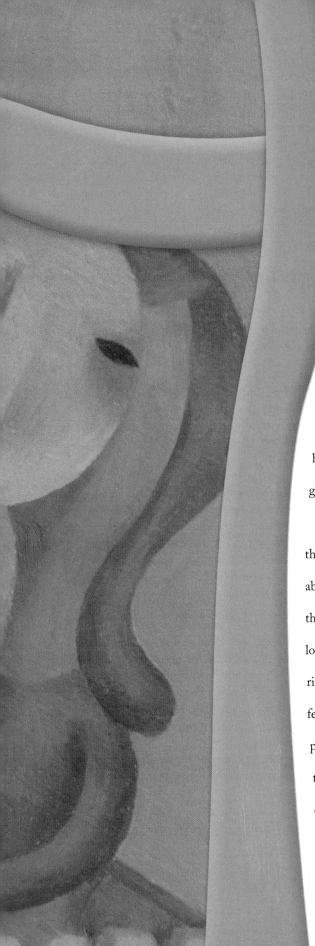

CASE IN POINT: DR. ROBERTO GOMEZ

As he approached the third-floor waiting room late in the evening, Dr. Gomez felt butterflies in his stomach. He was used to giving bad news to families, but he was especially troubled about telling Elise and Barry Camara that their baby girl was going to die soon. All he could think about was what it would be like to be told similar news about his 4-year-old daughter, Isabella. Entering the waiting room, he saw a fragile mother and father sitting on the arms of overstuffed chairs. He could tell the two had been crying by looking at their red eyes. Dreading the inevitable communication, the doctor took a deep breath and asked the parents to enter the private conference room. There, holding the mother's hand, he related the terrible news. He listened as the parents talked together, and he sensed the couple needed time alone.

Dr. Gomez left the conference room and looked down at his hands; they were trembling. He thought about his Isabella. He also thought about his other patients who were near death and how he handled giving this type of news to their families. As he walked into the physicians' lounge, Roberto Gomez kept hoping that the couple could see how terrible he felt. He didn't want to be viewed as a cold-hearted medical professional. He wished that the Camaras could see him as a compassionate person who was trying to overcome some of his own personal grief about the situation. He lay down, closed his eyes, and thought about his precious daughter and how lucky he was. ■

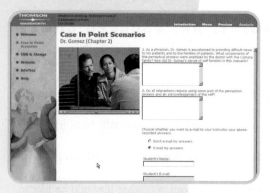

Use your Understanding Interpersonal Communication CD-ROM to watch a video clip of Dr. Gomez's interaction with the Camaras about their daughter. Click on the "In Action" icon in the menu at left, then click on "Conversation Menu" in the menu bar at the top of the screen. Select "Dr. Gomez" to watch the video (it takes a minute for the video to load). As you watch Dr. Gomez talk with the Camaras and think about his own daughter, consider his self-concept dilemma. Do you believe he handled the situation appropriately? You can respond to this and other analysis questions by clicking on "Analysis" in the menu bar at the top of the screen. When you've answered all the questions, click "Done" to compare your answers to those provided by the authors.

Look around you right now—at your apartment, office, or dorm room. Are people milling around? Is music playing? Is the television on? Is your computer turned on and logged on to a particular website? Is your cell phone ringing? What are you wearing? Do you hear noises outside? Are you sick or healthy? Are you fully awake?

Now think about how you felt the last time you had a heated argument with another person. What did you find particularly aggravating about the argument? How did you feel about yourself as you engaged in the conflict? What reactions did you receive from the person you were arguing with during the exchange? Did anyone "win" the argument? If so, how did that happen? How do you think you will handle the next conflict with this person?

You answered these questions based on two important topics in interpersonal communication: perception and the self. As you stopped to consider what was around you, you were perceiving your immediate surroundings. Some things you may have noticed before we prompted you to do so. However, you may not have thought about other things until we mentioned them. In both cases, you were engaged in the perception process.

As you thought about the last argument you had, you inevitably had to look at another critical part of interpersonal communication: the self. We asked you to think about your personal reactions to the conflict and how the conflict affected you. You probably thought about the effect of the conflict on your relationship with the other person. You also likely considered how your identity influenced the type of conflict and the way the conflict developed. These considerations are part of your "self."

We consider the perception process and an understanding of the self together in this chapter for a few reasons. First, we perceive the world around us with a personal lens (Stone, Patton, & Heen, 2002). Second, we can't talk about perception unless we talk about how those perceptions influence and affect our sense of self. Finally, we believe that perceiving requires an understanding of the self. In other words, we can't begin to unravel why we recognize some things and ignore others without simultaneously (sometimes unconsciously) figuring out how our individual identity functions within those realizations. We cannot discuss perception without also talking about how it relates to the self.

Our opening story of Dr. Gomez shows the interrelationship between perception and identity. We saw that the physician perceived the couple as grieving. He also sensed that the two needed some private time, so he left them alone. Dr. Gomez's realization that his hands were trembling shows that the physician was aware of his own physiological reactions to his news. Finally, think about how Dr. Gomez viewed the relationship of the grim news to his personal life. He seemed concerned about how the Camaras perceived him. It seems clear that their perception affects how Dr. Gomez views himself.

As Joseph Forgas (2002) states, perception and individual identity go hand in hand. This intersection is the focus of our chapter. We begin by explaining the perception process.

Understanding Perception: A Seesaw Experience

In most of our interpersonal encounters, we form an impression of the other person. These impressions, or perceptions, are critical to achieving meaning. The process of looking at people, things, activities, and events can involve many factors. For

Table 2.1 | **Stages of the Interpersonal Perception Process**

Stage	Description	Example
Attending and selecting	First stage in the perception process. It involves sorting out stimuli. We choose to attend to some stimuli and to ignore others.	Among the people, books, and activity at the campus library, Kendrick notices his friend talking to a woman in one of his classes he had wanted to meet and date.
Organizing	Second stage in the perception process. It involves categorizing stimuli to make sense of them.	Kendrick creates the belief that his friend and the woman are close.
Interpreting	Third stage in the perception process. It involves assigning meaning to stimuli.	Kendrick decides not to ask his classmate out for a date because she is already dating a friend.
Retrieving	Fourth stage in the perception process. It involves recalling information we have stored in our memories.	Kendrick remembers that the two were together at a concert on campus a few weeks earlier.

instance, in a face-to-face meeting with a teacher to challenge a low grade on a paper, you would probably notice not only your instructor's facial reactions and body position but also your own. You might also be attentive to the general feeling you get when going into the instructor's office. And you would probably prepare for the encounter by asking other students what their experiences with the instructor had been with respect to grade challenges.

Perceiving an interpersonal encounter, then, involves much more than hearing the words of another person. Perception is an active and challenging process that involves all five senses: touch, sight, taste, smell, and hearing. Through perception, we gain important information about the interpersonal communication skills of others and of ourselves. For our purposes, then, we define **perception** as a process of using our senses to respond to stimuli. The perception process occurs in four stages (attending and selecting, organizing, interpreting, and retrieving). Because perception is the foundation of all of our interpersonal communication, we spend some time describing each stage (see Table 2.1).

Attending and Selecting

The first stage, **attending and selecting,** requires us to use our visual, auditory, tactile, and olfactory senses to respond to stimuli in our interpersonal environment. When we are attentive and selective, we are **mindful.** Ellen Langer (1989) believes that mindful communicators pay close attention to detail. In other words, being mindful means being observant and aware of your surroundings. In the case of interpersonal communication, this includes engaging your senses. For example, take Dr. Gomez's mindfulness as he attended to the parents' grief, his own personal reaction to the news, and his perceptions of how the couple might perceive him as a medical professional. Further, he is attentive and focused. He saw the couple's sorrowful expressions (sight), held the mother's hand (touch), and listened as they talked about their situation (hearing).

Most of us are not as attentive as Dr. Gomez. We simply don't perceive every situation with complete mindfulness. We are constantly bombarded with stimuli that make it almost impossible to focus on every detail of an encounter. As a result, we use **selective perception.** When we selectively perceive, we decide to attend to things that fulfill our own needs, capture our own interests, or meet our own expectations. In selective perception, we pay attention to some things while ignoring others. You can explore this idea further in an article that discusses how we attend to and select what is important to us from the sometimes overwhelming number of messages we receive each day. Read "Bet You Can't Remember How to Tie the Bows on Your Life Jackets," available through InfoTrac College Edition. Use your Understanding Interpersonal Communication CD-ROM to access InfoTrac College Edition Exercise 2.1: Attending to What Is Important.

In our relationships with others, we use selective perception all the time. For example, let's say that Luke has decided to end his relationship with Melissa. He explains that he thinks it is in her best interest as well as his for them to break up. However, he says that he has learned a lot while in the relationship. Luke continues talking, telling Melissa several of the things he feels he learned from being with her, and explains that he was grateful to have spent time with her.

As Melissa selectively perceives this unexpected conversation, she will probably be attending to the reason why Luke is breaking up with her. Regardless of everything else Luke says, Melissa listens for a particular piece of information. As a result, she filters and ignores other information, such as what Luke learned while being in the relationship. As would most people in such a situation, Melissa wants to know what motivated Luke's decision to break up. In addition to selectively perceiving his words, Melissa also selectively attends to some of Luke's nonverbal signals while ignoring others. His eye contact and tone of voice, for instance, are especially important to her.

In this example, Melissa could consider a number of different stimuli—Luke's behaviors, the time of day, the noises in the room, and so on. But, she remains focused on fulfilling her need to hear why the relationship no longer works for Luke.

Organizing

After we are done selecting and attending to stimuli in our environment, we need to organize them in such a way that we can make sense of them. The **organizing** stage in the perception process requires us to place what are often a number of confusing pieces of information into an understandable, accessible, and orderly fashion.

We frequently categorize when we organize. For example, patients organize information they receive from physicians to reduce their uncertainty about their illness. Because doctors tend to use language that is highly abstract and usually technical, patients must organize the doctor's confusing information into specific and understandable bits of information. In doing so, the researchers found that patients' uncertainty is reduced and that they have a clearer understanding of their illness (Babrow, Hines, & Kasch, 2000).

When we organize, we usually use a **relational schema** (Andersen, 1993), which is a mental framework or memory structure that people rely on to understand experience and to guide their future behavior. We need a recognized way of understanding something or someone. Therefore, we use schema to help sort out the perception process. You may classify your boss according to *leadership style* (autocratic, diplomatic, yielding, and so forth), *work ethic* (hard-working, lazy, and so forth), or *personality characteristic* (rude, compassionate, insincere, and so forth). These schemas help us recognize aspects of our boss's communication effectiveness without our having to do a lot of thinking. Workers frequently use these types of classifications to help them organize the numerous messages given by a supervisor. For example, if the only types of messages that Jenny gets from her boss are insensitive and rude, she will inevitably categorize all of her boss's comments in that manner, regardless of whether the messages are framed that way.

When organizing, we look for consistencies rather than inconsistencies. Most of us would have a difficult time trying to communicate with each person we meet in the subway, in the elevator, on the street, and in the grocery store in an individual manner. We therefore seek out familiar patterns of classifications: seniors, children, men, women, and so forth. Your decision of which classification to use is a selective process because when you choose to include one category, you are necessarily ignoring or eliminating another.

Organizing is essential because it expedites the perception process. However, the impulse to lump people into recognizable categories can be problematic. Using broad generalizations to describe groups of people is considered stereotyping. **Stereotyping** occurs when we have fixed mental images of groups. Not all stereotypes are negative—for instance, many professors stereotype students as wanting to learn or willing to make sacrifices, and many of us view police officers as concerned for our safety. However, stereotypes generally get in the way of effective interpersonal communication. We discuss this problem further in this text because stereotyping affects many aspects of interpersonal communication. When we stereotype others, we use schema without being concerned with individual differences, and such categorization is problematic when we begin to adopt a fixed impression for a group of people. Consider the following dialogue between Jackson and Ryan, two students who happen to be on the school baseball team, as they talk about their first day of class:

JACKSON: What's with all these older students in class?

RYAN: What do you mean?

JACKSON: I mean I need to get an A in this class! It's not fair. They have more time to study because they take only one or two classes. And they keep to themselves.

RYAN: You're nuts! My fiction class last semester had some nontraditional students in there, and I loved it. They helped a lot in study groups come test time.

REVISITING CASE IN POINT

1. Discuss how Dr. Gomez used the process of organizing in his conversation with the Camara family.
2. Discuss how Dr. Gomez used the process of interpreting in his conversation with the Camara family.

 You can answer these questions online under Student Resources for Chapter 2 at the Understanding Interpersonal Communication website.

JACKSON: And they ruined the curve, right?

RYAN: Get rid of these issues, man. You certainly don't want other people to think that all baseball players are dumb jocks, right? Think about what you're saying.

In this scene, Jackson obviously uses a unique schema to communicate about non-traditional-aged learners in his class. What he does is stereotype this group of people as having free time, not wanting to help other students, and being uninvolved in campus activities. Ryan attempts to dispel Jackson's perceptions by focusing on the value of nontraditional students in class. Of course, many other stereotypes have damaging consequences, such as looking at homosexuals as promiscuous, the disabled as unqualified for a job, or the elderly as feeble.

We encounter problems when we act upon our stereotypes in the perception process. When we perceive people to possess a particular characteristic because they belong to a particular group, we risk communication problems. Perceiving men as lacking emotion, immigrants as recipients of public assistance, or car dealers as slick and dishonest makes it difficult for honest and ethical communication to occur. People who stereotype in this way oversimplify the complex process of perception. It's a delicate balance—we need some shortcuts so all the stimuli coming at us doesn't drive us crazy but not so many shortcuts that we treat people unfairly. For a surprising look at how people from other countries perceive people from the United States, use your Understanding Interpersonal Communication CD-ROM to access **Interactive Activity 2.1: Stereotypes about the United States.**

Interpreting

After the process of attention/selection and organization are complete, we are then ready to interpret. When we are **interpreting,** we are assigning meaning to what we perceive. Interpreting is required in every interpersonal encounter. Reflecting on the transactional nature of communication that we discussed in Chapter 1, we need to achieve meaning for interpersonal communication to occur. What should you think of the friend who tells you to "get lost" after an argument? Do you take him literally? Or, what about the neighbor who decides to build a fence and then proceeds to tell you that she loves being your neighbor? How do you assign meaning to the comment made by your sibling who says, "So, do you want a closer relationship with me or not?"

The process of interpreting something is not simple; it is influenced by relational history, personal expectations, and knowledge of the self and other. First, your relational history, a concept we addressed in Chapter 1, affects your perception. Consider how you would perceive a statement by a close friend with whom you have had a relationship for more than 11 years versus a coworker with whom you have had a professional relationship for about a year. Because of your previous relationship experiences, perhaps your friend can get away with being sarcastic or pushy. However, your past experiences with the coworker are limited, and you may not be so open to sarcasm or pushiness. This example reflects the impersonal-interpersonal continuum we addressed in Chapter 1.

Your personal expectations of an individual or situation can also affect how you interpret behavior. Let's say that you work in an office in which the department supervisor, Jonathan, is grouchy and intimidating. Consequently, whenever department meetings are held, workers avoid expressing their views openly, fearing verbal backlash. At one of these meetings, how would you talk about ways to improve efficiency in the office, fearing that Jonathan would react harshly?

In addition to relational history and personal expectations, your knowledge of yourself and others can greatly affect your interpretation of behavior. For instance, are you aware of your personal insecurities and uncertainties? Do they influence how you receive off-the-cuff or insensitive comments? What do you know about your own communication with others? Do you recognize your strengths and shortcomings in an interpersonal encounter? Finally, what do you know about the other person? What shared fields of experience can be identified in your encounter? What assumptions about human behavior do you and others bring into a communication exchange? Such questions can help you assess how much knowledge you have about yourself and about the other communicator.

Retrieving

So far, we have attended to and selected stimuli, organized them, and interpreted them to achieve meaning in the encounter. The final stage of perception, **retrieving,** asks us to recall information stored in our memories. At first glance, retrieving appears to be pretty straightforward. Yet, as you think about this further, you'll see that the retrieval process involves selection as well. At times, we use **selective retention,** a behavior that recalls information that agrees with our perceptions and selectively forgets information that does not. Here is an example that highlights the retrieval process and some potential conflict associated with it.

Crystal sits with her friends as they talk about Professor Wendall. She doesn't really like what she is hearing. They are talking about how boring the professor is and that his tests are too hard. They also make fun of his Southern drawl as they imitate his teaching. Crystal remembers that she had Professor Wendall for a class more than two years ago, but she doesn't recall him being such a bad professor. In fact, she remembers the biology course she took from him as challenging and interesting. It doesn't make sense that her friends don't like Professor Wendall.

So, why do Crystal's friends and Crystal perceive Professor Wendall differently? Crystal has retrieved information about her professor differently. He may have ridiculed students, but Crystal doesn't recall that. She remembers his accent, but she does not remember it causing any problems. She also recollects Wendall's exams to be fair; she never received anything below a grade of B. Crystal's retrieval process, then, has influenced her perception of Professor Wendall in the classroom. When we exercise selective retention in the perception process, then, it affects our communication with others.

So far, we have examined the perception process and its components. As we know, interpersonal communication can be difficult at times. Understanding how perception functions in those encounters helps clarify potential problems. We now turn our attention to several influences on our perception process. As you will learn, the accuracy of our perceptions is affected by a number of factors.

Factors such as our past relationships, personal expectations, and knowledge of other people influence how we interpret the behavior and messages of others. Madonna is an example of a celebrity whose words and actions are interpreted in many different ways. Some see her as an overly aggressive entertainer who's just out for more money. Others see her as a visionary trendsetter whose creativity has kept her in the public eye for more than two decades. What sort of past relationships and personal expectations do you think influence these varying interpretations?

Facing *Change*

Although we generally accept that most of us have similar life experiences, our cultural backgrounds influence those experiences. In fact, how we perceive a person, event, or activity is affected by culture. Further, self-concepts can be influenced by culture. Think about a newly arrived immigrant to the United States. How might his or her perception and self-concept be affected? In other words, discuss how cultural background affects an immigrant's perception and self-concept.

 Use your Understanding Interpersonal Communication CD-ROM to watch the CNN video clip "Accent Reduction," which highlights the fact that people speaking with a different accent or dialect often face discrimination or negative perceptions in professional and social settings. Click on the "CNN & Change" icon in the menu  at left, then click on "Video Menu" in the menu bar at the top of the screen. Select "Accent Reduction" to watch the video (it takes a minute for the video to load). As you watch the video, notice how newcomers to the United States work to reduce their "foreign" accents to fit into U.S. society. Have you ever felt that you needed to change something fundamental about yourself to improve the way others perceive you? You can respond to this and other analysis questions by clicking on "Analysis" in the menu bar at the top of the screen. When you've answered all the questions, click "Done" to compare your answers to those provided by the authors.

Influences on Perception

When we perceive activities, events, or other people, those perceptions are a result of many variables. In other words, we don't all perceive our environment in the same way because individual perceptions are shaped by individual differences. We now discuss five factors that shape our perceptions.

Culture

Culture is an important teacher of perception (Nakayama & Martin, 1999) and provides the meaning we give to our perceptions (Chen and Starosta, 1998). In Chapter 3, you will learn how culture pervades our lives and how communication is affected by culture. With regard to perception, culture dictates how something should be organized and interpreted. For instance, Bantu refugees from Somalia perceive time differently after they arrive in the United States. In Somalia, they did not have wall clocks or watches, but in the United States, they learn to be punctual and watch the clock. William Hamilton (2004) notes:

> Bantu parents learn that hitting their children is discouraged, though that was how they were disciplined in Africa. . . . they learn that Fourth of July fireworks are exploded to entertain not kill, and that being hit by a water balloon, as Bantu children were in one incident at school, is a game and not a hateful fight. (p. A14)

As another example, in the United States, we expect people to maintain direct eye contact during conversation. This conversational expectation is influenced by a European American cultural value. However, Japanese culture does not dictate direct eye contact during conversation, so we may feel a classmate from Japan is not listening to us during conversation when he or she doesn't maintain eye contact (Ishii-Kuntz, 1997). As a final illustration, although it may be difficult for someone without any religious connection to understand, Islam and Christianity guide many Lebanese American families in virtually every decision of life, including birth, death, education, courtship, marriage, divorce, and contraception (Hashem, 1997). For another example of how perceptions stemming from cultural beliefs affect people in important aspects of their lives, read the article "Asian-Americans Face Great Wall; Perceptions, Cultural Traditions Hinder Advancement to Top Corporate Ranks," available through InfoTrac College Edition. Use your Understanding Interpersonal Communication CD-ROM to access InfoTrac College Edition Exercise 2.2: Cultural Perceptions and the Glass Ceiling.

You can see, then, that cultural heritage affects how people perceive the world. In turn, that same cultural heritage affects how they communicate with and receive communication from others. So cultural variation is sometimes the reason we can't understand why someone does something or the reason that others question our behavior. Although it's natural to believe that others look at things the same way you do, cultures can vary tremendously in their practices, and these differences affect

Our culture influences how we perceive ourselves and others. By the same token, when we immerse ourselves in another culture, our perception of ourselves and others can evolve and change.

perception. We will delve further into the effects of culture on interpersonal communication in Chapter 3.

Sex and Gender

Sex refers to the biological make-up of an individual (male or female). **Gender** refers to the learned behaviors a culture associates with being a male or female. For example, we have a masculine or feminine gender. If we possess both masculine and feminine traits in equally large amounts, we are called *androgynous,* and possessing relatively low amounts of masculinity and femininity is termed *undifferentiated* (see Figure 2.1). It is possible to be a masculine female or a feminine male.

Research examining sex differences shows that men and women differ in their perceptions and perceptual ability. In an interesting study looking at perceptions of body type, researchers found that boys and girls in kindergarten and second grade differed in preferences for body types. Girls preferred a thinner figure than boys, and girls perceived thinness as both attractive and feminine. Boys preferred more athletic builds by kindergarten and were indirectly communicating "preferences for being smart, moderately strong, and somewhat prone to fighting" (Miller, Plant, & Hanke, 1993, p. 56).

Many of these differences are a result of the way men and women have been raised. **Gender role socialization** is the process by which women and men learn the gender roles appropriate to their sex (for example, being masculine if you are biologically a male). This socialization affects the way the sexes perceive the world. Messages about masculinity and femininity are communicated to children early in life, and these messages stick with us into adulthood. Sandra Bem (1993) notes that when we understand and organize our world around masculinity and femininity, we

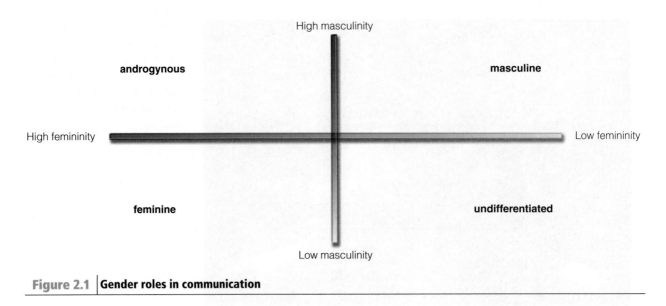

Figure 2.1 | **Gender roles in communication**

are using a **gender schema.** Specifically, she believes that through a schema, we process and categorize beliefs, ideas, and events as either masculine or feminine. If new information doesn't fit our gender schema, Bem maintains that we simply discard it.

Consider your perceptions of the following situations:

- A 5-year-old boy playing house with a 6-year-old neighbor girl
- A retired elderly male dancing with another male at a New Year's Eve party
- A newborn girl wearing a pink dress with flowers
- An adolescent female helping her father change the oil in his car

Did any of these situations contradict how you normally view male and female behavior? Did the age of the person make a difference? If so, why? What contributed to these perceptions? Parents? Teachers? Peers? Games? In all likelihood, each of these—in some way—has helped shape your current perceptions.

Men and women may look at things differently (Tannen, 1990), depending on what gender schema they bring to a circumstance. As people sort out the various stimuli in their environment, gender cannot be ignored nor devalued. Certainly, men and women can reject gender prescriptions and help society expand its perceptual expectations. However, most people continue to look at their worlds with rigid interpretations of the sexes, resulting in perceptions that may be distorted or inaccurate. To further explore the power of perception in relation to gender and communication, read the article "Exploring the Impact of Gender Role Self-Perception on Communication Style," available through InfoTrac College Edition. Use your Understanding Interpersonal Communication CD-ROM to access InfoTrac College Edition Exercise 2.3: Sex, Gender, and Perception about Communication.

Physical

Our physical make-up is another element that contributes to variations in perceptions. The physical factors affecting perception are wide in scope and include age, health, and ability, among others. For instance, *age* influences our perceptions; we seem to perceive things differently as we age because of our life experiences. Being

single and in debt at age 19 is different than being in debt as a single parent of three young children at age 45. No one is relying on a single teenager for sustenance, whereas a parent needs to consider the three children at home. The aging process allows us to frame our life experiences. Our *health*, too, helps shape perceptions. We broadly define health to include such things as fatigue, stress, biorhythms, and physical ability. For instance, women with HIV/AIDS (Cline & McKenzie, 1996), individuals who are terminally ill (Thompson, 1996), and alcoholics (Thomas & Seibold, 1996) have all been found to have limitations in their perceptual abilities. Some people are simply not physically able to see another person's behaviors or to listen attentively to his or her words. Others need some accommodation to be able to attend to stimuli in their surroundings. Our senses vary, often according to our physical limitations. Imagine the difficulty a wheelchair-bound individual has navigating nonaccessible curbs compared to someone who does not use a wheelchair. If you don't use a wheelchair, you won't perceive the curbs as potential obstacles.

To read an interesting article about how a particular physical factor, our hair, affects our perceptions of ourselves and others, use your Understanding Interpersonal Communication CD-ROM to access **Interactive Activity 2.2: Social Perceptions of Hair and Baldness.** And for dramatic—and fun—examples of how our visual capabilities affect our perceptions, use your Understanding Interpersonal Communication CD-ROM to access **Interactive Activity 2.3: Optical Illusions and Perception.**

Technology

Now more than ever, technology affects our perceptions. The Internet, in particular—which has little oversight and no accountability—requires us to be critical in our perceptions. We need to remember that websites have been created by a variety of people with different backgrounds (for example, psychiatrists, talk-show hosts, video store owners, and so on). Keep in mind that the trustworthiness of websites varies.

In addition, technology makes possible the cultivation of online relationships. However, keep in mind that, in contrast to interacting face to face, the perception process is influenced in these types of relationships (Barnes, 2003). Relying upon on-screen text and a downloaded picture is potentially problematic. First, the individual might provide false information (and a picture that might not be authentic). Second, we are unable to read the facial expressions, listen to the vocal characteristics, look at the clothing, watch the body movement, and observe the eye contact of the other person. In sum, we are relationally shortchanged because we can't perceive the whole picture. We are receiving only what the other person wants us to receive. Likewise, we communicate what we wish to communicate to the other person. As Sue Barnes (2003) observes, "screen names, signature lines, personal profiles, and personal Web pages can be carefully designed to present an image of self" (p. 133). With the Internet, then, trying to organize and interpret information is challenging.

The Internet is not the only technological development that affects our perceptions. For example, consider how our perceptions are altered when we observe people with cell phones, pagers, or palm organizers. Couple these technologies with other differences, and you'll inevitably witness perceptual influences. For instance, what do you think when you see a teenager talking on a cell phone? Now, consider your reaction to an older man in a suit talking on a cell phone while walking down the street. Do you experience any difference in perception?

We can't escape the influence that technology has on our perceptions. This influence occurs in both overt and covert ways. We may be conscious of how our perceptions change or be unaware of technology's influence. Nowadays, the reaction we have to electronic technology ranges from indifference to awe. At times, we expect everyone we meet to own some technology; other times, we are impressed by the latest technology, privately vowing to own it once we have enough money! We return to the topic of technology and interpersonal communication in Chapter 11.

Self-Concept

A final factor that shapes our perceptions is self-concept, which we discuss later in this chapter. For now, it's important to point out that the perceptions we hold of ourselves are influential in the perception process. We define **self-concept** as a relatively stable set of perceptions a person holds of himself or herself. Our self-concept is rather consistent from one situation to another. For instance, our core beliefs and values about our intellectual curiosity or charitable ways stay fairly constant. Self-concept is flexible, though; for example, our beliefs about our ability to climb a mountain may differ at age 30 and age 65. And imagine the self-concept of the man who tackled the Appalachian trail with a prosthetic leg!

Self-concept affects our perceptions. Generally, statements from people we trust and respect carry more weight than statements from those we don't trust and respect. Consider, then, the way you would perceive the same words depending on whether they came from a close friend or from a classmate. For example, if a classmate tells you that she thinks you don't listen well, you might not be as willing to consider changing your behavior as if a close friend makes the same observation. You would probably give the close friend's words more credibility. However, keep in mind that the close friend may not be accurate in his or her perceptions.

To further explore the factors that influence our perceptions, such as our needs, values, and education, use your Understanding Interpersonal Communication CD-ROM to access **Interactive Activity 2.4: Perception Filters**. To read an article that examines the link between perception and the self, particularly regarding our positive and negative impressions of others, read the article "Quality Interpersonal Communication—Perception and Reality," available through InfoTrac College Edition. Use your Understanding Interpersonal Communication CD-ROM to access **InfoTrac College Edition Exercise 2.4: Positive and Negative First Impressions.**

Thus far, we have given you a sense of what perception is, noted why it's important in interpersonal communication, and identified some significant influences on the perception process. Throughout our discussion, you have seen that it's virtually impossible to separate our sense of self from our perceptions. Now, we delve further into the self and explain the importance of the self in interpersonal communication. We start by explaining the self and its dimensions.

Understanding the Self: The "I's" Have It

How do you see yourself? This is the key question guiding our discussion of the self. Answering this question is not easy. Certainly, we realize that you can't answer this question in a word or two. Previously, we noted that our self-concept is both fixed and flexible. It makes sense, then, that you would inevitably begin your answer to this question with "well, it depends."

This chapter will help you formulate and clarify a response to this question. If you think "it depends," you're partially correct. However, there are ways to articulate a more thoughtful response. We hope that you you will think about this question as you read this section. We are guided by the following principle as we introduce this information: To have a relationship with someone else, you must first have a relationship with your self. In other words, communication begins and ends with you.

Self-Concept

Earlier, we defined self-concept as a relatively fixed set of perceptions we hold of ourselves. The self-concept is everything we believe about ourselves. We hold a collection of perceptions that are more stable than fleeting. However, that does not mean that our self-concept is permanent. It changes. One reason it changes is because self-concept emerges from our various interpersonal encounters with others. George Herbert Mead (1934), more than 70 years ago, posited that communication (with others) forms personal identity. His theory, called **symbolic interactionism,** suggests that our understandings of ourselves and the world around us are shaped by our interactions with those around us.

To begin our discussion, consider two versions of the following story regarding Terrence Washington.

Ethics & Choice

After living in an abusive home environment for nearly all her life, Karena Paulsen was looking forward to her upcoming marriage to Nick Corsetti. The two had dated for over two years and felt comfortable with each other and each other's values. Yet, Karena's feelings of self-worth became compromised one day as she and Nick discussed having a family. Karena wanted to wait a few years and try to get her footing at her new job. Nick wanted to have children immediately.

As the two discussed the issue, it became apparent that Karena's past would come into play. Nick told her that the real reason that she wanted to postpone a family had everything to do with her childhood. He reasoned that she had never worked out her "childhood demons," which would prevent her from really loving children of her own. Karena denied such an allegation, trying to explain to Nick her anxiety about discussing her past with him again.

The low-key conversation eventually turned into a shouting match. Karena accused Nick of resurrecting an old issue, and Nick responded by telling Karena that as long as she avoided going to counseling, she couldn't really move on with the subject. In fact, he felt that she needed to get in touch with who she was. He felt that her relationship with her father was significant in how Karena perceived herself.

Karena's and Nick's conflict underscores how important perceptions of the self are in interpersonal relationships. First, comment on whether or not Nick should push Karena to talk about her background with him again. Second, what ethical system of communication should be followed in this example (categorical imperative, utilitarianism, ethic of care, golden mean, significant choice)?

Use your Understanding Interpersonal Communication CD-ROM to access an interactive version of this scenario on the Understanding Interpersonal Communication website. Look under Student Resources for Chapter 2 and click on the "Ethics & Choice" menu at left. The interactive version of this scenario allows you to choose an appropriate response to this dilemma and then see what consequences your choice brings about. You can also compare your answers to the questions at the end of the scenario to those provided by the authors and, if requested, email your response to your instructor.

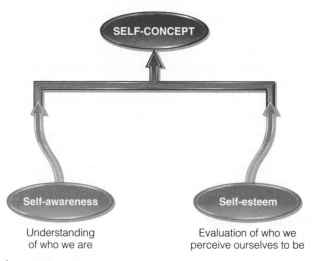

Figure 2.2 | **Components of self-concept**

As a self-employed painter, Terrence is completely reliant upon small projects to make a living. His recent surgery to correct tendinitis, though, has caused him to be laid up at home. As a result, he is unable to continue to paint homes. His inability to take on jobs has not only caused him some financial problems but has also affected his psychological well-being. Terrence now feels fairly useless and can't seem to shake his feeling of self-doubt.

Now consider Terrence's situation again. This time, though, Terrence is visited by his friends, who assure him that this circumstance is only temporary. One friend suggests that he help her figure out a color scheme for her living room. Another friend gets Terrence a temporary job advising customers in a local paint store. Although he is unable to paint homes, Terrence finds himself busier than ever. His self-doubts about his future begin to dissipate, and his feelings about himself take on a positive cast.

The two examples result in different self-concepts for Terrence. In the first example, we see a man who is beginning to doubt his own abilities. His self-concept will likely proceed into a negative spiral: He wants to get better, but to get better, he needs to feel good about himself. Because he doesn't feel good about himself, he won't get better. Our second example underscores the importance of others in our self-concept. Terrence's friends will positively affect both his self-concept and his career ambitions.

Terrence's self-concept is influenced by both an awareness of his self and an assessment of his potential. We call these influences self-awareness and self-esteem, the two primary components of self-concept (Figure 2.2). As we examine these two, keep in mind that, together, they help create our self-concept. You'll find that they overlap to some degree.

Self-Awareness

According to symbolic interaction theorists, we begin our lives as blank slates—that is, we are born with no consciousness of who we are. We rely on our parents, guardians, or family members to help us recognize our selves. **Self-awareness** is our understanding of who we are. We soon realize, for instance, that when we hear our parents cooing to us, we exist. The adults around us soon start talking, using all kinds of baby talk. This talk may not sound all that important, but it starts the process of self-awareness.

In Terrence Washington's case, his self-awareness stems from the belief that he is a painter who has successfully made a living painting other people's homes. Self-awareness serves as the first step toward understanding our self-esteem.

Self-Esteem

Self-esteem is a bit more complicated than self-awareness. Our **self-esteem** is an evaluation of who we perceive ourselves to be. In a sense, our self-esteem is our self-worth, or how we feel about our talents, abilities, knowledge, expertise, and appearance. Our self-esteem comprises the images we hold—that is, our social roles (for example, father, receptionist, electrician, and so on), the words we use to describe these social roles (for example, doting grandparent, courteous police officer, skilled nurse, and so on), and how others see us in those roles (for example, competent, negligible, thorough, and so on).

We develop our self-esteem as a result of overcoming setbacks, achieving our goals, and helping others in their pursuits (Sternberg & Whitney, 2002). Our feelings of self-worth may not be jeopardized if we think we have beaten obstacles along the way. Elizabeth Graham (1997; 2003) found that even ex-spouses following a divorce do not remain angry forever. So, what appeared to be an insurmountable relationship episode (divorce) has actually resulted in couples being able to not only talk to one another but also to retain some of the original feelings of affirmation they once held for each other.

Keep in mind that other people do not always enhance our feelings of self-worth. Regardless of how many family or friends surround us during difficult times, it might be the case that nothing helps us feel better about ourselves. In fact, at times, others may unwittingly contribute to our negative self-perceptions. For example, if you try to encourage someone after the loss of a relational partner by showering him with platitudes or cliche phrases (for example, "I'm sure you'll make it" or "Hey, not all relationships were meant to be"), you may unknowingly cause your friend to feel worse.

One more point about self-esteem. Like our self-concept, self-esteem may fluctuate. One day we consider ourselves to be excellent, and the next day we can change our opinion. This variation in esteem is often due to our interactions with others in our lives. We usually listen more carefully to those we admire or whose previous advice was worthwhile. We generally reject the opinions of those we don't know. Most of us are able to understand that one situation shouldn't necessarily affect our feelings of self-worth.

Self-Fulfilling Prophecy

In addition to a person's self-concept, the self is also formed, in part, by the predictions you make about yourself. When something happens because you expected it to happen, you have created a **self-fulfilling prophecy.** These prophecies may either be *self-imposed,* which occurs when your own expectations influence your behavior,

> **Your** *Turn*
>
> Think about a time when your self-concept was affected by your communication with another person. What were the circumstances of the communication? How did your dialogue influence your self-concept? Were your self-awareness and your self-esteem both affected? Use examples to describe and explain your experiences. If you'd like, you can use your student workbook to complete this activity.

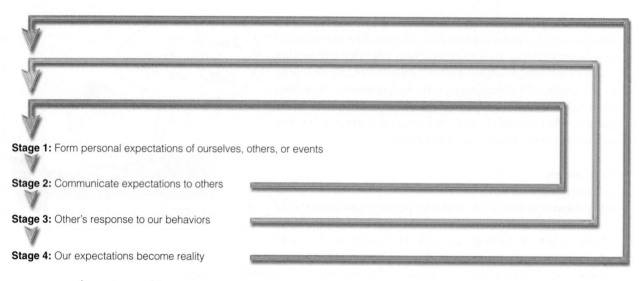

Stage 1: Form personal expectations of ourselves, others, or events

Stage 2: Communicate expectations to others

Stage 3: Other's response to our behaviors

Stage 4: Our expectations become reality

Figure 2.3 | Stages of self-fulfilling prophecies

or *other-imposed*, which occurs when the expectations of another person influence your behavior. Self-fulfilling prophecies can take place within a number of interpersonal situations, from the family to the workplace:

- Mario is nervous about talking to someone he respects and admires, thinking that he probably is going to blunder when he speaks with that person. When he meets the person, he trips over his words.
- A professor tells Sheila that he respects the comments she gave in class and that he anticipates an excellent final term paper. Sheila receives an A on the paper.
- Hank approaches a job interview thinking that his job expertise and communication skills will get him the job. The job is offered to him.

Although each of these prophecies is different, self-fulfilling prophecies usually follow a pattern. First, we form expectations of ourselves, others, or particular events. Next, we communicate those expectations to others. Third, others respond to our behaviors. Fourth, our expectations become reality, and our expectations confirm our original thinking about ourselves. However, each stage returns to the first stage, because the original perception prompted the prophecy itself (Figure 2.3). Here is an example of how self-fulfilling prophecies function in a person's life.

As a young child, Jennifer felt that she was awkward around groups of people. She wasn't particularly social and seemed to have a tough time talking to someone face to face, especially in social settings (Step 1: Form expectation of event). While attending a wedding reception, Rodney, one of the guests at her table, asked Jennifer to dance. She told him that she was not a good dancer, that she was not interested in making a fool of herself on the dance floor, and did not want to dance with Rodney (Step 2: Communicate expectation to other). When Rodney returned to his seat, he thought to himself: "Wow, she is shy! And talk about not wanting to hang out with people" (Step 3: Others respond to behavior). On the other hand, Jennifer thought that Rodney did not want to talk to her because she was not social or out-going (Step 4: Confirmation of original perception).

To read about a famous and interesting study that tested the power of self-fulfilling prophecies in an elementary school class, use your Understanding Interpersonal Communication CD-ROM to access **Interactive Activity 2.5: Pygmalion in the Classroom.** In addition, further explore how the ideas of self-concept and self-fulfilling prophecy can apply to the workplace by reading the article "Quality Interpersonal Communication—Managing Self-Concept," available through InfoTrac College Edition. Use your Understanding Interpersonal Communication CD-ROM to access **InfoTrac College Edition Exercise 2.5: The Self and the Workplace.**

As you can tell, the self doesn't simply develop without being influenced in some way. After you gain an understanding of your self, you can begin to address how you present your self to others. Researchers refer to this as identity management, which is the topic we explore in the next section.

Identity Management: Let's Face It

At the heart of the self is **identity management,** which refers to the ways we handle the various situations in which we find ourselves. When we manage our identities, we decide upon a particular communication behavior to influence how others perceive us. Another important reason to communicate our identities is to be active citizens. As Nikolas Coupland and Jon Nussbaum (1993) state, "to be our social selves, to be individuals functioning within social and political communities, we need to *voice* our identities and so participate in the reproduction of these communities" (p. 1).

One of the first people to discuss identity management was sociologist Erving Goffman (1959). Goffman believed that identity is best explained using an analogy to theatrical performances. He believed that "when an individual appears before others, he [or she] will have many motives for trying to control the impression they receive of the situation" (p. 15). Goffman goes on to say that we play characters in a performance and are concerned about "coherence among setting, appearance, and manner" (p. 25). In other words, we are actors who "perform" for the audiences around us.

This image of a theatrical production may seem a bit odd to you. After all, who wants to admit to "acting" in an interpersonal encounter? Yet, Goffman believes that we all take on particular social roles. We also manage these roles to achieve meaning in our relationships with others.

Identity management does not happen without some risk and consequence. For instance, suppose that Victor is a 25-year-old who decides to come back to live with his parents for financial reasons, one of a group of people researchers have called "boomerang kids" (Okimoto & Stegall, 1987). The rules that were once part of the household (for example, "No profanity" or "Clean up your room") may now seem pretty out of date to Victor. As he figures out how to act at home (establishing his identity), he may reject the household rules because he feels that he is too old to abide by them. Yet, what happens if his mom or dad requires adherence to the rules? Aren't they also managing their identity as Victor manages his? How he handles these different identities will affect the quality of the interpersonal communication Victor has with his parents.

Our need to present both a positive and a negative face in our interactions can have an enormous impact on our communication with others, particularly when we try to communicate effectively with someone who is very different from us.

Because identity management requires some risk, we may find ourselves in a situation that compromises our sense of self. Therefore, we become preoccupied with protecting the image we decide to present to others. In doing so, we are engaged in facework.

Identity Management and Facework

In interpersonal interactions, people shape their identities to display a particular sense of self. When we get into conversations with others, we offer our identity and hope that others will accept that identity. This is essential to our self-concept overall and to our self-esteem in particular. The image of the self that we present to others in our interpersonal encounters is called **face.** Generally, face is somewhat automatic (Cupach & Metts, 1994). We take it for granted that there is a give and take in maintaining face. In other words, following the transactional nature of communication that we identified in Chapter 1, both communicators in an interaction are responsible for facework. As Cupach and Metts (1994) conclude, "face is not merely what one individual dictates. Rather, partners negotiate (usually tacitly) who each other 'is' with respect to one another" (p. 96).

Typically, we present two types of face in our conversations with others: positive face and negative face. **Positive face** pertains to our desire to be liked by significant others in our lives. We have positive face when others make efforts to confirm our beliefs, respect our abilities, and value what we value. That's not to say that individuals have to agree with everything we have to say or with everything we believe (that would be impossible!). Most of us simply want to relate to people who make efforts to understand, to appreciate, and to respect our perceptions and competencies.

Negative face refers to our desire for others to refrain from imposing their will on us. Negative face is maintained when people respect our individuality and our uniqueness and others avoid interfering with our actions or beliefs. Again, this is not to say that people will simply become dutiful and obedient in our conversations without challenging us. Rather, we're suggesting that in our interpersonal encounters, we should be flexible enough to understand that people periodically have a need to be autonomous.

When we receive messages that do not support either our positive or negative face, our identities become threatened. Face threats can jeopardize meaning in an interpersonal encounter. As Joseph Forgas (2002) concluded, "to fail in a performance leads to loss of face, which upsets the pattern of social intercourse" (p. 29). If our positive face is threatened—such as when another person challenges our skills—we have to figure out how to deal with the threat to our identity. For instance, let's say that Pat is a hairstylist and that Nola, a client of 19 years, threatens Pat's positive face by asking Pat, "Where *did* you find this horrid color? In your attic?" Because Pat takes pride in her abilities, this insult may be pretty difficult to overcome. Pat will have to figure out a way to preserve her positive face with Nola. Indeed, this process happens frequently in our lives, and we have to learn how to handle these face threats. In the United States, we are normally not conditioned to help others "save" their face (Pan, 2000) although people in other cultures (for example, Asian cultures) are attuned to maintaining everyone's face in an interaction.

Strategies for Identity Management

Identity management is not an easy undertaking. A number of variables and issues must be considered: the type of relationship, the topic of conversation, the extent to which face is threatened, and so forth. How do we manage our identity and preserve threats to our face at the same time? Because managing our identities is so important, we now examine four strategies for handling those times when our individuality and face are threatened.

Pay Attention to Timing

Sometimes it's okay to stay silent in a conversation rather than asserting a particular identity with another. Being insensitive to the timing of identity management may complicate an already uncomfortable situation. For instance, imagine telling an interviewer that you are not the type of person who is interested in doing "meaningless jobs" for the boss. Consider what might happen if you wear clothing to the interview that you feel represents your identity but that is not appropriate for the job. You might think that such strategies help the interviewer perceive who you truly are before you accept the job. Yet, ignoring the timing of your identity management may not even get you the job!

Concentrate on the Message

Forget worrying about the future; commit to the conversation now. Show that you are involved in what is going on and focus on what's taking place. So, for example, if you meet a person to whom you're attracted, be less concerned with what impression you're making on the other person and more focused on the content of the message.

REVISITING CASE IN POINT

1. Discuss how identity management functioned in the interaction between Dr. Gomez and the Camara family.
2. How does "face" relate to the interaction between Dr. Gomez and Elise and Barry Camara?

You can answer these questions online under Student Resources for Chapter 2 at the Understanding Interpersonal Communication website.

Communication Assessment Test

Self-Monitoring Scale

Directions: The statements below concern your personal reactions to different situations. No two statements are exactly alike, so consider each statement carefully before answering. If a statement is *true* or *mostly true* as applied to you, place a T next to the question. If a statement is *false* or *mostly false* as applied to you, place an F next to the question. You can also take this test online under Student Resources for Chapter 2 at the Understanding Interpersonal Communication website.

_____ 1. I find it hard to imitate the behavior of people.

_____ 2. My behavior is usually an expression of my true inner feelings, attitudes, and beliefs.

_____ 3. At parties and social gatherings, I do not attempt to do or say things that others will like.

_____ 4. I can argue for only those ideas that I already believe.

_____ 5. I can make impromptu speeches even on topics about which I have almost no information.

_____ 6. I guess I put on a show to impress or entertain people.

_____ 7. When I am uncertain how to act in a social situation, I look to the behavior of others for cues.

_____ 8. I would probably make a good actor.

_____ 9. I rarely seek the advice of my friends to choose movies, books, or music.

_____ 10. I sometimes appear to others to be experiencing deeper emotions than I actually am.

_____ 11. I laugh more when I watch a comedy with others than when alone.

_____ 12. In groups of people, I am rarely the center of attention.

_____ 13. In different situations and depending who I am with, I often act as if I am different people.

_____ 14. I am not particularly good at making other people like me.

_____ 15. Even if I am not enjoying myself, I often pretend to be having a good time.

_____ 16. I'm not always the person I appear to be.

_____ 17. I would not change my opinions (or the way I do things) in order to please someone or win their favor.

_____ 18. I have considered being an entertainer.

_____ 19. To get along and be liked, I tend to be what people expect me to be rather than anything else.

_____ 20. I have never been good at games like charades or improvisational acting.

_____ 21. I have trouble changing my behavior to suit different people and different situations.

_____ 22. At a party, I let others keep the jokes and stories going.

_____ 23. I feel a bit awkward in company and do not present myself as well as I should.

_____ 24. I can look anyone in the eye and tell a lie with a straight face (if it is for a right end).

_____ 25. I may deceive people by being friendly when I really dislike them.

Scoring

Give yourself one point for each of the following questions that you marked with an F:

1, 2, 3, 4, 9, 12, 14, 17, 19, 20, 21, 22, 23

Give yourself one point for each of the following questions that you marked with a T:

5, 6, 7, 8, 10, 11, 13, 15, 16, 18, 24, 25

Add up the points. A score between 0 and 12 indicates that you are relatively low in your self-monitoring. A score between 13 and 25 indicates that you are relatively high in your self-monitoring.

From M. Snyder, 1974, Self-monitoring of expressive behavior. Journal of Personality and Social Psychology, 30, 526–537. Copyright © 1974 by the American Psychological Association. Reprinted by permission.

Stay Culturally Aware

As we discuss in Chapter 3, we need to pay attention to cultural differences in communication, particularly when we manage our identities. Because cultural identity has a profound effect on our interpersonal communication (Lustig & Koester, 2000), maintaining cultural awareness is paramount in identity management. For instance, some Spaniards address individuals by titles, such as *Profesor* for teacher, and *Ingeniero* for an engineer (Morrison, Conaway, & Borden, 1994), and some elderly African Americans prefer to be called Mr., Ms., or Mrs. to show respect (Stroman, 2000). Because culture affects who we are, what we believe, how we view the world, and with whom we communicate, it necessarily influences identity management.

Practice Self-Monitoring

People vary in their abilities to pay attention to their own actions and the actions of others (Snyder, 1979). The term **self-monitoring** refers to the extent to which people actively think about and control their public behaviors and actions. Self-monitoring is important in identity management because people who are aware of their behaviors and the effects of their behaviors in a conversation are viewed as more competent communicators (Hamacheck, 1992). Practicing self-monitoring too much will result in being preoccupied with details that may be unimportant. On the other hand, being ignorant of your strengths and shortcomings in a conversation is just as problematic. Finding a reasonable middle ground in self-monitoring is critical in identity management.

Perception, the Self, and Interpersonal Communication

Think back to Dr. Gomez and his communication with the grieving parents at the beginning of this chapter. Most of us will never be in this position; however, like the physician, a link exists between our perceptions, our sense of self, and our communication with others. The following four conclusions regarding perception, the self, and interpersonal communication illustrate how the three are closely related.

Each person operates with a personal set of perceptions. To understand this conclusion, consider **implicit personality theory,** which suggests we fill in the blanks when identifying characteristics of people. We use a few characteristics to draw inferences about others. We believe that certain traits go together and communicate with people on this basis. For example, consider how you fill in the following sentences (choose from the words in parentheses):

Dr. Hess is warm, sensitive, and (intelligent, dumb).
Dr. Aldine is rude, distant, and (compassionate, temperamental).

If you chose "intelligent" in the first sentence and "temperamental" in the second sentence, you are prone to the **halo effect,** which states that you will match like qualities with each other. A **positive halo** occurs when you place positive qualities (warm, sensitive, and intelligent) together. A **negative halo** exists when you place negative qualities (unintelligent, rude, and temperamental) together.

Implicit personality theory permits us to effectively manage a lot of information about another person. However, be careful of overusing this theory when communicating with others. Don't perceive characteristics in a person that don't exist. Responding to people according to such predispositions can lead to problems in interpersonal communication.

Perceptual problems can inhibit interpersonal communication. Perceptual errors can lead to problems in our communication with others. For example, **attribution theory** (Heider, 1958) examines how we create explanations or attach meaning to someone's behavior. Fritz Heider (1958) once said that we are all "naive psychologists" in that we try to uncover reasons for people's actions, yet we may have no real understanding of the person nor the circumstances surrounding the actions.

The attribution process can be problematic because our attributions are often influenced by our feelings for another person. For instance, have you ever arranged to meet someone for coffee and that person showed up late? What were your thoughts while waiting? If the person was someone you liked, you probably attributed the lateness to something out of his or her control, such as car trouble, congested traffic, disobedient children, and so forth. If the person was someone you didn't know well or didn't like, you probably attributed the delay to something within the person's control. Perhaps you viewed the person's behavior as intentional. Yet, the person might have been late for unforeseen circumstances. We may be "naive," then, to the number of different influences on behavior. In Chapter 4, we look further into how feelings and emotions affect our relationships with others.

The self undergoes a continual process of modification. Our sense of who we are changes as our relationships change. In other words, our identity is a process, not a constant. This conclusion implies that we and our relationships are changing. Consequently, our interpersonal communication should reflect these changes. Think about the way you were as a sophomore in high school. Now look at who you are now. Your perceptions of your own strengths and shortcomings have inevitably changed over the years. Imagine what it would be like if you didn't change or if others didn't change. You'd get pretty angry at someone who still treated you as an adolescent after you became an adult.

The self responds to stimuli. To understand this conclusion, consider the fact that we respond to people (father or mother), surroundings (noise level or lighting), and technology (Internet site or television program). Each has the capacity to affect the self. In other words, the self is vulnerable to a variety of stimuli.

Choices for Checking Perceptions and Improving Self-Concept

You should be developing a clear idea about the importance of perception and the self in our communication with others. How can you work toward checking your perceptions so that you don't make erroneous assumptions about others or their behavior? What can you do to improve your self-concept? How do our perceptions and self-concepts function in our interpersonal communication? Let's look at a number of skills to consider as you respond to these questions.

Improving Perception Checking

When we check our perceptions, we attempt to rid ourselves of predisposed biases and images of people that we hold. Checking our perceptions also helps build meaning in our relationships. Let's examine the five skills of perception checking.

Skill *Spotlight*

Distinguish Facts from Inferences

To improve our perception, we need to recognize that facts and inferences have different meanings. As we noted, facts are things we know to be true. Facts may be stated only after we have observed or experienced something.

Inferences, on the other hand, may be made at any time and can extend beyond our observations. Inferences can be presented by anyone, and they can reference the past, present, or future. The accuracy of inferences should be suspect because they are essentially subjective assumptions given by an individual.

Consider the following situation. Lonny, dressed in a suit and tie and carrying a briefcase, is standing in line at a coffee shop. He appears to be happy because he has a smile on his face. The first sentence is a statement of fact; you are able to observe Lonny's location, clothing, and accessories. The third sentence, though, is an inference. Just because Lonny is smiling, it doesn't mean he is happy. You cannot verify Lonny's emotional state through observation.

We need to take extra care to distinguish facts from inferences in our perceptions. It's impossible to avoid making inferences in our lives. And, at times, doing so is necessary in our relationships. Yet, when we evaluate the people and the world around us, making the distinction between facts and inferences will help us be more accurate in our perceptions. In turn, we will be less likely to jump to conclusions in our interactions.

Skills at Work At work, we need to pay particular attention to differentiating between facts and inferences. There are social, collegial, and legal implications to confusing these two. For instance, if Jennifer sees Scott staring at a coworker, she may make the inference that Scott is attracted to that coworker. Jennifer may, in turn, communicate her perception to another, who then may turn around and tell another employee. Soon, despite the fact that Scott was not attracted to the coworker at whom he was staring, a workplace rumor has started. This rumor may affect the working environment, the level of trust among coworkers, and may even influence how workplace policy is written. Can you identify other consequences of confusing facts and inferences in the workplace?

Understand Your Personal Worldview

Each of us enters a communication situation with a unique **worldview**, a personal frame for viewing life and life's events. Your worldview is different from your classmate's, which is different from your coworker's. You may believe that humans are basically good creatures; your classmate may have a more callous view of humanity, citing war, famine, and greed. We all enter interpersonal encounters with various worldviews, and we need to recognize the influence that these various views have upon our communication.

Realize the Incompleteness of Perception

There is no possible way for us to perceive our environment completely. By its nature, perception is an incomplete process. When we attend to certain aspects of our surroundings, as you learned earlier, we necessarily are not attending to something else. So, if you are working on a group project and think a group member is lazy,

CHOICES *for Improving Perception Checking*

- Understand your personal worldview
- Realize the incompleteness of perception
- Seek explanation and clarification
- Distinguish facts from inferences
- Be patient and tolerant

you should check your perception further. Perhaps there is some other issue, such as working a late-night job or caring for a sick relative, that is contributing to the group member's behavior. And don't forget that people, objects, and situations change, thereby making it important to update your perceptions periodically.

Seek Explanation and Clarification

We need to double-check with others to make sure that we are accurately perceiving a person, situation, or event. Seeking explanation and clarification requires us to foster a dialogue with others. Trying to understand whether or not your perceptions are accurate communicates to others that you are eager to gain an accurate understanding, which will help you achieve meaning in the interpersonal exchange.

Consider the following encounter between Wes and Lee. The two have dated for only one month, yet the differences between the two have prompted Wes to reconsider his future with Lee. Wes calls Lee at 10 p.m. to let her know that they had better stop dating. Lee is puzzled by the call because the last time the two were together—three nights earlier—Wes was talking about how happy he was with Lee. Lee wonders how things could have changed so quickly. Immediately, Lee feels defensive and thinks that Wes is breaking up with her because he is critical of her manner of communicating. She knows she talks a lot, and some of her previous boyfriends didn't like that. Yet, this isn't what is bothering Wes; he is troubled by their age difference; he is 15 years older than Lee.

Most likely, Lee could have avoided her feelings of confusion, frustration, and anger if she had sought out clarification and explanation of Wes's perceptions, and both could arrive at a more amicable end to their relationship.

Distinguish Facts from Inferences

One way to explain and to clarify is to distinguish facts from inferences. Facts are statements based on observations; inferences are personal interpretations of facts. Looking at the tense lips and angry look on a woman at the baggage claim at an airport may prompt you to draw the conclusion that she is unhappy that the airline lost her luggage. But this is your inference, not a fact.

During the perception process, we need to be careful not to confuse facts and inferences. Remember implicit personality theory, which we explained earlier? Take extra care and avoid filling in the blanks or extending a perception beyond the facts. At the very least, recognize when you are using an inference. It's not a question of if but when we are using an inference, and of whether or not we are aware of its use.

Be Patient and Tolerant

We cannot overemphasize the importance of being patient and tolerant in your perceptions. Because we live in an "instant society," we expect things to happen quickly. Being patient and tolerant, like many other recommendations, sounds easy. However, you can't expect to develop quality communication skills overnight; they take

© Brad Wrobleski / Masterfile

Our self-concept often changes as we grow older. Sometimes we want to change the way we see ourselves but we're not sure we can. By taking a calculated risk, you may find that the way you see yourself—and, in turn, the way you see others—can change dramatically.

time and practice to learn. The effort is worth it, because without patience and tolerance, you won't be able to check the accuracy of your perceptions.

Improving Self-Concept

When you improve your sense of self, you are on your way toward increasing your self-awareness and self-esteem. In turn, your relationships improve. In this section, we explore five skills necessary to improve your self-concept.

Have the Desire and Will to Change

As we mentioned earlier in the chapter, our self-concept changes as we grow. Therefore, we should be willing to change our self-concepts throughout our lifetimes. If you want to be more sensitive to others, make that commitment. If you'd like to be more assertive, take the initiative to change. Having the desire or will to change your self-concept is not always easy. We grow comfortable with ourselves, even when we recognize ways we'd like to change. We need to realize that a changing self-concept can help us grow just as much as it can help our relationships grow.

Decide What You'd Like to Change

After you establish a will to change, describe what it is specifically about yourself that needs to change. Further, describe why you feel a change may be needed. Are others telling you to change? If so, what significance do these individuals have in your life? Are their concerns legitimate, or are you simply engaging in a self-fulfilling prophecy?

Set Reasonable Personal Goals

Always strive to have reasonable goals. In other words, don't set goals that you cannot meet. Otherwise, you may feel a sense of failure. A reasonable goal for a college student might be to do all your assigned reading in each class for a semester. Studying hard, reading and rereading the classroom readings and/or textbook(s), participating in class when appropriate, and being a good listener seem reasonable . . . and attainable. Setting a goal of getting a perfect grade point average, writing error-free papers, and thinking you understand the content without asking questions seems unreasonable and pretty much impossible. And don't expect to be someone that you are not. Avoid societal expectations of perfection. Look beyond the superficial expectations that we find in the media.

Review and Revise

At times, you may make changes to your self-concept that are not entirely beneficial. Think about the implication of these changes and consider revising them if necessary. For instance, you may have tried to be more accommodating to your family members, but the result was that your integrity was trampled. Perhaps you made some changes at work, trying to engage people who annoy you daily, and now you're having trouble getting your work finished on time because these people stop to talk for long periods of time during the day. Perhaps some of your past behaviors now need to be refreshed.

Let's look further at this skill with an example. Consider Hillary, who, at age 18, described herself as a "really boring person." To bolster her self-esteem and to assert her independence, Hillary decided to get a tattoo, much to the surprise and shock of her parents. As an 18-year-old, she felt that she was an adult and did not have to abide by her parents' rules. Now, as a 30-year-old, Hillary is rethinking her image-boosting behavior. She thinks that the tattoo, located on her right forearm, communicates an image that is contrary to the one she wants to convey as a middle school teacher. Now, it seems, demonstrating independence is not as important to her self-concept as it used to be.

Occasions in which you revise past changes may force you to think about whether changes to your self-concept were justified in the first place or whether they are appropriate for you now. For Hillary, her reflections on whether or not the tattoo was important at age 18 no doubt occupy her mind from time to time. At age 30, she probably regrets being so impulsive in her behavior without thinking about the consequences of her behavior.

Surround Yourself with "Relational Uppers"

Think, for a moment, about the amount of stress in your life right now. You may be working full time, raising children, taking a full course load, not entirely healthy, or having a hard time with a particular course. Now, think about hanging around people who do nothing but tell you that you need to change. Or, consider interpersonal relationships with people who constantly tell you that you are deficient in this or that. You should stay clear of those people who agitate, whine, and complain. (For information about how others' moods affect your emotion, see Chapter 4.)

CHOICES *for Improving Self-Concept*

- Have the desire and will to change
- Decide what you'd like to change
- Set reasonable personal goals
- Review and revise
- Surround yourself with "relational uppers"

We believe that you need to avoid these types of people in favor of **relational uppers,** those people who support and trust you as you improve your self-concept. Take care to surround yourself with relational uppers because these individuals will be instrumental for you to achieve your potential.

Summary

A significant part of our interpersonal communication effectiveness is based upon our perceptions and on our self-concepts. Our perceptions are influenced by our self-identity, and our self-identity is influenced by our perceptions. The two are inseparable in our relationships with others.

Perception is the process of using our physical senses to respond to the world around us. The perception process occurs in four stages: attending and selecting, organizing, interpreting, and retrieving. In the attending and selecting stage, we use our senses to respond to our interpersonal environment, then decide which stimuli we will attend to. In the organizing stage, we order the information we have selected so that it is understandable and accessible. In the interpreting stage, we assign meaning to what we perceive, based on our relational history, personal expectations, and knowledge of ourselves and others. In the retrieving stage, we recall information we have stored in our memories, which affects how we communicate with others. Perception is influenced by many factors, including culture, sex and gender, physical factors, technology, and self-concept.

A person's self-concept is the relatively stable set of perceptions a person holds of himself or herself. Our self-concept is shaped by self-awareness, an understanding of who we are; by self-esteem, an evaluation of who we perceive ourselves to be; and by self-fulfilling prophecy, predictions we or others make about ourselves.

An important component of the self is identity management, or the ways we handle various interpersonal situations to influence how others perceive us. When we present our identity to others, we are presenting a particular sense of self. The image of the self we present to others is called face, and we typically present two types of face in our interactions with others: positive face and negative face. Positive face is our desire to be liked, understood, and respected by others. Negative face is our desire for others to respect our individuality and to refrain from imposing their will on us.

After ridding yourself of your predisposed biases, you can employ several skills to improve your perceptual abilities. First, understand your personal worldview, or personal frame for viewing life and life's events. Second, be aware of why you choose to select and attend to particular stimuli in your interpersonal environment over others, and check your perceptions as needed. Third, check in with others to make sure you are accurately perceiving a person, situation, or event. Fourth, distinguish facts from inferences. And fifth, practice being patient and tolerant.

In addition, you can implement five strategies to improve your self-concept. First, have the desire and will to work at changing your self-concept. Second, make the decision to change and be specific about what you will change. Third, set reasonable personal goals for changing so that you experience success and avoid a sense of failure. Fourth, review and revise your changing self-concept as needed, retaining those changes that are beneficial. And fifth, surround yourself with "relational uppers," people who support and trust you as you work to improve your self-concept.

Understanding Interpersonal Communication Online

Now that you've read Chapter 2, use your Understanding Interpersonal Communication CD-ROM for quick access to the electronic study resources that accompany this text. Your CD-ROM gives you access to the video of Dr. Gomez's interaction with the Camaras on pages 34–35, the CNN & Change video clip "Accent Reduction" on page 40, the Ethics & Choice interactive activity on page 45, the Communication Assessment Test on page 52, InfoTrac College Edition, and the Understanding Interpersonal Communication website. When you get to the Understanding Interpersonal Communication home page, click on "Student Book Companion Site" in the Resource box at right to access additional online study aids for this chapter, including a digital glossary, review quizzes, and chapter activities. ■

Terms for Review

attending and selecting 35	negative face 51	self-awareness 46
attribution theory 54	negative halo 53	self-concept 44
face 50	organizing 36	self-esteem 47
gender 41	perception 35	self-fulfilling prophecy 47
gender role socialization 41	positive face 50	self-monitoring 53
gender schema 42	positive halo 53	sex 41
halo effect 53	relational schema 37	stereotyping 37
identity management 49	relational uppers 59	symbolic interactionism 45
implicit personality theory 53	retrieving 39	worldview 55
interpreting 38	selective perception 36	
mindful 35	selective retention 39	

Questions for Understanding

Comprehension Focus

1. What are the stages in the perception process?
2. Define relational schema.
3. Differentiate between positive and negative face.
4. What is a self-fulfilling prophecy?
5. What are the two primary components of self-concept?

Application Focus

1. **CASE IN POINT**
   Look again at our chapter opening. Discuss your reaction to the perceptual and self-concept dilemma presented to Dr. Gomez. Do you believe the physician spoke to the family appropriately? Why or why not?

2. How might your personal insecurities or anxieties affect your perception of a college classroom?
3. Explain the perception process by examining how a child and parent may differ on the issue of curfew. Use all the stages of perception in your discussion.
4. Use implicit personality theory to explain how the dating process may function. In your discussion, be sure to include the halo effect and its relationship to dating.
5. Discuss how facework might function in a job interview. Look at face from both the perspective of the interviewer and the interviewee.

Interactive Activities and InfoTrac College Edition Exercises

Complete the Interactive Activities and InfoTrac College Edition Exercises for Chapter 2 online at the Understanding Interpersonal Communication website. Select the chapter resources for Chapter 2, then click on "Activities" or "InfoTrac College Edition." If requested, you can submit your answers to your instructor.

Interactive Activities

2.1 Stereotypes about the United States 38
2.2 Social Perceptions of Hair and Baldness 43
2.3 Optical Illusions and Perception 43
2.4 Perception Filters 44
2.5 Pygmalion in the Classroom 49

InfoTrac College Edition Exercises

2.1 Attending to What Is Important 36
2.2 Cultural Perceptions and the Glass Ceiling 40
2.3 Sex, Gender, and Perception about Communication 42
2.4 Positive and Negative First Impressions 45
2.5 The Self and the Workplace 49

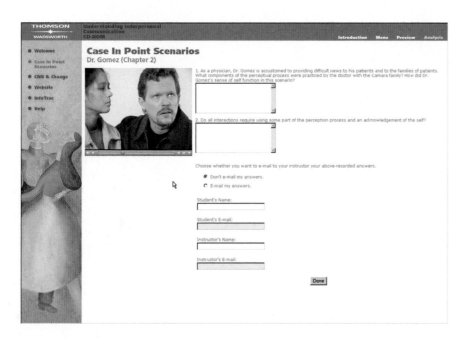

3

Communication, Culture, and Identity

Recognize and understand the complexity of culture

Identify reasons for the importance of intercultural communication

Explain the obstacles to achieving intercultural effectiveness

Employ strategies to improve intercultural communication

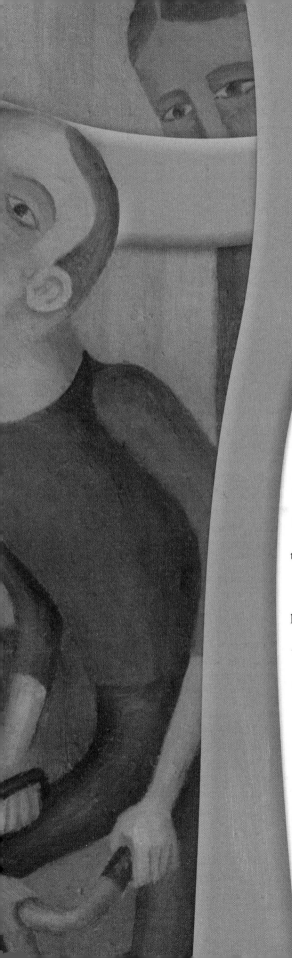

Brad Atchison wanted to get away. He had just graduated from college and, although he was in debt, he figured that he could afford a one-week vacation. He heard that it didn't cost that much to travel to Mexico, and the dollar was doing particularly well there. He figured that he would spend most of his time in the bars and on the beach, which shouldn't be too expensive. And he thought this was a once-in-a-lifetime opportunity to get away before job responsibilities set in.

As he waited at the airport for his plane to Mexico City, Brad sat next to Miguel, a 22-year-old Mexican who was going to college in the United States. Miguel and Brad hit it off immediately. They talked about college life, women, tattoos, and their mutual interest in cycling. But it was the following comment by Brad that prompted Miguel to reconsider his new acquaintance: "Man, you Mexicans know how to relax. I'd love to take a *siesta* every day!"

At first, Miguel did not know quite what to say to Brad, but he knew he had to say something. He didn't want to antagonize Brad, but he also felt that he shouldn't let Brad's comment die. So, Miguel spoke up: "Look, man, what you don't know about Mexico is obvious. That *siesta* stuff is so old. Don't you know anything about the country you're going to?" Brad replied, "Hey, sorry, man—I don't know a thing about Mexico. But, let's face it. I'm not on this trip to get a lecture. I'm going to have fun."

A bit of awkwardness now developed between the two men. But, Miguel wanted to take this chance to educate Brad. He didn't want

Use your Understanding Interpersonal Communication CD-ROM to watch a video clip of Brad's interaction with Miguel. Click on the "In Action" icon in the menu at left, then click on "Conversation Menu" in the menu bar at the top of the screen. Select "Brad" to watch the video (it takes a minute for the video to load). As you watch Brad and Miguel talk, consider Miguel's decision to educate Brad about Mexican culture. Do you think he handled the situation appropriately? You can respond to this and other analysis questions by clicking on "Analysis" in the menu bar at the top of the screen. When you've answered all the questions, click on "Done" to compare your answers to those provided by the authors.

to push the issue, but he thought that Brad was a good conversationalist and could take a little ribbing (and education). And, as a first-generation college student studying in the United States, Miguel was used to dispelling fictional images of his country. Why not take this chance to explain to Brad some cultural facts about Mexico? So he did. Miguel explained dating rituals, the roles of women and men, and the importance of the family in Mexico. Brad listened attentively, interested in what Miguel had to say about his culture. He also felt embarrassed. Brad realized that he should have informed himself about Mexican culture before leaving on the trip. He was grateful to Miguel and hoped he hadn't offended him too much by his ignorance. ■

Most people communicate with the belief that others will understand them. For instance, in the United States, most people don't think twice about using the English language to make their point, despite the fact that people who live in the United States speak different languages and are members of various cultural groups (Jandt, 2004). Also, most English speakers use their own nonverbal codes without thinking about how nonverbal communication differs across cultures. For example, looking someone directly in the eyes during a conversation is the norm in the United States but is viewed as disrespectful or a sign of aggression in many parts of the world, such as Africa (Samovar & Porter, 2004). In addition, many people in the United States value emotional expressiveness, yet research shows that some cultural groups, such as Chinese Americans, do not freely express their feelings (Gao & Ting-Toomey, 1998). Today more than ever, much of the meaning in our interactions with others depends on the cultural backgrounds of the communicators.

In our opening Case in Point, Brad's understanding of Mexico appeared to be based on outdated images of the country. Fortunately for Brad, Miguel taught him firsthand knowledge of Mexican culture. Miguel's information provided Brad with knowledge that made his subsequent encounters in Mexico much more pleasing than they would have been.

In the first two chapters, we noted that communication and identity are interrelated. In this chapter, we look at the role of culture in interpersonal communication. Because culture pervades virtually every component of interpersonal communication, cultural diversity is a fact of life. We can learn a lot about the ways we and others communicate by understanding culture.

The focus of this chapter is intercultural communication. For our purposes, **intercultural communication** refers to communication between and among individuals and groups whose cultural backgrounds differ. As you read and review the material, keep in mind two of the words in this book's title: "changing times." Indeed, times are changing. We live in a society that is more culturally diverse than ever. We describe this cultural complexity in this chapter and look at the significant issues associated with culture and communication. The words of Larry Samovar and Richard Porter (2004) underscore our rationale for this chapter: "What members of a particular culture value and how they perceive the universe are usually far more important than whether they eat with chopsticks, their hands, or metal utensils" (p. 24). Knowledge of others' cultural values and practices enhances intercultural communication.

For intercultural communication to occur, individuals don't have to be from different countries. In a diverse society such as the United States, we can experience intercultural communication within one state, one town, or even one neighborhood. Some researchers distinguish between communication across national cultures (for example, Japan and the United States) and communication between groups within one national culture (for example, African Americans and European Americans). They call the former *intercultural* and the latter *cross-cultural* communication. However, for our purposes in this text, we simply refer to all such encounters as intercultural.

The United States Census (2000) presents statistics that underscore the rich cultural heritage of the country. When provided an opportunity to identify with more than one race, 6.8 million, or 2.4 percent of the population, chose to do so. Those with mixed ancestry joined the ranks of celebrities with multiracial backgrounds, including golfer Tiger Woods (black, white, Thai, Native American), singer Joan Baez (white, Mexican American), musician Eddie Van Halen (white, Indonesian), and astronaut Franklin Chang-Diaz (Chinese, Costa Rican).

Trying to understand people who may think, talk, look, and act differently from us can be challenging at times. Just think about the words people use to describe those who may be culturally different from them: odd, weird, strange, unusual, and unpredictable. These associations have existed over centuries. Consider the words of fifth century Greek playwright Aeschylus: "Everyone is quick to blame the alien." As we discuss in this chapter, today, the "alien" takes many intriguing shapes and forms.

Intercultural communication theorists (for example, Jackson, 2002) argue that humans cannot exist without culture. Our individuality is constructed around culture. As we learned in Chapter 2, our identities are shaped by our conversations and relationships with others and vice versa. Our cultural background enters into this mix by shaping our identity, our communication practices, and our responses to others. We tend to use other people as "guideposts for normative behavior" (Jackson, p. 360). In doing so, we can focus on how others from diverse cultures differ from us. For instance, when Jean from the United States meets Lee from China in her philosophy class, she might notice how Lee smiles more frequently than her U.S. counterparts. Jean might also observe that Lee is much more deferential to the professor than she and her U.S. friends are. Yet, this comparison is incomplete. Intercultural scholars believe that despite their cultural differences, people continue to have a great deal in common. This chapter explores both what factors culturally bind us as well as what elements divide us. It also discusses how these influences affect our intercultural communication.

Diversity in the United States: A Nation of Newcomers

Intercultural contact is pervasive in the United States. This diversity affects family structure, corporations, religious institutions, schools, and the media. With more than 280 million citizens, our nation is a heterogeneous mix of various cultures (Calloway-Thomas, Cooper, & Blake, 1999). Fred Jandt (2004) notes that Latinos, many from Mexico, are the fastest growing cultural group in the United States, growing considerably over the past decade and constituting 12 percent of the population. He states that the migration from Mexico is "the largest sustained mass mi-

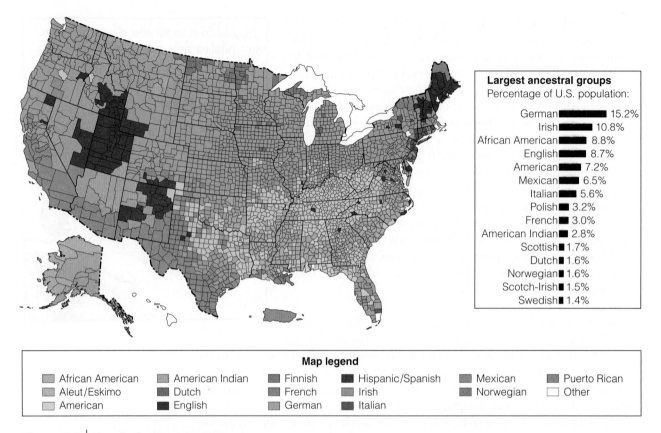

Largest ancestral groups
Percentage of U.S. population:

German	15.2%
Irish	10.8%
African American	8.8%
English	8.7%
American	7.2%
Mexican	6.5%
Italian	5.6%
Polish	3.2%
French	3.0%
American Indian	2.8%
Scottish	1.7%
Dutch	1.6%
Norwegian	1.6%
Scotch-Irish	1.5%
Swedish	1.4%

Map legend

African American	American Indian	Finnish	Hispanic/Spanish	Mexican	Puerto Rican
Aleut/Eskimo	Dutch	French	Irish	Norwegian	Other
American	English	German	Italian		

Figure 3.1 | Diversity in the United States

From *USA Today* July 1, 2004, p. 7A. Used by permission.

gration of one group to the United States" (p. 369). For additional information on ancestry across the United States, see Figure 3.1.

The increase in diversity is not without consequence. Rubin Martinez (2000) observes that our diversity can be challenging: "All across the country, people of different races, ethnicities, and nationalities, are being thrown together and torn apart . . . it is a terrifying experience, this coming together, one for which we have of yet only the most awkward vocabulary" (pp. 11–12). Relating to individuals rather than to the culture is an effective first step toward bridging intercultural relationships. We discuss this strategy in more detail later in this chapter.

With the exception of Native peoples, who were the first cultural group in the United States, we live in a nation of immigrants. The United States traditionally supports cultural newcomers. However, a backlash of sorts seems to be increasing. For example, an "English only" movement has gained momentum across the country. Politicians and activists, feeling that the arrival of new cultural groups in the United States risks dividing the country along language and cultural lines, continue to try to make English the official language of the country. In fact, in 1996, the United States House of Representatives passed the English Language Empowerment Act, which would have made English the official language of the United States. It never became law, but it highlighted feelings by some that multiple cultures with multiple languages can cost the United States economically (Hayakawa, 1990).

Almost 50 years ago, anthropologist Edward T. Hall (1959) noted that "culture is communication and communication is culture" (p.169). In other words, we learn how, where, why, when, and to whom we communicate through cultural teachings. Conversely, when we communicate, we are reproducing and reinforcing our cultural practices. Hall's words resonate even today. The United States is more diverse than ever, and almost everyone has been exposed to this growing diversity in some way. The nation's growing diversity has been hotly debated, with some writers believing that the increase in diversity results in honoring only those voices that support it (for example, McGowan, 2001). However, other writers (for example, Chang, 1999) contend that diversity allows for perspectives from many cultural backgrounds. Regardless of the divergent opinions on this matter, we cannot ignore the fact that we now live in a country with expanding cultural variability.

Learning how to communicate effectively with members of different cultures is a hallmark of a thoughtful and effective communicator. We can't venture too far in our lives without being introduced to cultural diversity in our personal, professional, spiritual, and familial lives. Let's explore this issue further by first examining the concept of culture and its underlying assumptions.

Defining Culture

Culture is a difficult concept to define, in part because it is complex, multidimensional, and abstract. Although there are hundreds of definitions of the term, for our purposes, we define **culture** as the shared, personal, and learned life experiences of a group of individuals who have a common set of values, norms, and traditions. The values of a culture are its standards and what it emphasizes most. Norms are patterns of communication. Traditions are the customs of a culture. These values, norms, and traditions affect our interpersonal relationships within a culture. It's almost impossible to separate values, norms, and traditions from any conversation pertaining to intercultural communication. Now, let's look at three assumptions embedded in our definition of culture.

Culture Is Learned

We aren't born with knowledge of the practices and behaviors of our culture. People learn the values, norms, and traditions of their culture through the communication of symbols for meaning. We learn about culture both consciously and unconsciously. We can learn about culture directly, such as when someone actually teaches us, and indirectly, such as when we observe cultural practices. In the United States, our family, friends, and the media are the primary teachers of our culture.

Let's look at an example of a ritual that varies depending on culture. Bradford Hall (2005) observes some differences in dating in New Zealand and the United States. In New Zealand, it is uncommon for someone to exclusively date another unless he or she has gone out with that person in a group of friends first. Even television shows in New Zealand suggest that romantic relationships begin in groups. Further, exclusive dating in New Zealand occurs only after the couple makes long-term relationship plans. As Hall observes (and as most of you already know), in the United States, exclusive dating does not have to be preceded by group interactions, and many people in exclusive dating relationships in the United States haven't made long-term plans.

For the most part, the United States embraces the notion of co-cultures. Although U.S. co-cultures often clash, most co-culture members balance their own cultural practices with those of the larger culture and sometimes even invite people outside their co-culture to participate in their traditions.

Culture Creates Community

Central to our definition of culture is the assumption that it helps to create a sense of community. We view **community** as the common understandings among people who are committed to coexisting together. Cultures create their own sets of values, norms, rules, and customs, which help them to communicate.

In the United States, communities are filled with a number of cultures within cultures, sometimes referred to as **co-cultures** (Orbe, 1998). For example, a Cuban American community, a Chinese American community, and a community of people with disabilities are all co-cultures within one larger culture (the United States). Each community has individual and unique communication behaviors and practices, but each community also subscribes to behaviors and practices embraced by the larger United States culture. Many times, the two cultures mesh effortlessly; however, sometimes a **culture clash,** or a conflict over cultural expectations, occurs. For example, Ling Chen (2004) points out that upon arriving in the United States, Chinese "sojourners" move about the country

> as if they know the ropes, going about their business as if they were still in their native culture. They deal with matters in ways they always do, until that moment when they find themselves in a problematic situation. Only then are they surprised, realizing that too much has been taken for granted; only then do they begin trying to understand the situation. (p. 267)

Ultimately, sometimes with the help of others from their co-culture, most members of co-cultures become adept at balancing their own cultural practices with those of the larger culture. However, being a member of more than one co-culture (for example, being a child with a mother who is African American and a father who is white) can pose a cultural identity challenge. Tina Harris (2004) calls this "cultural duality," emphasizing that the duality may result in a "lifelong and tumultuous journey" (pp. 204–205).

Culture Is Multileveled

On the national level of culture, we assume that people of the same national background share many things in common that bind them in a common culture: language, values, norms, and traditions. Thus, we expect Germans to differ from Hmong based on differing national cultures. However, as discussed in the previous section, cultures can be formed on other levels, such as generation, sexual identity, gender, race, and region, among others. For example, in many parts of the country, regionalisms exist. People who live in the middle of the United States (Kansas, Illinois, Iowa, Nebraska, Indiana, Wisconsin, and so on) are often referred to as "Midwesterners." People who live in Vermont, New Hampshire, Maine, Massachusetts, Rhode Island, and Connecticut are called "New Englanders." Both Midwesterners and New Englanders believe they have a special way of looking at things, but the reality is that the two regions share a great deal in common—namely, pragmatic thinking and an independent spirit.

Another example of a co-culture that is not based on nationality is a culture that develops around a certain age cohort. People who grow up in different time frames grow up in different cultural eras. This assumption allows us to attach names to various generations—for example, Depression Babies of the 1930s or Flower Children of the 1960s. The 1930s culture of the Great Depression did not make an effort toward inclusiveness; indeed, the country was trying to survive during the troubling financial times. In contrast, the 1960s ushered in an era in which individual rights began to take hold, and people with various life backgrounds were honored. As people age, they find it difficult to abandon many of the values that were taught during their childhood.

We have given you a general framework for understanding culture. To help you further understand the complexity of culture, let's turn our attention to the dimensions of culture. We present five dimensions in the next section.

Dimensions of Culture

Dutch management scholar Geert Hofstede (1980; 1984; 1991; 2001) examined work attitudes across 40 cultures. His work showed that four dimensions of cultural values were held by more than 100,000 corporate managers and employees in multinational corporations: uncertainty avoidance, distribution of power, masculinity-femininity, and individualism-collectivism.

Uncertainty Avoidance

Uncertainty avoidance is a tricky topic; it refers to how tolerant (or intolerant) you are of uncertainty. Those cultures that resist change and have high levels of anxiety associated with change are said to have a high degree of uncertainty avoidance. Because cultures with a high degree of uncertainty avoidance desire predictability, they need specific laws to guide behavior and personal conduct. The cultures of Greece, Chile, Portugal, Japan, and France are among those that tolerate little uncertainty. Risky decisions are discouraged in these cultures because they increase uncertainty.

Those cultures that are unthreatened by change have a low degree of uncertainty avoidance. The cultures of the United States, Sweden, Britain, Denmark, and Ireland tend to accept uncertainty. They are comfortable taking risks and are less aggressive and less emotional than cultures with a high degree of uncertainty avoidance. To test your understanding of high and low degrees of uncertainty avoidance, use your Understanding Interpersonal Communication CD-ROM to access **Interactive Activity 3.1: Degrees of Uncertainty Avoidance**.

Intercultural communication problems can surface when a person raised in a culture that tolerates ambiguity encounters another who has little tolerance. For instance, if a student from a culture with high uncertainty avoidance is invited to a party in the United States, he or she will probably ask many questions about how to dress, what to bring, exactly what time to arrive, and so forth. These questions might perplex a U.S. host, who would typically have a high tolerance for uncertainty, which might include a laid-back attitude toward the party—"Just get here whenever." Recall that cultures with high uncertainty avoidance prefer to have rules and clear protocol more than cultures with low uncertainty avoidance.

REVISITING CASE IN POINT

1. Embedded in Brad and Miguel's conversation are some assumptions of culture. Identify how at least one assumption relates to their dialogue in the airport.
2. One of the assumptions to consider when defining culture relates to culture creating community. Within that assumption is the notion of a culture clash. Discuss the presence of elements associated with a culture clash in Brad's discussion at the airport with Miguel.

You can answer these questions online under Student Resources for Chapter 3 at the Understanding Interpersonal Communication website.

Facing *Change*

The society in which we live will continue to experience vast and formidable cultural changes. Social relationships are also changing, whether in the office, at home, with our friends, or in the media. We are seeing both the benefits and the shortcomings of living in a culture composed of numerous co-cultures. What do you predict will happen as the United States grapples with increasing diversity? Will society become more or less welcoming to newcomers? What communication accommodations or changes will people have to make to accommodate cultural changes?

 Use your Understanding Interpersonal Communication CD-ROM to watch the CNN video clip "L.A. Diversity," which highlights the fact that Los Angeles has become the most diverse city in the world, boasting 140 nationalities and 96 languages. Click on the "CNN & Change" icon in the menu at left, then click on  "Video Menu" in the menu bar at the top of the screen. Select "L.A. Diversity" to watch the video (it takes a minute for the video to load). As you watch the video, think about how the level of diversity (or the lack of diversity) in your hometown influenced your social relationships. If you're going to school in a town different from the one you grew up in, has its level of diversity changed the way you approach social relationships? You can respond to this and other analysis questions by clicking on "Analysis" in the menu bar at the top of the screen. When you've answered all the questions, click on "Done" to compare your answers to those provided by the authors.

Distribution of Power

How a culture deals with power is called **power distance.** Citizens of nations that are high in power distance (for example, Philippines, Mexico, India, Singapore, and Brazil) tend to show respect to people with higher status. They revere authoritarianism, and the difference between the powerful and the powerless is clear. Differences in age, sex, and income are exaggerated in these cultures, and people accept these differences.

The caste system of the Hindu people in India is an example of a culture that is high in power distance. This social classification organizes people into four castes or categories: *Brahmins* (priests), *Kashtryas* (administrators/rulers), *Vaisyas* (businesspeople or farmers), and *Sudras* (laborers) (Hayavadana, 1996). Each caste has various duties and rights. This caste hierarchy inhibits communication among caste groups. In fact, only one group (the priests, who historically have been afforded full respect) has the prerogative to communicate with all other social groups.

The cultures that are low in power distance are the United States, Austria, Israel, Denmark, and Ireland. People in these cultures believe that power should be equally distributed regardless of a person's age, sex, or status. Cultures with low degrees of power distance minimize differences among the classes and accept challenges to power in interpersonal relationships. Although the United States ranks low in power distance, the culture is becoming higher in power distance because of the growing disparity between rich and poor (Jandt, 2004).

Intercultural encounters between people from high and low power distance cultures can be challenging. For instance, a supervisor from a high power distance culture may have difficulty communicating with employees who come from lower power distance cultures. Although the supervisor may be expecting complete respect and follow-through on directives, the employees may be questioning the legitimacy of such directives.

Masculinity-Femininity

Hofstede (2001) identifies the dimension of masculinity-femininity as the extent to which cultures represent masculine and feminine traits in their society. Remember from our discussion of masculinity and femininity in Chapter 2 that masculinity is not the same as "male," and femininity is not the same as "female," although use of these terms still reinforces stereotypical notions of how men and women should behave. **Masculine cultures** focus on achievement, competitiveness, strength, and material success—that is, characteristics stereotypically associated with masculine people. Money is important in masculine cultures. Further, masculine cultures are those where the division of labor is based on sex. **Feminine cultures** emphasize sexual equality, nurturance, quality of life, supportiveness, and affection—that is, characteristics stereotypically associated with feminine people. A compassion for the less fortunate also characterizes feminine nations.

Hofstede's (2001) research showed that countries such as Mexico, Italy, Venezuela, Japan, and Austria are masculine-centered cultures, where the division of labor is based on sex. Countries such as Thailand, Norway, the Netherlands, Denmark, and Finland are feminine-centered cultures, where a promotion of sexual equality exists. The United States falls closer to masculinity.

What happens when a person from a co-culture that honors such masculine traits as power and competition intersects with a person from a co-culture that honors such feminine traits as interdependence and quality of life? For example, suppose that a feminine person is asked to lead a group of masculine individuals. In Scandinavian countries, such as Denmark and Finland, such a task would not be problematic. Many political leaders in these countries are feminine (and female), and flexible gender roles exist. Yet, if you come from a masculine culture, you might view such leaders with skepticism and wish to challenge their leadership. In terms of marital interpersonal relationships, masculinity and femininity are not necessarily problematic, especially if both persons in the relationship are from the same culture.

Individualism-Collectivism

When a culture values **individualism,** it prefers competition over cooperation, the individual over the group, and the private over the public. Individualistic cultures have an "I" communication orientation, emphasizing self-concept and personal achievement. Individualistic cultures, including the United States, Canada, Britain, Australia, and Italy, tend to reject authoritarianism. Members of individualistic cultures usually don't touch or stand close to others. Individualistic cultures typically support the belief that people should "pull themselves up by their own bootstraps."

Collectivism suggests that the self is secondary to the group and its norms, values, and beliefs. Group orientation takes priority over self-orientation. Collectivistic cultures tend to take care of extended family members and value duty, tradition, and hierarchy. A "we" communication orientation prevails in collectivistic societies. Collectivistic cultures such as Columbia, Peru, Pakistan, Chile, and Singapore lean toward working together in groups to achieve goals. Families are particularly important in collectivistic nations, and people have higher expectations of loyalty to family.

Interestingly, the collectivistic and individualistic orientations intersect at times. For instance, in the Puerto Rican community, a collectivistic sense of family is in concert with the individualistic need for community members to become personally successful. Hector Carrasquillo (1997) observed that "a Puerto Rican is only fully a person insofar as he or she is a member of a family" (p. 159). Still, Carrasquillo points out that younger Puerto Ricans have adopted more independence and have accepted and adapted to the individualistic ways of the United States culture. We see, therefore, that even within one culture, the individualism-collectivism dimension is not static.

Hofstede's work regarding dimensions of culture is often applied to business settings. To read an interesting article about the dramatic influence of culture in the workplace, use your Understanding Interpersonal Communication CD-ROM to access **Interactive Activity 3.2: Culture in the Workplace.** And to read an article that discusses how Hofstede's dimensions of culture can be applied specifically to business negotiation, read "Next for Communicators: Global Negotiation," available through InfoTrac College Edition. Use your Understanding Interpersonal Com-

In many Asian countries, doing things together underscores the collectivistic nature of society. In the United States, people sometimes have trouble identifying with the collectivistic value of placing the group before the individual. At the same time, they often embrace collectivistic values, such as the importance of family and tradition.

munication CD-ROM to access **InfoTrac College Edition Exercise 3.1: Culture and Negotiation.**

Consider the summary of Hofstede's four dimensions of culture provided in Table 3.1. As we did in the previous sections, we provide representative cultures as identified by Hofstede. Keep in mind that because his results are based on averages, you will most likely be able to think of individuals you know who are exceptions to the categorization of nations. For another summary of these concepts and an even more extensive list of representative countries, use your Understanding Interpersonal Communication CD-ROM to access **Interactive Activity 3.3: Hofstede's Dimensions of Culture.**

One additional cultural dimension merits consideration: Context. Recall from Chapter 1 that context is the environment in which communication takes place. Intercultural communication theorists find that people of different cultures use context to varying degrees to determine the meaning of a message. Scholars have referred to this as "context orientation theory" (Hall & Hall, 1990). Context orientation theory answers the following question: Is meaning derived from the setting of a message or from the words in the message?

Researchers have divided context into two areas: high-context and low-context (Victor, 1992). In **high-context cultures,** the meaning of a message is primarily drawn from the surroundings. People in high-context cultures do not need to say much when communicating because there is a high degree of similarity among members of such cultures. Further, people read nonverbal cues with a high degree of accuracy because people share the same structure of meaning. Native American, Latin American, Japanese, Chinese, and Korean cultures are all high-context cultures.

Table 3.1 | **Hofstede's Cultural Dimensions**

Dimension	Description
Uncertainty avoidance	• Cultures high in uncertainty avoidance desire predictability (for example, Greece, Japan). • Cultures low in uncertainty avoidance are unthreatened by change (for example, United States, Great Britain).
Distribution of power	• Cultures high in power distance show respect for status (for example, Mexico, India). • Cultures low in power distance believe power should be equally distributed (for example, United States, Israel).
Masculinity-femininity	• Masculine cultures value competitiveness, material success, and assertiveness (for example, Italy, Austria). • Feminine cultures value quality of life, affection, and caring for the less fortunate (for example, Sweden, Denmark).
Individualism-collectivism	• Individualistic cultures value individual accomplishments (for example, Australia, United States). • Collectivistic cultures value group collaboration (for example, Chile, Columbia).

In **low-context cultures,** communicators find meaning in the messages, not the context. Low-context cultures lack well-developed networks of meaning. For this reason, nonverbal communication is not easily comprehended, and information must be explicitly related, usually in words. As a result, low-context communicators talk more than high-context communicators. In addition, members of low-context cultures tend to have elaborate verbal messages; very little of the conversation is left to interpretation. Examples of low-context cultures include Germany, Switzerland, the United States, Canada, and France.

Think about how cultural differences in context might affect interaction during conflict episodes, job interviews, or dating. If one person relies mainly on the spoken word and the other communicates largely through nonverbal messages, what might be the result?

Why Study Intercultural Communication?

Intercultural communication scholars Judith Martin and Thomas Nakayama (2004) note several reasons to study intercultural communication. We identify six "imperatives" based on Martin and Nakayama's work and provide their application to interpersonal relationships. At the heart of this discussion is our belief that intercultural communication has merit beyond the class you are taking.

Technological Imperative

The extent to which technology has changed the United States cannot be overstated. The advent of the personal computer more than twenty years ago was just the beginning of a technological revolution. Following computers, a number of other technologies (including faxes, palm organizers, videophones, and, of course, the Internet) helped propel the United States into the twenty-first century.

These technological changes increase opportunities for intercultural communication. For example, consider Yolanda's experience with eBay, an online auction site. When Yolanda finds out that she holds the high bid on an antique handkerchief she wants to buy, she discovers that the seller is from a small town in Italy. Yolanda emails the seller and tells him that her grandmother has relatives in a small town in northern Italy. He emails back to tell her that he, too, has relatives in that same small town in northern Italy. As the two continue to email each other, they realize that both sets of relatives in Italy know each other! Later that year, they all get together electronically, an event they decide to repeat each year.

The implications of technology on our intercultural relationships continue to change even as we write this chapter. We revisit the subject of technology and interpersonal communication in Chapter 11.

Demographic Imperative

Earlier in this chapter, we noted that the United States continues to be shaped and reshaped by cultural diversity, and we provided information about the demographic changes in the United States. Yet, many co-cultures within the country reject the notion that blending into the national culture is ideal. Since dialogues about diversity began, writers and scholars have referred to the United States as a "melting pot," a metaphor that evokes a unified national character formed as a result of immigration. In the past, immigrants frequently changed their names, clothes, language, and customs to "blend in."

In contrast, recent metaphors for diversity in the United States include a symphony, stew, or salad (Lustig & Koester, 1999a), suggesting that diversity provides for unique "tints, textures, and tastes" (p. 16). In these metaphors, different cultures retain their unique characters even while becoming a part of the U.S. culture. For many immigrants, this process results in a bicultural identity, or the balance of two cultural backgrounds that we spoke of earlier in this chapter.

These metaphors of a symphony, stew, or salad also provide a chance for the larger culture to accommodate and to appreciate the diversity of co-cultures (Hecht, Collier, & Ribeau, 1993; Lustig & Koester, 1999b). For example, food, dress, religion, and street signs now recognize individual cultural groups. We eat at Korean restaurants, witness Saudi men wearing a thawb (the ankle-length white shirt), and read greeting cards celebrating Kwanzaa, an African American holiday affirming African culture. In addition, despite efforts to make English the official language of the United States, signs and labels in some parts of the country are written in two languages—for example, Spanish and English in the Southwest, and French and English in northern New England.

Economic Imperative

Today, extremely few places on earth are completely out of touch with the rest of the world. This phenomenon is referred to as the **global village,** which means that all societies—regardless of their size—are connected in some way (McLuhan, 1964). No country is economically isolated any longer. More than 2,400 foreign firms now operate almost 6,000 businesses in the United States. The National Council on Economic Education (2000–2004) reports that the percentage of exports in this country hovered around 10.2 percent in 2001, and imports were at about 14 percent. Therefore, the United States depends on other countries for its economic sustainability. Today, because of the availability of cheap labor, U.S. firms continue to send work and workers overseas, a practice called **outsourcing.** People in business

© 2003 David Wells / The Image Works

As developing countries continue to supply the U.S. with imported goods, as more U.S. companies send workers to jobs overseas, and as more people from other countries emigrate and find work in the United States, the ability to communicate across cultures will become increasingly necessary and valuable. For example, tele-workers in India who are employed by U.S. companies learn about many aspects of U.S. culture, including finance, sports, and entertainment, so they can better communicate with customers in the United States.

and industry, education, media, and politics communicate with others of different cultures, if for no other reason than that it is cost-efficient to do so. All of these exchanges of human resources represent one piece of the process known as globalization. To explore the effects of globalization on cultural diversity, women, and more, use your Understanding Interpersonal Communication CD-ROM to access **Interactive Activity 3.4: Effects of Globalization**.

Workers from other countries who come to the United States often receive no training in intercultural similarities and differences (Palmer, 2002). The result can be problematic: "Foreigners can't be expected to learn our [United States] customs through osmosis" (Palmer, 2002, p. 13A). We would add that citizens of the United States can't be expected to learn about others through osmosis, either.

For another perspective on cultural diversity and its positive or negative impact on an economy, check out the article "Diversity and Development; The UN's Human Development Report; Is Cultural Diversity Good for Development?" available through InfoTrac College Edition. Use your Understanding Interpersonal Communication CD-ROM to access **InfoTrac College Edition Exercise 3.2: Diversity and Development**.

Peace Imperative

The Lakota Indians have a saying: "With all beings and all things we shall be as relatives." Yet, as Judith Martin and Thomas Nakayama (2004) ask, is it really possible for cultures to work together and get along on one planet? Our current state of world affairs makes it difficult to answer this question. On one hand, the Berlin Wall has been torn down, but on the other hand, other types of walls have been put up. For instance, violence in the Middle East, Africa, and Russia, coupled with tensions between China and Taiwan, make this a very challenging time for cultural understanding. We're not suggesting that if cultures understood each other, cultural warfare would end; rather, we believe that learning about other cultures aids in understanding conflicting points of view, perhaps resulting in a more peaceful world. Looking at an issue from another's perspective, as we learn in Chapter 5, is critical to interpersonal relationships.

Self-Awareness Imperative

As we mentioned in Chapter 2, each of us has a worldview, which is a unique way of seeing the world through our own lens of understanding. Worldviews originate in our culture (Samovar & Porter, 2004). Although these perspectives are often unconscious, they are directly derived from our cultural identity. When we have a clear understanding of who we are and what forces brought us to our current state, we can begin to understand others' worldviews. Consider the fact that many Japanese value *gaman,* which is perseverance in the face of adversity. Think about the importance of *gaman* when Japanese couples face marital conflict, financial problems, or natural disaster. Now, consider what many married couples in the United States do in the face of adversity: divorce. Finally, how do you handle adversity in your life? Becoming personally aware of your own worldview and the worldviews of others will inevitably improve your intercultural communication.

Ethical Imperative

Recall from Chapter 1 that ethics pertains to what is perceived as right and wrong. Culturally speaking, ethics can vary tremendously (Buber, 1970). That is, different fields of cultural experience dictate different opinions of what constitutes ethical behavior. For example, let's consider behavior associated with the family that may be viewed differently in the United States versus in China. In the Chinese culture, boys are valued more than girls (Galvin, 2004), and parents are required by Chinese policy to have only one child. As a result, when a mother gives birth to a girl in China, the child may be abandoned or given up for adoption to allow the parents to try again to have a boy.

You may agree or disagree with this practice based upon your ethical perspective(s). Regardless of our personal opinions, each of us has an ethical obligation to ensure that cultural behaviors are depicted in the context of cultural values. We also have an ethical obligation to ensure that we fully understand cultural practices before deciding whether to impose our own cultural will upon others.

We summarize the six imperatives in Table 3.2. Each imperative is accompanied by examples of how that imperative applies to the study of intercultural communication.

So far in this chapter, we have discussed why you need to understand intercultural communication. We're confident that you are beginning to appreciate the cultural diversity in your lives and that you are prepared to work on improving your intercultural communication skills. The first step toward understanding your culture and the cultures of others is to understand the problems inherent in intercultural communication. We examine five such challenges now.

Table 3.2 | **Reasons for Studying Intercultural Communication**

Imperative Type	Example
Technological imperative	*Email* is facilitating communication between and among cultures. The *Internet* facilitates cross-cultural understanding of societies around the world.
Demographic imperative	The *influx of immigrants* from Mexico, Russia, and Vietnam has changed the workforce in the United States.
Economic imperative	The *global market* has prompted overseas expansion of U.S. companies. *Business transactions and negotiation practices* require intercultural understanding.
Peace imperative	*Resolution of world conflicts,* such as those in the Middle East, requires cultural understanding.
Self-awareness imperative	*Self-reflection* of cultural biases aids in cultural sensitivity. Understanding personal *worldviews* promotes cultural awareness.
Ethical imperative	*Cultural values* are frequently difficult to understand and accept. We have an ethical obligation to appreciate the cultural variations in dating, marriage, and intimacy.

Challenges of Intercultural Communication

Although intercultural communication is important and pervasive, becoming an effective intercultural communicator is easier said than done. In this section, we explain five obstacles to intercultural understanding: ethnocentrism, stereotyping, anxiety and uncertainty, misinterpretation of nonverbal and verbal behaviors, and the assumption of similarity.

Ethnocentrism

When we personalize culture and view our world using a selfish cultural lens, we are practicing ethnocentrism. **Ethnocentrism** is the process of judging another culture using the standards of your own culture. Ethnocentrism is derived from two Greek words, *ethno,* or nation, and *kentron,* or center. When combined, the meaning becomes clear: nation at the center. Ethnocentrism is a belief in the superiority of your own culture. Myron Lustig and Jolene Koester (1999b) claim that cultures "train their members to use the categories of their own cultural experiences when judging the experiences of people from other cultures" (p. 146). Normally, ethnocentric tendencies exaggerate differences and usually prevent intercultural understanding.

At first glance, being ethnocentric may appear harmless. Few people even realize the extent to which they prioritize their culture over another. For instance, you will note that throughout this book, we avoid the use of the term *American.* Like many researchers and practitioners, we believe that *American* can refer to people in North America, Central America, and South America. To suggest that the word pertains only to those in the United States is ethnocentric.

We tend to notice when people from other cultures prioritize their cultural customs. For example, although many people in the United States value open communication, not all cultures do. Many Asian cultures (for example, China and Japan) revere silence. In fact, Chinese philosopher Confucius said that "Silence is a friend who will never betray." Now, consider what happens in conversations when the Western and Eastern worlds meet. Let's say that Ed, a business executive from the United States, travels to China to offer Yao, another executive, a business deal. Ed is taken aback when, after he makes the offer, Yao remains silent for a few minutes.

Communication Assessment Test

Revised Ethnocentrism Scale

Directions: Below are items that relate to the cultures of different parts of the world. Work quickly and record your first reaction to each item. There are no right or wrong answers. Please indicate the degree to which you agree or disagree with each item using the following five-point scale:

strongly disagree = 1   disagree = 2   neutral = 3
agree = 4   strongly agree = 5

You can also take this test online under Student Resources for Chapter 3 at the Understanding Interpersonal Communication website.

_____ 1. Most other cultures are backward compared to my culture.

_____ 2. My culture should be the role model for other cultures.

_____ 3. People from other cultures act strangely when they come to my culture.

_____ 4. Lifestyles in other cultures are just as valid as those in my culture.

_____ 5. Other cultures should try to be more like my culture.

_____ 6. I am not interested in the values and customs of other cultures.

_____ 7. People in my culture could learn a lot from people in other cultures.

_____ 8. Most people from other cultures just don't know what's good for them.

_____ 9. I respect the values and customs of other cultures.

_____ 10. Other cultures are smart to look up to our culture.

_____ 11. Most people would be happier if they lived like people in my culture.

_____ 12. I have many friends from different cultures.

_____ 13. People in my culture have just about the best lifestyles of those in any culture.

_____ 14. Lifestyles in other cultures are not as valid as those in my culture.

_____ 15. I am very interested in the values and customs of other cultures.

_____ 16. I apply my values when judging people who are different.

_____ 17. I see people who are similar to me as virtuous.

_____ 18. I do not cooperate with people who are different.

_____ 19. Most people in my culture just don't know what is good for them.

_____ 20. I do not trust people who are different.

_____ 21. I dislike interacting with people from different cultures.

_____ 22. I have little respect for the values and customs of other cultures.

Scoring

1. Recode questions 4, 7, and 9 with the following format:

   1 = 5   2 = 4   3 = 3   4 = 2   5 = 1

2. Drop questions 3, 6, 12, 15, 16, 17, and 19.
3. Add up the numbers you marked for the remaining responses. This is your composite ethnocentrism score. The higher the score, the more you are ethnocentric. The lower the score, the less you are ethnocentric.

From www.jamescmccroskey.com. Used by permission.

"Excuse me. We're Americans. Would you give us your table?"

Ed repeats the specifics of the offer, and Yao acknowledges his understanding. With such a standstill in the talk, Ed believes that Yao is going to reject the offer. However, if Ed had studied the Chinese culture before his trip, he would know that to the Chinese, silence means agreement. One speaks only if he or she has something of value to add. Ed's cultural ignorance may cost the company both money and respect. Ed's inability to look beyond his own Western view of silence represents ethnocentrism. To read an interesting article that discusses international competition and how some non-Western athletes feel pressure to adjust their cultural style to win higher marks with a Western-style performance, check out "Putting Patriotism on Ice: Top Figure Skating Duo Shen and Zhao Crave Gold—with Chinese Characteristics," available through InfoTrac College Edition. Use your Understanding Interpersonal Communication CD-ROM to access InfoTrac College Edition Exercise 3.3: Putting Patriotism on Ice.

Stereotyping

Consider the following statements:

> Japanese people love taking pictures. Old people are crabby.
> Boys don't cry. Italians love to use their hands
> while speaking.

These statements are stereotypes, the "pictures in our heads" (Lippman, 1922, p. 3) that we discussed in Chapter 2. We have all stereotyped at one point or another in our lives. Stereotypes are everywhere in U.S. society, including politics ("All politicians are crooked"), medicine ("Doctors know best"), entertainment ("Hollywood stars live perfect lives and have no problems"), journalism ("The media are so liberal"), and sports ("They're just dumb jocks"). Such statements generalize the qualities of some members of a group to the group as a whole.

Stereotypes can be good or bad. Think about the positive stereotypes of fire-fighters, police officers, emergency personnel, and other rescue workers after the September 11, 2001 terrorist attacks on the United States. Words like "heroic," "compassionate," "daring," and "fearless" have all been attributed to these groups of individuals, regardless of the cultural identification of the members of these groups. However, right after the attacks, many Arabs living in the United States were accused of being terrorists simply because of their ethnicity. People used hurtful and hateful speech while interacting with Arab Americans. The point is that we must be willing to look beyond the generalizations about a particular group and communicate with people as individuals.

Anxiety and Uncertainty

At times, we are simply nervous and anxious around people who are different from us. At other times, we may not know how to act around others who are different from us, leaving us filled with uncertainty. You may feel anxiety and uncertainty when you are introduced to people who speak, look, and act differently from you (Gudykunst & Kim, 1997). Our society has few guidelines to help us through some of the early awkward moments. People commonly question what words or phrases to use while discussing various cultural groups. Most of us want to be culturally aware and utilize language that doesn't offend, yet we frequently don't know what words might be offensive to members of cultures other than our own. For example, you might wonder whether you should refer to someone as Indian or Native American.

In Chapter 2, we observed that our family and friends usually influence our perceptions. Their observations and reactions to cultural differences are often passed on to us. And they can prompt us to either feel that we are members of an in-group or an out-group. **In-groups** are groups to which a person feels he or she belongs, and **out-groups** are those groups to which a person feels he or she does not belong.

Perceptions of belonging are directly proportional to the level of connection an individual feels toward a group. Let's say that Rob and Nate, a gay couple, meet Nate's best friend, Rose. Although Rose is not a lesbian, she feels that she has in-group affiliation with the gay men. Now suppose that Rob and Nate meet Rose's mom, Sandra, who is not accepting of the men's intimate relationship. Sandra will view Rob and Nate as an out-group because she does not feel a sense of belonging with gay men. Being a member of either an in-group or an out-group influences our degree of comfort in intercultural communication.

Misinterpretation of Nonverbal and Verbal Behaviors

Speakers expect to receive nonverbal cues that are familiar. However, nonverbal behaviors differ dramatically across and within cultures. For example, let's say that Lena is meeting a member of the Western Apache nation in Arizona or an immigrant from India. She will probably introduce herself and start some small talk. However, she may run into problems, because these cultures typically value silence in conversations. The Apache use silence when they meet strangers (Basso, 1990). For many Asian Indians, silence means agreement, is used as a sign of conversational respect, or is a way to show sensitivity to the speaker (Pais, 1997).

An Asian proverb states that "those who know, do not speak; those who speak, do not know." In this example, if Lena is a person who believes that communication must be constant to be effective, she may struggle with interpersonal exchanges with the Western Apache or the Asian Indian. However, as is true of other facets of culture, nonverbal communication varies within cultures as well as between cultures. For instance, although Italians might gesture more than people from the United States in general, not all Italians use expansive gestures. We could certainly find someone from Italy who gestures less than someone we pick from the United States. We return to the topic of culture and nonverbal communication in Chapter 7.

In addition to nonverbal differences, verbal communication differences exist between and among cultures and co-cultures. Aside from the obvious language differences that separate cultures, verbal communication styles can differ. For example, words used from one generation to the next vary in meaning. Words such as *smooching* and *necking* once referred to an act most people today refer to as *kissing*. We cover the use of language extensively in Chapter 6. We must understand nonverbal and verbal differences between cultures if we are to achieve meaning in our intercultural relationships.

When we learn to appreciate our differences and discover what we have in common, we increase our ability to communicate with one another in an effective and mutually beneficial way.

The Assumption of Similarity or Difference

We often have competing desires in our interpersonal relationships (Baxter & Montgomery, 1996) that result in contradictory tensions. These contradictions are called **dialectics.** For instance, in our relationships, we often find we want to have both independence and connection. Also, we want to be open with our relational partner but, at the same time, we want to maintain our privacy.

Dialectic thinking, with its focus on contradiction, helps us understand the final challenge to intercultural communication. On one end

© Ethel Wolkovitz / The Image Works

of the dialectic is the feeling that "people are people"—in other words, regardless of cultural background, everyone has the same universal concerns (family, health, friendships, and so on). This approach suggests that intercultural communication is possible because it simply requires honing in on people's inherent similarities. At the other end of the dialectic is the belief that people from different cultures are vastly different from one another, and, therefore, communication between them is difficult if not impossible. Assuming similarity fails to appreciate difference, and assuming difference fails to appreciate cultural commonalities.

In the United States, we need to be careful when we place a premium on the "American way." We are ethnocentric if we believe that other cultures should do things the way that we do things here or if we think that cultures that do things the way we do them here are imitating U.S. culture. For instance, consider the following conversation between Jasmine and Renny, two friends talking about an anthropology class:

JASMINE: So, I don't get it. You think that women should be forced to wear those veils over their heads. I don't. They want to be free to show their faces. Men don't have to do it, so why should women?

RENNY: You need to read more, Jasmine. I read that the veils are called *hijab* and they are part of the dress that women have worn for years. Some women wear them so that they can be treated as human beings instead of targets of beauty or objects of affection.

JASMINE: Okay, but don't they know that it can be seen as oppressive?

RENNY: Says who? You? Me? We live in the United States, a country where most women don't wear the hijab, but that doesn't mean that it's an oppressive thing. Look at our country. What about women in other countries who don't understand why married women here take their husband's name? What about women in other countries who laugh at how much women in the United States spend on cosmetics for their faces? What about . . .

JASMINE: Okay, okay, I get the point.

This conversation reflects the fact that simply because something is practiced or revered in the United States does not mean that it is similarly practiced or revered in other cultures. Renny helps us see through the problems of assuming similarity across cultures.

We have given you a number of issues to consider in this chapter so far. First, we defined culture and co-culture, and proceeded to outline several reasons for studying intercultural communication. Next, we addressed some of the most common challenges to intercultural communication. We now offer you some suggestions for improving your intercultural effectiveness in relationships.

REVISITING CASE IN POINT

1. Discuss how stereotyping is part of Brad's and Miguel's conversation.
2. Explain how cultural uncertainty and anxiety may have affected Brad's conversation with Miguel.

You can answer these questions online under Student Resources for Chapter 3 at the Understanding Interpersonal Communication website.

Choices for Intercultural Understanding

In this section, we present several ways to improve your communication with people from different cultures. Because most cultures and co-cultures have unique ways of communicating, our suggestions are necessarily broad. As we have emphasized in this chapter, communicating with friends, classmates, coworkers, and others from different cultural backgrounds is both exciting and challenging.

Know Your Biases and Stereotypes

Despite our best efforts, we enter conversations with biases and stereotypes. How do we know we have biases and stereotypes? Listening carefully to others' responses to our ideas, words, and phrases is an excellent first step. Have you ever told a story about a cultural group that resulted in a friend saying, "I can't believe you just said that!" That friend may be pointing out that you should rethink some culturally offensive language or risk facing challenges from others during conversations.

We need to avoid imposing our predispositions and prejudices on others. Perceptions of different cultural groups are frequently outdated or otherwise inaccurate and require a constant personal assessment. Facing your biases and even your fears or anxieties is an essential first step toward intercultural effectiveness.

Recall that ethnocentrism is seeing the world through your own culture's lens. We may like to think that our particular culture is best, but as you have seen through our many examples, no culture can claim superiority. We first need to admit that we all are biased and ethnocentric to some extent. Next, we need to honestly assess how we react to other cultures. As we previously mentioned, you can listen to others for their reactions. Looking inward is also helpful; ask yourself the following questions:

- What have I done to prepare myself for intercultural conversations?
- Do I use language that is biased or potentially offensive to people from different cultures?
- What is my reaction to people who use offensive words or phrases while describing cultural groups—am I silent? If so, do I consider my silence problematic?
- How have my perceptions and biases been shaped? By the media? By school? By talking to others?

These are among the questions you should consider as you begin to know yourself, your perceptions, and how you may act upon those perceptions. We all need to understand our outdated and misguided views of others that have falsely shaped our impressions of other cultures.

Tolerate the Unknown

Earlier in the chapter, we noted that some cultures easily tolerate uncertainty. Although we noted that the U.S. is one such culture, tolerating things of which you are unaware is not always that easy. We may wish to *think* we are tolerant, but the truth is that differences can bother us at times.

You may be unfamiliar with various cultural practices of coworkers, craftspeople you hire for home repair, and others whose backgrounds and fields of experience differ from yours. For instance, consider the Romanian who is accustomed to greeting people by kissing the sides of both cheeks. Or, think about the colleague who is Japanese and who may not shake your hand upon meeting. If you feel that an Arab from North Africa is too close to you while speaking, avoid being judgmental. These may be cultural behaviors that are simply different from yours. It will take time to understand the differences. Be patient with yourself and with others. If you encounter a cultural unknown, think about asking questions about a particular custom, practice, or behavior.

Your *Turn*

Think about the cultural diversity of the United States to which we refer in this chapter. For a week, read a particular newspaper or watch a television newscast. Keep a journal of the number of stories related to intercultural communication. How many of these stories did you perceive as positive? How many were negative? Write about your reactions to how the media contribute to stereotypes of various cultures. If you'd like, use your student workbook to complete this activity.

Skill *Spotlight*

Know Your Biases and Stereotypes

Biases are predispositions to thinking or behaving in a certain way. Stereotypes are fixed mental images of individuals or groups. We have a variety of biases and stereotypes, some good and some bad. For instance, when we positively stereotype, we may believe that our elected leaders care about the country's citizens and speak and act on their behalf. Of course, we realize that this is not true of all politicians. Yet, such a predisposition to view those who represent us in a favorable light may help us become less cynical and more receptive to politics.

Most of us are more familiar with the negative biases and stereotypes that endanger intercultural communication. We may find ourselves either consciously or unconsciously acting out a distorted view of a cultural group. For example, you may find yourself speaking loudly to seniors or using profanity with truck drivers.

Problems arise when biases and stereotypes become part of our intercultural relationships. Imagine doing business with a Russian businessman and prejudging him as cold, secretive, and authoritarian simply because he is Russian. Consider the consequences of living with an Irish American while believing that Irish people are loud and hot-tempered. Or, visualize how difficult a working relationship with a single mother would be if you think that most single moms are on welfare. These biases and prejudices obstruct the development of effective intercultural communication.

Skills at Work The use of biases and stereotypes at work can carry enormous consequences. Today's workplaces are increasingly diverse in terms of gender, race, ethnicity, sexual and religious identity, and other cultural markers. This diversity has prompted employers to modify the organizational policies and procedures that pertain to people's speech and behaviors. Furthermore, employees are no longer tolerating offensive communication while they are at work.

Suppose, for instance, that during a work break, Mindy and James are drinking a quick cup of coffee outside. During their conversation, James mentions that he thinks a lot of women workers in the company get a "free ride" because they can go home early when their children are sick or leave work if they have a family emergency. Mindy is outraged by the stereotypes James holds. She reminds him that company policies dictate personal time regulations for all employees and that men, too, care about their families and ask for time away from work for unexpected family events.

The interpersonal conflict between Mindy and James occurred in a private conversation. In some companies, if James had stated his belief in front of others, he would have found himself in more serious trouble. Staying clear of biases or stereotypes—even though you may have harbored them for years—is wise for both personal and professional reasons.

Practice Cultural Respect

Various traditions, customs, and practices allow cultures and co-cultures to function effectively. Skilled intercultural communicators respect those cultural conventions. No one culture can claim superiority over others in terms of knowing "the right way" to solve work problems, raise children, and manage interpersonal relationships. Practicing cultural respect requires us to show that we accept another culture's way of thinking and relating, even though we may disagree with or disapprove of it. Different societies have different moral codes, and judging a culture using only one moral yardstick can be considered both arrogant and self-serving.

When you practice cultural respect, you empathize with another culture. **Cultural empathy** refers to the learned ability to accurately understand the experiences of people from diverse cultures and to convey that understanding responsively (Ting-Toomey & Chung, 2005). When you are empathic, you are able to develop an emotional and psychological bond with another person or social group. In other words, you try to reach beyond the words to the feelings that the communicator is trying to show. You become other-oriented.

Developing cultural respect involves trying to look at a culture from the inside. As difficult as it sounds, we all must try to understand what it is like to be a member of another culture. Avoid reading verbal and nonverbal communication solely from your own cultural point of view. Refrain from becoming easily insulted if another person is not using your language or is having a hard time communicating.

Practicing cultural respect does not require us to practice complete cultural relativity, however. **Cultural relativity** means that an observer can never condemn any practice in which any culture engages. In other words, cultural relativity doesn't ever allow us to judge another culture. Cultural respect requires us to be aware that our own ways are not the only ways, but it allows us to judge other cultures when warranted. For example, some cultural practices may be inhumane. The challenge of cultural respect is that we must look at a culture and its practices from that particular society's perspective without totally giving up our own perspectives.

Educate Yourself

Aside from taking this course in interpersonal communication, you can take advantage of numerous opportunities to educate yourself about other cultures. First, simply reading about other cultures will give you a backdrop for future reference and will allow you to discover more about your own culture as well. Second, educating yourself requires that you learn about cultures through others. Listen to community lectures and discussions about cultural groups. Talk to people who represent another race, religion, nationality, or other cultural group. Be interested in their experiences, both good and bad, but avoid patronizing them.

In addition to reading about cultures and talking to others, visit Internet sites dedicated to co-cultural issues. For instance, the home site for Education World allows you to electronically visit a different culture. WorldBiz.com and Intercultural-Relations.com (click on the link "The Edge: The E-Journal of Intercultural Relations") provide links to information about cultures all over the world. For an international understanding of culture, check out the Society for Intercultural Education, Training and Research—Europe (click on the link "Doc Centre" at the top of the home page, then on the link "Newsletters & Journals Online"). To better understand religious diversity, visit Adherents.com. For information on tribal nations, NativeCulture.com is helpful. These are just a few of the active websites our students have chosen as important intercultural resources (you can find links to all these sites under Student Resources for Chapter 3 on the Understanding Interpersonal Communication website). Don't accept everything written about culture and communication as truth. Be rigorous in your reading and tentative in your acceptance. Be willing to seek out all available information that is based on both research and personal experience.

Ethics & Choice

Roberto, a Guatemalan exchange student, wasn't sure what to do about his living situation. He had been thrilled to be assigned to one of the best dorms on campus, and he had been excited about the roommate the computer had paired him with—a student from India. On move-in day, Roberto met his roommate, Eddy, for the first time. Roberto had limited exposure to speaking to anyone outside of his hometown in Guatemala, so his excitement about his new living arrangement was tempered by a little bit of nervousness.

Despite the cordial overtures in Roberto's and Eddy's relationship, Roberto's early excitement soon gave way to uncertainty. First, Roberto was bothered by the fact that Eddy constantly talked about Hinduism. He knew that Eddy was a devout Hindu, but he didn't know the extent to which Eddy's religion influenced his life. Second, although they hung out together at lunch, Roberto didn't really want to spend that much time with Eddy because he didn't care for the kind of music Eddy listened to and didn't like Eddy's friends.

Eddy, too, was having second thoughts about the living arrangement. He thought about Roberto's unkept promise of studying together. Eddy was also having trouble with the fact that Roberto often made food with some pretty powerful spices that would make the room smell for several days. Eddy was also getting irritated with Roberto's family's numerous late-night phone calls. Eddy was at his wits' end and wanted to figure out what to do next.

The roommates are clearly conflicted over what to tell each other (if anything). This intercultural dilemma raises a few important points. Would you advise Roberto or Eddy to say anything to the other? Are their concerns related to their different cultures or to the fact that they are roommates? What ethical system of communication that we discussed in Chapter 1 (categorical imperative, utilitarianism, golden mean, ethic of care, significant choice) do you believe is appropriate to consider in this story?

Use your Understanding Interpersonal Communication CD-ROM to access an interactive version of this scenario on the Understanding Interpersonal Communication website. Look under Student Resources for Chapter 3 and click on the "Ethics & Choice" menu at left. The interactive version of this scenario allows you to choose an appropriate response to this dilemma and then see what consequences your choice brings about. You can also compare your answers to the questions at the end of the scenario to those provided by the authors and, if requested, email your response to your instructor.

Be Prepared for Consequences

Although we may make a serious effort to be thoughtful and considerate, having a conversation with an individual from a different culture can be challenging. So many issues operate simultaneously in a conversation—verbal differences (word choice, dialect, syntax, and so forth), nonverbal differences (clothing, eye contact, conversation space, and so forth), nervousness, cultural customs, rules, and norms. We may try to attend to all these aspects of our conversation, but things still may go awry.

For instance, consider the experience of Mandy, a 29-year-old recent college graduate who interviews with a large health care company. After meeting her interviewer, Ms. Schultz, Mandy finds out that Ms. Schultz is a German who has just moved to the United States with the company after working for it in Germany for quite some time. Mandy, who thinks she is trying to be culturally responsive, attempts to engage Ms. Schultz with stories of her vacation in Germany, her two years of taking German language classes, and even proceeds to try to incorporate some German words and phrases in her interview. However, despite her best intentions, Mandy is viewed as patronizing and condescending. She may be nervous, but that serves as no excuse when Ms. Schultz finds her behavior insensitive and inappropriate.

In this scenario, Mandy clearly needed more cultural understanding. Mandy should have avoided talking about Germany altogether unless the topic was introduced by Ms. Schultz.

Relate to the Individual, Not the Culture

Although we are aware that we have necessarily had to draw upon generalizations to make some of the points in this chapter, we remain concerned about painting broad cultural strokes to define individuals. Identifying with the person and not the cultural group is paramount in intercultural communication.

Accepting individual cultural uniqueness is important. First, as we learned earlier, there are variations within cultures and co-cultures. For instance, not all Christians have the same beliefs, nor do all women support feminist views. Second, people's communication behaviors and skills can vary tremendously within cultures. Some people use a lot of personal space in conversations, whereas others use little. Some people are direct and forthright in their dialogues, but others are more reserved and timid. Some individuals may be reluctant to share personal tragedies; however, others may have no qualms with such disclosure. Constantly reminding yourself that not all members of a certain cultural group think alike, act alike, and talk alike allows you to focus on the person instead of the group to which he or she belongs.

CHOICES *for Intercultural Understanding*

- Know your biases and stereotypes
- Tolerate the unknown
- Practice cultural respect
- Educate yourself
- Be prepared for consequences
- Relate to the individual, not the culture
- Reevaluate and eliminate your prejudices

Reevaluate and Eliminate Your Prejudices

As we noted previously, knowing your biases is a good way to begin to improve your intercultural communication effectiveness. We expand this suggestion to encourage you to, while reevaluating your prejudices, rid yourself of some that you may have had for years. Recognizing that your family, friends, coworkers, school, and the media influence your prejudices is critical. Getting rid of the unwanted or misguided prejudices is essential if we are to begin to forge intercultural relationships with others.

We cannot understate the importance of actively eliminating harmful biases. Working toward eliminating those prejudices should be a priority. For example, because the media saturate our lives, they frequently influence our prejudices. We encourage you to be an engaged consumer of the media instead of consciously and unconsciously accepting as truth what the media present. Think about the thousands of websites that post hate-filled language and pictures. Newspapers frequently focus on cultural issues, but be on the alert for stereotypical and uninformed perspectives. Television, too, may communicate images that are less than authentic. Let the media know when they present faulty or inaccurate representations of cultural groups. At this point in your life, you have some foundation from which to argue your points.

Summary

Our cultural background shapes our identity, our communication practices, and our responses to others. Intercultural communication refers to communication between and among individuals and groups whose cultural backgrounds differ. As the populations of countries become more diverse, communicators today need to have knowledge of others' cultural values and practices to inform their communication.

The United States is a heterogeneous mix of various cultures, with 2.4 percent of the population identifying with more than one race. We can experience intercultural communication at the national level or at the small scale of a neighborhood. The United States generally supports cultural newcomers, including Latinos, the fastest growing cultural group.

Family, friends, and the media teach us culture. The national culture is made up of numerous co-cultures, or cultures within cultures, membership in which is determined by factors such as sexual identity, gender, and race. Cultures and co-cultures create a sense of community for members.

Culture has four dimensions. Cultures vary in the degree that they desire predictability (the uncertainty avoidance dimension) and how much they show respect for status (the distribution of power dimension). They also differ on what they value, such as competitiveness or quality of life (the masculinity-femininity dimension) and individual or group accomplishments (the individualism-collectivism dimension). Another important ingredient in culture is context; members of high-

context cultures draw the meaning of the message from the surroundings, whereas people in low-context cultures derive the meaning from the message itself.

In today's world, there are six reasons, or imperatives, to study intercultural communication. The technology imperative shows that technology makes communication with those in other countries easier than ever before. The demographic imperative recognizes that the United States is a symphony of cultures that should accommodate and appreciate each other. The economic imperative states that all societies—and their businesses—are interconnected in a global village. The peace imperative says that looking at world affairs from other countries' perspectives is a step in the right direction, especially if you have taken advantage of the self-awareness imperative, which encourages us to have a clear understanding of our own worldview. Finally, according to the ethical imperative, we have an obligation to ensure that cultural behaviors are depicted in the context of cultural values.

The chapter discusses five obstacles to intercultural communication. Ethnocentrism makes us judge other cultures using the standards of our own culture. Stereotyping is an often misguided process that associates certain traits with individuals just because they are part of a group. Anxiety influences our communication; feeling like a member of an in-group or out-group can affect our relationships. Nonverbal behaviors differ across cultures. Finally, if we assume we are similar to those in other cultures, we don't appreciate the differences between us, and the reverse is also true.

You can make positive choices to improve your intercultural understanding, including knowing and eliminating your biases, tolerating the unknown, practicing cultural respect, educating yourself, being prepared for consequences, and relating to the individual instead of the culture. Intercultural communication requires patience, knowledge, sensitivity, and respect. We hope that you work toward establishing and maintaining intercultural relationships with the information we outline in this chapter.

Understanding Interpersonal Communication Online

Now that you've read Chapter 3, use your Understanding Interpersonal Communication CD-ROM for quick access to the electronic study resources that accompany this text. Your CD-ROM gives you access to the video of Brad's interaction with Miguel on pages 63–64, the Ethics & Choice interactive activity on page 86, the CNN video clip "L.A. Diversity" on page 70, the Communication Assessment Test on page 78, InfoTrac College Edition, and the Understanding Interpersonal Communication website. When you get to the Understanding Interpersonal Communication home page, click on "Student Book Companion Site" in the Resource box at right to access the online study aids for this chapter, including a digital glossary, review quizzes, and the chapter activities.

Terms for Review

co-cultures 68	dialectics 81	intercultural communication 64
collectivism 71	ethnocentrism 77	low-context cultures 73
community 68	feminine cultures 70	masculine cultures 70
cultural empathy 85	global village 74	out-groups 80
cultural relativity 85	high-context cultures 72	outsourcing 74
culture 67	individualism 71	power distance 70
culture clash 68	in-groups 80	uncertainty avoidance 69

Questions for Understanding

Comprehension Focus

1. What is culture?
2. What are the dimensions of culture?
3. Differentiate between high-context and low-context cultures.
4. Define and explain stereotyping.
5. Define and explain ethnocentrism.

Application Focus

1. **CASE IN POINT**
   Examine our opening story of Brad Atchison. What advice would you offer to Brad when he returns to the United States after his visit to Mexico? Who would you suggest he speak to, and where could you direct him for additional information on cultural relationships?

2. Discuss the notion of cultural relativity and its relationship to the workplace, the classroom, or family life. Use examples from your personal and professional lives to support your views.

3. What would you say to someone who told you that too many cultural voices are being heard in society?

4. Explain how the media influence our perceptions, beliefs, and values associated with intercultural communication. Use examples from both print and nonprint media.

5. If you had a chance to talk to an intercultural communication researcher about some of the rules and laws in society pertaining to intercultural relationships, what would you talk about? What would guide your discussion?

Interactive Activities and InfoTrac College Edition Exercises

Complete the Interactive Activities and InfoTrac College Edition Exercises for Chapter 3 online at the Understanding Interpersonal Communication website. Select the chapter resources for Chapter 3, then click on "Activities" or "InfoTrac College Edition." If requested, you can submit your answers to your instructor.

Interactive Activities

3.1 Degrees of Uncertainty Avoidance 69
3.2 Culture in the Workplace 71
3.3 Hofstede's Dimensions of Culture 72
3.4 Effects of Globalization 75

InfoTrac College Edition Exercises

3.1 Culture and Negotiation 71
3.2 Diversity and Development 75
3.3 Putting Patriotism on Ice 79

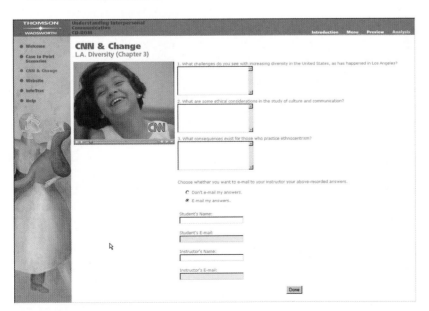

4

Communication and Emotion

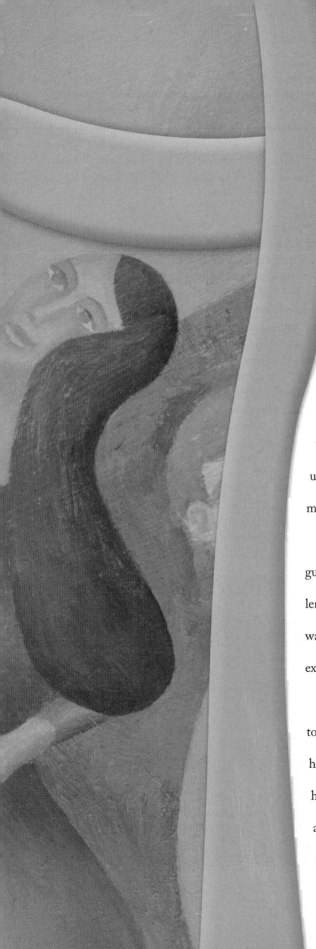

Tricia Nolan was enjoying her first full-time job as the secretary-receptionist for Four Star Construction Company. She had never dreamed she would work in such a beautiful environment and have such nice coworkers. The showroom, including her reception area, had been extensively remodeled just before she had begun working there a little more than two years ago, and it truly showcased the firm's construction skills. In addition, everyone in the company was so nice that she looked forward to going to work each morning. They all showed her respect and she enjoyed joking around with them. She also loved interacting with the customers because people coming into the showroom were usually happy and excited to be starting a construction project. That made the atmosphere at work very "up," which Tricia liked.

Tricia also loved her job because her boss, Theo Rankin, was a jovial guy who got along with people so well. Tricia knew he had a lot of problems at home because his daughter had juvenile diabetes, but he still always seemed to have a ready smile for those who worked for him. He was extremely kind as Tricia learned the business.

Although she had made a lot of mistakes when she was learning how to type up the proposals Theo gave her, he had never lost his temper. If he had been angry with her, he had never let his emotion show. It was a huge shock, then, when Tricia came in to the office early one morning and found Theo crying at his desk. When he saw her, he stopped immediately and tried to laugh it off, saying he had something in his eye.

Use your Understanding Interpersonal Communication CD-ROM to watch a video clip of Tricia's interaction with Mr. Rankin. Click on the "In Action" icon in the menu at left, then click on "Conversation Menu" in the menu bar at the top of the screen. Select "Tricia" to watch the video (it takes a minute for the video to load). As you watch the video, consider Tricia's response to Mr. Rankin's emotion. What do you think you might do in the same situation? You can respond to this and other analysis questions by clicking on "Analysis" in the menu bar at the top of the screen. When you've answered all the questions, click on "Done" to compare your answers to those provided by the authors.

He obviously didn't want to talk about it, and they both felt extremely uncomfortable. Tricia didn't know what to do or say, and she felt a mixture of emotions. Of course, she was concerned for Mr. Rankin and wished she could do something helpful. But she was also curious, upset, and fearful that this incident might change her wonderful workplace into a less comfortable environment. At the same time, she felt ashamed for thinking about herself at a time when Mr. Rankin obviously was in so much pain. ▇

We all experience the powerful impact of emotion: the joy of falling in love, the grief of losing a loved one, the pride we take in our accomplishments, the embarrassment we feel when we make a public mistake, the anger that boils up when someone fails to trust us, the jealousy that torments us when a loved one seems to prefer another, and so forth. In our opening Case in Point, Tricia's emotional reactions affected how she evaluated her workplace, how she interacted with her boss, and how she approached the dilemma of seeing him cry. Of course, emotion prompted Theo's tears. Emotion affects so much of our daily lives in a powerful way. Can you imagine interacting with others without emotion?

Our experiences of emotion and our communication about those experiences shape our daily lives and our relationships. Emotion is often what we remember about interpersonal encounters, and it forms the foundation for how we represent and judge our relationships. For example, when we think back to a friendship that has ended, we may be glad it's over because of all the arguments, which left us feel-

Emotion and interpersonal communication often go hand in hand. Not only does emotion influence how, when, and why we communicate with others, but our displays of emotion communicate messages themselves. For example, this family doesn't have to say a word to communicate their joy, gratitude, and relief when they receive a new house from Habitat for Humanity—their expressions say it all.

© Annie Griffiths/Corbis

ing angry most of the time. Or, we may remember a teacher fondly because she or he instilled a feeling of pride in us and left us feeling optimistic about the future.

Few of us would want to live without the richness provided through emotional experience. Emotions such as joy, love, and even rage and fear make us feel alive and aware and help define many people's lives and relationships. As a team of communication researchers observes, "clearly emotional experience and expression is part of a fabric of thoughts, feelings, and behaviors that blend together to characterize the tapestry of interpersonal interaction" (Guerrero, Andersen, & Trost, 1998, pp. 3–4). Feelings and communicating with others go hand in hand.

In this chapter, we investigate emotion and its relationship to the interpersonal communication process. We all know how important emotion is, but often we don't have enough information about emotion. When we neglect to learn about this topic, we experience an "obvious gap" in what we know about interpersonal communication (Planalp, 1999). For instance, emotional communication is often hard to interpret, so we need information about emotion to improve our accuracy in this regard. As with so many aspects of interpersonal communication, we need to gain adequate knowledge before we can develop our skills. Let's begin by defining emotion and emotional communication.

Defining Emotion: More Than Just a Feeling

Defining the term *emotion* is tricky because emotion is a thorny, complex concept. Some researchers observe that emotion forms the fundamental feeling states that guide our lives, especially our relationships with others (Planalp & Fitness, 1999). Others argue that only emotion that involves one person's feelings (like anger, fear, anxiety, happiness, and so forth) can be included in the definition. These researchers classify feelings involving more than one person (like love, hate, and jealousy) as social, so they fall outside their definition of emotion (for example, Fehr & Russell, 1984; Ortony, Clore, & Foss, 1987).

In this text, we take a middle position and define **emotion** as the critical internal structure that orients us to and engages us with what matters in our lives: our feelings about ourselves and others. Thus, in this text, the term *emotion* encompasses both the internal feelings of one person (for instance, anxiety or happiness) as well as feelings that can be experienced only in a relationship (for instance, jealousy or competitiveness).

To capture the complexity of emotion, some researchers have created category systems to classify common emotions. These systems focus on attributes of emotion, such as how intense it is, whether it reflects a positive or negative feeling (the **valence** dimension), or whether it implies action or passivity on the part of the person experiencing it. For example, an emotion such as hate is intense, negative, and implies some action, whereas an emotion like boredom is less intense, less negative, and rather passive.

Three Category Systems for Emotion

One category system (Russell, 1978, 1980, 1983) categorizes emotion along two dimensions: positive-negative and active-passive. This system allows us to see how specific emotions cluster together depending on whether they are active-negative, active-positive, passive-negative, or passive-positive (see Figure 4.1).

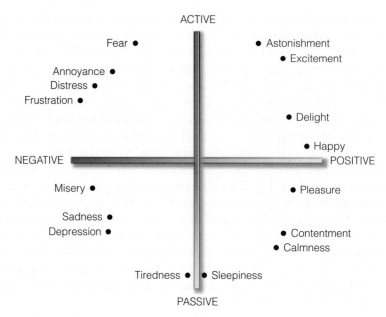

ACTIVE

Fear ●

● Astonishment
● Excitement

Annoyance ●
Distress ●
Frustration ●

● Delight

● Happy

NEGATIVE ━━━━━━━━━━━━━━━━━━━━━━━━━━ POSITIVE

Misery ●

● Pleasure

Sadness ●
Depression ●

● Contentment
● Calmness

Tiredness ● | ● Sleepiness

PASSIVE

Figure 4.1 | **Category system for emotions: positive-negative and active-passive**

From Guerrero, Anderson, Trost, eds. *Handbook of Communication and Emotion,* 1998, p. 14. Reprinted by permission of Elsevier.

Another way to classify individual emotion is based on its intensity. Robert Plutchik's (1984) emotion cone provides a graduated image of emotional range (see Figure 4.2). The lowest level of each vertical slice represents the mildest version of the emotion, and each successive level represents a more intense state. This system points to the impact of labeling an emotion with a particularly intense name. For example, if you say you are bored in a class, that carries a much different meaning, and is far less intense, than saying you loathe the class. For another look at Plutchik's emotion cone and the various dimensions of emotion, use your Understanding Interpersonal Communication CD-ROM to access **Interactive Activity 4.1: Emotion Cone.**

The third system, the prototype approach, builds on the importance of language in organizing our thoughts about emotion (see Figure 4.3). This system clusters specific emotions in a hierarchy so that families of emotions are arranged based on their level of generality. The first level is the most general, naming the overall category and stating the positive or negative nature of the emotion. Below that, the second level represents the core emotion of the category. The third level lists all the other individual emotions related to that prototype and shows similarities and differences between emotion families. For example, in Figure 4.3 we can see that under the core emotion joy, the individual emotions pride, triumph, and optimism are related to each other and are differentiated from contentment and pleasure.

Mixed Emotions

The category systems we've just described treat emotion as a series of individual, separate states. However, in life, people usually experience blends of several emotions. You may notice that so far in this chapter we usually refer to *emotion* rather than *emotions.* We do this intentionally because we think part of the definition of

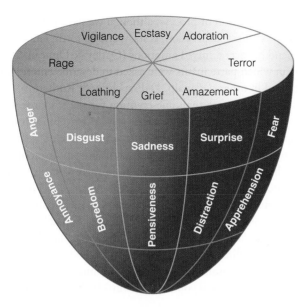

Figure 4.2 | **Emotion cone**

Plutchik, R. "Emotions: A general psychoevolutionary theory." In K. R. Scherer & P. Ekman, eds., Approaches to Emotion, 1984, p. 203. Reprinted by permission of Lawrence Erlbaum Associates.

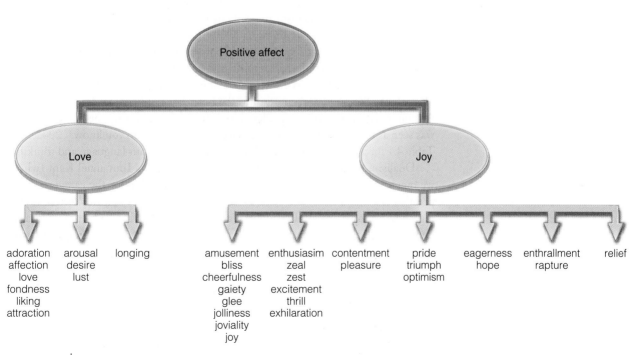

Figure 4.3 | **Category system for emotions: prototypical approach**

From Guerrero, Anderson Trost, eds. *Handbook of Communication and Emotion*, 1998, p. 20. Reprinted by permission of Elsevier.

emotion rests on the notion of process; although we have names for discrete emotions such as fear, sadness, depression, ecstasy, and so forth, emotion is often experienced as a blend of several mixed emotions (Oatley & Duncan, 1992).

In a study in which participants were asked to describe emotional communication they observed in others (Planalp, DeFrancisco, & Rutherford, 1996), the participants usually picked more than one emotion for the response even though the question was phrased to elicit a single emotion ("What emotion did you observe, e.g. anger, happiness, fear, etc.?"). Forty-five percent of the respondents chose two emotions for their answer, and 22 percent used three or more emotions. As the narrator states in the novel *Middlesex*, "emotions, in my experience, aren't covered by single words. I don't believe in 'sadness,' 'joy,' or 'regret'. . . . I'd like to have at my disposal complicated hybrid emotions, Germanic traincar constructions like, say, 'the happiness that attends disaster'" (Eugenides, 2002, p. 217).

Think about the last time you engaged in conflict or expressed affection to someone. Were you feeling only one emotion or a blend of two or three? Was your emotional response and communication easily summed up as a single event, or was it part of the ongoing process of your relationship? It's hard to point to only one feeling, isn't it?

Emotion, Cognition, and the Body

From the preceding discussion, you can see the complexity associated with the term *emotion*. Another reason that defining emotion is a difficult task is that Western thought has been historically grounded in dualisms. **Dualism** refers to a way of thinking that constructs polar opposite categories to encompass the totality of a thing. For example, dualism prompts us to think about all of temperature as either hot or cold; all of gender as either feminine or masculine; all of a person as either good or bad. Further, dualism prompts us to think about things in an "either/or" fashion. Thus, when we are thinking dualistically, we consider a person to be split into two parts—mind and body—that operate completely independently.

The historic division between mind and body is further split when the mind is seen, in another dualism, as either reason or emotion. Interestingly, the assignment of reason to the brain and emotion to the heart has not been consistent over time. Although the heart is now considered foolish and fickle, during the Middle Ages it was seen as the seat of human intelligence and wisdom ("Do you know?" 2002). See Table 4.1 for a listing of common dualisms that pervade our language and thinking.

Dualism, a legacy of eighteenth century philosophers Immanuel Kant (whom we mentioned in Chapter 1 as the philosopher responsible for the categorical imperative as a moral code) and Rene Descartes, is often seen today in Western thinking. For example, recall President George W. Bush's frequent comment after September 11, 2001, that countries had to decide: They were either allied with

Table 4.1 | **Common Dualisms in Western Thought**

hot	⟷	cold	strong	⟷	weak
male	⟷	female	right	⟷	wrong
good	⟷	bad	public	⟷	private
mind	⟷	body	black	⟷	white
reason	⟷	emotion	thinking	⟷	feeling
liberals	⟷	conservatives	active	⟷	passive

the United States against terrorism, or they were against the United States and implicitly a part of terrorism themselves. Thinking about emotion as separate from reason and the body is also reflected in medical school curricula. Many courses teach students to treat physical symptoms, but relatively few address the thoughts and feelings of patients and their families. And dualism is illustrated whenever someone says to another in a conflict: "Stop being hysterical about this! Just be reasonable."

However, despite these examples, on some level we also understand that emotion, the body, and reason are inextricably linked:

> Every day in this divided world of mind and body, our language [betrays] the limitations of our categories. "Widow Brown must have died of a broken heart—she never got sick until after her husband was gone. "My parents talked about our friend the grocer, who "worried himself sick". . . . (Moyers, 1993, p. xi)

Our language can help us see connections among emotion, mind, and body. Think about words we use to describe emotion: *heartache, heartsick, heartened, bighearted, heartless, heartfelt, light-hearted.* All these words indicate our instinctive knowledge of the connection between mind and body.

Further, experiencing emotion seems to affect people's physical functioning in ways that are not simply physical manifestations of the emotion. Journalist Bill Moyers (1993) interviewed Margaret Kemeny, a psychologist with training in immunology (the study of the immune system). She told him that evidence suggests that experiencing emotion has an effect on health. Based on her studies, she theorizes that prolonged depression makes people vulnerable to heart attacks and other debilitating diseases.

Psychiatrist Ana Fels concurs. A cardiologist referred a patient to her after a heart attack because the doctor hoped that treating the patient's depression would help stabilize the heart disease. Fels observed the relationship between body and emotion by stating, "not only had his heart attack set off his depression, but his depression could worsen his heart disease" (Fels, 2002, p. D5). To read an interesting article about how the brain and body changes when recalling emotional experiences, use your Understanding Interpersonal Communication CD-ROM to access **Interactive Activity 4.2: Feeling Emotion**. For more about the links among emotion, the body, feeling, and the mind, use your Understanding Interpersonal Communication CD-ROM to access **Interactive Activity 4.3: Emotions, the Body, and the Mind**.

In terms of the relationship between emotion and reason, communication researcher Sally Planalp (1998) offers the following story. A woman goes to the airport to pick up a friend. While she waits for the plane to land, she goes to a cafe, buys a candy bar, and sits down at a lunch counter to eat it. She is seated next to a man. After she takes a bite of her candy, much to her surprise, the man leans over, breaks off a piece of the candy, and eats it while giving her an odd look. They proceed to eat the entire candy bar by alternating bites until it is gone. During this process, the woman becomes more and more irritated until she finally gets up and leaves in a fury. After leaving, she opens her purse and finds her uneaten candy bar. Now her anger changes to embarrassment. As Planalp observes, new information altered her emotion.

Planalp also argues that the reverse is true: reason is dependent on emotion. Hunches and gut reactions show emotion in service of reason. Emotion helps us to decide between competing alternatives when all else is equal. How do you choose

Table 4.2 | **Emotions, Physical Reactions, and Cognitions**

Emotions	Physical Reactions	Cognitions
Joy	Warm temperature Fast heartbeat	Recognition of incoming stimuli
Anger	Fast heartbeat Tense muscles	Processing
Sadness	Lump in throat Tense muscles	Using the meaning of these stimuli to guide thoughts and actions
Shame	Hot flushes Fast heartbeat	Conscious awareness

between a brown scarf and a black scarf when both look equally good with your coat? How do you choose whether to visit your friend Mark or your friend Sam, when you like them each the same? We would be paralyzed by indecision if we didn't have emotional responses to help us make decisions (de Sousa, 1987).

Therefore, when we define emotion, we must take cognitive or rational and physical aspects into consideration. For example, let's examine the emotional process of fear. Information comes to you that you are being threatened in some way and that your safety is at risk. This involves cognition. You must notice that something dangerous is happening (for example, Mike is scowling at you and advancing toward you). In this step, you compare your knowledge of a nondangerous event to what is actually happening, and you see the discrepancy (for example, you say to yourself, "I could be walking down the street with no one bothering me, but I'm not"). You also have to determine the importance of this behavior and evaluate the context (for example, you and Mike are friends playing football, or you are walking down a dark street and Mike is a stranger). All these judgments are part of the cognitive element of emotion.

In addition, while Mike is coming toward you with a scowl, you're experiencing physiological symptoms such as accelerated heart rate, breathing changes, a lump in your throat, and tense muscles. These reactions comprise the physiological component of emotion. Table 4.2 presents a listing of common emotions with their accompanying cognitive and physical elements.

Emotion about Emotion

Before we leave the definition of emotion, let's take a look at a related topic: meta-emotion. **Meta-emotion** means emotion about emotion. People who study emotion tend to focus on the process of emotion and specific emotions, but they have not paid much attention to how people feel about expressing certain emotions. For example, in the case of anger, "some people are ashamed or upset about becoming angry, others feel good about their capacity to express anger, and still others think of anger as natural, neither good nor bad" (Gottman, Katz, & Hooven, 1997, p. 7).

Differences in the effects of emotion may vary in part because of meta-emotion. For example, compare the emotions of two couples who have been dating for a year: Andrea and José, and Marla and Leo. Andrea's expression of love for José is accompanied by the meta-emotion pride in her ability to engage in a committed relationship. José feels the same way. On the other hand, when Marla expresses love to Leo, she experiences the meta-emotion shame for becoming so vulnerable in a relationship. Transactions between Andrea and José should differ significantly from

REVISITING CASE IN POINT

1. How does Tricia's response to Theo illustrate the concept of meta-emotion?
2. How do you think Tricia's meta-emotion might affect how she'll communicate with Mr. Rankin?

You can answer these questions online under Student Resources for Chapter 4 at the Understanding Interpersonal Communication website.

those between Marla and Leo because one couple is proud of their commitment whereas one part of the other couple (that is, Marla) feels shame.

Models of Emotion: Biology and Social Interaction

Let's look at two models of emotion that illustrate how emotion operates: the biological and social models of emotion (Hochschild, 1983). These models will help us understand emotion more comprehensively and will further refine our definition of emotion.

The Biological Model of Emotion

Proponents of the biological model agree with Charles Darwin and others (Hochschild, 1983) that emotion is mainly biological, related to instinct and energy. Because advocates of this view believe that emotions are similar across many types of people, they propose that people from a variety of cultures should experience feelings in the same manner.

Further, this model assumes that emotion exists separately from thought and that we need thought only to bring a preexisting emotion to our conscious awareness. For example, let's say that Maura is arguing with her friend Barbara about how to plan a campus event. While they talk, Maura is thinking about advancing her ideas in the argument and is not paying any attention to the emotion she is experiencing. However, as she walks away from Barbara, she notices that she's slightly irritated because Barbara disagrees with her about the best way to advertise the event. Although Maura had been experiencing these emotions during the argument, she needed introspection, or thought, to bring them to the surface.

Our biology has a tremendous effect on our emotional expression. Smiling is a good example of an inherent human behavior—we don't have to be taught to smile to express happiness, pleasure, and many other emotions.

© Reuters/Corbis

Darwin placed importance on observable emotional expressions, not the meaning associated with them. Darwin argued that these "gestures" of emotion were remnants of prehistoric behaviors that served important functions. For instance, when we bare our teeth in rage, our behavior is a remnant of the action of biting. When we hug someone in an expression of love, our action is a remnant of the act of copulation. And when our mouths form an expression of disgust, our action is a remnant of the need to regurgitate a poisonous substance or spoiled food. Thus, in the biological model, "emotion . . . is our experience of the body ready for an imaginary action" (Hochschild, 1983, p. 220). Furthermore, Darwin argued that people enact these gestures as a result of experiencing emotion. However, he also asserted that the opposite is true—that is, when people enact a certain gesture, they experience the related emotion. Darwin also believed that these emotive gestures (with a few exceptions, such as weeping and kissing) are universal, meaning that they cross all cultures.

The Social Model of Emotion

The social model, attributed to Hans Gerth and C. Wright Mills (1964), among others, acknowledges that biology affects emotion and emotional communication. However, proponents of this model are also interested in how people interact with their social situation before, during, and after the experience of emotion. In this way, the model adds social factors to the biological basis for explaining emotion.

For example, let's say that Catherine finds out on Tuesday that her best friend, Lola, is having a party on Friday. Lola hasn't invited Catherine. The social model is interested in the following questions: What elements in Catherine's cultural milieu contribute to how she perceives being left off the guest list? That is, do any contextual elements affect her experience of emotion? For example, if Catherine's birthday is coming up, she might think Lola is giving her a surprise party. The biological model of emotion considers these questions unimportant, but they are central to the social model.

Like Darwin, Gerth and Mills were interested in gesture. However, their interest was founded in how the reactions of others to our gestures help us define what we are feeling. For example, let's say that Catherine tells another friend, Allen, about not being invited to the party, and she starts to cry because she feels hurt. Allen interprets Catherine's tears as a manifestation of anger, saying to Catherine, "You must be really mad!" Catherine hears this and agrees, "Yes, I can't believe that jerk didn't invite me after all the times she's been to my parties!" Catherine's sense of her own emotional experience may have been confused before she talked to her friend, but his interpretation swayed her and influenced how she labeled her emotion.

See Table 4.3 for a comparison of the biological and social models.

Table 4.3 | **The Biological and Social Models of Emotion**

	The Biological Model	**The Social Model**
Definition of emotion:	Biological processes	Feeling states resulting from social interaction
Relationship of emotions to cognitions:	Separate	Interrelated
Assumption of universality:	Yes	No
Concern with subjective meaning:	No	Yes

To take a look at several other models of emotion, including the "common sense" model, use your Understanding Interpersonal Communication CD-ROM to access **Interactive Activity 4.4: Models of Emotion.**

Now that we have discussed the definition of emotion, noting its complexity, we are ready to address our primary concern in this chapter: how emotion relates to interpersonal communication.

Emotion and Communication

In examining the relationship between interpersonal communication and emotion, we address the communication of emotion. We intentionally use the phrase *communication of emotion* or *emotional communication* rather than *expression of emotion* or *emotional expression* because we wish to highlight the importance of the communication process. The first part of this section focuses on the language used in the United States to portray emotion—that is, the metaphors we employ that center on emotion. The second part of this section discusses the communication of emotion through a variety of verbal and nonverbal cues.

Talk about Emotion

People often employ figurative language, especially metaphors, to talk about emotion. Further, people use metaphoric language to distinguish among various emotions as well as "the subtle variations in a speaker's emotional state (e.g., *get hot under the collar* refers to . . . [a] less intense state of anger than does *blow your stack*" [Leggitt & Gibbs, 2000, p. 3]). Table 4.4 lists some common metaphors for emotion.

Our figurative language also implies that emotion has a presence independent of the person experiencing it—as in the phrase "she succumbed to depression." Emotions are frequently framed as opponents ("he struggled with his feelings") or as wild animals ("she felt unbridled passion") (Koveçses, 2000). We speak of guilt as something that "haunts" us, fear as something that "grips" us, and anger as something that "overtakes" us (Hochschild, 1983).

Although these phrases are evocative of the feelings that various emotions engender, they leave the impression that people are not responsible for their emotion—that is, that people are acted upon by emotional forces beyond their control. This way of talking about emotion fits in with our earlier discussion of the division between emotion and reason. Such language depicts emotion as something that makes us lose our minds completely as we are overwhelmed by forces beyond our rational control.

Emotional Communication

In discussing how we talk about emotion, we must define three terms:

- **Emotional experience** refers to the feeling of emotion.
- **Emotional communication** means actually talking about the experience.
- **Communicating emotionally** suggests that the emotion itself is not the content of the message but rather a property of it.

Consider the following example of communicating emotionally. Let's say that Roberto yells at his wife, Tessa, without actually telling her that he's upset. In this case, the emotion—anger—is a property of the message. However, when we com-

Table 4.4	Common Metaphors and Emotions
Anger	
A hot fluid in a container	She is boiling with anger.
A fire	He is doing a slow burn.
Insanity	George was insane with rage.
A burden	Allison carries her anger around with her.
A natural force	It was a stormy relationship.
A physical annoyance	He's a pain in the neck.
Fear	
A hidden enemy	Fear crept up on him.
A tormentor	My mother was tortured by fears.
A natural force	Mia was engulfed by fear.
An illness	Jeff was sick with fright.
Happiness	
Up	We had to cheer him up.
Being in heaven	That was heaven on earth.
Light	Anna brightened up at the news.
Warm	Your thoughtfulness warmed my spirits.
An animal that lives well	Tess looks like the cat that ate the canary.
A pleasurable physical sensation	I was tickled pink.
Sadness	
Down	He brought me down with what he said.
Dark	Phil is in a dark mood.
A lack of vitality	That was disheartening news.
A natural force	Waves of depression swept over Todd.
An illness	Lora was heartsick.
A physical force	The realization was a terrible blow.

Adapted from Kovecses, 2000.

municate emotionally, we need to send and receive the reason for the emotion—as well as the emotion itself—accurately. If Roberto is upset because Tessa hasn't been listening to him, Roberto must communicate both messages (that he's upset and the reason for it), which are inseparable. Roberto wouldn't be upset if Tessa listened, and her lack of listening wouldn't be a problem if Roberto weren't upset by it.

Another issue related to emotion and communication involves the effect of emotional states on communication behavior (Burleson & Planalp, 2000). Communicative performance can be marred by emotions such as anxiety, fear, embarrassment, anger, and depression. As we mentioned in Chapter 1, many of us have suffered from some type of communication apprehension, such as "stage fright," which made our communication less effective than we wanted it to be. For example, when Sophie ran into her friend Alexa at the mall and accidentally called her Deanna, the name of another friend, Sophie was so embarrassed and flustered that she was unable to fluently conduct the rest of the conversation with Alexa.

How Emotion Is Communicated

Among the many tools for communicating emotion are facial expressions, vocal cues, gestures, and verbal cues. In this section, we discuss each of these cues briefly in turn. Keep in mind that people often use a combination of cues.

Facial Expressions

Facial expressions, the most researched cues to emotion, are obviously one of the most important means for communicating emotion. When people view photos of facial expressions for a variety of emotions, they are accurate in their ability to discern one emotion from another (Gosselin, Kirouac, & Dore, 1995). Probably the most researched facial expression is the smile. Smiles usually indicate warmth and friendliness, but smiles can be false and sneering as well. For example, Donna's boss, Melanie, often uses a smile as a mocking gesture. Therefore, when Melanie approaches Donna's office with a smile on her face, Donna braces herself for some type of unpleasant interaction. For an interactive look at the nature and types of emotion, influences on emotion, and facial displays of emotion, use your Understanding Interpersonal Communication CD-ROM to access **Interactive Activity 4.5: Expression of Emotion**. Also, to read an article about how brain signals determine facial expressions, check out "The Face of Feeling," available through InfoTrac College Edition. Use your Understanding Interpersonal Communication CD-ROM to access **InfoTrac College Edition Exercise 4.1: The Face of Feeling.**

Vocal Cues

Although it is not as well researched as the face, the voice is probably equally important in conveying emotion. How loudly people talk, how high-pitched their tone, how fast they talk, how many pauses they take, and so forth give clues to emotion. In addition, "the voice also carries information about whether emotions are positive and negative because, based on vocal cues alone, pride is more likely to be confused with elation, happiness, and interest than it is with the negative emotions" (Planalp, 1999, p. 46).

For example, when Jack calls his coworker Ely one morning before work, Ely can tell right away by the way Jack says "hello" that something is wrong. Before Jack explains his problem verbally, Ely is cued by the tone in Jack's voice. To read a fascinating article about how culture affects emotional communication, read the article "Stop That Laughing, Please," available through InfoTrac College Edition. Use your Understanding Interpersonal Communication CD-ROM to access **InfoTrac College Edition Exercise 4.2: Stop That Laughing.**

Gestures

Sally Planalp (1999) observes that emotions are "embodied," that "people scratch their heads, clench their fists, shake, gesture wildly, hug themselves, pace the floor, lean forward, fidget in their seats, walk heavily, jump up and down, slump, or freeze in their tracks" (pp. 46–47). However, there isn't a great deal of research on gestures and body movement. Some research has indicated that depressed people gesture less than those who are not depressed (Segrin, 1998).

Verbal Cues

People rarely state a specific emotion directly (Shimanoff, 1985, 1987). Instead, they use indirect cues as they communicate emotionally. For example, Max infers that Russ is angry with him when Russ calls Max an idiot and tells him that he wants to be alone. Russ doesn't tell Max any direct information about his emotion, but calling him a name and saying that he wants to be by himself are indirect verbal indicators of Russ's emotional state.

We often infer people's emotional states when they use sarcasm or rhetorical questions (Leggitt & Gibbs, 2000). For instance, let's say that Isabella invites Ruth over for dinner, and Ruth shows up an hour late. When Isabella greets Ruth by saying, "Nice of you to show up on time," Ruth gets the idea that Isabella is angry. Ruth would also probably get the same message about Isabella's emotional state if she asked Ruth rhetorically, "Do you ever look at your watch?" In neither case did Isabella say she was angry directly, but her comments were indirect indicators of anger. Later in this chapter, we show you how to use I-messages to verbalize your emotions, which can prevent the confusion that might result from indirect communication.

Combinations of Cues

Although we have discussed these cues separately, people usually communicate emotion through a mixture of cues. People often use verbal and vocal cues while gesturing and smiling. For example, when Dwight surprises Pat with a vacation to Acapulco, Pat tells him that she's happy in a high-pitched voice while grinning and giving him a hug. However, in contrast to these matching cues, sometimes cues are conflicting or incongruent. For example, when Sandy tells her son, Jake, that she is angry that he hasn't put away all his toys, she laughs indulgently. Especially in cases of conflicting cues, people rely on other information to try to discern the meaning. We discuss some of these other influences in the next section.

Influences on Emotional Communication

In this section, we briefly review research on three of the many factors that influence emotional communication. As you will observe in our examples, the three factors—culture, gender, and context—overlap a great deal.

Culture

Remember from our discussion of the biological model of emotion that Darwin asserted that emotions are primarily universal—that is, people of all cultures respond to the same emotions in the same way. Few people agree with that assertion today. Although some emotional states and expressions—such as joy, anger, and fear—are thought to be universal, the current focus of research is on differences in emotional communication across cultures. The brief review in this section will give you an overview of how different cultures think about emotion and how emotion is communicated in various cultures. In Chapter 3 we discussed the topic of culture more completely.

Thinking about Emotion

Sally Planalp and Julie Fitness (1999) observe that cultures differ in how much they think and talk about emotion. For example, according to these researchers, 95 percent of Chinese parents report that their children understand the meaning of shame by age 3, whereas only 10 percent of U.S. parents say their children do. Because of this difference, Planalp and Fitness argue that shame plays a more important role in Chinese culture than it does in U.S. culture.

Planalp and Fitness (1999) note that the opposite situation exists with the emotion of love; the Chinese think less about love than do those in the United States. Further, when the Chinese do think of love, they have a cluster of words to describe "sad-love," or love that does not succeed; such words are absent in U.S. culture. Other research (Lazarus, 1991) points to a similar dynamic in Japanese culture. In Japanese stories, when a conflict exists between a couple and the families of the couple, it is resolved in favor of the families, even when that means the couple has to give each other up. In Japan, stories that end with the lovers separating because of family objections are celebrated as showing the triumph of right. In contrast, in the United States and other Western European cultures, many of the stories in books, magazines, and movies end with the couple staying together against the wishes of their families. In these cultures, listeners cheer the lovers on, enjoying the triumph of romantic love.

How Emotion Is Communicated across Cultures

People of different cultures express emotion differently (Aune & Aune, 1996). For instance, people from warmer climates have been found to be more emotionally expressive than those from colder climates. In addition, people from collectivistic cultures (like Korea, China, and Japan), which we discussed in Chapter 3, are discouraged from expressing negative feelings for fear of their effect on the overall harmony of the community. Thus, people from these cultures are less inclined to express negative feelings.

This does not mean that people from collectivistic cultures do not have negative feelings; it simply means that emotional restraint in communication is a shared cultural value (Johnson, 2000). People from individualistic cultures like the United States have no such cul-

Ethics & Choice

Marco Petrillo felt conflicted, and he wasn't sure where to turn for help. He had studied hard during his first three years of college to keep his grades up and to make connections so that he could land a choice internship for his senior year. His hard work had paid off; he had recently begun working for Jones and Markum, one of the best advertising agencies in the city. He was initially overjoyed about the position and had been patting himself on the back for landing it. He thought his advertising classes had prepared him well for this experience, and he wanted to be successful so he had a chance of being offered a job with the agency after graduation.

Everything seemed to be going well until he was assigned to a group working on a campaign for a video game targeted at kids ages 9 to 13. The game was offensive to Marco because it seemed to glorify violence and was disrespectful of women. In the game, the player received points for beating up people encountered in the street, including a prostitute. The player got double points for picking her up and then throwing her out of the car. Marco had grown up in a pretty rough neighborhood, and he had never found violence fun—he had seen too much at close range.

When Marco reported for the group's first meeting, he was surprised to discover that none of the other group members had a problem with the game. In fact, two of them had come up with what they thought were some great emotional appeals to sell it. They argued that the game should be surrounded with bright colors that kids in the target age group liked to achieve an immediate nonverbal response. They then proceeded to present a clever series of print ads and television commercials that played on kids' desires and fears. Marco had to give them credit; the ads were good. They pushed a lot of emotional buttons and implied that owning this game would resolve the emotional confusion that the ads themselves created.

What would you advise Marco to do? Should he talk to his advisor at the college? Should he raise his concerns in his work group or with his bosses at the ad agency? Should he quit? Should he stick with the group but try to get it to tone down the emotional appeals in the ad? Or should he just keep quiet and go along with the group? What would be the consequences of each of these decisions?

In answering these questions, think about the five ethical systems described in Chapter 1 (categorical imperative, utilitarianism, ethic of care, golden mean, significant choice). Explain how your answers regarding the consequences relate to these systems. Do you prefer one course of action over the other? Explain.

Use your Understanding Interpersonal Communication CD-ROM to access an interactive version of this scenario on the Understanding Interpersonal Communication website. Look under Student Resources for Chapter 4 and click on the "Ethics & Choice" menu at left. The interactive version of this scenario allows you to choose an appropriate response to this dilemma and then see what consequences your choice brings about. You can also compare your answers to the questions at the end of the scenario to those provided by the authors and, if requested, email your response to your instructor.

tural value—in fact, emotional openness is valued—so they are more expressive of negative emotions.

Gender

Gender differences in emotional communication are widely researched. The U.S. culture, which divides many activities according to sex, is interested in the ways in which men and women are presumed to differ (Tannen, 1995). For example, although gender stereotypes are in flux in the United States, parenting is still seen as primarily the responsibility of women, whereas men are expected to work to pay the bills. The two sexes are expected to do different things and have different strengths in the workplace and at home (Buzzanell, Sterk, & Turner, 2004). In this section, we review research that examines emotion and gender stereotypes and then explore research on the expression of emotion and gender.

Emotion and Gender Stereotypes

Of course, the stereotypical view holds that women are more emotional, more emotionally expressive, and more attuned to the emotions of others than are men. Agneta Fischer (2000) wonders why women are thought to be the emotional sex while men are perceived to be unemotional. She asserts:

> As far back as I can remember I have encountered emotional men; indeed, I have met more emotional men than emotional women. My father could not control his nerves while watching our national sports heroes on television (which made watching hardly bearable); my uncle immediately got damp eyes on hearing the first note of the Dutch national anthem; a friend would lock himself in his room for days when angry; a teacher at school once got so furious that he dragged a pupil out of the class room and hung him up by his clothes on a coat-hook; one of the male managers at our institute was only able to prevent having a nervous breakdown by rigidly trying to exercise total control over his environment; and a male colleague's

How do gender stereotypes influence your perception of how men and women should communicate emotion and how you yourself should communicate emotion? What have been the main social or cultural influences that led you to accept or reject gender stereotypes in regard to emotion: your family, your friends, school, the workplace, the media?

© Michelle D. Bridwell/PhotoEdit

constant embarrassment in public situations forced him to avoid such set-tings altogether. (p. ix)

Fischer's point is not that men are more emotional than women but that all these instances of emotional men go unnoticed because they do not support the stereotypes we have of emotional women and stoic men.

Stephanie Shields (2000) makes a similar point when she argues that emotional expression (or lack of it) defines the essence of femininity and masculinity. She notes that people even use gender stereotypes to make judgments about their own emotions. Shields reports on an earlier study she and her colleagues conducted (Robinson, Johnson, & Shields, 1998, as cited in Shields, 2000), in which participants played a competitive word game. In the study, participants were asked about their emotional experience both immediately after playing and then a week later. The researchers found that the reports about the emotions matched gender stereotypes more closely the longer the reports were recorded after the event. The researchers concluded that when the participants forgot exactly how they felt, they used stereotypes (that is, men are stereotyped as more stoic and women as more emotional) to provide an answer.

Shields participated in another study that showed the power of gender stereotypes of emotion. This study (Shields & Crowley, 1996) asked college students to read an emotion-provoking scenario and then to answer open-ended questions about the scenario. The scenario was identical for all participants except that in some cases the protagonist was male and in others female. The scenario stated one of the following:

"Karen was emotional when she found out that her car had been stolen."

"Brian was emotional when he found out that his car had been stolen."

The researchers found that the respondents judged the word *emotional* in the scenario differently depending on whether they read the Karen version or the Brian version. If participants thought the protagonist was Karen, they attributed the cause of her emotions more to her personality than to her situation, and they imagined her reaction was extreme and hysterical. Respondents who thought Brian's car was stolen downplayed the word *emotional* in the story and described his emotion as what any rational person might feel who had worked hard making money to buy the car. The researchers concluded that the respondents used gender stereotypes to answer the questions.

To read more about stereotypes concerning gender and emotion, read the article "Speaking from the Heart: Gender and the Social Meaning of Emotion," available through InfoTrac College Edition. Use your Understanding Interpersonal Communication CD-ROM to access InfoTrac College Edition Exercise 4.3: Gender, Emotions, and Stereotypes.

Emotional Expression and Gender

Researchers are interested in the differences between men and women in nonverbal expressions of emotion, such as smiling. Three differences are well documented and may be caused by men and women conforming to stereotyped gender roles (Hall, Carter, & Horgan, 2000). Women smile more than men in social situations (Hall et al., 2000). Men and women also differ in nonverbal expressiveness, or facial animation and the liveliness of gestures. Again, women are more expressive than men (Hall et al., 2000). Women are also more accurate than men in figuring out what others' emotional states are based on nonverbal cues (Hall et al., 2000).

"Federal Bureau of Feelings, sir. It seems that last night you neglected to ask your wife how her day was. You have the right to remain silent."

REVISITING CASE IN POINT

1. How do you think Mr. Rankin's sex affects Tricia's response to him?
2. How do you think being a male affects Mr. Rankin's own feelings about Tricia discovering him crying?

 You can answer these questions online under Student Resources for Chapter 4 at the Understanding Interpersonal Communication website.

As people age, these gender stereotypes seem to exert less influence on their behaviors. Men tend to become more emotionally expressive, and women become more instrumental or task oriented. A study of 20 married couples over the age of 60 who had been married on average for 42 years shows this change. The researchers interviewing the couples found the men to be expressive about their emotions (saying things like they fell in love with their wives at first sight and reporting how nervous they'd been to meet her parents), whereas wives were more matter-of-fact in their accounts (Dickson & Walker, 2001).

To further explore gender and emotion and how they relate to context, read the article "Gender-Emotion Stereotypes Are Context Specific," available through InfoTrac College Edition. Use your Understanding Interpersonal Communication CD-ROM to access **InfoTrac College Edition Exercise 4.4: Gender, Emotion, and Context.**

Context

The contexts in which we express emotion are infinite: We express emotion at work, with friends, in our families, at school, over the phone, in person, and so on. We discuss three specific contexts here: online emotional expression, historical period, and the feelings of those around us.

Online Communication

As we discussed in Chapter 1, the channel for a communication transaction influences the communication. Because more and more of our communication time is spent in electronic communication or computer-mediated communication (CMC), online emotional communication is a worthwhile subject of study. You might won-

Table 4.5	Emoticons
:) or :-)	Happiness, sarcasm, or a joke
: (or :-(	Unhappiness
:] or :-]	Jovial happiness
: [or :-[	Despondent unhappiness
:D or :-D	Jovial happiness
: I or :-I	Indifference
:-/ or :-	Indecision, confusion, or skepticism
:Q or :-Q	Confusion
:S or :-S	Incoherence or loss of words
:@ or :-@	Shock or a scream
:O or :-O	Surprise, a yell, or realization of an error ("uh-oh!")

Common emoticons (n.d.)

der how email users and frequenters of chat rooms can express emotion without nonverbal cues. As you probably know, the answer to that question is the emoticon. **Emoticons** are icons that can be typed on the keyboard to express emotions. They are used to compensate for the lack of nonverbal cues in CMC.

Emotional communication is obviously vital to online interactions; a preliminary online search yielded more than 100,000 sites in at least five languages that deal with emoticons. Most emoticons look like a face (eyes, nose, and mouth) when rotated 90 degrees clockwise. See Table 4.5 for examples of commonly used emoticons and their translations.

Some research (Rourke, Anderson, Garrison, & Archer, 2001) argues that when people become experienced users of CMC, it is just as rich a communication process as any other, including face to face. Further, CMC doesn't inhibit emotional expression; a study found that 27 percent of the total message content consisted of emotional communication (Rourke et al., 2001).

A recent study investigated emoticon use by males and females (Wolf, 2000). The study showed that when people moved from a same-sex newsgroup to a mixed-sex newsgroup, men adopted the female standard and began expressing more emotion as evidenced by a greater use of emoticons. We explore the topic of technology and interpersonal communication further in Chapter 11.

Facing *Change*

Technological changes offer many new communication options, and some people argue that technology may be fundamentally altering the way we communicate. For example, the Internet may not simply be another, different communication channel—it may actually change the structure, meaning, content, and effect of communication. How do you think emotional communication is affected by using email, chat rooms, instant messaging, and so forth? Do you think expressing emotion through new technologies such as those mentioned will somehow change the ways we feel emotion? How might that happen? For example, does using emoticons online alter how you are experiencing the emotion you are representing?

Historical Period

In his book *American Cool,* Peter Stearns (1994) traces the changes in emotional communication in the United States from the Victorian period (beginning approximately in the 1830s) to the 1960s. His main thesis is that the Victorians were much more emotionally expressive than U.S. citizens of the 1960s. According to Stearns, the 1960s North American favored "cool" over the emotional excesses of the Victorians. Stearns states that culture is governed by **feeling rules,** or "the recommended norms by which people are supposed to shape their emotional expressions and react to the expressions of others" (p.2). He notes that the feeling rules of U.S. culture changed considerably during the time span he examines.

Stearns observes that in the 1890s, men in the United States were instructed to express their anger. However, 70 years later, child-rearing experts warned parents not to encourage boys to express anger, arguing that an angry man is possessed by the devil. In the area of romantic love, Victorian men were also encouraged to be expressive, in contrast to the 1960s vision of male love as primarily sexual and silent. Stearns quotes from a love letter written by a man of the Victorian era:

> "I don't love you and marry you to promote my happiness. To love you, to marry you is a mighty END in itself. . . . I marry you because my own inmost being mingles with your being and is already married to it, both joined in one by God's own voice." (p. 3)

Obviously, a man in Victorian times would be influenced by the feeling rules of his time and would express himself much differently than a man of the 1960s, who would be equally influenced by a very different set of feeling rules. Today, we have different feeling rules as well, although the influence of "cool" is still strong in contemporary U.S. society.

Others' Feelings

The influence of the feelings of those around us is manifested in what has been called **emotional contagion,** or the process of transferring emotions from one person to another. Emotional contagion occurs when one person's feelings "infect" those around him or her. You have probably experienced emotional contagion yourself. You can probably remember a time when you were with a friend who was nervous. Didn't you find yourself becoming nervous, too, just watching your friend fidget? Or you may have become depressed yourself after spending time with a friend who was down in the dumps. Conversely, if you are around someone who exudes positive feelings, you usually find your own mood brightening.

The Dark Side of Emotional Communication: We Always Hurt the Ones We Love

As we discussed earlier in this chapter, some classification systems of specific emotions use positive and negative (that is, valence) as a primary dimension for typing those emotions. We are all familiar with the emotions that fall on the dark side: embarrassment, guilt, hurt, jealousy, anger, depression, and loneliness, to name a few. When we discussed the dark side of communication in Chapter 1, we mentioned that hurtful messages are part of the dark side. Indeed, hurtful messages have received recent attention from researchers exploring how this type of emotional communication operates in relationships (for example, Vangelisti & Young, 2000; Young & Bippus, 2001). One study found that if hurtful messages were phrased humorously, they were perceived as less intentionally hurtful and thus caused fewer wounded feelings (Young & Bippus, 2001).

Some dark side emotions are the polar opposites of bright side emotions. For example, empathy, a bright side emotion, is the opposite of the dark side emotion *schadenfreude.* Later in this chapter, we suggest empathy (a skill we discuss more in Chapter 5) as a recommended practice for becoming an effective communicator. On the other hand, *schadenfreude* is a German word that, loosely translated, means to take pleasure in another's misfortune. The term is derived from the words *damage* and *joy.* In 2002, some reporters used *schadenfreude* to describe how many people felt when they saw Martha Stewart's image tarnished by her suspected involvement with insider trading (St. John, 2002).

The fact that *schadenfreude* blends two emotions should come as no surprise. As we mentioned earlier in this chapter, emotions are often experienced in blends, and bright and dark, love and hate, are entangled with one another. Another emotional blend is strategic embarrassment. Although embarrassment is an unpleasant emotional state, people often plan embarrassing situations for others, and planning an embarrassing moment for someone else is often socially acceptable (Bradford & Petronio, 1998). For example, it is a common practice among adolescents to use strategic embarrassment in the following way (Bradford, 1993): Tom knows his friend, Jesús, is interested in Amy. He also knows that Jesús is shy and won't introduce himself to her. As Amy and Jesús pass in the school hallway, Tom purposely pushes Jesús into Amy. Jesús is embarrassed but recognizes that Tom actually helped him connect with Amy.

Another way that negative emotional communication can have a bright side is that negative expressions of anger can be functional in certain contexts, including the following example from Tavris (2001):

> A 42-year-old businessman, Jay S., described how his eyes were opened when he overheard his usually even-tempered boss on the phone one afternoon: "I've never heard him so angry. He was enraged. His face was red and the veins were bulging on his neck. I tried to get his attention to calm him down, but he waved me away impatiently. As soon as the call was over, he turned to me and smiled. "There," he said. "That ought to do it." If I were the guy he'd been shouting at, let me tell you, it would have done it, too. (p. 251)

In this example, Tavris (2001) points out that yelling and showing anger accomplished a goal. She argues that there are no simple guidelines specifying when talking is better than yelling because the context, the receiver, the sender, and the social goal all make a difference. According to Tavris, the categorization of an emotion or even a mode of emotional communication as either dark or bright is problematic because it all depends on whether the context called for the emotion, the sender and the receiver expected the emotion, and the social goals of the situation were accomplished through the emotional communication.

As Tavris (2001) states, "the calm, nonaggressive reporting of your anger (those "I messages" that so many psychologists recommend) is the kindest, most civilized and usually most effective way to express anger, but even this mature method depends on its context" (p. 250). Tavris then goes on to relate the case of a 40-year-old woman who cannot get her husband to pay attention to her anger unless she screams and rants. He won't believe that she is really angry if she speaks to him in I-messages and in a calm manner.

The Bright Side of Emotional Communication: Happy Talk

Communication that offers comfort, social support, warmth, affection, forgiveness, or desire falls on the positive end of the emotional spectrum. However, like the dark side, the bright side of emotional communication does not present a simplistic picture. Some of the research on social support provides a glimpse at the mixture of bright and dark that are expressed simultaneously. David Spiegel and Rachel

Your *Turn*

In your journal, reflect on the dark and bright sides of emotional communication. Which side do you experience most when you undergo emotional arousal? Does one side predominate when you talk about your emotions or when you communicate emotionally? How do the dark and light sides combine in an emotional situation? Does your answer vary depend on the type of emotion you are experiencing or communicating? Explain using examples. If you'd like, you can use your student workbook to complete this activity.

Kimerling (2001) introduce an example from a support group for family members of breast cancer patients by saying, "the expression of positive feelings often brackets the expression of painful sadness" (p. 101). Following is the vignette they quote:

> A 20-year-old daughter was tearfully coming to terms with the sudden downhill pre-terminal course of her mother's breast cancer: "I see this black hole opening up in my life. I don't think I will want to live without my Mom. She would stay up at 2 A.M. and talk me through my misery for two hours. She won't be there, but I don't want to make her feel guilty for dying." Her father, also at the family group meeting, held her hand and tried to comfort her, but he clearly was overwhelmed by his own sadness and his lifelong fear of strong emotion and dependency on him by others. The husband of another woman whose breast cancer was progressing rapidly started to comfort her but found his voice choked with emotion: "I am sure you will get through this—there's so much love in your family." "Why are you crying?" the father asked. "I don't know," he replied, and everyone, tearful daughter included, found themselves laughing. (p. 101)

The mix of bright and dark shows a complex tapestry of emotion. Another instance that shows a mixture of bright and dark was reported in the *Annals of Behavioral Medicine* (Ullrich & Lutgendorf, 2002). When college students were asked to write their feelings about a traumatic event as well as their efforts to understand and make sense of it, they became more aware of the benefits of the trauma, such as improved relationships, greater personal strength, spiritual growth, and a greater appreciation of life. The authors concluded that the process of communicating their thoughts and emotion made a negative event seem brighter.

Yet another example of the complexity involved in classifying emotional communication as dark or bright can be seen in the emotional communication of forgiveness. Forgiveness, which is based in numerous religious teachings, represents the bright side because it allows for peace and reconciliation.

However, even proponents of forgiveness acknowledge how difficult it can be in practice. Archbishop Desmond Tutu (1999), who wrote a book about reconciliation in South Africa titled *No Future Without Forgiveness,* places a high priority on forgiveness. To stress the importance of reconciliation, he invokes the African concept of *ubuntu,* which means that a person is only a person through other people. Archbishop Tutu

When we experience traumatic events as a community, such as the hurricanes that hit Florida in 2004 or the terrorist attacks of September 11, 2001, we express emotions not only on the negative side of the emotional spectrum but often on the positive side as well. In helping others, receiving assistance, and talking about the experience, we may express gratitude at our ability to stay strong in a crisis, we may experience a greater sense of closeness to our families and friends, and we may feel a heightened appreciation for those things in life that matter to us most.

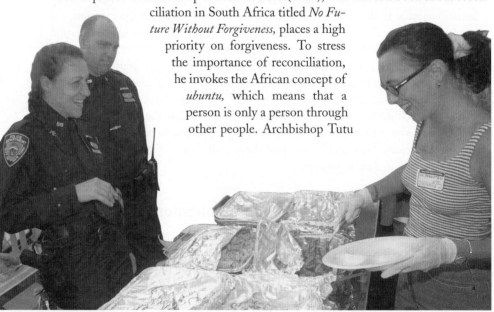

© AP/Wide World Photos

chaired South Africa's Truth and Reconciliation Commission, which stressed forgiveness as an alternative to racial hatred. The commission presided over hundreds of hearings in which blacks and whites spoke of past grievances and asked forgiveness for those they had harmed. Archbishop Tutu claims in his book that the commission and the process of forgiveness it supervised spared South Africa from the violence and civil unrest that many expected after years of white-minority rule. However, even Archbishop Tutu admits that forgiveness is difficult to achieve in some instances.

Dean Murphy (2002) writes in the *New York Times* about the power and problematic nature of forgiveness. He cites Roger W. Wilkins, a civil rights activist and history professor at George Mason University, who notes that people need to forgive for their own sense of self-preservation. Mr. Wilkins observes,

> After a while you figure it out for yourself: you can't be consumed by this stuff because then your oppressors have won. . . . If you are consumed by rage, even at a terrible wrong, you have been reduced. (Murphy, 2002)

However, Mr. Wilkins recognizes the limits of forgiveness when he reflects on the bombing of the 16th Street Baptist Church in Birmingham, Alabama, in 1963, which killed four young black girls. In 2002, Bobby Frank Cherry was convicted of the bombing deaths and sentenced to life imprisonment. He has not asked for forgiveness and continues to deny his guilt. The prosecutor notes that this makes forgiveness complicated and states that forgiveness requires participation from both sides. In this case, Mr. Wilkins suggests that people can purge hatred from their hearts without actually forgiving.

Murphy (2002) relates another difficult case: a Fulbright scholar was murdered in South Africa, and her parents managed to forgive. Californian Amy Biehl was stoned and stabbed to death in South Africa in 1993. Her parents quit their jobs to work for racial reconciliation. They testified in favor of political amnesty for the killers and offered two of them jobs. They stated that they found it liberating to forgive.

Forgiveness highlights the bright and dark sides in tandem. To experience the liberation of forgiveness, the Biehls had to suffer the torment of grief. Figure 4.4 illustrates the interdependence of the bright and dark sides of emotional communication.

Figure 4.4 | **The interdependence of the bright and dark sides of emotion**

Choices for Developing Emotional Communication Skills

Competence in expressing emotion and in listening and responding to the emotional communication of others is critical to your success as an interpersonal communicator. Some have called this competence *emotional intelligence.* This concept has received a great deal of attention since the 1995 publication of Daniel Goleman's best-selling book with that title. Goleman notes that communicative skills are central to emotional intelligence (E-IQ) and that E-IQ is required to be effective in contemporary society.

We agree with Sally Planalp (1999), who says that although emotional communication does require intelligence, *emotional intelligence* might be more accurately labeled *emotional competence.* Planalp makes the argument that intelligence connotes a relatively unchanging aptitude rather than a skill set that can be improved and developed. As she states, "we may not all be emotionally brilliant, but most of us are competent—we get along" (p. 70). Further, we can develop our competence so that we'll get along better than we do currently. Practicing to become better and enacting these skills requires effort. Some researchers (for example, Buzzanell & Turner, 2003) have called the effort or energy involved in maintaining emotional competence **emotion work.** To help you develop emotional communication competence, we provide several skills for you to consider.

Know Your Feelings

Competence in emotional communication begins with your ability to identify the emotion or mix of emotions you are experiencing at a particular time. This skill requires you to do several things:

1. Recognize the emotion you're feeling.
2. Establish that you are stating an emotion.
3. Create a statement that identifies why you are experiencing the emotion. (You may or may not choose to share this statement with anyone else; it is sufficient that you make the statement to yourself.)

Recognizing Your Emotion

This step requires you to stop for a moment and ask yourself what your emotional state is at the present. In other words, you are to take a time out from the ongoing process and take your emotional temperature. It is important not to skip this step, because it involves making a link between yourself and outer reality. To name your feelings signals how you perceive them and alerts you to what your expectations are. For instance, when you recognize that you are irritable, that cues you that you have less patience than usual, and you may expect others to make allowances for you. The opposite process occurs as well. When you give a feeling a name, you respond to that label, which triggers perceptions and expectations.

This step is difficult for several reasons. First, in the heat of an emotional encounter, you may not be prepared to stop and take a time out. Second, we are often so detached from our feelings that it is difficult to name them. And third, some people are simply less aware than others of their emotional states. If you are "low affective-oriented" (Booth-Butterfield & Booth-Butterfield, 1998), you will be relatively unaware of your own emotional experiences.

Communication Assessment Test

Emotional Intelligence (E-IQ)

Although there is no current, valid pencil-and-paper test for your E-IQ that works as reliably as the IQ test, the following test was devised by Daniel Goleman, author of the best-selling 1995 book *Emotional Intelligence.* Answering these questions will give you a rough idea of what your E-IQ might be. You can also take this test online under Student Resources for Chapter 4 at the Understanding Interpersonal Communication website.

_____ 1. You're on an airplane that suddenly hits extremely bad turbulence and begins rocking from side to side. What do you do?
A. Continue to read your book or magazine, or watch the movie, paying little attention to the turbulence.
B. Become vigilant for an emergency, carefully monitoring the flight attendant reading the emergency instructions card.
C. A little of both A and B.
D. Not sure—never noticed.

_____ 2. You've taken a group of 4-year-olds to the park, and one of them starts crying because the others won't play with her. What do you do?
A. Stay out of it—let the kids deal with it on their own.
B. Talk to her and help her figure out ways to get the other kids to play with her.
C. Tell her in a kind voice not to cry.
D. Try to distract the crying girl by showing her some other things she could play with.

_____ 3. Assume you're a college student who had hoped to get an A in a course, but you have just found out you got a C- on the midterm. What do you do?
A. Sketch out a specific plan for ways to improve your grade and resolve to follow through on your plans.
B. Resolve to do better in the future.
C. Tell yourself it really doesn't matter how you do in the course, and concentrate instead on other classes where your grades are higher.
D. Go to see the professor and try to talk her into giving you a better grade.

_____ 4. Imagine you're an insurance salesperson calling prospective clients. Fifteen people in a row have hung up on you, and you're getting discouraged. What do you do?

A. Call it a day and hope you have better luck tomorrow.
B. Assess qualities in yourself that may be undermining your ability to make a sale.
C. Try something new in the next call, and keep plugging away.
D. Consider another line of work.

_____ 5. You're a manager in an organization that is trying to encourage respect for racial and ethnic diversity. You overhear someone telling a racist joke. What do you do?
A. Ignore it—it's only a joke.
B. Call the person into your office for a reprimand.
C. Speak up on the spot, saying that such jokes are inappropriate and will not be tolerated in your organization.
D. Suggest to the person telling the joke that they go through a diversity training program.

_____ 6. You're trying to calm down a friend who has worked himself up into a fury at a driver in another car who has cut dangerously close in front of him. What do you do?
A. Tell him to forget it—he's okay now, and it's no big deal.
B. Put on one of his favorite tapes and try to distract him.
C. Join him in putting down the other driver as a show of rapport.
D. Tell him about a time something like this happened to you and how you felt as mad as he does now, but then you saw the other driver was on the way to the hospital emergency room.

_____ 7. You and your life partner have gotten into an argument that has escalated into a shouting match; you're both upset and, in the heat of anger, making personal attacks you don't really mean. What's the best thing to do?

(continued)

Communication Assessment Test (*continued*)

A. Take a 20-minute break and then continue the discussion.

B. Just stop the argument—go silent, no matter what your partner says.

C. Say you're sorry and ask your partner to apologize, too.

D. Stop for a moment, collect your thoughts, then state your side of the case as precisely as you can.

_____ 8. You've been assigned to head a working team that is trying to come up with a creative solution to a nagging problem at work. What's the first thing you do?

A. Draw up an agenda and allot time for discussion of each item so you make the best use of your time together.

B. Have people take the time to get to know each other better.

C. Begin by asking each person for ideas about how to solve the problem, while the ideas are fresh.

D. Start out with a brainstorming session, encouraging everyone to say whatever comes to mind, no matter how wild.

_____ 9. Your 3-year-old son is extremely timid and has been hypersensitive about—and a bit fearful of—new places and people virtually since he was born. What do you do?

A. Accept that he has a shy temperament and think of ways to shelter him from situations that would upset him.

B. Take him to a child psychiatrist for help.

C. Purposely expose him to lots of new people and places so he can get over his fear.

D. Engineer an ongoing series of challenging but manageable experiences that will teach him he can handle new people and places.

_____ 10. For years you've been wanting to get back to learning to play a musical instrument you tried in childhood, and now, just for fun, you've finally gotten around to starting. You want to make the most effective use of your time. What do you do?

A. Hold yourself to a strict practice time each day.

B. Choose pieces that stretch your abilities a bit.

C. Practice only when you're really in the mood.

D. Pick pieces that are far beyond your ability, but that you can master with diligent effort.

Scoring

1. Anything but D—that answer reflects a lack of awareness of your habitual responses under stress.
   A = 20, B = 20, C = 20, D = 0

2. B is best. Emotionally intelligent parents use their children's moments of upset as opportunities to act as emotional coaches, helping their children understand what made them upset, what they are feeling, and alternatives the child can try.
   A = 0, B = 20, C = 0, D = 0

3. A. One mark of self-motivation is being able to formulate a plan for overcoming obstacles and frustrations and follow through on it.
   A = 20, B = 0, C = 0, D = 0

4. C. Optimism, a mark of emotional intelligence, leads people to see setbacks as challenges they can learn from, and to persist, trying out new approaches rather than giving up, blaming themselves, or getting demoralized.
   A = 0, B = 0, C = 20, D = 0

5. C. The most effective way to create an atmosphere that welcomes diversity is to make clear in public that the social norms of your organization do not tolerate such expressions. Instead of trying to change prejudices (a much harder task), keep people from acting on them.
   A = 0, B = 0, C = 20, D = 0

6. D. Data on rage and how to calm it show the effectiveness of distracting the angry person from the focus of their rage, empathizing with their feelings and perspective, and suggesting a less anger-provoking way of seeing the situation.
   A = 0, B = 5, C = 5, D = 20

7. A. Take a break of 20 minutes or more. It takes at least that long to clear the body of the physiological arousal of anger—which distorts your perception and makes you more likely to launch damaging personal attacks. After cooling down, you'll be more likely to have a fruitful discussion.
   A = 20, B = 0, C = 0, D = 0

(continued)

Communication Assessment Test (*continued*)

8. B. Creative groups work at their peak when rapport, harmony, and comfort levels are highest—then people are freer to make their best contribution.
A = 0, B = 20, C = 0, D = 0

9. D. Children born with a timid temperament can often become more outgoing if their parents arrange an ongoing series of manageable challenges to their shyness.
A = 0, B = 0, C = 0, D = 20

10. B. By giving yourself moderate challenges, you are most likely to get into the state of flow, which is both pleasurable and where people learn and perform at their best.
A = 0, B = 20, C = 0, D = 0

200 is the highest score, and 100 is average.

From D. Goleman, Emotional Intelligence: Why it can matter more than IQ, 1995. Reprinted by permission of Bantam Books, a division of Random House.

You need to practice this skill and work on methods to overcome these obstacles. For example, in a highly charged emotional interaction, you can repeat a phrase like "it's time to take a time out," or you can make a prior agreement with a relational partner that you will check every half hour to see if a time out is needed. You might want to list emotions in a journal so you can consult the list to remind yourself of the variety of emotion you might be experiencing. You can also monitor your physical changes to check for signals of emotion. As we noted in Table 4.2, emotion is often accompanied by physiological conditions such as a hot flush, a lump in the throat, and so on. And you can monitor your thoughts to see how they might relate to feelings.

Establishing That You Are Stating an Emotion

This step in the process provides a check to see that you are really in touch with emotion language. It isn't enough to simply say "I feel"; you must be sure that what follows really is an emotion. For instance, if you say "I feel like seeing a ball game," you are stating something you want to do, not an emotion you are experiencing. A better phrasing would be: "I feel restless because I have been working on this project all weekend and I'd like to get out and see a game."

Creating a Statement that Identifies Why You Are Feeling the Emotion

This step involves thinking about the antecedent conditions that are contextualizing your feelings. Ask yourself, "Why do I feel this way?" and "What led to this feeling?" Try to put the reasons into words. For example, statements such as the following form reasons for emotion:

- "I am angry because I studied hard and I got the same grade on the exam that I got when I didn't study."
- "I am feeling lonely. All my friends went to spend the weekend upstate and left me alone at home because I couldn't take time off from work."
- "I am feeling really happy, proud, and a little anxious. I finally got the job I wanted, and I worked especially hard to make a good impression at the interview. All the prep work I did paid off. But now I have to actually make good on everything I said I could do!"

- "I'm feeling guilty. I told my boyfriend I couldn't see him tonight because I had to study, but I really just felt like having a night to myself."

Going through this exercise should help you to clarify why you are experiencing a particular emotion or emotional mix. Further, it should point you in a direction to change something if you wish to. For instance, if you wish to reduce your guilt, tell your boyfriend that you need some time to yourself occasionally without having to give him a reason.

Analyze the Situation

After identifying your emotion, you analyze the situation by asking yourself these questions:

1. *Do you wish to share your emotion with others?* As we mentioned previously, some emotional experiences are not ready for communication—that is, you may not completely understand the emotion yet or you may feel that you would quickly slide into conflict if you communicated the emotion. Or, you might decide that you are comfortable with the emotion and that you don't ever need to share it. For example, if you are looking through your high school yearbook and feel nostalgia for the time you spent there, you might enjoy your reminisces and not feel the need to talk about it with anyone. If you wake up early one morning and experience a beautiful sunrise, you may feel joy without needing to tell anyone about it.

2. *Is the time appropriate for sharing?* If you decide you want to communicate an emotion to someone else, an analysis of the situation helps you decide if the time is right. If your partner is under a great deal of stress at work, you might wait until the situation improves before talking about your unhappiness at how little time you spend together. If you just found out you are pregnant with a wanted baby and your best friend has recently suffered a miscarriage, you also might decide to wait to share your joy.

3. *How should you approach the communication?* Analyzing the situation helps you think about how to share your emotion. If you are angry with your boss, you need to consider if and/or how to express your anger. Obviously, anger at a boss and anger at a partner provide entirely different situational constraints. Because the workplace climate is not conducive to emotional communication, you may decide not to tell your boss how you feel even though you would like to do so.

4. *Is there anything you can do to change the situation if needed?* Your analysis allows you to think about how and whether to change the situation. In the case of a workplace issue, you might consider instituting new norms at work, accepting the way things are, or looking for a new job.

Own Your Feelings

Owning is the skill of verbally taking responsibility for your feelings. Owning is often accomplished by sending **I-messages,** which show that speakers understand that their feelings belong to them and aren't caused by someone else. I-messages take the following form:

"I feel _____ when you _____, and I would like _____."

Skill *Spotlight*

Identifying Your Emotion

It takes practice to name and express emotions. Mic Hunter (2000) suggests that to get in touch with your emotion, you need to take time out of your everyday routines to think about which emotion you are experiencing. Hunter advocates keeping a list of emotion and placing copies of it in strategic places as a reminder to notice your feelings and to label them appropriately.

For instance, you can tape one list to your bathroom mirror so you can think about what you are feeling as you prepare for your day. After you acknowledge what you are feeling, you can then ask yourself how and to whom you will express this feeling. You can keep another copy of the list at work or in your briefcase or backpack. Then, during a break in your day you can glance at the list and identify the emotion you have experienced thus far.

Finally, you can place another copy of the list on your bed. Before you go to sleep, review your day and specify the emotion you have experienced. Hunter also suggests that it may be helpful to keep an emotion journal where you can record the emotion you've felt by making daily or weekly entries. Writing about your emotion in the journal will provide valuable information about emotion that you are having difficulty identifying.

In addition to journaling about your own emotion, you can gain practice in the skill of identifying emotion by writing about emotion revealed in books or the media. When you go to see a movie, you can record in the journal the emotion you observed that the characters expressed. After reading a passage in a novel, record the feelings you think are behind the dialogue. By faithfully noting the emotion you feel and observe, you will become skilled at identifying and getting in touch with emotion.

Skills at Work As we have shown in previous examples, many emotional communication skills have an impact on communication in the workplace. One work scenario in which the skill of owning feelings is particularly important is on group projects. For example, let's say that Bill works on a project with a coworker, Angela. If he believes that he is not being acknowledged for his contributions and that Angela is taking credit for his work, he may feel angry and upset. Feeling he is working hard without getting the appropriate credit taps into concerns about fairness and loyalty and can stir powerful emotions. However, expressing these emotions can be tricky in the workplace. If Bill decides to do so, it is critical that he own them. If he speaks to Angela in a defensive, accusatory fashion, conflict may result that ultimately might affect their working relationship, might darken the workplace climate, and might even result in disciplinary actions for one or both employees. Can you think of a way that Bill could use owning statements to avoid these potential problems but still communicate his concerns?

For example, let's say that Vanessa is unhappy that her boyfriend, Charles, spends more time with his buddies than with her. Vanessa's I-message would be something like the following:

> "I feel unhappy when you spend four nights a week with your friends, and I would like you to spend one of those nights with me."

I-messages differ from you-messages, in which I place the responsibility for my feelings on you. If Vanessa had sent a you-message to Charles, she might have said:

> "You are so inconsiderate. All you do is hang out with your friends. I can't believe I am staying with you!"

You can see that Charles's reaction might be more positive to the I-message than to the you-message. Using I-messages does not guarantee that you will get what you ask for. Charles could still tell Vanessa that he wants to spend four nights with his friends. But I-messages help to ensure that Charles hears what Vanessa wants and that he doesn't get sidetracked into a defensive spiral where he argues with her characterization of him as inconsiderate. The I-message focuses on Vanessa's emotion, which is what she wants to talk about with Charles.

Reframing is a particularly useful skill for keeping anger in check. For example, if you start to succumb to road rage, think of the other driver as rushing to see a desperately sick relative in the hospital rather than as just a jerk who cut you off.

© Tony Freeman/PhotoEdit

Reframe When Needed

Reframing refers to the ability to change the frame surrounding a situation to put it in a more productive light. When Jane Brody (2002) wrote about suggested methods for reducing hostile tendencies, she alluded to the skill of reframing. Brody quotes Dr. Norman Rosenthal, a psychiatrist in the Washington, DC, area who specializes in depression and anger. Rosenthal comments that a friend often grew angry when waiting in his car at long red lights. The friend's wife reframed for him by reminding him that "the red light doesn't care, so he might as well save his fury" (p. D7). Rosenthal suggests that it is easier for people to reframe their thinking about something than it is to change the world. He goes on to say that after you discover what makes you mad, you can reframe those irritants by changing the messages you give yourself. If you think of other people as rude, that frame may cause hostility. If you change the frame to respecting yourself for being polite, you will feel less anger and hostility.

Carol Tavris (2001) talks about a similar process when she recounts what Ray Navaco advises clients who come to him for help in anger management. Navaco points out that "anger is fomented, maintained, and inflamed by the statements we make to ourselves and others when we are provoked—'who does he think he is to treat me like that?' 'What a vile and thoughtless woman she is!'" (Tavris, 2001, p. 252). He teaches his clients to reframe and to substitute other statements, such as "Maybe he's having a tough day" and "She must be very unhappy if she would do such a thing."

Empathize

As you will learn in the next chapter, **empathy** is the ability to put yourself in another's place so you are able to understand his or her point of view. Empathy is often accomplished through the skill of **active listening,** which calls for you to suspend your own responses for a while so you can concentrate on the other person. In active listening, you usually allow the other person a full hearing (no interruptions), and when it's your turn, you say something like, "You sound really troubled by your relationship with your dad. Tell me more about how you're feeling." This skill is valuable when you are the receiver of another person's emotional communication. For example, when Rob comes storming into his fraternity house, throwing his books on the table, and swearing about his problems with his girlfriend, Chloe, he needs someone to listen to him with empathy.

CHOICES *for Developing Emotional Communication Skills*

- Know your feelings
- Analyze the situation
- Own your feelings
- Reframe when needed
- Empathize

Often our response to hearing someone's emotional outburst is to attempt to solve his or her problem ("here's what you should say to her the next time you see her"), question the person ("how long has she been acting like this?"), tell a story about a similar problem that you have had ("hey, I know just how you feel, my girlfriend does the same thing! That's why I dumped her") or evaluate the person's problem ("you know, all couples fight—it's not that big a deal"). Although some of those responses might prove useful later in the conversation, empathizing is the best approach for early in the talk because it keeps the focus on the person who is expressing the emotion and allows that person to set the pace and the content of the conversation. In this way, that person can explore how he or she really feels while you lend a listening ear.

Although these skills take practice, knowing your feelings, recognizing your emotion, being able to identify reasons for your emotion, phrasing an emotion statement, analyzing the situation, owning, reframing, and empathizing all will contribute to your communication competence in emotional encounters.

For more about emotional competence and its role in a specific context—the workplace—read the article "Your Emotional Skills Can Make Or Break You," available through InfoTrac College Edition. Use your Understanding Interpersonal Communication CD-ROM to access InfoTrac College Edition Exercise 4.5: Emotional Skills at Work.

Summary

Emotional language and emotional communication are inevitable in our daily interactions. *Emotion,* a complex term, is the critical internal structure that orients us to what matters in our lives, our feelings about ourselves and others. Emotion relates to the affective, or feeling tone, of our experiences.

Three systems of categorization allow us to classify specific emotions based on their attributes. One system uses positive-negative (valence) and active-passive dimensions, one classifies emotions according to their intensity, and one uses prototypes to arrange emotions so that they are clustered in a hierarchy. Although these classification schemes treat emotions as separate states, people often experience more than one emotion at once.

Western thought encourages dualistic thinking, which prompts us to see emotion as separate from reasoning. However, such thinking is fallacious because emotion, reason, and physiology are interconnected. To add to the complexity of emotion, meta-emotion, or how people feel about expressing certain emotions, influences people's interactions.

The biological model of emotion, based mainly on Darwin's ideas, states that emotions are related to instinct and are universal. This view places emphasis on observable emotional expressions, or "gestures" of emotion. On the other hand, the social model of emotion, attributed mainly to Hans Gerth and C. Wright Mills, states that the social situation, as well as biology, affects the experience of emotion. This view studies how the reactions of others to our gestures help us define our feelings.

People often use metaphors to talk about emotion, many of which make it seem as if emotional forces are beyond our control. When people communicate emotionally, the emotion is a property of the message rather than its content. Tools for emotional communication include facial expressions, vocal cues, gestures, and verbal cutes. Culture, gender, and context are three of the many factors that influence emotional communication. Emotional communication has a dark side and a bright side, which often overlap.

Becoming competent in emotional communication requires practicing the following techniques: knowing your feelings, analyzing the situation, owning your feelings, reframing when needed, and empathizing. Emotional communication is a complex activity that involves sensitivity, awareness, insight, and empathy. Just like any proficiency, emotional communication requires patience and persistence, but the rewards are worth the effort.

Understanding Interpersonal Communication Online

Now that you've read Chapter 4, use your Understanding Interpersonal Communication CD-ROM for quick access to the electronic study resources that accompany this text. Your CD-ROM gives you access to the video of Tricia's interaction with Theo on pages 91–92, the Ethics & Choice interactive activity on page 105, the Communication Assessment Test on page 115, InfoTrac College Edition, and the Understanding Interpersonal Communication website. When you get to the Understanding Interpersonal Communication home page, click on "Student Book Companion Site" in the Resource box at right to access the online study aids for this chapter, including a digital glossary, review quizzes, and the chapter activities.

Terms for Review

active listening 120	emotional	feeling rules 109
communicating	communication 101	I-messages 118
emotionally 101	emotional contagion 110	meta-emotion 98
dualism 96	emotional experience 101	owning 118
emoticons 109	emotion work 114	reframing 120
emotion 93	empathy 120	valence 93

Questions for Understanding

Comprehension Focus

1. Define emotion.
2. Compare and contrast the biological and social models of emotion.
3. Distinguish among emotional experience, emotional communication, and communicating emotionally.
4. List three factors that influence emotional communication.
5. Define owning and provide an example.

Application Focus

1. **CASE IN POINT**
   Examine our opening story of Tricia Nolan and Theo Rankin. What advice would you offer Tricia? What should she say to Theo? What advice would you offer Theo? What should he say or do at this time? Does an understanding of emotional intelligence help you understand this case? Explain how it does or why it does not.

2. Discuss the relationship among thought, feeling and the body. Do you see them as separate or intertwined? Use examples to support your opinion.

3. Provide your own definition of emotional communication. How does it differ from the definition presented in the chapter? Explain the reasons for those differences. Does emotional communication differ from emotions? Explain your answer.

4. Evaluate the models of emotion that we presented in the chapter. Explain what you see as the strengths and weaknesses of each.

5. Discuss the research on culture as a factor that influences emotions and emotional communication. To what degree do you think that emotions are universal or transcend culture? Justify your answer with evidence and examples.

Interactive Activities and InfoTrac College Edition Exercises

Complete the Interactive Activities and InfoTrac College Edition Exercises for Chapter 4 online at the Understanding Interpersonal Communication website. Select the chapter resources for Chapter 4, then click on "Activities" or "InfoTrac College Edition." If requested, you can submit your answers to your instructor.

Interactive Activities

4.1 Emotion Cone 94
4.2 Feeling Emotion 97
4.3 Emotions, the Body, and the Mind 97
4.4 Models of Emotion 101
4.5 Expression of Emotion 103

InfoTrac College Edition Exercises

4.1 The Face of Feeling 103
4.2 Stop That Laughing 103
4.3 Gender, Emotions, and Stereotypes 107
4.4 Gender, Emotions, and Context 108
4.5 Emotional Skills at Work 121

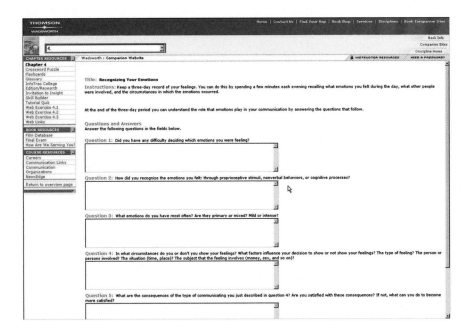

5

Effective Listening

CHAPTER GOALS

Understand the complexity of the listening process

Recognize social and personal obstacles to listening

Identify your personal style of listening

Describe several habits of poor listening

Explain how culture affects listening

Utilize a variety of techniques to enhance your listening effectiveness

CASE IN POINT: JACQUELINE MITCHELL

Jacqueline Mitchell, age 25, had been the director of volunteers for a local political campaign for almost a month. She knew that she was perceived as an important gatekeeper because both political and community leaders considered the campaign to be a critical one.

Jacqueline's responsibilities consisted primarily of coordinating the schedules of the candidate's nearly 20 campaign volunteers. She also answered about 50 phone calls a day for the campaign. With a degree in communication and public policy, Jacqueline thought this was the ideal job. She wasn't paid a lot, but she thought she would gain beneficial experience working on the campaign. At one point, the campaign director, Mara, asked Jacqueline to do some quick research to prepare the candidate for an upcoming interview. Although Jacqueline felt unqualified for this task, she listened to Mara's directions and did her best. Successfully completing this assignment made Jacqueline feel even more confident about her job performance, but she soon learned that even the most self-assured can make mistakes.

Jacqueline scheduled a few important appointments for her candidate at the precise time that the candidate would be attending a rally. In addition, Jacqueline told a campaign secret to one of her volunteers, who then told a member of the media.

When the campaign director verbally reprimanded Jacqueline for scheduling appointments when the candidate would be busy at a rally,

Use your Understanding Interpersonal Communication CD-ROM to watch a video clip of Jacqueline's situation. Click on the "In Action" icon in the menu at left, then click on "Conversation Menu" in the menu bar at the top of the screen. Select "Jacqueline" to watch the video (it takes a minute for the video to load). As you watch Mara scold Jacqueline, consider some strategies Jacqueline might have used to help her listen better. You can respond to this and other analysis questions by clicking on "Analysis" in the menu bar at the top of the screen. When you've answered all the questions, click on "Done" to compare your answers to those provided by the authors.

Jacqueline was confused because she thought she remembered hearing that there were no rallies scheduled for several weeks. Mara also admonished Jacqueline for not keeping campaign secrets. Mara told Jacqueline that she might not be cut out for the fast pace of politics. Jacqueline, too, wondered whether she was suited to the job or whether her listening skills needed a major overhaul. Mara told Jacqueline that she would be given one more chance because she was new to the job.

At times, failing to listen attentively and passionately is not all that devastating. In fact, in the course of an average day most of us don't listen perfectly to the barrage of messages from the media, our friends, family, and coworkers. Some of these messages are useless or meaningless to us, others we've heard over and over again, and still others don't make sense to us.

Most of the time, though, failing to listen to a message has consequences. When interpersonal communication becomes difficult, we, like Jacqueline, may be concerned about whether or not we are listening well. In Jacqueline's case, more than a relationship was at stake—her job was on the line.

Think of scenarios in which listening is crucial. For example, how would you feel if your physician didn't listen to your health problems? Or, how would you feel if your psychotherapist didn't listen to your psychological troubles? Consider the effects of a supervisor not listening to a colleague who knows of unethical practices in the company. What would happen if your best friend failed to listen when you were recounting an important problem? This chapter discusses the importance of listening, explores reasons why we don't always listen, and suggests ways we can overcome our bad listening habits.

The Importance of Listening

Although we like to think that we are good listeners, the truth is that we all need help in this area. Listening is an ongoing interpersonal activity that requires lifelong training. Active listening, a behavior we discuss in more detail later in the chapter, is particularly crucial. Because we listen for a variety of important reasons (see Figure 5.1), listening needs to be a high priority in our lives (Brownell, 2002).

Figure 5.1 | **Why we listen**

Listening is essential to our relationships with others, especially in the workplace. Employers rank listening as the most important skill on the job (Career Solutions Training Group, 2000). Listening expert Michael Purdy suggests that hourly employees spend 30 percent of their time listening, managers 60 percent, and executives 75 percent or more (Purdy, 2004). Liz Simpson (2003), a writer for the *Harvard Management Communication Letter,* offers the following advice to those in the workplace: "To see things from another's point of view and to build trust with her [him], you have to listen closely to what she [he] says" (p. 4).

Listening has been called a twenty-first century skill (Bentley, 2000; Grau & Grau, 2003). Sheila Bentley (2000) remarked that "new technology and changes in current business practices have changed whom we listen to, what we are listening for, when we listen to them, and how we listen to them" (p. 130). Years ago, we took the skill of listening for granted, but today, we need to be aware that we will encounter negative consequences if we don't listen well. Listening errors can influence relational intimacy and worker productivity (Barker & Watson, 2001).

A significant amount of corporate time is dedicated to training employees in listening (Wolvin & Coakley, 2000). Writing from a corporate vantage point, Jennifer Grau and Carole Grau (2003) note that "expanding listening capability and well-developed conflict management skills are not dispensable management tools" (p. 3). To read an article about the importance of listening in the workplace and to check out listening skill training offered to business managers, use your Understanding Interpersonal Communication CD-ROM to access **Interactive Activity 5.1: Listening in the Workplace.**

Good listening skills are valuable in other types of interpersonal relationships as well. For example, successful medical students must develop effective listening skills because, on average, a medical practitioner conducts approximately 150,000 medical interviews with patients during a 40-year career (Watson, Lazarus, & Thomas, 1999). In the educational context, researchers have found that effective listening is associated with more positive teacher-student relationships (Wolvin & Coakley, 2000). And on the home front, many family conflicts can be resolved by listening more effectively (Gottman, 1994; Turner & West, 2006).

Although it dates to the 1940s (Nichols, 1948), the topic of listening is clearly relevant today. You would have trouble thinking of any interpersonal relationship in your life that doesn't require you to listen. Improving your listening skills will help improve your relational standing with others. We hope you agree that the power of listening cannot be overstated. To read an interesting article that reinforces the importance of listening and that offers steps to effective listening, use your Understanding Interpersonal Communication CD-ROM to access **Interactive Activity 5.2: The Importance of Listening.**

Before we discuss the listening process, we need to point out that not everyone has the physical ability to hear. Although our discussion in this chapter focuses on those who are able to hear physiologically, we are aware that many individuals rely on another communication system to create and share symbols: **American Sign Language (ASL).** ASL is the third most popular language in the United States after English and Spanish. A visual rather than auditory form of communication, ASL is composed of precise hand shapes and movements. According to the "About ASL" page of a website dedicated to American Sign Language (www.aslinfo.com), approximately half a million people communicate in this manner in the United States and Canada alone. In fact, ASL is seen as a natural communication method

Your *Turn*

Think about how being a good listener affects your family relationships. Write about the different situations in which listening is important or about a time that you failed to listen to a family member. Also comment on what happens when other family members don't listen to you. Do you use any specific listening strategies with family members that may not necessarily work in other relationship types? If you'd like, you can use your student workbook to complete this activity.

Take a moment to notice all the auditory stimuli around you. On an average day, how much stimuli do you think you ignore so that you can concentrate on a task or on another person's message?

© Bill Aron/Photo Edit

for visual learners who aren't hearing-impaired, making it commonplace in many schools across the country (Toppo, 2002). The hard-of-hearing and deaf community have embraced ASL, and it is used to create and to sustain these communities.

We continue our discussion by differentiating listening from hearing. Although some people interchange the two terms, hearing and listening are different processes and mean different things, as our discussion of ASL begins to illustrate. Let's talk first about hearing.

Hear Today: The Hearing Process

Hearing occurs when a sound wave hits an eardrum. The resulting vibrations or stimuli are sent to the brain. For our purposes, we define **hearing** as the physical process of letting in auditory stimuli without focusing on the stimuli. For instance, when Polly sits at The Coffee Bean drinking coffee and reading the morning paper, she hears all types of noises, including people ordering coffee, couples laughing, the door squeaking as it opens and closes, and even the hum of the fluorescent lights. However, she is not paying attention to these background noises. Instead, she is hearing the stimuli without thinking about them. Polly must be able to tune out these stimuli because otherwise she wouldn't be able to concentrate on reading the paper.

Like Polly, we find ourselves hearing a lot of stimuli throughout our day, whether it's the buzz of lights, music in a restaurant, or the sound of cars passing on the street. Most of us are able to continue our conversations without thinking about these noises. To a large extent, people have grown accustomed to communicating without attending to the noises they hear in the background.

We now turn our attention to what encompasses listening. Being a good listener is much more than letting in audible stimuli. Listening is a communication activity that requires us to be thoughtful. The choices we make when we listen affect our interpersonal encounters.

Listen Up: The Listening Process

People often take listening for granted as a communication skill in interpersonal relationships. As Harvey Mackay (2001) of the International Communication Association concluded, "listening is the hardest of the 'easy' tasks." Unlike hearing, listening is a learned communication skill. People often have a difficult time describing what being an effective listener is, but people seem to know when another person is not listening. Within this framework, we define **listening** as the dynamic, transactional process of receiving, recalling, rating, and responding to stimuli and/or messages from another.

Listening is dynamic because it is an active and ongoing way of demonstrating that you are involved in an interpersonal encounter. Further, listening is transactional because both the sender and the receiver are active agents in the process, as we discussed in Chapter 1. In other words, listening is a two-way street. Merely showing that we are listening is a necessary but insufficient way to maintain relationships. We need others to show us they know we are listening.

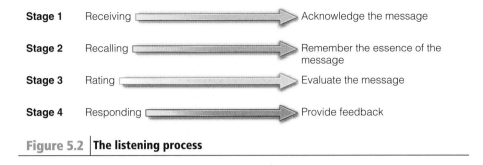

Figure 5.2 | **The listening process**

The remaining four concepts of the definition require a more detailed discussion. The "four Rs" of listening—receiving, recalling, rating, and responding—make up the listening process (see Figure 5.2). Each of the following sections discusses a component of the listening process and the specific skill it requires, including a few recommendations for improving that skill.

Receiving

When we receive a message, we hear and attend to it. **Receiving** involves the verbal and nonverbal acknowledgment of communication. We are selective in our reception and screen those messages that are least relevant to us. Perhaps one reason we don't receive every message is that our attention spans are rather short, lasting from around two to twenty seconds (Wolvin & Coakley, 1996). Our short-term memory, then, affects the receiving process.

When we are receiving, we are being mindful (Langer, 1989; Ting-Toomey, 1999), which means that we are paying close attention to the stimuli around us. We can also become mindless, which means we aren't paying attention to the stimuli around us. Imagine what your life would be like if you were always mindful—you would be overwhelmed in your communication activities. Being mindless at times is necessary, but keep in mind that some stimuli that are perceived as unimportant can be beneficial (think about listening to the rain falling as a way to reduce stress).

The following suggestions should improve your ability to receive messages effectively. First, eliminate unnecessary noises and physical barriers to listening. If possible, try to create surroundings which allow you to receive a message fully and accurately. Talking on a cell phone, watching MTV, or cleaning house while receiving a personal message are poor listening habits. Second, try not to interrupt the reception of a message. Although you may be tempted to cut off a speaker when he or she communicates a message on which you have a strong opinion, yield the conversational floor so you can receive the entire message and not simply a part of it.

Recalling

Recalling involves understanding a message, storing it for future encounters, and remembering it later. We have sloppy recall if we understand a message when it is first communicated but forget it later. When we do recall a conversation, we don't recall it word-for-word; rather, we remember a personal version (or essence) of what occurred (Bostrom, 1990). Recall is immediate, short-term, or long-term (Bostrom & Waldhart, 1988), and people's recall abilities vary.

Suppose another person criticizes you for recalling a conversation incorrectly. You might simply tell the other person that he or she is wrong. This is what happens in the following conversation between Lee and Dale. The two have been good friends for years. Lee is a homeowner who needed some painting done, and Dale verbally agreed to do it. Now that Dale has given Lee the bill, the two remember differently their conversation about how the bill will be paid:

DALE: Lee, I remember you said you'd pay the bill in two installments. We didn't write it down, but I remember your words: "I can pay half the bill when you give it to me and then the other half two weeks later." Now you're telling me you didn't say that. What's up with that?

LEE: That's not it at all. I recall telling you that I would pay the bill in two installments *only* after I was satisfied that the work was finished. Look, I know this is not what you want to hear, but the hallway wall is scratched and needs to be repainted. I see gouges on the hardwood floors by the living room, and look at the paint drips on the molding in the dining room.

DALE: I told you that I would come in later to do those small repairs, and you said you'd pay me.

LEE: I don't remember the story that way.

Lee and Dale clearly have different recollections of their conversation. Their situation is even more challenging because both money and friendship are involved.

Using the following strategies while listening can help improve your ability to later recall the message:

- *Repeat information.* In the case of Lee and Dale, in their initial conversation, it might have been useful for both of them to repeat the information they heard. Sometimes when you repeat information, the exact wording (if wording is important) will be better remembered later by both people. Repeating also clarifies confusing terms.

- *Use mnemonic devices.* Mnemonic (pronounced "nimonic"), or memory-aiding, devices include abbreviations because abbreviations are easier to remember than longer titles. For example, the abbreviations MADD (for Mothers Against Drunk Driving) and ACT-UP (for AIDS Coalition to Unleash Power) use acronyms as mnemonic devices.

- *Visualize items as you listen to them.* Later, the items will be easier to recall if they are associated with images.

- *Chunk information.* **Chunking** means placing pieces of information into manageable and retrievable sets. For example, if Lee and Dale discussed several issues and subissues—such as a payment schedule, materials, furniture protection, paint color, timetables, worker load, and so on—chunking those issues into fewer, more manageable topics (for example, finances, paint, and labor) may have helped reduce their conflict.

Rating

Rating means evaluating or assessing a message. When we listen critically, we rate messages on two levels: We decide whether or not we agree with the message, and we often place the message in context.

You don't always agree with messages you receive from others. However, when you disagree with another person, you should do so from the other's viewpoint. Rating a message from another's field of experience allows us to distinguish among facts, inferences, and opinions (Brownell, 2002). We briefly explored facts and inferences in Chapter 2. As a refresher, **facts** are verifiable and can be made only after direct observation. **Inferences** are a conversation's "missing pieces" and require listeners to go beyond what was observed. **Opinions** can undergo changes over time and are based on a communicator's beliefs or values.

When we evaluate a message, we need to understand the differences among facts, inferences, and opinions. Let's say, for example, that Maggie knows the following:

- Her best friend, Oliver, hasn't spoken to her in three weeks.
- Oliver is healthy and calling other people.
- Maggie has called Oliver several times and has left messages on his answering machine.

These are the facts. If Maggie claims that Oliver is angry at her, doesn't care about her well-being, or has redefined the relationship without her knowledge, she is not acting on facts. Rather, she is using inferences and expressing opinions. Maggie's conclusions may not be accurate at all.

Here are two recommendations that will help you improve your ability to rate messages. First, detect speaker bias, if possible. At times, you may find it difficult to listen to a message and to evaluate its content. The cause of this problem may be the speaker's bias; information in a message may be distorted because a speaker may be prejudiced in some way. Second, listeners should be prepared to change their position. After you have rated a message, you may want to modify your opinions or beliefs on a subject. Avoid being the know-it-all and try to become more flexible in your thinking.

Responding

When individuals are **responding,** they provide observable feedback to a speaker. Responding, which lets a speaker know that the message was received, happens during and after a conversation. We provide both nonverbal and verbal feedback to someone as he or she talks and, at times, our feedback continues even though the conversation has ended.

Our nonverbal behaviors can provide important feedback to others about whether or not we're really listening to what they're saying. Compare the nonverbal behavior of the man in the photo on the left and the man in the photo on the right. Which person do you think is listening effectively?

Feedback, as you learned in Chapter 1, can be nonverbal, verbal, or both. Margaret Imhof (2003) differentiated between good and bad listeners in a pool of U.S. and German communicators. Good listeners provided feedback while maintaining frequent eye contact, displaying an open body position, and paraphrasing or restating relevant statements. Poor listeners jumped to conclusions, talked only about themselves, displayed a closed body position, and interrupted.

You can enhance the way you respond in several ways. Adopting the other's point of view is important. This skill (which we talk about later in this chapter) is particularly significant when communicating with people with cultural backgrounds different from your own. Also, take ownership of your words and ideas. Don't confuse what you say with what the other person says. Finally, don't assume that your thoughts are universal; not everyone will agree with your position on a topic.

So far, we have introduced you to the components of the listening process. We have distinguished listening from hearing and have provided some insight into the complexity of the listening process. To read about another listening model (prepare, receive, process, store, and respond), read the article "Power Up Your Listening Skills," available through InfoTrac College Edition. Use your Understanding Interpersonal Communication CD-ROM to access **InfoTrac College Edition Exercise 5.1: Listening Model.**

At this point, you can see how important the skill of listening is in our interpersonal communication with others. Yet, for a number of reasons, people don't listen well. We now present several reasons that we don't listen in our relationships with others.

REVISITING CASE IN POINT

1. Explain how hearing a message, rather than listening to a message, in a campaign office can have lasting effects.
2. How might Jacqueline have been a more effective listener by practicing the "four Rs" of listening?

 You can answer these questions online under Student Resources for Chapter 5 at the Understanding Interpersonal Communication website.

The Barriers: Why We Don't Listen

People are often poorer listeners than they think they are. As we present the following context and personal barriers to listening, try to recall times when you have faced these obstacles during interpersonal encounters. We hope that making you aware of these issues will enable you to avoid them or deal with them effectively. Table 5.1 presents examples of these obstacles in action.

Noise

As we mentioned earlier in Chapter 1, the physical environment can affect our listening skills. Environmental noises that prevent effective listening are everywhere. These distractions include physical, semantic, and psychological noise we encounter that prevent a listener from receiving the sender's message. Noise, you will remember, is anything that interferes with the message. Suppose, for instance, that a deaf student is trying to understand challenging subject matter in a classroom. Attempting to communicate the professor's words, the signer begins to sign words that are semantically incorrect because the signer may not understand the content. Or, the signs are slurred or incoherent because the signing is too fast. These distractions would certainly influence the reception of the message by the deaf student.

Physical distractions can take place anywhere. We may have difficulty listening to our boss at work because a printer is running. Maybe a friend is not able to listen to you at a bar because the music is too loud. Perhaps the noisy dishwasher at home interferes with a parent-child conversation. Or, a signer may be signing too quickly

Table 5.1	Barriers to Listening
Barrier Type	**In Action**
Noise (physical, semantic, psychological)	Marcy tries to listen to Nick's comments, but his racist words cause her to stop listening.
Message overload	As a receptionist for a church, Carmen's daily tasks include reading about 20 emails, listening to approximately 10 voice mails, opening nearly 50 pieces of mail, and answering about 40 phone calls. When the minister approaches her with advice on how to organize the church picnic, Carmen's message overload interferes with receiving the minister's words accurately.
Message complexity	Dr. Jackson tells her patient Mark that his "systemic diagnosis has prevented any followup"; Mark tunes out because he doesn't understand what she means.
Lack of training	Jamie is asked to supervise a task force at work. He has never taken a course on communication, and he does not have any formal training in listening. He struggles with wanting to listen to the group and wishes he better understood how to listen.
Preoccupation	As Sara talks with Kevin, a coworker, she tries to listen to him talk about his job, but she is thinking about what time she will need to leave work to get to her little brother's graduation that evening.
Listening gap	As Loretta tells her grandkids how she and her husband met, the 6- and 7-year-olds grow impatient and tell their grandma to hurry up.

for hearing-impaired communicators. We run into physical distractions on a daily basis.

Message Overload

Senders frequently receive more messages than they can process, which is called **message overload.** With the advent of more and more media and advanced media technology, **multitasking,** or the simultaneous performance of two or more tasks, is now commonplace both at work and home. The average worker in the United States handles about 200 messages in one day ("In the News," 1999). We used to visit a coworker's desk just a few feet away, but now we email her. Before, we'd visit a neighbor to borrow something; now we call him instead. In the home, nearly 28 million people have virtual offices, a work arrangement referred to as "telecommuting" (Telework America, 2004). We now find ourselves talking on the phone while downloading a document, sending an email while chatting with a roommate, and checking our email while watching a movie with a partner. With all of this technological maneuvering, who wouldn't be tired of listening at some point during the day?

Message Complexity

Messages we receive that are filled with details, unfamiliar language, and challenging arguments are often hard to understand. Many in technical professions (for example, computing, engineering, biological sciences, and so on) are changing their behaviors. For example, because others don't understand the technical language of the engineering profession, engineers have begun to change their explanations to respond to different types of people (Darling & Dannels, 2003). However, most

"I'm sorry, I didn't hear what you said. I was listening to my body."

people who use technical jargon are less aware of the fact that their language is cumbersome and unfamiliar to others. Therefore, when these people speak to us, they usually make us feel as though we're walking through a conversational maze.

Lack of Training

Both the academic and corporate environments include opportunities to learn about listening, but more could be done. Although listening is a learned activity, only a few schools—such as the University of Northern Iowa, Nassau Community College (New York), and the University of Maryland—offer courses on the topic. Most students' preparation in listening is limited to a chapter such as the one you are reading now. Similarly, only a few companies offer training in listening (Brownell, 2002).

Preoccupation

Even the most effective listeners become preoccupied at times. When we are preoccupied, we are thinking about our own life experiences and everyday troubles. Those who are preoccupied may be prone to what Anita Vangelisti, Mark Knapp, and John Daly (1990) call *conversational narcissism.* When people engage in an extreme amount of self-focusing to the exclusion of another person, they are said to be using **conversational narcissism.** Those who are narcissistic are caught up in their own thoughts and are inclined to interrupt others. Most of us have been narcissistic at one time or another; think of the many times you've had a conversation with someone while you were thinking about your rent, your upcoming test, or your vacation plans. Although such personal thoughts are important, they can obstruct our listening.

Listening Gap

We generally think faster than we speak. In fact, research shows that we speak an average rate of 150 to 200 words per minute, yet we can understand up to 800 words per minute (Wolvin & Coakley, 1996). That is, we can think about three or four times faster than we can talk. The **listening gap** is the time difference between your mental ability to interpret words and the speed at which they arrive to your brain. When we have a large listening gap, we may daydream, doodle on paper, or allow our minds to wander. This drifting off may cause us to miss the essence of a message from a sender. It takes a lot of effort to listen to someone. Closing the listening gap can be challenging for even the most attentive listeners.

Check out how college students in a study at Valdosta State University analyzed their perception of their listening skills. They believed that they were effective listeners, but they did identify some barriers to effective listening. Use your Understanding Interpersonal Communication CD-ROM to access **Interactive Activity 5.3: Students Analyze Their Listening Skills.**

Poor Listening Habits

The six behaviors set out in Table 5.2 and described in this section are poor listening habits that we may have picked up over the years. Although some of these occur more frequently than others in conversations, each is serious enough to affect the reception and meaning of a message.

Selective Listening

You are **selective listening,** or spot listening, if you attend to some parts of a message and ignore others. Typically, you selectively listen to those parts of the message that interest you. For an example of how spot listening can be problematic, consider what happens when jurors listen to a witness's testimony. One juror may listen to only the information pertaining to *where* a witness was during a crime to assess the witness's credibility. Another juror may selectively listen to *why* a witness was near the crime scene. Their spot listening prevents them from receiving all relevant information about the crime. Controlling for selective listening first requires us to glean the entire message. Attending to only those message parts that interest you or tuning out because you believe that you know the rest of a message may prompt others to question your listening skills.

Table 5.2 | **How to Overcome Poor Listening Habits**

Poor Listening Habit	Strategy for Overcoming Habit
Selective listening	Embrace entire message
Talkaholism	Become other-oriented
Pseudolistening	Center attention on speaker
Gap filling	Fill gap by mentally summarizing message
Defensive listening	Keep self-concept in check
Ambushing	Play fair in conversations

"I'm sorry—here I am going on and on and I haven't asked you a thing about being caught in a trap."

Talkaholism

Some people become consumed with their own communication (McCroskey & Richmond, 1995). These individuals are **talkaholics,** defined as compulsive talkers who hog the conversational stage and monopolize encounters. When talkaholics take hold of a conversation, they interrupt, directing the conversational flow. Take, for example, the talkaholic in the Norella family. The nearly thirty members of the Norella clan who gather each Thanksgiving dread engaging Uncle Jake in conversation because all he does is talk. And talk. Some family members privately wonder whether Uncle Jake understands that many of his more than two dozen relatives would like to speak. But without fail, Uncle Jake comes to dinner with story after story to tell, all the while interrupting those who'd like to share their stories, too.

Not all families have an Uncle Jake, but you may know someone who is a talkaholic—that is, someone who won't let you get a word in edgewise. If you are a talkaholic and have the urge to interrupt others, take a deep breath and remain silent while the other person finishes speaking. If you find yourself talking in a stream of consciousness without much concern for the other person, you are susceptible to becoming a talkaholic. Remember that other people like to talk too.

Pseudolistening

We are all pretty good at faking attention. Many of us have been indirectly trained to **pseudolisten,** or to pretend to listen by nodding our heads, by looking at the speaker, by smiling at the appropriate times, or by practicing other kinds of attention feigning. The classroom is a classic location for faking attention. Professors have become adept at spotting students who pseudolisten; they usually laugh a bit later than others in the class and have a glazed look. You can correct this poor listening habit by making every effort to center your attention on the speaker.

Gap Filling

Listeners who think that they can correctly guess the rest of the story a speaker is telling and don't need the speaker to continue are called **gap fillers.** Gap fillers often interrupt; when this happens, the listener alters the message, and its meaning may be lost. Although an issue may be familiar to listeners, they should give speakers the chance to finish their thoughts.

Defensive Listening

Defensive listening occurs when people view innocent comments as personal attacks or hostile criticisms. Consider the experiences of Jeannie. As the owner of a small jewelry shop in the mall, she is accustomed to giving directions to her small staff. Recently, one of her employees commented: "Look, Jeannie, I think you could increase the volume of traffic here if you brought in some rainbow beads. The young girls love them." Jeannie's response was immediate: "Why don't you leave my store, find a lot of money, get your own store, and then you can have all of the rainbow beads you want! I've been in this business for almost ten years, and I think I know what to buy and what not to buy!"

Jeannie's response fits the definition of defensive listening. Those who are defensive listeners often perceive threats in messages and may be defensive because of personal issues. To ensure that you are not a defensive listener, keep your self-concept in check. Don't be afraid to ask yourself the following question: Am I too quick to defend my thoughts?

Ambushing

People who listen carefully to a message and then use the information later to attack the individual are **ambushing.** Ambushers want to retrieve information to discredit or manipulate another person. Gathering information and using it to undercut an opponent is now considered routine in politics. Divorce attorneys frequently uncover information to discredit their client's spouse. Ambushing in this manner should be avoided; words should never be viewed as ammunition for a verbal battle.

What are some of your poor listening habits? To help you identify areas in which you can improve your listening, use your Understanding Interpersonal Communication CD-ROM to access Interactive Activity 5.4: Identify Your Listening Problems. To read about strategies you can use to become a better listener, access Interactive Activity 5.5: Overcome Bad Listening Habits.

By now, it should be obvious that your listening skills affect your personal and professional relationships with others. Next, we focus on the styles of listening and then on the influence of culture on the listening process.

Styles of Listening

Typically, we adopt a style of listening in our interpersonal interactions. A **listening style** is a predominant and preferred approach to the messages we hear. We adopt a listening style to understand the sender's message. Researchers have identified four listening styles (Johnston, Weaver, Watson, & Barker, 2000): people-centered, action-centered, content-centered, and time-centered. We call this a P-A-C-T between communicators (see Figure 5.3).

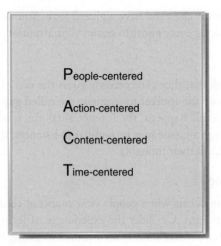

Figure 5.3 | **Styles of listening**

People-Centered Listening Style

The style associated with being concerned with other people's feelings or emotions is called the **people-centered listening style.** People-oriented listeners try to compromise and find common areas of interest. Research shows that people listeners are less apprehensive in groups, meetings, and interpersonal situations than other types of listeners (Sargent, Weaver, & Kiewitz, 1997; Watson & Barker, 1995). People-centered listeners quickly notice others' moods and provide clear verbal and nonverbal feedback.

Action-Centered Listening Style

The **action-centered listening style** pertains to listeners who want messages to be highly organized, concise, and error-free. These people help speakers focus on what is important in the message. Action-centered listeners want speakers to get to the point; they grow impatient when people tell stories in a disorganized or random fashion. They also **second-guess** speakers—that is, they question the assumptions underlying a message (Kirtley & Honeycutt, 1996). If a second-guesser believes a message is false, he or she develops an alternative explanation which they view as more realistic.

Action-centered listeners also clearly tell others that they want unambiguous feedback. For instance, as an action-centered listener, a professor may tell her students that if they wish to challenge a grade, they should simply state the facts about why they deserve a grade change and what grade they feel is appropriate. Such a person would not appreciate random or disorganized responses.

Content-Centered Listening Style

Individuals who engage in the **content-centered listening style** focus on the facts and details of a message. Content-centered listeners consider all sides of an issue and welcome complex and challenging information from a sender. However, they may intimidate others by asking pointed questions or by discounting information from those the listener deems to be nonexperts. Content-centered listeners are likely to play devil's advocate in conversations. Therefore, attorneys and others in the legal profession are likely to favor this style of listening in their jobs.

Time-Centered Listening Style

When listeners adopt a **time-centered listening style,** they let others know that messages should be presented succinctly. Time-oriented listeners discourage wordy explanations from speakers and set time guidelines for conversations, such as prefacing a conversation with "I have only five minutes to talk." Some time-centered listeners constantly check their watches or abruptly end encounters with others.

So, which style is the best? It depends on the situation and the purpose of the interpersonal encounter. You may have to change your listening style to meet the other person's needs. For example, you might need to be a time-centered listener for the coworker who needs information quickly, but you might need to be person-centered while speaking to your best friend about his divorce. However, remember that just because you adjusted your style of listening does not mean that the other person adjusted his or her style. You will both have to be aware of each other's style. Know your preferred style of listening, but be flexible in your style depending on the communication situation.

Our listening style is often based on our cultural background. We now turn our attention the role of culture in listening. When speakers and listeners come from various cultural backgrounds, message meaning can be influenced.

Culture and the Listening Process

As we learned in Chapter 3, we are all members of a culture and various co-cultures. We understand that cultural differences influence our communication with others. Because all our interactions are culturally based, cultural differences affect the listening process (Brownell, 2002).

Recall from Chapter 3 our discussion of individualistic and collectivistic cultures. We noted that the United States is an individualistic country, meaning that it focuses on an "I" orientation rather than a "we" orientation. Individualistic cultures value direct communication, or speaking one's mind. Some collectivistic cultures, such as Japan, respect others' words, desire harmony, and believe in conversational politeness (Lewis, 1999). While listening to others, communicators need to remember that differences in feedback (direct or indirect) may affect message meaning.

Richard Lewis (1999) suggests that listening variations across cultures affect the ability to be an effective salesperson. For example, Lewis points out that for the French, listening for information is the main concern. For citizens of several Arab countries, however, Lewis indicates that listening is done for know-how or for gain. And Lewis indicates that people in some cultures, such as Germany, do not ask for clarification; asking a presenter to repeat himself or herself is seen as a sign of dis-

---

Ethics & Choice

Four fraternity brothers were sitting in the lounge of their fraternity house on a cold winter day. Gabe Walther listened to his friends talk about their roommates, and he wondered who was telling the truth. First, Patrick related a story about how his roommate had tried to commit suicide but couldn't work up the guts to swallow all of the sleeping pills. Gabe then listened to Victor's tale about his roommate stealing a copy of the biology final exam. And then Chris told the group about his roommate's financial problems.

Finally, Patrick spoke directly to the group: "Listen, guys, I've got to tell you something that I don't want repeated to anyone. This story is something I heard about a week ago, and it's about Professor Weinberg." Gabe knew that he was about to hear another story based on gossip. He was fed up with all of the stories and what he felt were violations of trust among the guys in the house.

Gabe Walther was obviously struggling with an ethical dilemma: Should he continue to sit through the gossip and listen to the stories, or should he excuse himself and leave? He didn't want his friends to think he was a prude, but he also didn't want to hear all that gossip. He thought to himself: "Man, these guys have got to get a life. I just can't sit here and listen to this stuff."

What would you advise Gabe to do? Should he politely leave the lounge? Or, should he tell his housemates that he disliked their gossip? What ethical system of communication should be followed in this example (categorical imperative, utilitarianism, ethic of care, golden mean, significant choice)?

Use your Understanding Interpersonal Communication CD-ROM to access an interactive version of this scenario on the Understanding Interpersonal Communication website. Look under Student Resources for Chapter 5 and click on the "Ethics & Choice" menu at left. The interactive version of this scenario allows you to choose an appropriate response to this dilemma and then see what consequences your choice brings about. You can also compare your answers to the questions at the end of the scenario to those provided by the authors and, if requested, email your response to your instructor.

REVISITING CASE IN POINT

1. Choose one style of listening and apply it to Jacquelyn and her volunteer work in a political campaign.
2. Consider the listening styles and discuss whether one style is more useful than another for Jacquelyn, who serves as a director of volunteers.

You can answer these questions online under Student Resources for Chapter 5 at the Understanding Interpersonal Communication website.

Facing *Change*

Culture is identified as an influential agent in listening. Keeping in mind that the United States is experiencing significant cultural changes, comment on the different challenges that cultural groups experience with respect to listening. What cultural universals can you think of that could apply to most cultures? Frame your response with respect to race, religion, ability, and gender.

respect and impoliteness. Recognition of these cultural differences by salespeople is likely to have a positive effect on the bottom line.

Donal Carbaugh (1999) offers additional information on ways that culture and listening work together. He cites an example of the Blackfeet Indians, whose listening process is intertwined with their physical surroundings:

> Blackfeet listening is a highly reflective and revelatory mode of communication that can open one to the mysteries of unity between the physical and spiritual, to the relationships between natural and human forms, and to the intimate links between places and persons. (p. 265)

The common thread in these examples is the notion that cultures vary in their value systems and patterns of communication. Staying culturally aware of these variations as you consider the message of another person is important.

What strategies can you use to better communicate with individuals from different cultures? First, don't expect everyone else to adapt to your way of communicating. Second, accept new ways of receiving messages. Third, wait as long as possible before merging another's words into your words—don't define the world on your terms. Finally, seek clarification when possible. Asking questions in intercultural conversations reduces our processing load, and we are better equipped to translate difficult concepts as they emerge (Hall, 2005).

We spend the rest of the chapter reviewing effective listening skills you should practice. Improving your listening habits is not easy, pervades every occupation and profession, and is a lifelong process, so you shouldn't expect changes to your listening behaviors to happen overnight.

Choices for Effective Listening

This section outlines six primary skills for improving listening. Whether we communicate with a partner, boss, friend, family member, coworker, or others, we all must choose whether we will develop good or bad listening habits. Let's explore the following guidelines for effective listening.

Evaluate Your Current Skills

The first step toward becoming a better listener is assessing and understanding your personal listening strengths and weaknesses. First, think about the poor listening habits you have seen others practice. Do you use any of them while communicating? Which listening behaviors do you exhibit consistently, and which do you use sporadically? Also, which of your biases, prejudices, beliefs, and opinions may interfere with receipt of a message?

In addition, we have stresses and personal problems that may affect our listening skills. For example, if you were told that your company was laying off workers, how would this affect your communication with people on a daily basis? Could you be an effective listener when conversing with others, even though you would find yourself preoccupied with the financial and emotional toll you would experience if you were downsized? In such a situation, it would be nearly impossible to dismiss your feelings, so you should just try to accept them and know that they will probably affect your communication with others. To take a listening quiz that was developed for insurance agents but that is applicable to everyone, read the article "Are

You a Good Listener? Take the Skills Quiz," available through InfoTrac College Edition. Use your Understanding Interpersonal Communication CD-ROM to access InfoTrac College Edition Exercise 5.2: Are You a Good Listener?

Prepare to Listen

After you assess your listening abilities, the next step is to prepare yourself to listen. Preparation requires both physical and mental activities. You may have to locate yourself closer to the source of the message (of course, depending on who the speaker is, your physical proximity will vary). If you have problems concentrating on a message, try to reduce or remove as many distractions as possible, such as the TV or stereo. Place yourself in a situation where you will not be distracted by looking out a window or watching other people interact.

To prepare yourself mentally, do your homework beforehand if you are going to need information to listen effectively. For example, if you want to ask your boss for a raise, you would want to have ready a mental list of the reasons why you deserve a raise and possible responses to reasons why you do not. If you are a student, reading the material before class will make the lecture or discussion much more meaningful because you will have the background knowledge to be able to offer your thoughts on issues as they arise. In your personal relationships, you should be mentally prepared to consider other points of view as well as your own. This will entail some empathic communication, which we discuss in the next subsection.

Provide Empathic Responses

When we use empathy, we are telling other people that we value their thoughts. Empathy is the process of identifying with or attempting to experience the thoughts, beliefs, and actions of another. Empathy tells people that although we can't feel their exact feelings or precisely identify with a current situation, we are trying to cocreate experiences with them. As Judi Brownell (2002) observed: "you do not *reproduce* the other person's experiences. Rather, you and your partner work together to *produce,* or cocreate, meanings" (p. 185). Further, we show we're responsive and empathic by giving well-timed verbal feedback throughout a conversation, not simply when it is our turn to speak.

Empathy is an important component of listening. By providing empathic responses, we show that we value another person's thoughts and feelings. In the process, we may even help alleviate that person's anxiety, which is a useful emotional support skill.

Doing so suggests a genuine interest in the sender's message and has the side benefit of keeping us attentive to the message. To show empathy, we must also demonstrate that we're engaged nonverbally in the message. This can be accomplished through sustained facial involvement (avoiding a blank look that communicates boredom), frequent eye contact (maintaining some focus on the speaker's face), and body positioning that communicates interest.

Learning to listen with empathy is sometimes difficult. We have to show support of another while making sure that we are not causing unnecessary negative feelings. For instance, consider the following

© Richard Lord/The Image Works

Nonjudmental listening allows for good interpersonal relations. Accepting someone's feelings without judging them is a useful skill that supports strong relationships.

dialogue between two friends, Camilla and Tony. Camilla is angry that her boss did not positively review her work plan:

CAMILLA: He's self-righteous, that's all there is to it. He didn't even tell me that my idea made sense. I think he's just jealous because he didn't come up with it first.

TONY: Yeah, I bet you're right. He really didn't show you any respect. And because he's the boss, I'm sure he wanted to take credit.

Although Tony meant to show empathy, he may have unintentionally perpetuated the idea that Camilla's boss was a "bad" man. Because Tony seems to be supporting her thoughts, Camilla will have a difficult time changing her perception of her boss. This negative view won't help Camilla in future conversations with her boss. Now, consider an alternative response from Tony that doesn't reinforce Camilla's negative perception:

CAMILLA: He's self-righteous, that's all there is to it. I didn't even tell me that my idea made sense. I think he's just jealous because he didn't come up with it first.

TONY: I know you're pretty frustrated and angry at him. You sound like you want to quit. I know that it has to be pretty rough for you, but hang in there.

In this example, Tony not only demonstrated some empathic listening skills but helped Camilla redirect her thinking about her boss. When Tony changed the direction of the conversation in this way, Camilla could consider less resentful impressions of the situation. Helping others alleviate their anxiety is a necessary emotional support skill for many interactions (Burleson, 2003). To read an article that reinforces the notion that empathy is key to effective listening, check out "Leaders Know How to Listen," available through InfoTrac College Edition. Use your Understanding Interpersonal Communication CD-ROM to access **InfoTrac College Edition Exercise 5.3: Empathy and Listening.**

Use Nonjudgmental Feedback

Most of us provide feedback without any concern for how the receiver will interpret it. When we give **nonjudgmental feedback,** we describe another's behavior and then explain how that behavior made us feel. As we discussed in Chapter 4, centering a message on your own emotions without engaging in accusatory finger-wagging can help reduce interpersonal conflict.

Consider the difference between the following statements:

- "You are so rude to come in late. You made me a nervous wreck! You're pretty inconsiderate to make me feel this way!"

- "When you come home so late, I really worry. I thought something had gone wrong."

In heated moments, taking ownership of your feelings and perceptions, as in the second statement, is difficult. Owning your feelings rather than blaming others for your feelings results in more effective interpersonal communication.

Practice Active Listening

We define active listening as a transactional process in which a listener communicates reinforcing messages to a speaker. When we actively listen, we show support for another person and his or her message. Active listeners *want to* listen rather than feel *obligated to* listen. Particularly in close relationships with others, demonstrating that you are actively involved in the conversation will help both your credibility as a communicator and your relationship standing with others. Additional elements of active listening are paraphrasing, dialogue enhancers, and silence. We briefly discuss each of these in the following subsections.

Paraphrasing

Active listening requires **paraphrasing,** or restating the essence of another's message in our own words. Paraphrasing is a perception check in an interpersonal encounter; it allows us to clarify our interpretation of a message. When paraphrasing, try to be concise and simple in your response. For instance, you can use language such as "In other words, what you're saying is . . ." or "I think what I heard is that you . . ." or "Let me see if I get this right." Such phrases show others that you understand the intended meaning of a message. To read an article that reinforces the benefits of paraphrasing, check out "Practice Listening Skills as a Leader," available through InfoTrac College Edition. Use your Understanding Interpersonal Communication CD-ROM to access InfoTrac College Edition Exercise 5.4: Paraphrasing and Listening.

Dialogue Enhancers

Active listening requires us to show the speaker that even though we may disagree with his or her thoughts, we accept and are open to them. As we noted earlier, speakers need support in their conversations. **Dialogue enhancers** take the form of supporting expressions such as "I see" or "I'm listening." Dialogue enhancers should not interrupt a message. They should be used as indications that you are involved in the message. In other words, these statements enhance the discussion taking place.

The value of silence is not lost on monks who take a vow of silence as part of their spiritual practice. In such a tradition, practicing silence is not meant as a way to reject others but as a means to clear away noise so the monks are better able to listen.

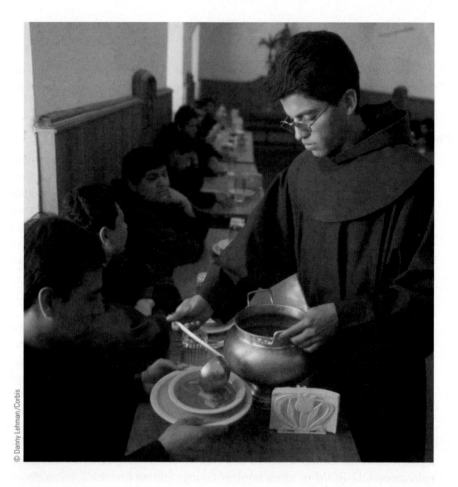

© Danny Lehman/Corbis

Silence

Author Robert Fulghum comments in *All I Really Need to Know I Learned in Kindergarten* that silence is a big part of a satisfying life (Fulghum, 1989). It may seem strange to talk about the importance of being silent in interpersonal communication. In fact, in the self-help book sections in U.S. book stores, we rarely find books on the importance of keeping quiet because the culture rewards talkativeness (McCroskey & Richmond, 1995). Silence is a complicated concept in conversations. As communication ethicist J. Vernon Jensen (1997) stated, "silence can warmly bind friends together, but can chillingly separate individuals" (p. 151). We live in a society in which overt communication is embraced—just look at television talk shows for proof.

We should honor silence when another person is struggling with what to say. We need to allow the entire message to be revealed before jumping in. We also need to be silent because, at times, words are not needed. For example, after a conflict has been resolved and two people are looking at each other and holding each other's hands, they don't need to speak to communicate. Silence in this context may be more effective than words in making the people in the relationship feel closer.

However, silence can also be used to manipulate or coerce another person in an interpersonal exchange. This is an example of the dark side of communication that we discussed in Chapter 1. For instance, giving someone "the silent treatment"—that is, refusing to talk to someone—may provoke unnecessary tension. Also, imposing your own code of silence in an encounter may damage a relationship. For ex-

Skill *Spotlight*

Active Listening

Although all of our listening behaviors are important, active listening in particular is especially critical in our conversations. The skill embraces both verbal and nonverbal communication and is particularly relevant to nearly every conversation we have.

Active listening is a process that requires us to demonstrate three primary supporting behaviors: paraphrasing, using dialogue enhancers, and honoring silence when necessary. When we paraphrase, we may include our own words, but we should ensure that our restatement is accurate and concise. Dialogue enhancers such as "I get your point" or "I see" tell the person who is speaking to you that his or her message is clear and that you are involved in the conversation taking place. The use of silence as an active listening skill may have caught you by surprise, but remember that our nonverbal behavior can be as important as our verbal behavior. Keeping quiet may be difficult for some people, especially because our society values the spoken word. However, periodically substituting quiet times for the spoken word will enhance our listening potential.

Skills at Work Perhaps no other skill is more important in the workplace than active listening. Unlike most behaviors, active listening applies to nearly every job. Although its importance is generally recognized by both employees and supervisors, few workplaces take the time to train their employees to become more active in their listening.

The consequences of failing to listen actively in a variety of work environments can be significant. For example, a physician who doesn't actively listen to a patient may miss out on important health habits of that patient. A contractor who doesn't listen actively to the wishes of a homeowner will likely find out that neglecting to do so was a costly mistake. And a client who fails to listen actively to his or her accountant during a tax audit may later encounter unexpected stress.

There is no substitute for being an active listener while at work. It is hard work, and you may not always be prepared to paraphrase, use conversational enhancers, and maintain silence while interacting with colleagues. However, after you start practicing this skill at work, others will find you more competent and will regard you as a more thoughtful communicator.

CHOICES *for Effective Listening*

- Evaluate current personal listening skills
- Prepare to listen
- Provide empathy
- Use critical and nonjudgmental feedback
- Practice active listening techniques

ample, if you chose to remain silent in an interpersonal conflict, you would most likely exacerbate the problem.

Listening is one of the keys to success in all areas of your life. In addition to reading the advice given in this chapter, check out seven strategies to better listening by using your Understanding Interpersonal Communication CD-ROM to access **Interactive Activity 5.6: Keys to Better Listening.** And for more techniques for better listening, including active listening, read the article "Improving Your Listening Skills," available through InfoTrac College Edition. Access **InfoTrac College Edition Exercise 5.5: Guidelines for Better Listening.**

Communication Assessment Test

The Listening Inventory

To get a general understanding of your beliefs about listening, complete the following assessment. Be sure to consider your general response to a question rather than a specific episode. Complete each sentence as honestly as possible. You can also take this test online under Student Resources for Chapter 5 at the Understanding Interpersonal Communication website.

1. Listening is not taught in our society because . . .

2. One job that does not require you to be a good listener is . . .

3. One big reason why I'm not the best listener is . . .

4. My family members listen . . .

5. Listening is as important as speaking because . . .

6. I would like to improve my listening skills because . . .

7. The ways in which listening will help me at school include . . .

8. The ways in which listening will help me at work include . . .

9. One person whom I consider a great listener is . . .

10. I can overcome many listening obstacles by . . .

Now review your responses. Which responses surprised you? Based on what you learned in this chapter, what would you change about your listening behaviors?

Summary

Listening is called a twenty-first century skill because it is essential in all arenas, including home, school, and work. Indeed, employers rank listening as the most important skill on the job, and listening is important in our friendships and other personal relationships. When we listen effectively we are communicating to senders that their messages are important to us.

Whereas hearing is the process of letting in, but not attending to, audible stimuli, listening is the dynamic, transactional process of the four Rs: receiving, recalling, rating, and responding to stimuli and/or messages from another. When we receive messages, we are being mindful and acknowledging them verbally and nonverbally. When we recall the message, we understand it and store it for later retrieval using the following strategies: repetition, use of mnemonic devices, visualization, and chunking. When we rate messages, we have to be sure we don't confuse facts with inferences and opinions. When we respond, we provide nonverbal and verbal feedback to the speaker.

There are many barriers to listening. Physical distractions such as semantic, psychological, or physiological noise interfere. Modern phenomena such as multitasking, telecommuting, and being bombarded by many messages from numerous media can lead to message overload. Messages that are too complex—such as those filled with unfamiliar jargon or challenging arguments—can be difficult to listen to and to understand. Businesses and schools seldom offer listening training or courses. Preoccupation with personal issues, including extreme self-focusing (conversational narcissism), can inhibit the processing of messages. Lastly, the time difference between the mental ability to interpret words and the speed at which they arrive at the brain (the listening gap) can cause the mind to wander.

Our poor listening habits also interfere with listening. When we selectively listen, we don't attend to those parts of the message that are uninteresting to us. Talkaholics hog the conversational stage, resulting in one-sided conversations. We may or may not fool others when we pseudolisten, or pretend to listen, to a message. Gap fillers interrupt because they believe they know the rest of the message. When we defensively listen, we perceive innocent comments as hostile in intent. Ambushers retrieve information so they can later use it to discredit or manipulate another person.

Researchers have identified four listening styles. Your listening style may vary depending on the situation and the purpose of the personal encounter. People-centered listeners are concerned with other people's feelings or emotions. Action-centered listeners are listeners who want messages to be highly organized and who sometimes second-guess, or question, the assumptions underlying the message. Content-centered listeners focus on the facts and details of a message and are likely to play devil's advocate. Time-centered listeners discourage wordy explanations from speakers and set time guidelines for conversations. In addition to noting a communicator's listening style, keep in mind that people from different cultures give different types of feedback (direct or indirect), which may affect message meaning.

To improve your listening skills, you need to evaluate your current skills, prepare to listen, provide empathic responses, use nonjudgmental feedback, and practice active listening. When we actively listen, we communicate reinforcing messages to the speaker through paraphrasing (restatements), dialogue enhancers (supporting expressions), and the use of silence. When you work on your listening skills, you are striving to become a more engaged and competent communicator.

Understanding Interpersonal Communication Online

Now that you've read Chapter 5, use your Understanding Interpersonal Communication CD-ROM for quick access to the electronic study resources that accompany this text. Your CD-ROM gives you access to the video of Jacqueline's situation on pages 125–126, the Ethics & Choice interactive activity on page 139, the Communication Assessment Test on page 146, InfoTrac College Edition, and the Understanding Interpersonal Communication website. When you get to the Understanding Interpersonal Communication home page, click on "Student Book Companion Site" in the Resource box at right to access the online study aids for this chapter, including a digital glossary, review quizzes, and the chapter activities.

Terms for Review

action-centered listening style 138

ambushing 137

American Sign Language (ASL) 127

chunking 130

content-centered listening style 138

conversational narcissism 134

defensive listening 137

dialogue enhancers 143

facts 131

gap fillers 137

hearing 128

inferences 131

listening 128

listening gap 135

listening style 137

message overload 133

multitasking 133

nonjudgmental feedback 142

opinions 131

paraphrasing 143

people-centered listening style 138

pseudolisten 136

rating 130

recalling 129

receiving 129

responding 131

second-guess 138

selective listening 135

talkaholics 136

time-centered listening style 139

Questions for Understanding

Comprehension Focus

1. Differentiate between hearing and listening.
2. What are the four components of the listening process?
3. What are the barriers that prevent us from listening well?
4. Explain the styles of listening and provide an example of each.
5. Identify at least one way that culture relates to the listening process.

Application Focus

1. **CASE IN POINT**
   Look at our opening story of Jacqueline Mitchell. If you were Jacqueline, how would you rate your personal listening skills? Do you believe that she should be penalized for her blunders? Why or why not?
2. Are there any times in a relationship when you would be justified practicing any of the six poor listening habits (selective listening, talkaholism, pseudolistening, gap filling, defensive listening, and ambushing)? Indicate why or why not with examples to support your view.
3. Describe times when you felt that your best friend wasn't listening to you. What were the circumstances surrounding the event, and what types of behaviors did your friend engage in? How did you respond?
4. During a job interview, what would you say to a prospective employer about your listening skills? Be specific and use examples.
5. Defend or criticize the following statement: Listening should be taught in grade schools alongside writing, speaking, and reading. Provide examples to defend your position.

Interactive Activities and InfoTrac College Edition Exercises

Complete the Interactive Activities and InfoTrac College Edition Exercises for Chapter 5 online at the Understanding Interpersonal Communication website. Select the chapter resources for Chapter 5, then click on "Activities" or "InfoTrac College Edition." If requested, you can submit your answers to your instructor.

Interactive Activities

InfoTrac College Edition Exercises

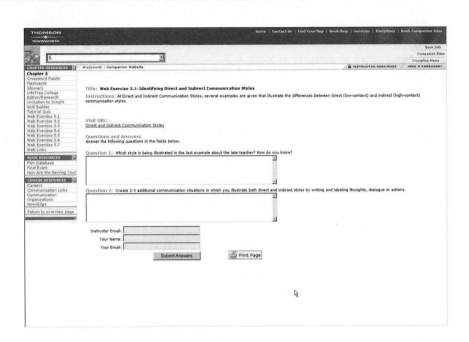

6

Communicating Verbally

CHAPTER GOALS

Develop an understanding of the nature of verbal symbols and their relationship to language and meaning

Identify factors such as gender and culture that affect verbal symbols

Explain the ways in which verbal symbols may be used positively, negatively, and ambiguously

Demonstrate skill and sensitivity in using verbal communication

CASE IN POINT: CARLOS PADILLA AND LIZ CARSON

Carlos Padilla saw Liz Carson every Monday, Wednesday, and Friday while walking to his part-time job after his philosophy class at Midtown University. He liked the way she smiled at him and gave him a small wave as they passed. Carlos wanted to talk to her, but he wasn't sure exactly what to say. Carlos was afraid Liz was just being polite when she smiled at him; in fact, he was pretty sure she didn't even know his name. However, he hoped that if she had a chance to talk with him he could win her over with his sense of humor and quick wit. Carlos decided he would stop the next time they passed each other and engage her in conversation.

When they next encountered each other, Carlos walked up to Liz, smiling broadly. She smiled back and slowed her pace. Soon they were standing facing each other and looking at one another a little awkwardly. "Hi," Carlos finally managed. "Buenos días," Liz replied. Carlos was taken aback. Was Liz mocking him? Did she think he couldn't speak English? He turned away slightly. Liz sensed his discomfort but she wasn't sure what had happened. She frowned and leaned forward slightly. Then she asked, "Is something wrong, Carlos?" Carlos smiled again; she did know his name. "No, nothing's wrong, Liz. I'm happy to have a chance to talk with you because I wondered if we could get together for coffee sometime. I hope you don't think it's untoward of me." Liz looked at Carlos for a moment, trying not to laugh. "Untoward?" she repeated. "Have you been reading the dictionary?" she asked with a gentle laugh. Carlos shook his head, cleared his throat, and decided to make a joke

Use your Understanding Interpersonal Communication CD-ROM to watch a video clip of Carlos and Liz's interaction. Click on the "In Action" icon in the menu at left, then click on "Conversation Menu" in the menu bar at the top of the screen. Select "Carlos" to watch the video (it takes a minute for the video to load). As you watch the video, ask yourself what Carlos could have said to Liz before he left her so that he would have walked away feeling better about their encounter. You can respond to this and other analysis questions by clicking on "Analysis" in the menu bar at the top of the screen. When you've answered all the questions, click on "Done" to compare your answers to those provided by the authors.

of it. "I am trying out new vocabulary words, but I'd really like to get together," he said, laughing. "Well, Carlos, I'd like that, but I can't make it today. I'm working in the library after class and then I have a ton of work—I have a huge paper due tomorrow. But I'd love to another time." Carlos backed away one step, saying, "Uh, okay, Liz, maybe another time then." He turned and walked away thinking that the encounter had been a failure. Liz left hoping they'd have a chance to get together another time. ■

Carlos and Liz experienced some of the problems we all encounter when we communicate with one another. When we interact with others, we use verbal and nonverbal symbols, which are often imprecise. Misunderstandings, misinterpretations, and inaccuracies often result from our necessary dependence on verbal and nonverbal symbol systems. For example, in the opening Case in Point, Liz failed to realize that Carlos was offended by her response to his use of the word *untoward*, and Carlos believed that Liz's laughter meant she was ridiculing him and didn't want to go out with him.

Verbal messages can have dramatic (even if unintended) effects. When Liz greeted Carlos using the Spanish phrase "Buenos días," Carlos was upset. He felt she was belittling his Mexican American heritage or insulting him by indicating she thought he couldn't speak English. The simple use of the Spanish words prompted powerful emotions in Carlos and almost ended the encounter altogether.

Certainly, verbal symbols are important to social life. According to Robin Dunbar (1998), language serves to cement social relationships. Dunbar estimates that approximately 63 percent of human interaction centers on sociality. Further, Dunbar argues that language developed as a means to differentiate the members of an in-group from those of an out-group, a topic we examined in Chapter 3. People who don't understand or can't use the language of an in-group are defined as part of an out-group. This boundary management function of language can cause communication problems. For example, people who are familiar with computer technology will be defined as part of an in-group when they use and understand statements like this one, taken from a Dell computer instruction manual:

> The only two valid memory configurations are: a pair of matched memory modules installed in connectors RIMM1 and RIMM2 with continuity modules installed in connectors RIMM3 and RIMM4 or a pair of matched memory modules installed in connectors RIMM1 and RIMM2 and another matched pair installed in connectors RIMM3 and RIMM4.

Those who are puzzled by such jargon will be assigned out-group status.

The use of the word *queer* is another example of how language distinguishes members of an in-group from those of an out-group. In this case, the word's use has evolved. Those in gay communities used to avoid the word because of its negative connotation. However, the word *queer* was recently reclaimed by many in gay communities, thereby neutralizing any stigma previously associated with the term (Levinson, 1996-2004). In fact, it became an in-group word; those outside a gay community were frowned upon if they used the word *queer*. However, in 2003, the media expanded the in-group when it presented television shows like *Queer Eye for the Straight Guy*. Now the word *queer* has become appropriate for everyone to use.

Young people are masters of language that assigns in-group and out-group status, particularly slang. Slang is most often used within the in-group by speakers to distinguish themselves from an out-group (such as parents or other authority figures), to fit in with the in-group, and to express common social and emotional experiences in efficient shorthand.

In this chapter, we define verbal symbols, illustrate their unique attributes, clarify the factors that affect them, examine their dark, bright, and ambiguous sides, and provide guidelines for their effective use. In Chapter 7, we explain nonverbal messages in a similar fashion. Although we have separated our presentation of each of these message systems into two chapters, verbal and nonverbal messages are inextricably intertwined, and the interplay between them is what makes meaning. For example, Carlos's disappointment when interacting with Liz resulted from how he "heard" both her verbal messages (using a Spanish phrase and saying she's too busy for coffee) and her nonverbal messages (laughing at him for using an uncommon word).

Understanding Verbal Symbols

To begin our discussion, we need to distinguish between two related terms: *language* and *verbal symbols*. We borrow from linguistics, the formal study of languages, to see where verbal symbols fit into the language system. From the linguistic perspective, **language** is the ability to transmit thoughts from the mind of one individual to another through the process of encoding. **Encoding** refers to the process of putting thoughts and feelings into **verbal symbols** (words) and/or nonverbal messages. As Nicolas Wade (2003) observed, "language, as linguists see it, is more than input and output, the heard word and the spoken. It's not even dependent on speech, since its output can be entirely in gestures, as in American Sign Language" (p. D4). The language system works by using words and **grammar,** or the rules that dictate the structure of language, to encode our thoughts and emotions into verbal messages others can understand.

Verbal symbols are important to the language system, but they must be accompanied by grammatical rules instructing us on their arrangement. If a man walked up to you and said, "Look on sky balloon is hanging," you would assume that he was not a native English speaker or that he was mentally ill. The words in the sentence are all recognizable as part of the English vocabulary, but their arrangement does not follow any rules for a sentence in English. To further explore grammar and the structure of the English language, use your Understanding Interpersonal Communication CD-ROM to access **Interactive Activity 6.1: Linguistics.**

Verbal symbols work to form the building blocks of interpersonal communication. To further expand our understanding, let's consider some specific characteristics, or attributes, of verbal symbols.

Attributes of Verbal Symbols

In this section, we outline five attributes of words: they are symbolic, their meanings evolve, they are powerful, their meanings may be denotative or connotative, and they vary in levels of abstraction. These five attributes help us understand how verbal symbols and language convey meaning in interpersonal communication.

Words Are Symbolic

As we discussed in Chapter 1, symbols are arbitrary, mutually agreed upon labels or representations for feelings, concepts, objects, or events. Because words are arbitrary symbols, there is not necessarily a relationship between the word and the thing. For instance, there is no direct relationship between the letters *c-a-t* used to represent the English word *cat* and the actual furry animal English speakers call a cat. The Spanish word *gato* and the German word *katze* are equally arbitrary symbols used to represent the same animal. Figure 6.1 illustrates this concept by graphically representing the thought, the thing, and the word that stands for the thing on the three points of the triangle of meaning, a classic model by Ogden and Richards (1923). As some researchers have said, "the map is not the territory." Stated another way, the word is *not* the thing but merely a symbol we have agreed to use to stand for it. By agreeing on symbols, we can engage in communication with one another about things.

Usually, a group of speakers (or a culture) records an agreement about verbal symbols in a dictionary that catalogs the meanings attached to verbal symbols. However, a dictionary is not a static statement on meanings because language and the verbal symbols that constitute it keep evolving.

Language Evolves

In the English language, as time passes, some words fall out of favor and cease to be used, the meaning of some words changes, and new words are added to the lexicon. Archaic words such as *petticoat, girdle, dowry, courtship,* and even *typewriter* are no longer used because they name things that are obsolete. Some expressions that were popular in earlier times have simply ceased to be spoken, illustrating that language is susceptible to fads and fashion. For example, if you are younger than 80 years old, you probably have never used or heard the phrase *the bees' knees,* 1920s slang that meant something was wonderful or "hot."

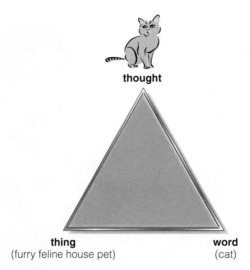

thought

thing
(furry feline house pet)

word
(cat)

Figure 6.1 | **The triangle of meaning**

Sometimes words that were popular during an earlier era experience a revival. For example, the word *groovy* was popular in the 1960s, fell out of favor, and then became trendy again in the late 1990s with the Austin Powers movies.

Social changes prompt changes in the lexicon, a process some people disparage with the label *political correctness.* But as Sara Mills (2003) observes, political correctness "is wrongly characterized as an excessive attention to the sensibilities of those who are seen as different from the norm (women, gays and lesbians, Black people, the disabled)" (p. 89). As Mills points out, confusing political correctness with important language reform is a mistake. Renovating the language to give people respect and enable accurate speech is a worthy goal that should not be trivialized. Mills contends that because verbal symbols are so powerful, they can symbolize prejudicial attitudes that we should eliminate.

For instance, the words *colored, negro, Afro-American,* and *African American* reflect changes in the position of black people in the United States. The language to describe people with disabilities has similarly evolved. For example, when Dale tells his parents about his friend Abby, who uses a wheelchair because of muscular dystrophy, he calls her a person with a disability. Dale doesn't use the word *handicapped* because language reform has helped him see people in wheelchairs as people first. He knows Abby as a great friend with a biting sense of humor who uses a wheelchair to get around. To further explore language reform, use your Understanding Interpersonal Communication CD-ROM to access **Interactive Activity 6.2: Politically Correct Language**.

Some college campuses are making efforts to accommodate transgender students, including using pronouns that have evolved in the transgender community: *ze* in place of *he* or *she* and *hir* instead of *him* or *her* (Bernstein, 2004). This accommodation is important for ease and accuracy of communication. For example, when Natalie wants to refer to a friend, Noel, who identifies as transgender, she can simply say, "ze is a friend of mine" instead of "he or she is a friend of mine." Verbal symbols continue to evolve. For example, people with good intentions disagree about whether to use the term *blind* or *visually impaired.*

Every day, the media coin or report on new words introduced into the English language via the Internet. Interestingly, many of these new words relate directly to interpersonal relationships, such as Friends and Family virus, *a computer virus that infects a machine and then replicates by emailing copies of itself to people in the user's address book. Another example is the term* Googling; *originally, it meant searching the web for information, but its meaning has evolved in some contexts to mean searching the web for information about a new or potential girlfriend or boyfriend.*

© Mitch Wojnarowicz/The Image Works

Other verbal symbols are still in use, but their meanings have changed. For instance, the words *calling card* used to mean an engraved card that you left at the home of someone whom you had just visited. Today, we still use the term *calling card,* but now it refers to prepaid cards for making phone calls. Similarly, the word *gay* used to refer to being happy and lighthearted, as in "we'll have a gay old time." Today, *gay* is a sexual identity. The term *gay* was chosen intentionally by people in gay communities because of the positive associations it carried from its former meaning.

People have coined words such as *weapons of mass destruction, metrosexual, embedded journalist, LOL* (an email-speak abbreviation for "laugh out loud"), and *blog* (a log or journal kept online), to name a few, to give labels to recent innovations. As Paul McFedries (2004) observes, "when there's a new invention, service, trend or idea, we need a new way to describe these things. The emerging vocabulary becomes a mirror to the culture" (p. 12). You can probably add other new words to this list.

New words reveal a great deal about our society. The second edition of the *Oxford Dictionary of English,* published in August 2003, contained 3,000 new words, and the themes they expressed centered on terrorism, technology, and television ("Are you suffering from data smog?" 2003). The new words included *24/7* (all the time), *counterterrorism* (military or political activities designed to thwart or prevent terrorism), *dirty bomb* (a conventional bomb containing material that is radioactive), *egosurfing* (searching the Internet for references to oneself), and *bada bing* (a term used to emphasize that something will happen effortlessly and predictably).

Some theorists (for example, Kramarae, 1981) use the term **lexical gaps** to refer to experiences that are not named. They argue that these gaps indicate that language does not always serve its users well. Cheris Kramarae (1981) calls people whose experiences are not well represented in verbal symbols **muted groups,** meaning that they have trouble articulating their thoughts and feelings verbally because their language doesn't give them an adequate vocabulary. For example, Fern Johnson (2000) argues that expressions from sports ("hit it out of the park") and war ("he attacked all his opponents' ideas") show that English is shaped more by the experiences of men than women. Kramarae is interested in women as a muted group, but other researchers suggest that African Americans (Orbe, 1998) and fathers (Chopra, 2001) are also muted by the English language. For instance, African Americans can be muted when language labels their experiences and behaviors in pejorative ways. When black speakers are said to be "aggressive" or "confrontational," they are being judged by white standards. Further, when black English is marginalized and considered substandard, black speakers are muted. When parenting is assumed to be mainly a woman's experience and the words "parent" and "mother" are used interchangeably, fathers are muted. Have you ever been unable to find a word to describe a particular experience? How did that make you feel?

Yet, language is flexible, and people can coin words to fill lexical gaps that muted groups experience. In the English language, people invent words all the time. However, acceptance of new words isn't always an easy process. For example, feminists point to the trouble they have had getting people to use "Ms." instead of "Miss" and "Mrs."

Words Are Powerful

When we use words to label something we've experienced, we make the experience important by talking about it. When we can't find a word to name our experience, it may make the experience seem unimportant or trivial. In addition, certain words (contrary to the old schoolyard rhyme, "Sticks and stones can break my bones, but words can never hurt me") have the power to affect people dramatically because people have agreed to give certain words power.

For example, in 2004, CNN.com reported that the state of Georgia was considering banning the word *evolution* in the science curriculum in the public schools ("Georgia considers banning 'evolution'," 2004). The school superintendent, Kathy Cox, said that the *concept* of evolution would still be taught but that the *word* would no longer be used. This case points to the power that Georgians gave the term *evolution.*

As another example, in 2002 President George W. Bush labeled North Korea, Iraq, and Iran an "axis of evil." Some critics thought Bush began a war of words with that phrase. On its editorial page, *USA Today* said that Bush's rhetoric was inflammatory as well as inaccurate because the three countries' political positions differed from one another. The editorial concludes by stating that "treating Iran, Iraq and North Korea as a unified, monolithic axis—vulnerable to the same rhetoric and tactics—is a formula for failure, not to mention an invitation to a multifront war" ("'Axis of evil' remark sparks damaging backlash," 2002, p. 16A). Others might argue that Bush's phrase was an example of strong, motivational rhetoric. Either way, it's a dramatic example of the power of words. To read an interesting student editorial about the media's use of the terms *terrorist* and *suicide bomber,* use your Understanding Interpersonal Communication CD-ROM to access **Interactive Activity 6.3: The Power of Words.**

Celia Kitzinger (2000) examined the rhetorical power of words in the English language when she studied how the phrase *think positive* affected breast cancer pa-

Facing*Change*

Verbal symbols are still important in an age of technology. For example, when we communicate on the Internet, we mainly use words to encode our messages. Do you think that this will change? Do you think we will eventually use all visual symbols or mainly visual symbols rather than words? If not, explain why not; if so, explain how you think these changes might take place. How have technological changes (cell phones, pagers, computers, TiVo, and so forth) changed our vocabulary? What new words have been added to the vernacular, and what words have been lost? How does gaining and losing words at a rather rapid pace affect our communication practices?

Use your Understanding Interpersonal Communication CD-ROM to watch the CNN video clip "Jargon," which highlights the extensive jargon used by the telecommunication and technology industries. Click on the "CNN & Change" icon in the menu at left, then click on "Video Menu" in the menu bar at the top of the screen. Select "Jargon" to watch the video (it takes a minute for the video to load). As you watch the video, consider your own use of jargon. If you use jargon in your job or when you communicate online, how does it help you convey certain ideas? You can respond to these and other analysis questions by clicking on "Analysis" in the menu bar at the top of the screen. When you've answered all the questions, click on "Done" to compare your answers to those provided by the authors.

tients. Kitzinger found that her respondents had some strategies for resisting the power of the phrase, such as "simply withholding any affiliative response whatsoever, resulting in a gap in the conversation" (Kitzinger, 2000, p. 130) or making a weak or token agreement when told to "think positive." However, she acknowledged that, in general, the phrase *think positive* sent a message that if you don't get better it's because you're not being positive enough. Kitzinger observed that this phrase had a great deal of power, often making patients feel inadequate or responsible for their own illness.

Sarah A. Meyers and Ellen Berscheid (1997) talk about the power of the word *in* for expressing the language of love. They observed that the English word *love* is used "promiscuously" for many purposes (for example, "I am madly in love with Todd," "I love my red sweater," "I just love that song"). The researchers asked 224 university students (112 women and 112 men) to fill out a packet of materials about their social relationships. Ninety-four percent of the respondents had a clear sense of the meaning of the statement "I love you, but I am not in love with you." The respondents observed that *love* in that sentence meant cared about, while *in love* meant cared about with a sexual attraction. Meyers and Berscheid argued that the word *in* has power because it can create a new connotation when paired with the word *love*.

Diane Ravitch (2003) documents the words that groups of conservative and liberal persuasions have requested to be banned from student texts. Words such as *devil, dogma,* and *cult,* and words that make comparisons, such as *economically disadvantaged,* have all been seen as dangerous, and groups have asked to ban them. As Ravitch observes, the fact that people label a word as taboo indicates that they think that word is highly charged and powerful.

Furthermore, after a word becomes taboo, it often becomes more powerful because it is forbidden. For instance, Robin's daughter Kate was 10 years old before she knew that all families didn't ban the word *fat.* Robin had struggled with her weight all her life and was very sensitive about her body. As a result, the family never used the word *fat,* and it became a very powerful word. While visiting a friend, Kate was surprised when she heard the family joking around about gaining weight and calling each other fat. Even though her friend's family found it acceptable to use the word *fat,* Kate couldn't bring herself to use the word.

Communication Assessment Test

Vocabulary Test

Sharpen your vocabulary by testing yourself with the following sentence-completion questions. Aft[e] making your choice, explain why you think it is correct. You can also take this test online under Stu[d] Resources for Chapter 6 at the Understanding Interpersonal Communication website.

_____ 1. Scrooge, in the famous novel by Dickens, was a _____; he hated all humankind.
A. misanthrope   D. hedonist
B. hypochondriac   E. sybarite
C. philanthropist

_____ 2. Businesspeople must widen their horizons; a _____ attitude will get them nowhere in this age of globalization.
A. moderate   D. diversified
B. petrified   E. comprehensive
C. parochial

_____ 3. Our bookshelves at home display a range of books on wide-ranging subjects in many languages, reflecting the _____ tastes of our family members.
A. anomalous   D. furtive
B. limited   E. eclectic
C. arcane

_____ 4. Plastic bags are _____ symbols of consumer society; they are found everywhere you travel.
A. rare   D. fleeting
B. ephemeral   E. covert
C. ubiquitous

_____ 5. Although some people think that only poor and poorly educated people use slang, this idea is _____.
A. accurate   D. widespread
B. popular   E. ineffectual
C. erroneous

_____ 6. Dr. Stuart needs to _____ his thesis with more data; as it stands, his argument is _____.
A. support, profound
B. bolster, acceptable
C. refine, satisfactory
D. buttress, inadequate
E. define, succinct

_____ 7. Through the nineteenth century, the classics of Western civilization were considered to be the _____ of wisdom and cul-

ture, and _____ people, by definition, knew them well.
A. foundation, average
B. epitome, uneducated
C. cornerstone, obtuse
D. font, ecclesiastical
E. repository, educated

_____ 8. In this biography, we're given a glimpse of the writer _____ pursuing the path of the poet despite _____ and rejection slips.
A. doggedly, disappointment
B. tirelessly, encouragement
C. sporadically, awards
D. successfully, acclaim
E. unsuccessfully, failure

_____ 9. In keeping with his own _____ in international diplomacy, Churchill proposed a personal meeting of heads of government, but the effort was doomed to failure because the temper of the times was _____.
A. ideas, pluralistic
B. predilections, inimical
C. aversions, hostile
D. impulses, amicable
E. maxims, salacious

_____ 10. The subtle shades of meaning, and still subtler echoes of association, make language an instrument which only very skilled users can employ with _____ and _____.
A. confidence, aloofness
B. self-assurance, certainty
C. sincerity, hope
D. conservatism, alacrity
E. eloquence, ruthlessness

Answers

1. A	3. E	5. C	7. E	9. B
2. C	4. C	6. D	8. A	10. B

Modified from "Sentence Completion Minitest 4" from www.takeSAT.com, 2004. Test created by Helen Mathur.

Meanings for Verbal Symbols May Be Denotative or Connotative

Denotative meaning refers to the literal, conventional meaning that most people in a culture have agreed is the meaning of a symbol. Denotation is the type of meaning found in a dictionary definition. For instance, Merriam-Webster Online (2004) defines the word *gun* as follows:

> **1 a:** a piece of ordnance usually with high muzzle velocity and comparatively flat trajectory
> **b:** a portable firearm (as a rifle or handgun)
> **c:** a device that throws a projectile
>
> **2 a:** a discharge of a gun especially as a salute or signal
> **b:** a signal marking a beginning or ending

These definitions form the denotative meaning of the word *gun.* Denotative meanings can be confusing; because the dictionary provides more than one meaning for *gun,* your listener must decide if you are using definition 1a, 1b, 1c, 2a, or 2b.

The **connotative meaning** of a term varies from person to person. Connotative meanings derive from people's personal and subjective experience with a verbal symbol. For example, someone who had a close friend or relative shot to death would have a different emotional or connotative meaning for *gun* than would a hunter or a member of the National Rifle Association. Although both of these people would be aware of the denotative meanings of *gun,* their definition of the word would be colored by their personal connotative meanings.

Words Vary in Level of Abstraction

You can place a word on a continuum from concrete to abstract. If a word is **concrete,** you are able to detect its **referent** (the thing the word represents) with one of your senses. Stated another way, concrete words are those that you can see, smell, taste, touch, or hear. The more a word restricts the number of possible referents, the more concrete the word is. For instance, if Sara has 15 relatives but only 3 brothers, *brother* is a more specific, concrete term than *relative,* and *Scott* (the name of one of Sara's brothers) is more specific than either of the two other terms. The word *relative* is the term with the fewest restrictions, so it is the most **abstract.** We can envision a ladder of abstraction (see Figure 6.2) that begins with the most concrete symbol for a referent and moves to the most abstract.

Some referents are, by their nature, somewhat abstract. Ideas like love and democracy do not have terms that correspond to the lower rungs of the ladder of abstraction. Language skills allow humans to talk about the concepts involved in abstract terms. For example, when we speak about *justice,* we use other abstract terms, such as *fairness,* to get our message across. To make our ideas more concrete so others can better understand our meaning, we use figures of speech such as metaphors and similes. Metaphors equate two terms—for example, "*Love* is a *roller-coaster ride.*" Similes make comparisons using the word *like* or *as*—for example, "*Justice* is like *redistributing portions of a pie.*" Although they do not provide perfect descriptions, figures of speech can be powerful and beautiful, allowing language to soar to poetic heights.

When referents are not right in front of us, we can visualize them through the **process of abstraction** (the ability to move up and down the ladder of abstraction from specific to general and vice versa). For instance, let's say that Jay wants to tell his friends about his fabulous new red and white Mini Cooper. As he uses descrip-

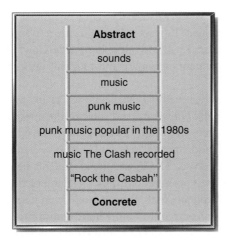

Figure 6.2 | **The ladder of abstraction**

tors to talk about his car in its absence, his friends are able to imagine his purchase with some degree of clarity. Later that day, Jay sees a friend, Lois, who just totaled her car. Jay decides to tell Lois about his new car, but he uses words that are less concrete, leaving out the brand name and color so that Lois won't be too envious. To read an interesting article that examines how journalists tend to move up and down the ladder of abstraction, check out "The Ladder of Abstraction," available through InfoTrac College Edition. Use your Understanding Interpersonal Communication CD-ROM to access InfoTrac College Edition Exercise 6.1: Moving Up and Down the Ladder of Abstraction.

Factors Affecting Verbal Symbols

We understand and use words differently depending on a variety of factors. In this section, we discuss the relationships between verbal symbols and each of the following: culture and ethnicity, gender, generation, and context. Although we discuss these factors in isolation, they can form many combinations. For example, an elderly African American man living in the United States who is talking to his granddaughter at home uses verbal symbols quite differently than a young Asian woman living in Korea who is speaking to a group of business associates at an annual meeting.

Culture and Ethnicity

On the most basic level, culture affects language (and vice versa) because most cultures develop their own language. Thus, people of Kenya tend to speak Swahili, and Polish people usually speak Polish. This subsection addresses some of the many other permutations of culture and ethnicity in relation to language.

Let's first look at idioms. An **idiom** is a word or a phrase that has an understood meaning within a culture, but that meaning is not derived by exact translation. Thus, people who are learning a language have to learn the meaning of each idiom as a complete unit; they cannot simply translate each of the words and put their meanings together.

For example, in English we say "it was a breeze" when we mean that something was easy. If someone tried to translate "it was a breeze" without knowing its idiomatic function, they would mistake the statement's meaning. The listener also has to pay attention to context. If "it was a breeze" is the response to the question "What messed up all the papers I had laid out under the window?" English speakers know not to access the statement's idiomatic meaning but rather to rely on the meaning of each word.

Let's look at another example. Madeline works for the International Student Center at Western State University, and some of the international students tell her that U.S. students are unfriendly. They told her that when they left a group of U.S. students, those students said "see you later"; however, the U.S. students didn't make any attempt to do so. The international students believed that the U.S. students failed to keep their promise for future social interactions. Madeline explained to the international students that "see you later" is an example of a particular type of idiom called phatic communication. **Phatic communication** consists of words and phrases that are used for interpersonal contact only and are not meant to be translated. This type of communication can be thought of as content-free because listeners are not supposed to think about the meaning of the statement; rather, they are expected to respond to the polite contact the speaker is making. When you see someone and say "hi, how are you doing?" you probably don't really want to know how the other person is doing—you're just making contact. "How's it going?" or "how are you doing?" should elicit a response such as "Okay—how about you?" If you said "how's it going?" to your acquaintance Katy, and she started to tell you about her recent breakup or the big fight she had with her brother, you would be surprised and probably think that Katy was odd.

With clever, ironic references to societal traditions and pop culture, such as "gimme some suga', I am your neighbor" and "shake it like a Polaroid picture," Outkast lyrics are examples of the black speech that is a staple in rap and hip hop songs.

Let's now discuss some verbal behaviors thought to characterize two specific groups, African Americans and Mexican Americans. There are many other groups we could examine, but these two are the most studied in terms of the effects of ethnicity on language. Although the findings do not apply to every member of these two groups, African Americans and Mexican Americans are often considered distinct language groups. Fern Johnson (2000) notes that African Americans spend a great deal of time with one another in social and neighborhood settings, and that most African Americans identify with race as a way of establishing identity. Her statements can be generalized to Mexican Americans as well. Let's look at the way language and ethnicity interact within each of these groups.

Some research suggests that African American speech is more assertive than European American speech (Ribeau, Baldwin, & Hecht, 2000). So, according to this research, in a conversation between Tisha, an African American, and Lee, a European American, Lee might say "Is everything okay between us?" and Tisha might respond "You know something is wrong—just say it out loud."

African Americans and European Americans may truly differ in how assertive their speech is, or this finding may be complicated by perceptions. Robert Shuter and Lynn Turner (1997) found that African American women think European American women are highly conflict avoidant. European American women reported their belief that African American women are assertive and confrontational. However, women in both groups did not characterize themselves as highly avoidant or confrontational.

Geneva Smitherman (2000) chronicles black speech and its vibrant and enduring qualities. She traces the evolution of words that have come to be known as black speech, many of which have found their way into the vocabulary of white speakers as well. For example, when white speakers say, "She can talk the talk, but can she walk the walk?" or use words like *hip, phat,* or *testify,* they owe a debt to African American speakers. Smitherman argues that, in addition to being rooted in tradition, black speech is humorous, witty, and wise.

In January 1997, the Linguistic Society of America issued a resolution asserting this same contention. They passed this resolution in support of the Oakland School Board's decision to recognize black English (variously known as African American Vernacular English [AAVE] or Ebonics). The Linguistic Society stated,

> The systematic and expressive nature of the grammar and pronunciation patterns of the African American vernacular has been established by numerous scientific studies over the past thirty years. Characterizations of Ebonics as "slang," "mutant," "lazy," "defective," "ungrammatical," or "broken English" are incorrect and demeaning (Linguistics Society of America, 1997).

To further explore views in support and in opposition to the use of Ebonics, read the article "Q: Would Ebonics Programs in Public Schools Be a Good Idea?" available through InfoTrac College Edition. Use your Understanding Interpersonal Communication CD-ROM to access **InfoTrac College Edition Exercise 6.2: Ebonics: Opposing Viewpoints.**

Chicano English, spoken by Mexican Americans, is perhaps less commonly known but is also studied by researchers. Mexican Americans form only a part of the Latino/Latina culture, sometimes known as Hispanic culture. This culture includes Cubans, Puerto Ricans, Chileans, Peruvians, Columbians, and many more. It is difficult to generalize about all Hispanics, but Fern Johnson (2000) observes that national, ancestral, and language ties are important to all Latinos/Latinas and that "the Spanish language also functions to create and cement cultural unity" (p. 167).

Mexican Americans, like other Hispanics, exhibit great variety in terms of their bilingualism. Some Mexican Americans speak English or Spanish exclusively, others speak Spanish in private and English in public, whereas still others engage in **code-switching,** or shifting back and forth between languages in the same conversation. When Luís says to José, "Yo no le creí, you know" ("I didn't believe him, you know") (Silva-Corvalán, 1994), he demonstrates code-switching by saying the statement in Spanish and ending with the slang English phrase "you know," just as a native English speaker would.

In Chapter 2, we discussed self-concept and symbolic interactionism. This theory explains how words relate to culture (Blumer, 1969; Mead, 1934). Symbolic interactionism says that cultures are held together by their common use of symbols and that things do not exist in an objective form; they exist based on cultural agreement about them. In short, "all the 'things' which make up our world, including ourselves, are products of symbolic actions, constituted and created through the communication process" (Trenholm, 1986, p. 37). Symbolic interactionism, then, points us to an understanding of how culture or society is tied to words. To read an article that examines the connection between a particular culture in Vermont and its language, check out "Vermont Area Struggles to Keep Welsh Culture Alive," available through InfoTrac College Edition. Use your Understanding Interpersonal Communication CD-ROM to access InfoTrac College Edition Exercise 6.3: The Ties between Language and Culture.

Another approach that links culture and verbal symbols is linguistic determinism, a theory put forth simultaneously by anthropologists Benjamin Whorf and Edward Sapir (Hoijer, 1994; Whorf, 1956). **Linguistic determinism** argues that words determine our ability to perceive and think. Both Sapir and Whorf believed that culture affects our thinking (through the vehicle of language). Researchers have suggested that without a word for something in the environment, a person has difficulty perceiving that thing or thinking that it is important. Daniel Nettle and Suzanne Romaine (2000) observe that Pacific Islanders' languages in the past had hundreds of names for the fish that were so crucial to their livelihood. However, some of these languages are disappearing and, as a result, the knowledge of the diversity of fish is also lost. As Nettle and Romaine state,

> Much of what is culturally distinctive in language—for example vocabulary for flora, fauna—is lost when language shift takes place. The typical youngster today in Koror, Palau's capital, cannot identify most of Palau's native fish; nor can his father." (p. 16)

The principle that language determines what you perceive and think about is apparent in the comments of Elizabeth Seay (2004), who studied Native American languages in Oklahoma. As she observes,

> Learning new languages can bring unnoticed ideas into focus. The Comanches have a word for the bump on the back of the neck which is thought to be a place where the body is centered. The Muscogee-Creeks single out the particular kind of love that children and their parents and grandparents feel for each other, using a word that also means "to be stingy." These words convey information the way cups carry liquid, giving a shape to the contents. (p. 17)

These examples, along with many others (such as the fact that the Chinese have no word for *privacy*) support the idea that language determines how we think and that speakers of different languages perceive the world in different ways.

However, not all researchers agree with linguistic determinism. Even Benjamin Whorf wondered if linguistic determinism might be overstating the case. He devised another theory, **linguistic relativity** (Whorf, 1956), which states that language influences our thinking but doesn't determine it. Both linguistic determinism and linguistic relativity point to the connections among culture, language, and thought, and they are sometimes referred to together as the strong and weak forms of the **Sapir-Whorf hypothesis.**

Further, even though compelling examples illustrate both theories, empirical evidence hasn't completely supported the theories' assertions. In fact, one of the most famous examples illustrating the Sapir-Whorf hypothesis has been called into question. Whorf (1956) said that linguistic relativity was supported by the fact that the Inuit have many words for *snow* because it is so crucial to their everyday lives. In addition, Whorf argued that the Inuit perceive snow differently from others whose lives are not as dependent on snow. (Whereas English speakers simply see monolithic white "stuff," due to having only one word, *snow,* the Inuit see all the va-

rieties their language allows.) Whorf didn't specify how many Inuit words for *snow* exist; some say about two dozen, but the numbers vary, and the *New York Times* once mentioned that there were 100 (Pullum, 1991). Geoffrey Pullum (1991) shows that this example is inaccurate. He argues that although the Inuit do use many different terms for snow, other languages allow their speakers to perceive the same variety through phrases and modifiers (fluffy, slushy, good-packing, and so forth).

Another example that refutes the Sapir-Whorf hypothesis is the fact that the Arabic language doesn't have a single word for *compromise,* which some have said is the reason that Arabs seem to be unable to reach a compromise. Geoff Nunberg (2003) relates that Arabic does provide several ways to articulate the concept of compromise, noting that the most common expression translates in English to "we reached a middle ground." This example illustrates an issue called **codability,** which refers to the ease with which a language can express a thought. When a language has a convenient word for a concept, that concept is said to have high codability. Thus, the word *compromise* gives that idea high codability in English. When a concept requires more than a single word for its expression, it possesses lower codability. It is accurate, then, to say that the idea of compromise has lower codability in Arabic than in English. As Nunberg explains, having a phrase rather than a single word to express an idea does not mean that the idea is nonexistent in a given culture, only that it is less easily put into the language code.

Cultures dictate attitudes toward language and certain language practices. For example, in the United

Ethics & Choice

When Andrea Madison entered Oklahoma City University, she was proud to follow in the footsteps of both her parents and her paternal grandparents. She loved everything about OCU—her classes, the parties, and the close relationships she was able to develop with faculty and friends.

One thing she especially enjoyed was going to the basketball games and cheering the outstanding OCU team—the Warriors—to victory. Andrea's grandfather had played on the OCU basketball team that went to the Sweet Sixteen, and her father's basketball team had been NCAA champions. Andrea and her best friends, Molly Byer and Sam Goodwin, spent a lot of time talking about the basketball team and organizing their schedules around basketball games. They hoped that the team would make it to the Final Four in March, and they were already planning how they could make the trip to the tournament to root for their team. Andrea had heard about March Madness all her life, and she was really excited that she might have her own stories to tell after this season. Andrea didn't know too much about Indian history, but she loved the traditions associated with being a fan, including doing war chants along with the team's Indian brave mascot during the exciting parts of the games.

As Andrea enjoyed a basketball game one evening, elsewhere on campus, OCU students Michael Whitefeather and Todd Olden attended a meeting of the First Peoples Association, a student group for the Native American students on campus. The students at the meeting appreciated the opportunity to talk about the situations they faced on campus as the smallest minority group. The discussion at the meeting centered on the fact that OCU still used symbols of Native culture in a disrespectful way by having a brave as a mascot and screaming a war chant during games. The speaker at the meeting, Paula Redfern, said that she cried each time she saw the mascot. She said that her feelings at OCU games were similar to how Catholic students would feel if the team mascot were dressed like the Pope and people bought toy crucifixes to wave whenever the team scored. The students at the meeting decided that they would stage a demonstration at the next basketball game. They wanted to peacefully, but firmly, get across

(continued)

Ethics & Choice (continued)

their message that it was wrong to appropriate another culture's symbols and use them for sport. Michael and Todd, who were moved by the speaker, agreed to be at the demonstration.

As the team's successful season continued, Andrea got more and more excited, so she was surprised when she saw Molly and Sam at the student union looking depressed. Molly told Andrea that a group of Native American students was planning to demonstrate at the next game to protest the team's name, mascot, and the use of the war chants, which the students said were disrespectful of their traditions. Andrea's jaw dropped. She had never thought that anyone could feel that way. She started forming arguments in her mind against the demonstration. She wondered if changing this tradition would mean that other revered OCU traditions would crumble, too.

What would you advise Andrea to do? What are the ethical implications in this scenario and in the choices Andrea has to make? Is it possible to respect the traditions of both Oklahoma City University and the Native Americans? Why is a name so important to Andrea and her friends and to the Native American students? What are the ethical issues for Michael and the other Native American students? In answering these questions, think about the five ethical systems we described in Chapter 1 (categorical imperative, utilitarianism, ethic of care, golden mean, significant choice). Explain how your answers relate to these systems. Do you prefer one of these ethical systems over the others for resolving this dilemma? Explain.

Use your Understanding Interpersonal Communication CD-ROM to access an interactive version of this scenario on the Understanding Interpersonal Communication website. Look under Student Resources for Chapter 6 and click on the "Ethics & Choice" menu at left. The interactive version of this scenario allows you to choose an appropriate response to this dilemma and then see what consequences your choice brings about. You can also compare your answers to the questions at the end of the scenario to those provided by the authors and, if requested, email your response to your instructor.

States, speech functions primarily as a vehicle for expressing one's ideas clearly and forcefully. On the other hand, the Chinese have the attitude that actions are more powerful than words, exemplified in proverbs such as "Talk does not cook rice." Other language traditions include the following:

- In the Lakota tradition, it is sacrilegious to say the name of a dead person in public.
- Jewish people believe that children should not be named for any living person.
- The Japanese avoid saying words in wedding toasts that refer to home or going back home.

Gender

Gender, especially with regard to language and verbal symbols, has been studied extensively. However, despite decades of research examining and comparing men and women's communication behaviors, we still don't have definitive information because the research has been contradictory. Early research held that women and men spoke differently. Robin Lakoff (1975) argued that women used a different vocabulary from men that included, among other things, more words for colors (for example, *mauve*), more polite words and phrases (for example, "would you please open the door" rather than "open the door"), and more modifiers (for example, *very* and *so*).

Some researchers theorized that children played in sex-segregated groups, and that the different ways of interacting within the groups resulted in different speech behaviors (Maltz & Borker, 1982). Little girls tended to play in small groups where it was difficult to gain entry; however, after a girl was accepted in the group, it was easy for her to speak up and be heard. Further, the preferred play activities for girls were creative interactions like house and school, which involve the players in setting the rules. In contrast, little boys played in large groups where it was easy to gain access but difficult to be heard. These boys played baseball, war, and soccer, which have set rules. Thus, whereas girls learned negotiation and cooperation, boys learned assertive communication behaviors and that little talk is necessary for play.

Daniel Maltz and Ruth Borker's belief that gender operated in the same way as culture in establishing different rules, norms, and language patterns for men and women came to be known as the two culture theory. This theory was grounded in the notion that "differences in men's and women's language use reflects different experiences, different worlds ..." (Mulac, Bradac, & Gibbons, 2001, p. 121). Much of Deborah Tannen's (for example, 1995) research comparing women and men's language use stems from the two culture theory. For instance, she argues that women prefer "rapport" talk, or talking for pleasure, while men prefer "report" talk, or talk that accomplishes a task.

Although some research in the last two decades has supported the idea that men and women speak differently in the ways that Robin Lakoff, Daniel Maltz and Ruth Borker, and Deborah Tannen speculated they would (for example, Coates & Cameron, 1989; Mulac, et al., 2001; Treichler & Kramarae, 1983; Wood, 1998), other studies (for example, Canary & Hause, 1993; Goldsmith & Fulfs, 1999; Turner, Dindia, & Pearson, 1995) question whether women and men actually differ much in their speech. For example, in an analysis of more than 1,200 research studies, researchers found that the differences in communication behavior attributable to gender totaled only around 1 percent (Canary & Hause, 1993).

Do women and men really communicate differently? That question is difficult to answer. However, keep in mind that gender makes a big difference in U.S. society. People in the United States consistently remark on gender even when gender distinctions aren't important to the situation. For example, a grade school teacher commands, "Quiet, boys and girls!" rather than "Quiet, students!" or "Quiet, children!" Similarly, a performer's usual greeting to the audience is "Good evening, ladies and gentlemen." Given this interest in dividing people based on gender, the fact that some sense of language community based on gender arises in the United States is not surprising. Perhaps more tellingly, men and women's language use is perceived differently even when it's essentially the same (Mulac, Incontro, & James, 1985). Gender continues to be a factor that affects language as it's spoken, heard, or both.

REVISITING CASE IN POINT

1. Do you think that the conversation between Carlos and Liz was more complicated by language issues relating to culture or to gender? Why?
2. Give an example of a U.S. idiom in the conversation between Liz and Carlos.

You can answer these questions online under Student Resources for Chapter 6 at the Understanding Interpersonal Communication website.

Generation

As we discussed earlier in this chapter, one of the functions of language is differentiating in-group members from those on the outside. One of the tasks of each generation is to distinguish itself from the generation that came before it. Generational differences form age cohorts that, to some extent, share experiences and beliefs. The members of any age cohort—for example, GenX, the Baby Boomers, or the Greatest Generation—share a popular culture, which leads to a common language. Slang such as *cheaters* (eyeglasses), *gams* (a woman's legs), *none of your beeswax* (none of your business), *the cat's meow* (something wonderful), and *hitting on all sixes* (giving 100% effort) peppered the talk of youth in the 1920s but is not heard much today. Explore how new words like these are coined by reading the article "How New Words Come to Be," available through InfoTrac College Edition. Use your Understanding Interpersonal Communication CD-ROM to access InfoTrac College Edition Exercise 6.4: How Words Come to Be.

Technological changes may affect language across generations as well. Yahoo news posted a story recently ("British girl baffles teacher," 2003) that noted how text messaging shorthand caused a communication dilemma between a 13-year-old girl and her teacher in Britain. The teacher commented that she could not translate an essay the student had turned in describing her summer holidays. The teenager had written, in part:

My smmr hols wr CWOT. B4, we used 2go2 NY 2C my bro, his GF & thr 3 : kids FTF. ILNY, it's a gr8 plc.

In translation, the above reads:

My summer holidays were a complete waste of time. Before, we used to go to New York to see my brother, his girlfriend and their three

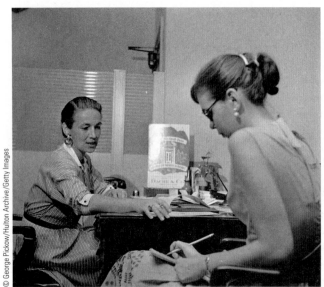

Language use varies from generation to generation, as do the systems used to record and transmit language. For example, if your grandmother was a secretary in the 1940s or 1950s, she probably learned shorthand, a system of hand-written symbols used to transcribe the spoken word. You probably never had to learn shorthand and don't know how to decipher it. But if you use your cell phone to send text messages, you use a newer form of shorthand that consists of numbers, abbreviations, and acronyms that are easy to type from a tiny keypad.

screaming kids face to face. I love New York. It's a great place.

Email addresses may also indicate age differences. Younger people often opt for email names that are punchy and creative, like Venus-chick, hot guy, Juliais-coolia, and so forth. However, as Nicole Sweeney (2004) observes, what seems cool to a 16-year-old can seem embarrassing a few years later, especially because colleges often take emailed applications. She describes one young woman, whose current email name is "artzy-fartzygirl." The girl noted that the moniker was rather embarrassing now because she is emailing colleges; she says she plans to change the name soon.

The *Chicago Tribune* (Warren, 2004) featured an article discussing what Baby Boomers who are becoming grandparents wish to be called by their grandchildren. The consensus of the grandparents interviewed for the article was that "Grandma" or "Grandpa" sounded too old. They were opting for younger sounding names such as Zsa Zsa, Moogie, Muna, Mima, Gigi, Boo-Boo, and LaLa. Ellen Warren says that Baby Boomers becoming grandparents are "launching a small semantic revolution to avoid the traditional label of senior citizen status" (Section 5, p.1). Warren says that Norah Burch, who tracks options for first-time grandparents at www.namenerds.com, observes that Baby Boomers generally don't think of themselves as old, so they are coming up with new names to avoid the connotations of the "blue-haired old granny stereotype" that come with the name "Grandma."

Context

Contextual cues subsume all the other elements we have discussed because the culture, ethnicity, gender, and generation of the people who are interacting factor into the context. Generally, in communication literature, the context involves the setting or situation in which the encounter takes place. Thus, as we discussed in Chapter 1, context means the people, location, proximity, communication behavior, roles, and goals of the interactants (Gudykunst, Ting-Toomey, Sudweeks, & Stewart, 1995; Trenholm & Jensen, 2003). Here, we briefly address the following contextual cues: situation, time, relationship, and nonverbal cues.

You can understand the impact of situation if you think of the same statement, "you have good legs," being said in any one of the following situations:

- By construction workers to a woman walking by a construction site
- By a coach to an athlete running on a track
- By a doctor to a child in the doctor's office

Although the words remain the same, each of these situations would create a different sense of the meaning of the statement. As we discussed previously in this chapter, the meanings of words can change over time. In the 1940s and 1950s, females over the age of 18 referred to themselves as *girls* without seeing a negative connotation. In the 1970s, some feminists rejected the word *girl* as demeaning when applied to adult females. In the 1990s and more recently, some feminists have reclaimed that word and use the term *girl power* with positive connotations. However, many women in their 40s and 50s still reject the term *girl* and do not use it or like to hear it, retaining the negative connotations for it.

Relationships between speakers also contribute to the contextual cues that affect meaning. People who are close to you can say things that would be considered impolite if said by mere acquaintances. Teasing, joking, and various forms of humor such as "loving abuse" (R. Shuter, personal communication, October 15, 2001) depend on a strong prior relationship between the speakers. If the relationship isn't positive, these types of interactions would probably be judged as insulting rather than friendly. Of course, even among good friends or family members, people can go too far, and a comment that was intended to be humorous can be interpreted as insulting.

Rhunette Diggs and Kathleen Clark (2002) discuss how a comment meant to be a joke between friends can be complicated by racial considerations. Diggs and Clark write an autoethnographic account of their own interracial friendship, begun in graduate school and sustained over several years after graduation. At a birthday party for Diggs, Clark, who was the only white person present, made a joke about Diggs being obedient. Although Clark meant it as a humorous jibe between friends, Diggs framed the comment as problematic, in large part because of the interracial context. Diggs saw the comment as giving her outsider status, being labeled by a white person.

As we discuss in Chapter 7, people depend on nonverbal cues to interpret verbal codes. If someone comments that you look nice, you probably check their tone and facial expressions to confirm that their verbal comment is sincere. If the speaker sounds sarcastic in tone, you will undoubtedly believe that you don't look good in their eyes. The nonverbal part of the context is powerful and persuasive in helping people make sense of verbal codes.

Leonard Shlain (1998) notes that although we don't know exactly when speech began, we can cautiously speculate that gestures preceded vocalizations. He says that one explanation for the fact that humans are the only primates that lack pigment on their palms is that this coloration may have helped the hands of early humans communicate. As Shlain states, "before the full development of spoken language, our ancestors sat around the fire speaking and gesturing to each other. It would have been a distinct advantage for the palms to be pale and thus more visible in dim light" (p. 41). In this example, we can see some evolutionary evidence of the importance of nonverbal behaviors in contextualizing verbal symbols.

In sum, when we communicate, we are doing much more than exchanging words. The verbal symbols we use are powerful, ever-evolving abstractions that have both denotative and connotative meanings. Further, they are affected by culture, gender, generation, and context. You can see, then, that the meaning of a statement often goes beyond the simple definitions of each word. For example, when Rick tells Lynette that he is bored, she must take into account many factors to see if he is referring to a temporary state or whether their relationship is in jeopardy. We will now address how verbal symbols may be problematic in interpersonal communication.

The Dark Side of Verbal Symbols

Verbal symbols are not inherently positive or negative. Rather, the value of verbal symbols is determined by how people use them. Verbal symbols in the English language may be easily used for negative ends; they may be exclusionary and derisive, and they can promote stereotypes. As you remember from Chapter 2, stereotypes are fixed mental pictures of groups that are applied to each member of the group. As we discussed in that chapter, some stereotypes may be positive, but in this section we focus on negative images conveyed by language.

Sexist Language

Sexist language refers to language that is demeaning to one sex. Most of the research has examined how language can be detrimental to women. For instance, some researchers assert that the fact that English uses the generic *he* is an example of sexism in language. The **generic *he*** refers to the rule in English grammar, dating from 1553, that requires the masculine pronoun *he* to function generically when the subject of the sentence is of unknown gender. For instance, in the following sentence, *his* would be the correct word to fill in the blanks using the generic *he* rule: "A person should do _____ homework to succeed in _____ classes." Researchers have argued that this rule excludes women because *he* isn't truly generic; rather, it conjures up images of male people (Gastil, 1990; Ivy, Bullis-Moore, Norvell, Backlund, & Javidi, 1995; Martyna, 1978).

Another example of language that some people think is sexist is **man-linked words.** These words—such as *chairman, salesman, repairman,* and *mankind*—include *man* but are supposed to operate generically to include women as well. Man-linked expressions such as *manning the phones* and *manned space flight* are also problematic. In addition, the practice of referring to a group of people as *guys,* as in "hey, you guys, let's go to the movies," reinforces sexism in language. Relatively easy alternatives to these exclusionary verbal symbols are becoming more commonplace (see Table 6.1). Test your skills at replacing man-linked words with gender-neutral terms by taking the Gender-Free Language Quiz. Use your Understanding Inter-

Table 6.1	Eliminating Sexism in Language
Sexist Language	**Nonsexist Alternative**
The scholar opened his book.	The scholar opened a book.
The pioneers headed West with their women and children.	The pioneer families headed West.
You're needed to man the table.	You're needed to staff the table.
Beth was salesman of the month.	Beth was the top seller this month.
Playing computer games cost the company a lot of man hours.	Playing computer games cost the company a lot of productive time.
Manhole cover	Sewer access cover
Freshman	First-year student
Postman	Letter carrier
A person needs his sleep.	People need their sleep.
Mankind	Humankind, humanity

Table 6.2 | **"Parallel" Terms for Women and Men**

Female	Male	Female	Male
mistress	master	majorette	major
stewardess	steward	waitress	waiter
governess	governor	comedienne	comedian
actress	actor	hostess	host
spinster	bachelor	songstress	singer
slut	stud	sculptress	sculptor

personal Communication CD-ROM to access Interactive Activity 6.4: Gender-Free Language.

Another example of sexism in language is the practice of renaming a woman after marriage. The courtesy title *Mrs.* has no male counterpart; men remain *Mr.* regardless of marital status. In addition, referring to a married woman by her formal married name (for example, Mrs. John Jones) obscures her identity under her husband's. Some researchers have pointed to the fact that there are more derogatory terms for women than there are for men and that parallel terms for men and women are not, in actuality, parallel (Pearson, West, & Turner, 1995). Further, as Table 6.2 illustrates, many of the feminine words exist only to mark the person as a female.

Jeffrey Stringer and Robert Hopper (1998) point out that language offers opportunities to "gender-tag human referents more or less automatically, that is, without stopping to consider how such usages reinforce the importance of gender-categorization" (p. 218). They note that we have a network of grammatical "resources" that allow us to sort the subjects we speak of by sex and that most of these resources "effortlessly emphasize men over women" (p. 218). To read an article that focuses on sexist language commonly—and often unconsciously—used in the workplace, read the article "Benefiting from Nonsexist Language in the Workplace," available through InfoTrac College Edition. Use your Understanding Interpersonal Communication CD-ROM to access InfoTrac College Edition Exercise 6.5: Sexist Language in the Workplace.

Racist Language

The feminist movement has sensitized us to sexism in language, but we have to remain alert to language that systematically offends one group, including racist language (language that demeans those of a particular ethnicity). In the twenty-first century, most people avoid overt racial slurs, but language can be racist in other, more subtle, ways. The practice of associating negativity with black ("Black Monday," the bad guys wear black hats," "you're blackening my good name") perpetuates racial stereotypes on a subtle level. When Miranda, a white woman, met Lyle, a black man, she hadn't known too many black people before. She tried to speak in a way that wouldn't offend him. It didn't even occur to her that Lyle would find her use of the terms *blackmail* and *blackball* troubling.

Some researchers argue that racism comes from being taught language that reflects a thought system that values one race over another. For example, when whites are taught from an Eurocentric perspective and don't learn anything about African or Asian history or accomplishments, racism flourishes (Asante, 1998).

Static Evaluation

Language reflects **static evaluation** when it obscures change. When we speak and respond to people today the same way we did ten years ago, we engage in static evaluation. To a degree, we need to think that people and things are stable. If we recognized that everything is in a constant state of flux, it would be difficult to talk or think because we would be paralyzed by the notion of how little control we have. However, if we ignore change, we cause problems, too. Language contributes to these problems because labels don't usually get updated to indicate the changes that take place over time.

For instance, *Mom* is what you call your female parent when you are 4, 18, and 40. However, your relationship with your mother, as well as you and your mother herself, all change greatly over time. When parents say to their children, "No matter how old you get, you will always be my little baby," they are naming the very problem that exists with static evaluation.

Polarization

Polarization occurs when people utilize the either-or aspect of language and speak of the world in extremes (another person is either *good* or *bad*). When we refer to people as *smart* or *dumb, nice* or *mean, right* or *wrong,* we are polarizing. Polarization is troubling because most people, things, and events fall somewhere between the extremes named by polar opposites. Most people are good some of the time and bad some of the time. Labeling them as one or the other fails to recognize their totality. For example, when Kayla tells her friend Marsha about her Professor, Dr. Lee, she focuses on how much she dislikes Lee. Kayla says, "He is such a sarcastic jerk! I cannot stand his class. All he ever does is make fun of students. He doesn't even realize how many stupid things he says!" Although Kayla is entitled to her opinion of Dr. Lee as a poor teacher, her use of such words as *jerk* and *stupid* is polarizing.

Polarization is also problematic because of static evaluation. If we settle on an extreme label for someone at one time and then encounter the same person later, we will probably not take into account the possibility that the person may have changed over time. For example, let's say that Christie briefly dated Rick in high school when they were both juniors, but she broke it off because he was too immature. Two years later, they meet at a party in college. Christie remembers Rick from high school and immediately thinks of the polarizing term *immature.* Keeping this word in her mind will hinder Christie's ability to see Rick's changes and interact appropriately. Polarization also causes communication problems because of reification, which we address next.

Reification

Reification is the tendency to respond to words, or labels for things, rather than the things themselves. Thus, if we call someone by an extreme label, reification suggests that is how we will respond to them, often regardless of what they might do. Reification is often referred to as a confusion between the symbol and the thing. When

We often see static evaluation, polarization, and reification at work in language used to describe crime. Criminals are seen as "scumbags" or "monsters," and people affected by crime are called "victims." Yet, not all people who commit crimes are inherently bad, and not all people affected by crime are inherent victims. Through mediation and counseling, sometimes criminals and victims can come to see themselves and each other as complete human beings rather than simply "monster" or "victim." This process was illustrated in the film Dead Man Walking, *which told the story of Sister Helen Prejean's work counseling a convicted murderer before he was executed.*

people have a strong reaction to a symbol such as a national flag or a school mascot, they are fusing the symbol (flag or mascot) with the thing itself (their country or their school). Although symbols are potent, they are not the same as the things they represent. People who cut up the U.S. flag or burn it may be as patriotic as those who fly the flag in front of their home each day.

The Bright Side of Verbal Codes

Although language can cause the problems we just discussed, it (along with nonverbal communication) is our only means to connect with others. Through language, we can express **confirmation,** or the acknowledgment and support of another. Through the use of confirmation, we can build supportive relationships with others. Confirming messages help another person understand that you are paying attention to him or her and that you recognize that person as an equal. You don't have to agree with a person to confirm him or her—you simply have to express that you are hearing that person and paying attention. For example, when Maddy listens intently to her sister, Charlene, complain about their mother, she confirms that she cares enough about Charlene to pay attention. Even though Maddy doesn't agree

Table 6.3 | **Confirming and Disconfirming Communication**

Disconfirming	Confirming
Ignoring	Attending
Silence	Appropriate talk
"You don't matter to me."	"You matter to me."
"You're on your own."	"We're in this together."
"You shouldn't feel that way."	"I hear how you feel."

with Charlene (Maddy has a positive relationship with their mother), Charlene feels confirmed.

In contrast, **disconfirmation** occurs when someone feels ignored and disregarded. Disconfirmation makes people feel that you don't see them—that they are unimportant. See Table 6.3 for examples of confirming and disconfirming responses to others.

We can also use language to develop inclusion rather than exclusion. Using the language of inclusion means that you are thoughtful and attentive to when others seem to be offended and that you ask what in your language might have given offense. Although we might accidentally exclude someone from time to time, through careful language use, we can build supportive relationships. In addition, as we discussed in Chapter 5, we can use empathic language to connect with others. When we try to understand another's feelings, we show we care enough about that person to spend time and energy listening, and we can establish genuine relationships.

Lastly, verbal codes help us solve problems. When we use open-ended questions (for example, "What do you think is the problem?" or "How would you like me to respond to you?"), we can work toward problem solving in our interpersonal relationships. Language helps us explain our position while conveying that we're also interested in the other person's position.

Ambiguity in Verbal Codes

Sometimes language is indirect or ambiguous, not directly positive or negative. This ambiguity may be unintentional or strategic. For instance, if Jane lacks the verbal skills of clarity and audience analysis, her communication may seem vague, which is unintentional on Jane's part. However, sometimes it may serve a purpose to be ambiguous. Researchers have described this phenomenon in two ways: strategic ambiguity and equivocation.

Strategic ambiguity is a term with a history in political discourse. In the field of communication, organizational researcher Eric Eisenberg (1984) popularized the term when he wrote that people in organizations do not always want others to completely understand their intentions. Sometimes, they leave out cues on purpose to encourage multiple interpretations by others. Eisenberg believed that the tensions in an organization are moderated by ambiguity. According to Eisenberg, to promote harmony, leaders of organizations have to be abstract (or ambiguous) enough to allow for many interpretations while simultaneously encouraging agreement. This strategy can also be used by a person in a conflict. Saying something like "I am not sure about that" allows several interpretations and may achieve the end of the argument.

Equivocation is a type of ambiguity that involves choosing your words carefully to give a listener a false impression without actually lying. Equivocation also allows the equivocator "deniability" after the fact. For example, if your grandmother sends you a birthday gift that you don't like, but you value your relationship with your grandmother, you might equivocate in your thank-you note. You might say: "Thanks so much for the sweater. It was so thoughtful of you to think about keeping me warm in the cold Wisconsin winters!" You have not said the sweater was attractive, nor have you said you liked it, so you haven't lied overtly. However, if you are a good equivocator, you have given your grandmother the impression that you are really pleased with a sweater that you, in fact, dislike. Keep in mind that such a tactic could have long-term consequences. In this case, you could receive similar unwanted sweaters for several subsequent birthdays.

Equivocating involves saying things that are true but misleading. It should be no surprise that the language of advertising makes use of equivocation. When an ad says that a car's seats "have the look and feel of fine leather" that means that they are *not* made of fine leather, but the use of the words *fine leather* leads an unsuspecting listener to think that they are. In addition, the word *virtually* is a good equivocal word. The phrase *virtually spotless* means that the described item has some spots on it, but the phrase leads you to believe otherwise.

Choices for Improving Verbal Communication

To improve your verbal communication skills, we suggest cultivating an attitude of respect for others. To do so, you need to engage in **perspective-taking,** which means acknowledging the viewpoints of those with whom you interact. For example, if you talk frequently with a friend who is a different ethnicity than you, perspective-taking requires you to understand that ethnicity matters and that your friend will have somewhat different experiences from yours as a result.

Marsha Houston (2004) writes that she doesn't like it when white women friends try to empathize with her by saying that they know exactly how she feels about racism because they have experienced sexism (or some other "ism"). Houston says that it erases her experience to state that your experience is just like it. Listen-

Your *Turn*

In your journal, reflect on ambiguity in verbal symbols. For a week or two, keep track of the language you hear in conversation and in the media. Pay special attention to political speeches and advertising. Record examples of ambiguous language and note whether you think the effect of each is positive or negative. When you see an example as negative, speculate about how verbal symbols could have been used differently to achieve a more positive result. When you see an example as positive, explain your evaluation. Overall, what do you think about ambiguity in the English language? Is it a positive force or is it somewhat troubling? Explain your position. If you'd like, you can use your student workbook to complete this activity.

ing to others before assuming that you already know exactly what their experience is will help you in perspective-taking.

In addition to developing respect for others and working on perspective-taking, you can practice four skills to help you be more effective in using verbal symbols: owning and using I-messages, understanding the ladder of abstraction, indexing, and probing the middle ground.

Owning and Using I-Messages

Each of us must take responsibility for our own behaviors and feelings in communication with others. Owning, which refers to our ability to take responsibility for our own thoughts and feelings, is often accomplished through I-messages. As we discussed in Chapter 4, I-messages acknowledge our own positions, whereas you-messages direct responsibility onto others, often in a blaming fashion. For example, if you are bored during a lecture, you could communicate your thought to the professor with a you-message ("Your lecture is boring") or an I-message ("I'm having trouble getting interested in this material"). See Table 6.4 for more examples of how to change you-messages to I-messages.

Understanding the Ladder of Abstraction

Earlier in the chapter, we mentioned that you can engage in the process of abstraction by using words at different levels on the ladder of abstraction—for example, vehicle, car, red 1960 Chevy convertible. The first term allows the listener to imagine a wide range of vehicles, the second term narrows the field somewhat, and the third restricts the referent much more. The more abstract you are, the more you allow a listener to interpret what you mean. The more concrete you are, the more you direct the listener to your precise meaning.

Being skillful in this area requires you to diagnose when a situation needs specificity and when general information might suffice. A simple guideline suggests that the better you know someone, the less concrete you have to be. For example, when two people have a developed relationship, they may understand each other without providing a concrete description. For example, when Tom tells Martha that he wants to spend some time relaxing, she knows from her five years' experience with him that he means he wants to go into his workshop and would appreciate not being disturbed. Tom doesn't need to tell her concretely what the abstract term *relaxing* means to him at this point in their relationship. However, when Tom is at work and tells a new coworker that they need to get a project finished as soon as possible, he probably should specify that *as soon as possible*, in this case, means by the end of the week. Otherwise, the coworker could spend eight hours working to finish the project, only to discover that Tom didn't need the project finished that soon.

Indexing

A way to avoid static evaluation, one of the problems we mentioned earlier, involves dating your statements to indicate you are aware something may have changed (Korzybski, 1958). **Indexing** requires that you acknowledge the time frame of your judgments of others and yourself. For example, if Alex notes that Rucha is self-centered, he would index that by saying, "Yesterday, when she wouldn't stop talking

Table 6.4 | **You-Messages and I-Messages**

You-Messages	I-Messages
You are insensitive.	I need you to pay attention to me.
You make me mad.	I get angry when you ignore me.
You don't understand anything.	I don't feel understood when you interrupt me.
You never listen to me.	I want you to put down the paper when I talk to you.
You are so rude.	I was hurt when you said you thought my hair looked bad.
You're a liar.	I need to be able to trust you, and I feel betrayed because you didn't tell me the truth about the car accident.

about herself, Rucha was self-centered." Indexing reminds us that the way people act at one given time may not be the way they are for all time.

Probing the Middle Ground

Probing the middle ground is a skill that helps you avoid polarization in your verbal communication. When you are tempted to label something with an extreme judgment, try to explore the shades of gray that might be more descriptive of the behavior. For instance, if you think someone is against you, try to discover the places where you agree so you can see that the person disagrees with you on some things, but not on all things. If you are tempted to label someone as irresponsible, try to discover the areas where the person has acted responsibly so you can see that they are not completely at one extreme on the responsibility scale. Thinking about the middle ground will help restrain you from polarizing or using extreme labels that can easily become inflammatory.

Probing the middle ground might involve more than simply one middle choice. For example, a study conducted in 1974 (Loftus & Palmer, 1974) showed that people responded to an accident report differently depending on what word was used to describe it. When people were told that there had been an accident involving two cars and then asked what speed the cars were traveling, their answers varied depending on whether the word used to describe the crash was *contacted, collided, bumped, hit,* or *smashed.* Those that were told that the cars "contacted each other" thought the cars were traveling the slowest, and the speed increased with each word listed. This study also illustrates how powerful words can be, so we should choose them carefully.

CHOICES *for Improving Verbal Effectiveness*

- Use I-messages to own your thoughts and feelings
- Understand how the ladder of abstraction applies to your messages
- Index to acknowledge the time frame of your judgments
- Probe the middle ground to avoid polarization

Skill *Spotlight*

Semantic Conjugations

One important skill in language use is the ability to capitalize on the flexibility of language to express different meanings. Word connotations provide some of the flexibility of language. To sharpen your skills in using words to express different shades of meaning, take each of the following descriptions and find a term that expresses the concept more positively and one that expresses it more negatively. Here's an example:

slender	thin	skinny
1. _____	having money	_____
2. _____	overweight	_____
3. _____	friendly	_____
4. _____	gets good grades	_____
5. _____	studies hard	_____
6. _____	tidy	_____
7. _____	fearful	_____
8. _____	tall	_____
9. _____	funny	_____
10. _____	serious	_____
11. _____	likes to party	_____
12. _____	likes computers	_____
13. _____	reads a lot	_____
14. _____	quiet	_____
15. _____	talkative	_____
16. _____	creative	_____
17. _____	speaks loudly	_____
18. _____	short	_____
19. _____	easy to please	_____
20. _____	hard to please	_____

Skills at Work At work, we need to pay particular attention to the words we choose to express our thoughts. Word choice can have social and job advancement implications. For instance, if Helen approaches her boss, Martha, about changing her vacation dates, how Helen phrases her request is important. If Helen says, "Martha, I need to take my vacation on February 10–21 instead of March 10–21," Martha might find Helen's directness too terse. Martha might want to show deference in her request ("Is it all right with you if I change my vacation?") or include an explanation ("I have had an unexpected event in my family").

Word choice affects both outcome and process. That is, Helen might get her vacation time (outcome) but at the expense of annoying her boss (process), or her request might be denied altogether because Martha feels Helen is being too direct (outcome and process). Of course, words don't determine all outcomes in the workplace, but careful word choice is a good start to getting what you want. Can you identify other consequences of word choice in the workplace?

Summary

We use words, or verbal symbols, to achieve our ultimate goal: sharing meaning with others. Verbal symbols are only symbolic representations, but they still can be quite powerful and flexible. As we use language, we are both expressing our thoughts and creating our thoughts, even deciding what is worth thinking about.

The lexicon is ever-changing; new words are coined as new technology emerges or are created to express the thoughts of muted groups (those who cannot find words in the language to convey their experiences). Other words are discarded because the things they refer to are obsolete or because the words of one generation are ignored by the next, replaced by language that characterizes a generational in-group. In addition, the meanings of existing words evolve. For example, although a word's denotative meaning (its dictionary definition) might stay the same, its connotative meaning (the ideas or feelings people associate with a term) might change.

Words are affected by factors such as culture and ethnicity. Idioms (words or phrases that have an understood meaning in a culture) such as phatic communication (words not meant to be literally translated) complicate communication between people of different cultures. Some people who navigate two cultures engage in code-switching, or shifting between languages in the same conversation. Other variables, such as gender, generation, and context, also influence our use of verbal symbols.

Our use of verbal symbols or language can be explained in many ways. Symbolic interactionism holds that the meanings of words are determined by cultural agreement, not by anything inherent in the words themselves. Linguistic determinism states that words determine our ability to perceive and think, and linguistic relativity proposes that language influences, but doesn't determine, our thinking.

Words can be inflammatory. Language can be perceived as sexist, such as use of the generic *he* (using the pronoun *he* for all people, male and female) and the prevalence of man-linked words (such as *salesman*). Other words, such as *blackmail*, can be considered racist. Language can be problematic when it encourages speakers to ignore change (static evaluation), to characterize another person as either good or bad (polarization), and to respond to the symbol rather than the thing itself (reification).

On the other hand, language can be restorative. We can use it to express confirmation and to develop inclusion. When we practice perspective-taking, we acknowledge the viewpoints of those with whom we interact. We can also use I-messages to own our behaviors and feelings. We can choose to communicate using concrete or abstract terms, depending on the circumstances. In addition, we can index the time frame of our judgments to avoid static evaluation. Lastly, we can probe the middle ground to avoid polarization.

Understanding Interpersonal Communication Online

Now that you've read Chapter 6, use your Understanding Interpersonal Communication CD-ROM for quick access to the electronic study resources that accompany this text. Your CD-ROM gives you access to the video of Carlos and Liz's encounter on pages 151–152, the CNN video clip "Jargon" on page 157, the Communication Assessment Test on page 159, the Ethics & Choice interactive activity on page 165, InfoTrac College Edition, and the Understanding Interpersonal Communication website. When you get to the

Understanding Interpersonal Communication homepage, click on "Student Book Companion Site" in the Resource box at right to access the online study aids for this chapter, including a digital glossary, review quizzes, and the chapter activities.

Terms for Review

abstract 160	grammar 153	polarization 172
codability 165	idiom 161	process of abstraction 160
code-switching 163	indexing 176	referent 160
concrete 160	language 153	reification 172
confirmation 173	lexical gaps 156	Sapir-Whorf hypothesis 164
connotative meaning 160	linguistic determinism 164	sexist language 170
denotative meaning 160	linguistic relativity 164	static evaluation 172
disconfirmation 174	man-linked words 170	strategic ambiguity 174
encoding 153	muted groups 156	verbal symbols 153
equivocation 175	perspective-taking 175	
generic *he* 170	phatic communication 162	

Questions for Understanding

Comprehension Focus

1. Distinguish between language and verbal symbols.
2. Define each of the five attributes of verbal symbols.
3. Define idioms and provide an example.
4. Explain how context affects verbal messages.
5. Compare and contrast the dark and bright sides of verbal messages.

Application Focus

1. **CASE IN POINT**
   What verbal skills could Carlos and Liz practice that might make their encounter more satisfactory? Where do you think Liz got the idea that Carlos would call her? Where do you think Carlos got the idea that they didn't have much of a chance for a relationship? What verbal symbols played a role in each of their conclusions?
2. Is it ethical to be equivocal or to use strategic ambiguity? Explain your answer. Think about the ethical systems we introduced in Chapter 1 as you formulate your answer.
3. Explain the theories of linguistic determinism and linguistic relativity. What are the differences between them? Which one do you think is more accurate in describing the relationship between language/culture and thought/perception? Explain your answer.
4. How do gender, ethnicity, and age affect language use and understanding? Is it fair to say that people of different genders, ethnicities, and ages speak different languages? Why or why not?
5. How can a speaker avoid the dark side of verbal codes? Is there any way to speak to others who are different from you are and not offend them at one time or another? Is the effort given to speaking in inclusionary terms misplaced? Explain your answer.

Interactive Activities and InfoTrac College Edition Exercises

Complete the Interactive Activities and InfoTrac College Edition Exercises for Chapter 6 online at the Understanding Interpersonal Communication website. Select the chapter resources for Chapter 6, then click on "Activities" or "InfoTrac College Edition." If requested, you can submit your answers to your instructor.

Interactive Activities

InfoTrac College Edition Exercises

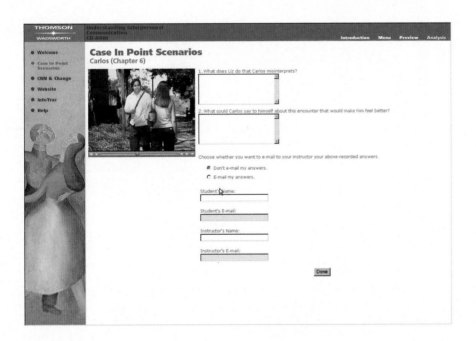

7

Communicating Nonverbally

CHAPTER GOALS

Understand nonverbal communication and its importance in human interaction

Identify the primary principles of nonverbal communication

Explain and exemplify the types of nonverbal communication

Articulate the relationship between nonverbal communication and culture

Apply a variety of strategies to improve skills in nonverbal communication

CASE IN POINT: MARK MATTSON

Watching his mother, Julia, get up from a chair in her kitchen, Mark Mattson knew her days of living independently were numbered. Today, in particular, Mark thought his mom looked every one of her 75 years. As she got up from the chair, she staggered and held onto its back. And she appeared more disheveled than ever; her hair wasn't brushed, she had on her bathrobe (which looked dirty), and she was muttering to herself even more than she had in past weeks. The two had never spoken to each other about an alternative living arrangement for Julia, but Mark knew the time may now have arrived.

Each day since his father's death three years ago, Mark had picked up two cups of coffee and the *Los Angeles Times* and driven fifteen minutes to his mom's house. There, he and his mother would sit, frequently in silence. The two didn't often feel the need to say anything to each other; they both enjoyed just being around the other. Julia had never spoken to Mark about her husband's death, a fact that saddened and even annoyed Mark.

This morning, Mark's dominant emotion was definitely sadness. As he and his mother each read a section of the paper, Mark snuck glances at his mother. He tried to ignore her unkempt look and think about what a great mother she had been. Her soft voice and hugs came rushing back to Mark. He wanted to make things like they used to be, but he knew that no hug could change the difficult days that were ahead for him and his mother. ◾

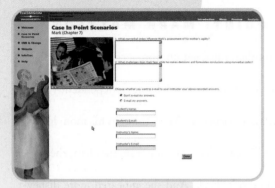

Use your Understanding Interpersonal Communication CD-ROM to watch a video clip of Mark and his mother. Click on the "In Action" icon in the menu at left, then click on "Conversation Menu" in the menu bar at the top of the screen. Select "Mark" to watch the video (it takes a minute for the video to load). As you watch the video, can you identify the nonverbal signals Julia sends that trigger sadness in Mark? You can respond to this and other analysis questions by clicking on "Analysis" in the menu bar at the top of the screen. When you've answered all the questions, click on "Done" to compare your answers to those provided by the authors.

We all communicate without saying a word; we all "speak" without talking. Nonverbal communication has been called the "unspoken dialogue" (Burgoon, Buller, & Woodall, 1996), and scholars have noted its importance in conversations. Some researchers report that around 65 percent of overall message meaning is conveyed nonverbally (Hickson, Stacks, & Moore, 2004) (see Figure 7.1). Other researchers assert that nearly 93 percent of emotional meaning is conveyed nonverbally (Mehrabian & Ferris, 1967).

When we attend to nonverbal behaviors, we draw conclusions about others, and others simultaneously draw conclusions about us. This process is part of the transactional nature of communication we discussed in Chapter 1. For instance, consider our opening story of Mark Mattson and his mother, Julia, who clearly have a close relationship. Instead of overtly speaking to Julia, Mark notes her nonverbal cues and makes various judgments. When deciding whether or not Julia should consider leaving her home, he observes her difficulty getting out of the chair and her dirty bathrobe. As he sits and reads the paper with her, he recalls an earlier time, and he remembers her voice and hugs.

The influence of nonverbal behavior on our perceptions, conversations, and relationships cannot be understated. Although we are frequently unaware of our use of nonverbal communication, that doesn't mean that nonverbal communication is absent in our interactions. As Mark Knapp and Judith Hall (2002) explain, nonverbal communication is "an inseparable part of the total communication process" (p. 31).

This chapter explores nonverbal communication and its importance in our lives. We focus our discussion on how nonverbal behavior functions, both directly and

"Say what's on your mind, Harris—the language of dance has always eluded me."

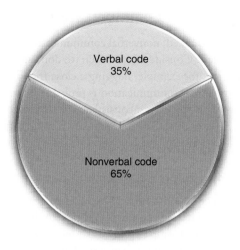

Figure 7.1 | **Communication of interpersonal meaning**

indirectly, in our daily activities. Before we move on in our discussion about non-verbal communication, let's spend a few moments interpreting it. We define **non-verbal communication** as all behaviors—other than spoken words—that communicate messages and have shared meaning between people. This definition has three associated parameters. First, electronic communication (a subject we return to in Chapter 11) is not included in our definition. Second, when we note that there is "shared meaning," we are saying that a national culture agrees on how to construe a behavior. For example, in many co-cultures in the United States, when a parent sees a child do something unsafe, the parent might wag his or her index finger. The child must know the meaning behind this nonverbal shaming technique to respond to the parent's reprimand. Third, as we mentioned in Chapter 6, verbal and non-verbal communication usually work together to create meaning.

Nonverbal communication competence requires us to be able to encode and de-code nonverbal messages (Burgoon & Hoobler, 2002). In our relationships with others, we must be able to detect the meaning of another's message through non-verbal communication as well as use this form of communication to get across our own meaning. In addition, being able to adapt to people around you is a hallmark of a competent nonverbal communicator. **Interaction adaptation theory** suggests that individuals simultaneously adapt their communication behavior to the com-munication behavior of others (Burgoon, Stern, & Dillman, 1995). Thus, the bet-ter we are able to adapt, the better we are able to understand the meaning of a message. Suppose, for example, that Rosa and her roommate, Nadine, are in a noisy place talking about a conflict they've had pertaining to their apartment's cleanliness. Nadine is practicing interaction adaptation if, when Rosa leans forward to talk about the topic, Nadine simultaneously leans forward to listen to the story. This "postural echo" suggests that Nadine is not only mirroring Rosa's behavior but that she is also trying to understand Rosa's meaning.

With our definition of nonverbal communication established, we're now ready to explore some of the principles of nonverbal communication before moving on to discuss nonverbal communication codes and cultural variations in nonverbal communication.

Principles of Nonverbal Communication

Although it is often overlooked, nonverbal communication is a vital aspect of interpersonal communication. Consider times when we don't say a word but manage to "say" so much. Imagine, for example, hugging a close friend at her father's funeral. In this situation, nonverbal communication is probably more comforting than any words you could say. This apparent inconsistency of efficient communication without words is what makes nonverbal communication so important in our conversations with others. We now explore four principles of this type of communication.

Nonverbal Communication Is Often Ambiguous

One reason nonverbal communication is so challenging in our relationships is that our nonverbal messages often mean different things to different people, which can lead to misunderstandings. Compared to verbal messages, nonverbal messages are usually more ambiguous. For example, suppose that Lena and Todd hold hands on a first date. Does that mean that they feel similarly about each other?

Mark Hickson, Don Stacks, and Nina-Jo Moore (2004) capture the challenge of nonverbal communication by noting that nonverbal communication "tends to be more elusive, is more intangible, is more difficult to define, and is more 'natural' than verbal communication" (p. 7). A major reason that this ambiguity exists is that many factors influence the meaning of nonverbal behaviors, including our shared fields of experience, current surroundings, culture, and so forth. Consider the following conversation between a father and son as they talk about the son staying out past his curfew:

FATHER: Look, I told you to be home by 11! It's past midnight now. And get that smirk off your face!

SON: First, dad, you might have told me 11, but you also didn't say anything when I asked if I could stay out till 12. You didn't say anything for sure. I mean, like, you were changing the oil on the truck when I asked you. You didn't even, like, look at me. I couldn't hear you that much while you were under the car. And, how am I . . .

FATHER: You heard what you wanted to hear. I told you . . .

SON: I swear, Dad. I thought my curfew was midnight. And I've stayed out till midnight before.

This conversation suggests a few things about the ambiguous nature of communication. First, the father seems to be annoyed by the son's smirk. Would he have noticed his son's smirk if he weren't mad at him? Second, the son didn't feel his dad was serious about the 11 p.m. deadline because his father never looked at him. In addition, the son felt that his dad hesitated on the time, and he also claimed that he didn't clearly hear his father. Finally, the son used his past experience in staying out till midnight to justify coming in past 11 p.m.

Nonverbal Communication Regulates Conversation

People use nonverbal communication to manage the ebb and flow of conversations. Nonverbal regulators allow speakers to enter, exit, or maintain the conversation. Who talks when and to whom, referred to as **turn-taking,** is based primarily on nonverbal communication. For instance, if we want a chance to speak, we usually lean forward, toward the speaker. When we don't want to be interrupted in a conversation, we may avoid eye contact with another and keep our vocal pattern con-

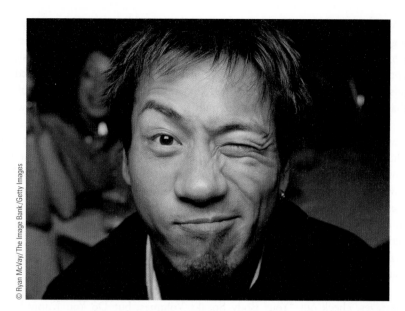

The ambiguity of nonverbal gestures can lead to misunderstandings. For example, if someone winks at you, is he flirting with you, letting you in on a joke, showing affection, or does he simply have something in his eye?

sistent so that others don't interrupt. When we are ready to yield the conversation to another, we typically stop talking, look at the other person, and perhaps make a motion with our hands to indicate that it is now okay for the other person to respond.

As we mentioned earlier, we are often unconscious of our nonverbal cues. For example, let's say that Bruce, a student in Dr. Brownstone's biology class, decides to challenge a grade. When Bruce arrives at Dr. Brownstone's office, he is so nervous about his verbal message that he is not thinking about his nonverbal communication. In other words, he is not worrying about when to speak, when to defer the conversation to the professor, when to sit back, when to bow his head, when to lower his voice, or when to interrupt. His nonverbal communication may contradict his verbal message or detract from it because he's not monitoring it.

Nonverbal Communication Is More Believable than Verbal Communication

Although, as we noted earlier, nonverbal communication is often ambiguous, people believe nonverbal messages over verbal messages. You've no doubt heard the expression "actions speak louder than words." This statement suggests that someone's nonverbal behavior can influence a conversational partner more than what is said. For instance, a job candidate being interviewed may verbally state her commitment to being professional, yet if she wears jeans and arrives late to the interview, these nonverbal cues will cause the interviewer to regard her statement with skepticism.

Consider how Esther reacts to the nonverbal communication of her customers at a local gas station. She makes judgments about people based on their appearance. For example, Esther is more inclined to give the store's restroom key to someone who appears calm than to someone with a rushed, nervous, and sweaty demeanor. However, as we learned in Chapter 2, her perception may be inaccurate or incomplete.

Nonverbal Communication May Conflict with Verbal Communication

Although nonverbal and verbal communication frequently operate interdependently, sometimes our nonverbal messages are not congruent with our verbal messages. We term this incompatibility a **mixed message.** When a friend asks you,

REVISITING CASE IN POINT

1. Identify one principle of nonverbal communication and apply it to Mark Mattson's perception of his mother.
2. How has Julia Mattson's appearance regulated any conversation between Mark and her?

 You can answer these questions online under Student Resources for Chapter 7 at the Understanding Interpersonal Communication website.

"What's wrong?" after observing you with tears in your eyes, and you reply "Nothing," the contradiction between your nonverbal and verbal behavior becomes evident. When a physician frowns as she reveals to her patient that the prognosis "looks good," the mixed message is clear. Or, consider a wife, who after being asked by her husband if she loves him, shouts, "Of course I love you!" Most of us would agree that when we love someone, we generally don't yell it in such an angry way.

When confronted with a mixed message, people have to choose whether to believe the nonverbal or the verbal behaviors. Because children are generally not sophisticated enough to understand the many meanings that accompany nonverbal communication, they rely on the words of a message more than the nonverbal behaviors (Morton & Trehub, 2001). However, most children understand nonverbal messages such as shaking the head for "no" and a finger to the lips for "keep quiet." In contrast, adults who encounter mixed messages pay the most attention to nonverbal messages and neglect much of what is being stated. The multiple messages that originate from the eyes, voice, body movement, facial expressions, and touch usually overpower the verbal message.

To further explore how our nonverbal behaviors often conflict with our verbal messages, check out "Your Body Speaks Volumes, but Do You Know What It Is Saying?" available through InfoTrac College Edition. Use your Understanding Interpersonal Communication CD-ROM to access **InfoTrac College Edition Exercise 7.1: What Is Your Body Language Saying?** To read about mixed messages in a specific context, business negotiations, use your Understanding Interpersonal Communication CD-ROM to access **Interactive Activity 7.1: Mixed Messages in Negotiations.**

Nonverbal Communication Codes

The study of nonverbal communication is vast and we employ several different forms of nonverbal codes in our conversations with others. Later in the chapter, we will look at a number of these nonverbal types and discuss their cultural implications. In this section, we examine a classifying system articulated by Burgoon et al. (1996), which is set out in Table 7.1. This system includes visual-auditory codes, contact codes, and place and time codes.

Visual-Auditory Codes

As their name reflects, visual-auditory codes include categories of nonverbal communication that you can see and hear. These categories are kinesics (body move-

Table 7.1 | **Categories of Nonverbal Communication**

Code	Nonverbal Category
Visual-auditory	Kinesics *(body movement)*
	Physical appearance *(body size, body artifacts, attractiveness)*
	Facial communication *(eye contact, smiling)*
	Paralanguage *(pitch, rate, volume, speed, silence)*
Contact	Haptics *(touch)*
	Space *(personal space, territoriality)*
Place and time	The environment *(color, lighting, room design)*
	Chronemics *(time)*

Many people use gestures to communicate nonverbally on the job, particularly when they work in a noisy environment or need to communicate with one another silently. Do you commonly use gestures in your workplace? What do they communicate?

ment), physical appearance (such as attractiveness), facial communication (such as eye contact), and paralanguage (such as pitch and whining).

Kinesics (Body Movement)

Body communication is also called **kinesics,** a Greek word meaning "movement." Kinesics refers to the study of body motions and how people use them to communicate. Kinesic behavior is wide-ranging; it can include anything from staying put at a party after being asked to leave, to gesturing during a speech.

The primary components of kinesics are gestures and body posture/orientation. Gestures have been talked about for almost 2,500 years. For example, writings by the Greek philosopher Aristotle explained that gestures are important when delivering a public speech. Further, Michael Corballis (2002) notes that gestures preceded verbal communication by tens of thousands of years.

What can we learn from gestures? We need to consider the context to understand them. Consider the gestures that the following individuals would use: parking lot attendant, nurse, radio disc jockey, landscaper, and auctioneer. What gestures would they have in common? What gestures are unique to these occupations? In the classroom setting, gestures such as raising a hand, writing on a chalkboard, pointing, and waving at a student to come sit in a particular seat are common. Janet Bavelas (1994) describes the following gesture types:

- **Delivery gestures** signal shared understanding between communicators. Clifton, for example, nods his head to let his friend, Kaitlin, know that he understands what she is talking about.
- **Citing gestures** acknowledge another's feedback. For instance, in a conversation with her employee, Ms. Rasmussen uses a citing gesture when she disagrees with what her employee is saying; she raises her hand, palm flat to receiver, index finger extended upward.

REVISITING CASE IN POINT

1. Identify several areas of nonverbal communication pertaining to Mark and Julia Mattson.
2. Looking at physical appearance specifically, how does Mark make a decision associated with his mother's mental and physical competency? Do you believe his impending decision is appropriate?

You can answer these questions online under Student Resources for Chapter 7 at the Understanding Interpersonal Communication website.

- **Seeking gestures** request agreement or clarification from the speaker. For instance, we may extend both our arms out, keep our palms flat, and shrug. This gesture is used when someone is communicating "I don't know what you mean."

- **Turn gestures** indicate that another person can speak or are used to request the conversation floor. We referenced this nonverbal communication earlier in the chapter when we discussed the regulating function of nonverbal messages. Turn gestures include pointing at another to indicate it is his or her turn, or extending your hand outward and rotating your wrist in a clockwise position to show that the other person should continue speaking.

In addition to gestures, our body posture and orientation reveal important information. Posture is generally a result of how tense or relaxed we are. For example, your body posture would differ depending on whether you were reading this chapter while you were alone in your room or in the campus library. **Body orientation** is the extent to which we turn our legs, shoulders, and head toward (or away) from a communicator. Albert Mehrabian (1981) found that body orientation affects conversations. For example, when people communicate with those of higher status, they tend to stand directly facing him or her. Conversely, those with higher status tend to use a leaning posture when speaking to subordinates.

 To further explore how we use our bodies to convey interpersonal feelings and attitudes, use your Understanding Interpersonal Communication CD-ROM to access **Interactive Activity 7.2: Feelings, Attitudes, and Kinesics.**

Physical Appearance

In interpersonal exchanges, physical appearance plays a role in our evaluations of others. Physical appearance encompasses all of the **physical characteristics** of an individual, including body size, skin color, hair color and style, facial hair, and facial features (for example, nose size, skin texture, and so on).

How does physical appearance influence our interpersonal communication? Although we are unable to discuss every aspect of physical appearance, a few thoughts merit attention. Certainly, one's skin color has affected the communication process. Even today—decades after civil rights legislation took effect—some people won't communicate with people of a different race. Body size, too, can influence our interpersonal relationships. Do you find yourself making judgments about people who appear overweight or too thin? What is your first assessment of a person who is more than six feet tall? What is your initial impression of a bodybuilder? Do you evaluate differently women who shave their body hair and women who choose not to shave?

Body artifacts also have the potential to communicate. Clothing can convey social status or group identification. In the corporate world, tailored clothing bolsters one's status among many peers. During Kwanzaa, a holiday celebration in African American communities, participants frequently wear traditional African clothing, which serves as a nonverbal connection among African Americans. Other body artifacts or adornments are also communicative. People who wear religious symbols, such as a crucifix or the Star of David, may be exhibiting religious commitments. Military clothing is usually accompanied by medals or stripes to depict rank, which connotes military accomplishment. Body piercings and tattoos can communicate many different messages, and those who have them are typically viewed as nonconformists and independent, and they are rated poorly by employers (Acor, 2001; Forbes, 2001).

Physical appearance also includes the attractiveness of the interpersonal communicators. Each culture has its own ideal of physical beauty, its own interpretation of what is attractive. Much research exists on interpersonal attractiveness. Mark Knapp and Judith Hall (2002) have compiled a number of conclusions based on their review of the research findings. Two seem particularly pertinent to our discussion. First, generally speaking, people seek out others who are similar to themselves in attractiveness, just as they seek out others who are similar to themselves in other characteristics. If you are a nonsmoker, are you likely to be compatible with a smoker? If you are vegetarian, will you be attracted to a carnivore? Although people are not so narrow and simplistic that they use only one behavior to determine attractiveness, it is true that we are interested in being around those people who are similar to us.

Second, Knapp and Hall (2002) found that physically attractive people are often judged to be more intelligent and friendly than those not viewed as attractive. This conclusion resonates in a number of different environments, including the classroom. For example, researchers note that physically attractive students are viewed as more intelligent and friendly than less attractive students (Ritts, Patterson, & Tubbs, 1992). However, in the business setting, "more attractive women in executive roles are often the victims of prejudice, taken less seriously and often resented, thus feeling the pressure to come up with glasses and hairstyles that project a more severe aura" (Jones, 2004, p. 3B). Thus, we have to be careful in our interpretations of attractiveness.

Facial Communication

More than any other part of the body, the face gives others some insight into how someone is feeling. Our facial expressions cover the gamut of emotional meaning, from eagerness to exhaustion. We often have difficulty shielding authentic feelings from others because we usually don't have much control over our facial communication. This fact further explains the point we made earlier in this chapter, that people tend to believe our nonverbal codes over our verbal codes—it's tough to hide our feelings. While looking at an infant or toddler, try suppressing a smile. When talking to a parent who has lost a child in a war, repressing a sad look on your face is probably impossible. It's simply too challenging to control a region of our body that is so intimately connected to our emotions.

The part of the face with the most potential for communication is the eye. Eye contact is a complex part of human behavior. For most of us, a single eye movement

© Baby Blues. Reprinted with special permission of King Features Syndicate.

communicates on multiple levels. Brian Bates and John Cleese (2001) underscore this thinking: "In the right context, even a glance held a fraction longer than normal may be perceived as an act of intimacy. The glance can penetrate the psychological space of the other, and also reveals our own" (p. 113). We can look directly into someone's eyes to communicate interest, power, or anger. We roll our eyes to signal disbelief or disapproval. We avoid eye contact when we are uninterested, nervous, or shy. Our eyes also facilitate our interactions. We look at others while they speak to get a sense of their facial and body communication. Simultaneously, others often look at us while we speak. We also make judgments about others simply by looking at their eyes. We may decide if someone is truthful, uninterested, tired, involved, or credible by looking at them. Although our conclusions may be erroneous, most people rely on eye contact in their conversations.

Finally, smiling is one of the most recognizable nonverbal behaviors worldwide. Although in some contexts a smile can have a negative effect, it usually has a positive effect on an encounter. In an experiment testing the effects of smiling on helping behavior, Nicolas Gueguen and Marie-Agnes De Gail (2003) report that smiling at others encourages them to assist in tasks. Studying 800 passersby, the research team had eight research assistants ask others for help. One group of assistants smiled at some of the people exiting a grocery store. A few seconds later, passersby had an opportunity to help an assistant who dropped a computer diskette on the ground. Results showed that the previous smile of a stranger enhanced later helping behavior. That is, those who were smiled at earlier were more likely to help the stranger with the computer disk.

Smiling at another nearly always results in a more pleasant encounter. However, smiling at ill-conceived times may prompt others to react unfavorably. In conflict, for instance, smiling is often perceived as an inappropriate behavior. Smiling during a heated exchange can aggravate an already difficult situation, unless the smile is well timed. Smiling has multiple meanings (for example, a smirk and a sneer communicate two different things), so context is definitely important when we interpret another's smile.

For an interactive look at how our eyes, mouth, and tilt of the head provide clues about our emotions, use your Understanding Interpersonal Communication CD-ROM to access **Interactive Activity 7.3: Eyes, Mouth, and Tilt of Head.** And to read an interesting article about emotions that are recognized across cultures, check out "Emotions Revealed: Recognizing Facial Expressions" available through InfoTrac College Edition. Use your Understanding Interpersonal Communication CD-ROM to access **InfoTrac College Edition Exercise 7.2: Universal Facial Expressions.**

Paralanguage (Voice)

To introduce the concept of paralanguage, let's examine the story of Charles. A few years ago, Charles contracted HIV, the virus that can lead to AIDS. Charles is frequently an upbeat man, and everyone around him enjoys his company. However, sometimes his best friend, Melissa, can hear a "voice" that is different from the one Charles normally expresses. For example, sometimes when Charles says that he feels fine and that no one should be concerned about his health, Melissa hears a different message. During such conversations, Charles is frequently silent. He uses awkward pauses as he talks about his doctor's appointments. He laughs at odd times, convincing Melissa that he is nervous, anxious, and still very afraid of what the future holds.

This story underscores a vocal phenomenon called **paralanguage,** or vocalics, which is the study of a person's voice. Paralanguage refers not to *what* a person is saying but *how* a person is saying it. Paralanguage covers a vast array of nonverbal behaviors such as pitch, rate, volume, inflection, tempo, and pronunciation, which we call **vocal qualities.** For our purposes, **vocal segregates** (the "ums" and "ers" of conversation) and the use of silence are also vocal qualities. Paralanguage also encompasses such nonverbal behaviors as crying, laughing, groaning, muttering, whispering, and whining; we call these **vocal characterizers.** Don't underestimate the usefulness of studying these paralinguistic behaviors. They give us our uniqueness as communicators, help us differentiate among people, and influence people's perceptions of us and our perceptions of them.

Our vocal qualities include the rate (speed), volume (loudness/softness), inflection (vocal emphasis), pitch (highness/lowness), intensity (volume), tempo (rhythm), and pronunciation associated with voices. Vocal qualities lead listeners to form impressions about a speaker's socioeconomic status, personality type, persuasiveness, and work ethic (Griffin, 2004). One way to tap into these vocal nuances is to practice saying the same sentence with various rates, volume, inflection, and tempo. For example, try saying the following statement to connote praise, then blame, then exasperation:

You really did it this time.

The next time you want to borrow a friend's car, tell your mother a secret, ask your professor a question, or engage in a debate with your roommate about religion or politics, you will probably utilize a number of different vocal qualities.

The "uhs," "ers," and "ums" in our conversations may seem unimportant and may be viewed as "white noise" (Erard, 2004, p. B7), but these vocal segregates compose an increasingly researched area of vocal qualities because they can predict whether a conversation will continue and the fluency of that conversation. Further, how do you react when you hear a speaker use these disfluencies? You may find them appropriate for many social situations, but what happens in more professional settings, such as formal presentations at work, job interviews, or class oral reports? When vocal segregates are used excessively, people view them as bad habits that can jeopardize credibility.

We include silence in our discussion of the vocal qualities of paralanguage because a person's use of his or her voice includes the decision whether or not to use it. Strange as it may sound, in our relationships, we should all exercise our right to remain silent. However, how many of us do? Society seems to have a love affair with talking. Self-help books exclaim that communication is the way to relational bliss and long-lasting happiness. Therapists tell their patients to open up and communicate. And what adolescent doesn't hear from a parent: "Talk to me!" We live in a culture that places a premium on the spoken word.

Yet, at times, as we touched on in Chapters 3 and 5, honoring silence may be the most powerful way to communicate to another person. Silence communicates and informs the communication process in a number of ways. First, silence indicates that we need some time for reflection. Silence gives us a chance to think about the circumstances or events surrounding an interpersonal relationship. For instance, if you have been battling with your sibling, taking some time to withdraw from the conversation can help you refocus on the original issue and how you want to go about resolving it.

Silence is also part of the dark side of communication between people. At times, silence serves as an interpersonal weapon (Hickson, Stacks, & Moore, 2004). Suppose that Andrew and Jessica, who have been married for six months, are having a fight about whether or not they can afford to have a child. Because Andrew is not comfortable talking about this topic so early in their marriage, he remains silent on the issue. On the other hand, Jessica wants to talk about this topic because she feels that having children is an important part of being married. Each time Jessica tries to bring up the subject, Andrew simply says he doesn't want to talk about it and leaves the room.

You may have been the target of this "silent treatment" or may have decided yourself that giving this sort of punishment in a relationship was necessary. Silence can be a frustrating nonverbal behavior to respond to, as Jessica probably knows all too well. What does a person say or do when another person is not saying or doing anything? A sort of communication spiral ensues: Someone wants to jump-start the conversation to get the issues clarified and resolved, but after the issues are clarified, the fighting continues, resulting in one or both people shutting down. Unfortunately, using silence to hurt or undermine another person is commonplace. Understanding when silence is effective and when it sabotages the interpersonal communication process takes time and experience.

Vocal characterizers such as laughing, moaning, or whining also communicate a great deal about how to interpret verbal messages. For example, if Rhonda tells José, "I'm so over you," but does so with laughter, José probably can infer that the comment should not be taken seriously. Or, suppose Ron is a member of a task group at work. Each time the group meets, his coworker Linda always complains about the time it takes to get the group together, the assignment, and the time constraints. Linda's moaning about the task will certainly affect Ron's conversations with Linda.

To read an interesting article about one culture's use of paralanguage, check out the article "A Whistle a Day Keeps Globalization Away," available through InfoTrac College Edition. Use your Understanding Interpersonal Communication CD-ROM to access InfoTrac College Edition Exercise 7.3: A Whistle a Day. You can also test your accuracy in interpreting another's paralanguage by using your Understanding Interpersonal Communication CD-ROM to access Interactive Activity 7.4: Test Your Paralanguage Skills.

Contact Codes

Contact codes include touch (haptics) and space (such as personal space).

Touch (Haptics)

Touch communication, or **haptics,** is the most primitive form of human communication. Research has concluded that touch has lasting value. Ben Benjamin and Ruth Werner (2004) support this claim:

> Human touch can completely change the way the body functions. From your heart rate to your blood pressure to the efficiency of your digestive system, welcomed touch can make your body work better. Humans need touch. We crave it, we hunger for it, and we get sick and can even die from the lack of it. (pp. 30, 31)

Touch behavior is the ultimate in privileged access to people. That is, when you touch another person, you have decided—whether intentionally or unintentionally—to invade another's personal space (a subject we return to later in this chapter). When forced into circumstances where everyone is close—for example, standing in a crowded elevator, sitting next to someone on the train or bus, or standing in a line—we normally offer an apology or an excuse if we accidentally touch someone. Interestingly, at public celebrations like Mardi Gras and New Year's Eve parties, touching another person doesn't seem as intrusive. In fact, some people enjoy it!

Touch behavior is an ambiguous form of communication because touching has various mean-

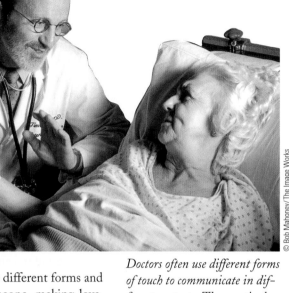

Doctors often use different forms of touch to communicate in different contexts. They routinely touch patients to examine or treat them. They may greet a patient or a patient's family with handshakes or pats on the back. And sometimes they touch patients to comfort them.

ings depending on the context. Touching another person takes different forms and signals multiple messages. Shaking hands upon meeting someone, making love, slapping an old friend on the back, physically abusing a partner, and tickling a small child are all examples of touch behavior.

Stanley Jones and A. Elaine Yarbrough (1985) review several functions of touch:

- Touch is used for *positive affect,* which includes support, appreciation, inclusion, and affection. The mother who hugs her child after he falls off his bike exemplifies positive affect through touch.
- Touch has a *playful* function; it serves to lighten an interaction. This type of touch is apparent when two kids wrestle each other or when baseball players slap each other on the butt after a home run.
- Touch is used to *control* or to direct behavior in an encounter. Touching another person while saying "move aside" is an example of touching to control.
- *Ritualistic* touch refers to the touches we use on an everyday basis, such as a handshake to say hello or goodbye.
- The *task* function pertains to touch that serves a professional or functional purpose. For instance, hairstylists and dentists are allowed to touch you to accomplish their tasks.
- A *hybrid touch* is a touch that greets a person and simultaneously demonstrates affection of that person. For instance, kissing a family member hello is an example of a hybrid touch.
- Touch that is *accidental* is done without apparent intent. This type of touching includes touching in closed spaces, such as intimate restaurants, in elevators, at graduation ceremonies, or at a religious service.

Touch is only part of a larger nonverbal (and verbal) system of behaviors. For example, when talking to an ailing relative, many people not only hold the other's hand but also speak softly and use calming language.

Space

Spatial communication is important in conversation. **Proxemics,** the study of distance, is historically related to how people use, manipulate, and identify their space. **Personal space** is the distance we put between ourselves and others. We carry informal personal space from one encounter to another; think of this personal space as a sort of invisible bubble that encircles us wherever we go. Our personal space provides some insight into ourselves and how we feel about other people.

Regardless of our unique thoughts about personal space, sometimes decisions about spatial communication are made for us. Over the past 20 years, corporate environments in particular have become quite strict with respect to spatial communication between employees. Guidelines or rules exist in many companies that dictate where and when you can stand with others. Although such rules may sound odd to you, think about the clear differences in power and status in most companies and the sexual, ethical, and legal implications of not respecting another's personal space.

Anthropologist Edward T. Hall (1959) was the first to devise categories of personal space. His system suggests that in most co-cultures in the United States, people communicate with others at a specific distance, depending on the nature of the conversation. Starting with the closest contact and the least amount of personal space, and moving to the greatest distance between communicators, the four categories of personal space are intimate distance, personal distance, social distance, and public distance (Figure 7.2). Examine Hall's categories and think about your own interpersonal encounters.

Intimate distance covers the distance that extends from you to around 18 inches. This spatial zone is normally reserved for those people with whom you are close—for example, close friends, romantic partners, and family members. Of course, in some situations, you have little choice but to allow others within an intimate distance (for example, attending a movie or theater production, sitting on a train, watching a rock concert, and so forth). If you let someone be a part of your intimate distance zone, you are implying that this person is meaningful to you. In fact, zero personal space—in other words, touch—suggests a very close relationship with someone because you are willing to give someone part of your private space.

Personal distance, ranging from eighteen inches to four feet, is the space most people use during conversations. This distance allows you to feel some protection from others who might wish to touch you. The range in this distance type allows those at the closest range to pick up your physical nuances (such as dry skin, acne, body odor or breath odor). However, we are still able to conduct business with those at the far range—which Hall (1959) calls "arm's length"—but any signs of nonverbal closeness are erased. Examples of relationships accustomed to personal distance are casual friends or business colleagues.

Social distance, which is four to twelve feet, is the spatial zone usually reserved for professional or formal interpersonal encounters. Some office environments are arranged specifically for social distance. Tables are aligned in a particular way, and cubicles are set up specifically to encourage social distance (rather than intimate distance or personal distance). As a result, many business transactions take place within social distance. Water-cooler chat or conversations in a break room at work also characterize the social zone. Whereas in the intimate and personal spatial zones we can use a lower vocal volume, social distance typically requires increased volume.

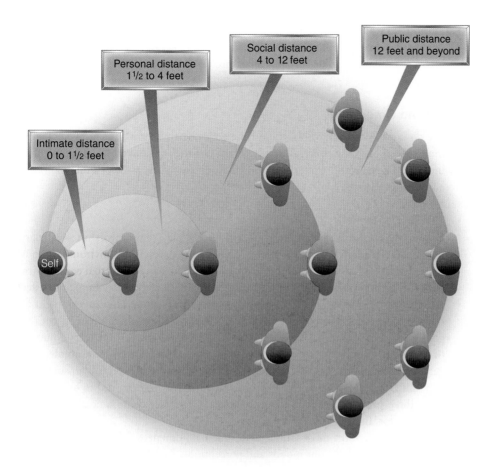

Figure 7.2 | **Edward T. Hall's four types of personal distance**

At the **public distance,** communication occurs at a distance of twelve or more feet. This spatial zone allows listeners to scan the entire person while he or she is speaking. The classroom environment exemplifies public distance. Most classrooms are arranged with a teacher in the front and rows of desks or tables facing the teacher. Of course, this setup can vary, but many classrooms are arranged with students more than twelve feet from their professor. Public distance is also used in large settings, such as when we listen to speakers, watch musicals, or attend television show tapings.

Before moving on, we'd like to address one final point about space. Whereas personal space is that invisible bubble we carry from one interaction to another, **territoriality** is our sense of ownership of space that remains fixed. Humans mark their territories in various ways, usually with items or objects that are called **territorial markers.** For example, a relative may have a favorite chair in the living room where she sits each time the family gathers. Or, perhaps you go to a coffee shop each morning and stake out your table with a newspaper. Although one doesn't really own a particular territory, we nonetheless presume "ownership" by the sheer frequency with which we occupy a space. In a sense, we believe we have proprietary rights over some particular location. If, for example, you take the train each morning to work and sit in the same seat, you have claimed your territory. If someone were to occupy your seat one day, there really is nothing you could do about it except experience some sort of displeasure (aside from wanting to tell the person to leave).

Place and Time Codes

We do not often think of place and time codes when we think of nonverbal communication, but they affect us deeply. The categories of nonverbal communication included in place and time codes are environment (such as color and smell) and chronemics (time).

The Environment

Where you sit, sleep, dance, climb, jog, write, sing, play, sew, or worship are all parts of your **physical environment.** How we utilize the parts of the environment, how we manage them, and their influence upon us are all part of nonverbal communication. Or, as Burgoon et al. (1996) succinctly noted, "it is typically human to affect and change the environment. . . . Humans have always altered the environment for their purposes, interpreted meaning from it, and relied on environmental cues for guides to behavior" (pp. 109–110). Our physical environment includes a number of features, including the smell (for example, restaurant), clutter (for example, attic, garage, basement, closet), and sounds (for example, music, chatter) of our surroundings. But what do we do to the environment, and what does it "do" to us? Let's explore three prominent environmental factors that affect communication between people: color, lighting, and room design.

Color is one of the most subtle environmental influences. Most researchers conclude that color affects our moods and perceptions. In other words, color has symbolic meaning in the environment and in our society (Sadka, 2004). Red, for instance, embodies an interesting contradiction: It both facilitates togetherness and incites anger. Couples share their (red) hearts of candy on Valentine's Day; later, this same couple may see red in each other's eyes when they get into a fight. The color blue also has several meanings. Many people associate blue with calmness (think about lakes and oceans), whereas others feel "blue" when they are sad or depressed. Yellow, black, and purple are much less paradoxical in that they normally convey joy, sadness, and wisdom, respectively.

Our perceptions of color, which can be based on cultural interpretations, can affect our perception of the physical environment. Do you feel that a certain color is most conducive to learning? Now, notice what color your communication classroom is. At work, do you believe that the color of your work environment affects yours or others' productivity? Regarding your living environment, do you like bold and bright colors, or are you more of an earth tone person? One reason that so many educational and work environments remain neutral in coloring is because we cannot universally agree upon what color is best.

In addition to color, the *lighting* of the environment can modify behavior (Meer, 1985). The effect of lighting on worker productivity has been investigated for many decades (Roethlisberger & Dickson, 1939). Lighting levels also seem to affect behavior within interpersonal interactions. Next time you're in a department store, look at how the lighting level varies in the different departments. Some departments, such as cosmetics, have soft lighting because it makes the customer look

Beachfront tourist areas, such as those in Miami, often feature brightly colored buildings to convey a sense of fun and relaxation. Tourists wear brightly colored bathing suits or Hawaiian shirts, which indicate freedom from the more conservative colors and expectations of the workplace. Bright neon signs attract crowds at night with the promise of excitement and abandon.

good and thus be more inclined to buy the store's beauty products. Or, think about how lighting in dimly lit restaurants affects our behavior; it may prompt us to feel relaxed, causing us to prolong our evening (and increase our dinner tab). Brightly lit restaurants, such as McDonald's or Wendy's, may increase people's rate of eating (thus, the term *fast food*).

Finally, *room design,* including room size, affects communication. For example, many retirement villages are now being designed to allow for both independence and interaction. Individual living units similar to small condominiums are built to promote privacy, but the units converge to form a meeting room where activities, events, and group functions can take place. To further explore room design and how one company is changing its space to be more consistent with its mission and goals, read the article "Lessons from Frank Lloyd Wright," available through InfoTrac College Edition. Use your Understanding Interpersonal Communication CD-ROM to access InfoTrac College Edition Exercise 7.4: What Does Office Space Communicate?

Time (Chronemics)

Chronemics, the study of a person's use of time, helps us to understand how people perceive and structure time in their dialogues and relationships with others. Time is an abstract concept that we describe using figures of speech (which we discussed in Chapter 6)—for example, "time is on your side," "time well spent," "time to kill," "time on your hands," "don't waste time," "on time," and "quality time." Dawna Ballard and David Seibold (2000) observed the reciprocal relationship between time and communication: "Communication creates persons' views and understanding of

Ethics & Choice

As Kyle Wood navigated the icy streets in his car, he glanced at the dashboard clock. 9:50 a.m. He couldn't imagine arriving on time for his 10 a.m. job interview. Kyle, a newly minted graduate, really wanted this job, which seemed like a perfect match for him. The company was highly recommended by Kyle's best friend, Lou, who had worked there for almost three years.

As he continued driving, Kyle thought about calling Ms. Littleton, the human resources director, on his cell phone to inform her that he would be late. He hesitated, recalling his friend's warning that Ms. Littleton was a stickler about punctuality who didn't believe in excuses for being late. However, he knew that he would never get to her office in ten minutes, so he decided to call her.

As he waited to be connected to human resources, Kyle began to wonder whether he should tell the truth about the slippery roads or simply make up an entirely different excuse, such as a sick sister or mother. He even considered saying that his mother had just been rushed to the hospital, so he needed to reschedule the appointment. Then, as quickly as he thought about that scenario, Kyle thought about how hard it was for him to lie to another person. He just couldn't do it. In fact, when his best friend, Bud, had cheated on the midterm exam last year, Kyle had been angry at him for a week. Kyle had chastised Bud about how low his friend's ethics had gone. Kyle remembered Bud's shaky voice and fidgety body movements when Kyle confronted him. Would Kyle have the same reaction as he lied to Ms. Littleton over the phone? Would she be able to tell he was lying by his voice? What would be his physical reaction during his rescheduled interview, if he was ever given another chance? Would he be able to finish the deceptive story when he was face to face with the human resources director? Ms. Littleton was now on the phone, and Kyle had to make a decision.

As you reflect on Kyle Wood's situation, consider the dilemma he faces. He wants to be interviewed for the job so badly that he is considering lying. What is your reaction to Kyle's ethical challenge? Should he tell the truth to Ms. Littleton, who has a reputation as a punctuality czar? If not, what would you advise him to do? What ethical system of communication should be followed in this example (categorical imperative, utilitarianism, ethic of care, golden mean, significant choice)?

Use your Understanding Interpersonal Communication CD-ROM to access an interactive version of this scenario on the Understanding Interpersonal Communication website. Look under Student Resources for Chapter 7 and click on the "Ethics & Choice" menu at left. The interactive version of this scenario allows you to choose an appropriate response to this dilemma and then see what consequences your choice brings about. You can also compare your answers to the questions at the end of the scenario to those provided by the authors and, if requested, email your response to your instructor.

time, yet our sense of time enables and constrains communication in important ways" (p. 219).

Edward T. Hall (1959) noted three time systems. *Technical time* is the scientific measurement of time. This system is associated with the precision of keeping time. *Formal time* is the time that society formally teaches. For example, in the United States, the clock and the calendar are our units of formal time. For example, we know that when it is 1 a.m., it is usually time to sleep; however, 1 p.m. refers to the time that we find ourselves at work or school. Further, in the United States, our arrangement of time is fixed and rather methodical. We learn to tell time based on the hour, and children are usually taught how to tell time by using the "big hand" and the "little hand" as references. *Informal time* is time that includes three concepts: duration, punctuality, and activity:

- Duration pertains to how long we allocate for a particular event. In our schedules, we may earmark forty minutes for grocery shopping or an hour for a religious service. Some of our estimates are less precise. For instance, what does it mean when we respond "be there right away"? Does that mean we will be there in ten minutes, one hour, or as long as it takes you? And, despite its vague and odd-sounding nature, the statement "I want it done yesterday" is clear to many.

- Punctuality is the promptness associated with keeping time. We're said to be punctual when we arrive for an appointment at the designated time. Despite the value placed on punctuality in the United States, friends may arrive late to lunch, professors late to class, physicians late to appointments, and politicians late to rallies. (In fact, with the tendency of some people to always be tardy, we may question why we even make appointments in the first place.)

- Activity is a somewhat chronemic value. People in Western cultures are encouraged to "use their time wisely"—in other words, they should make sure their time is used to accomplish something, whether it's a task or a social function. Simultaneously, they should avoid being so time-occupied that others view them as focused and obsessive."

Our use and management of time is associated with status and power. For example, the old adage "time is money," which equates an intangible (time) with a tangible (money), suggests that we place a value on our use of time. And as a country with individualistic values (see Chapter 3), the United States is a society that supports the belief that time is intimately linked to status and power.

Suppose, for instance, that Joan arrives at an interview five minutes late. Joan probably won't get the job because punctuality is an important value to communicate to a future boss. However, let's say that the interviewer, Mr. Johansen, is five minutes late for the interview. Of course, he would not lose his job. Similarly, John's optometrist could be late for his appointment with no consequence, but if John is late for his own appointment, he might have to pay a "no show" fee.

Let's look at a few more examples. Some professors are regularly late for class, but these same professors have policies about student punctuality. And many of you have waited in long lines for a school loan, concert tickets, or a driver's license. If you truly had power, you wouldn't have to spend time waiting in line. Time is clearly related to status and power differences between individuals (Hickson et al. 2004).

We have spent a great deal of time identifying the primary types of nonverbal communication so you can better understand the comprehensive nature of nonverbal behaviors. We close this chapter by considering how culture affects nonverbal messages. As we learned in Chapter 3, culture influences virtually every aspect of interpersonal communication. Understanding various cultural influences on nonverbal behavior helps you realize that not everyone shares your beliefs, values, and meanings. Particularly in the area of nonverbal communication—which, as we noted earlier in the chapter, is often ambiguous and open to interpretation—remembering cultural variations helps us become more competent communicators.

Cultural Variations in Nonverbal Communication

We could write an entire text about the influence of culture on nonverbal behavior. In fact, several books on this topic already exist (for example, Martin & Nakayama, 2004; Samovar & Porter, 2004). To provide you with a sense of how culture affects nonverbal behavior, let's explore conclusions related to body movement, facial expressions, personal space, and touch.

Body Movement

Research has shown that greetings vary from one culture to another. For instance, most Westerners are accustomed to shaking hands upon meeting. In other cultures, however, the handshake is not common. In Japan, for instance, individuals bow when they meet (Morrison, Conaway, & Borden, 1994). The person with the lower status initiates bowing and is expected to bow deeper than the individual with higher status. The person with elevated status decides when the bowing will end.

Gesturing has also been studied across cultures. For instance, while speaking, Mexicans, Greeks, and people from many South American countries are dramatic and animated. Mexicans use lots of hand gestures in their conversations, and Morrison et al. (1994) note that Italians "talk with their hands" in expressive gestures. However, people in a number of Asian cultures consider such overt body movements rude, and Germans consider bold hand gestures too flashy.

Another cultural difference in nonverbal communication is the way the concept of "two" is communicated. For example, in the United States, people use the forefinger and the middle finger, whereas Filipinos hold up the ring finger and the little finger.

Your *Turn*

Choose one type of nonverbal communication. Now, consider all of the close relationships you have, and write about how that specific nonverbal behavior functions in those relationships. For each relationship, describe the relationship (for example, work, personal, friendship, romantic) first and then explore the presence of the behavior you chose in that relationship. After you are finished making notes about all your relationships, consider these questions: Did you use the chosen behavior differently, depending on the relationship? Were there differences in the frequency with which you used the behavior? Did you not use the behavior at all in certain relationships? What similarities in usage of the behavior existed? Discuss the pervasiveness of the behavior by using specific examples. If you'd like, you can use your student workbook to complete this activity.

Facial Expressions

One much-studied facial display is eye contact. As mentioned in Chapter 3, the extent to which a person looks at another during a conversation is culturally based. Members of most co-cultures in the United States are socialized to look at a listener while speaking (Burgoon et al., 1996), and it's common for two people from the United States to look at the other's eyes while communicating. In this country, frequent eye aversion may communicate a lack of trust in another. However, in other cultures, such as Japan and Jamaica, direct eye contact is rejected because it is perceived as communicating disrespect for another.

Personal Space

Spacial distances have been the focus of research in intercultural communication. In the United States, as previously discussed, we tend to clearly demarcate our territory. Edward Hall and Mildred Reed Hall (1990) discuss the territoriality of Germans and the French:

> Germans . . . barricade themselves behind heavy doors and soundproof walls to try to seal themselves from others in order to concentrate on their work. The French have a close personal distance and are not as territorial. They are tied to people and thrive on constant interaction. (p. 180)

In addition, interpretations of personal space vary from culture to culture. People in many South American countries, such as Brazil, require little personal space in an interaction. Arabs, Hungarians, and Africans similarly reduce conversational distance (Lewis, 1999). Generally speaking, people from individualistic cul-

The reduced conversational distance expected by people in collectivistic cultures can be disconcerting to people who require greater distance. How much conversational distance do you require when you're talking to someone? Does the amount of distance you require depend on the situation, with whom you're talking, or the information you're trying to convey?

tures (for example, United States, Germany, Canada) require more space than do those from collectivistic cultures (Costa Rica, Venezuela, Ecuador). The personal space requirements of people from collectivistic cultures can be partially explained by the fact that people from those cultures "work, play, live and sleep in close proximity to one another" (Andersen, 2003, p. 239).

Touch

Researchers have also investigated touch behavior within a cultural context. For example, Tiffany Field (1999) found that adolescents from the United States touched each other less than adolescents from France did. Field observed friends at McDonald's restaurants in Miami and Paris and found that the U.S. teenagers did less hugging, kissing, and caressing than their French counterparts. However, the U.S. adolescents engaged in more self-touching, such as primping, than the French adolescents.

Some cultures accept more same-sex touching than others. For example, men frequently hold hands in Indonesia, and men frequently walk down the street with their arms around each other in Malaysia. Such overt touching, however, would be frowned upon in Japan or in Scandinavia.

In the United States, touching in usually avoided. To get a sense of the extent to which you avoid touch, complete the Touch Avoidance Inventory.

As you can see from the variety of cultural differences in nonverbal behavior discussed in this section and summarized in Table 7.2, nonverbal behaviors should always be understood within a cultural context. We cannot assume that others automatically understand our nonverbal displays because their meanings can differ significantly within and across cultures. Further, as we pointed out in Chapter 3, the U.S. population continues to grow more diverse. Being sensitive to cultural communication differences and seeking clarification will help you in your interpersonal relationships. If you'd like to explore how your nonverbal behaviors compare with those used by people in another country, use your Understanding Interpersonal Communication CD-ROM to access **Interactive Activity 7.5: Nonverbal Behavior in Japan.**

Table 7.2 | **Culture and Nonverbal Communication**

Nonverbal Type	Nonverbal Behavior	Cultural Difference
Kinesics	Greeting another	***United States*:*** Varies; generally, shaking hands ***Japan:*** Bowing
Facial expression	Eye contact during conversation	***United States*:*** Varies; generally, direct ***Cambodia:*** Indirect
Proxemics	Personal space during conversation	***United States*:*** Varies; generally, large ***Costa Rica:*** Small
Haptics	Same-sex touching during conversation	***United States:*** Taboo ***Malaysia:*** Same-sex hand-holding is common

*Due to the co-cultural differences in the United States, broad cultural generalizations about the behavior are difficult.

Communication Assessment Test

Touch Avoidance Inventory

Use the following scale to respond to the statements. Try to record your first reaction, and don't go back and change your responses. You can also take this test online under Student Resources for Chapter 7 at the Understanding Interpersonal Communication website. ⬤➤

strongly disagree = 1   disagree = 2   undecided = 3

agree = 4   strongly agree = 5

_____ 1. A hug from a same sex friend is a true sign of friendship.

_____ 2. Opposite sex friends enjoy it when I touch them.

_____ 3. I often put my arm around friends of the same sex.

_____ 4. When I see two people of the same sex hugging, it revolts me.

_____ 5. I like it when members of the opposite sex touch me.

_____ 6. People shouldn't be so uptight about touching persons of the same sex.

_____ 7. I think it's vulgar when members of the opposite sex touch me.

_____ 8. When a member of the opposite sex touches me, I find it unpleasant.

_____ 9. I wish I were free to show emotions by touching members of the same sex.

_____ 10. I'd enjoy giving a massage to an opposite sex friend.

_____ 11. I enjoy kissing persons of the same sex.

_____ 12. I like to touch friends that are of the same sex as I am.

_____ 13. Touching friends of the same sex does not make me feel uncomfortable.

_____ 14. I find it enjoyable when I and a close friend of the opposite sex embrace.

_____ 15. I enjoy getting a back rub from members of the opposite sex.

_____ 16. I dislike kissing relatives of the same sex.

_____ 17. Intimate touching with members of the opposite sex is pleasurable.

_____ 18. I find it difficult to be touched by members of my own sex.

_____ 19. Touching between people of the opposite sex bothers me.

_____ 20. I am comfortable around members of the same sex who are touching.

There is no particular touch avoidance score in this inventory. Rather, look at those items where you responded with a "5" and those items where you responded with a "1." Do you see consistencies in your responses? For instance, questions 13 and 20 ask about your comfort level with same sex touching. Did you respond similarly to these questions? Also, does it make a difference whether you (or others) are touching relatives, friends, or intimate partners? Looking at the personal, social, and legal implications of touch, what sorts of conclusions can you draw from these questions and your responses?

From Berko, Wolvin & Wolvin, *Communicating,* 9th ed. Copyright © 2004 by Houghton Mifflin Company. Used with permission.

Choices for Increasing Nonverbal Communication Effectiveness

As we have previously stated, nonverbal behavior is difficult to pin down with precision. We may think we understand what a person's hand gesture or eye behavior means, but there are often multiple ways to interpret a particular nonverbal behavior. Therefore, we must be cautious when we interpret messages. We now turn our attention to identifying five skills for improving nonverbal communication effectiveness. As you practice these skills, keep in mind that culture affects nonverbal communication.

Recall the Nonverbal-Verbal Relationship

Throughout this chapter and Chapter 6, we have reminded you that nonverbal communication is often best understood with verbal communication. That is, we need to pay attention to what is said in addition to the nonverbal behavior. Most of us blend nonverbal and verbal messages. We raise our voice to underscore something we've said. We frown when we tell a sad story. We motion with our hands when we tell others to get going. And, when young toddlers are angry, we see them jump up and down on the floor while they scream "No." These examples illustrate the integration of nonverbal and verbal messages. We need to remain aware of this relationship to achieve meaning in our conversations. In addition, we need to be prepared for incongruity between nonverbal and verbal behavior.

Be Tentative When Interpreting Nonverbal Behavior

In this chapter, we have reiterated the ambiguous nature of nonverbal communication, including cultural differences in nonverbal expressions. Because of individual differences, we can never be sure what a specific nonverbal behavior means. For example, when Gene walks into Professor Laura Crumb's office, he may be confident in thinking that she is busy. After all, there are books everywhere, the phone is ringing, and Dr. Crumb is seated behind a desk with many papers on it. However, these environmental artifacts and conditions may not be accurately communicating the professor's availability. Gene needs to clarify his interpretation of this nonverbal communication by asking the professor if she has time to talk to him.

In addition, consider the cultural background of communicators. Be especially aware of your own biases, because they may not reflect the views of another.

Monitor Your Nonverbal Behavior

Being a self-monitor is crucial in conversations (Snyder, 1979). Becoming aware of how you say something, your proximity to the other person, the extent to which you use touch, or your use of silence is just as important as the words used. This self-monitoring is not easy. For example, let's say that Maria is in a heated exchange with her roommate, Sue, who refused to clean the apartment. When Maria tries to make her point, it's not easy for her to think about how she is saying something or whether or not she is screaming or standing too close. Like most people, Maria simply wants to make her point! However, Maria's nonverbal communication can carry significance, particularly if Sue is focusing on it and Maria is ignoring it. You need to look for meaning in both your behavior and the behavior of another.

Facing *Change*

Culture influences how people communicate nonverbally and how people interpret the nonverbal behavior of others. Within and outside the United States, various aspects of one's identity—including age, family background, personality, and profession—can be gleaned through nonverbal communication. How might various co-cultures communicate their identities through nonverbal codes? Provide both abstract and concrete examples of communicating identity through nonverbal communication.

Skill *Spotlight*

Ask Others for Their Impressions

The skill of asking others for their impressions of us implies that we believe others can help us become more effective communicators. The significant issue inherent in this skill is clear: Whom should we consult to ensure accuracy in our nonverbal communication?

The easy answer is that we should ask someone with whom we are close. They can give us valuable information, such as that our silent reactions to others' disclosures make them uncomfortable or that our constant eye rolling during a conflict causes others duress. Or, perhaps they can let us know that our verbal and nonverbal behaviors are not congruent, such as when a spouse yells to another, "Of course I love you!" Those who are close to us are more likely to inform us about problems in our nonverbal communication.

However, we can gain important information about our nonverbal communication from those with whom we don't have an intimate relationship. Your physician or dentist could comment on your nonverbal communication during office visits, and a work colleague might be able to explain why some of our nonverbal behaviors are misunderstood. In fact, many acquaintances may be able to offer their impressions, including friends of friends, distant family members who see us once a year at holiday gatherings, and even neighbors. We should seek out those who are willing to offer suggestions or advice pertaining to our nonverbal communication.

Skills at Work Sometimes what is perceived as an easy thing to do is often difficult. For instance, when we ask others for their impressions of us, the request suggests that there are areas we need to work on. While communicating at work, asking others for their impressions is not only important for your personal understanding; it also allows your work colleagues to believe you are genuinely interested in improving your communication at work.

Consider, for example, two supervisors—Manuel and J. T.—who are jointly responsible for a company task plan that affects nearly 300 employees and four million dollars. Although Manuel has been with the company for over fifteen years and J. T. has been with the company for only three years, the two have developed a cohesive working relationship. On more than one occasion, Manuel has asked J. T. whether Manuel tends to get too loud while defending his ideas. And J. T. has asked Manuel for advice on becoming more assertive and less reactionary on the job. J. T. has also sought out Manuel's perception of whether other employees view J. T. as a pushover because J. T. is rather soft-spoken and dresses casually. Both Manuel and J. T. are seeking the other's impression. Despite the fact that both are supervisors, their wishes to become more effective in their leadership positions are laudable.

Whether you are in charge or simply following the lead of others, asking for other people's thoughts can be informative and helpful in the workplace. Asking others for their impressions of your vocalics, physical appearance, body movement, use of space, or other nonverbal behaviors can make you more aware of idiosyncrasies that coworkers may find challenging. Improving these aspects of your communication can improve your productivity and your overall job satisfaction.

Ask Others for Their Impressions

When applying for a job, we ask others for their interview strategies. When going out on a date, we ask friends how we look or smell. When choosing a class, we may ask our friends about their experiences with a particular professor. Yet, when we try to improve our communication with others, we generally neglect to ask others about our effectiveness. We need to consult others as we decide whether or not we're achieving meaning in our interpersonal relationships. See the Skill Spotlight for more on this topic.

Place Nonverbal Communication in Context

We live in a society that embraces simplistic notions associated with nonverbal communication. For instance, in the 1970s and 1980s, John Molloy (1978) made millions of dollars from his book *Dress for Success*. This simplistic source told business professionals how to dress to look "professional" and to be taken seriously in the workplace. Scores of companies embraced the basic suggestions of the book and used its conclusions to mandate changes to corporate attire.

However, when discussing human behavior, we need to avoid such superficial ideas about our nonverbal communication. We should pay attention to nonverbal cues, but we should place them in appropriate context. Be careful of assigning too much meaning to a wink, a handshake, a pair of dangling earrings, or a voice that sounds uptight. These may carry no significant meaning in a conversation. To acquire meaning, you must consider the entire communication process, not just one element of it.

CHOICES *for Improving Nonverbal Effectiveness*

- Keep in mind the relationship between verbal and nonverbal messages
- Be tentative when interpreting nonverbal behavior
- Monitor your own nonverbal behavior
- Check in with others about their impressions of your nonverbal behavior
- Place nonverbal communication in context

Summary

Nonverbal communication plays a significant role in our interpersonal relationships. It is often ambiguous, meaning different things to people of different cultures and co-cultures. People use nonverbal cues to regulate conversation, such as using body language to facilitate turn-taking. Nonverbal communication is more credible than verbal communication because it is harder to mask. Sometimes, nonverbal and verbal communication are at odds, resulting in mixed messages.

Nonverbal communication manifests itself in many forms. Kinesics includes gestures and body posture/orientation. Physical appearance encompasses the physical characteristics of an individual (including attractiveness) and body artifacts such as clothing, jewelry, and tattoos. Facial expressions, especially the eyes and smiling, are the nonverbal cues that give the most insight into how someone is feeling.

Paralanguage, or vocalics, involves vocal qualities such as vocal segregates (the "ums" and "ers" of conversation), the use of silence, and pitch, rate, volume, inflection, tempo, and pronunciation. Paralanguage also encompasses vocal characterizers such as crying, laughing, whining, and so on. Touch communication, or haptics, the most primitive form of communication, represents the ultimate in privileged access to people, and can perform diverse functions.

Proxemics, the study of distance, involves people's personal space (which can vary by circumstance and culture) as well as their territoriality, or their need to "own" certain spaces. Aspects of the physical environment, such as color, lighting,

and room design, can affect our nonverbal communication. And chronemics, or the study of a person's use of time, explains how people perceive and structure time, including how the management of time is associated with status and power.

Culture affects nonverbal behavior and interpretation of nonverbal behavior. People of different cultures vary in their mode of greeting and gesturing, how much they engage in eye contact, the personal space they require, and their acceptance of touching.

To improve our nonverbal communication, we must remember that verbal and nonverbal communication work together. We also need to avoid jumping to conclusions about what certain nonverbal cues mean. Furthermore, we need to monitor our nonverbal behavior and ask others for their impressions of our nonverbal cues. Finally, we must interpret nonverbal communication within its context.

Understanding Interpersonal Communication Online

Now that you've read Chapter 7, use your Understanding Interpersonal Communication CD-ROM for quick access to the electronic study resources that accompany this text. Your CD-ROM gives you access to the video of Mark and his mother on page 183, the Ethics & Choice interactive activity on page 200, the Communication Assessment Test on page 204, InfoTrac College Edition, and the Understanding Interpersonal Communication website. When you get to the Understanding Interpersonal Communication home page, click on "Student Book Companion Site" in the Resource box at right to access the online study aids for this chapter, including a digital glossary, review quizzes, and the chapter activities. ■

Terms for Review

body artifacts 190	mixed message 187	social distance 196
body orientation 190	nonverbal communication 185	territorial markers 197
chronemics 199	paralanguage 193	territoriality 197
citing gestures 189	personal distance 196	turn gestures 190
delivery gestures 189	personal space 196	turn-taking 187
haptics 194	physical characteristics 190	vocal characterizers 193
interaction adaptation	physical environment 198	vocal qualities 193
theory 185	proxemics 196	vocal segregates 193
intimate distance 196	public distance 197	
kinesics 189	seeking gestures 190	

Questions for Understanding

Comprehension Focus

1. Explain how nonverbal communication is a part of every personal message a communicator delivers.
2. Identify at least three principles of nonverbal communication.
3. Define paralanguage and explain its importance in conversations.
4. What are the consequences of touch in our society?
5. Describe the influence of culture on at least two types of nonverbal communication.

Application Focus

1. **CASE IN POINT**
   Reread the opening story of Mark Mattson and his mother, Julia. If you found yourself in Mark's situation, what do you think you would discuss with your mother (or father)? Discuss the importance of "reading" someone's nonverbal communication and its affect on a relationship similar to that of Mark and Julia.
2. Identify several nonverbal behaviors during the dating (courtship)

stage of an interpersonal relationship.

3. Spend some time during the day interacting without using any gestures or touch behavior. Was it possible? If not, why not? If so, what did it feel like?

4. Defend or criticize the following statement: Touch is a double-edged sword in close relationships. Use examples as you explain your view.

5. Write a brief dialogue between a married couple in a conflict and insert appropriate nonverbal codes that you believe would be part of that conflict. (Assume the couple has been together for 10 years.) What patterns do you see with respect to conflict and nonverbal communication? What sorts of nonverbal behaviors accompany the conflict? Explain.

Interactive Activities and InfoTrac College Edition Exercises

Complete the Interactive Activities and InfoTrac College Edition Exercises for Chapter 7 online at the Understanding Interpersonal Communication website. Select the chapter resources for Chapter 7, then click on "Activities" or "InfoTrac College Edition." If requested, you can submit your answers to your instructor.

Interactive Activities

7.1 Mixed Messages in Negotiations 188
7.2 Feelings, Attitudes, and Kinesics 190
7.3 Eyes, Mouth, and Tilt of Head 192
7.4 Test Your Paralanguage Skills 194
7.5 Nonverbal Behavior in Japan 203

InfoTrac College Edition Exercises

7.1 What Is Your Body Language Saying? 188
7.2 Universal Facial Expressions 192
7.3 A Whistle a Day 194
7.4 What Does Office Space Communicate? 199

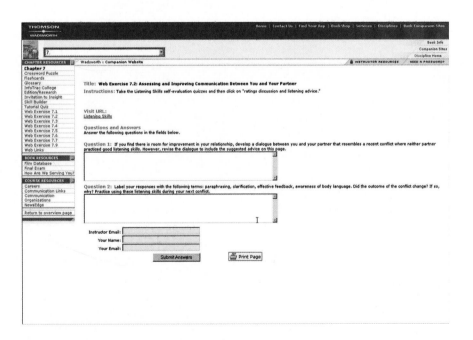

8 Sharing Personal Information

CASE IN POINT: ROBERTA GILBERT AND PHILIP JERMAINE

Roberta Gilbert and Philip Jermaine had lived together for ten years, and both were happy with their relationship. They met when Roberta was 27 and Philip was 30, and they moved in together two years later. Before they bought their condo together, they spent a lot of time talking. Philip always said that one of his favorite things about Roberta was how easy it was to talk to her. They had told each other their likes and dislikes and confided about past relationships. They had discussed at length their views on marriage, agreeing that it was a patriarchal institution that they wished to avoid.

However, in those discussions twelve years ago, Roberta hadn't been completely honest with Philip. She hadn't told him that she had been married briefly when she was 19. The marriage was a hasty one, entered into on the spur of the moment, and Roberta honestly didn't know what she'd been thinking. It was almost like she and Carl just ran off and got married to have something to do on their date. Roberta's parents found out about the marriage and had it annulled almost immediately, to the relief of both Roberta and Carl. Now it had been so long since she had seen Carl that, frankly, Roberta hardly even remembered she'd actually been married.

When she and Philip met, it didn't seem important to tell him about Carl at first, and after Philip spent so much time expounding on the evils of marriage (which she mainly agreed with), it would have been awkward to mention it. So, time went by and Roberta simply kept the information to herself. She reasoned that it didn't really make a difference whether she told Philip about this ancient history because she was totally honest with him about everything else. However, Roberta's past was about to catch up with her.

Yesterday at the grocery store, Roberta ran into Carl! It was a shock to see him after so long. He said that he and his family had just moved into town. Because the town was so small, Roberta knew she had to tell Philip about their past relationship or he would find out some other way. She was nervous, but she decided to tell him that night—she'd kept this secret long enough. She made a lovely candlelit dinner and, after they'd eaten, she nervously mentioned that she'd seen an old friend at the store the day before. Philip looked mildly interested, and, after a few false starts, she finally just blurted out her story. There was a long pause. Finally, Philip cleared his throat and pushed away from the table.

Philip told Roberta that he wasn't upset that she'd had a brief marriage, but he couldn't understand why she hadn't told him before. Roberta had to admit she couldn't understand it herself. She swore she'd never keep anything like this from Philip again. He looked serious, shrugged, and told her he hoped there wouldn't be anything else like this to tell. He seemed to be making light of the situation, but privately he wondered if their relationship was as solid as he'd thought. He hoped they could get over this, and he told her he was glad she'd finally disclosed her secret. ■

Self-disclosure is arguably the most researched behavior in the communication discipline. Most researchers believe self-disclosure is a critically important communication skill because it helps relationships develop and contributes to the maturation and revision of self concept. Some people judge the strength and intensity of their relationships by the frequency and level of intimacy of the disclosures that occur within them. Ample evidence shows that greater disclosure is related to greater emotional involvement in a relationship (Finkenauer & Hazam, 2000) and that "disclosure is central to people's definitions of intimacy" (Lippert & Prager, 2001 p. 294).

In our opening scenario, Roberta and Philip's relationship may be in danger as a result of the twelve-year delay in Roberta's disclosure. Philip's sense of his intimate knowledge of Roberta is shaken. Further, Roberta's sense of herself seems to be in question. Roberta sees herself as an honest person, and keeping this secret from Philip causes her to doubt this self-assessment. Yet, both Philip and Roberta are glad to finally have this secret out in the open.

Researchers and nonresearchers alike believe that self-disclosure and relationship development are intertwined. Every day we encounter numerous examples of self-disclosures in our own relationships and in more public venues such as talk shows, classrooms, and religious settings. Because self-disclosure is integral to interpersonal relationships, we need to examine this communication skill more closely. What does it really mean to self-disclose? Is it always a helpful behavior? What are the risks? What exactly are the boundaries between intimate information and information we're willing to make public? How can we become skillful self-disclosers?

Definition of Self-Disclosure: Opening Up

We begin our inquiry into self-disclosure with a definition. Generally speaking, *self-disclosure* is communication about your self. Specifically, self-disclosure occurs when you intentionally tell another something about yourself that the person would be unable to easily learn otherwise. For example, if Sandra gives her brother, Fred, a present that she had received from a friend, Fred will most likely not discover this unless Sandra decides to tell him.

There are at least two types of self-disclosures. We use **evaluative disclosures** to tell another how we judge other people ("I like Dan"), things ("I hate squash"), and events ("I am sick of family gatherings"). On the other hand, **descriptive disclosures** are self-revelations, such as "I am really obsessed with John—I can't get him out of my mind," "I used to box professionally," or "I am concerned about our relationship—I am having trouble trusting you as I once did."

Self-disclosure, then, is evaluative and descriptive information about the self, shared intentionally, that another would have trouble finding out without being told. Implicit in this definition is the fact that self-disclosures are verbal behavior. We do reveal information about ourselves nonverbally—for example, by dressing in certain clothes, wearing a wedding ring, or making facial expressions—but these types of revelations do not fit our definition of self-disclosure because they don't have the same intentionality as revelations told to a specific person. In other words, nonverbal behaviors are more generally sent—for example, everyone we come in contact with sees what we wear. Many researchers (for example, Rosenfeld, 2000) define self-disclosure in this way, focusing only on verbal communication. However, note that verbal communication doesn't have to be oral or face to face; we could self-disclose in a letter or an email, although not much research has investigated written self-disclosures.

Features of Self-Disclosure: Expanding the Definition

Our definition highlights several important features of self-disclosing: *intentionality, choice, intimacy, risk,* and *trust.* In this section, we expand on each of these features.

Intentionality and Choice

Disclosures are intentional communication. When you engage in self-disclosure, you choose to tell another something about yourself. For example, when Mike tells Elizabeth that he fears he isn't smart enough to make it in medical school, his disclosure is a conscious, voluntary decision to confide a vulnerability to a friend. Mike isn't coerced into telling Elizabeth his concerns; rather, he freely discloses them. Although disclosures sometimes slip out unintentionally (for example, when someone is drunk, overly tired, or otherwise impaired), these "slips" don't meet our definition for real self-disclosure.

Implicit in the feature of choice is the idea that there are varying degrees of self-disclosures. We choose whether to tell something and we also choose how to tell it and how much detail to provide in the telling. For instance, Mike may tell Elizabeth about his fear of failing in medical school, but he may withhold the information that he did poorly on the GMAT (the entrance test for medical school). Mike is in control of how much he tells and, therefore, how vulnerable he allows himself to be in his relationship with Elizabeth.

Intimacy and Risk

Because a self-disclosure is information another would not be easily able to discover without being told, the information involved must be personal. Although telling someone that you were born in Ohio is a disclosure, most people don't consider it a significant one. The state where you were born is not critical information, nor is it private, because this fact could be discovered without your help through public birth records.

On the other hand, telling someone that you were adopted is a more personal disclosure, and this is where risk comes into play. Self-disclosure is a frightening notion. It involves sharing who we really are with another and letting ourselves be truly known by them. Of course, the scary part is that we may be rejected by the other person after we have made ourselves vulnerable in this fashion.

Public versus Private Information

The discussion of intimacy and risk brings up the issue of public and private information. **Public information** consists of facts that we make parts of our public image—the parts of ourselves that we present to others. Usually, people strive to present socially approved characteristics as public information. Some researchers use the metaphor of the theater to refer to life, and they refer to public information as what is seen "on stage."

Private information reflects the self-concept, as we discussed in Chapter 2. Private information consists of the assessments—both good and bad—that we make about our selves. It also includes our personal values and our interests, fears, and concerns. In the "life as theater" metaphor, private information is referred to as what is kept "backstage." When we're backstage, we can forget about some of the social niceties that are important for public information. The following dialogues illustrate the concepts of public and private conversation. The first conversation is between Gwen and her boss at Clarke Meat Packing Plant, Ms. Greene; the second is between Gwen and her best friend, Robin, who doesn't work at the plant.

Although it is tempting to think that we can know what this person might self-disclose based on what he looks like, the image he is trying to project via his use of nonverbal signals may differ quite dramatically from what he would disclose about himself in a personal conversation with a friend. Our nonverbal signals can reveal a lot about us, but real self-disclosure involves intentionality, choice, intimacy, risk, and trust.

GWEN: Ms. Greene, I need to take a personal day a week from Friday.

MS. GREENE: That's a problem, Gwen. Our new plant policy is that we don't allow personal days if they'll result in having to pay other workers overtime. As I look at the work flowchart, I see that there are only two workers scheduled for your shift a week from Friday. So, I'm afraid I'll have to deny your request.

GWEN: I'm kind of surprised to hear that, Ms. Greene. When did that policy go into effect?

MS. GREENE: It's been our policy for the past six months now, Gwen. Didn't your union rep inform you?

GWEN: No, I don't think he did, but I may have missed the meeting— I can check with the rep myself. In the meantime, what do you suggest I do about my problem a week from Friday?

MS. GREENE: I suggest you come to work, Gwen. You know, if you don't like the conditions here, you can always look for another job.

GWEN: I like working here, Ms. Greene. I don't want another job.

In this dialogue, Gwen displays public information. She tries to show her supervisor that she is a cooperative, dedicated worker who enjoys working at the plant and who takes responsibility for her own problems (for example, she volunteers to talk to the union rep, and the fact that she needs a personal day implies she is taking care of her personal affairs). In the next dialogue, Gwen is free to exhibit private information with her best friend.

GWEN: Oh, Robin, I'm so mad!! That witch, Greene, won't let me have a personal day. The entire plant is now being run just for the convenience of the bosses!

ROBIN: Hey, Gwen, slow down. What happened?

GWEN: I asked that jerk for a personal day a week from Friday, and she said no because it would mean she would have to pay someone else overtime. I hate my job. But Greene came out and told me if I didn't like it I could take a walk. I really wish I could—I should start looking for a new job, but I hate getting out and looking for work, and to be honest, I hate change, too. It would serve them right if I did leave and I didn't give any notice. I can't stand that place!

When displaying private information, Gwen is unconcerned about presenting herself as competent and responsible. Instead, she vents her emotions and reveals some of her less than positive self-assessments: she doesn't like change or job seeking.

As an interesting side note, Lawrence Rosenfeld (2000) points out that our notions of public and private information have changed over time. He notes that in Germany in the sixteenth century, a newlywed couple was expected to consummate their marriage in front of witnesses who could testify to the validity of the marriage. However, although the sexual aspect of marriage was seen as public information, private communication between couples was formal, not differing from how strangers or acquaintances would address one another.

Trust

Trust explains why we decide to take the plunge and reveal ourselves through self-disclosure. When we are in a relationship with a trusted other, we feel comfortable self-disclosing because we believe that our confidante can keep a secret, will continue to care for us, and won't get upset when we relate what we are thinking (Derlega, Metts, Petronio, & Margulis, 1993). Also, when we trust someone, we are likely to provide more intimate disclosures (Taylor & Altman, 1987). Our perception of trust is a key factor in our decision to self-disclose, and most self-disclosures take place in the context of a trusting relationship.

For information about how to disclose private information about your health, use your Understanding Interpersonal Communication CD-ROM to access **Interactive Activity 8.1: Disclosing Health Information.** And for suggestions concerning how to disclose information about a disability to a potential employer, use your Understanding Interpersonal Communication CD-ROM to access **Interactive Activity 8.2: Disclosing about a Disability.**

REVISITING CASE IN POINT

1. How does Roberta's self-disclosure illustrate the quality of intentionality?
2. How does Roberta's self-disclosure illustrate the quality of risk?
3. How does Roberta's self-disclosure illustrate the quality of trust?

You can answer these questions online under Student Resources for Chapter 8 at the Understanding Interpersonal Communication website.

Ethics & Choice

Theo Henley was on his way to his third job interview for a position he really wanted. After making it through the first and second rounds of interviews, Theo was feeling good about himself and thought he had a real chance at getting an offer. On the previous two occasions, he had gotten along well with all the members of the company who had interviewed him, and the more he learned about the job and the company, the better he liked them. He thought that the fit between himself and the job was just about perfect.

However, despite his high hopes, he was worried. He faced the same old dilemma: Should he reveal anything about his disability to the prospective employers? Theo had Multiple Sclerosis (MS). When he had been diagnosed seven years ago, it had seemed like a death sentence, but he'd learned to live with the disease. His situation was complicated by the fact that he had what his doctors called "invisible symptoms." Although he sometimes suffered because of the MS, no one knew he had it unless he told them. His worst symptom was excessive tiredness.

For the past three years, he had been experiencing a remission, and his condition was much improved. However, he lived with the knowledge that the symptoms could return at any time. The doctors knew little about this unpredictable disease.

This complicated situation made interviewing for the job complex. He knew he could do the job. He was sure he could do it even if the symptoms returned, because he had held down a job through the seven years of his illness. Occasionally he had called in sick because of the fatigue and disorientation brought on by the MS, but he didn't think he was absent more than anyone else. And he always got good performance reviews.

But he wasn't sure if it was right to keep this information from a prospective employer. Moreover, what if the MS returned and became even worse? If that happened, he would need to ask for some assistance at work. If he hadn't told the company before, he might be in a bad position if he needed help. In addition, he wanted to be honest. But he wasn't sure how this information would be received or if he needed to reveal this personal problem.

What do you think Theo should do? In answering this question, what ethical system of communication informs your decision (categorical imperative, utilitarianism, ethic of care, golden mean, significant choice)?

Use your Understanding Interpersonal Communication CD-ROM to access an interactive version of this scenario on the Understanding Interpersonal Communication website. Look under Student Resources for Chapter 8 and click on the "Ethics & Choice" menu at left. The interactive version of this scenario allows you to choose an appropriate response to this dilemma and then see what consequences your choice brings about. You can also compare your answers to the questions at the end of the scenario to those provided by the authors and, if requested, email your response to your instructor.

Self-Disclosure as a Subjective Process: Making It Real

As you've probably noticed, whether information is considered a self-disclosure depends on subjective assessments made by the discloser. For example, the degree of risk involved is a somewhat personal judgment. For example, what one person considers to be a risky disclosure might be information that someone else would find easy to tell. Taking this fact into consideration, some researchers make a distinction between history and story.

History consists of information that may sound personal to a listener but that is relatively easy for a speaker to tell. Disclosures that are classified as history may be told easily because of the teller's temperament, changing times, or simply because the events happened a long time ago and have been told and retold. For instance, Nell was in a serious car accident when she was 19. The story of the accident and its aftermath is a dramatic one, but it doesn't feel risky to tell it anymore because she has told it so many times that it has become routine. In another example, Melanie, who married Jeff in 1970, used to feel nervous about telling people that her husband had been married once before. By 1990, when she and Jeff had been married for 20 years and the divorce rate in the United States had reached almost 50 percent, Melanie stopped being concerned about revealing that information.

In contrast, **story,** or what some researchers call true self-disclosure, exists when the teller *feels* the risk he or she is taking in telling the information. A disclosure should be considered story (or authentic) even if it doesn't seem personal to the average listener. For instance, when Marie told her friend, Miguel, that she had never known a Mexican American person before, Miguel thought that she was simply making a factual observation. However, to Marie, that admission felt very risky. She was afraid that Miguel would think less of her and judge her as provincial because she was unfamiliar with people other than white Anglo-Saxons like herself. Marie was engaging in story even though Miguel heard it as history.

Another way to think about history and story relates to the topic of a disclosure. Some topics seem to be inherently more personal than others. For example, you could share a great deal of information about a topic like sports without seeming to become very personal ("I love the Green Bay Packers," "I think the Bears are the most improved team in the NFL," "I believe that professional athletes make too much money"). However, topics such as sex or money seem to be more personal. Thus, disclosures are typed based on **topical intimacy.** However, a person can reveal an actual disclosure (that is, story) about what seems to be a low-intimacy topic. For instance, Jill might feel she's taking a risk to tell her feminist friends that she's a football fan. The reverse is also true; a person can reveal little personal information about a high-intimacy topic. For example, when Mike says he wants to take a course in the sociology of sex, he may not think he's risking much. It all depends on the risk the teller feels while disclosing to a listener.

At this point in our discussion, you may be thinking of self-disclosure as an event in which one person tells another something of consequence. In fact, this is the way many researchers have talked about self-disclosure. However, some people think that disclosures aren't discrete, finite events; rather, they are viewed as processes that occur on a continuum. For instance, Kathryn Dindia (1998) observed that the gay men she and her colleague interviewed saw self-disclosing as an ongoing process. Dindia quotes one of her participants as saying, "I . . . am in the process of coming out. . . . When you say, 'heh, I'm gay.' That's the beginning. Yeah, [first you come] out to yourself and then [you] slowly [come] out to other people as well" (p.87). Self-disclosures are unfinished business because there is always something more to tell or someone else to disclose to.

Factors Affecting Disclosure

Although the initial definition of self-disclosure is fairly straightforward, the discussions of history and story, as well as considerations of self-disclosure as a process, show that it is not a simple concept or skill. A complete understanding of self-disclosure requires consideration of many factors, including individual differences, relational issues, cultural values, gender, and the receiver of the disclosure.

Individual Differences

People have different needs for openness. Whereas Karl has no problem telling his friends all about his personal feelings, Selena saves disclosures of that nature for only her family and most intimate friends. Think about your own tendencies to share information with others in your life. Do you believe that some things are better left unsaid, or do you think friends and family should know all about you?

Even people who have a high need to disclose don't wish to tell everyone everything. Although Deanna might tell her partner, Eric, about the fact that she was sexually abused by her stepfather, she may have no problem keeping that information secret from her friend Trish.

Relational Issues

People have expectations about the need for, and the appropriate amount of, self-disclosure based on their definitions of their relationships with significant others. These needs vary depending on the relationship. When we engage in interpersonal encounters, we negotiate the boundaries between privacy and openness through self-disclosing or keeping quiet. Sandra Petronio (2000) observes that being both known by others and yet unknown "is essential to our communicative world" (p. xiii). Selectively self-disclosing helps us as we create the balance between what is

Communication Assessment Test

Exploring Your Approach to Self-Disclosure

Directions: Complete the following sentences about your approach to self-disclosure. There are no right or wrong answers for this assessment, and there is no method of scoring. Rather, simply taking a moment to think about your approach to self-disclosure can help you make thoughtful choices about when and how you self-disclose in future interactions. You can also complete this assessment online under Student Resources for Chapter 8 at the Understanding Interpersonal Communication website.

1. Intimate communication to me means . . .
2. The hard thing about intimate communication is . . .
3. Sometimes I withdraw from intimate communication when . . .
4. When I disclose, I do so because . . .
5. One of the things I'd like people to know about me is . . .
6. When I try to talk about things that are important to me . . .
7. When I try to express intimate feelings . . .

8. If I were more open about expressing my feelings and opinions . . .
9. When people try to talk with me, sometimes I . . .
10. If I weren't concerned about the listener's response . . .
11. Sometimes I become blocked when . . .
12. One of the ways I sometimes make it difficult for people to disclose to me is . . .

Adapted from Michigan State University Counseling Center, 2003.

private only to ourselves, what is shared only with intimates, what is disclosed only to close friends, and what is known to many others.

 To assess your own willingness to self-disclose in various situations, use your Understanding Interpersonal Communication CD-ROM to access **Interactive Activity 8.3: Self-Disclosure Assessment.**

Self-disclosures wax and wane over the life of a relationship. Telling each other all secrets may be important early in the relationship, but in long-term friendships, marriages, or partnerships, self-disclosures account for a much smaller amount of the communication time. Mark Knapp and Anita Vangelisti (2005) observe that the longer people know each other, the less time they spend in disclosing. "Getting to know you" is an important part of developing a new relationship, but as relationships endure and stabilize, the participants need to disclose less because they already know a great deal about one another.

Researchers have suggested that some general patterns of self-disclosure behavior may be related to the life of a relationship (see Figure 8.1). The first pattern pictured represents the general scenario we previously described: People meet, get to know each other, begin to tell each other more and more personal information, and then decrease their disclosures as the relationship endures. In other words, this pattern shows a gradual increase in self-disclosing that parallels the growth of the relationship until the relationship stabilizes; at that point, self-disclosures decrease. One study (Huston, McHale, & Crouter, 1986) found that after one year of marriage, couples were less self-disclosing than they had been as newlyweds, yet they were still satisfied with their relationships. The researchers postulated that perhaps as relationships endure, discussion of other more practical topics becomes important, and time available for self-disclosing decreases.

The second pattern pictured in Figure 8.1 represents two people who know each other as casual friends for a long time before escalating the relationship with self-disclosures and increasing intimacy. The long-term relationship is characterized by low self-disclosures and then a spike up before a leveling off of openness. Let's look at an example. Steven, an emergency room nurse at a local hospital, has worked for four years on the same shift as Beth, an intern at the hospital. They have spoken to

Figure 8.1 | **Three patterns of self-disclosure in relationships**

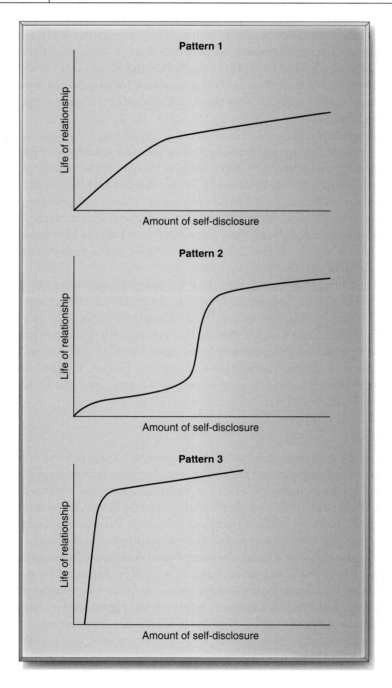

each other a lot about the working conditions and about the fine points of emergency health care, but they seldom work on the same cases. Although Steven and Beth don't know each other well, they like each other and respect each other's medical skills and steadiness in an emergency. One night, Steven's father suffers a stroke and is brought into the emergency room. When he dies a few hours after being admitted, Steven finds comfort in sharing his feelings with Beth. This tragedy leads to increased disclosures between Beth and Steven. One year later, they refer to each other as best friends. This pattern shows that, as was the case with the first pattern, Beth and Steven's disclosures will eventually decrease over time.

The third pattern pictured in Figure 8.1, sometimes referred to as "clicking," shows a high incidence of self-disclosing almost immediately in the relationship. Researchers refer to these relationships as ones that just "click" from the start rather than needing a gradual build. For example, Ben and Marcus met twenty years ago as 12-year-olds at football camp. They immediately found each other easy to talk to and enjoyed being together. Now, two decades later, they still enjoy an openness and a deep friendship.

Researchers explain the clicking process by suggesting that people carry around relationship scripts in their heads, and when they find someone who fits the main elements of that script, they begin acting as though all the elements were there (Berg & Clark, 1986). In other words, let's say that Ben expects a friend to have the same interests he has, resemble him physically, be open and attractive, and have a good sense of humor. When he finds all those characteristics in Marcus, he quickly begins acting as though they have a developed friendship. If Marcus has a similar response, we should see the clicking pattern. Again, in this third pattern, we see a leveling off of self-disclosures over time.

Thus, in all three patterns in Figure 8.1, self-disclosures eventually level off—and, in many cases, they eventually decrease dramatically if relationships last a long time. However, when new issues arise, even longtime friends or couples who have been together a long time self-disclose. Another time self-disclosures may increase is when people feel their relationship has fallen into a rut, and they wish to bring back some of its earlier excitement and intensity. Further, if self-disclosures decrease suddenly and radically between people, that may signal that a relationship is in trouble (Baxter, 1987).

Culture

Like all the behaviors we discuss in this text, self-disclosing behavior is moderated by cultural prescriptions and values. For example, Asian Indians' sense of appropriate self-disclosure differs from those of North Americans and Western Europeans. Asian Indians would be considered overly private by North American or Western standards (Hastings, 2000). Parents and children in Pakistan self-disclose to each other less often than parents and children who are native to the United States do. The Japanese also self-disclose less than North Americans do, primarily because harmony and privacy are Japanese cultural values. Most Asians believe that successful persons do not talk about or exhibit feelings and emotions, whereas most North Americans and Western Europeans believe, as we suggest in this chapter, that a willingness to disclose feelings is critical to relationship development.

Some researchers have observed that scholars, students, and teachers focus on self-disclosure because of a Western bias that favors openness over privacy and disclosure over withholding information. These researchers (Bochner, 1982; Parks, 1982) have criticized the cultural biases that cause Westerners to value disclosure more highly than privacy and secrecy.

Further, the level of self-disclosure of a culture relates to whether it is a high-context or low-context culture. As we discussed in Chapter 3, high-context cultures (such as China and Japan) derive meaning mainly from activity and overall context, not verbal explanation; the reverse is true in low-context cultures (such as the United States). Thus, explicit verbal disclosures are unnecessary in high-context cultures. For example, some research confirms that the Chinese value actions rather than talk in developing relationships (Chen, 1995).

North Americans are thus seen as more disclosive than Asians, yet it is important to recognize that within the United States, different ethnic groups vary in their frequency of disclosure (Klopf, 1998). For instance, European Americans are generally more disclosive than Latinos.

Gender

Many people believe that gender or sex is a major factor in self-disclosing behaviors. We are all familiar with the stereotypes of women engrossed in conversation and men remaining strong and silent. In general, in the United States, women seem to self-disclose more than men, and they value self-disclosures more (Ivy & Backlund, 2000; Wood, 2000). In an analysis of 205 studies examining sex differences in self-disclosure, Dindia and Allen (1992) found that women disclosed more than men, but the difference was rather small. Maccoby (1998) observed that when women friends talked, they usually related emotional disclosures. Tannen (1990) found that even at a young age (second graders), girls talked easily with one another and shared personal stories.

Women seem to expect that close relationships involve exchanging intimate knowledge (Bate & Bowker, 1997; Johnson, 1996). Men may prefer to relate to their friends through actions rather than words. Further, men and women may choose different topics for their self-disclosures. Women are more inclined to discuss intimate topics and are more willing to disclose shortcomings (Johnson, 2000).

Research indicates that women and men both believe establishing close relationships is important. However, they differ a bit in how they think closeness is achieved (Rose & Asher, 2000). In general, men choose to do things together, and women favor talking things over (Tannen, 1990). Some research shows that men do express closeness through talking, just not as much as women do (Canary & Dindia, 1998). Further, some researchers have noticed, that when the goal in a situation is clear (for example, developing a relationship or impressing a partner who has high status), men can disclose as much or more than women (Derlega, Winstead, Wong, & Hunter, 1985; Shaffer & Ogden, 1986).

Thus, the actual difference in self-disclosure between the sexes is probably much smaller than our stereotypes would indicate (Floyd & Parks, 1995). Further, gender role may influence self-disclosure more than biological sex. For example, men who are androgynous (that is, they embody both masculine and feminine traits) share the women's perspective that self-disclosure characterizes close relationships (Jones & Dembo, 1989). Androgynous men desire friends who want to share themselves through talk, and they want to do the same.

© Jason Harris

The common stereotype holds that women disclose a great deal about themselves and men disclose very little. However, research shows that the differences between men and women's self-disclosures are not that dramatic. For example, although men tend to establish close relationships by doing things together more than women tend to, men can disclose as much or more than women do, particularly in certain situations, such as when they are establishing a relationship.

Because the way in which gender or sex influences self-disclosing behavior is complex and confusing, you might be tempted to fall back on stereotypes depicting chatting women and grunting men. However, most of the research doesn't support such a definitive conclusion. As Katherine Dindia (2000) observes, the overall differences between women and men as self-disclosers are relatively small, and they are more likely to be differences of degree rather than kind.

The Receiver

Although we may disclose the same information to several people, the way we frame our disclosure may vary based on the person involved. For example, Jim tells both his mother and his good friend, Rose, that he has cancer. When Jim tells his mother, he concentrates on how hopeful his doctor is and how early the cancer was detected. When Jim tells Rose, he focuses on his fears and vulnerability.

Some receivers of disclosure may be physicians or counselors. In such cases, disclosures are made because the receivers are "licensed" to receive them. Disclosers may be more detailed and complete in the doctor's or therapist's office because they are paying for care. In other cases, the recipients of disclosure may not realize the gravity of what they are hearing, as we observed when discussing history and story. For instance, when children tell parents about teasing they endure on the playground, the parents may not understand the full intimacy of the disclosure. A dismissive "kids will be kids" response might influence the child to keep quiet about this topic in the future. Thus, the recipient of the disclosure has an impact on the process as well as on the sender.

To read an interesting article about how the fear of self-disclosure prevents some people from seeking psychological help, use your Understanding Interpersonal Communication CD-ROM to access **Interactive Activity 8.4: Fear of Self-Disclosure**. And to examine the relationship between what we expect will happen when we disclose personal information and what actually happens, read the article "Expected versus Actual Responses to Disclosure in Relationships of HIV-Positive African American Adolescent Females," available through InfoTrac College Edition. Use your Understanding Interpersonal Communication CD-ROM to access **InfoTrac College Edition Exercise 8.1: Expected versus Actual Responses.**

Models of Self-Disclosure: Seeing the Big Picture

People have suggested many ways to picture the process of self-disclosure so that we can understand it more clearly. We discuss three models in this section: social penetration, dialectics, and the Johari Window.

Social Penetration

The **social penetration model,** developed by Irwin Altman and Dalmas Taylor (1973), says that people, like onions, have many layers. A person's layers correspond to all the information about them ranging from the most obvious to the most personal. For example, when two strangers meet, some information—like a person's sex, approximate height and weight, and hair color—is easily observable. This information makes up the outer layer. Other information—like sexual identity, how a person feels about his or her height and weight, and whether his or her hair color is natural or dyed—is less accessible; conversation is necessary to "peel" these layers of the onion. Through interaction, people may choose to reveal these deeper layers of themselves to one another and, in so doing, deepen their relationship.

The social penetration model pictures all the topics of information about a person—such as their interests, likes, dislikes, fears, religious beliefs, and so forth—along the perimeter of an onion that has been sliced in half (see Figure 8.2). We can have a relationship with a casual friend where the only topics we discuss are at the surface layer of the onion. For example, our friend may know that we are interested in communication, like cats, don't like jazz, are afraid of snakes and belong to the Catholic church.

In this example, our relationship has a fair degree of **breadth** (that is, we have covered several topics) but not much depth. **Depth** occurs when we tell our friend how we feel about the topics—for example, that we're experiencing a crisis in our Catholic faith. Some relationships have a great deal of breadth without depth, and vice versa. Other relationships have a great deal of both; for example, an extremely close friend or partner would probably know a lot about us in a variety of areas. And yet other relationships involve not much of either, as when a distant relative knows only a few things about us not in much depth. The degree to which you self-disclose controls the social penetration described by the model. Using Figure 8.2 as an example, you could draw a separate diagram for each of your friends and relatives to determine how much depth and breadth you have in each relationship.

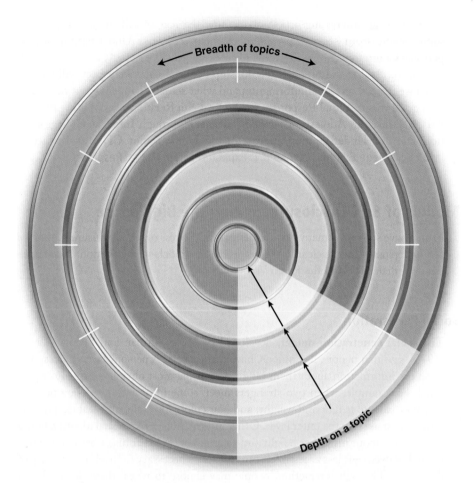

Figure 8.2 | **The social penetration model**

Dialectics

As we mentioned in Chapter 3, dialectics explains relational life as full of push-pull tensions resulting from the desire for polar opposites. In this chapter, we discuss the tension between wanting to be open with our relational partners and the opposing desire of wanting to maintain our privacy. In Chapter 10, we discuss some other tensions that dialectics theorists say people experience in relationships.

Before we discuss dialectics specifically, we need to talk about the polar oppositions of openness and privacy. In early research on self-disclosure, theorists asserted that self-disclosures created our sense of self and contained the essence of being human. Sidney Jourard (1971) is probably the researcher who most influenced our positive response to self-disclosure. He suggested that we must engage in self-disclosure to be psychologically and physically healthy. His position came to be known as the "ideology of intimacy" (Bochner, 1982; Parks, 1982) because he believed disclosing to create intimacy with another was the most important thing a person could do.

More recently, people have rejected this idea in favor of emphasizing the benefits of privacy and even deception. Some researchers now contend that concealing information can have positive effects on relationships. For example, Leda Cooks (2000) writes about discovering that the man who had raised her was not her birth father. Her mother told her this secret when Cooks was 30, revealing that no other members of the family, not even the man Cooks considered her father, knew the truth. Cooks was dumbfounded, but she eventually decided to keep the secret, believing that in doing so she would preserve her relationship with her custodial father and, more importantly, with her brother, to whom family meant everything. Cooks thought that her brother would be destroyed by this information.

The dialectics model tries to integrate these opposing positions. Dialectics explains how we wish to have conflicting, seemingly incompatible things (in this case, being known and staying private) at the same time and how we try to deal with the tensions raised by this conflict. Dialectic thinking assumes that we all want to have *both* privacy *and* the closeness that comes from being known by others, even though these two things seem like polar opposites. We feel conflict over our desire to both "let it all out" to a friend or relative and to keep it in to avoid the risks inherent in telling. According to dialectics, the real core of relational life consists of "communicators seeking a variety of important, yet apparently incompatible goals" (Rosenfeld, 2000, p. 5). Dialectics theory says that to reduce the tension of this process, communicators use several coping strategies: cyclic alternation, segmentation, selection, and integration (Baxter, 1988).

REVISITING CASE IN POINT

1. Before Roberta tells Philip about Carl, what strategy for coping with dialectic tension is she using?
2. After Roberta tells Philip about Carl, what strategy for coping with dialectic tension is she using?

You can answer these questions online under Student Resources for Chapter 8 at the Understanding Interpersonal Communication website.

- **Cyclic alternation** helps communicators handle tension by featuring the oppositions at alternating times. For instance, if Eileen discloses a great deal with her mother when she is in high school and then keeps much more information private from her mother when she goes to college, she is engaging in cyclic alternation. By sometimes being open and other times keeping silent, cyclic alternation allows Eileen to satisfy both goals.

- **Segmentation** allows people to isolate separate arenas for using privacy and openness. For example, if Mac Thomas works in a business with his father, Joe, they may not disclose to one another at work but do so when they are together in a family setting.

- **Selection** means that you choose one of the opposites and ignore your need for the other. To follow up on the previous example, Mac might decide to use selection and simply stop disclosing to his father altogether, making their relationship less open and more businesslike.

- **Integration** can take one of the following three forms:
  - **Neutralizing** involves compromising between the two oppositions. If Mac decided to use neutralizing, he would strive to disclose a moderate amount to his father both at home and at work. Neutralizing copes with the tension by creating a happy medium.
  - **Disqualifying** allows people to cope with tensions by exempting certain issues from the general pattern. Thus, Mac might make some topics, like his love life, off limits for disclosure with his dad but otherwise engage in a lot of self-disclosure. This coping strategy creates **taboo topics,** or issues that are out of bounds for discussion. Most relationships contain topics that are not talked about by unspoken mutual consent. Many families avoid discussing sex and money. Even couples who engage in the most intimate of sexual behavior may not talk about sex to each other. Another example of a taboo topic might be a family member's alcoholism.

- **Reframing** refers to rethinking the notion of opposition. In doing so, people redefine the dialectic. For instance, couples may say that they actually feel closer to each other if they don't tell each other everything. Reframing is illustrated in a couple's belief that if they keep some secrets, that makes what they do tell more significant.

The Johari Window

The Johari Window is another model that can be used to examine the self-disclosure process. Although "Johari" sounds like a term that comes from a mystical language, it is simply a combination of the first names of its creators, Joseph Luft and Harry Ingham (Luft, 1970). Luft and Ingham were interested in the self, and the model they created can help us understand more than just self-disclosure (for example, it can be used as a tool for self-awareness). For our purposes here, we examine how the window can be applied to the self-disclosure process.

The **Johari Window** is a device that provides a pictorial representation of how "known" you are to yourself and others. As Figure 8.3 illustrates, the model is a square with four panels. The entire, large square represents your self as a whole. It contains everything that there is to know about you. The square is divided by two axes: one representing what you know about yourself and one representing what you have revealed about yourself to others. The axes split the window into four panes: the open self, the hidden self, the blind self, and the unknown self.

- The **open self** includes all the information about you that you know and that you have shared with others through disclosures. Whenever you tell someone a piece of information about yourself (for example, your opinion or your concerns), the open self increases.
- The **hidden self** contains the information that you are aware of but that you have chosen not to disclose. When you decide that it is too soon to tell your friend that you feel like a bit of an outsider at school, that information remains in the hidden self.
- The **blind self** encompasses information that others know about you although you yourself are unaware of this information. For example, if you have a tendency to twist the rings on your fingers or chew gum loudly when

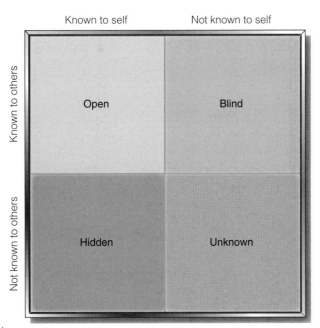

Known to self   Not known to self

Known to others

| Open | Blind |
| Hidden | Unknown |

Not known to others

Figure 8.3 | **The Johari Window**

you are nervous, others watching you know this, but you aren't conscious of your habit.

- The **unknown self** consists of the information that neither you nor others are aware of about you. Neither you nor any of your friends or family might know that you have a capacity for heroism. If you're never tested, that information might remain forever in the unknown self. Luft and Ingham believed that there is always something about each person that remains a mystery. So, there are always things about you to learn and discover.

In Figure 8.3, all the quadrants are the same size, but the Johari Window is a person-specific model, meaning that we need to draw a different window for each person with whom we interact. For instance, your Johari Window for you and your mother will differ from your Johari Window for you and your professor. Also, the sizes of the panes can change as your relationships evolve. For example, after you disclose something personal to a professor, in redrawing the window of your relationship with that professor, your open self panel will increase and your hidden self panel will decrease. See Figure 8.4 for an illustration.

The Johari Window helps us understand self-disclosure in many ways. First, self-disclosures emanate from the parts of the self that are known to us: the hidden self and the open self. Second, self-disclosures regulate the relative sizes of the open and the hidden selves. As we choose to disclose, the open self becomes larger, and the hidden self becomes smaller; when we decide to withhold disclosures, we achieve the opposite result. Third, as others provide us with feedback, we learn more about our selves, which increases our ability to self-disclose (should we choose to do so). Finally, as we have new experiences and learn more about ourselves, the unknown self decreases, and we have more available information that we may chose

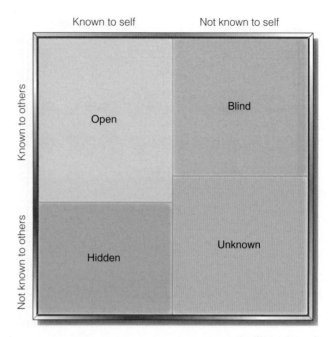

Figure 8.4 | **The Johari Window after self-disclosure**

to disclose to others. To explore some uses of the Johari Window in professional contexts, use your Understanding Interpersonal Communication CD-ROM to access **Interactive Activity 8.5: The Johari Window in a Professional Setting** and **InfoTrac College Edition Exercise 8.2: Pruning the Grapevine.**

Principles of Self-Disclosure

From our discussion so far, you should have a picture of the self-disclosure process—even though that picture is complicated by factors we have mentioned, such as gender, culture, and the receiver. To try to sharpen our picture, we now examine four principles, or norms, of self-disclosure.

We Disclose a Great Deal in Few Interactions

This principle suggests that self-disclosures are somewhat rare if we examine our total communication behavior. Some researchers estimate that only approximately 2 percent of our communication can be called self-disclosure (Dindia, Fitzpatrick, & Kenny, 1997; Pearce & Sharp, 1973; Rosenfeld, 2000). We generally spend a lot more time in small talk than in the relatively dramatic behavior of self-disclosure.

For instance, think about a typical day. Maybe you get up at 7 a.m. and mumble a morning greeting to those you live with as you hurry to get ready for your day. You may grab a fast-food breakfast at a drive-through and then go to your part-time job. At work, you may have to give guidance to and take instructions from a variety of people. You might spend a little bit of time complaining to your coworkers that you are tired and have a great deal to do. You may make some phone calls and place orders, type up a report, and file some paperwork. For lunch, you meet a friend, and the two of you chat about the movie you saw together last week and engage in some

Your *Turn*

Keep a record of self-disclosures you make and receive for the next two weeks. Record the entries using the following categories:

- Who disclosed
- Who listened
- Subject of disclosure
- Context in which disclosure took place

At the end of the two weeks, see if you can discern a pattern in the disclosures. Try to apply one of the models from this chapter (social penetration, dialectics, or the Johari Window) to explain your observations. If you'd like, you can use your student workbook to complete this activity.

trivial gossip about another friend who might be getting divorced. You leave lunch to hurry over to campus to take two classes. You don't speak much in class because you are busy taking notes during the lectures. After the classes, you head over to the library to check out a book. You ask the reference librarian for some help finding a source you need. You stop at the store on the way home to pick up the ingredients for a quick dinner. You run into a friend at the grocery and exchange a few words before hurrying home. When you get home, you turn on the television and watch a game show while you put dinner together. Over dinner the TV remains on, then you clean up the dishes and watch the news. You fall into bed by 10:40 p.m.

In that scenario of a typical day, you probably have not self-disclosed at all, even though you did talk to many people. The kinds of interactions in the day described were routine, phatic, or instrumental and did not involve sharing much personal information. However, on another day, you might call a friend and spend an hour telling her or him about a problem that has been bothering you. Therefore, this generalization about self-disclosure says that we disclose a large amount in a few interactions. Most of our interactions are short, routine, and relatively impersonal. Only a few of our interactions are truly self-disclosive. Yet, because of the emotional impact self-disclosure has on us and on our relationships, it receives more attention from researchers and ourselves than some of our other communication behaviors, which actually take up more of our time.

Self-Disclosures Occur between Two People in a Close Relationship

Although it is possible for us to tell personal information to small groups of people (or even to large groups, like on television talk shows), generally self-disclosure occurs when only two people are present. Further, how much and how frequently we self-disclose depends in great part on the nature of our relationship with another. Some research suggests that people disclose the most in relationships that are close (for example, in marital, cohabiting or family relationships, and close friendships). In a study examining why people tell family secrets, the researchers found that people had to think their relationships were secure to feel comfortable enough to self-disclose (Vangelisti, Caughlin, & Timmerman, 2001). This finding illustrates the principle that self-disclosure takes place in close, secure relationships.

However, a principle is only true *most* of the time, and there are some exceptions to this generalization. The exceptions include self-disclosing in public forums and "the bus rider phenomenon."

People on TV talk shows daily disclose very private information to millions of others whom they do not know at all. Some research argues that television disclosures are a different sort of self-disclosure than those that occur in interpersonal relationships (Priest, 1995). Victoria Orrego and her colleagues (2000) suggest that TV disclosures break the norm of self-disclosure by taking place in public to strangers who don't respond. However, these disclosures may still provide benefits to the discloser, including correcting stereotypes and educating the public; achieving fame (even if only briefly); and getting a forum to speak, including being able to market a book or business idea (Priest, 1995).

Another exception to the principle that self-disclosure takes place in close relationships is "the bus rider phenomenon," also called "strangers on a train" (Thibaut & Kelley, 1959). This notion refers to self-disclosures made to strangers rather than to close friends or relatives. The phenomenon derives its name from the fact that

such self-disclosures may often occur on public transportation like buses, planes, or trains where two people are confined together for a period of time with not much to do but talk to each other. In such cases, the relationship between the people is temporary and transient rather than close and ongoing. We're sure that many of you have heard a stranger's life story while traveling across the country on public transportation, or you have disclosed to strangers.

Self-Disclosures Are Reciprocal

This principle refers to **reciprocity,** or the tendency to respond in kind. Most research suggests that the self-disclosures of one member of a dyad will be reciprocated by self-disclosures by the other. The **dyadic effect** describes the tendency for us to return another's self-disclosure with one that matches it in level of intimacy. For example, if Leila tells her friend Alicia that she was raped when she was 18 by a guy she was dating, Alicia's reciprocal disclosure would have to be about something equally serious and intimate. The norm of reciprocity suggests that Alicia would be unlikely to respond by simply telling Leila that at one time she dated a basketball player. As we discuss in more detail in a moment, Alicia doesn't have to reciprocate immediately; she may simply listen with empathy (see Chapter 5) while Leila tells her story.

On an everyday basis, we tend not to disclose too much about ourselves to total strangers. However, when we're traveling for a long period of time, we may be willing to disclose quite a bit to someone we've just met. Have you ever disclosed personal information to a stranger while traveling? Did you disclose things you wouldn't have mentioned if you had struck up a conversation with the same person while standing in line to register for classes?

Reciprocity is sometimes explained by noting that it keeps people in the relationship on an equal footing. If two people have reciprocated disclosures, they have equalized the rewards and the risks of disclosing. In addition, researchers observe that disclosure reciprocity may be governed by global conversational norms such as the requirement that a response has to be relevant to the comment that preceded it (Grice, 1975). As Valerian Derlega and his colleagues (1993) noted:

> When a speaker self-discloses, the recipient has to generate a response that is not only sensitive to the discloser's self-imposed vulnerability but also responsive to the conversational demand to be topically relevant. The recipient may find that self-disclosing in return addresses both needs. (p. 34)

Thus, when Leila tells Alicia her story about date rape, Alicia responds with a story about how she narrowly escaped date rape herself. In doing so, Alicia matches Leila's intimacy level and keeps the conversation on the same topic.

However, we know that conversations involving self-disclosures do not always contain immediate responses of reciprocal self-disclosures like the one we described between Leila and Alicia. A typical transaction might include Leila's self-disclosure and Alicia's expressions of concern rather than a reciprocal self-disclosure. Alicia, instead of telling about her own experience after hearing about Leila's, might encourage Leila to tell her more about what happened, about how she feels about it now, and so forth. Further, Alicia may express empathy for Leila as she encourages her to speak more about the rape. John Berg and Richard Archer (1980) found that expressing concern for the speaker was actually a better response (because it made a more favorable impression on the discloser) than responding with a matching self-disclosure.

Does this mean that the norm of reciprocity is wrong? Not exactly, according to Kathryn Dindia (2000). After examining many studies of self-disclosure, she concludes that people in close relationships don't have to engage in immediate reciprocity but that they should reciprocate within the conversation at some point. In other words, Leila would be unhappy about the conversation (and maybe her relationship with Alicia) if Alicia never revealed anything personal about herself. But Alicia's self-disclosures don't have to come immediately after Leila's to satisfy the norm of reciprocity.

When people are just getting to know one another, the need for immediate reciprocity is strong (Derlega, Metts, Petronio, & Margulis, 1993). In developed relationships, however, this need is relaxed, and reciprocal disclosures may not even need to occur within the same conversation. In these cases, the participants simply trust that disclosures will equalize over the course of their relationship. For example, Sarah might simply listen to her sister, Miranda, as she discloses that she is about to divorce her husband, without disclosing anything to Miranda at all. But Sarah has disclosed a lot to Miranda in the past and will continue to do so in the future as needed.

Self-Disclosures Occur in the Context of Time

Disclosures generally happen incrementally over time. We usually tell a low-level self-disclosure to a relationship partner first and then increase the intimacy level of our disclosures as time goes by and our relationship with that person continues and deepens. In our example of Leila and Alicia, this suggests that Leila would make her disclosure about date rape after she had already disclosed other, lower-level personal information about herself (for example, that she had flunked calculus and still had a teddy bear she'd gotten as a 3-year-old). Therefore, although initially self-disclosure is a message or a single event, it is also a process that develops as a relationship develops (Spencer, 1994). Self-disclosures change the relationship, and the nature of the self-disclosures changes as the relationship matures or deteriorates.

This principle also specifies that time affects the meaning of disclosure. For example, the first time Todd tells his partner a piece of personal information, it may be a sign of their relational growth. However, after they have been together for many years, that same information may be seen as a part of the overall pattern of their relationship. Valerian Derlega and his colleagues (1993) give the example of the disclosure "I don't feel like my life is going anywhere," stated early in the relationship of two college students. Derlega and colleagues point out that this disclosure may be heard with empathy and support; however, if this couple stays together, the same disclosure 30 years later could be heard as an indictment of the relationship and would not be met with empathy and support. Therefore, the function and meaning of disclosures vary within the context of time.

Reasons to Self-Disclose: I Want You to Know Me

Several specific motivations encourage people to take the risk and reveal themselves to another. Some of the reasons represent factors specific to an individual, whereas others relate to the relationship between people. Table 8.1 presents these motivations, and this section briefly discusses each of them.

Table 8.1 | **Reasons to Self-Disclose**

Individual Reasons	Relational Reasons
• To achieve catharsis (therapeutic release of tensions) and to maintain psychological health • To maintain physical health • To attain self-awareness	• To aid relationship development • To maintain or enhance a relationship • To satisfy expectations for a close relationship • To achieve relational escalation (can be manipulative)

To Experience Catharsis and Improve Psychological Health

One reason psychologists are so interested in the concept of self-disclosure is probably because individuals experience **catharsis,** or a therapeutic release of tensions and negative emotion, through disclosing (Omarzu, 2000). In general, engaging in self-disclosure is seen as a method for helping individuals achieve psychological health. For example, some research suggests that although gay and lesbian adolescents find coming out to their parents difficult, doing so offers those adolescents many psychological benefits (Waldner & Magruder, 1999).

The field of psychotherapy is predicated on the psychological healing function of self-disclosing. Recently, therapists have advanced the idea that some self-disclosure on the part of the therapists themselves could be healing and helpful. Erica Goode (2002) reported that although psychotherapists have traditionally been

The notion that self-disclosure can lead to catharsis and can improve psychological health is so captivating that we often see portrayals of therapists and their patients in movies and on television. Examples include Good Will Hunting, American History X, Girl Interrupted, The Sixth Sense, The Sopranos, *and, of course, virtually any Woody Allen movie. In* The Sixth Sense, *we see a troubled young Cole famously reveal, "I see dead people." Interestingly, in this movie Cole's revelation brings about not only his own catharsis, but also that of his therapist Malcolm.*

taught not to self-disclose any information to their patients, a new study suggests that revealing personal information is not harmful to patients and may actually improve the bond between patient and therapist, making a better atmosphere for psychological healing. For example, when Linda was counseling her client, Paul, one of his central issues was that he believed he wasn't a good father. He was concerned about his son's brushes with the law, his drug use, and his disrespect for authority. After Linda told Paul about her son's similar experiences, Paul felt better about himself.

The adage "A trouble shared is a trouble halved" contains the common wisdom that self-disclosing about troubles provides some relief from those troubles. In one study that tested that assumption, 243 Chinese workers in Hong Kong filled out questionnaires about occupational stress and disclosing to a best friend (Hamid, 2000). The researcher found that disclosing to a best friend did reduce the workers' perception of occupational stress. People engage in self-disclosure to receive psychological support for their problems.

To Improve Physical Health

Evidence supports the belief that self-disclosure provides physical as well as psychological benefits for disclosers. In a 1959 article in the *Journal of Mental Hygiene*, Sidney Jourard stated that self-disclosure promotes physical health and that failure to disclose may cause ill health. This was a controversial position in 1959, and few others followed up on Jourard's thesis. Yet, as Charles Tardy (2000) observes, it is a viable argument today because a great deal of evidence supports the relationship between self-disclosing and physical health.

Examples of the connection between disclosure and physical health abound in the research. For example, a study of Holocaust survivors found that people who disclosed the most about their experiences showed better physical health than those who concealed more (Pennebaker, Barger, & Tiebout, 1989). Other researchers conducted a nine-year study of gay men with HIV positive status (Cole, Kemeny, Taylor, Visscher, & Fahey, 1996). They found that men who concealed their sexual identity and their health issues had more deterioration in their immune systems, a quicker onset of AIDS, and lived a shorter time with AIDS than did men who self-disclosed. In addition, a large body of research supports the contention that disclosing has a positive impact on blood pressure levels and resistance to cardiovascular disease (for example, see Tardy, 2000).

An episode of the old sitcom *Spin City* illustrated this benefit in a humorous fashion. When one character accidentally found out that two of his coworkers were having an affair, they told him he could not tell anyone else. He begged to be able to disclose this secret, but they refused permission. As he struggled to keep this information private, he broke out in hives. Throughout the show, his hives got worse and spread until he was completely covered. Then his nose began bleeding profusely. Unable to withstand all this physical trauma, he blurted out the secret to all the other coworkers and immediately his nose stopped bleeding and his hives completely disappeared!

To explore self-disclosure from the point of view of the medical professional rather than the patient, read the article "How Medical Students View Their Relationships with Patients," available through InfoTrac College Edition. Use your Understanding Interpersonal Communication CD-ROM to access **InfoTrac College Edition Exercise 8.3: The Private and Public Selves of Medical Students.**

To Achieve Self-Awareness

Self-disclosures provide us with the means to become more self-aware. We are able to clarify our self-concepts by the feedback we receive from others when we disclose and by the process of hearing ourselves disclose. For example, when Bethany discloses to her sister, Martha, that she feels stupid for not learning how to swim till she was an adult, Martha responds by praising Bethany for having the courage to tackle a new skill later in life. Martha tells Bethany that she is really proud of her and feels that she is setting a good example for their children that it's never too late to learn. Bethany is pleased to hear her sister's comments. As she reflects on them, she realizes that persisting with swimming lessons was worthwhile, even though it was more difficult to learn at age 35 than it would have been at age 5. After talking to Martha and thinking about their conversation, Bethany feels really good about herself.

In another example, when George discloses to his friend Julia that he is thinking about quitting his job and starting his own business, he surprises himself. Although he had been feeling discontented with work, until he hears himself tell Julia that he wants to start his own business, he hadn't really been sure of this. When he puts that thought into words for Julia, he begins to clarify his feelings for himself. This process is pictured in the Johari Window, which we described earlier; as we listen to ourselves disclose and receive feedback, we increase the side of the window that is known to us.

Facing *Change*

Some people have suggested that current U.S. culture encourages a fast movement toward intimacy in communication; people push to know each other quickly and move to self-disclosures before much time has passed. This rate of disclosure seems to be a change from a more leisurely pace in the past. Discuss the implications this change has for relationship development, and speculate what social changes have caused this change.

 Use your Understanding Interpersonal Communication CD-ROM to watch the CNN video clip "Dating," which features dating workshops that teach people assertiveness in interpersonal relationships. Click on the "CNN & Change" icon in the menu at left, then click on "Video Menu" in the menu bar at the top of the screen. Select "Dating" to watch the video (it takes a minute for  the video to load). As you watch the video, think about whether or not the workshops encourage people to rush into intimate relationships. You can respond to this and other analysis questions by clicking on "Analysis" in the menu bar at the top of the screen. When you've answered all the questions, click on "Done" to compare your answers to those provided by the authors.

To Initiate a Relationship

As we discussed previously, disclosers are prompted to tell private information as a way of developing a new relationship with someone who seems interesting. Jeffrey Vittengl and Craig Holt (2000) conducted a study that supported the idea that self-disclosures help develop new relationships. As the researchers state, "self-disclosure within get-acquainted conversations is accompanied by liking or feelings of social attraction to conversational partners and by an increase in positive emotions" (p. 63). Here it is important to remember that "social attraction" includes friends, partners, coworkers, and so forth, not simply romantic and/or sexual attraction.

To illustrate Vittengl and Holt's findings, let's examine the case of Anita and Zoe. Anita is a working single mother. She attends the local community college part time and holds down two part-time jobs: hostess in a nice restaurant downtown and administrative assistant at a local law firm. Because her numerous responsibilities keep her so busy, she hasn't made many friends at school or at work. One day when she is rushing to finish a project at the office, she bumps into Zoe. Anita had met Zoe, who is also a single mother, during her orientation to the law office. Zoe works full time at the law firm and, beginning this year, has taken on the responsibility of mentoring new employees to help them adjust to working for the firm.

When they had met, Anita had thought that it would be nice to get to know Zoe, but she just hadn't had time to do so. When

Self-disclosure is an integral part of initiating a relationship. When we want to get to know someone better, we often also want them to know us better, so we disclose information that we might not disclose to just a casual acquaintance.

they bump into each other, Anita is worrying about her son, Brad, who has been getting into fights at preschool. The teacher has just called her to tell her about the problem and to work out a plan for dealing with Brad. Anita is concerned about Brad's fighting but is also worried that she doesn't have the time to stay on top of him like she promised the teacher she would. She is trying to figure out how she will talk to Brad about stopping his bad behavior.

Anita's mind is racing with her "to do" list for the day, Brad's behavior, and general concerns she has about all three of her kids. Zoe says "hi" in a friendly way and asks if Anita would like to have coffee later. Although Anita really doesn't have the time, she says yes and is surprised when, over coffee, she finds herself telling Zoe about some of her concerns about Brad. Zoe listens with empathy and then responds that her son had some behavior problems when he was Brad's age, too, and that she, like Anita, had worried that her work schedule might have been partly to blame. Zoe mentions that she and her son had benefited from some counseling sessions with the school psychologist. When Zoe and Anita part, they both think they have begun a friendship. Anita and Zoe illustrate Vittengl and Holt's study results: When we self-disclose to others we like, it's probable we'll develop new relationships.

To Maintain Existing Relationships

Existing relationships also benefit from self-disclosures. In an interesting study examining why people tell others about their dreams, Karen Ijams and Larry Miller (2000) found that 100 percent of their participants attributed their disclosures to some type of relational goal. People said they told a relational partner about a dream to enhance closeness, warmth, and trust. The authors quote one of their respondents, who explained why revealing dreams was important:

> "My brother and I have a good sibling relationship. We tell each other everything that goes on in our dreams. Each time we reveal something, the bond between us strengthens. It seems melodramatic, but there is a strong bond between us." (p. 141).

To Satisfy Expectations of What Constitutes a Good Relationship

As we mentioned previously, the ideology of intimacy dictates that we should be completely open and self-disclosive with people in intimate relationships. If we fail to do so or if we consciously keep secrets from intimate others, we often believe that our relationships are flawed or not as good as we want them to be. Self-disclosing allows us to see our relationships in a positive light.

As an example, in the study referred to in the previous subsection (Ijams and Miller's, 2000), some study participants said they told a partner about their dream because the partner was already close to them, and the participants' expectation was that in a close relationship people tell each other everything, including their dreams. As one of their respondents stated: "'He knows everything about me. I love him and trust him and pretty much share everything with him'" (p. 141).

To Escalate a Relationship

As previously mentioned, self-disclosing provides a way to get to know another and to allow that person to know you. This process escalates a relationship, often moving it from one stage to another. Casual acquaintances may become close friends after they spend some time telling each other personal information about themselves. For example, when Laurie tells her friend Javier that she used to suffer from bulimia and that she still worries every day that she might slip back into her old binge-and-purge habits, Javier feels honored that Laurie trusts him with this information. Her self-disclosure makes him feel closer to her and advances their relationship to a more intense level.

However, as we discussed earlier in the text, communication can be used for dark purposes as well as positive goals. Indeed, self-disclosures can be used to manipulate a relational partner. For example, a person can offer a self-disclosure we would label history (or inauthentic) to manipulate a relational partner, through the norm of reciprocity, into revealing something truly personal. In this manner, the relationship may escalate faster than it would have otherwise, which might be the devious objective of the first discloser. Or, one person may say "I love you" early in a relationship simply to advance the intimacy of the relationship.

Reasons Not to Self-Disclose: Why Am I Afraid to Tell You Who I Am?

Although opening up ourselves to another provides many benefits, there are also compelling reasons to keep our secrets to ourselves. The dialectics model we discussed earlier in this chapter argues that in any relationship, both desires are extremely important. We want to be open with our partners, but at the same time, we want to maintain our secrets. Sometimes, keeping silent puts us in the position of deceiving our relational partners. Although ethical questions arise when we keep something that is critically important from another, most of the time, maintaining privacy is ethical.

Table 8.2 | **Reasons to Avoid Self-Disclosure**

- To avoid hurt, rejection, or both
- To avoid conflict, protect a relationship, or both
- To keep one's image intact, maintain individuality, or both
- To reduce or forget about stress

Some of the reasons people choose to be silent rather than to disclose are outlined in Table 8.2 and discussed in this section. As you read the examples, think about the ethical implications of choosing to keep silent in these situations.

To Avoid Hurt and Rejection

Perhaps the most common reason for keeping a secret is because we believe that the person we reveal it to may use the information to hurt us or may reject us when they know our inner selves. For example, Mick doesn't tell his friend, Marci, that he served time in a juvenile detention center for possession of drugs because he fears that she will be angry, respect him less, or bring it up in a taunting way in an argument. All of these negative outcomes are reasons for keeping a secret private.

If we share a really critical piece of information, even with a sympathetic friend, we have given this friend some potential power over us, and we can't be absolutely sure that our friend would never use this power against us or in a way that we would not like. For instance, when Belle confides in Allen that she thinks she is a lesbian, she figures that Allen is a trustworthy confidante because he is a longtime friend who is gay himself. However, she doesn't realize that Allen feels strongly that being homosexual is nothing to hide. Allen tells several mutual friends about Belle's disclosure and feels no regrets about "outing" Belle. Although Belle doesn't believe that being a lesbian is shameful, she wasn't ready to tell all their friends yet; she was still getting used to the idea herself. She was extremely hurt by what she saw as Allen's betrayal.

To Avoid Conflict and Protect a Relationship

As we mentioned when we discussed the dialectics perspective, some secrecy may provide a good balance for openness in a relationship. For example, Lois might think that she doesn't need to tell her friend, Raymond, that she has some affectionate feelings for him and may want more than a friendship. Lois might fear that if she takes the risk and discloses this, the news would cause a big conflict that could harm their relationship. She decides it's better to have a good friend for sure than take a chance for something more and end with no relationship at all.

As another example, Marsha does not like her brother's wife. When Marsha chooses not to tell her brother, Hal, this fact, she figures that her silence keeps the relationship between her and Hal more peaceful. Because Marsha knows that Hal is happy with his wife, it seems irrelevant to reveal that she isn't. This secret does not affect their relationship much, because they live in different cities separated by thousands of miles, and Marsha and Hal keep in touch mainly by email and phone. So, Marsha doesn't often have to interact with Hal's wife, and she decides that what Hal doesn't know won't hurt him; in fact, the secret probably helps Marsha and Hal's relationship.

As discussed previously in this chapter, culture influences people's views of self-disclosures and whether they help or harm a relationship. A study of Chinese business people (Hamid, 2000) found that disclosing to one's mother was negative for

"You never tell me anything. Keep up the good work."

the relationship because it increased feelings of stress in both parties. As the author concludes:

> In Chinese families, open expression of emotion, either positive or negative, is not encouraged. The Chinese believe that excessive emotion is harmful to one's mental and physical health and that one can maintain good health and achieve maturity by keeping emotions under control and well-balanced. (p. 1081)

Finally, some research indicates that if you disclose to someone who responds in a negative fashion, you are likely to feel badly about the interaction, the other person, and about your relationship with the other person (for example, see Afifi & Guerreo, 2000; Roloff & Ifert, 2000). Some people may believe disclosing isn't worth that risk.

To Keep Your Image Intact and Maintain Individuality

Some people withhold self-disclosures because they are concerned that if they begin disclosing, they will lose control and be unable to stop disclosing. Further, these people fear that disclosures will bring with them unrestrained emotionality, perhaps causing the discloser to cry uncontrollably. Thus, people may choose to keep their secrets to avoid engaging in uncontrolled behaviors. Some research indicates that men more than women cite this reason as a rationale for not disclosing (Hatfield, 1984). In a related vein, some people worry that self-disclosing will cause them to lose their sense of mystery and individuality. For instance, Caitlin may fear that if Nolan knows all about her, she won't seem interesting to him any longer. And Gary's fear is that if he tells his friend Lyle all about himself, Gary may become so much a part of this friendship that he'll disappear as a separate individual. Such concerns may keep people from telling their private disclosures.

Further, if someone has established a particular role in a relationship, they may fear changing that role and their image. For example, Lucy and Rebecca have been friends for five years. In their relationship, Rebecca often turns to Lucy, who has been married for 15 years, for advice when Rebecca has problems with a boyfriend. When Lucy and her husband fight, she doesn't feel comfortable confiding in Rebecca because it seems to negate her identity as a happily married person who gives support but doesn't need to ask for it.

To Reduce Stress

In the previous section, we mentioned that people often engage in self-disclosures to reduce stress. Although this is frequently the case, some evidence indicates that the opposite is also true. For instance, Valerian Derlega and his colleagues (1993) give the following example:

> Bill, 20, and Mark, 21, are juniors at a state university. They are flying together to Florida for spring break. Bill is uncomfortable about flying, and he tells Mark about being nervous. Mark, in turn, describes an unpleasant experience when, on another flight, his plane had mechanical problems. As the plane takes off, neither of them is feeling very good. Somehow, talking about their fears made them feel worse rather than better. (p. 103)

Similarly, Anita Vangelisti and her colleagues (2001) observe that continuing to think and talk about stressful issues can result in more stress. They note that stress is reduced only when the disclosures begin to reflect a positive outlook.

To explore the possible consequences of choosing not to reveal personal information, read the article "The High Costs of Hidden Conditions," available through InfoTrac College Edition. Use your Understanding Interpersonal Communication CD-ROM to access InfoTrac College Edition Exercise 8.4: The Cost of Choosing Not to Disclose.

Choices for Effective Disclosing

Although we may have good reasons for keeping silent at times, we need to refine our self-disclosing skills for those times when we wish to open up to another. In this section, we outline important techniques for building our self-disclosing skills.

Use I-Statements

Owning, or the use of I-statements, which we discussed in Chapter 6, is the most basic verbal skill for self-disclosing. Saying "I think," "I feel," "I need," I believe," and so forth indicates that you accept that what you are talking about is your own perception, based on your own experiences, and affected by your value system. When you self-disclose using owning, you take responsibility for your feelings and experiences. In addition, your listener realizes that you are speaking for yourself and not trying to make a generalization. Let's take a look at an example of an owned self-disclosure. Edward tells Mike, "I don't know if I will really be happy going to

Skill *Spotlight*

Honesty and Clarity

- **Make your disclosures clear.** Don't ask a question when you really want to express an opinion, a feeling or a need. For example, if you are angry at your partner, asking "How could you spend that much money?" isn't a clear statement of how you feel.
- **Don't send double messages.** For example, if you want to tell a friend that you feel you are drifting apart, don't say "Of course, I'd like to be with you, but you wouldn't like the crowd I'm going out with."
- **Avoid hidden agendas and dishonesty.** Don't use self-disclosure to impress others, to get sympathy, to provide excuses for your behavior, or to manipulate others into disclosing. Deceiving and manipulating others eventually hurts or drives them away.
- **Don't assume that others understand what you think, feel, and want** without your saying anything. We must repeatedly say and show "I love you." We must tell our parents and our children "I appreciate your help" and thousands of other feelings, views, and needs.

Remember: **No one can read your mind!**

Skills at Work At work, honesty and clarity are essential. Dishonesty and lack of clarity can have many serious consequences. Of course, sometimes you wish to be thoughtful and tactful rather than brutally honest, but it is still important to be honest and clear. For instance, let's say that your coworker Tanya asks your opinion about a report she needs to turn in next week. If you think that Tanya can improve the report significantly, you should let her know the ways in which it can be strengthened in specific language. You don't need to be unkind, but you do need to tell her exactly what the report lacks. If you are not clear, Tanya may leave your conversation not knowing if she needs to change the report or not. Can you identify other consequences of lack of clarity in the workplace?

college in New York. It's so far away from my family—I know I'll be homesick." This is different from Edward stating, "It's important to stay near home for college. It's not good to put too much distance between family members." When Edward uses this phrasing, he doesn't own his feelings; instead, he presents them as a general rule that all people should consider when deciding where to go to college.

Be Honest

Honesty in self-disclosure refers to being both clear and accurate. If you are too ambiguous and unclear, your self-disclosures may not be "heard" as real disclosure. Yet, if you and your partner know each other very well, you may be able to offer disclosures more indirectly (Petronio, 1991). For instance, if you know your partner is struggling with several deadlines at work, you will be able to hear a disclosure in your partner's sarcastic comment: "I had a great day at work today. What a pleasure palace that job is!" Generally speaking however, you need to be clear and accurate in your disclosures. If you are dishonest or inaccurate while disclosing, you are defeating the purpose of self-disclosure. You won't help yourself or your relationship by receiving feedback for a problem that doesn't actually exist.

Be Consistent with Your Verbal and Nonverbal Communication

Consistency means that, as we discussed in Chapter 7, your nonverbal communication should reinforce, not contradict, your verbal communication. For example, if Shannon tells Josie that she is really upset about her grades for the semester, but she smiles while saying it, Josie may be confused about whether Shannon is upset or not.

Focus Your Nonverbal Communication

Try to focus your nonverbal communication on the issue at hand and provide nonverbal cues that add meaning rather than ones that distract from your message. For instance, if Mia continually taps her pencil against a table while telling her mother that she wants to quit school, her mother may be distracted by the gesture and have trouble concentrating on Mia's disclosure.

Be Sure Your Content Is Relevant

Relevancy to the context refers to an assessment of the appropriateness of the disclosure to the situation itself. For example, if Ron is at a company picnic, he may decide that it isn't the time or place to tell his boss that he is unhappy at work and wants more responsibility. In this chapter's opening Case in Point, Roberta tried to make a good context for her disclosure. She prepared a nice dinner to set the stage for telling Philip her secret.

Be Sure Your Topic Is Relevant

Relevancy to the topic means that you are able to weave your disclosure naturally into the conversation. When Jeff and Noel go out bowling together for the first time, they begin talking about their involvement in sports in the past. Thus, the situation and the topic seem to invite Jeff to tell Noel that he is insecure about his athletic abilities. If Jeff and Noel were at a restaurant talking about a movie they had both recently seen, the topic would not have been so inviting for Jeff's disclosure.

Estimate the Risks and Benefits

To be competent in self-disclosure, you need to be able to estimate and balance its risks and benefits. As mentioned previously, there are compelling reasons to reveal and to withhold disclosures, many of which pertain to issues of self-identity. To be effective at self-disclosing, you need to practice judging when the benefits outweigh the risks, and vice versa.

Predict How Your Partner Will Respond

Your ability to decode messages of warmth, concern, and empathy on the part of the other person will help you make judgments about when to tell and when to be silent. For instance, in this chapter's opening Case in Point, Roberta knew that Philip was a sympathetic listener. Therefore, although Roberta felt some fear about revealing such a serious disclosure, she felt that Philip was ready to hear her confession.

Be Sure the Amount and Type of Disclosure Are Appropriate

Although as mentioned previously in this chapter there are a few exceptions to this rule, the amount and type of disclosure should match the perceived intimacy level of the relationship. Thus, on a first date, it may be unwise to tell your date about all your insecurities and past indiscretions. Further, early in your relational life, you and your partner should share talk time. Therefore, you don't want to dominate the

"You just self-deprecated yourself right out of a job."

conversation with long self-revelations. You should attempt to pace your disclosures so that they roughly match the developing intimacy of your relationship.

Estimate the Effect of the Disclosure on Your Relationship

Think about how the disclosure might affect the relationship. For example, Jake asks himself if telling Rochelle about his growing interest in her will actually cause the end of their friendship. Jane considers whether telling Marc about her trouble with commitment in the past will hurt or intensify their relationship. Of course, you can never know for sure what effect a disclosure will have, but making well-founded assessments of effects is an important skill to develop.

To read an interesting article that likens disclosure to a dance of veils and offers suggestions for making disclosure easier, check out "The Art of Self-Disclosure," available through InfoTrac College Edition. Use your Understanding Interpersonal Communication CD-ROM to access **InfoTrac College Edition Exercise 8.5: Disclosure as a Dance of Veils.**

CHOICES *for Effective Self-Disclosure*

- Use I-statements.
- Be honest and clear.
- Use consistent verbal and nonverbal communication.
- Focus your nonverbal cues.
- Be sure the context is relevant.
- Be sure the topic is relevant.

- Estimate the risks and benefits.
- Predict how your partner will respond.
- Match the disclosure to your relationship's level of intimacy.
- Estimate the effect of the disclosure on your relationship.

Summary

Self-disclosure is a complex, well-researched communication process. We define it as verbal communication that intentionally reveals personal information about our selves that our listener would be unlikely to discover without being told. This means that self-disclosing is a choice we make; we always have the option of not telling.

We generally choose to disclose in the context of a close, trusting relationship because self-disclosure is scary and implies risk. Not everyone self-discloses in the same way or at the same rate. Our disclosures are affected by individual differences, the stage of the relationship, cultural values, gender, and the receiver we've chosen. We wish to emphasize that our knowledge of and attitude toward self-disclosure is heavily influenced by cultural norms; for example, in the United States, the culture favors openness over secrecy.

One way we can understand the process of self-disclosing is through the notion of social penetration. This theory pictures relational development as a gradual, incremental process facilitated by self-disclosures (like peeling back layers of an onion). We can also get a handle on self-disclosure from a dialectics perspective. This approach encourages us to see self-disclosure as a way to regulate our conflicting desires for privacy and openness in our relationships. Finally, the Johari Window provides information about self-disclosure by showing how the four panes of the window (the open self, the hidden self, the blind self, and the unknown self) shrink or expand as we disclose and get feedback.

One norm of self-disclosures is that we disclose a great deal in a few interactions; only about 2 percent of our communication time is involved in this activity. Another principle is that self-disclosures occur between two people in a close relationship; however, exceptions to this rule include self-disclosing in public forums (such as on a TV talk show) or to a stranger while traveling ("the bus rider phenomenon"). Another guideline self-disclosures follow is that they are reciprocal; the dyadic effect describes the tendency for us to return another's self-disclosure with one that matches it in level of intimacy. Lastly, self-disclosures occur in the context of time—that is, self-disclosures get more intimate as a relationship progresses, and time affects the meaning of disclosure.

People have both individual and relational reasons for disclosing to others. Reasons that provide primarily individual benefits include catharsis, psychological health, physical health, and self-awareness. Reasons involving relational life encompass developing a new relationship, maintaining a relationship, fulfilling the expectations for what should happen within a relationship, and exerting control over a relationship.

Reasons for not engaging in self-disclosure include avoiding hurt and rejection, avoiding conflict and protecting a relationship, keeping our image intact and maintaining our individuality, and thinking more about an issue. Dialectic thinking shows us that we are constantly doing a balancing act in our relationships related to providing and withholding information.

Understanding self-disclosure contributes to an understanding of interpersonal communication. To engage in skillful self-disclosure, you need to learn how to use I-statements, and you must be honest and consistent with your verbal and nonverbal communication. Remember to focus your nonverbal communication, and be sure your content and topic are relevant. Practice estimating the risks and benefits of self-disclosure and predicting how your partner will respond. Be sure the amount and type of disclosure are appropriate, and try to estimate the effect of the disclosure on your relationship.

Understanding Interpersonal Communication Online

Now that you've read Chapter 8, use your Understanding Interpersonal Communication CD-ROM for quick access to the electronic study resources that accompany this text. Your CD-ROM gives you access to the Ethics & Choice interactive activity on page 216, the Communication Assessment Test on page 218, the CNN video clip "Dating" on page 234, InfoTrac College Edition, and the Understanding Interpersonal Communication website. When you get to the Understanding Interpersonal Communication home page, click on "Student Book Companion Site" in the Resource box at right to access the online study aids for this chapter, including a digital glossary, review quizzes, and the chapter activities.

Terms for Review

blind self 226	history 216	segmentation 225
breadth 223	integration 225	selection 225
catharsis 232	Johari Window 226	self-disclosure 213
cyclic alternation 225	neutralizing 225	social penetration model 223
depth 223	open self 226	story 216
descriptive disclosures 213	private information 214	taboo topics 225
disqualifying 225	public information 214	topical intimacy 217
dyadic effect 230	reciprocity 230	unknown self 227
evaluative disclosures 213	reframing 226	
hidden self 226		

Questions for Understanding

Comprehension Focus

1. Define self-disclosure and elaborate on each of the important elements in the definition.
2. Define public information and private information and give an example illustrating each.
3. Distinguish between history and story.
4. Describe the three patterns of self-disclosure.
5. List the four principles of self-disclosure.

Application Focus

1. **CASE IN POINT**
   Specifically, how does Roberta's disclosure fit our definition of self-disclosure? Use each of the attributes of the definition and show how Roberta's comments illustrate (or don't illustrate) the definition.
2. Do you agree with the criterion that self-disclosure has to be verbal? How important to the definition of self-disclosure is this assertion? Make a case for or against

including nonverbal behaviors in the definition. Provide examples to strengthen your case.

3. What are some important cultural issues to consider when thinking about self-disclosure? Why do you think people in the United States, Western Europe, and other Western countries are so interested in a communication behavior that people may engage in for only 2 percent of their total communication time?
4. What are some of the factors that you think about before you tell someone something personal about yourself? How do your factors compare to the ones discussed in this chapter?
5. Which model of self-disclosure (social penetration, dialectics, or the Johari Window) do you think best explains the self-disclosure process? Defend your position and provide examples. How can the three models work together to help us understand the process?

Interactive Activities and InfoTrac College Edition Exercises

Complete the Interactive Activities and InfoTrac College Edition Exercises for Chapter 8 online at the Understanding Interpersonal Communication website. Select the chapter resources for Chapter 8, then click on "Activities" or "InfoTrac College Edition." If requested, you can submit your answers to your instructor.

Interactive Activities

InfoTrac College Edition Exercises

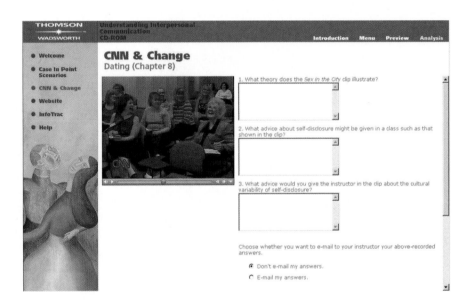

9

Communicating Power and Conflict

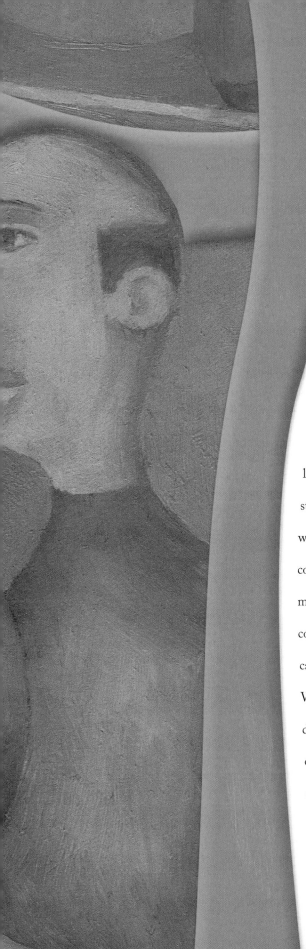

CASE IN POINT: TAMARA WILEY AND JEFF HARRIS

Tamara Wiley glanced in the mirror before leaving her apartment and heading to her 8 a.m. English class. She was having a major bad hair day, so she had thrown on a scarf. Her quick check in the mirror told her the scarf covered most of the problem.

After class she was supposed to meet her best friend, Jeff Harris, for coffee, but she was hoping he would understand if she canceled because she was way behind on her physics assignment. On her way to English class, she called and left Jeff a voice mail message.

Meanwhile, Jeff was having a bad morning of his own. He was really looking forward to seeing Tamara for coffee because she always understood him and cheered him out of his depression. Jeff admired Tamara as well as liked her. He knew she was the first person in her family to go to college, and he thought that was truly commendable. It was especially remarkable because he knew Tamara didn't get much support at home; in contrast, his family gave him a great deal of support for his college and career plans, and he couldn't imagine where he would be without that. When Jeff got to the coffee shop, he scanned the room for Tamara but didn't see her. He bought a latte for each of them and settled into an overstuffed chair to wait for her. When Tamara's latte got cold, Jeff started to get anxious. He called her apartment but there was no answer.

Jeff waited for another hour and finally left in disgust. Not only had he wasted a lot of time waiting, he missed talking to Tamara, so now he was feeling even worse than he had earlier. Later that evening when he

Use your Understanding Interpersonal Communication CD-ROM to watch a video clip of Tamara and Jeff. Click on the "In Action" icon in the menu at left, then click on "Conversation Menu" in the menu bar at the top of the screen. Select "Tamara" to watch the video (it takes a minute for the video to load). As you watch the video, consider how Tamara and Jeff could have handled their conflict more effectively. You can respond to this and other analysis questions by clicking on "Analysis" in the menu bar at the top of the screen. When you've answered all the questions, click on "Done" to compare your answers to those provided by the authors.

finally reached her on the phone, he spoke rather harshly, asking her where the hell she'd been when she was supposed to meet him. Tamara was taken aback by his tone and she replied rather coldly, "I left you a message that I had to do an assignment and that I couldn't make it to the coffee shop." Jeff yelled back that he hadn't checked his messages and she knew that he rarely listened to voice mail: "You know I hate voice mail, Tamara. If you had really wanted to let me know, you should have stopped by the coffee place and just told me. I guess our relationship means more to me than it does to you!" Tamara frowned and raised her voice, too. "Hold on, Jeffrey," she said. "You are making a huge deal out of nothing. I just couldn't make it for coffee. Get over it and don't make something out of nothing." Jeff's voice grew cold: "Call me when you want to get together sometime—at your convenience, of course." Jeff slammed down the phone. Tamara was left holding the receiver, listening to the dial tone, and wondering what had just happened. ■

It's difficult to imagine relating to others without ever experiencing conflict; it's simply a normal, unavoidable part of relational life. Some researchers (for example, Lloyd, 1987) estimate that couples in happy, stable relationships may engage in conflict twice a week on average. Some relationships have a lot of conflicts and others have fewer, but if you have a relationship of any consequence, you're bound to eventually engage in conflict.

Conflicts are common in relationships because we are all different, unique individuals, and conflicts occur when differences between people become a problem. Sometimes, people recognize differences between them that do not matter. For example, let's say that Patrice likes cats and her cousin Melissa hates them. If Patrice and Melissa don't live together and don't bring animals along when they see each other, this difference will probably not precipitate conflict.

However, most of the time, our differences do cause friction. For instance, in our opening story, Jeff and Tamara perceive their differences on that particular day as a dilemma. Jeff really wants to talk to Tamara and is hurt and troubled when she doesn't seem to reciprocate. Tamara is angered and puzzled by Jeff's reaction to a missed meeting—a response that she feels is different from how she would behave if the roles were reversed. In this scenario, we see that their differences challenge Jeff and Tamara, and conflict results.

When your coworker wants to rework a project you consider sufficiently completed, when your roommate wants to entertain and you want to sleep, when your parent wants you to help more around the house than you deem necessary, when you believe your paper deserved a better grade than your professor gave it, when you think you did the lion's share of the work on a joint project—in such cases, differences matter, and conflict may quickly follow. Conflict is a fact of life in relationships because when we interact, we become aware of both our similarities and our differences. If we never differed with another, we would never experience conflict. Even if we get to know someone well and feel we have a lot in common, we will still differ in some respects, so there is always the potential for conflict.

Think back to the first time you met someone you later became good friends with or dated. Your early encounters with this person probably had fewer conflicts than your later interactions. When people first meet, they usually focus on their similarities, thus reducing opportunities for conflict. Part of the fun of getting to know

Throughout our lives, the nature of many of our relationships implies differing interests, concerns, and bases of power. As such, conflict is inevitable. Learning how to handle conflict in a constructive way is one of the tricks to cultivating healthy interpersonal relationships.

someone is discovering the things you have in common. However, later in the relationship, you may notice and discuss differences. For example, in the scenario we presented at the beginning of the chapter, even though Jeff and Tamara have known each other for a while, this occasion was their first opportunity to see how they differ in their commitment to keeping appointments.

In some relationships, the people involved notice differences relatively quickly because the nature of the relationship implies differing interests, concerns, and bases of power. For example, in a relationship between a worker, Carlos, and a boss, Manuel, the job titles indicate that despite the fact that the two work for the same company, they have divergent perspectives. Manuel's job dictates that he be responsible for maximizing productivity and minimizing expense. This goal may run counter to Carlos's needs and desires. Further, the power relationship between the two is not symmetrical. Manuel has the power to punish or reward Carlos in ways that are not reciprocal. These inherent differences make boss-worker friendships or romances tricky (although not impossible) to negotiate. Parent-child and teacher-student are other types of relationships where the intrinsic differences between the roles played offer ripe arenas for difference and, thus, conflict. Some people suggest that relationships between people of different cultures and even relationships between men and women maximize difference and provide opportunities for more conflicts than do relationships between more similar people. Certainly, interpersonal conflict occurs when people recognize differences and are challenged, threatened, inconvenienced, and/or troubled by them.

As your own experiences and this introduction have established, experiencing conflict in your relationships is inevitable. However, what is not preordained is how you and your partner deal with the normal conflicts of relational life. You have some control in this crucial arena and can exercise some skills that may determine the course of your relationship. However, before we can learn how to manage conflict, we need to define the term and understand what exactly constitutes interpersonal conflict.

Defining Conflict: Knowing It When You See It

We have all experienced conflict, but often it is a surprise, as it was for Tamara in our opening example. Like Tamara, we're left scratching our heads, wondering what just happened. Knowing what conflict is all about won't stop you from experiencing discord, but it's the first step in helping you manage conflict better. Later in the chapter, we present specific ways to manage conflict.

Interpersonal conflict is commonly defined as "the interaction of interdependent people who perceive incompatible goals and interference from each other in achieving those goals" (Folger, Poole, & Stutman, 2001, p. 5). Several key parts of this definition, discussed in the following subsections, can help us understand the meaning of conflict.

Interaction

In the context of the definition, **interaction** means that conflicts are created and sustained through verbal and nonverbal communication. The interaction that conflicting parties exhibit ranges greatly. Some conflicts involve yelling, crying, swearing, and screaming. Other conflicts consist of icy silences, cold shoulders, frowns, and withdrawal. However, regardless of the behaviors, remember that the definition specifies that conflict is interaction *between* people. In other words, if Cate talks to Jim just as she has always done, even though internally she is angry with him, they aren't in conflict by our definition. They enter into conflict only when she does something overt.

Because this text is focused on explaining interpersonal communication, we emphasize the expression of conflict through verbal and nonverbal cues. Many researchers agree that communication is central to understanding conflict (Canary, Cupach, & Serpe, 2001; Roloff, 1987). However, this focus doesn't mean that we are not interested in the thoughts that people have during conflicts. Our emphasis is on how thoughts influence talk; interaction is in the foreground, and cognition is in the background, or they work together, each affecting the other.

A recent study by Alan Sillars and his colleagues (Sillars, Roberts, Leonard, & Dun, 2000) examined the relationship between thoughts and communication behaviors in marital conflict. The researchers asked 118 married couples to discuss a current issue that caused conflict for them and then to watch the videotapes of their discussion. As the researchers noted when detailing the relationship of thought and talk, "To appreciate the subtlety and complexity of communication in conflict, it is helpful to consider what people are thinking as they interact" (pp. 480–481).

Sillars and his colleagues found that in severe conflicts especially, husbands and wives tended to construct individual accounts that didn't agree with each other. Thus, as wives watched the tapes and recalled what they were thinking, they generated a very different picture than did their husbands. The researchers comment that selective perception is a central dynamic in conflict interactions; interactants were thinking very different things and attributing very different motives to one another as they watched their tapes.

If you're standing at a checkout counter and annoyed that the sales clerk is chatting on the phone and ignoring you, do you have conflict? What if another clerk can help you with your purchases, but the chatty clerk still annoys you? No matter how much the sales clerk gets on your nerves, conflict exists only when there is an interaction and an interdependence between two people. So, unless the chatty clerk is the only person who can help you, and you confront her about ignoring you, there is no conflict.

Interdependence

Interdependence means that the people involved in the conflict rely on one another, need each other, and are in a relationship with one another. Parties must feel some degree of interdependence to experience conflict. If you have no relationship with a person, that person isn't important enough to you for conflict to exist. For example, let's say that Louise meets Justin at a party. Justin doesn't interest Louise much, and Louise finds herself disagreeing with his loudly stated political views. Louise decides to talk to someone else and politely excuses herself. In another example, it doesn't affect you if a stranger likes heavy metal and you like rap music, so there is no need to argue about it. On the other hand, if your roommate, your sibling, or your partner has different musical tastes than you do, a conflict over what CDs to play may result.

Interdependence issues bring up one of the striking ironies of conflict. Robin Kowalski (2001) notes that although people's need for others is a basic, fundamental human desire, people rank conflicts with others one of the most critical stressors that they experience. Kowalski comments that "it is ironic that the same relationships that people seek so eagerly are the source of many, perhaps most, of their greatest frustrations and unhappiness" (p. 297). Our connection to others provides us both pleasure and pain, both the joy of merger and the conflict of differentiation.

For example, when Marty thinks of his happiest moments, he usually thinks of the times he has spent with his best friend, Ray. However, Marty's unhappiest time was also associated with Ray. Ray had thought that Marty was flirting with Ray's girlfriend, and Ray had been furious, not speaking to Marty for a week, even when they were at basketball practice and classes together. Marty had felt a lot of pain because he had thought that their friendship was over. Finally, Ray realized that Marty wasn't really guilty, and they were able to resume their friendship. Marty thought it was odd that the same person he had so much fun around could also make being around him feel like torture.

Interdependence is the main reason that conflict is a natural and inevitable part of life. The more we rely on another, the more potential there is for observing differences and being affected by them. In addition, conflict orients us to others and, in some cases, even helps define our relationships with others (Lulofs & Cahn, 2000).

Perception

Perception refers to the psychological process involved in sensing meaning (recall our discussion of perception in Chapter 2). The definition of conflict states that for conflict to exist, the interdependent people have to perceive that they have incompatible goals. For example, Nola wants to go on a family vacation to Florida. She misunderstands a statement that her husband, Dave, makes and jumps to the conclusion that he disagrees with the vacation destination. Even though Nola and Dave really agree on where to take their vacation, if they believe they disagree, they will come into conflict. This type of conflict persists until the parties come to understand that their goals really are similar.

Dan Canary and his colleagues (Canary et al., 2001) emphasize the importance of perception to the conflict process when they apply a competence model to interpersonal conflict. The model suggests that people judge themselves and their conversational partners based on how well they communicate and how successful they are in reaching their goals in an interaction (Spitzberg & Cupach, 1984, 1989). When applying this model to conflict, Canary et al. (2001) observed that people's perceptions of how competently they and their relationship partners handled the conflict directly affected the relationship. For instance, if Josie and Bill have an argument about cleaning the apartment, and each perceives that both of them are competent in their conflict, they will be more satisfied and happier with one another than they would be if they'd had the exact same conflict but thought they'd behaved less competently. Therefore, Canary and his team argue that perception of communication competence is an extremely important dimension of interpersonal conflict.

Incompatible Goals

The definition of conflict specifies that friction results when people's goals differ (as in "I want to study, but Jorge wants me to go to a party with him") and when people think that others stand in the way of the achievement of personal goals (as in "I want to get promoted at work, but my boss doesn't seem to like me"). These conditions (incompatible goals and interference from another in achieving goals) are rather broad and cover a range of conflict types, including image conflicts, content conflicts, value conflicts, and relational conflicts.

Types of Conflict

We can define conflict further by describing these various types of conflict. Understanding them helps us to gain a better sense of what conflict means.

Image Conflicts

Image conflicts concern self-presentation. For example, if Enid considers herself a competent adult, she may engage in conflict when her mother offers suggestions

SIPRESS

*"Well, if it doesn't matter who's right and who's wrong,
why don't I be right and you be wrong?"*

about how to manage her career. Enid may feel that her mother is not respecting her as an adult and, as such, isn't allowing Enid's image of herself to exist uncontested. This type of conflict is especially difficult when two different images are in play. For instance, if Enid's mother still views her as a child, Enid and her mother actually do have two competing images. A similar problem can exist when a parent pushes a child to grow up faster than the child feels comfortable. In that case, the parent's image of the child is of an adult, whereas the child may still see herself or himself as a child. Sometimes, image conflicts may masquerade as another type of conflict (such as content conflict), but at the core is a disagreement about one's sense of oneself.

Content Conflicts

Content conflicts are often called "substantive" because they revolve around an issue. Interdependent people fight about myriad topics. Maeve calls her Internet provider to complain about the service, and the service provider tells her there is no evidence to support her complaint. Nanette likes a tree on her property line, but her neighbor Dwayne thinks its roots are responsible for cracking the driveway. Matt hates to bowl, and his best friend, Tom, loves bowling. Ginna wants to spend some savings on a vacation, and her husband, Sean, thinks that would be a waste of money. Penny thinks that the data for her work group's presentation should be rechecked, and the other members of the group think they've been checked sufficiently. Marcus thinks that even though he works part time, he should be respected as a member of the company and allowed a say in company policies; however, the full-time workers believe that the part-time employees shouldn't be involved in those matters. Although all of these examples involve topics of disagreement, some of these content conflicts have undertones of the other types of conflicts within them. As we discuss the subsequent types, we will point out this overlap.

Amy Johnson (2002) observes that content conflicts can be subdivided. Some content conflicts focus on what she terms **public issues,** or issues outside the relationship. Other content conflicts involve **personal issues** and relate more closely to the relationship. For instance, when Stan and Frank disagree about whether Bill Clinton was a great president, they are debating a public issue. When Stan complains that Frank has no time to hang out with him anymore because he is always spending time with his new girlfriend, Miranda, they are tackling a private issue. Not surprisingly, Johnson found that people enjoy arguments about public issues more than conflicts about private issues.

Value Conflicts

Value conflicts can be considered content conflicts in which the content is specifically a question of right and wrong. The neighbors who are arguing about the tree on their property line may be having a values conflict if they are discussing it in terms of ecosystems and environmental protection. When people disagree about war in Iraq, abortion, or capital punishment, they may be engaging in value conflicts because opinions on those topics largely depend on value judgments made by the participants. For example, arguments about capital punishment often hinge on the value placed on human life and the value placed on punishment and retribution.

Relational Conflicts

Relational conflicts focus on issues concerning the relationship between two people. For example, when Marge argues with Percy, telling him that the way he speaks to her makes her feel disrespected, they are engaging in relational conflict. Couples who argue about how much they should tell their in-laws and how much they should keep private also exemplify relational conflict. In a previous example, Ginna and Sean's fight about whether to spend savings on a vacation would be a re-

Table 9.1 | **Types of Conflict**

Image Conflict	
MARILYN:	Mom, why do you still treat me like a child although I am 22 years old?
MOM:	Marilyn, you are always going to be my little girl.
Content Conflict	
FRED:	Jeff, I don't think that New York has the largest population of any state in the United States. I am sure I read that it was California.
JEFF:	I don't think so, Fred. But we can look it up.
Value Conflict	
AMY:	Travis, I can't believe we're so close to getting married, and I am just finding out that you don't want to have kids! To me, that's what marriage is all about.
TRAVIS:	Are you kidding, Amy? I certainly don't believe that marriage is all about having kids. What about love, companionship, and fun? Aren't those the things that marriage is all about?
Relational Conflict	
ANGELA:	Marlee, I know this sounds funny to bring up, but I am feeling kind of left out when you and I are together with Justine. You and I used to be best friends, and now it seems like you don't even want to be around me if you have the chance to hang out with Justine.
MARLEE:	That's not exactly true, Angela. Maybe I have been spending a lot of time with Justine, but that's just because we have the same major and are in a lot of classes together.

REVISITING CASE IN POINT

1. How would you type the conflict Tamara and Jeff had about the missed coffee date? Is it an image, content, value, or relational conflict? Or is it some combination?

2. How does typing this conflict help in managing it?

You can answer these questions online under Student Resources for Chapter 9 at the Understanding Interpersonal Communication website.

lational conflict if it centers on how they make decisions in their relationship. The disagreement would be a values conflict if it underscores a difference in how the two value money.

To read short dialogues that illustrate each of the four types of conflict, see Table 9.1. Figure 9.1 presents a dialogue and picture that show how these conflict types overlap. Even though the types cannot be completely separated, being able to identify what kind of conflict you are having is useful because this knowledge helps you decide how to manage it.

To check out a number of links about conflict in a variety of contexts, use your Understanding Interpersonal Communication CD-ROM to access Interactive Activity 9.1: Conflict in Context. And for information about other causes of conflict, access Interactive Activity 9.2: Causes of Conflict.

Power: Who's Got It, Who Wants It, and How to Deal with It

As you may have noticed in the preceding discussion, our understanding of interpersonal conflict is enriched through insight into another concept: power. **Power** can be defined as the ability to control the behavior of another. In conflict situations, power often influences the outcome as well as the process of the interaction. Some researchers believe that all communication contains a power dimension, even simple conversations used to exchange demographic or superficial information (see, for example, Dillard, 1990; Marwell & Schmitt, 1967, 1990; Miller & Parks, 1982). Whether or not you agree that all communication rests on power differentials, conflict communication utilizes power in a variety of ways. The following sections discuss the modes and sources of power as well as the concept of empowerment.

Modes of Power

Joseph Folger, Marshall Scott Poole, and Randall Stutman (2001) discuss four modes of power that operate in many conflict interactions: direct application, direct and virtual use, indirect application, and hidden use.

Direct application of power in a conflict situation involves using any resources at your disposal to compel the other to comply, regardless of their desires. When Marla spanks her 2-year-old son, Jerry, and sends him to his room, she is using direct application of power. Related to this mode, **direct and virtual use of power** involves communicating the *potential* use of direct application. Folger et al. refer to the use of threats and promises as good illustrations of this mode of power. For example, when Dr. Moore says he will fail Lorna in his Introduction to Communication class unless she rewrites a paper to his satisfaction, he is exercising a threat. When Dr. Seltzer promises the students in his Communication Theory class that they will all receive A's if they complete all the written work on time, he is offering a promise. Threats and promises are two sides of the same coin.

The **indirect application of power** concerns employing power without making its employment explicit. For instance, if Jeff has heard his boss, Colleen, mention

Conflict Dialogue

Andre: "I am so happy George W. Bush won the 2004 election. He is strong where Kerry would have been weak on terrorism. And besides, he's a born-again Christian, so I know he has good values."

Michael: "Wow, Andre, I thought I knew you and now I am blown away that I knew you so little. Bush is a horrible person who supported the death penalty in Texas and got us into an immoral war. That's hardly good values! I am not sure I can be friends with someone who holds your views."

Figure 9.1 | **Overlap in types of conflicts**

that she likes all office memos to be cc'ed to her, and he does that even though it's not an official office policy, Colleen has used indirect application of power. One example of the indirect application of power is seen in relational messages. When people send **relational messages,** they define the relationship (and implicitly state that they have the power to do this). For instance, when Tim tells Sue how much he gave up so they could move to Ohio to be near her parents, he sends a message that in their relationship, Sue is indebted to him. Of course, partners may accept or contest the implicit message. If Sue agrees that Tim has done her an enormous favor at some cost to himself, she accepts his relationship definition and his power. If she argues with him that he really wanted to move, too, or that he didn't give up that much, they will conflict over the relationship definition.

Most of the time we think of power as the ability to force someone else to comply with a decision, but in the case of **hidden use of power** (also called "unobtrusive power"), decisions are suppressed or avoided in the interest of one of the parties. As Folger and his colleagues (2001) observe, "If an issue never even materializes and nothing happens, it seems as though power has never come into play when, in fact, it is responsible for the lack of action" (p. 136). For example, if Sammy doesn't bring up a topic for discussion because he knows his friend, Dale, won't agree with him, Dale is exercising hidden power. And when Maria complies with her mother's wishes for a big, lavish wedding, although she and her fiancé really want a small, more conservative ceremony, Maria succumbs to her mother's hidden power. Maria doesn't even broach the subject; Maria lets her mother be in charge without argument even though she doesn't agree with her plans.

Throughout this discussion, we adopt a relational perspective on power. In other words, we see power, like conflict, as a process that is co-constructed by the relational partners. Thus, although one partner may try to utilize direct application of power or any of the other power modes we have discussed, the power loop is not closed until the other partner responds. For instance, when Marla spanks her son, Jerry and sends him to his room, she checks in on him later to find that Jerry has thrown all his toys on the floor and ripped all the pages out of his books. Thus, the mother's direct application of power is not met with compliance; rather, it encounters resistance in the form of an exercise of direct power on Jerry's part.

See Table 9.2 for a summary of the modes of power.

Table 9.2	Modes of Power
Direct application	
Direct and virtual use	
Indirect application	
Hidden use of power	

Sources of Power

People are able to utilize the modes of power in conflict situations because they draw power from a variety of sources. We identify six sources of power: referent, legitimate, expert or information, persuasive, reward, and coercive (French & Raven, 1968).

Referent power derives from the charisma and attractiveness a person possesses. For instance, Amy has referent power in her sorority if all the other sisters wish to be like her and look up to her. A person who seems to light up the room when they enter it has referent power because everyone wants to be identified with and spend time with that person.

Legitimate power usually is based in the positions people occupy. If Nicole is the president of her company, she has legitimate power over her employees. Parents have legitimate power over their children. Judges, doctors, police officers, teachers, ministers, and so forth all have legitimate power in certain contexts. However, not all employees, children, parishioners, and so forth respect legitimate power. Fur-

We often interact with people who have legitimate power over us, such as parents, teachers, and employers. When we experience conflict with authority figures like these, they are often able to exercise their power to take control of the conflict. However, at times, we may find that we don't respect an authority's power and may choose to create a conflict in an effort to establish a more even balance of power.

ther, depending on their personalities, people differ in the ways in which they occupy positions of power. For example, Jenn is a committee chair who tells the committee, "I don't like to lead groups, so I expect you all to do your work on your own." This leadership style differs from the way Bobbi, a chair of another committee, conducts business; she calls frequent meetings, sets detailed agendas, and assigns tasks to the members. Both chairs have legitimate power, but they enact it quite differently.

Expert or information power refers to the knowledge a person possesses. If Mark is a plumber, when Des needs a plumbing problem solved, he will defer to Mark's expertise. Anyone who knows something that another needs has a source of expert power. Note that the key is the need on the part of another. If Rachel has a large store of knowledge about gorillas but no one needs to know anything about gorillas, she won't develop expert or information power.

Persuasive power comes from being seen as a good, logical communicator who can sway others to a certain point of view. If Mario is known by his brothers and sisters to have persuasive power, he will be the one they ask to talk their parents into letting them go on a ski vacation.

Reward power originates from the ability to reward others. Teachers have reward power over students because they can award them with good grades and write glowing letters of recommendation on their behalf. However, if students are not motivated by grades or do not need letters of recommendation, teachers' reward power diminishes. Rewards may be material (for example, money, possessions) or social (for example, friendship, respect). Bosses have reward power over their employees; they can offer both material rewards such as raises and social rewards such as respect.

Coercive power derives from the ability to punish others and usually accompanies reward power because if you have the ability to reward someone, you probably have the ability to punish that person as well. Teachers can give students poor grades and refuse to write letters of recommendation, or they can write negative ones. Bosses can fire employees or make the workplace inhospitable for them. Table 9.3 provides an overview of the sources of power.

Table 9.3	Sources of Power
Referent	
Legitimate	
Expert or information	
Persuasive	
Reward	
Coercive	

Empowerment

A final consideration concerning the relationship between power and conflict revolves around **empowerment,** or helping to actualize people's power. Stephen Littlejohn and Kathy Domenici (2001) note that some mediators refer to empowerment as "power balancing," or the efforts of a third party to equalize the power distribution so that the participants in the conflict can both listen and be heard. However, Littlejohn and Domenici find the term "power balancing" problematic:

> The problem is that the mediator, who is really an outsider, cannot know what sources of power parties might have available to them. It might look as though a man is out-powering a woman by dominating the conversation, but the woman may have a great deal of power in her silence. It may look as though a well-to-do businessperson has more power than a blue-collar customer, but the customer may have connections and buying power that give him or her a great deal of power. It may look as though a parent has more power than a teen, but anyone who has raised teenagers might disagree. . . . Rather than judge who has the power, we want to empower both parties to do and say what needs to be done and said, to identify the problem in their own terms, to establish what a successful outcome would mean for them, and to create ideas for achieving that outcome. (pp. 78–79)

Whether you call the intricate power dynamics within our relationships power balancing or empowerment, managing conflict necessitates that each party is listened to and really heard.

Conflict Models: Seeing the Big Picture

In this section, we review two models that help us sort us out the complex phenomenon of conflict by diagramming its component parts. Although Virginia Satir's (1972) four-part model and A. C. Filley's (1975) process model are each more than 30 years old, they remain useful, and people still think about interpersonal conflict in the manner suggested by these models.

Satir's Four-Part Model

Virginia Satir conceived of conflict as a circle divided into four sections that represent the critical parts of any conflict (see Figure 9.2): you, me, the context, and the subject. For Satir, *you* refers to one of the participants in the conflict and *me* refers to the other. *Context* comprises the emotional background surrounding the conflict—for example, whether it's the first conflict on this topic, whether the two participants are highly and equally invested in the conflict, whether the topic is ex-

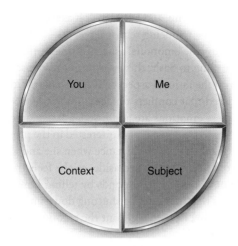

Figure 9.2 | **Satir's four-part conflict model**

tremely important to the relationship between the two parties, and so forth. *Subject* means what the parties are arguing about—for example, whether to move, whether to have children, whether to go to the basketball game or to the movies, whether abortion is wrong, whether the household chores are distributed fairly, and so forth.

Satir argued that effective conflict management requires that each part needs to be considered completely. She maintained that all four parts are equally important and that if each part is not attended to, the conflict will fester. Therefore, her model assumes that the nature of conflict focuses on the interdependence of all these parts; if one segment is ignored, the overall conflict cannot be completely resolved. Satir noted that people generally fear or dislike conflict interaction and, as a result, will try to resolve conflicts as quickly as possible. However, in our haste to conclude conflict interactions, Satir explained, we usually ignore one or more of the four integral segments, resulting in ineffective conflict management. Let's take a look at the results of ignoring or disqualifying each portion of the conflict.

Satir stated that when people disqualify the *me* in a conflict, they are being passive or ignoring their own needs in the situation. According to Satir, this passive response, which cancels out one's own position in a conflict, is called **placating.** For example, when George wants to compete with his coworker, Dina, for a promotion, but instead decides to tell her that he'll defer in her favor, George is placating. Satir's model does not mandate that George has to fight Dina for the promotion; it is possible to opt out of competition with another for various reasons. For example, George might think that Dina is more qualified or might acknowledge that she has more seniority with the company than he does. Or it's possible that George is having problems at home, and he realizes that now isn't the right time to assume a more demanding position. However, if deferring to Dina is George's first response, exercised simply to avoid a conflict, Satir's model suggests that course of action is a mistake because it doesn't pay attention to the full circle of conflict.

When people disqualify the *you* in a conflict, they respond in an aggressive manner without acknowledging the needs of the other person in the conflict. Satir called this **pouncing.** If George tries to undermine Dina's application for the promotion by talking behind her back and spreading gossip about her at work, he is pouncing. Anything that George might do to ignore Dina's side of the conflict and advance his own is considered pouncing, and Satir labels it as ineffective. Again, the full conflict is not reflected in the pouncing response.

The *context* contains the emotional aspects of the conflict. If someone disqualifies the context, according to Satir, this **computing** response ignores the emotional aspects and focuses on the rational aspects. Although Satir didn't advocate irrational responses, she observed that conflicts touch emotions deeply and that they cannot be resolved unless these emotions are addressed. For example, let's say that Dina is upset when she learns that George is also interested in the promotion. She raises her voice, pointing out that in a previous instance when she and George both competed for something at work, she had stepped aside, so she feels that, in fairness, George needs to step aside now. If George responds by telling Dina not to yell and not to feel upset, Satir argues that he would be shutting down an important aspect of their conflict. George and Dina have to confront the emotions involved in their conflict to be able to manage it.

If Dina comes into George's office to discuss her interest in the promotion, and George interrupts her to talk about a different topic, Satir said George would be disqualifying the subject of the conflict. She called this response **distracting** because it involves keeping the parties distracted from the subject of a conflict.

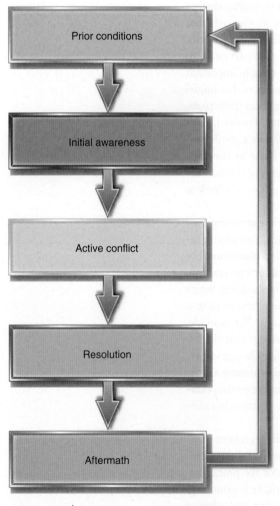

People who laugh, cry, change the subject, run out of the room, and so forth when presented with a conflict engage in distracting responses.

In each case, according to Satir's model, one portion of the conflict is ignored or disqualified. In so doing, the conflict interaction is rushed or skipped altogether. This accomplishes the immediate goal of minimizing the time that two people spend in conflict. However, Satir asserts that, in the long run, none of these responses is capable of doing justice to the conflict because all four of the segments of the conflict circle are equally important, and if one is ignored, the conflict is not managed properly.

Filley's Process Model

Satir's model pictures each of the elements of a conflict as occurring simultaneously within a conflict interaction. In contrast, Filley (1975) models conflict as a process that occurs in the following stages: prior conditions, initial awareness, active conflict, resolution, and aftermath. In this section, we discuss each of these stages in turn. See Figure 9.3 for an illustration of how the stages fit together to form the conflict process.

Prior conditions form the first stage of Filley's conflict process. **Prior conditions,** which are similar to the context in Satir's model, set the stage for conflict and contain the history between the two parties, the areas of disagreement they have discussed in the past, and so forth. For example, when Ryan and Geoff become roommates, they have a history going back to the second grade. Geoff knows that Ryan is messier than he is and that Ryan doesn't care about his physical surroundings nearly as much. They had talked about how they would deal with this difference before moving in together.

The second stage consists of an **initial awareness** of a problem. During this stage, Geoff might remind Ryan of their agreement

Figure 9.3 | **Filley's process conflict model**

© Bonnie Kamin /PhotoEdit.

Satir's four-part model and Filley's process model provide us with valuable information about how we can manage conflict effectively. Although it's not always easy to do during a conflict, practicing effective interpersonal skills, such as really listening to what another person has to say or sensitively addressing another person's emotion, can help us maintain good relationships over a lifetime.

about tidying up the apartment. Ryan could admit that he hasn't been keeping up his end and promise to do better. However, it is possible that during this stage, only one of the roommates might experience frustration. Geoff could become concerned that the apartment is not up to his standards of neatness while Ryan is blissfully unaware that there is a problem brewing.

The next stage is the **active conflict** stage. Geoff tells Ryan how he is feeling, and Ryan responds. Our original definition of conflict comes into play in this stage, when the two engage in interaction around their differences. Conflict experts suggest that the active conflict stage should follow the initial awareness stage rather quickly. Otherwise, Geoff might build up a lot of resentment against Ryan before the two actually talk about the problem.

The active conflict stage may last for a long time, and the next stage—resolution—may or may not be reached. In the **resolution** stage, the parties decide on a way to manage the conflict. Some conflicts recur because the parties don't go through this stage, and some relationships end because the partners are unable to resolve their conflicts. For instance, Ryan and Geoff might decide that they don't want to be roommates any longer because they can't come up with a plan to clean the apartment that satisfies them both. Or they might get sick of arguing about it and ignore the problem for a while until Geoff can't stand the mess anymore, and then the conflict begins again. However, in Filley's model, the ideal is that the parties reach a mutually agreed-upon solution. For example, Ryan and Geoff might decide that Ryan will pay for a cleaning person to come in once a month.

Finally, Filley's model shows that conflicts are never completely over. The results of the resolution stage form the conflict aftermath. The **aftermath** includes the residue of having engaged in the conflict and the feelings that both of the participants have about their interaction. For instance, Geoff and Ryan might feel really proud that they came up with a great idea that pleases them both—Geoff is glad that he gets to live in a clean apartment, and Ryan is relieved that he doesn't have to change lifelong habits. Alternatively, Ryan could feel a little resentful about the agreed-upon solution. Even though he said he would do it, he might feel that it's unfair that he has to pay a monthly fee beyond the rent just to keep Geoff happy.

In addition to the parties' responses to the solution, they both have feelings about the ways they interacted during the conflict. Geoff, for example, might be

REVISITING CASE IN POINT

1. In the conflict between Tamara and Jeff, what is the context?
2. In the conflict between Tamara and Jeff, what is the resolution?

 You can answer these questions online under Student Resources for Chapter 9 at the Understanding Interpersonal Communication website.

congratulating himself on not losing his temper and on confronting Ryan before building up too much resentment. Geoff might also be feeling grateful to Ryan for listening to his point of view and empathizing even though Ryan can't see the point of thoroughly cleaning the apartment. For his part, Ryan might think he did a great job of listening and might feel happy that Geoff explained his position in such a way that it began to make sense to him. It is also possible that both men could feel a bit resentful about the way the conflict interaction unfolded. One or both of them might feel that he got pushed around by the other.

As Figure 9.3 illustrates, the aftermath feeds into the prior conditions for the next conflict between the two. For instance, if Geoff is feeling grateful to Ryan for his behavior during the conflict about cleaning the apartment, that will set the stage for how a later conflict—whether they should pitch in together to buy a big-screen TV—unfolds. Geoff may be inclined to listen more carefully to Ryan's point of view in this conflict because he feels Ryan was so cooperative in their previous conflict. Thus, we see in Filley's model how conflicts affect relationships and even define relational life.

For more on conflict models and the role of negotiation in conflict, read the article "Models of Conflict Management," available through InfoTrac College Edition. Use your Understanding Interpersonal Communication CD-ROM to access InfoTrac College Edition Exercise 9.1: Models of Conflict Management.

Myths about Conflict

Because you now know much about what conflict *is,* in this section we spend some time discussing what it *is not.* As noted previously, conflict is an unavoidable, normal fact of relational life that many people find distasteful and unpleasant. As such, conflict is an important communication behavior that people talk a great deal about. This process generates myths that many people subscribe to, including conflict is always bad, conflict is just miscommunication, all conflict can be resolved through good communication, and it is always best to talk through all conflicts.

Conflict Is Always Bad

One myth states that conflict is completely negative and implies that relational life would be perfection if only the partners could eliminate all conflicts. Research on metaphors for conflict (Buzzanell & Burrell, 1997; Turner & Shuter, 2004) indicates that when people think of comparisons for interpersonal conflict, their choices are overwhelmingly negative (conflict is like war, hell, disease, a natural disaster, and so forth). Yet, as previously discussed, relationships cannot exist without conflict. Further, there are many positives to engaging in conflict with a relational partner.

Researchers have shown that managing conflict with sensitivity leads to evaluations of communication competence (Lakey & Canary, 2002). In addition, research suggests that dealing productively with conflict in marriage promotes physical and mental health (Gottman, 1999). In addition, other researchers have claimed the following benefits for conflict: getting feelings out in the open and increasing knowledge of one another, promoting feelings of confidence in relationships that survive conflicts, promoting genuine human contact, increasing the depth of a relationship, maximizing the chances of making a good decision, and shaking a relationship out of a rut.

As Robin Kowalski (2001) observes when speaking about aversive behaviors in general, "given the inevitability of these negative social behaviors, it is fortunate that they sometimes have positive features and are sometimes even motivated by efforts to establish camaraderie and connections with others" (p. 307). Although all conflict doesn't automatically produce positive outcomes for relationships, it is a myth that conflict is all bad.

To read an interesting article about the different styles people use in communicating about conflict, use your Understanding Interpersonal Communication CD-ROM to access **Interactive Activity 9.3: Conflict Styles.**

Conflict Is Just Miscommunication

This myth suggests that all conflict results from people not clearly communicating their goals and wishes to one another. However, sometimes people communicate clearly to each other and, in fact, they disagree. For instance, if Jim wants to go to Harvard, and his parents tell him they do not want him to go to school so far away from home, Jim and his parents may continue to argue about this topic even though they know exactly what each other's positions are. The problem in this case is not that they haven't been clear; rather, they disagree about whose goal is most important and, possibly, who has the power in their relationship to make such a decision.

All Conflicts Can Be Resolved through Good Communication

This myth tells us that if we master a certain set of skills, we can resolve all conflicts. Although we offer a set of skills later in this chapter, we recognize that some conflicts persist, and partners may have to agree to disagree. For example, no amount of good communication practices will convince Harry to vote Democratic even though his son, Michael, tries to persuade him that the Democrats advocate better policies than the Republicans do. Harry simply states that he has voted Republican his whole life and he is proud to continue to do so.

It Is Always Best to Talk through All Conflicts

This myth represents the commonly held belief that increasing communication solves conflicts. Relational partners often believe that they simply need to communicate more to reach a mutually satisfying solutions to their conflicts. However, many scholars believe that this myth obscures the benefits that sometimes occur

Communication Assessment Test

Argumentativeness Scale

Argumentativeness may be thought of as contributing to the negative aspects of conflict, but research by Dominic Infante and Andrew Rancer (1982) suggests that this is not always the case. They define argumentativeness as a willingness to argue for your point of view on significant issues. Infante and Rancer distinguish between argumentativeness and verbal aggressiveness, a more negative trait, by saying that whereas argumentativeness focuses on ideas, verbal aggressiveness focuses on winning an argument, even if it means verbally attacking the other person.

Directions: This questionnaire contains statements about arguing about controversial issues. Indicate whether a statement describes you according to the following scale:

almost never true = 1   rarely true = 2   occasionally true = 3
often true = 4   almost always true = 5

You can also complete this assessment online under Student Resources for Chapter 9 at the Understanding Interpersonal Communication website.

_____ 1. While in an argument, I worry that the person I am arguing with will form a negative impression of me.

_____ 2. Arguing over controversial issues improves my intelligence.

_____ 3. I enjoy avoiding arguments.

_____ 4. I am energetic and enthusiastic when I argue.

_____ 5. After I finish an argument, I promise myself that I will not get into another.

_____ 6. Arguing with a person creates more problems for me than it solves.

_____ 7. I have a pleasant, good feeling when I win a point in an argument.

_____ 8. When I finish arguing with someone, I feel nervous and upset.

_____ 9. I enjoy a good argument over a controversial issue.

_____ 10. I get an unpleasant feeling when I realize I am about to get into an argument.

_____ 11. I enjoy defending my point of view on an issue.

_____ 12. I am happy when I keep an argument from happening.

_____ 13. I do not like to miss the opportunity to argue a controversial issue.

_____ 14. I prefer being with people who rarely disagree with me.

_____ 15. I consider an argument an exciting intellectual challenge.

_____ 16. I find myself unable to think of effective points during an argument.

_____ 17. I feel refreshed and satisfied after an argument on a controversial issue.

_____ 18. I have the ability to do well in an argument.

_____ 19. I try to avoid getting into arguments.

_____ 20. I feel excitement when I expect that a conversation I am in is leading to an argument.

Scoring

1. Add your scores for questions 2, 4, 7, 9, 11, 13, 15, 17, 18, and 20. These questions represent your willingness to engage in arguments.

2. Add 60 to this total.

3. Add your scores for questions 1, 3, 5, 6, 8, 10, 12, 14, 16, and 19. These questions represent your tendency to avoid arguments. Subtract this total from the total you obtained in the first two steps. This number represents your argumentativeness score.

Use the following guidelines for interpreting your score:

73–100   High argumentativeness
56–72   Moderate argumentativeness
20–55   Low argumentativeness

Remember, moderation is probably the most skillful position. Does the score you received seem to reflect how you operate in discussions of controversial issues? If your score is not in the moderate category, what do you think you can do to compensate for the problems you might face in conflict?

From D. A. Infante and A. S. Rancer, "A conceptualization and measure of argumentativeness," Journal of Personality Assessment 46: 72–80, 1982. Reprinted by permission of Lawrence Erlbaum Associates, Inc.

when people avoid topics rather than talk about them in great detail (see for example, Baxter & Wilmot, 1985; Guerrero & Afifi, 1995; Petronio, 2002). Some arguments are not that important and if you ignore them, they really will go away. On the other hand, talking about them just exaggerates and prolongs the problem. For instance, when Mel broke the rain gauge in their backyard, Tina was angry. However, because she realized that it was just a $3.00 item and that getting into a big discussion about it wouldn't be productive for their relationship, she didn't say anything.

Although we acknowledge that many people subscribe to these four myths about conflict, from our perspective, they name four characteristics that don't accurately describe interpersonal conflict. Remember that not all interpersonal conflict is negative, that it's not always based on misunderstandings, that it's not always resolvable, and that it's not always best to deal with it through more communication.

Factors Influencing Interpersonal Conflict

In this section, we briefly discuss two factors that affect conflict interaction: gender and culture. Although we review them separately, these two variables most often act in concert to affect conflicts. For example, a German American man and a Chinese American woman who work together in a small software company may have a disagreement over how to invest their limited research and development budget. In this case, there are cultural forces and gendered messages interacting to influence their conflict. All conflicts take place between people who are gendered and who come from a specific cultural background. These factors interact and have an impact on conflict interactions.

Gender and Conflict

As we discussed in Chapter 2, when we talk about gender, we are referring to gender socialization. Men and women are not inherently different in their orientations to conflict or in their conflict behaviors; rather, they have been taught a set of responsibilities and norms that affect their conflict interactions. Further, not all men nor all women are socialized to the same degree (Bem, 1993). Thus, we see great variety in how women and men enact gendered social norms.

Because women are taught to be keepers of relational life and men are socialized to pay attention to public life (Sullivan & Turner, 1996), women often want to talk about relationship issues, and men do not. This imbalance may cause conflict within relationships. For example, when Moira tells Jack that she wants to talk about their relationship, Jack may perceive her statement as an indication that their relationship is in trouble and, as a result, try to avoid the problem. Moira may not have intended to imply that she wanted to discuss a specific problem; she just wanted to connect with Jack about the topic of their life together.

Facing *Change*

One suggestion for coping constructively with conflict advocates a cooling-off period, a time out when the participants won't say anything to each other in the heat of anger that they might regret. During this period, the people involved in the conflict shouldn't speak and might even profit from being apart. Later, when their emotions aren't so aroused, they can reconvene to discuss the conflict. How do you think our growing communication technologies might affect this suggestion? Does it make it more difficult to take a time out when you can reach people through beepers, cell phones, e-mail, and the like at any time? Explain your answer.

 Use your Understanding Interpersonal Communication CD-ROM to watch the CNN video clip "Internet Watchdogs," which highlights chat room hosts who monitor online conversations to avert potential conflict. Click on the "CNN & Change" icon in the menu at left, then click on "Video Menu" in the menu bar at the top of the screen. Select "Internet Watchdogs" to watch the video (it takes a minute for the video to load). As you watch the video, think about the pros and cons of trying to avert conflict. You can respond to this and other analysis questions by clicking on "Analysis" in the menu bar at the top of the screen. When you've answered all the questions, click on "Done" to compare your answers to those provided by the authors.

Some research suggests that women are more collaborative and men are more competitive in conflict interactions. However, recent studies call this generalization into question. A relatively recent study examining college students found that women were more likely than men to report that they used both cooperative and competitive conflict strategies (Rudawsky, Lundgren, & Grasha, 1999). Another study (Messman & Mikesell, 2000) found that women and men in romantic relationships did not differ in their use of competition as a conflict strategy.

Robert Shuter and Lynn Turner (1997) found that European American women as a group were evaluated by African American women and by themselves as highly conflict avoidant. However, when the researchers asked individual women from both groups to talk about their own approaches to conflict, the responses did not differ significantly. Shuter and Turner concluded that people are affected by stereotypes when asked to talk about a group but that they see themselves as not necessarily representative of the group to which they belong.

Some evidence does point to more enduring differences between women and men in conflict. For instance, Levenson and Gottman (1985) showed that men and women react differently to the stress of relational conflict. Whereas women seemed to be able to tolerate high levels of the physiological arousal found in conflict with a partner, men were more bothered by this arousal and sought to avoid it. In a more recent test of that conclusion, Ann Buysse and her colleagues in Belgium (Buysse,

De Clercq, Verhofstadt, Heene, Roeyers, & Van Oost, 2000) found that men desired to avoid marital conflict more than women.

For more about gender and conflict, check out the study "Gender-Related Effects in Emotional Responding to Resolved and Unresolved Interpersonal Conflict," available through InfoTrac College Edition. Use your Understanding Interpersonal Communication CD-ROM to access **InfoTrac College Edition Exercise 9.2: Gender and Conflict.**

Culture and Conflict

As we have discussed many times throughout this text, we live in a world of increasing diversity. In the twenty-first century,

> Direct contact with culturally different people in our neighborhoods, schools, and workplaces is an inescapable part of life. With immigrants and minority group members representing nearly 30% of the present workforce in the United States, an understanding of competent conflict management is especially critical in today's society.
> (Ting-Toomey & Oetzel, 2001, pp. 1-2)

Differing cultural practices and norms may put us in conflict with one another. Even though all humans wish to be respected and shown approval, the ways in which respect and approval are expressed often differ from culture to culture.

Even the meaning of the word *conflict* may differ across cultures. Stella Ting-Toomey and John Oetzel (2001) observe that for the French the term means warlike opposition. The negative connotations of conflict are extremely strong for the French; consequently, although the French like to debate, they do not enjoy engaging in conflict. Further, for the Chinese, the meaning of the word *conflict* involves intense struggle and fighting. Not surprisingly, the Chinese do not like conflict, which they consider disruptive to the harmoniousness of interpersonal relationships. Although those in the United States may not enjoy conflict either, they define the word more broadly than the French or the Chinese do, allowing for more possible responses to the interaction itself. The Spanish word for conflict doesn't have so many negative connotations, and many Hispanic cultures consider conflict an interesting exercise, allowing for dramatic flair that is enjoyable.

Culture affects our conduct of interpersonal conflict in myriad ways. A person whose primary orientation is toward individualism might conflict with a

Ethics & Choice

When Daryl Mills left home to attend Metro College, she felt uncertain and afraid. Although everyone probably has some trepidation about leaving home and starting college, Daryl's fears were compounded by the fact that she had pink hair, two nose rings (as well as various other piercings), and several large tattoos. She hoped people at college would be more accepting of her than her classmates at Fairhurst High School had been. A lot of people in high school had whispered behind her back, and she could still feel the sting of hearing "freak" every time she passed by a group of kids.

She was hoping that there would be people like her at Metro, but after a few weeks there, Daryl was feeling nostalgic for high school. Metro College was five times as bad as Fairhurst High had been. At Fairhurst kids had whispered about her, but here they yelled right in her face. Daryl actually feared for her safety because the abuse was so strong, and the threat of violence was clear. The teachers turned away when they saw the students menacing her, and Daryl felt she had nowhere to go for help. Finally, she decided to call home and talk to her mother about the problem.

Daryl told her mother there was no way she could continue at Metro College—she was too scared. Just walking around campus put her in a panic, and she always had to be in "survival mode." Daryl's mother was sympathetic, but she counseled Daryl that she had to learn to get along with people who were more conservative in their dress and looks. Her mother told her, "You have to be tough and be able to withstand other people's disapproval if you choose to be different from the mainstream."

What do you see as the ethical implications of this story? What ethical responsibilities did Daryl, her mother, the students, teachers, and administrators at Metro College have? How is power an ethical issue in this story? What do you think Daryl should do? In answering this question, what ethical system of communication informs your decision (categorical imperative, utilitarianism, ethic of care, golden mean, significant choice)?

Use your Understanding Interpersonal Communication CD-ROM to access an interactive version of this scenario on the Understanding Interpersonal Communication website. Look under Student Resources for Chapter 9 and click on the "Ethics & Choice" menu at left. The interactive version of this scenario allows you to choose an appropriate response to this dilemma and then see what consequences your choice brings about. You can also compare your answers to the questions at the end of the scenario to those provided by the authors and, if requested, email your response to your instructor.

person whose primary orientation is toward collectivism because of their different values. An individualistic orientation leads to a concern with one's own image (self-face), whereas a collectivistic orientation leads to a concern for the other person's image (other-face). The individualist wishes to resolve a conflict so that the solution is equitable or fair. The collectivist wishes to resolve a conflict so that the solution benefits the community. The two people will have opposing communication behaviors (for example, competition vs. avoidance) during conflict, probably leading to an escalation of conflict and misunderstanding.

To read an article about a study that compared the emotional responses of European American and Chinese American dating couples involved in interpersonal conflict, check out the study "Cultural Influences on Emotional Responding," available through InfoTrac College Edition. Use your Understanding Interpersonal Communication CD-ROM to access **InfoTrac College Edition Exercise 9.3: Culture and Conflict.**

Communication Patterns in Conflict

Relational partners often notice that their communication behaviors form repeating patterns (Turk & Monahan, 1999). Although these patterns are sometimes negative and the participants wish to break out of them, they generally find it difficult to do so. Other times, the patterns are more productive. In this section, we review three negative and one positive conflict pattern.

Symmetrical Escalation

Symmetrical escalation exists when each partner chooses to increase the intensity of the conflict. When Mike yells at Sally and she yells back at him, they begin the symmetrical escalation pattern. If Mike then advances on Sally with a menacing look, she might slap his face. Each partner matches the other's escalating fight behaviors. Sometimes this pattern is called "fight-fight" (Knapp & Vangelisti, 2005). Obviously, this pattern cannot go on indefinitely, or it would end in the destruction of the two partners. Because the amount of escalation that can exist is limited, this pattern is a futile one for communicators.

Symmetrical Withdrawal

Symmetrical withdrawal means that when conflict occurs, neither partner is willing to confront the other. Thus, one person's move away is reciprocated by the other's move away. For example, if Jolene stops speaking to Marianne because she feels she did all the work for their joint presentation in Organizational Communication, and Marianne responds in kind, they both withdraw from their relationship. This pattern, like symmetrical escalation, spells the end of the relationship if it's carried to its logical conclusion. If both partners move away from each other when conflict happens, they will soon be so far apart that they will have difficulty reuniting.

Pursuit-Withdrawal/Withdrawal-Pursuit

These patterns, unlike the previous two, are asymmetrical. This means that the behavior of one partner is complemented by the other's behavior rather than one partner mirroring the behavior of another. In the **pursuit-withdrawal** pattern,

The pursuit–withdrawal and withdrawal–pursuit patterns are quite common, yet they are extremely unsatisfying for both participants in conflict—it can be maddening when one person wants to pursue a conflict and the other wants only to flee. Have you ever engaged in either of these patterns? If so, what was the outcome of the conflict, and did you feel good about it? If not, what could you have done to more effectively manage the conflict?

when one partner presses for a discussion about a conflictual topic, the other partner withdraws. For example, Pam tells her son, Nicky, that they have to talk about his staying out so late on school nights, and Nicky disappears into his room and shuts the door. **Withdrawal-pursuit** is just the opposite. In this pattern, a partner's withdrawal prompts the other's pursuit. For example, when Anthony absents himself in the attic to work on a project and Sissy runs up to the attic several times to try to get him to discuss buying a new car, they experience this pattern.

These patterns are extremely unsatisfying to the participants; they have the quality of a dog chasing its tail. Gregory Bateson (1972) referred to these types of conflicts as *schismogenesis:* both partners do what they wish the other would do for them, and both are rebuffed. Sissy wants Anthony to come talk to her about their conflict, so she pursues him. Anthony wants to avoid talking about it, so he withdraws. Anthony's withdrawal spurs Sissy to advance more, which in turn causes Anthony to withdraw further. Caughlin and Vangelisti (2000) noted that even though these patterns are so unsatisfying and are related to discord within relationships, they are extremely common in conflict behavior. The researchers suggest that personality characteristics such as extroversion and introversion might be related to the use of this pattern; in general, the extroverts pursue, and the introverts withdraw.

Symmetrical Negotiation

Symmetrical negotiation is the one positive pattern we discuss. In this pattern, each partner mirrors the other's negotiating behaviors. They listen to each other and reflect back what they have heard. They offer suggestions for dealing with the

© Jason Harris

Your*Turn*

In your journal, note the times you engage in interpersonal conflict during a week. Record the following information about your conflicts:

- The persons involved
- The relationships between/ among the persons involved
- The context surrounding the conflict
- The topic of the conflict
- A rating of how important that conflict was to you (not very important = 1 to very important = 7)
- A brief description of what was said during the conflict
- A rating of how satisfied you were with the conflict (not at all satisfied = 1 to very satisfied = 7)
- A brief explanation of how this conflict relates to the material in this chapter

If you'd like, you can use your student workbook to complete this activity.

conflict and are willing to talk as much or as little as necessary to come to a mutually satisfying resolution of the conflict.

You need to recognize that people in relationships don't use only one of these patterns exclusively to communicate. Even satisfied couples may use a negative pattern, but they are likely to break out of it and get back to discussing the problem in a more positive manner fairly quickly, using techniques we discuss in the following section.

Choices for Conflict Management: Working It Out

To manage conflict, you need to keep in mind several strategies. Remember that just because you have conflict in your interpersonal relationships does not mean that those relationships are destined to fail. Consider the following strategies for conflict management in your conversations with others.

Lighten Up and Reframe

Lightening up refers to your ability to stay cool-headed when others get "hot." The techniques which help you to do this include staying in the present and acknowledging that you have heard what your relational partner just said. Maintain eye contact and nod to show that you heard their contribution. You can say, "I understand you have a concern," or you can reframe by changing something that has a negative connotation to something with a more positive connotation. This is similar to what we discussed in Chapter 8 about dealing with dialectic tensions. (See the Skill Spotlight for more specifics on reframing.) Finally, lightening up might involve your asking permission to state your views: "May I tell you my perspective?" Keep your nonverbal communication genuine—avoid sarcasm.

Presume Good Will and Express Good Will

Go into each conflict interaction believing that you and your partner both want to come to a constructive resolution. Build rapport by focusing on the areas where you do agree. Reach out to your partner and expect that your partner will do the same for you. While you are engaging in conflict, tell your partner the things about him or her that you respect. Keep it real, but mix in praise with your complaints.

Ask Questions

Focus on the other. After you both have had a chance to speak, ask your partner if he or she has anything further to add. Reflect back what you have heard stated and ask if you got it correctly. Ask: "What would make this situation better?" "What would you like to see happen now?" "How can I understand your position better?" "What can you tell me that I seem to be misunderstanding?"

Listen

We detailed the role of listening in Chapter 5 and again highlight its importance here. A conflict is difficult to manage unless we spend time listening to the other. Remember to practice all of the behaviors associated with effective listening,

Skill *Spotlight*

Reframing Statements

Stephen Littlejohn and Kathy Domenici (2001) are mediators. They write about how they help people in conflict by acting as third-party interveners in the conflict. Mediators help change the pattern of communication between people "to alter their interaction in some way, and to open an opportunity for new ways of thinking about the situation in which they are embroiled" (p. 7). Reframing is one of the tools mediators use to accomplish this goal. Sometimes the participants in a conflict can act as their own mediators and engage in reframing themselves.

We can practice the skill of reframing by understanding the variety of ways to enact it.

1. We can reframe from negative to positive. In conflict, people often voice complaints ("I can't stand how loudly you blare your music on the CD player!"). Complaints are, by definition, negative statements. To reframe the parenthetic statement to a positive statement, we could say, "I would like more peace and quiet in the house."

2. We can reframe from the past to the future. Complaints often focus on past behaviors ("You didn't show up when you said you would last night"). To reframe, we could say "If you always meet me when you say you're going to in the future, we won't have trouble like this."

3. We can reframe from hostile statements to ones that are positive or at least neutral. Conflict situations are usually highly emotional, and communicators often make comments that reflect strong negative emotions ("You are a liar, and I can't stand liars—I won't work with sneaky, lying good-for-nothings!"). To reframe, we could say, "I feel I wasn't told the truth, and I want to work in an environment where honesty is valued."

4. We can reframe from individual interests to community interests. In conflicts, we often speak about what we want and need individually ("I can't stand all this prying into my affairs. I need some privacy in this family!"). Reframing to say, "I think our family might get along better if everyone had a bit more privacy" may be helpful.

5. We can reframe from complaint to request. Conflicts often become bogged down by repeated complaints ("You haven't been home for dinner in two weeks! You don't care about me—you're not around!"). To reframe we could say, "I would really like to have more time for us to be together. Could you make it home for dinner tonight so we could have a pleasant evening with one another?"

Skills at Work Reframing can make the difference between enjoying the workplace and dreading going to work. For instance, if Raphael's boss asks him to rewrite a few sections of a report that Raphael had thought was finished, Raphael has many options. He could complain to his coworkers about how unreasonable the boss is; he could redo the work while privately steaming; he could refuse to work on the report again, telling the boss it didn't need further revision; or he could reframe by deciding to look at the boss's request as an opportunity to really check that he'd done the best work he could on the report. Raphael could comment to his boss that he thought the report was complete, but that he was happy to take another look at it, because it's always important to double-check. Can you identify other instances where reframing might be used in the workplace?

including looking at the other person, focusing on the words, and being prepared to allow the full story to unfold. In conflict situations, listening to another person is more than just hearing the words spoken; it's a way to show the other that the conflict is important to resolve and that the relationship is valuable in your life.

Practice Cultural Sensitivity

Be mindful and tune into your own culture's norms and assumptions first before evaluating others (Ting-Toomey & Oetzel, 2001). Slow down your judgments of others; suspend your evaluations until you have had a chance to engage in an internal dialogue. Ask yourself questions such as: Am I respectful of the different cultural background of the other person? Am I using my own cultural lens to understand what is being said? What types of strategies am I using to make sure that I don't inadvertently evaluate the person rather than the message? These and many other questions should be considered as you remember the cultural backgrounds of others.

To practice techniques that can help you deal with conflict effectively, use your Understanding Interpersonal Communication CD-ROM to access **Interactive Activity 9.4: Techniques for Resolving Conflict.** To read a couple of articles that provides tips for managing conflict in relationships and in groups, check out "Relationships: How to Manage Conflict" and "Conflict Resolution—A Key Ingredient in Successful Teams," both available through InfoTrac College Edition. Use your Understanding Interpersonal Communication CD-ROM to access **InfoTrac College Edition Exercise 9.4: Managing Conflict in Relationships** and **Exercise 9.5: Conflict in Groups.**

CHOICES *for Conflict Management*	
■ Lighten up and reframe.	■ Ask questions.
■ Presume good will and express good will.	■ Listen.
	■ Practice cultural sensitivity.

Summary

Interpersonal conflict is a pervasive fact of relational life. Conflicts are interactions about important differences between interdependent people. These interactions can focus on image, content, values, and/or relational questions. Two factors that often influence conflict are gender and culture. Although conflict is often viewed as solely negative, conflict can have benefits, such as helping us clarify a relationship, its goals, and its values.

Power often influences the outcome as well as the process of the interaction. The four modes of power are direct application, direct and virtual use, indirect application, and hidden use. The six sources of power are referent, legitimate, expert or information, persuasive, reward, and coercive.

We can conceptualize conflict by using Satir's (1972) model, which has four basic, interdependent parts: you, me, context, and subject. Ignoring even one of these components results in ineffective conflict management. Another approach that is helpful in thinking about conflict is Filley's (1975) model, which explains conflict as a process with five stages (prior conditions, initial awareness, active conflict, resolution, and aftermath). Conflicts sometimes cause the relationship to rupture before the final stages are reached.

Common myths that don't accurately describe interpersonal conflict are that conflict is always negative, based on misunderstandings, resolvable, and best dealt with through more communication. During conflicts, communication partners often repeat patterns of behavior, including symmetrical escalation, symmetrical withdrawal, withdrawal-pursuit or pursuit-withdrawal, and symmetrical negotiation. The only one of these patterns that is positive is symmetrical negotiation, in which each partner mirrors the other's negotiating behaviors.

To manage your conflicts, use the following strategies: lighten up and reframe, presume and express good will, ask questions, listen, and practice cultural sensitivity. Although no one can avoid conflict, these techniques should improve your satisfaction in conflict encounters. Effectively managed conflict will help you acquire necessary tools for satisfaction in your interpersonal interactions.

Understanding Interpersonal Communication Online

Now that you've read Chapter 9, use your Understanding Interpersonal Communication CD-ROM for quick access to the electronic study resources that accompany this text. Your CD-ROM gives you access to the video of Tamara and Jeff on pages 247–248, the Communication Assessment Test on page 264, the CNN video clip "Internet Watchdogs" on page 265, the Ethics & Choice interactive activity on page 267, InfoTrac College Edition, and the Understanding Interpersonal Communication website. When you get to the Understanding Interpersonal Communication home page, click on "Student Book Companion Site" in the Resource box at right to access the online study aids for this chapter, including a digital glossary, review quizzes, and the chapter activities.

Terms for Review

active conflict 261
aftermath 261
coercive power 258
computing 260
content conflicts 253
direct and virtual use of
   power 255
direct application of
   power 255
distracting 260
empowerment 258
expert or information
   power 257
hidden use of power 256

image conflicts 252
indirect application of
   power 255
initial awareness 260
interaction 250
interdependence 251
interpersonal conflict 250
legitimate power 256
personal issues 254
persuasive power 257
placating 259
pouncing 259
power 255

prior conditions 260
public issues 254
pursuit-withdrawal 268
referent power 256
relational conflicts 254
relational messages 256
resolution 261
reward power 257
symmetrical escalation 268
symmetrical negotiation 269
symmetrical withdrawal 268
value conflicts 254
withdrawal-pursuit 269

Questions for Understanding

Comprehension Focus

1. Define interpersonal conflict. Discuss each of the component parts of the definition.
2. List and describe the four types of conflict.
3. List the six sources of interpersonal power and define each briefly.
4. Describe Satir's model of conflict. What underlying assumption about conflict does the model reveal?
5. Describe Filley's model of conflict. What underlying assumption about conflict does the model reveal?

Application Focus

1. **CASE IN POINT**
   Is gender an issue in the case of Tamara and Jeff? If yes, explain how. If not, what other factors might be influencing their conflict? What skills might be useful in managing their conflict more productively? Rewrite the scenario so that both Jeff and Tamara can be more satisfied with their interaction.

2. Think about your general beliefs about conflict. Does your response reflect a belief in one or more of the myths we described? What factors form your concept of conflict?
3. Explain the relationship between power and conflict. Is it possible to have power differences without conflict? Is it possible to have conflict when there are no critical power differences? How do cultural differences affect your answers?
4. What does it mean to you to take a communication perspective on conflict? Do you agree that although you may typically respond to conflict in a certain way, your behavior is really most influenced by the interaction? Explain with examples.
5. Remember an instance when you think you took a productive approach to an interpersonal conflict. Map the productivity of your conflict.

Interactive Activities and InfoTrac College Edition Exercises

Complete the Interactive Activities and InfoTrac College Edition Exercises for Chapter 9 online at the Understanding Interpersonal Communication website. Select the chapter resources for Chapter 9, then click on "Activities" or "InfoTrac College Edition." If requested, you can submit your answers to your instructor.

Interactive Activities

InfoTrac College Edition Exercises

THOMSON
WADSWORTH

Understanding Interpersonal
Communication
CD-ROM

Introduction   Menu   Preview   Analysis

- Welcome
- Case In Point
  Scenarios
- CNN & Change
- Website
- InfoTrac
- Help

Case In Point Scenarios
Tamara (Chapter 9)

1. According to Satir's model, what aspect of the conflict does Tamara need to focus on to be more effective?

2. How do you suppose the aftermath of this conflict will affect future conflicts between Tamara and Jeff?

Choose whether you want to e-mail to your instructor your above-recorded answers.

○ Don't e-mail my answers.
● E-mail my answers.

Student's Name:

Student's E-mail:

Instructor's Name:

Instructor's E-mail:

Done

10

Communicating in Close Relationships

CASE IN POINT: RANDY TANAKA AND HOPE REYNOLDS

Randy surveyed his work in Hope's kitchen and was pleased with what he saw. He thought Hope would like the job he had done, too. He smiled as he thought about how nervous he had been the first day he had come to work for her. He had just started his own construction company. Hope had seemed like a demanding woman, and he was afraid he wouldn't be able to meet her high expectations. He needn't have worried—the two of them hit it off right away. After he'd been working at her house for a couple of weeks, they were more like friends than worker and customer.

Randy remembered the first time she had offered him coffee, and they sat at the breakfast table and talked. He had found himself telling her about his divorce from Laura, his new marriage to Beth, and his problems getting along with Beth's oldest son. Hope understood the complexities of stepfamilies—her husband had been married before, and they shared custody of his three children from his previous marriage. Randy and Hope spent almost an hour chatting about the challenges and joys of stepparenting. Every day after that, when Randy came to work, Hope had the coffee on, and they spent a little time talking. Hope was such a great listener.

First, Randy had created some built-ins for the living room, and then Hope had found other jobs for him to do. Hope's husband traveled a great deal and just didn't have time to do much around the house, so Hope found many chores for Randy. Her husband, Ned, even joked

Use your Understanding Interpersonal Communication CD-ROM to watch a video clip of Hope and Randy. Click on the "In Action" icon in the menu at left, then click on "Conversation Menu" in the menu bar at the top of the screen. Select "Hope" to watch the video (it takes a minute for the video to load). As you watch the video, think about the fact that Hope and Randy would like to continue their friendship. How could they best communicate this to each other? You can respond to this and other analysis questions by clicking on "Analysis" in the menu bar at the top of the screen. When you've answered all the questions, click on "Done" to compare your answers to those provided by the authors.

about Randy being his biggest rival for Hope's affections. It was all in good fun; Randy and Hope shared a lot and enjoyed talking with each other, but both were devoted to their marriages. Finally, Randy had tackled a kitchen remodel. Randy was excited about showing the kitchen to her, and her reaction did not disappoint him—Hope was delighted with the results of his labor. Now, Randy had come to the end of the work. Hope's house was beautiful.

They looked at each other and smiled. Both were so happy, yet they both privately wondered if the end of the job would mean the end of the great friendship they had forged over months of coffee, conversation, and shared goals. They both certainly hoped their relationship wouldn't end because they had become such important friends to one another. ■

Relationships give importance and meaning to people's lives. Randy and Hope cherish the friendship they shared over the months of remodeling. They want to continue being friends even though the job is over. We are all social beings, and we need relationships to satisfy our desires for connection and community. Abraham Maslow's (1968) famous hierarchy of needs (see Figure 10.1) is an illustration of how people's needs are ranked in importance. Maslow believed that people are basically good and unselfish but need to satisfy certain lower-level needs before they can demonstrate their goodness. Maslow's model places our social needs on the third level, just after physical and safety needs. Thus, Maslow tells us that after we have satisfied our hunger and thirst, and we feel safe, the next thing we strive for is establishing relationships with others. The anthropologist Walter Goldschmidt (1990) calls satisfying social needs "the human career."

A 1998 Gallup survey showed that 83 percent of people between the ages of 18 and 34 rated a close-knit family as their highest priority, and 64 percent of all the adults surveyed said that "relationships with loved ones are always on their minds" (cited in Harvey & Weber, 2002, p. 4). The phenomenal growth of websites like Match.com, Yahoo personals, and Matchmaker.com point to people's need for connections with others. For example, even though its parent company, Ticketmaster, lost $46 million in the fourth quarter of 2001, Match.com earned $7.6 million during that same period. In addition, Match.com had 3.8 million monthly visitors in 2002 and more than 382,000 subscribers (Tedeschi, 2002). We discuss the relationship of technology and interpersonal communication in more detail in Chapter 11.

Some people assert that friendships and close relationships can even improve some of society's social problems. For example, when talking about the problems of segregation and poor race relations in Milwaukee, Wisconsin, Robert Shuter (personal communication, Oct. 15, 2001) said the question can boil down to who your friends are and whom you invite over for dinner. Shuter comments that such social contacts can increase trust and understanding, improving race relations.

Brandeis University in Waltham, Massachusetts, implemented an unusual scholarship program grounded in the same belief. The program encourages young Jews and Palestinians to create friendships. In a *New York Times* article, Claire Hoffman (2003) observes that Maisa Khshaibon, a Palestinian, and Marina Pevzner, an Israeli Jew, became best friends through this program. She notes that they and the other students in the program "say they are convinced that peace must begin from friendships like their own, and from the recognition that their futures are intertwined" (p. A22). Ms. Pevzner noted that her family in Israel had become more mil-

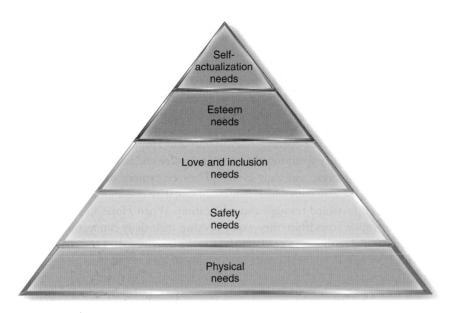

Figure 10.1 | **Maslow's hierarchy of needs**

itant as the fighting had escalated, yet they were still able to welcome Ms. Khshai-bon warmly when Ms. Pevzner brought her home for a visit. Small seeds of change such as these are what the program's founder, Brandeis's president, Jehuda P. Rein-harz, says he had hoped the program would achieve.

As discussed in Chapter 1, another benefit of close relationships is that they can improve health. A growing body of research shows this link. In one study (Berk-man, Leo-Summers, & Horowitz, 1992), chances for survival after a heart attack were more than twice as high when the patient was emotionally supported by two or more people. Marjorie Getz (2002) found that significant improvements in gross and fine motor skills in elderly arthritic women were correlated with an increase in social activities and the strengthening of their social ties. And after surveying a number of studies examining the effect of close relationships on mental health, Duncan Cramer (1998) concluded that having any type of close relationship—friendship, marriage, church contacts, and so forth—increased one's mental and emotional health. In sum, relationships have a critical impact on our lives.

However, the presence of other people in our lives is not solely responsible for our health and happiness; the *quality* of our relationships plays a crucial role. James Coyne and his colleagues (2001) found that a good marriage can give people a rea-son to stay alive after a heart attack. Coyne et al.'s research showed that both men and women in good marriages recovered better from congestive heart failure than those in bad marriages did. This effect was even stronger for women than for men. Coyne and his colleagues visited homes of couples in which one partner had heart disease and videotaped the couples' discussions. They then classified the tapes based on the negativity of the interactions. Heart patients whose conversations with their partners were more negative were 1.8 times as likely to die within four years as those whose conversations were less negative. For more about how close relationships can affect health and recovery, read the article "Shorter Stays for Patients Treated by Hospitalists," available through InfoTrac College Edition. Use your Understanding

Interpersonal Communication CD-ROM to access **InfoTrac College Edition Exercise 10.1: Relationships and Recovery.**

Clearly, communication is central to relationships. As Kathryn Dindia (2003) observes, "to maintain a relationship, partners must communicate with one another. Conversely, as long as people communicate, they have a relationship" (p. 1). Relationships are constructed through communication, and our judgments about our interactions shape both the consequences of our relationships and our overall satisfaction with them. In our opening story, Randy and Hope developed their friendship over the time they spent together drinking coffee and talking about home improvements, their lives, and daily events. Their enjoyment of their relationship stemmed from the ease with which they could talk with one another. Similarly, relationships are sustained through communication. When Hope and Randy think about their future friendship, they worry because their daily connection will soon end. They fear that they won't talk much after the job is finished and that, without talk, their friendship will be jeopardized. To take an online quiz that may help you better understand the nature of your own communication in your relationships, use your Understanding Interpersonal Communication CD-ROM to access **Interactive Activity 10.1: Relationship Communication Quiz.**

Healthy relationships play a crucial role in our lives, communities, and societies. The nature of our close relationships and our communication within them influence how we see the world and interact with others. What role do your own close relationships play in your life? How do you think they benefit you, your community, and your society?

Communication Assessment Test

Relational Communication Scale

This test, adapted from work done by Judee Burgoon and Jerry Hale (1987), is meant to measure the eight themes that characterize communication in interpersonal relationships, which the researchers identified as the following:

- Immediacy (being involved in the conversation)
- Depth (caring what the other thinks)
- Trust (expressing that trust is desirable)
- Composure (acting in a calm manner)
- Formality (making the interaction formal)
- Dominance (talking more and deciding the topics discussed)
- Equality (treating the other person as an equal)
- Orientation (expressing a social or task orientation in the conversation).

Use the Relational Communication Scale (RCS) to determine how you and a selected partner rate in terms of each of these themes.

Directions: Think of a recent conversation you have had with a person who is in a close relationship with you. That person is the "they" in each item on the RCS. Focusing on this specific conversation, answer the following questions using the scale below. For example, if you strongly agree that the statement describes your impression of the conversation, rate it a 5; if you strongly disagree, rate it a 1; and so forth. Answer all the questions.

strongly disagree = 1   disagree = 2   neutral or unsure = 3

agree = 4   strongly agree = 5

You can also complete this assessment online under Student Resources for Chapter 10 at the Understanding Interpersonal Communication website.

_____ 1. They were intensely involved in the conversation.

_____ 2. They wanted to stick to the main purpose of the interaction.

_____ 3. They made me feel similar to them.

_____ 4. They attempted to persuade me.

_____ 5. They considered us equals.

_____ 6. They were sincere.

_____ 7. They felt very tense talking to me.

_____ 8. They made the interaction very formal.

_____ 9. They did not want a deeper relationship between us.

_____ 10. They wanted to cooperate with me.

_____ 11. They were more interested in social conversation than the task at hand.

_____ 12. They communicated coldness.

_____ 13. They acted like we were good friends.

_____ 14. They seemed to care that I liked them.

_____ 15. They were willing to listen to me.

_____ 16. They seemed nervous in my presence.

_____ 17. They wanted the conversation to be informal.

_____ 18. They had the upper hand in the conversation.

_____ 19. They were very work-oriented.

_____ 20. They acted bored by our conversation.

_____ 21. They tried to move the conversation to a deeper level.

_____ 22. They wanted me to trust them.

_____ 23. They were comfortable interacting with me.

_____ 24. They didn't attempt to influence me.

_____ 25. They were honest in communicating with me.

_____ 26. They seemed very relaxed talking with me.

_____ 27. They tried to control the conversation.

(continued)

Communication Assessment Test (*continued*)

Scoring

Add all the numbers you gave as answers. However, for items 7, 9, 11, 12, 16, 17, 20, and 24, reverse your numbers; change 5 to 1, 4 to 2, 3 stays the same, 2 to 4, and 1 to 5. For example, if you gave yourself a 5 on item 7, add it in your total as a 1; if you gave yourself a 2, add it in your total as a 4. The higher your score, the more you were using all these themes of communication to structure your relationship in the conversation with the person you were thinking about.

Specific questions of the RCS relate to each theme. You can add your scores on each theme individually, as shown below (again using your reverse scores for items 7, 9, 11, 12, 16, 17, 20, and 24). Comparing your scores in each area will tell you which themes were most prevalent in the conversation.

- Immediacy (being involved in the conversation): 1, 9, 12, 20
- Depth (caring what the other thinks): 2, 13, 14, 21
- Trust (expressing that trust is desirable): 6, 15, 22, 25
- Composure (acting in a calm manner): 7, 16, 23, 26
- Formality (making the interaction formal): 2, 8, 17
- Dominance (talking more and deciding the topics discussed): 4, 18, 24, 27
- Equality (treating the other person as an equal): 5, 10
- Orientation (expressing a social or task orientation in the conversation): 2, 11, 19

Adapted from Burgoon & Hale, 1987.

The type of relationship people have is reflected in and created by talk. For instance, Hope wouldn't talk to Randy in exactly the same way that she speaks to her husband, Ned. She wouldn't be as familiar with Randy, she wouldn't touch on certain topics, and she would probably be more polite and more careful of Randy's feelings. Research supports the notion that intimate partners talk to each other with less consideration than they accord less intimate friends and acquaintances (Emmers-Sommer, 2003). Think about your most recent conversations with the people you feel closest to and interactions you've had with less intimate friends. What were some of the communicative differences that marked these conversations?

We have talked so far about the importance and benefits of close relationships, as well as the way they are entwined with communication behavior. Throughout this introduction, we have spoken as though everyone has the same understanding of what constitutes a close relationship. Although we do have an intuitive definition for close relationships because they are such an important and ubiquitous part of our lives, we need to establish a more specific and coherent definition so we can make sure we're all on the same page.

Understanding Close Relationships: What Do We Mean, Anyway?

As we discuss the definition of close relationships in this section, think about the following relationship elements:

- Close relationships are ongoing, with a past, present, and future.
- Close relationships are characterized by:
  - The partners' psychological and emotional concerns; their feelings of affection and conscious knowledge of one another

- The cultural/social expectations and demands on the partners
- The partners' communication practices that negotiate between their private and public contexts

Some people suggest that close relationships consist of specific characteristics. For example, Robert Hinde (1995) defined close relationships in terms of ten factors:

- **The content of the interactions:** What people talk about and do together. Hinde might say that Robert and Nelson have a close relationship if they hang out together, engage in conversations that are beyond the superficial, and discuss a variety of topics.
- **The diversity of interactions:** The number of different experiences people have together. Melanie and Lorraine might be considered close if they go to the movies together, play together on the basketball team, study together, and spend time talking about their futures and their jobs with one another.
- **The qualities of the interactions:** Do the partners shout, talk lovingly, and so forth? If Geoff and Blaine speak in a friendly fashion more often than they yell at one another, Hinde would suggest that they have a close relationship.
- **The relative frequency of the interactions:** Are the interactions repetitive or more variable? George and Ted's relationship can be considered close because they interact frequently and their conversations contain both some routine repetition ("Hi, how's it going?") as well as more varied communication that is specific to their friendship ("What's happening with your Organic Chem class? I know you were worried about the test last Tuesday.").
- **The nature of the interactions:** Are the interactions complementary (opposite) or reciprocal (the same), or some combination? Mya and Nels have a close relationship if they exhibit a mix of these types. So sometimes Mya tells Nels she doesn't feel like deciding where to go out, and he responds that he doesn't either (reciprocal). However, sometimes he responds by deciding for the two of them (complementary). Another variation is that sometimes the roles are reversed, and Mya makes the decision when Nels doesn't want to do so.
- **The quality of power in the interactions:** Do the partners agree on the power distribution? Roger and Lynette have a close relationship if they agree that Lynette has the power to decide about household spending under $500, and Roger has the power to decide about car purchases. They agree that all other purchases and budget decisions they will make together.
- **The intimacy of the interactions:** How much self-disclosure do the partners engage in? As we discussed in Chapter 8, self-disclosing makes relationship partners feel closer to each other. Robin and Theo have a close relationship when they tell each other personal disclosures that they choose to reveal.
- **The partners' perception of the interactions:** Are the partners' perceptions in agreement? How do they see each other and the outside world? Kelly and Ray are in a close relationship because they see each other in a similar fashion and feel understood by each other. In addition, they hold similar political beliefs and generally see the world in a similar way.
- **The commitment reflected in the interactions:** Do the partners each see the other as committed to the relationship? Diana and Cal have a close relation-

ship because they speak openly of how committed they are to one another, and each know that the other is devoted to their relationship.

- **The satisfaction expressed in the interactions:** How closely do their interactions fit their ideal? Camille and Pat have a close relationship because they frequently say that they couldn't want a better friend than each other. By contrast, Edie and Dick don't have as close a relationship because they are often heard expressing discontent with one another, saying, "I don't know why we ever got together! I can't take much more of the way we fight."

Hinde's list allows us to form a beginning definition of a relationship. The characteristics that Hinde described allow us to see a **relationship** as a bond between two people that is reflected in their interaction patterns and their perceptions of these patterns.

Are Relationships Performances?

Leslie Baxter and Dawn Braithwaite (2002) take a different approach from Hinde to understanding close relationships. In their study of marriage renewal rituals, Baxter and Braithwaite assert that marriages (and, by extension, all relationships) are cultural performances. What they mean by this is that relationships consist of the ongoing processes between the partners. These exchanges include myriad communication practices, including private conversations, public rituals like weddings and commitment ceremonies, as well as public discourse by politicians and others indicating what marriages, families, and other relationships should be like and what values should define them. Thus, relationships are both defined and enacted in the culture that surrounds them.

If we use Baxter and Braithwaite's approach, we can see that Brea and Tal have a close relationship because they do things that people in close relationships do. They go to parties together, own a home together, make budgets, take out loans, and sign jointly for their bank accounts and other financial considerations. Further, they had a wedding and publicly vowed that they were in a close relationship, labeled marriage. Thus, Brea and Tal have a close relationship because they are performing a close relationship according to the social and cultural rules of the United States.

Are Relationships in Our Heads?

Some research examines the notion of relationship scripts, which are cognitive structures that contain a pattern for the key events that we expect in a relationship (Holmberg & MacKenzie, 2002). People seem to have both narrow scripts (for example, what should happen on a first date) and broad scripts (for example, how a friendship generally should progress). Diane Holmberg and Samantha MacKenzie reviewed research showing that people in North American culture exhibit broad agreement on the order of events in dating relationships. They argue that these relationship scripts serve several functions for people: They conserve our brain's energy, allowing us to process information about the relationship efficiently and rapidly; they help guide our behavior, making it easier for us to know what to do in certain relational situations; and they enhance our satisfaction when there's a match between our scripts and our lived relationship.

William Wilmot (1995) also takes this approach, arguing that close relationships exist when both participants have a mental construct of the relationship. Wilmot asserts that these mental images occur on at least two levels. At a basic level, people are simply aware of each other and the fact that they are in a relationship with one another. The second level is more complex. On this level, according to Wilmot, several things happen to establish the mental construct of the relationship. In order, they are the following:

1. The communication between the partners becomes patterned, and they can imagine with some predictive accuracy what the other will say or do in a variety of situations.
2. The partners perceive a past, present, and future together. They are able to bring the past forward into the present and future by holding a mental image of what the partner has done in the past and generalizing it to the present or the future ("when I brought her flowers before, she liked it, so she'll probably like it again"). Wilmot calls this "carrying the relationship with you" and suggests that it happens whenever people imagine what a relational partner's reaction to something might be.
3. People label their relationship ("this is my best friend," "this is my daughter," or "this is my girlfriend"). In the following section, we address

© Bill Aron / PhotoEdit

Relationship scripts, such as what should happen in a dating relationship, are useful because they allow us to process information about a relationship quickly and efficiently, help us know how to behave in certain relational situations, and make us feel good when our scripts and our lived relationships match. What are some of your relationship scripts? Where do you think they came from? Do some of your scripts differ from those of the mainstream U.S. culture?

the question of language and the definition of close relationships in more detail.

Are Relationships in Our Language?

As we just mentioned, language influences our sense of close relationships. Giving a relationship a label (friendship, love, and so forth) helps us to feel "in relationship" to another. Yet, as we discussed in Chapter 6 when we addressed lexical gaps, some relationships don't have convenient labels. What do you call your father's second wife, her children by her first marriage, your brother's former wife, or a person you are dating when both of you are in your 50s? What do children of gay parents call their two mothers or fathers? Some people think that it's difficult for men and women to be friends because the English language has so many terms for heterosexual love, romance, and sex that it is difficult to talk about friendship across the sexes. Language has not always kept pace with our relationships.

Another way that relationships exist in language relates to figurative language, another subject we mentioned in Chapter 6. Figurative language—specifically, metaphors and similes—helps us understand relationships by comparing them to other phenomena (Lakoff & Johnson, 1980). In such linguistic comparisons, the qualities of the phenomenon to which a relationship is linked shed light on the qualities of the relationship itself. Thus, some researchers have argued that metaphors give us a sense of reality (Burrell, Buzzanell, & McMillan, 1992; Foss, 1988; Turner & Shuter, 2004) suggesting that metaphors "'compose the building blocks of any group's social reality'" (Darrand & Shupe, 1983, pp. 2–3).

Metaphors and figurative language offer a vocabulary for understanding our relationships but they also *shape* our understanding. This is the case because they throw some elements of the relationship into sharper relief than others and downplay other elements. For example, the metaphor of relationship-as-dance features the coordination and enjoyment elements of a relationship while it downplays the conflicts and struggles in relationships. We use metaphors to compare relationships to many things: gardens, leaky rowboats, quilts, circuses, roller coasters, old shoes, and so forth. (See Table 10.1 for a list of common relational metaphors.) How do these metaphors affect your thinking about relationships?

Researchers argue that metaphors do affect thinking and, further, that they also influence our communication in relationships (Owen, 1989). For instance, if Ben and Leslie picture their marriage as a "well-oiled machine," they may adopt communication behaviors that focus on efficiency ("keeping the wheels turning") and functioning ("we don't want a breakdown in communication") at the expense of emotional communication. Some people talk about their families using a corporate metaphor, calling the mother the CEO of the family (Peel, 1997).

Recently, researchers have criticized corporate metaphors because of the way they affect our thinking about the family. Organizational communication scholar Stan Deetz (1992) calls this phenomenon "corporate colonization," or the values of the marketplace taking over in other places, and he warns that it erodes family values and practices. Caryn Medved and Erika Kirby (in press) agree, noting that stay-at-home moms may feel that they have to come up with some type of corporate way of defining themselves to justify staying at home. For instance, if Sabrina decides to leave her high-powered job at a law firm to stay at home with her son, Eddie, she

REVISITING CASE IN POINT

1. How does Randy and Hope's relationship illustrate relational scripts?
2. What metaphor might Hope and Randy use for their relationship?

You can answer these questions online under Student Resources for Chapter 10 at the Understanding Interpersonal Communication website.

Table 10.1	Common Metaphors Used to Describe Close Relationships
Nature	Thunderstorm
	Volcano
	Sunny day
	Meadow with flowers
	Tree with deep roots
Machines	Well-oiled machine
	Leaky boat
	Merry-go-round
	Roller coaster
	Broken record
Food	Stew
	Gooey cake with ice cream
	TV dinner
	Milkshake
	Tossed salad
Clothing	Ripped sweater
	Comfortable old shoes
	Tie that's choking me
	Pair of pants with an elastic waist
	Party outfit

may redefine herself as the "Chief Home Officer" and think of her different role as a new job for her to tackle.

Are Relationships Face to Face?

So far in our discussion of close relationships, our examples have centered on friends, family, dating partners, and so forth. As you've been reading this chapter, you have probably been picturing people you see regularly in your own relationships. Most of the research on close relationships focuses on partners who see each other face to face. Of course, many people maintain long-distance relationships, but even in such relationships, the expectation is that at some point, the partners will interact in person. Two types of relationships, online and parasocial, contradict the assumption that to qualify as a close relationship, the partners have to interact face to face.

Online Relationships

With the increasing use of the Internet, many relationships begin online and evolve into face-to-face relationships, whereas others remain online without becoming face to face. For instance, Melissa, based in San Francisco, works with a colleague based at her company's German office. The two complete three projects together and feel they know each other well, but they never meet face to face. All the work they do is conducted via email, fax, overnight mail, and the phone.

We discuss this topic of technology's effect on interpersonal communication in greater detail in Chapter 11. For now, we simply note that online relationships can provide a sense of closeness even if the relationship partners never actually meet

Your *Turn*

In your journal, spend two weeks collecting metaphors you hear in daily conversation referring to relationships. You can gather metaphors from television or other popular media as well as from conversations you participate in or overhear. For instance, if you hear a friend say that they had to break up with someone because "they were stuck in a rut," that would be a metaphor. The relationship partners weren't literally stuck in a rut—that's a figurative way of describing the feeling your friend had in the relationship. At the end of the two weeks, look over your metaphors and answer the following questions: How do metaphors guide our thinking about relationships? How do metaphors influence the way we actually communicate in our relationships? If you'd like, you can use your student workbook to complete this activity.

Facing *Change*

Mary Pipher (2003) has written that community is where you have friends and know the names of many people that you encounter in your daily routines. She says that when you sit down to talk in your community, you don't have to discuss movie stars or public figures—you have real people in common. Further, she notes that in real communities in the twenty-first century, fostering strong interpersonal relationships is both threatened and necessary. We are witnessing colossal social changes, including globalization, telecommuting, and demographic changes that have seen some small towns struggle for viability. Do you think these changes have affected the type and quality of personal relationships? How have changes such as these made an impact on how we communicate in our relationships with others?

 Use your Understanding Interpersonal Communication CD-ROM to watch the CNN video clip "Commuter Couples," which highlights couples whose careers make it necessary for them to maintain long-distance relationships. Click on the "CNN & Change" icon in the menu at left, then click on "Video Menu" in the menu bar at the top of the screen. Select "Commuter Couples" to watch the video (it takes a minute for the video to load). As you watch the video, consider the challenges these couples face in maintaining their relationships. Have you ever been in a long-distance relationship? If so, what were some of the challenges you faced? Were you able to overcome them? You can respond to this and other analysis questions by clicking on "Analysis" in the menu bar at the top of the screen. When you've answered all the questions, click on "Done" to compare your answers to those provided by the authors.

in person. Some would argue that not seeing the other face to face can even intensify the relationship because "words have the power to connect disparate souls from distant lands minus the weighty significances of physicality" (Tamosaitis, 1995, p. 46). Further, some research (Tidwell & Walther, 2002) suggests that computer-mediated communication may be more direct, which results in greater conversational effectiveness by the partners.

Of course, online relationships also offer a greater opportunity for deception and fantasy, which may make them illusory and even dangerous. A famous case of deception online involved a male psychiatrist who posed as a handicapped woman named Joan in an online support group for disabled women (VanGelder, 1990). "Joan" became a beloved and important virtual friend to the other members of the group. When she wrote that she was dying and then eventually faked "her" death, people were devastated. They became enraged when the psychiatrist was exposed and Joan was revealed as a phony identity.

Parasocial Relationships

A **parasocial relationship** (Horton & Wohl, 1956) consists of a one-way relational tie with a media personality or character that reminds us of face-to-face interaction. For example, if Simon watches the television show *The O.C.* often, he may begin to think he has a relationship with the characters Ryan, Seth, Marissa, Sandy, or Julie. If Kate watched *Friends* regularly, she may have felt she "knew" the characters Phoebe, Monica, Rachel, Joey, Chandler, and Ross as well as she did the people in her daily life. Frequent viewers of soap operas often establish parasocial relationships with the characters. In speaking about soap operas' appeal, James E. Reilly—one of the writers for *Days of Our Lives* (NBC) and *Passions* (NBC)—noted, "We have created an alternative universe. Sort of like *The Truman Show.* And these characters, with their heartaches and joys and marriages, become friends of yours. They're part of your life. These people are real to the viewers" (quoted in Weinraub, 2004, p. B8). You can also have parasocial relationships with public personalities whom you frequently watch in the media, such as a local newscaster or a movie star.

To conclude our section on understanding close relationships, we admit that the definition is subject to negotiation. Everyone in a close relationship defines it somewhat differently. Scholars who study the subject also take different perspectives. Some view close relationships as social institutions, embedded in cultural norms, whereas others see them as psychological structures or scripts that provide guidelines for the individuals involved. Overarching both these viewpoints is the notion that language and communication behaviors define and maintain close relationships. Further, technology affects our definition of close relationships, even though the research on relationship development in online and parasocial relationships continues to evolve.

To check out an interesting website that may help you learn more about your own close relationships, use your Understanding Interpersonal Communication CD-ROM to access **Interactive Activity 10.2: Assessing Close Relationships.**

Explaining Communication in Close Relationships: What's It All About?

Given the importance of communication to our understanding of close relationships, it's understandable that so many theories have been offered to explain it. Also, trying to explain communication and our relationships is something we all spend a lot of time doing ourselves. As Heider (1958) says, we are all "naïve psychologists" engaging in "implicit theory making." We often ask why relationships develop the way they do and why some types of communication helps relationship woes and some kinds make them worse. For instance, when Mel gives Tania a surprise gift for no apparent occasion, Tania may spend some time thinking about why Mel did that and what that means about their relationship. In this section, we review the basic tenets of four major theories advanced by researchers. Theories help us answer puzzling questions, and they point us toward the right questions to ask. Some of these theories can work together to help us understand communication in close relationships, but others differ so significantly that they can't be used jointly.

Systems Theory: We're All Connected

When trying to understand communication in close relationships, some people find it helpful to compare relationships to something else. As we previously mentioned, using a metaphor enables us to view more clearly how communication in relationships works. In systems theory (von Bertalanffy, 1968), relationships are compared to living systems, which have six important properties:

- Wholeness
- Interdependence
- Hierarchy
- Boundaries or openness
- Calibration or feedback
- Equifinality

Researchers who like systems theory find that understanding how each of these six properties of living systems works allows them to apply that knowledge to how communication in relationships works. This section briefly explains each of the properties.

Wholeness means that you can't understand a system by simply picking it apart and understanding each of its parts in isolation from one another. Wholeness indicates that knowing Bert and Ernie separately is not the same as knowing about the relationship between Bert and Ernie. The relationship between people is like a third entity, which extends beyond each of the people individually. If you think of a specific relationship that you are in, the concept of wholeness becomes quite clear. The way you act and communicate in that relationship is probably different from the way you act and communicate in other relationships. The other person's reactions, contributions, and perceptions of you make a difference in how you behave, and vice versa. Further, the way you perceive the relationship between the two of you makes a difference. If you are longtime friends with someone, you don't have to explain things to them the same way you might to someone who is a newer friend of yours. So, just because Karen knows Cara and Susie individually doesn't mean she knows them *in relationship* to each other.

Figure 10.2 | **Hierarchy as a systems principle**

Interdependence builds on the notion of wholeness by asserting that members of systems depend on each other and are affected by one another. If Kyle's sister is injured in a car accident, his life is affected because of his relationship with her, not because he himself is injured. When you talk to the people in your close relationships, you monitor their behavior and respond to it—you are affected by their shifts in mood and tone, and your communication shifts accordingly.

Hierarchy states that these shifts and accommodations don't exist in a vacuum. Kyle's relationship with his sister is embedded in the larger system of his family (all of the members of which are interdependent), and his family is embedded in the larger system of his extended family, his neighborhood, his culture, and so forth. Lower-level systems are called **subsystems,** and higher-levels are called **suprasystems.** Kyle and his sister form a subsystem of his family. Kyle's neighborhood is a suprasystem around his family. (See Figure 10.2.)

Boundaries or openness refers to the fact that hierarchy is formed by creating boundaries around each separate system (Kyle and his sister, the family as a whole, and so forth). However, human systems are inherently open, and information passes through these boundaries. (Therefore, some researchers call this element "openness," and some call it "boundaries.") For example, Marsha and Hal are best friends who have a very close relationship, and they tell each other things that they don't tell their families. This closeness forms the boundary around their relationship. Yet, if Marsha confides something to Hal that he finds disturbing, like that she is abusing drugs or feeling suicidal, Hal might ask members of his family or other friends for help. In so doing, Hal would violate and expand the boundaries of their subsystem. Boundaries exist to keep information within the subsystem. However, in human systems, the boundaries can never be completely closed, so the system has the property of openness.

Calibration centers on how systems set their parameters, check on themselves, and self-correct. For example, Maggie and her grandmother have a close relationship, and the two of them form a subsystem of Maggie's extended family. When Maggie was 10, she and her grandmother calibrated their system by setting a weekly lunch date. As Maggie got older, she found it harder to meet her grandmother every Saturday for lunch because she wanted to do more activities with her friends. She provided feedback to her grandmother expressing this, and they **recalibrated** by changing their lunch date to once a month. When systems experience such a change, it's a result of **positive feedback.** If they stay the same, the feedback is judged as **negative feedback.** If Maggie and her grandmother had not changed their ritual, the feedback Maggie gave would be called negative feedback.

Equifinality means the ability to achieve the same goals (or ends) by a variety of means. For instance, you may have some friends with whom you spend a lot of time and other friends with whom you spend less time. Some of your friends may be people you play tennis with, and others may be those you like to go to movies with, and so forth. Each of these friendships may be close, but you become close (and maintain your closeness) in different ways.

Table 10.2 provides an example of how each of the six properties of systems theory relates to communication behaviors. Systems theory doesn't explain all communication with our relational partners; it isn't specific enough to give us answers to questions like why some couples argue more than others or why some communication in friendships is more satisfying than others. However, it does give us a good overall impression of how relationships work and how communication behaviors function within relationships.

Dialectics Theory: It's a Push-Pull Feeling

A different explanation for communication in close relationships comes from dialectics theory, which we discussed in Chapter 8 (Baxter & Montgomery, 1996). This approach focuses on the tensions that relational partners feel as a result of desiring both opposing poles of a contradiction. Dialectic thinking rejects either/or approaches in favor of both/and. As Baxter and Montgomery (1996) state, "dialectical thinking is not directed toward a search for the 'happy mediums' of compro-

Table 10.2 | **System Properties and Communication**

Property	Communication Outcome
Wholeness	Mary is so different with Tom than she is with me.
Interdependence	I can't talk to you when you act like that!
Hierarchy	Jake has to talk to his son, Marcus, about his problems at school.
Boundaries or openness	Frieda tells a secret to only her best friend, Laya, and trusts her not to tell their other friends.
Calibration	Hap tells Miles that they can't play basketball every Wednesday because he needs to spend more time with his son.
Equifinality	Laura and Roy are happily married, and they tell each other everything. Nadine and Bob are happily married, and they keep many things private and don't confide in each other as much.

mise and balance, but instead focuses on the messier, less logical, and more inconsistent unfolding practices of the moment" (p. 46).

Common Relational Dialectics

To clarify this position, let's discuss three of the common dialectics that are thought to characterize relational life:

- Autonomy and connection
- Openness and protection
- Novelty and predictability

The contradiction between **autonomy and connection** centers on our desire to be independent or autonomous while simultaneously wanting to feel a connection with our partner. For example, this tension is apparent when Desiree wants to be with her own friends while also wanting to spend time with her boyfriend, Shane. The second dialectic, between **openness and protection,** revolves around our desire for self-disclosures, which make us transparent to another, and our desire for withholding disclosures, which keeps us safe from another's disapproval. This tension exists whenever you debate the pros and cons of telling a friend something personal about yourself. As we discussed in Chapter 8, you want to tell because that may bring you closer, but you are afraid to tell because it might actually drive you apart. Finally, the tension between **novelty and predictability** manifests in our simultaneous desires for excitement and stability. For example, Malcolm feels bored with the everyday routines he's established in his relationship with Tom, but he also feels comforted and reassured by them. It's scary to leave familiar routines, even when you might find them tedious. These three basic contradictions or dialectics are all seen as dynamic. This means that the interplay between the two opposites pole permeates the life of a relationship and is never fully resolved.

Additional Dialectics Found in Friendships

Although the three dialectics just discussed are thought to be common in many relationships, most of the research they are derived from examined romantic relationships. Williams Rawlins (1992) examined friendships from a dialectics perspective

and, in addition to autonomy and connection, openness and protection, and novelty and predictability, he found a few different tensions that seemed specific to the friendship context. Rawlins' four new tensions were the following:

- Judgment and acceptance
- Affection and instrumentality
- Public and private
- Ideal and real

The tension between **judgment and acceptance** involves criticizing a friend as opposed to accepting a friend for who or she is. Rawlins found that people were often torn between offering (unwanted) advice and accepting a friend's behavior. For instance, if Maria has a friend, Josh, who is dating someone Maria thinks is wrong for him, or someone who is dishonest or untrustworthy, should she offer her opinion or simply accept Josh's choice? Most people, according to Rawlins, want both things simultaneously; they want to be able to make and hear judgments, but they also want unconditional acceptance. The next dialectic, **affection and instrumentality,** poses a tension between framing your friendship with someone as an end in itself (affection) or seeing it as a means to another end (instrumentality). This dialectic suggests that in close friendships, people want to both just enjoy their friends and get some help from them. For example, if Tony often gets a ride to work from his close friend, Michael, that friendship serves an instrumental function, but Tony also values the friendship for other, affectional reasons as well, such as the fun they have talking to each other on the way to work.

Rawlins calls the two previous tensions **internal dialectics** because they focus on how the partners communicate with one another. The next two he labels **external dialectics** because they have to do with how friends negotiate the more public aspects of their friendship. For instance, the dialectic between **public and private** specifically centers on how much of the friendship is demonstrated in public and what parts are kept private. Some emblems of friendship are fine for public consumption (like the fact that Kelly and Amy both like horror movies and always race to see the newest releases) while other things (like the silly nicknames they have for one another) might be kept between them. Some friendships, especially in adolescence, are kept more private than public. For instance, Terry, the football team captain at Metropolitan University, doesn't always share publicly that he's friends with Paul, a computer geek. In private, Terry and Paul get along well, but neither wants to tell all their other friends about their friendship.

Finally, the dialectic between the **ideal and real** reveals the tension between an idealized vision of friendship and the real friends that one has. For example, we may carry images in our heads of how self-sacrificing, other-oriented, and altruistic friends should be. We get these mental images in large part from popular culture: television shows, buddy movies, books, and magazines that show examples of friendships. For example, although Georgia recognizes that these idealized images of friendship are fantasies, she can't help feeling some tension when her best friend, Alma, goes on a ski trip, even though Georgia can't make it. Somehow, Georgia had kept hoping that Alma would refuse to go without her. (See Table 10.3 for a summary of the dialectics.)

REVISITING CASE IN POINT

1. How does Randy and Hope's relationship illustrate the autonomy-connection tension?
2. How does Randy and Hope's relationship illustrate the affection-instrumentality tension?

You can answer these questions online under Student Resources for Chapter 10 at the Understanding Interpersonal Communication website.

Table 10.3 | **Summary of Dialectics**

Most Common Relational Dialectics	
1.	Autonomy and connection
2.	Openness and protection
3.	Novelty and predictability
Additional Dialectics Found in Friendships	
1.	Judgment and acceptance
2.	Affection and instrumentality
3.	Public and private
4.	Ideal and real

Strategies for Managing Relational Dialectics

Despite the constant presence of these contradictions, people in relationships devise strategies for dealing with the tensions that they cause. As we discussed in Chapter 8, Leslie Baxter (1988) identified several methods that people use in managing relational dialectics. Baxter says that some people may respond to dialectic tension through cyclic alternation, which means choosing different poles of the contradiction at different times in the life of the relationship. For example, Ethan and Chad, who are brothers, might feature autonomy in their relationship when they are young and then alternate to connection as they get older.

A second approach for dealing with the tensions is segmentation, or highlighting each of the polar opposites in different settings. For example, two friends who work for the same company might be very close outside of work but focus on their independence at the workplace. A third strategy, selection, calls for making a choice between the oppositions. In this approach, the true dialectic nature of the tensions is ignored, and the partners feature just one in their interactions. For instance, an uncle who rarely sees his nieces and nephews and who is uninvolved in their lives has chosen autonomy and ignored connection.

Baxter's final strategy is termed integration because it involves some type of synthesis between the opposites. Integration takes three forms: disqualifying, neutralizing, and reframing. Disqualifying works by exempting certain areas from the general pattern. For example, Joe and Beth are good friends who have a relationship in which they rarely make plans but do a lot of things together on the spur of the moment. They value the novelty in their relationship, and they are always telling stories about the crazy things they have done because they were ready for anything. However, they employ a disqualifying approach on each of their birthdays; they routinely go to the same restaurant and order the same meals, and they always give each other a small joke gift. They have established a fixed routine around this one event that is different from their usual, unpredictable way of relating.

Neutralizing strikes a compromise between the opposites. Sometimes people neutralize out of necessity. According to Elizabeth Graham (2003), divorced couples who have children cannot completely become autonomous of one another. Thus, they create a separate-togetherness which strikes a middle ground between being close and being autonomous. Finally, reframing means redefining the opposition so it doesn't seem like it's opposing any longer. For instance, when people say

Table 10.4 | **Managing Relational Dialectics**

Cyclic Alternation	Segmentation	Selection	Integration
Alternating between the opposing tensions at different times.	Alternating between the opposing tensions in different settings.	Choosing between the opposing tensions.	Synthesizing the oppositions (three forms).
			• *Disqualifying:* Making some things exempt from the general way of handling the oppositions.
			• *Neutralizing:* Finding a middle ground between the oppositions.
			• *Reframing:* Redefining the oppositions so they no longer seem opposing.

they can't truly love another unless they love themselves first, they are transforming autonomy into a critical part of connection.

Like systems theory, the dialectics approach is rather general. Although it provides a framework for understanding how people struggle with oppositions in relationships and helps us understand some communication behavior as strategies for dealing with these tensions, it doesn't clearly predict which strategies people will use, nor does it tell us why some relationships are more stressed than others by these tensions. However, dialectics theory is a good starting place for revealing some of the undercurrents that guide communication in close relationships. See Table 10.4 for a summary of the strategies people use in managing relational dialectics.

Social Exchange Theories: If You Rub My Back, I'll Rub Yours

Social exchange theories come from a different line of thinking than the systems and dialectics approaches do. Rather than providing a large framework for understanding communication in close relationships, social exchange theories are a bit more specific and point us more directly toward testable predictions about the topic. Social exchange isn't just a single theory (Roloff, 1981); instead, several theories all advance the same general assumptions of social exchange. We will talk briefly about these assumptions and then profile one particular social exchange theory, John Thibaut and Harold Kelley's (1959) theory of interdependence.

Assumptions of Social Exchange

The heart of social exchange thinking lies in the concepts of costs and rewards. **Costs** constitute those things in relational life that people judge as negative. Examples could include having to do favors for friends, having to listen to Uncle Al's boring stories at family gatherings, or having to baby-sit for a younger, bratty cousin. On the other hand, **rewards** are those parts of being in a relationship that are pleasurable to people. Examples might include having your spouse listen to your problems and offer empathy, having a friend to share your favorite activities with, and sharing private jokes with your brother. Social exchange theories assume that all people do mental calculations about the costs and the rewards they experience in relationships. People judge their relationships, according to social exchange prin-

© Image 100/Royalty-Free/Corbis

The social exchange theory assumes that we stay in relationships that provide us with more rewards than costs. What are some of the rewards and costs of your own close relationships? What rewards would cause you to stay in a relationship despite the costs? Conversely, what costs would cause you to leave a relationship despite the rewards?

ciples, by subtracting their costs from their rewards. The theories assume that when costs exceed rewards, people will leave the relationship, if possible. Implicit in this discussion are three basic assumptions about human nature: people are motivated by rewards and wish to avoid punishments, people are rational, and people evaluate costs and rewards differently. The first assumption states that people want to obtain rewards (things that are pleasurable to them) and that they want to avoid punishments (things that they view as negative). For example, exchange theorists believe that friends Jennifer and Laurie each want to do things they find rewarding (like going to the movies together) and that neither want to do things that seem punishing (Jennifer wouldn't want to do Laurie's laundry, for example). The social exchange perspective asserts that people are motivated to maximize their rewards while minimizing their costs (Molm, 2001).

The next assumption clarifies the first by asserting that people are thinking rationally most of the time, so they can calculate what the costs and rewards of any given relationship might be. Social exchange theorists assert that people keep mental balance sheets about relational activities (for instance, "I had to spend two hours helping Dan with his economics homework, but he paid me back by buying my lunch yesterday"). Finally, social exchange theories assume that what is costly for one person might seem rewarding for another. For example, Matt finds baby-sitting for his cousin a drag, but if Meg majored in early childhood education and doesn't have a chance to spend time with any children, she might welcome an opportunity to practice some of her classroom knowledge by baby-sitting for a cousin. Further, both people in a relationship may see their costs and rewards differently. For instance, Hillary thinks that the fact that her parents don't like Pat is a huge cost to their relationship, but Pat isn't concerned about parental approval, so he ranks the cost much lower.

Theory of Interdependence

Thibaut and Kelley's (1959) theory of interdependence builds on these assumptions and adds an ingredient from systems theory—that is, the idea that relationships are interdependent. Whatever one person does in a relationship affects the other and their relationship as a whole. Further, Thibaut and Kelley added a calculation to their theory to explain why people stay or leave relationships. The general principle of social exchange says that people stay in relationships where rewards outweigh costs. However, we know that sometimes people stay in relationships that seem pretty bad, and some seemingly good relationships end.

Thibaut and Kelley proposed two concepts to help clarify these situations: comparison level and comparison level for alternatives. The **comparison level** is a person's standard level for what types of costs and rewards should exist in a given relationship. People learn from a variety of sources—like the media, their families, and their past experiences—what to expect from relationships. So your comparison level might tell you that friendship is a relationship where you should expect to give and take in equal proportions. whereas love relationships require more giving than taking. Thibaut and Kelley argued that people will be satisfied in relationships where the actual costs and rewards match what we expect from our comparison level.

Comparison level for alternatives refers to how you compare the costs and rewards of a current relationship to the possibility of doing better in a different relationship. As an example, Melanie calculates that she has more costs than rewards in her relationship with her husband, Erik. However, she still might stay with Erik if she also calculates that her chances of doing better without him, either by finding a better relationship or being alone, are poor. Some researchers (for example, Walker, 1984) have used this theory as an explanation for why women stay in abusive relationships.

For more on social exchange theory, particularly how it relates to emotions and the emotional process, read the article "Bringing Emotions into Social Exchange Theory," available through InfoTrac College Edition. Use your Understanding Interpersonal Communication CD-ROM to access **InfoTrac College Edition Exercise 10.2: Emotions and Social Exchange.**

Stage Models: Step by Step

The three explanations we have just reviewed previously hold somewhat differing beliefs about relationships: that they operate like systems, that they are fraught with tensions and contradictions, or that they are developed through self-interest. In contrast, stage models are concerned with how relationships develop and how communication changes as we deepen or weaken our relational ties with another. Perhaps the best known of the many stage models that describe relational life was originated by Mark Knapp (1978). Knapp actually built his model on social exchange theories; he argues that costs and rewards are the general motivating force for relational movement. However, his work differs from social exchange theories in that it further clarifies *how* the movement in relationships takes place and how communication characterizes relational growth and decay.

Mark Knapp and Anita Vangelisti (2000) said that Knapp's original model answers the following questions: "Are there regular and systematic patterns of communication that suggest stages on the road to a more intimate relationship? Are there similar patterns and stages that characterize the deterioration of relationships?" (p. 36). The model provides five stages of coming together and five stages of coming apart. See Table 10.5 for a summary of the model.

Knapp and Vangelisti (2005) noted that the model is useful for all kinds of relationships because it provides for relationships that end after only a couple of stages as well as relationships that do not move beyond an early stage. In addition, the researchers stated that the model explains the movement of friendships as well as love relationships, although most of the discussion of these stages uses heterosexual romantic relationships as examples. As you read about the stages, try to imagine how they work in a variety of relationships.

Some people have criticized all stage models for presenting a linear picture of relationship development. These critics note that relational development doesn't happen neatly in stages and that the model doesn't clarify what happens when one partner moves to a stage and the other doesn't do the same. Knapp and Vangelisti

Table 10.5 | **Knapp's Model of Relationship Development**

Coming Together	
Stage	**Sample Communication**
Initiating	"Hi, how are you?"
Experimenting	"Do you like water polo?"
Intensifying	"Let's take a vacation together this summer. We can play water polo!"
Integrating	"You are the best friend I could ever have!"
Bonding	"Let's wear our team shirts to the party. I want everyone to know we're on the same team!"

Coming Apart	
Stage	**Sample Communication**
Differentiating	"I am surprised that you supported a Republican. I am a longtime Democrat."
Circumscribing	"Maybe we'd be better off if we didn't talk about politics together."
Stagnating	"Wow, I could have predicted you'd say that!"
Avoiding	"I have too much homework to meet you for coffee."
Terminating	"I think we shouldn't hang out together anymore. It's just not fun now."

(2000) admitted that stage models simplify a complicated process. They noted that "each stage contains some behavior from other stages. . . . Stages are identified by the proportion of one type of communication behavior to another" (pp. 36-37). Further, they observed that people sometimes slide back and forth between stages as they interact in their relationship. Thus, stage models give us a snapshot of the process of relationship development, but they don't tell the entire story. In the following sections, we briefly discuss each of the stages in Knapp's model.

Initiating: Getting Started

This stage, the first stage of the coming together part of the model, is where a relationship begins. In the **initiating stage,** two people notice one another and indicate to each other that they are interested in making contact: "I notice you, and I think you're noticing me, too. Let's talk and see where it goes." Initiation depends on attraction, which can be seen as either short-term or long-term.

Short-term attraction, a judgment of relationship potential, propels us into the initiation stage. **Long-term attraction,** which makes you want to continue a relationship and move through the subsequent stages, sustains and maintains relationships. Sometimes the things that attract you to someone in the short term may be the things that turn you off in the long term. For example, Marge may have initially struck up a friendship with Anita because she saw Anita as outgoing and friendly. However, later in their relationship, Marge may come to resent how much Anita talks to others because it means less time for the two of them to interact.

Both types of attraction are based on several elements, such as physical attractiveness, charisma, physical closeness, similarity, complementary needs, positive outcomes, and reciprocation. Especially initially, people are attracted to others who fit their cultural ideal of attractiveness, but they will probably initiate relationships with others who tend to match their own level of attractiveness (Cash & Derlega, 1978; Hinsz, 1989; White, 1980). We feel more comfortable talking with people who are about as physically attractive as we see ourselves to be. We also like people who are confident and exude charisma. Furthermore, it's more likely that we'll be attracted to those who are in physical proximity to us than to those who are more distant, because it's more difficult to enter the initiating stage with someone who is far away.

We are also motivated to initiate conversations with those who share some of our own attributes, values, and opinions. In a study investigating why people are attracted to one another, Peter Buston and Stephen Emlen (2003) found that a "likes-attract" rule was much stronger than an "opposites-attract" rule for heterosexual couples in Western cultures. Yet, too much similarity can be boring, so we seek some complementarity in our relationships as well. For example, if Chris is quiet and Glenn is talkative, they may want to initiate a conversation because they complement each other. Finally, we are attracted to others who seem attracted to us, or who reciprocate our interest. For instance, when Renny smiles at Natalie at a party and she doesn't smile back, Renny probably will not move any further with the relationship.

Some of our relationships stay in the initiating stage. You may see the same person often in a place you frequent, such as a grocery, bookstore, or coffee shop. Each time you see this person, you might exchange smiles and pleasantries. You may have short, ritualized conversations about the weather or other topics but never move on to any of the other stages in the model. Thus, you could have a long-term relationship that never moves out of initiating.

Experimenting: Finding Out More

If a relationship progresses beyond initiating, the second stage, **experimenting,** is where people become acquainted by gathering information about one another. They engage in **small talk**—interactions that are relaxed, pleasant, uncritical, and casual. Through small talk, people learn about one another, reduce their uncertainties, find topics that they might wish to spend more time discussing, "test the waters" to see if they want to develop the relationship further, and maintain a sense of community.

Mark Knapp and Anita Vangelisti (2005) point out that many of our relationships stay in the experimenting stage. We have many friends whom we know through small talk but not at a deeper level. If you see a friend in the coffee shop and go beyond "hi, it sure is nice to see sunshine today" to small talk, you have deepened the relationship some, but you still have kept it at a low level of commitment. Further, Knapp and Vangelisti observe that even people in close relationships spend time in this stage, perhaps in an effort to understand their partner more, to pass the time, or to avoid uncomfortable feelings stirred up by a more intense conversation.

Intensifying: I Think I Like You

This stage begins to move the relationship to a closeness not seen in the previous stages. **Intensifying** refers to the intensification of intimacy in the relationship. During this stage, partners self-disclose, forms of address become more informal, and people may use nicknames or some form of endearment to address one another ("Hi, honey"). Relational partners begin to speak of a "we" or "us," as in "we like to go to the basketball games" or "it'll be nice for us to get a break from studying and go for a walk."

In this stage, people begin to develop their own language based on private symbols for past experiences or simply knowledge of each other's habits, desires, and beliefs. For instance, Missy and her mother still say "hmmm" to each other, because that's what Missy said when she was little to mean "I want more." And Neil says, "it's just like walking on a rocky path" when he wants Ana to do something because when they first became friends, he made Ana take a walk along a path scattered with rocks when Ana wanted to go the movies instead.

Further, this stage is marked by more direct statements of commitment—"I have never had a better friend than you," or "I am so happy being with you." Often these statements are met with reciprocal comments—"Me neither," or "Same here." In intensifying, the partners become more sophisticated nonverbally also. They are able to read each other's nonverbal cues, they may replace some verbalizations with a touch, and they may mirror one another's nonverbal cues—how they stand, gesture, dress, and so forth may become more similar. In the 2003 movie *13*, one way the main character signifies her new friendship is to stop dressing like her old friends and to start wearing clothes and makeup that make her look like her new friend.

Integrating: Becoming a Couple

In this fourth stage, the partners seem to coalesce. **Integrating** has also been called "coupling" (Davis, 1973) because it represents the two people forming a clear identity as a couple. This coupling is often acknowledged by the pair's social circles; the pair cultivates friends together, and they are treated as a unit by their friends. They are invited to places together, and information shared with one is expected to be shared with the other.

Sometimes the partners designate common property. They may pick a song to be "our song," they may open a bank account together, buy a dog together, or move into an apartment together. In the case of the authors of this book, coauthoring a series of books together has created a couple identity for us. We are often referred to together, and if people ask one of us to do something (such as make a presentation at a convention), they usually assume that the other will come along as well.

Bonding: Let's Tell the World

The final stage in the coming together part of the model is **bonding,** which refers to a public commitment of the relationship. Bonding is easier in some types of relationships than in others. For heterosexual couples, the marriage ceremony is a traditional bonding ritual. As Knapp and Vangelisti (2000) note, "the institutionalization of the relationship hardens it, makes it more difficult to break out of, and

probably changes the rhetoric that takes place without a contract" (p. 44). In addition, bonding provides a certain social sanction for the relationship.

Other relationships don't have a well-recognized ritual to gain social sanction or public recognition. However, because bonding is important to many people, some have worked to create ceremonies. Examples include commitment ceremonies for gay and lesbian couples, naming ceremonies for new babies to welcome them to the family, and initiation ceremonies to welcome new "sisters" or "brothers" to sororities and fraternities.

Differentiating: We're Not the Same

The first stage in the coming apart section of the model, **differentiating** refers to how couples begin to notice ways in which they differ. In this stage, individuality is highlighted. This emphasis is unlike the coming together stages, which featured the partners' similarities. The most dramatic episodes of differentiating involve conflict, discussed in Chapter 9. However, people can differentiate without engaging in conflict. For example, the following seemingly inconsequential comment exemplifies differentiation: "Oh, you like that sweater? I never would have thought you'd wear sweaters with Christmas trees on them. I guess our taste in clothes is more different than I thought."

People switch from "we" to "I" in this stage and focus more on themselves as individuals than on the relationship. Furthermore, they may spend a lot of time talking about how they differ. Knapp and Vangelisti (2005) position this stage as the beginning of the relationship's unraveling process. However, we know that all relationships can oscillate between differentiation and other stages, like intensifying. No two people can remain in a coming together stage such as intensifying, integrating, or bonding without experiencing some differentiating. Dialectics theory illustrates this notion quite well. People want both to bond with close partners and to be their own individual selves. However, if the conflicts and the differences mount without enough connection, the relationship may move to the next stage of coming apart.

Circumscribing: I Don't Want to Talk about It

The next stage, **circumscribing,** refers to restraining communication behaviors so fewer topics are raised (for fear of conflict), more issues are out of bounds, and the couple actually interacts less. This stage is characterized by silences and comments like "I don't want to talk about that anymore," "let's not go there," "it's none of your business," and so forth. Again, relationships in all stages of the model may experience some taboo topics or behaviors that are typical of circumscribing. But Knapp and Vangelisti (2005) argue that when relationships enter this stage (in other words, if the biggest proportion of their communication is of this type), that is a sign of a decaying relationship. If measures aren't taken to repair the situation—sitting down and talking about why there's a problem, going to counseling, taking a vacation, or some other remedy—the model shows that people enter the next stage.

Stagnating: We're in a Rut

The third stage of coming apart, **stagnating,** consists of extending circumscribing so far that the couple no longer talks much. They express the feeling that there is no use to talk because they already know what the other will say. "There's no point in bringing this up—I know she won't like the idea" is a common theme during this

stage. People feel "stuck," and their communication is effortful, awkward, stylized, and unsatisfying

Each partner may engage in **imagined conversations** (Honeycutt, 2003), which means that one partner plays the parts of both partners in a mental rehearsal of the negative communication that characterizes this stage. Me: "I want to go visit my parents." Me in Role of Partner: "Well, I am much too busy to go with you." Me: "You never want to do stuff with my family." Me in Role of Partner: "That may be true, but you certainly can't stand my family!" After this rehearsal, people usually decide it's not worth the effort to engage in the conversation for real.

Avoiding: Keep Away

If a relationship stagnates for too long, the partners may decide that the relationship is unpleasant. As a result, they move to **avoiding,** a stage where partners try to stay out of the same physical environment. Partners make excuses for why they can't see one another ("Sorry, I have too much work to go out tonight;" "I will be busy all week;" "I have to go home for the weekend," and so forth). If people used to meet at a particular restaurant or a certain spot on campus, they change their routines and no longer stop by these places. They may vary their habits so that they do not run into their partner as they used to.

Sometimes it isn't possible to physically avoid a partner. If a couple is married and unable to afford two residences, or if siblings still live in their parents' home, it's difficult for the partners to be completely separate. In such cases, partners in the avoiding stage simply ignore one another or make a tacit agreement to segregate their living quarters as much as possible. For example, the married couple may sleep in separate rooms, and the siblings may come into the den at different times of day. When partners in the avoiding stage accidentally run into one another, they turn away and don't speak.

Terminating: It's All Over Now

This stage comes after the relational partners have decided, either jointly or individually, to part permanently. **Terminating** refers to the process of ending a relationship. Some relationships enter terminating almost immediately: You meet someone at a party, go through initiating and experimenting, and then decide you don't want to see them anymore, so you move to terminating. Other relationships go through all or most of the stages before terminating. Some relationships endure in one stage or another and never go through terminating. And other relationships go through terminating and then begin again (people remarry and estranged friends reunite). Further, some relationships terminate in one form and then begin again in a redefined way. For example, when Scott and Virginia get divorced, they end their relationship as married partners. However, because they have two children, they redefine their relationship so that they become friends.

Terminating a relationship can be simple ("I have to go") or complicated (involving lots of discussion and even the intervention of third parties like counselors, mediators, and attorneys). It may happen suddenly or drag out over a long time. It can be accomplished with a lot of talk that reflects on the life of the relationship and the reasons for terminating it, or it can be accomplished with relatively little or no discussion.

For more about Knapp's relational stages model and information about strategies for terminating relationships, use your Understanding Interpersonal Communication CD-ROM to access Interactive Activity 10.3: Knapp's Relational Stages Model. For an article that attempts to more quantitatively define the various stages of Knapp's model, check out the article "Development of Relationship Stage Measures," available through InfoTrac College Edition. Use your Understanding Interpersonal Communication CD-ROM to access InfoTrac College Edition Exercise 10.3: Knapp's Model Revisited.

Factors Affecting Communication in Relationships

Many factors affect how we communicate in close relationships. In this section, we examine the effects of gender and culture. Close relationships are susceptible to issues related to gender and culture because relationships draw on both our conceptions of sexuality and cultural meaning. We understand love and friendship based on our understandings of what it means to be a man or a woman and based on what our culture has taught us about such relationships.

Gender

As we have mentioned in all our chapters, differences between men and women, both in terms of the ways they communicate and the ways they are heard, permeate our understanding of interpersonal communication. Close relationships are just another context in which gender differences (or perceived differences) have an impact. As we have said before, we take the perspective that differences between the genders are learned through cultural instructions guiding girls to behave in ways that society has deemed feminine and teaching boys to engage in masculine behaviors (McGeorge, 2001). Further, our notions of sex and gender are somewhat fluid, and they can change over time.

This perspective does not deny that sex and gender make a difference in our thoughts and behaviors in close relationships. In fact, some recent research (Marano, 2004) indicates that biological differences between men and women, like responses to stress and propensity to depression, may affect communication in close relationships. Yet, when we critically examine this impact, we conclude, as Julia Wood (2002) did, that the differences between what women and men want from close relationships, and how they act in them, are differences of degree, not quality.

For example, some research by Catherine Reissman (1990) investigating why people divorced found that men became dissatisfied with their marriages when their wives stopped doing certain things for them, like fixing dinner and greeting them at the door. Women's dissatisfaction came from a different source—they felt their marriages were headed for divorce when they and their husbands stopped talking to one another. Yet, both women and men attributed their dissatisfaction to the same overarching reason—they no longer felt cherished in the relationship. Thus, both sexes desired the feeling of being cherished, but men tended to feel that way when their wives did concrete favors for them, whereas women felt most cherished when they experienced good communication with their husbands.

Wood (2002) notes women and men "both place a priority on emotional expressiveness" (p. 204), although men are slightly more likely than women to feel that emotional expressiveness comes through shared activities. Women are slightly more likely than men to believe that emotional expressiveness is achieved through verbal communication. However, when Loreen Olson (2003) interviewed ten married men to get a sense of their definition of love and compared her results with past research on women's expressions of love, she found a great deal of overlap between how men and women expressed love. This finding caused her to conclude that there may be a "universal, non-gender specific [experience] of love" (p. 42).

The stereotype that women are relational experts and men are relational idiots is common in the United States—check out most TV commercials. Yet, research shows that although women and men do differ in what they learn about relationships, ultimately what they want from relationships is quite similar. Interestingly, this similarity in relational goals is increasingly reflected in some of the relationships portrayed on popular television shows such as ER *and* Sex and the City.

James Honeycutt, James Cantrill, Pamela Kelly, and David Lambkin (1998) observed that evidence exists of men and women possessing a different relational awareness. They found support for the notion that men were more reticent in communicating and monitoring their relationships, and women were more tuned in to relational goals. However, this difference was slight, and it seems easily explained by social teaching, which categorizes women as relational experts.

Although women and men do differ in what they have learned about relationships, what they expect from them, and do have some differing experiences within close relationships, popular writers like John Gray (who wrote *Men are from Mars, Women are from Venus* in 1992) have taken our cultural interest in gender differences to an extreme, constructing some differences where none really exist, overestimating the differences that do appear, and failing to talk about the cultural context framing gender differences. To read an interesting study about communication in same-sex versus other-sex relationships, particularly self-disclosure and emotional intimacy, check out the article "Close Emotional Relationships with Women versus Men," available through InfoTrac College Edition. Use your Understanding Interpersonal Communication CD-ROM to access InfoTrac College Edition Exercise 10.4: Who Are You Closer to Emotionally?

Culture

As we discussed in Chapter 3, cultural norms, values, and expectations shape us in important ways. Thus, it should come as no surprise that culture plays a role in how we communicate in close relationships—and even in how we define close relationships. For example, Steven Miura (2000) notes that traditional Hawaiian culture is fundamentally collectivistic. He states,

> Whenever we greet one another in the [continental] U.S., we typically ask, "How are you?" When members of the traditional Hawaiian culture greet one another in their native language, they ask, *"Pe hea kou piko?"*—"How is the center of your life?" The "center" of one's life, of course, refers to the family *'ohana*. (p. 19)

Miura goes on to explain that the family is extended and expanded; *'ohana* consists of the immediate family (people with blood and marital ties), those who have been adopted into the family (a common practice), and the spiritual ancestors. Further, communication practices differ as a result of this definition and the value of harmony in traditional Hawaiian culture. When conflict in the *'ohana* threatens its harmony, the members call in a third party or *haiku* (usually a healer or family doctor) to mediate the flow of communication, to monitor the contributions of those in the conflict, and to provide a safe space for the conflict to be resolved. The practice is ritualized; it begins with the *haiku* reciting a prayer, moves on to a discussion of each point in the conflict, then each person involved discusses his or her feelings about the conflict, then the *haiku* guides them to a resolution, and the process finally concludes with another prayer and a snack or meal, which all share together.

Co-cultures also affect communication in close relationships. Charlton McIlwain (2002) observes a salient difference between African American and European American families' communication behaviors around death rituals. Specifically, McIlwain notes that African American families engage in much greater emotional expression than European American families at funerals. Furthermore, he explains that "in black funerals, more than whites [sic], such emotional outbursts are customary, almost expected—they are allowed, considered 'normal' and appropriate" (p. 2). Although McIlwain found that in many other ways blacks and whites performed death rituals similarly, this difference points out a piece of cultural identity that influences communication behaviors in close relationships.

Communicating in Close Relationships: The Dark Side

As we have discussed throughout this chapter, having close relationships is critically important to people and affects their physical and emotional health and well-being. Yet, some close relationships are toxic and unhealthy. In fact, some psychiatrists advocate creating a new category of mental illness called relational disorders (Vedantam, 2002). This category suggests that individuals may be perfectly healthy except when it comes to specific relationships. Currently, this movement is focusing only on family relationships. Shankar Vedantam (2002) states that "if the new category is created, couples who constantly quarrel and parents and children who clash could be diagnosed with mental illness and treated, possibly with drugs.

Troubled relationships between siblings could be the next large group" (p. 1G). This thinking is rooted in systems thinking, which sees the interdependency in relationships as a reason for never looking at one part of the system in isolation (the property of wholeness).

Certainly, one type of toxic close relationship is that of abuse. Violence and abuse are relatively common in the United States. John Harvey and Ann Weber (2002) observe that "FBI statistics showed that 32% of the 3,419 women killed in the United States in 1998 died at the hands of a husband, a former husband, a boyfriend, or a former boyfriend" (p. 145). If you adopt a less extreme definition of abuse or violence, the numbers are even higher. Michael Johnson (1995) talked about common couple violence, which includes minor acts of violence (like pushing and shoving) used when conflicts get out of hand. Some researchers (for example, Olson, 2002) believe that as many as 50 percent of couples in the United States experience common couple violence. For more on abusive relationships and information that can help you recognize when a relationship is unhealthy, use your Understanding Interpersonal Communication CD-ROM to access **Interactive Activity 10.4: Toxic versus Healthy Relationships.**

Another group of psychologists is examining the concept of bad friendships. Harriet Lerner (2001) states that friendship can be very painful. She notes that jealousy, envy, anger, and a whole host of difficult emotions can be present in friendships. Lerner observes that it may be better to end these friendships before they damage your health. Jan Yager (2002) has surveyed friends and found that there are twenty-one types of bad friendships, including friendships that lead you into antisocial or illegal activities (for example, the friendship portrayed in the movie *13*, in which one friend led another into shoplifting and dangerous sexual behavior, or Martha Stewart's friendship with Sam Waksal, who told her to sell her ImClone stock), as well as friendships with people who are betrayers, insulters, abusers, meddlers, and liars.

In addition to relationships that are completely toxic, all relationships can have negative phases or be characterized for a time by negative communication patterns.

When we think of toxic relationships, we often think of the physical and emotional abuse that define domestic violence. Communication in abusive relationships is often controlled by the abusive partner and can include minimizing or denying the abuse, belittling the victim of the abuse, blaming the victim for the abuse, using the silent treatment as a means of punishment, or using coercion or threats to control the relationship.

© Lon C. Diehl/PhotoEdit

In addition, sometimes positive outcomes in relationships are accomplished by communicating in "bad" ways. For instance, gossip may be seen as both aversive and bonding (Bergmann, 1993). Monique Turner and her colleagues (Turner, Mazur, Wendel, & Winslow, 2003) point out that gossip is associated with relational ruin when it's negative and communicated to strangers, but they term gossip "social glue" when it's communicated to friends and/or it's positive. Ralph Rosnow (2001) observed that although gossip has a dark side, it may also be a way to establish intimacy. Sharing secrets together is a way to advance a relationship and to build cohesion and emotional ties.

Alaina Winters and Steve Duck (2001) make the same claim about swearing. They observe that "willing collusion in a social practice that is otherwise aversive can be used to signal bonding and acceptance" (p. 73). Thus, if Rusty and Kim swear a lot around each other, they may be signaling that they have a relationship bond that defies social conventions. Winters and Duck note that swearing is considered bad behavior because of the negative charge that swear words have in our society. But in this bonding function, swearing is a positive behavior for close relationships.

Ethics & Choice

Connie and Eli Miller had been married for four years, and they were very happy. They wished to have children, but after trying unsuccessfully to conceive for almost a year, they were becoming discouraged. They finally consulted a fertility expert, who told them the sad news that they would never be able to conceive because Eli's sperm count was too low. However, the doctor did offer one intriguing possibility to the couple—the possibility of a sperm donor. If they chose this option, Connie could carry the baby and give birth. They went home to think about it.

After the two of them talked about it endlessly, they still weren't sure what to do. They decided to ask their family and friends what they thought of such a method of conception. They were a little afraid that they would be seen as strange or freakish if they had a child using this technology. They knew that the procedure was common, but they did not personally know anyone who had used a sperm donor, and the idea still seemed like science fiction to them.

At a family gathering one evening, Connie and Eli made seemingly offhand comments about how a friend was considering conception via sperm donor, and they were happy to find that no one seemed to consider the prospect too weird. The day after the family dinner, Eli got a call at work from his brother, Lucas. Lucas told Eli that he had guessed that Connie and Eli had broached the topic because they themselves were thinking about using a sperm donor to conceive. Eli was actually relieved that Lucas knew the truth, and by the end of their conversation, Lucas had volunteered to be the donor.

Connie and Eli accepted Lucas's offer gratefully, and soon Connie was carrying a child who was born healthy and perfect. The baby, whom they named Hannah, was a pure delight, and the Millers were completely happy. Yet, as Hannah got older, Connie began to wonder whether they should tell her that half of her genetic makeup was contributed by her uncle, not Eli. At first, they hadn't planned to tell her. Lucas hadn't asked them to do so, and he was very comfortable in his role as Hannah's uncle. Because Lucas and Eli were brothers, Hannah resembled her father, and there didn't seem to be any obvious reasons to make the disclosure.

However, lately Connie had been wondering if keeping a secret so big might cause some problems down the road for her family. She thought that Hannah had a right to know how she came into the world. Yet, Connie worried about how telling Hannah the truth might change the relationships among herself, Hannah, Eli, and Lucas, not to mention Eli's parents, who had never been told. Things seemed to be going so well, and Connie didn't want to disrupt her family's harmony.

Eli was very proud of his daughter, and Connie definitely didn't want to change how they regarded each other. Wrestling with this decision was keeping her up at night. What do you think Connie should do in this situation? How should she broach the subject with Eli, Lucas, and her in-laws? What are the implications of keeping family secrets? Do you agree that keeping secrets creates a toxic situation that erodes trust and ultimately damages relationships? Is it ethical to tell something that you know will hurt someone else, at least in the short run? In answering these questions, what ethical system of communication informs your decision (categorical imperative, utilitarianism, ethic of care, golden mean, significant choice)?

Use your Understanding Interpersonal Communication CD-ROM to access an interactive version of this scenario on the Understanding Interpersonal Communication website. Look under Student Resources for Chapter 10 and click on the "Ethics & Choice" menu at left. The interactive version of this scenario allows you to choose an appropriate response to this dilemma and then see what consequences your choice brings about. You can also compare your answers to the questions at the end of the scenario to those provided by the authors and, if requested, email your response to your instructor.

Communicating in Close Relationships: The Bright Side

Positivity in communicating to relational partners is extremely important. John Gottman (2004) observes that although happily married couples disagree the same amount as unhappily married couples, the happily married couples disagree in a more positive manner. Gottman observed that in happily married couples, there is a 5 to 1 ratio between positive and negative comments, even in conflicts.

When thinking about close relationships, we usually imagine the positive results of our communication: continued or increased closeness, support, romance, and connection, for example. In addition, we think of communication as both an indicator of our closeness with another ("I would tell only you this secret") and a means for developing this sense of closeness ("I feel so much closer to you now that we've talked about this"). Many behaviors accomplish this dual function. We spoke in detail about one of them, self-disclosure, in Chapter 8. We now discuss two related behaviors that are usually associated with the bright side of close relationships: expressions of affection and private languages.

As Kory Floyd and Mark Morman (2000) observed, most people agree that affectionate communication is extremely important in close relationships and "often serve[s] as critical incidents by which relational development is gauged" (p. 287). Affection can be expressed in a variety of ways—directly ("You are my best friend," "I love you") or indirectly (through giving support, compliments, or planning future activities together). As we mentioned previously in our discussion of the intensifying stage in relationship development (Knapp & Vangelisti, 2005), one way people express affection indirectly is by developing a private language that identifies them as part of a unique, closed circle.

As a result of sharing a history together, people in close relationships often develop inside jokes or private idioms. They may develop new words or names to call each other, or they may come up with new meanings for commonly used words or phrases. For example, Carla and Kevin, who have been friends since second grade, call one another private nicknames that came from their elementary school experiences. Carla is "Tootsie" because Tootsie Rolls were her favorite candy, and Kevin is "Slurps" because he was famous for slurping his milk in the cafeteria. In Trina's family, when someone doesn't understand what the other has just said, the listener says, "Look on sky, balloon is hanging." Trina's father once heard a non-native English speaker say that phrase, and he introduced it to the family, where it became a favorite.

Mark Knapp and Anita Vangelisti (2005) note that personal idioms arise out of a desire to say things in a different way to mark a relationship as unique. They observe that private languages are perhaps the most important distinction between the communication of those in close relationships and those who have more casual acquaintances.

Choices in Communicating in Close Relationships

This section presents several ways to improve communication in close relationships. Because many factors affect relationship development, we are necessarily broad in offering these suggestions. As we have emphasized in this chapter, communicating with people in close relationships is our source of greatest pleasure and greatest grief.

Communication Skills for Beginning Relationships

Beginning a relationship requires a fair amount of skill, although you may not think about developing these skills. Most people meet new people fairly frequently, and they don't consciously think about how they go about striking up conversations and cultivating new friends. One study (Douglas, 1987) examined the skills needed to initiate relationships; these techniques are described below.

Networking
Networking means finding out information about the person from a third party. If you ease into a relationship with the help of a third person, William Douglas (1987) found that you are behaving efficiently and in a socially acceptable fashion.

Offering
Offering means putting yourself in a good position for another to approach you. If you sit near a person you'd like to get to know better, or walk along the same route that they do, you're putting proximity to work for you.

Approaching
Approaching means actually going up to a person or smiling in that person's direction to give a signal that you would like to initiate contact. Approaching allows the relationship to actually begin, with both parties involved in some interaction.

Table 10.6 | **Affinity-Seeking Strategies**

1.	**Altruism**	Help the other person and offer to do things for him or her.
2.	**Assume control**	Take a leadership position.
3.	**Assume equality**	Don't show off. Treat the other as an equal.
4.	**Comfort**	Act at ease.
5.	**Concede control**	Allow the other to be in charge.
6.	**Conversational rules**	Follow the cultural norms for a conversation.
7.	**Dynamism**	Project excitement and enthusiasm.
8.	**Elicit disclosure**	Ask questions and encourage the other to talk.
9.	**Inclusion**	Include the other in activities and conversations.
10.	**Facilitate enjoyment**	Make time together enjoyable.
11.	**Closeness**	Indicate that the two of you have a close relationship.
12.	**Listening**	Lean in, listen intently, and respond appropriately.
13.	**Nonverbal immediacy**	Display good eye contact, appropriate touching, and so forth.
14.	**Openness**	Disclose appropriate personal information.
15.	**Optimism**	Display cheerfulness and positivity.
16.	**Personal autonomy**	Project independence.
17.	**Physical attraction**	Try to look good.
18.	**Present self as interesting**	Highlight past accomplishments and things of interest about self.
19.	**Reward association**	Offer favors and remind about past favors.
20.	**Confirmation**	Flatter the other.
21.	**Inclusion**	Spend time with the other.
22.	**Sensitivity**	Display empathy appropriately.
23.	**Similarities**	Point out things you have in common.
24.	**Supportiveness**	Be encouraging of the other and avoid criticism.
25.	**Trustworthiness**	Be dependable and sincere.

Adapted from Bell & Daly, 1984.

Sustaining

Sustaining means behaving in a way that keeps the initial conversation going. Asking appropriate questions is a way to employ sustaining.

Affinity Seeking

Affinity seeking means emphasizing the commonalities you think you share with the other person. Sometimes affinity seeking goes hand in hand with asking appropriate questions; you first ask questions to determine areas of common interest or experience, and then you comment on them. "Do you like reality shows?" "No kidding? I'm a big fan, too." Robert Bell and John Daly (1984) discovered that people use a variety of affinity-seeking strategies to get others to like them (see Table 10.6 for a summary of their strategies).

Communication Skills for Maintaining Relationships

Some people focus all their attention on beginning a relationship, thinking that after they have a friend, a boyfriend, or a girlfriend, they're set. They fail to realize that close relationships need attention, and sometimes work, to keep them functioning.

"We really need to talk about our relationship, so I've booked us on a TV show."

Of course, close relationships aren't all work, or we wouldn't enjoy them so much. But if you ignore your closest relationships, they will begin to falter and perhaps deteriorate. **Preventative maintenance** involves paying attention to your relationships when they are not experiencing troubles. Both partners need to attend to this. We review three skills that are useful for maintenance: openness, supportiveness, and humor.

Openness

As we mentioned in our discussion of systems theory, openness is one half of a dialectic tension. We all want to be transparent and yet protected in interpersonal relationships. So, we aren't recommending ignoring protection. Yet, it is helpful in close relationships to share feelings with a partner appropriately. We maintain relationships by telling our partners how we feel about things that don't relate to them and by sharing how we are feeling in the relationship. When we are willing to share our feelings about things and people outside the relationship, we self-disclose and let the other know that we trust them. In addition, we give them information to let them know us fully. When we share our feelings, our emotional reactions to our partner and our relationship we can strengthen our relational ties. The feelings we share need to be both positive as well as negative and, according to research (Gottman, 2004), the more the balance is weighted toward the positive, the better.

Supportiveness

A supportive communication climate, which encourages relational growth and maintenance, is conducive to maintaining relationships. However, supportive climates do not happen by chance; skillful communication is necessary to build this type of climate. In the "Skill Spotlight," we elaborate some of the specific skill sets that contribute to a supportive climate in relationships. The overall guidelines (Gibb, 1961, 1964, 1970) are as follows:

- Make *descriptive* rather than evaluative comments
- Speak in *provisional* ways rather than in a certain manner

Skill *Spotlight*

Establishing a Supportive Climate

Use Description
When we describe, we use the I-messages that we have talked about previously in the text, and we don't activate defensive feelings in the partner as easily. For example, if Josie says to her friend Carole, "I was disappointed that you forgot my birthday," which describes how Josie feels rather than blames Carole, Carole is likely to respond in a non-defensive manner. For example, Carole might say, "I'm sorry, I don't know what happened this year. I would like to celebrate your birthday now, if it's okay," providing a positive resolution to the situation. Although we don't mean to imply that you should never make an evaluative statement, remember that others may find evaluation comments difficult to hear, even when they are positive (Partner A: "What a good job you did cleaning up the kitchen." Partner B: "Do you think I am 12? Why do you have to comment on that like it's the first time I've ever cleaned up anything!").

Be Provisional
If you are absolutely certain about something ("This is the only restaurant worth going to in town" or "There's no way I can be persuaded that George W. Bush is a good president"), you cut off further conversation with your partner if your partner has a different viewpoint. Why bother trying to convince someone to try a different restaurant if that person has already stated that there are absolutely no other places worth trying? Provisional ways of speaking indicate that, although you have an opinion, you are open to discussing the topic if your partner wants to do so ("I've always enjoyed going to Louie's Place, and I haven't found a better restaurant anywhere—but, of course, I haven't tried every restaurant in town" or "The way I see George W. Bush is pretty negative; to me, he wasn't able to implement the good ideas he did have").

Be Spontaneous
Although strategic thinking is useful in some situations (in a job interview, in a negotiation, and so forth), in close relationships, strategic communication generally makes people feel defensive, on guard, and less trusting. These feelings defeat the goal of building a supportive climate between partners. More open and spontaneous communication is preferred. If you want to ask your partner for a favor, asking directly is generally more supportive than introducing it in a less forthright manner. If you begin by reminding your partner of the last favor you did for him or her, your partner may feel manipulated when you pounce on him or her with your request. If you simply ask, "Would you be able to run these errands for me on your way to class today?" you will probably build a more supportive climate than if you hint around before asking.

Take a Problem-Solving Orientation
Speaking about conflicts or decisions as problems for the two of you to solve together rather than as power struggles between you helps foster a supportive climate. If, for example, Max wants to go to sleep, but his roommate, Dexter, wants to have the lights on so he can study, Max could argue for his point of view in an attempt to control the outcome of the conflict. Some people refer to this as a win-lose perspective (Dexter wins because he gets to keep the lights on, and Max has to suffer with it, so he loses). A problem orientation helps lead to a win-win outcome. Instead of arguing for why it's fair to leave on the lights or turn them off, the two roommates brainstorm a solution that allows both of their goals to be satisfied. Can Dexter study in the lounge? Can Max sleep with a room-darkening mask on? Can Dexter have the lights on later on Mondays, Wednesdays, and Fridays, turning them off earlier on other days? When you adopt a problem orientation, you try to look at the conflict as a problem to be solved (how can we both get what we want?) rather than an opportunity to assert power and control over your relational partner.

(continued)

Skill *Spotlight* (continued)

Exhibit Empathy

Empathy is not needed in every interaction between partners, and part of the mastery of this skill involves learning when to use it. If Brad and Peg are having a casual conversation about how their school's football team is doing in the standings, or Stan is talking to his wife about something he just read in the newspaper, empathy (or active listening) may not be needed. However, if Stan's wife comes home from work and tells him what a terrible day she had, or Brad calls Peg to say he's afraid his girlfriend wants to break up with him, showing empathy is definitely called for and helps build a supportive climate. When you empathize, you want to let the other person know that you are there for him or her and that you are willing to settle in and really listen to what your partner has to say. You don't want to say something like "everyone has a bad day once in a while" or "girlfriends come and go," because both of these statements make it seem as though you are an objective, neutral observer, oblivious to the feelings the other is expressing. Empathy says you care about the other so much so that you will suspend what you are doing and focus while that person talks about his or her feelings.

Express Equality

Communication that expresses equality says that we respect one another. When people feel that they are not respected in a relationship, that feeling contributes to defensiveness. At times, someone you relate with may know more about an issue or a skill than you do. But even when one friend teaches another something, the teaching process can be done in a manner that shows respect. For example, if Maria knows a lot more about computers than her friend Ellie, Maria can teach Ellie some computer skills if Ellie asks. However, Maria shouldn't say to Ellie that's she's surprised that Ellie hasn't learned how to use the computer yet or speak to Ellie in sophisticated computer-speak, which would make Ellie feel stupid and hopeless about ever learning what Maria knows.

Skills at Work At work, we may not feel that a supportive atmosphere is necessary or even possible. And, of course, there are boundaries in the workplace concerning pursuing personal relationships. Yet, it is possible to adapt some of the elements we've discussed for supportive climates to the work context. For instance, taking a problem-solving orientation is a skill that's critical on the job. If Alma and Mel are working together on a project, and they encounter a dilemma before the project is completed, they need a problem-solving approach to be productive. If they begin blaming one another or attempting to exert power over each other, they will not be able to finish the project efficiently. Instead of attacking each other, a more helpful strategy would be for Alma and Mel to brainstorm and focus on resolving the problem. Can you identify other instances where a supportive climate can be helpful in the workplace?

- Be more *spontaneous* than strategic
- Strive for a *problem orientation* rather than a control orientation
- Provide *empathy* instead of neutrality to your partner
- Establish *equality* between partners rather than superiority of one over the other

Using Humor

Finally, humor in close relationships serves a maintenance function. Joking and kidding are both indicators of enjoyment. Research supports the notion that humor promotes bonding and cohesion as well as stress management (Axmaker, 2002–

2004). You can probably think of a time when you shared a joke with a friend or broke the tension with a humorous statement. Humor is a way of bringing people together (Young & Bippus, 2001). Bonding over something that's seen as amusing by both partners helps maintain relationships.

For more about understanding relationships and building successful relationships with others, use your Understanding Interpersonal Communication CD-ROM to access Interactive Activity 10.5: Building Relationships That Last.

Communication Skills for Repairing Relationships

When relationships run into trouble, you and your partner are faced with the difficult task of **corrective maintenance,** or repair (Dindia, 1994). Remember that relational repair is the job of both partners. Repair skills are more difficult to implement than maintenance skills because repair involves correcting a complication, whereas maintenance is simply aimed at keeping things moving.

Metacommunication

Metacommunication means communicating about communication. If communication is the problem in the relationship, the partners need to address how to improve their communication. For example, if Mary tells her friend Mike that she doesn't like it when he raises his voice to her, she is engaging in metacommunication. Mike might respond that he raises his voice when he gets excited. Mary can then tell him that she interprets it as anger. After the two define the problem through metacommunication, they can work on figuring out how to repair the problem.

Apology

An **apology** is a simple statement like "I am really sorry." Sometimes apologies are accompanied by **accounts,** or explanations for the transgression. For example, Keisha and Maya had been really close friends all through high school. They had kept in touch after graduation, even through they had moved to opposite ends of the country. For several years, they exchanged Christmas cards, and they even saw each other from time to time. Each time they met, it was as if they had just been together. However, one year, Keisha sent Maya her usual Christmas card, and Maya didn't respond. After a couple of years, Keisha stopped sending the cards, and the two ceased contact.

Three years later, Maya called and apologized. She told Keisha that problems she had been having with her family had demanded all her concentration. Maya just

---

CHOICES *for Beginning, Maintaining, and Repairing Relationships*

To begin:
- Network
- Offer or make yourself approachable
- Approach others yourself
- Sustain the conversation
- Engage in affinity-seeking behaviors

To maintain:
- Express yourself openly
- Develop a supportive communication climate
- Use humor

To repair:
- Metacommunicate
- Offer apologies and accounts

hadn't had the energy for keeping up any of her long-distance friendships. Keisha felt a lot better when she heard Maya's explanation, and the two were able to resume their friendship.

Summary

In this chapter, we tackled a huge topic: communication in close relationships. According to Maslow's hierarchy of needs, establishing relationships is the third most important human need, after physical and safety needs. People's close relationships are both public (and thus knowable) and private (and therefore subjective, difficult to study, and idiosyncratic). Researchers have been drawn to studying communication in the context of close relationships because the two have been shown to be inextricably intertwined and because close relationships are powerful forces for both good and ill in people's lives. As a result, we have a lot of information about communication in close relationships.

To organize the information, we reviewed many definitions of close relationships and examined the important role that language plays in establishing an understanding of what constitutes close relationships. We illustrated this point with a brief discussion of how metaphors for close relationships ("I felt like I was being smothered in this relationship," "We burned with passion," "Our relationship always left me hungry for more," and so forth) give us ways to think about relationships and perhaps affect the ways we communicate in them as well.

We reviewed four frameworks (systems, dialectics, social exchange, and Knapp's model of relationship development) that offer some explanation for how we communicate in close relationships. We discussed systems thinking, which allows us to see close relationships as highly interdependent, open, self-adjusting systems. We illustrated seven common relational dialectics—autonomy-connection, openness-protection, novelty-predictability, judgment-acceptance, affection-instrumentality, public-private, and real-ideal—and talked about some strategies to manage them. We explored the central premise of social exchange: relationships are governed by self-interest or a desire to keep costs down and rewards high. Lastly, we considered the ten stages in Mark Knapp's model of coming together and coming apart.

We addressed the importance of factors such as gender and culture—variables that make generalizing about communication in close relationships difficult. Although there are some universals of close relationships, some differences—for example, differences across cultures, such as collectivism versus individualism—affect how friendships and family relationships are constituted and communicated.

We examined both dark and bright sides of communication in close relationships. The dark side includes toxic relationships, such as those characterized by violence. Ironically, some "bad" behaviors, such as swearing, can actually have a positive affect on relationships. The bright side includes increased closeness and connection. And even when partners in a close relationship disagree, they may do so in a positive manner.

Some guidelines for communicating in close relationships are helpful. In beginning relationships, you need to engage in networking, offering, approaching, sustaining, and affinity seeking. When maintaining relationships, you should focus on openness, be supportive, and use humor. Metacommunication and apology are useful strategies for repairing relationships. As was the case throughout this book, all these skills provide suggestions, not prescriptions. Given the variety of close relationships and the factors that influence them, no one can come up with a single list of skills that will always be successful in every relationship across all cultures. Yet, we believe that the more we understand about communicating in close relationships, the more successful and life-enhancing our relationships will be.

Understanding Interpersonal Communication Online

Now that you've read Chapter 10, use your Understanding Interpersonal Communication CD-ROM for quick access to the electronic study resources that accompany this text. Your CD-ROM gives you access to the video of Hope and Randy on pages 277, the Communication Assessment Test on page 281, the CNN video clip "Commuter Couples" on page 288, the Ethics & Choice interactive activity on page 307, InfoTrac College Edition, and the Understanding Interpersonal Communication website. When you get to the Understanding Interpersonal Communication home page, click on "Student Book Companion Site" in the Resource box at right to access the online study aids for this chapter, including a digital glossary, review quizzes, and the chapter activities.

Terms for Review

accounts 313
affection and instrumentality dialectic 293
affinity seeking 309
apology 313
approaching 308
autonomy and connection dialectic 292
avoiding stage 302
bonding stage 300
boundaries or openness 290
calibration 291
circumscribing stage 301
comparison level 296
comparison level for alternatives 297
corrective maintenance 313
costs 295

differentiating stage 301
equifinality 291
experimenting stage 299
external dialectics 293
hierarchy 290
ideal and real dialectic 293
imagined conversations 302
initiating stage 298
integrating stage 300
intensifying stage 299
interdependence 290
internal dialectics 293
judgment and acceptance dialectic 293
long-term attraction 298
metacommunication 313
negative feedback 291
networking 308
novelty and predictability dialectic 292

offering 308
openness and protection dialectic 292
parasocial relationship 288
positive feedback 291
preventative maintenance 310
public and private dialectic 293
recalibrated 291
relationship 284
rewards 295
short-term attraction 298
small talk 299
stagnating stage 301
subsystems 290
suprasystems 290
sustaining 309
terminating stage 302
wholeness 289

Questions for Understanding

Comprehension Focus

1. Describe the difference between defining close relationships from a performance perspective and defining close relationships from a psychological perspective.
2. List the characteristics that Hinde believes characterize a close relationship.
3. List the stages of coming together and coming apart. How does communication differ depending on the stage you are in?
4. List the main dialectics that researchers think characterize close relationships, including friendships.
5. What is the main metaphor that social exchange theory applies to communication in close relationships?

Application Focus

1. **CASE IN POINT**
   How can Hope and Randy stay friends after the reason that began their friendship has ended? What skills for relationship maintenance would it be useful for them to employ?
2. What do you think best explains communication in close relationships: dialectics, social exchange,

systems, or Knapp's model of relationship development? Can you combine these to come up with a better explanation than any one theory on its own can offer? Explain your answer with communication examples.

3. In your experience, how do factors like gender affect communication in friendships? Be specific. Do you think it's possible to generalize about women's and men's communication in friendships? Explain.
4. Do you agree that close relationships have a dark side as well as a bright side? Do you think relationship ills are "in the relationship" or in the person? Explain your answer. How would a systems theorist answer the question? Would your answer (or the question itself) be different if you looked at cultures other than the culture in the United States? Explain.
5. Describe the metaphor inherent in a stage model approach to explaining relationships. What information does it bring with it, and how does it guide us to perceive relational life? Why do people think of relationships as needing movement?

Interactive Activities and InfoTrac College Edition Exercises

Complete the Interactive Activities and InfoTrac College Edition Exercises for Chapter 10 online at the Understanding Interpersonal Communication website. Select the chapter resources for Chapter 10, then click on "Activities" or "InfoTrac College Edition." If requested, you can submit your answers to your instructor.

Interactive Activities

InfoTrac College Edition Exercises

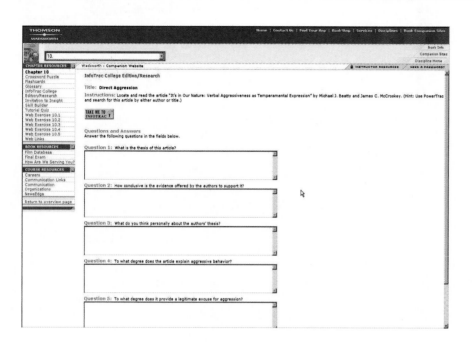

THOMSON
WADSWORTH

Home | Contact Us | Find Your Rep | BookShop | Services | Disciplines | Book Companion Sites

Book Info
Companion Sites
Discipline Home

10.

Wadsworth : Companion Website

CHAPTER RESOURCES
Chapter 10
Crossword Puzzle
Flashcards
Glossary
InfoTrac College
Edition/Research
Invitation to Insight
Skill Builder
Tutorial Quiz
Web Exercise 10.1
Web Exercise 10.2
Web Exercise 10.3
Web Exercise 10.4
Web Exercise 10.5
Web Links

BOOK RESOURCES
Film Database
Final Exam
How Are We Serving You?

COURSE RESOURCES
Careers
Communication Links
Communication
Organizations
NewsEdge

Return to overview page

INSTRUCTOR RESOURCES   NEED A PASSWORD?

InfoTrac College Edition/Research

Title: **Direct Aggression**

Instructions: Locate and read the article "It's in Our Nature: Verbal Aggressiveness as Temperamental Expression" by Michael J. Beatty and James C. McCroskey. (Hint: Use PowerTrac and search for this article by either author or title.)

TAKE ME TO
INFOTRAC

Questions and Answers
Answer the following questions in the fields below.

Question 1: What is the thesis of this article?

Question 2: How conclusive is the evidence offered by the authors to support it?

Question 3: What do you think personally about the authors' thesis?

Question 4: To what degree does the article explain aggressive behavior?

Question 5: To what degree does it provide a legitimate excuse for aggression?

11

Technology and Interpersonal Communication

Marjorie Gillespie couldn't imagine life without Carrie, her only child, and yet the time had come for Carrie to leave for college. Marjorie had known that this day would come, but the butterflies in her stomach caught the single mom by surprise. Marjorie looked out her bedroom window and saw the packed car. It seemed like only yesterday when she had taught Carrie how to drive, and now the car would be taking Carrie away. Marjorie was dreading that final goodbye.

As Carrie came upstairs, she saw her mother sitting next to the window. Carrie went over to her mom, put her arm around her, and reminded her that she was an adult now. Carrie said: "Look, Mom—I'm not a little girl anymore. You have got to stop thinking of this as the end of our relationship. We'll always stay in touch. Hey, with today's technology, we could literally stay in touch twenty-four hours a day!"

Marjorie thought about Carrie's words. Stay in touch, she thought—whatever that means. Marjorie knew that as a single mother with only one child, she had always felt a bit protective of Carrie. She had volunteered in every class of Carrie's and had served on the local school board to oversee what took place in her daughter's school. When she thought about what it meant to keep in touch, Marjorie wondered how that would be possible when they would be so far apart.

Carrie continued: "Mom, we both have cell phones. You can call me anytime. We have email; you can write me anytime you need to, and I'll write you back. I have a pager, just in case you need to get in touch with me when I'm in class. I'm in the new 'tech generation,' and now you're a part of it, too. You can't turn back now, Mom!" Marjorie began to smile and confessed, "And to think I had trouble with the VCR!"

As the two walked downstairs, they vowed to stay in contact every day. Carrie thought that constant communication would help her mom get over living in an empty house. When Carrie drove away, Marjorie ran into the house, picked up the phone, and called her daughter's cell phone. Carrie answered. "What is it, Mom?" Marjorie admitted that it was going to be tough to let her daughter go, but she knew she could talk to her anytime. So the two women began their long-distance relationship, each relying on communication technology to get them through this challenging time. ■

We have been using technology to communicate for more than 100 years. The invention of the telephone in 1875 allowed people to talk to a next-door neighbor or a distant cousin. And 100 years later, the invention of the telephone answering machine in the 1980s gave many people even more comfort in calling because a message could be left even when the receiver was not home.

Today, the telephone may seem like an antiquated technology, despite its continued popularity and the continuing changes and updates on the basic model. We now have an assortment of technologies available for making electronic connections: palmOne organizers, pagers, beepers, iPods, videoconferencing, email, and fax machines, to name just a few. And cell phones in particular are everywhere. As Michael Bugeja (2004) notes, "cell phones remind us that we dwell in more than one place at most times, splitting consciousness in parks, cars, schools, restaurants, and malls" (p. B5). We employ these communication technologies in our personal and professional lives. In fact, they help shape our lives in many ways, and the effect of this communication upon us is the focus of this chapter.

The members of our society have different technological fields of experience. Your classroom is likely a microcosm of society. Some of you grew up with a full awareness of, and expertise in, technology. Using the computer, setting the VCR, talking on a cell phone, and using other technology are second nature. For others of you, figuring out how to change the tape in the telephone answering machine is a challenge. Regardless of our backgrounds in using technology, there is always something new to learn and something coming soon.

And it appears that we can't acquire technology fast enough. We are becoming a society that is impatient with just one technological innovation at a time; we always want new technology and technology that can be used in conjunction with our current technology. Responding to that need, "technologies continue to converge" (Jones, 1998, p. xiv). **Convergence** is the integration of various technologies. We are living in a time where many technologies are morphing and interacting with other technologies. Think about voice-activated computers or cell phones that take pictures. Or consider the evolution of the phone-fax-answering machine. The newest handheld organizer (called BlackBerry) is a cell phone, computer, and personal calendar all in one.

As a society, we have grown accustomed to convergence. We tend to expect technologies to evolve so that they are more efficient and less cumbersome. Most of us cannot afford a new technology when it first comes out, so we wait for prices to decrease. For example, when the plasma television came on the market, it cost more than $10,000. In recent years, the price has dropped by almost 70 percent.

Since the advent of the personal computer and the mobile phone in the 1980s, the use of communication technology has exploded. Everywhere you look, someone is accessing email via a wireless connection, talking on a cell phone, or recording an appointment on a handheld organizer. What technologies do you use to communicate with your family, friends, and coworkers?

The lower the cost, the more affordable technology becomes. The more affordable, the more people will own it. And, the more people own it, the more they will tend to use it.

Perhaps the convergence of technology has made us a population that brings people closer together. In our opening story, Marjorie Gillespie, unlike some parents, doesn't appear too anxious about the technology available. Knowing the effects of her daughter's departure on her personally, Marjorie will likely consult all available technology to keep the lines of communication open with her daughter, Carrie. In fact, Alcestis Oberg (2003) comments that families who use technology are more likely to remain close:

> My children and I all have moved together into cyberspace. It no longer matters anymore where we are physically. If home is where the heart is, then our hearts have moved into the invisible realm of mobile and wireless communications, and into the ethereal hometown called the Internet. There, we can be—and always will be—together. (p. 11A)

As we write this chapter, some of it may quickly become out of date because advances in technology continue to dominate our culture, and what is new today becomes obsolete tomorrow. Yet, like the telephone, some communication technology remains with us forever. And this technology has the potential to affect who we are, what we do, and how we interact with others.

This chapter examines the role that technology plays in our interpersonal communication. Specifically, we focus on **computer-mediated communication (CMC),** which refers to the use of various technologies to facilitate communication with others. A valuable theoretical framework to consider as you read this chapter is **technological determinism,** which suggests that technology is irreversible, inevitable, and inescapable (McLuhan & McLuhan, 1988). In other words, it's hard to ignore the impact that communication technologies have had upon us—and, according to technological determinists, we have no choice but to deal with that impact.

We noted earlier that you and your classmates probably have various levels of experience and exposure to technology. Therefore, to ensure that we all have the same foundation of knowledge in this area, we begin with a discussion of the characteristics of technology.

Characteristics of Communication Technology

As we have discussed, technology affects our conversations and relationships with others. Without an understanding of communication technology and the language used to discuss it (see Table 11.1 on page 325), you won't be prepared to make effective choices when dealing with those who may or may not embrace technology. Consider the three characteristics of technology: It is pervasive, paradoxical, and powerful.

When we state that technology is pervasive, we are saying that it is everywhere. We cannot escape nor ignore technology in our lives. We wake with an alarm clock. We make telephone calls to our family. We fax reports at work. We take digital pictures on our vacations. We are beeped by our children, who ask what's for dinner. Those same children sit down in front of the television to play video games. And some of us try to organize our day's activities on a BlackBerry®.

Because technology is everywhere, we rely on it as a matter of course. Consider, for instance, how you would make it through the day without technology. Most of us would feel overwhelmed if we were deprived of the convenience that technology offers us. As communication and culture scholar Siva Vaidhyanathan (quoted by Neil Swidey, 2003), said, "It's the collapse of inconvenience. It turns out inconvenience was a really important part of our lives and we didn't realize it" (p. 11).

Technology is paradoxical, meaning that it is conflicting, inconsistent, and ironic. To understand this concept, consider what communication theorist Marshall McLuhan (1964) called the **global village.** McLuhan coined this term to describe how communication technology ties the world into one political, economical, social, and cultural system. Although the phrase *global village* is almost a cliché these days, McLuhan is the one who, more than 40 years ago, expressed the idea that technology has the ability to bring people together. McLuhan stated that "the globe is no more than a village" (p. 5). The paradox is evident; the term *global* suggests an expansive view of the world, whereas the term *village* suggests a small community. The idea that technology, a large and cumbersome thing, can bring people together seems paradoxical.

When we say that technology is powerful, we mean that it influences people, events, and entire cultures. Technology can affect how people think, what they think about, when they develop relationships, and how they process their emotions with others (Kakutani, 2001). For instance, let's say that Jana is a student who decides to skip a group presentation. She emails the group members to let them know about an unplanned doctor's appointment. The group members read the email and reach different conclusions about her not being at the presentation. Some may think Jana is lazy, others may view her as self-serving, and others may de-

cide not to waste energy worrying about her motivations. Technology has the power to cause others to make judgments, even though the communicators are not face to face.

The Accessibility of Technology

Accessibility refers to the availability of technology to everyone. Accessibility helps eliminate the technological gap that exists between people and between cultural communities. Some have called this gap the "digital divide" (e.g., U.S. Department of Commerce, 1999). Many commonly refer to this as the battle between the information "haves and have-nots." On a global scale, researchers estimate that about 90 percent of Internet use occurs in richer and industrialized countries (Thurlow, Lengel, & Tomic, 2004). On a local level, Mike Wendland (2002) contextualizes this topic. He argues that if you live in a suburb, make lots of money, and are highly educated, you most likely have no problem understanding the Internet. If you dwell in a large city, have a low income, and possess a limited education, you're probably not connected to or benefiting from the Internet.

Additionally, racial and geographic differences concerning Internet use further illustrate the digital divide. The Pew Foundation's study of Internet use and race, for example, found that among the major racial groups, more than half of white people (58 percent), 43 percent of African Americans, and 50 percent of Hispanics have used the Internet (Spooner & Rainie, 2000). Finally, looking at rural and urban use, Sandra Guy (2004) sees accessibility to technology as the same as seeking out friends and neighbors: "Rural residents go online [for instance] for information and to seek support groups, sports leagues, and civic groups—communities they cannot find in their neighborhoods."

The digital divide is evident with nearly all communication technology. Even telephones—one of the most ubiquitous of technologies—vary in their accessibility. The National Telecommunications and Information Administration (1999),

REVISITING CASE IN POINT

1. Explain the relevancy of the phrase *global village* to the relationship between Marjorie and Carrie Gillespie.
2. Apply all three characteristics of communication technology to the closeness of Carrie and Marjorie's relationship.

You can answer these questions online under Student Resources for Chapter 11 at the Understanding Interpersonal Communication website.

for example, notes that there is a significant divide among racial communities. The national survey showed that overall, households headed by white individuals have a higher telephone availability and usage (95.0 percent) than African American households (85.4 percent) and households headed by Hispanic individuals (84.6 percent). And across the world, vast differences in telephone accessibility exist. Consider the observation of Allen Hammond (2001), Senior Scientist at the World Resources Institute: Half of the world's population has never even made a phone call.

For an alternate look at the current state of the digital divide in the United States, use your Understanding Interpersonal Communication CD-ROM to access **Interactive Activity 11.1: What Digital Divide?**

What does accessibility to communication technology have to do with interpersonal communication? First, if everyone does not have access to all technology, language barriers may exist. In conversations with others, we cannot refer to meeting someone online, finding out information about Alzheimer's disease on the Internet for a relative, leaving a voice mail if no one is at home, reading an online profile, or "welcoming" someone in a chat room, because not everyone will understand our language and be able to avail themselves of these multiple technologies. Consistent communication without equal access to technology is difficult. What many of you may take for granted (for example, a telephone call, a message on an answering machine, an instant message, and so forth) may not be universally accepted nor understood because of accessibility issues. Consequently, think twice before assuming a classmate has access to a certain technology.

Second, accessibility to communication technology has many positive benefits: It increases safety, creates a sense of play, and improves psychological well-being between and among people. Making phone calls in case of emergencies seems instinctive to most of us. Playing chess on the computer or having a technological conversation in a discussion group with other dog owners helps increase the element of play. We explore how technology can improve psychological well-being when we discuss the bright side of technology a bit later in this chapter.

We have been discussing communication technology such as the Internet as if each of you knows its meaning. To make sure we have a common understanding, let's briefly talk about the background of the Internet as well as its dark and bright sides.

The Internet: Connecting Now

Imagine being on the streets of New York City. All the streets, from the major arteries to the small alleys, comprise a complex network. Now, imagine you are in the office of the city's Director of Streets and Sanitation looking at a lighted grid of every street in Manhattan. The grid encompasses the 22.4 square miles of the island.

This image should help you understand what the Internet is. When we send electronic communication, our information is transported by the **Internet,** which is an extended network of smaller computer networks interconnected with each other. The Internet

Facing *Change*

In this chapter, we discuss the notion that technology is often framed within a "haves" and "have-nots" framework. This issue centers on whether or not everyone has equal access to communication technology. Considering the wave of immigration in our country and our country's response to it, do you believe that the percent of people with accessibility to technology will increase or decrease? What impact, if any, will newly arrived immigrants have upon communication technology? Will online relationships be influenced in any way? Explain with examples.

Use your Understanding Interpersonal Communication CD-ROM to watch the CNN video clip "France and Cyberspace," which discusses France's response to Internet terminology that is based in U.S. culture and idiom. Click on the "CNN & Change" icon in the menu at left, then click on "Video Menu" in the menu bar at the top of the screen. Select "France and Cyberspace" to watch the video (it takes a minute for the video to load). As you watch the video, consider the "cyberspeak" you've seen on the Internet. Was it easy to interpret, or did you find yourself completely confused? What do you think of France's response to current Internet terminology? You can respond to this and other analysis questions by clicking on "Analysis" in the menu bar at the top of the screen. When you've answered all the questions, click on "Done" to compare your answers to those provided by the authors.

Table 11.1   Coming to Terms with the Internet

Term	Definition	Example
World Wide Web	Internet sites are called websites, and websites are part of the **World Wide Web** (abbreviated *WWW*), an extravagant collection of Internet servers that give users visual access to documents. Websites contain web pages, and the first page of a website is the **home page** (a term often used to refer to an entire website).	www.wadsworth.com, the homepage of the publisher of this text.
Hyperlink	The World Wide Web is organized around links. An image or text on a web page that is linked to another web page or another part of the same web page is a **hyperlink.** An external link takes users who click on it to another web page, and an internal link takes users who click on it to a different spot on the same page. Hyperlinks make your search for information more comprehensive by enabling you to easily move between web pages.	Go to the U.S. census website (www.census.gov) to find numerous hyperlinks. For example, the menu items in the lefthand column and at the bottom of the page are hyperlinks, as are the items in the middle column of the page.
Spam	A kind of junk mail on the Internet, **spam** is unsolicited and may take the form of promotions that clog your email inbox. Generally, spam is an annoyance, and email users try to block it with filtering software.	Unsolicited email that encourages you to buy "Xanax for less" or lets you know that "Britney Spears loves Rolex watches."
Search engine	Most computers have software installed that allows the user to locate content on the web. This software is called a **search engine.** Search engines are like libraries; they store and categorize information or graphics for future use. Search engines, like websites, come and go. Search engines vary in how they cluster and organize the information sought by users.	www.google.com www.yahoo.com www.dogpile.com
Browser	You view websites using a **browser,** which is a program that determines how documents are displayed on your computer. The first web browser was called Mosaic, and was conceptualized by an undergraduate student at the University of Illinois. When browsers are user-friendly (that is, easy to navigate and visually appealing), they help increase web traffic.	Netscape Navigator Internet Explorer Opera
Cookies	**Cookies** are small data files that are left and stored on your computer by your browser. Cookies allow for online tracking of your activities, whether you're searching for online dates, purchasing magazines, or researching medical websites. Most browsers allow cookies to be deleted, and others let the user know that a cookie is being stored.	
Chat room	When individuals come together in an electronic gathering "place," they are said to be in a chat room. **Chat rooms** are live online dialogues with other people who share similar interests. Chat room participants may meet at the same time each day, or they may engage in spontaneous conversations. Chat rooms span thousands of topic areas.	If you're interested in the Boston Red Sox, you could enter a chat room dedicated to this World Series–winning team (http://groups.msn.com/boston redsox).
Uniform resource locator	The addressing scheme used by browsers on the World Wide Web is called the **uniform resource locator,** or **URL.** The URL is basically the address of the web page. Every web page has its own web address.	www.songtitle.info, the URL to the fun site Songtitle.Info: Music from TV commercials.

(or "the Net") has been called a "network of networks" because of its embedded connections and because it "has changed the way people work, learn, play, and communicate" (Barnes, 2003, p. 3).

Background of the Internet

The Internet was called the "information superhighway" when it first appeared in the late 1970s, but this metaphor has lost its luster. Michael Noll (1997) observes that the information superhighway "has not been as super as many have promised. The many potholes and washed out bridges have jolted our sense of reality" (p. 191).

So many have traveled this electronic highway that it is in need of significant attention and repair.

Although the Internet didn't live up to the super-high expectations, it continues to be an important presence in communication technology. The number of people connected to the Internet has grown exponentially. Worldwide, approximately 934 million people use the Internet, including about 200 million in Canada and the United States (ClickZ Stats staff, 2004). The Pew Internet and American Life Project (2004) found that just under half of adults in the United States accessed the Internet in 2000; in 2003, that number had grown to 59 percent. In terms of age differences, the Pew Project discovered that in the United States, 22 percent of those over age 65 go online compared to 75 percent in the 30-to-49 age bracket. Finally, the regions of the country with the highest rates of Internet use are along the Pacific seaboard (the Pacific Northwest has 68 percent; California has 65 percent) and the Atlantic seaboard (66 percent of New England is connected to the Internet). These numbers clearly show that, despite our earlier discussion of accessibility, millions of people are electronically connected, although some differences across generations and locations exist.

The Dark Side of the Internet: Proceed with Caution

Communication technologies such as the Internet should be approached cautiously. Like nearly any technology, there is always the opportunity for something to go wrong. With more than 275 million web pages and a growth rate of nearly 20 million pages per month (Bharat & Broder, 1998), it is impossible to control web content because anyone can put up a website. In fact, as Verlyn Klinkenborg (2004) writes in the *New York Times*, "Make no mistake. The web is still a place where you find every kind of fraud, deceit, obscenity, and insanity—more of it than ever" (p. A24). In other words, a lot of stranger danger lurks on the Internet. Let's examine three significant issues to consider as you use the Internet: accountability, hate, and flaming. (See Table 11.2 on page 328 for examples of each of these dangers.)

Little Accountability

It's easy to develop a web page. All you have to do is figure out a possible web address, find out if the name has been taken, and follow through accordingly. Robert Danford (1999) writes,

> Users of the Web must approach the plethora of Web sites with the skills of a good consumer to see if the product offered is indeed what it purports to be, to see if the site will fulfill the user's need, to see which of the sites is available is the "best" in a given situation so that the user will be able to count on the information or services offered. (p. xiii)

In other words, there must be accountability. Accountability is being responsible. We demand accountability with our banks, employers, and schools, yet to demand accountability with the Internet is entirely different because without Internet accountability, we have the potential to be misguided, misinformed, and manipulated.

When using the Internet, we caution you to embrace accountability when at all possible. For example, suppose Damian is interested in trying online dating. He has had little luck meeting interesting people in person and has heard success stories from his roommate, so Damian decides to go to the Internet. Although Damian may be inclined to start surfing the web for dating sites, he should first ask himself a few questions. What criterion is he using to locate a particular website? What evidence shows that the site he accesses is legitimate? Does the site have a sponsor? Will Damian have to pay fees, or does the site's revenues come from advertisements? What protections are in place to ensure his privacy? How do others looking for dates contact you? Is there a way of verifying the credentials of potential dates? What sorts of ads appear on the website? Are they sexually explicit or professional? Are there restrictions for downloading pictures or personal information? And, most important for Damian's purposes, what is the site's record for successful matches? As Leonard Shedletsky and Joan Aitken (2004) aptly note, "while some people find their love, a soul mate online, others find the nightmare of a lifetime" (p. 157).

The list of questions to ask is endless. We encourage you to be bold in your accountability pursuits. Doing anything less may result in relational consequences that you did not expect.

Fostering Hate

Certainly, websites have the potential to positively affect your conversations and relationships with others. Yet, the dark side of communication technologies suggests that hate on the Internet is alive and proliferating. **Hate speech** can be defined as extremely offensive language that is directed toward a particular group of people. Although hate speech is protected by First Amendment rights, such extremist communication has the potential to negatively affect another's communication.

Websites that use hate speech have proliferated over the years. They cover the spectrum, focusing on everything from anti-abortion sites that promote the death of abortion providers to websites ridiculing the existence of the Holocaust. Shedletsky and Aitken (2004) conclude that "through the Internet, disturbed minds effectively fuel hatred, violence, sexism, racism, and terrorism" (p. 108). Because offensive points of view are protected by First Amendment free-speech rights, hate speech on the Internet is probably here to stay. Websites that promote gay bashing, anti-Semitic views, the reinstitution of slavery, and so forth will continue. One way to combat this hatred is to visit sites that are dedicated to wiping out cultural hate. For example, the Southern Poverty Law Center (www.splcenter.org) promotes the development of community coalitions to combat hate. And a relational step you can take to combat hate is to speak up to others to educate them about why their biases are misplaced.

Flaming

At times, relationships with others online can get tense. **Flaming** occurs when people exchange malicious, hostile, or insulting comments. This lack of civility is like electronic road rage—it has the capacity to escalate. Flaming may simply be an exercise of control over others or a bold attempt at aggression (Thurlow, et al., 2004). Regardless of how long you may have known the flamer, flaming is best dealt with by disengaging and using more subtle ways of communicating. Avoiding capital letters, extreme punctuation (such as exclamation marks or ellipses), and accusatory language may help prevent further incivility. Consider the difference between the following two examples in a chat room of gay men:

© Reuters/Corbis

In the weeks following the terrorist attacks of September 11, 2001, many anti-Arab sites went up on the Internet, erroneously labeling some prominent Arab Americans as Islamic terrorists. The harmful effects of the misinformation spread by these sites illustrate the need for accountability on the Internet—not only were innocent people unfairly targeted, but many Internet providers spent time and money deleting these sites.

Situation 1

FLAMER: U F*GS R GONNA BURN IN HELL!:))))))))

PARTICIPANT 1: UR the freakn @-hole!

FLAMER: STAY 2UNED...MORE>>ONS!!

PARTICIPANT 2: And we're afraid of what? A PIG ^ 0 ^ like you?

FLAMER: DIE F*GS!

Situation 2

FLAMER: U F*GS R GONNA BURN IN HELL!

PARTICIPANT 1: Get LOST!!!!!!

FLAMER: CAN'T TAKE IT? FEEL THE HEAT?

PARTICIPANT 2: Taking off JT. Come back L8R.

Striving for disengagement and not becoming personally antagonistic, which is the strategy shown by Participant 2 in the second situation, should help you remove yourself from flaming and the flamer.

Consider how this interaction might have differed if it had happened in person instead of online. Some people find it easier to be uncivil in electronic than in face-to-face settings. Perhaps technological interactions provide a higher comfort level because a hateful person can be anonymous while cowardly hiding behind a computer screen. Remember the wizard in *The Wizard of Oz?* He lost all of his composure, aggressiveness, and anger when the curtain was literally pulled open. Would cyberhate be limited if individuals were required to communicate in person?

Table 11.2 | **The Dark Side of Internet Usage**

Little Accountability

Example: Chad decides to go online to a website that promotes itself as "the only website for single men who wish to meet accountants." After logging in, Chad meets a woman who claims to be an accountant for a large firm in the Midwest. After several email exchanges, he is favorably impressed and decides to give her his cell phone number. The problem is that Chad's online conversational partner is not an accountant; rather, she is an advertiser who wants to find out what sorts of hair care products he uses. The website was created by a large advertising company who specializes in men's cosmetics.

Fostering of Hate

Example: Lena is assigned to examine various websites on "spiritual values" for her Modern History class. When she types that phrase into a search engine, thousands of websites match that description. However, one website, called "Spiritual Values for the New Century," catches her attention. As appealing as that title sounds, Lena soon figures out that the website is filled with hate. The home page of the website states that "abortionists will burn in hell" if they don't "repent." Further, some links on the site allow Lena to read essays with such titles as "Why Abortionists Should Die," "What God said about the Abortion Doctors," and "Killing the Fetus Slowly." Lena soon discovers that the website promotes the execution of doctors who perform abortions.

Flaming

Example: David can't believe what he is reading. As a new parent, he had wanted to learn a bit more about temper tantrums. But, as his experience in a chat room on parenting is teaching him, people can be awfully vicious in their attacks. First, he reads the comments of one participant, who has no children, that every parent is a "selfish b**tard" and that "kids just boost egos!" A parent responds by telling the childless participant, "too bad your mom didn't fall down the steps carrying u!" David sits sadly by. He wants to jump in, but knows that he would probably just provoke even more incendiary remarks. He can't believe that people would discuss a topic such as parenting with such hostile and aggressive comments.

The Bright Side of the Internet: New Opportunities

Although the Internet certainly has its dark side, it also offers us unique opportunities. Generally speaking, we can communicate with people we might not have been able to communicate with otherwise. Further, such communication is quick and seamless, and even those with little technological know-how can quickly learn to communicate via the web. Let's look at two areas of Internet opportunities: widening your social network and enhancing your educational accessibility. (See Table 11.3 for examples of each of these benefits.)

Widening Your Social Network

With the Internet, you can widen your social circles tremendously in a short period of time—something you can't do with face-to-face communication. Computer-mediated communication allows individuals to seek out information and to maintain their relationships.

Earlier, we identified chat rooms as an important term to understand (see Table 11.1). In many ways, chat rooms are excellent venues to discover information about a particular subject—for example, the qualifications of political candidates, how to start a small business, or where to go on a cruise. In addition, information-seeking web users can facilitate online discussions with professionals who have credentials in a particular area. For example, let's say Marcie was recently diagnosed with diabetes and has no idea what the disease is all about. Marcie's first step will probably be to go to the Internet to find information using a search engine. After she discovers that there are literally hundreds of websites available on the topic, she has to decide which one to visit first. Inevitably, she will discover some chat rooms where physicians who specialize in the disease are able to answer her questions or respond to her concerns. However, keep in mind the important information about accountability that we discussed a bit earlier. Marcie should not be misled by those who are not qualified to offer suggestions in this area.

We already talked about the fact that some people use online interactions to facilitate the development of their relationships. Barnes (2003) also noted that CMC can aid in the maintenance and expansion of our relationships, both romantic and professional. In fact, Joseph Walther (1994) noted that the building and maintenance of relationships occurs all the time via CMC.

How can our relationships be maintained via electronic means? First, we live in a mobile society, with people transferring jobs or working across the miles; communication technology can bridge the geographic divide. According to Daniel Wood (2004), over 40 million people moved in 2002–2003, comprising about 14 percent of the population. Whether moving across town or across the country, migration usually requires adaptation to new surroundings and maintenance of existing relationships. Past friends and current family members, for example, will likely expect ongoing communication, and email can facilitate keeping in touch.

A second way in which our relationships are maintained via technology pertains to supporting others. In fact, some research indicates that entire communities are built and maintained online. For instance, Elena Larsen (2004) notes that faith communities in particular are flourishing and that individuals are using the Internet to show their support for each other and each other's religious identity. Larsen concludes that "more than 90% of online congregations reported that their members email each other for fellowship purposes" (p. 47). Individuals can seek out others for prayer requests, spiritual assistance and advice, and even facilitate spiritual relationships that were previously nonexistent. With technology, individuals who were once strangers can become linked in ways unimagined prior to the Internet.

Enhancing Your Educational Accessibility

We argued earlier that everyone cannot access the Internet. Susan Barnes (2003) asserts that "there is unequal access to the Internet in the United States" (p. 325). Crispin Thurlow, Laura Lengel, and Alice Tomic (2004) observe that "women have historically had little access to media" (p. 130). And Karen Riggs (2004) notes that "even though computer-user rates are growing fastest among Americans 50 and over, this age group remains the least likely to use computers and the Internet" (p. 227). Claims such as these make it increasingly important to look at how web accessibility increases the education of people who go online.

Earlier in this chapter, we talked about how the digital divide cuts across various racial groups. Another type of divide exists as well—a division between younger and older generations in terms of their Internet usage. Simply put, those who are younger (say, under the age of 50) tend to use the web much more frequently than those who are older (say, those over 50 years old). Why is this the case? Karen Riggs (2004) believes that ageism may be at play. Many people—from employers to physicians—maintain stereotypes of older adults, including the belief that they are unable to adapt to new technology. Yet, Riggs argues that with some training and enough tenacity, older adults are able to rapidly and competently deal with any technological challenge.

Just because older adults may not go online as frequently as younger adults does not mean that those over 50 remain technologically ignorant. When older adults do go online, they increase their opportunities to be informed about issues that relate

Table 11.3	The Bright Side of Internet Usage
Widen Your Social Network	
Example: As a newcomer to Chicago, Ramona isn't prepared to deal with the millions of people in the city. Her hometown has only 300 people, and although her previous job had taken her to the Windy City, she has never felt so alone in her life. Ramona isn't in the habit of going out; when she isn't at work, she usually stays home and watches television or emails her sister. However, one night Ramona decides to surf the Internet. She soon finds herself in a local chat room reading messages about one of her favorite topics, Hispanic history. She particularly likes reading about the history of mask making in Mexico. After several weeks in the chat room (during which she interacts with some of the other participants, sharing some of her thoughts on the topic), Ramona decides to meet several people from her chat room at a local museum that is featuring Aztecan masks. One person in particular catches Ramona's eye, they hit it off, and she soon thinks Chicago is one of the best cities in the world!	
Enhance Your Educational Accessibility	
Example: Morgan stands in his dining room looking at pictures of his wife. She has been dead for nearly a year now, and he still finds himself crying all the time. He decides that he can either cry every day or make something out of the rest of his life. Not wanting to let his emotions control him, Morgan decides to do something he has been wanting to do for many years but had been reluctant to tackle because he was uncertain how to proceed—he decides to start his own handyman business. So, he goes to the Internet and types "starting a business" in his search engine. Morgan soon begins to learn about self-employment tax, state regulations, and other matters small business owners need to know. He trusts the government's Small Business Administration website and downloads all of the information he can digest in one sitting. Morgan is excited about finding an opportunity to learn about an area he had never thought he would understand.	

directly to their professional and personal well-being. For example, Jackson, a 55-year-old father of two, decides to use the Internet to obtain information about employment discrimination. Leo, a 70-year-old father of five, browses the web for volunteer jobs. Cassandra, a 59-year-old single woman, goes online to find out about her recent diagnosis of ovarian cancer. And Rodney, a 65-year-old single man, seeks out potential mates on a website for single senior citizens.

The new economy requires a host of technological experiences and expertise (Neff & Stark, 2004). Further, the Internet continues to be a dominant source of information and entertainment for people of all ages. Therefore, communication technology cannot be reserved for those who have immediate access because they are Internet-active or because they happen to be recent college graduates with a wealth of web knowledge. The Internet affords people of all ages a number of professional and personal opportunities.

Now that you better understand the characteristics of technology and the dark and bright sides of the web, we turn our attention to how people present themselves online and then to more specific forms of communication technology and how they affect interpersonal communication.

The Presentation of the Self Online

In Chapter 2, we emphasized the role of the self in interpersonal communication. In this section, we describe the way individuals present themselves online. We begin with a brief examination of a few assumptions associated with the way identities are managed online, and then we sort out some of the identity markers available to those in electronic relationships.

Assumptions of Online Presentations of the Self

Understanding a few assumptions of how individuals present themselves online will expand your thinking about the self and its relationship to technology. Sherry Turkle (1995) reminds us that people online develop a "cyberself" and that in "virtual reality, we self-fashion and self-create" (p. 180). With each of the assumptions we describe, we draw comparisons to face-to-face encounters.

Assumption 1: The Computer Screen Can Deceive

When people are online, they often pretend to be someone or something they are not. Online dialogues can lead to deceitful presentations. Men can become women who want to talk to other women. Convicted felons can pose as young teenagers interested in Paris Hilton or Colin Farrell. The unemployed can become corporate CEOs, and CEOs can present themselves as unemployed. Generally speaking, people want to create a positive impression to manipulate their images to the maximum extent possible. What you see and read on the computer screen, then, may not be entirely accurate.

In face-to-face encounters, being deceitful to such an extent is usually much tougher. We can't lie about our biological sex, and we can't claim to be a tall and toned person when we are short and stocky. Our conversations with others are in the present; they are not delayed or responded to later, as are our online dialogues. If we ask a question, we expect a response. If we don't get a response, we may walk away from the encounter. Although chat rooms are in "real time," people can choose

Ethics & Choice

Bernadette Amarosa sat staring blankly at her computer screen. She had just done something she rarely did: she had lied. She hadn't meant to, she thought to herself, but she had gotten carried away with her online conversation with Michael and had typed in the lie before she thought it through.

As a divorced woman, Bernadette was not in the habit of going online to seek out a relationship. As a matter of fact, she laughed at her close friends—all of whom are married—when they encouraged her to visit some online dating websites. She thought that guys who placed personal ads online were rather desperate, and she certainly didn't want to date a desperate man! Yet, for some reason on this hot summer evening, Bernadette had decided to search for a website that specialized in dating. She had soon found herself entering some personal information, including her screen name ("Dot") and some other details, such as her dating preferences, including sex ("man"), age ("25–40"), profession ("be employed"), and location ("southeastern United States").

As she searched the personal ads, Bernadette was attracted to a profile of a man named Michael. She read his "stats" and felt something in common with him. She also thought that Michael, smiling with his baseball cap on backward in the picture, was cute. Bernadette finally worked up the nerve to email Michael. After a few minutes, he responded and said he was happy she connected. He said he had looked at her picture and profile and found her attractive.

Soon the two started emailing each other. Bernadette was not entirely truthful in her emails—for example, she didn't tell Michael that she was divorced and that she had two adult sons. Further, although she told Michael that she was in her 40s, she really was 53. As time went on, Bernadette grew more nervous about her deception. She thought she might have gotten herself in way too deep with her lies.

Bernadette faces a number of options in this technological predicament. She could tell Michael her real age and the fact that she has two children. Or, she could reveal part of this information to him. Or, she could choose to continue to conceal her true age and her children's existence. Are there other alternatives? What ethical issues are inherent in this circumstance? Reflecting on the five ethical system of communication we identified in Chapter 1 (categorical imperative, utilitarianism, ethic of care, golden mean, significant choice), explain your response with these frameworks in mind. Is one system more relevant than another? Explain.

Use your Understanding Interpersonal Communication CD-ROM to access an interactive version of this scenario on the Understanding Interpersonal Communication website. Look under Student Resources for Chapter 11 and click on the "Ethics & Choice" menu at left. The interactive version of this scenario allows you to choose an appropriate response to this dilemma and then see what consequences your choice brings about. You can also compare your answers to the questions at the end of the scenario to those provided by the authors and, if requested, email your response to your instructor.

when they'd like to respond. There is an immediate consequence and important difference, then, when one communicates via a computer screen versus when one communicates face to face.

Assumption 2: Online Discussions Often Prompt Introspection

Imagine that Bob and Shelly email each other about what they thought of the midterm exam. Shelly tells Bob that she thought it was pretty easy, but Bob thought it was pretty tough. As Bob reads Shelly's email, he starts to think about why he and Shelly each had different perceptions. They had studied together, after all. Before responding to the email, Bob starts to think about the material he didn't understand. "Yeah," he thinks, "there was some stuff I just didn't get." Email, in this situation, inspired Bob to think about his own study habits, an introspective behavior that may not have occurred without his friend's prompting.

Not every email elicits this self-assessment. Yet, when we do email another, we frequently engage in something similar to an internal dialogue. Think about when a supervisor emails an employee requesting a meeting as soon as possible but offers no specifics. Or, consider a time when a partner sends you an email wanting to break up, yet fails to explain why. These instances provoke us to reflect on both the message and our response to that message.

In face-to-face interactions, this same introspection and self-dialogue is not as apparent. First, we often don't take the time to think about the words of another *while they are being stated*. In fact, imagine what would occur if—in the middle of a conversation—you decided to stop to think about what another person was saying. Second, we are not trained nor conditioned to pause or stop conversations in this way. Most of our interpersonal encounters move rather freely from one point to another, with little reflection time.

Assumption 3: Online Discussions Promote Individualism

In Chapter 3, we looked at individualism, which is a cultural orientation that favors the self over the group. When communicating online, we tend to value our individuality; working on and with the computer is essentially a personal endeavor. We search out people, websites, and chat rooms in which we are interested. If others wish to contact us, we make a choice whether or not we want to respond to their

overture. In electronic relationships, keep in mind that one or both individuals may either choose to reply or not to reply. Because we have no physical proximity, we are not compelled to interact. People communicate at their own convenience.

In face-to-face interactions, we typically must be collaborative in our conversations. Although we can choose to say nothing, our silence—as we learned in Chapter 7—can communicate a great deal. In addition, when we are speaking in person, there is give and take, questions require answers, and our answers usually result in further dialogue. People cannot avoid the ongoing and transactional nature of communication in face-to-face conversations.

Assumption 4: Self-Disclosure Occurs Online

The process of revealing aspects of yourself to another is not confined to face-to-face conversations. Research shows that self-disclosure occurs online and that some people reveal quite a bit through electronic communication (Joinson, 2001). As we learned in Chapter 8, when people self-disclose, they are inclined to give people important pieces of information about themselves. Further, we know that self-disclosure tends to increase intimacy.

Some people feel comfortable disclosing online because they don't have to deal with immediate reactions of disgust, disappointment, or confusion. Individuals may find it easier to reveal emotionally laden information in a technological medium. The problem, according to Susan Barnes (2003), is that **postcyberdisclosure panic** **(PCDP)** can set in. PCDP is a situation in which someone discloses personal information in an email message only to experience significant anxiety later because the discloser begins to think about the number of people who could have access to that message. For instance, if Fran emails a coworker about her past problems with alcohol, that information has the potential to be passed (even inadvertently) to others, both in and out of the workplace. Interestingly, people may reveal information about themselves online that they would never reveal while face to face, perhaps because the computer screen is an impersonal object that doesn't have the capacity to show emotion.

The self-disclosive conversations we have with people while face-to-face can be dramatically different from those we engage in via email. In face-to-face interactions, we have to contend with facial reactions. We are often asked to clarify our thoughts or disclosures, and we may find it difficult to simply leave. We can't "turn off" another person as easily as we can turn off our computer screen. Self-disclosure in person generally causes an immediate reaction, which is something we don't necessarily have to deal with while online.

To read an interesting article that discusses self-disclosure on the Internet and how some people fared moving from online to face-to-face relationships, check out "Relationship Formation on the Internet: What's the Big Attraction?" available through InfoTrac College Edition. Use your Understanding Interpersonal Communication CD-ROM to access InfoTrac College Edition Exercise 11.1: Self-Disclosure Online. To read another article, "Can You See the Real Me?" which discusses the presentation of the true self online, access InfoTrac College Edition Exercise 11.2: Can You See the Real Me—Online?

Identity Markers on the Internet

On the Internet, individuals typically communicate who they are through identity markers. An **identity marker** is an electronic extension of who someone is. In other words, an identity marker is an expansion of the self. Two primary identity markers exist on the Internet: screen names and personal home pages.

Your screen name and home page can tell others a lot about who you are and what you're all about. Maybe you're into a particular celebrity, or you're an advocate for animal rights, or you're interested in weight lifting. These two roommates are what we could call music "freaks." What would be good screen names for them?

© Thomson Higher Education

Screen Names

As in face-to-face relationships, online relationships inevitably require introductions. Yet, unlike in interpersonal relationships, we can introduce ourselves online by using names which are odd, silly, fun, editorial, or outright offensive. These nicknames, called **screen names,** often serve to communicate the uniqueness of the sender of a message. Many screen names function as a way for communicators to protect their identities from others until more familiarity and comfort develops.

People use a wide variety of screen names. Some are shaped by fiction (>madhatter< or >hobbit<), others by popular culture (>AmIdol< or >TRUMPthis<), and still others by a desire to reinforce personal values (>WARRingOUT<). Haya Bechar-Israeli (1996) observes that many people place a great deal of importance on their screen names and nicknames and that they invest a great deal of thought in their creation. According to Bechar-Israeli, "References to collective cultural, ethnic, and religious themes in nicknames might indicate that the individual belongs to a certain social group." Her research shows that rather than frequently changing their names, people tend to keep their names for a period of time, which underscores the fact that people commit themselves to a screen identity.

At first glance, screen names may seem unimportant in building an electronic discussion and relationship. However, unlike your name (which was probably given to you at birth), screen names are created by the individual. And despite the relative stability of screen names, people can change their names much more easily in virtual life than in real life. If you encounter someone who is verbally offensive online, you can leave a chat room, establish a different name, and reenter the chat room under an entirely different alias. Even wigs and cosmetic surgery can't achieve such a transformation so quickly! Finally, unless you are a member of an ethnic community in which names are rooted in family lineage, most of our given names at birth (for example, Joe, Luisa, Natalie) communicate little to others. On the other hand, screen names give others insight into people's interests or values. A screen name such as >STALKU< can tell others a lot. As we noted in our Chapter 6 discussion of email addresses, screen names that are appropriate for some aspects of our life may be inappropriate for others.

Personal Home Pages

If an individual wants to communicate a great deal of personal information, a personal home page may be the first step. A **personal home page** is a website that provides online viewers an opportunity to better know an individual. Personal home pages, sometimes called web pages, present a number of features that depict who the person is, such as information on personal hobbies and genealogy; photographs of the person and his or her family members, friends, pets, and home; and links to groups with advocacy causes or contacts.

Communicating one's identity via a personal home page is often enlightening to others. In their 1999 book, *Web Wisdom,* Janet Alexander and Marsha Ann Tate note that personal websites can contain information that may be deliberate or accidental. First, as is the case with personal interactions, people may strategically present themselves in a certain way on their personal web pages. Digital photos, slick graphics, funky fonts, interesting links, and creative screen names may communicate a sense of organization, creativity, insight, and invitation. These sorts of intentional markers may be consciously presented on web pages so that others have a comprehensive understanding of who the person is and can find out a bit about his

Your *Turn*

Identity markers are prevalent on the Internet. Examine different types of identity markers by surfing some chat rooms. Go to chat rooms on topics that interest you and be particularly careful of chat rooms that may be potentially offensive. What conclusions you can draw from the identity markers you reviewed? What consistencies exist across different types of chat rooms? What differences did you encounter? Explain with examples. If you'd like, you can use your student workbook to complete this activity.

REVISITING CASE IN POINT

1. Discuss what sorts of identity markers or other technology Carrie Gillespie might use in her communication with her mother.
2. What cautions would you provide to Carrie and Marjorie as they work toward maintaining their interpersonal communication through technology?

You can answer these questions online under Student Resources for Chapter 11 at the Understanding Interpersonal Communication website.

or her attitudes, beliefs, and values. The message is clear: "I'm a person you want to meet. I've got it together online. You can imagine how together I will have it when you meet me."

However, some personal home page designers would do well to remember a corollary of Murphy's law: If nothing can go wrong, it will anyway! Someone may have the best intentions of communicating clarity and authenticity, but they go awry. Consider the following greeting on a personal home page: "Welcome to my home page. I hoop you get a kick out of reading the different stories me." Or, what about the web page that had inadvertently been linked to a pornographic website? And then there are personal home pages that have so much personal information on them that it feels as though you've stumbled onto an *Oprah* set! When people encounter spelling errors, accidental links to websites, and over-disclosing, they may skip over a home page rather than engage it. As in face-to-face encounters, although we mean well, the words (and pictures and links) sometimes come out wrong.

Screen names and home pages are just two ways that individuals communicate their identity on the Internet. By now, you should have a clear sense of how the Internet functions in online dating and how the self influences the process of electronic relationships. We now explore the interplay between communication technology and our interactions with others.

Communication Technology and Interpersonal Communication

Communication between and among individuals is forever changed because of technology. People are now able to initiate, maintain, and terminate conversations and relationships through technological means. Years ago, to get a date with someone, you had to meet in a common place, such as a laundromat, church, grocery store, bar, or classroom. Today, if you're *wired* with the right *hardware*, a *mouse* will help you *google* a date on *cupid.com*. The effects of technology on our interpersonal communication is unprecedented, unstoppable, and unpredictable. We begin our discussion of how to engage in electronic interpersonal communication in an informed way by examining some of the wording associated with developing a relationship over the Internet.

Relational Tech: More than Words

We observed in Chapter 6 that language is the primary way that people communicate with each other. We also concluded that the language of the Internet is unique. When we put that language in the context of interpersonal relationships, we have a recipe for an interesting electronic relationship. We capture some of this uniqueness here by exploring abbreviated language, graphic accents, and blogging.

Abbreviated Language

Because technology is often used while people are on the go, it makes sense to use **abbreviated language** for efficiency in online relationships. People commonly use abbreviations such as ASL (age/sex/location), AFK (away from keyboard), PAW (parents are watching), HAND (have a nice day), S^ (s'up—what's up?), A3 (anyplace, anytime, anywhere), SETE (smiling ear to ear), and one of our favorites, FMTYEWTK (far more than you ever wanted to know). The challenge with abbreviated language is that both the sender and the receiver have to understand the abbreviations. And if you don't understand an acronym, will you ask its meaning? How do you go about getting clarification?

Graphic Accents

In Chapter 4, we mentioned that emoticons, such as smiley faces, are used to communicate emotions. An **articon** is a picture used in an electronic message; it can be downloaded from a website or compiled of keyboard characters. Researchers have discovered that using graphic icons can elaborate on the words being used. For example, Diane Witmer and Mary Lee Katzman (1997) discovered that emoticons and articons helped clarify for the reader the meaning of the written word. They also concluded that both men and women use graphic accents sparingly. Perhaps they feel that their words and abbreviations are sufficient. The use of emoticons and articons will become more frequent as computer graphic programs become more sophisticated and Internet users continue to download websites filled with faces, bodies, and objects depicting various emotions. In fact, on the horizon is an ever-growing list of artwork that does not require you to tilt your head, but rather look at the icon straight on:

(::[ ]::)	@(*0*)@	=^.^=
Band-Aid for comfort	koala for playfulness/cute	cat for frisky

These kinds of graphic accents show creativity and, when used by both communicators, allow for shared meaning. Although it may be easier for some to express their feelings via technological displays, eventually two people have to meet before they can facilitate an intimate bond.

Blogging

In our electronic relationships with others, we may also keep or read blogs. As we noted in Chapter 6, a **blog** is a running commentary—a journal on the Internet—that usually includes personal thoughts and feelings about a particular topic or individual. Warren St. John (2001) reports that blogs detail everything, including information about family, work, and personal heartaches. Andrew Sullivan (2002) notes that blogs are "imbued with the temper of the writer." Blogging is a technological intrapersonal and interpersonal experience. It is intrapersonal in nature because the authors are communicating something about themselves every time they write something for others to read. Blogging is also an interpersonal experience because others may comment on what is written or may be directed to Internet links relevant to the conversation taking place.

Writing your thoughts and feelings for public consumption should be done cautiously. Imagine, for instance, blogging about a coworker's decision to elope or a family member's mental illness. There are ethical considerations associated with such disclosures.

You've Got Mail (and a Relationship)

Leonard Shedletsky and Joan Aitken (2004) believe that interpersonal communication and our relationships with others are positively influenced by online technology. Indeed, communication technology is changing the way we look at relationships. In that spirit, we first explain the role that online relationships play in our

Communication Assessment Test

A Chat Self-Test

Internet users in chat rooms frequently create personal identities. To get a sense of whether you engage in identity management, answer the questions below. Make sure you respond spontaneously and select an honest reaction; try not to think too much about a question before answering it. Use the scale to respond to the statements. You can also complete this assessment online under Student Resources for Chapter 11 at the Understanding Interpersonal Communication website.

YES	yes	?	no	NO

_____ 1. It's important for me to make sure people know my real name while I communicate with them online.

_____ 2. If chat room participants refuse to reveal their real names, they have something to hide.

_____ 3. I believe "cutesy" or "childish" screen names say a lot about a person.

_____ 4. When people start to make fun of others in a chat room, they are really creating a sense of play.

_____ 5. Using screen names creates an expressive connection.

_____ 6. Using emoticons or articons is an effective way to provide others some insight into who you are.

_____ 7. Chat rooms and other e-groups generally draw those who have nothing else to do with their time.

_____ 8. The typical person in a chat room tries to create a false identity of who he or she is.

_____ 9. All email in chat rooms should be archived and available to anyone.

_____ 10. There should be explicit rules of behavior for chat room participants.

Interpretation of Results

If you found yourself answering YES or NO to any of these questions, look at the individual statements. What guided your thinking for each? What online experiences have you had in chat rooms that would have influenced your responses? If you responded with a "?" to any of the statements, think about why you are not sure about your response. Does identity management play a role in your decisions? If so, in what capacity? Be sure to reflect on the importance of online identity in your response.

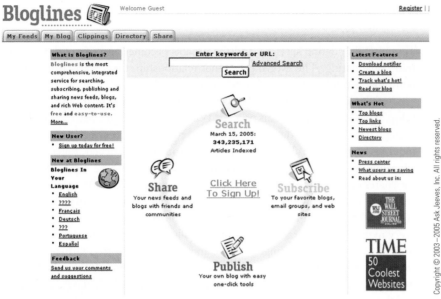

Blogs have become an increasingly influential method of communicating ideas—both personal and public—via the Internet. Here is the homepage of bloglines.com, a free online service for searching, creating, and sharing news, blogs, and other web content. Two of the main attractions of blogs are that they allow the poster to write about his or her thoughts and feelings about a topic, and they often allow other people to respond to the poster.

lives, and then look at how people develop their virtual relationships into face-to-face relationships.

Researchers have examined the association between electronic and interpersonal communication (Barnes, 2001; Booth & Yung, 1996; Parks & Floyd, 1996). This scholarship has helped to differentiate between online relationships and traditional relationships. Succinctly noting why online dating is a good idea, Judith Silverstein and Michael Lasky (2004) observe that "traditional dating is fundamentally random" (p. 10). What they mean is that during the dating stage, people tend to "stumble" onto others at a social gathering by luck. You might find yourself in the right place at the right time and meet the right person. Or, you won't. Regardless, this way of meeting people involves a little bit of good timing and a lot of luck.

However, developing an online relationship is not as random; online dating "reverses the standard rules of dating" (Shin, 2003, p. D2). Silverstein and Lasky (2004) note a number of advantages of meeting someone online:

- Many people online are available and seeking companionship.
- Before you exchange personal information, you have the power to secure a profile of the other person.
- You know something about how another thinks and writes.
- You know how to contact him or her.
- You have the chance to exchange email and talk on the phone without ever revealing your identity.

- You can do all of this for less than what it might cost for dinner at a moderately priced restaurant.

Toss in online dating services, and the process becomes even more different from traditional dating. The evolving Internet relationship, then, starts from a vantage point that is unlike a face-to-face relationship.

Let's look at an example to help explain how an online relationship might develop. After a breakup with his partner, Willy decides to post a personal ad and photograph with an online dating service. In a few days, he receives more than twenty inquiries from women all over the state. One woman in particular, Lena, is especially appealing to Willy. He emails Lena, she emails back, and he soon discovers that she shares one of his interests—she, too, is an amateur skier. After an ongoing exchange of email (in which they communicate their dating history, feelings about family, and other personal details), they swap phone numbers. Soon, they are talking every night. After several weeks of phone calls, Willy and Lena decide to set up a time to meet. Meeting strangers online and forming the sort of virtual relationship that Willy and Lena have formed is what Warren St. John (2001) calls "**hyperdating**," which is the development of an online relationship at "lightning speed" (p. D1).

Not everyone who is turned on by the Internet may be turned on by hyperdating; some people develop an online conversation that never materializes into online intimacy. Discussing personal views about exterior painting, politics, or the environment may occur in a virtual chat room. Friendships form rather easily this way. In *USA Today*, Janet Kornblum (2003) relates that even if there is no chemistry between online partners, individuals are finding lifelong friends. S. Lee Jamison (2003) also notes that websites such as www.thelunchclub.com have facilitated thousands of friendships. This online service in New York City brings together strangers for meals and conversations. These discussions may result in establishing an online dialogue rather than in a romantic relationship.

At what point does a virtual relationship become a "real" relationship? In other words, how do we move from an online relationship to a face-to-face relationship? First, the all-important telephone call begins the process of moving from the com-

puter screen to a live voice. Phone calls inevitably allow people to move from a sur-real relationship to a real relationship. However, wise use of the phone is critical. As Silverstein and Lasky (2004) conclude, "The phone can hurt you or help you in on-line dating" (p. 237). As with all communication technology, the effectiveness and usefulness of the telephone can vary. Necessary cautions such as caller ID blocking and not disclosing personal details about one's self are essential. Ensuring that another person is not lying to you is also paramount. Remember, all communication has the potential to have a dark side.

Yet, if discussions over the phone go well, two people may agree to meet. Upon meeting, the two will have a chance to discover a great deal about each other. Each person will be able to acquire some knowledge of the other's physical appearance. Each will also have a chance to listen—face to face—to the other, attending to the various verbal and nonverbal cues. Finally, in time, the two will inevitably get a sense of each other's beliefs, attitudes, and values. Ultimately, trust must be an ingredient for a close relationship to take place.

As we noted, not all online discussions evolve into interpersonal relationships, and you should always err on the side of caution when communicating with another online. Some people may be feigning interest, manipulating you to gain information, or simply having a good time at your expense. Online dating is still a relatively new phenomenon, and not everyone wants to engage in this "relational tech."

For a list of safety tips and warnings of potential dangers when meeting and communicating with potential friends or romantic partners online, use your Understanding Interpersonal Communication CD-ROM to access Interactive Activity 11.2: Safe Online Relationships. And for a good reminder that we are responsible for and can control our own safety on- and offline, check out the article "Finding Love Online—How to Be Safe and Secure," available through InfoTrac College Edition. Use your Understanding Interpersonal Communication CD-ROM to ac- cess InfoTrac College Edition Exercise 11.3: Finding Love Online the Safe Way.

Learning the language of the Internet, understanding the cautions with its use, appreciating how people create an online identity, and exploring the interplay between online relationships and face-to-face interactions will provide you an important base of technological know-how. We close our chapter with specific skills to consider as you think about online relational connections.

Choices for Improving Online Communication Skills

Your ability to function effectively in social and professional settings depends a great deal on your ability to be competent with communication technology. As we have seen, individuals utilize technology to cultivate online relationships with others. We close our discussion by exploring several skills to consider as both a sender and a receiver of electronic communication. We begin with the sender of electronic messages, move to the receiver, and then—following our transactional model of interpersonal communication, explained in Chapter 1—we expand our discussion to both sender and receiver.

Sender Skills for Electronic Messages

The following sender skills apply to the source of an electronic message. If you are an avid consumer of communication technology, you might try to identify additional skills that are not explained here.

Be Succinct When Necessary

You have probably written or received an email that goes on and on and on. This stream-of-consciousness writing is easy to do because the sender doesn't have to organize his or her thoughts before sending a message. For example, if you want to email another person about your likes and dislikes, your hobbies, and what you do in your spare time, your message could continue for several pages! Learn to abbreviate your thoughts. The longer the message, the more the receiver will be inclined to emphasize parts of your message that may not deserve such attention. Stay on point. Consider the following example:

> Hi. I'm really not all that excited about writing U. I waz nervous the first time we "talked" online. Of course, I realize that we weren't really talking, but it's strange anyway. So, HOW RU? I'm OK! So much 2 tell u. DAH! I should SU so U can talk!!!

The sender appears to be babbling aimlessly, which communicates some nervousness on the sender's part. The receiver may read far more into this stream-of-consciousness writing than the message warrants. Now, look at an alternate, more succinct opening:

> Hi. this online stuff is new to me, so help me out if i mess up. i hope you're OK. being online keeps me thinking . . . what am i gonna say next?

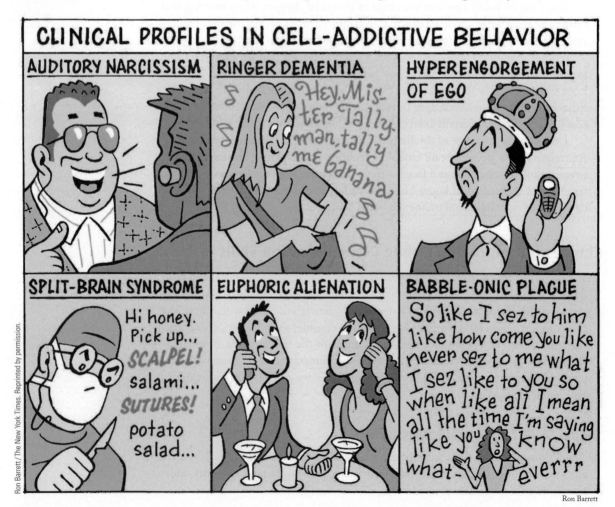

Ron Barrett / The New York Times. Reprinted by permission.

Ron Barrett

This is a much more concise way of opening up the dialogue and letting the receiver know that you're new to electronic discussions.

Write Literally

Regardless of whether communication is electronic or face to face, we must be precise in our wording to others. Using concrete and precise language avoids ambiguous and convoluted thoughts. Because a sender of an electronic message isn't privy to the recipient's facial reactions, body movements, and eye expressions, it is important to be as clear as possible when sending a message so that it is less likely to be misinterpreted.

Senders of email messages need to be especially careful in communicating feelings; an emoticon or articon isn't always sufficient. In fact, if you use one during a challenging discussion, the receiver might view it negatively. For example, sticking in a frowning face while talking about a family member's illness may be viewed by the receiver as flippant, which is probably a different message than what the sender intended.

Stay Polite

Although it's easy for us to suggest politeness, it's frequently difficult to practice. As in face-to-face conversations, when someone communicating online is passionate about a topic, he or she may blunder and be offensive. Keep in mind the permanency of the written word and the fact that communication is irreversible; after we write something mean or offensive, we can't take it back.

Let's look at an example. Breanna is mad that she didn't get the Friday night off from work that she requested, so when her boss emails her asking if she can work a double shift on Wednesday, Breanna sends the following message: "Sorry, can't do. I have to rest from being required to work Friday night!" Clearly, Breanna isn't the most polite sender of information! Now, consider an alternative response from Breanna: "I need to get back to you. Let me check it out, and I'll talk to you on Tuesday when I work." Courtesy and deference when communicating online are far more constructive than rudeness. Also Breanna asks for a face-to-face conversation so that she can fully explain herself. Doing so will likely result in less misinterpretation than an email exchange would.

We are not suggesting that you simply roll with the punches all the time and avoid sticking up for yourself when matters become heated. At times, you do have to be direct in your email communication. Yet, we suggest that you temper your eagerness to make a point by recalling the power of words and their lasting effect upon both senders and receivers.

Take a Deep Breath

This suggestion is both literal and figurative. When you inhale and release your breath, you reduce stress. Figuratively speaking, taking a deep break means thinking about what you want to write before you actually write it and press "Send." Reflect on your message. Reread it. In electronic discussions, we always recommend taking a deep breath before responding too quickly or taking action without first thinking about the ramifications.

Taking a deep breath takes many forms. Imagine how different the results would be if people paused and considered their words before sending them to others. Consider the following examples. Neil sent an email and forgot to delete the original draft of the email at the bottom of the message, which blasted a colleague for not responding quickly enough to a previous email. Marla, a student who received a poor grade on a midterm, wrote an email to the professor telling him that his questions didn't make sense and that the exam was way too long. And Tavo disclosed his entire life story in one email to a potential future partner online, unaware that his disclosure revealed that his ex-wife was the best friend of the woman he was dating! We can't urge you enough to take a deep breath before any online dialogue begins.

Receiver Skills for Electronic Messages

The receiver of information must also be savvy in the ways of online communication. Here, we explore receiver skills of online dialogues. As with the sender skills, think about additional receiver skills that may be needed.

Check In with the Sender

The receiver should always make sure that what he or she is responding to is what the sender intended. Checking in may be as simple as asking the sender to clarify. Or, a receiver may simply want to send out a brief **electronic trial balloon,** which is an overture that briefly responds to a sender's message. For example, when asked what she "does for fun" from someone responding to an online personal ad, Kia responds this way: "If U mean, what do I do in my spare time, I love animals. I volunteer at an animal shelter. What DID U mean?"

What Kia offered was an electronic trial balloon. She briefly responded to the question but then asked for more clarification. Checking in is an efficient form of communication because the receiver can avoid responding with unnecessary or irrelevant information. Checking in saves time and allows for clarity.

Show Empathy When Possible

When we discussed listening in Chapter 5, we addressed the need to be empathic. Empathy, as you recall, means to put yourself in another's position. In face-to-face conversations, empathy may take the form of hugging another when he's down and out or giving a "high-five" and shouting "yeah!" when a friend tells you she just got engaged. In our online discussions, we don't have the benefit of showing empathy in such ways. However, we can still show empathy for someone even though we aren't sharing the same physical space.

Being empathic online can take various forms. You might use articons (sparingly) to express how you feel about the situation in conjunction with words that show how you feel. For example, when Keith gets laid off from his job, Lee's written response should show some level of comfort: "We've all been there, buddy. You'll pull through this one (::()::) I know you will." Lee's words accompanied by the symbol of comfort (a Band-Aid) provide some degree of empathy that Keith will appreciate.

Listen beyond the Words

Listening applies to electronic conversations as well as those we conduct in person. When you listen to others online, you need to read between the lines to figure out the intention, emotion, and intuition. Yet, we need to be careful since we may be attributing too much detail to words, and we may come to an inaccurate conclusion. That's why we need to check in with the sender, a skill we noted previously.

Listening beyond the words is difficult. Recall Chapter 5 where we stated that listening is easier said than done, particularly on topics about which we have strong beliefs or opinions. Further, during our online conversations, we may have more distractions than during our face-to-face interactions. For example, while online, you may choose to answer the door, make breakfast, talk to a roommate, pay your bills, clean your bedroom, change a light bulb, or do a number of other things that you feel need attention. Of course, your online partner doesn't necessarily know you are doing anything else except communicating with him or her.

New technologies allow us to communicate with loved ones more quickly and more efficiently than ever before. For example, parents can take pictures of their new baby with a digital camera and email them the same day to anyone in the family who has access to email—no photo developing or scanning required. And friends and family can easily email empathy and support to people in places where mail delivery is slow.

Sender and Receiver Skills for Electronic Messages

In Chapter 1, we introduced the transactional model of communication, which suggests that a sender and receiver simultaneously engage in the communication process. Like face-to-face interactions, online conversations are transactional in nature. Let's explore a few skills needed by both sender and receiver while online with each other.

Take Responsibility for Your Own Words

Many people tend to forget that they "own" the words they choose to use. That is, whether we are in front of a person or a computer screen, we need to take responsibility for what we say or write. When communicating with someone online, this language ownership becomes important when we consider that the written word has the power to be permanent; it's not available to only you for future use—it's available to virtually anyone!

We recommend that you adopt a mantra that places responsibility for what is written solely within yourself, regardless of whether you are a sender or a receiver. Consider an earlier skill we identified that encouraged you to reflect before writing anything. And if you write something you didn't mean to write, try to reframe the situation by placing your words in context. Try not to cast blame on another for the words you chose to use.

Build Your Dialogue

We can think of a face-to-face conversation as a play. The scene may need to be set up, the characters have to be notified about their parts, and the setting should be clear to the audience. In online relationships, a similar metaphor seems reasonable. Plays don't begin in the middle. You don't expect a cast member to know what happens next unless you give some sort of background. You present ideas and concerns as a process, not as an ultimatum.

Building a dialogue online ensures that topics and ideas are arranged in order of importance. Subordinate ideas should be given less attention than primary ideas. For instance, if Tess is concerned that her online conversation is taking a turn to the highly intimate with J. C., she might inform J. C. about her feelings first and then proceed to explain why she is concerned. Perhaps Tess feels that too much personal information is being shared early in the development of the electronic conversation. If so, she needs to clearly state her belief.

To read an article that discusses building a dialogue online by asking questions that can help you reduce your uncertainty of others, check out "Interrogative Strategies and Information Exchange in Computer-Mediated Communication," available through InfoTrac College Edition. Use your Understanding Interpersonal Communication CD-ROM to access InfoTrac College Edition Exercise 11.4: Reducing Uncertainty Online.

Recall the Challenge of Online Communication

Both senders and receivers of electronic messages must always remember that this type of communication is frequently ambiguous and fraught with misinterpretation. Even if you have extensive experience meeting people online, remember that others may not share your electronic expertise. Be careful when it comes to using abbreviations that are not universally understood. Think before stating too much too soon; others may be put off by your level of comfort.

Finally, don't assume that your words will be taken as you intended. Consider Carol, the mother of Laura, who is herself a mother of three children. As a 70-year-old, Carol is a relative newcomer to email. Yet, early on, she learned that online conversations can be easily misconstrued. While communicating with her daughter, she indicates that she misses her grandchildren and wants to see them by writing her daughter the following message:

> IT MUST BE NICE TO HAVE CHILDREN AROUND. I WISH I COULD SEE MY GRANDKIDS!

Her daughter responds:

> Why do you get mad every time you talk about my children? Just because you don't see them doesn't mean I'm somehow "protecting" them from you. CHILL OUT, mother. I'll make sure you see them next month.

The challenge of online communication is demonstrated in this online dialogue through the use of capital letters. Although Carol used capital letters because she simply forgot to turn off the "Caps Lock" command on the keyboard, her daughter, Laura, took the capitalized words as an intentional personal affront. Realizing the potential for confusion while online is essential for everyone in the communication process.

As we continuously note throughout this book, the communication process is transactional. Both the sender and receiver, then, become responsible for meaning making. In our electronic conversations with others, the transactional nature of communication becomes more critical because we don't have the privilege of a face-to-face interaction. Practicing the skills discussed in this section—whether as a sender or receiver—becomes paramount when we cultivate online interactions.

For a useful site that contains links to articles about netiquette (the rules of common courtesy for online communication) and a quiz you can take to help you better understand the do's and don'ts of communicating online, use your Understanding Interpersonal Communication CD-ROM to access Interactive Activity 11.3: Netiquette Quiz.

Skill *Spotlight*

Maintain Focus on the Challenge of Online Communication

Although the Internet has been around for more than 30 years, we are still living in an electronic age that often renders its use challenging. Electronic communications are prone to ambiguity, vagueness, and technical difficulties. Consequently, meaning is often sacrificed.

One reason that meaning may become clouded is that all aspects of the content of the message may not be understood by the receiver. For example, emoticons are not universally available to all computers, and language abbreviations may not be understood by both individuals. Imagine speaking Spanish to someone who doesn't know Spanish; little meaning making would occur. Now, consider using words and phrases such as LOL (laughing out loud) and SUL8R (see you later); even some experienced Internet users may not understand such nuanced phrasing.

In addition to these language barriers, the technical aspects of online communication contribute to a challenging technological climate. For example, if you find yourself emailing one person, that person may decide to forward your email to someone else. Privacy, therefore, becomes arbitrary. Internet servers break down and email addresses change, which may result in your message being undeliverable. Finally, people have schedules that may prohibit promptness. In face-to-face conversations, we can excuse ourselves if we have an appointment or if there is an emergency. In our online relationships, if our schedules get busy and we don't respond to an email within a few days, our online partner might be offended or concerned.

Skills at Work The twenty-first century workplace relies on communication technology more than ever. In fact, online communication has found its way into nearly every aspect of organizational life. Despite this pervasiveness, like face-to-face interactions, our technological interactions can break down. The challenge of dealing with online communication cannot be understated. For example, consider what happens when— in a fit of anger about being assigned too many tasks—Alyse decides to write to a colleague to complain about her workload. Unfortunately, that email is later inadvertently forwarded to the very same supervisor about whom Alyse was complaining. Or, think about Jay's technological dilemma. After being reminded about an appointment he was about to forget, Jay writes the following abbreviated email to his administrative assistant, Jacqui: "Thanx for all U do. Your ☺ always makes my day." Yet, Jacqui did not receive Jay's emoticon in the same spirit as he intended, and he was later warned by human resources to be careful in communicating with such ambiguous emoticons as a smiley face.

Despite our best intentions and life experience, online communication can become problematic at work. Most work environments put legal, ethical, and professional guidelines in place. Because communication technology can challenge those guidelines, we need to pay special attention to our online dialogues with others. If you were charged with establishing guidelines for online communication at work, what would you advise? What criteria would you choose to establish those guidelines?

| CHOICES | *for Improving Online Communication Skills* |

For senders:	■ Show empathy
■ Be succinct	■ Listen beyond the words
■ Write literally	**For senders and receivers:**
■ Stay polite	■ Take responsibility for your own words
■ Take a deep breath	■ Build your dialogue
For receivers:	■ Recall the challenge of online
■ Check in with the sender	communication

Summary

We live in a time of unprecedented technological change. One new technology quickly replaces another and we talk about it, work with it, and engage it in ways never before seen in society. This technological evolution has also affected our interpersonal communication. The use of computer-mediated communication is now commonplace among people of various races, ages, and cultures.

Technology plays an integral role in our communication with others. Because technology is pervasive, we rely on it. It is paradoxical that such a large, cumbersome entity as technology can draw people together—a concept encompassed by the idea of the *global village*. Another important characteristic of technology is that it is powerful; it influences people, events, and entire cultures. Lastly, the accessibility of technology varies depending on people's age, race, culture, and geographical setting—a phenomenon called the *digital divide*.

The Internet, a giant network of computers, has both a bright side and a dark side. Users should be wary of online sources until they are sure of those websites' accountability. Other websites might be filled with hate speech, or users might encounter flamers in a chat room. The anonymity of the web makes some users less civil than they would be in face-to-face interactions. The bright side of the Internet includes the opportunity to widen your social network; in fact, entire communities are developed and maintained online. You can also educate yourself by searching online via search engines for informational websites and chat rooms with professionals who give advice.

Keep in mind that people can lie or pretend to be someone else online. On the plus side, online discussions can prompt introspection and individualism. And by self-disclosing online, people can increase intimacy and avoid immediate reactions of disgust, disappointment, or confusion. However, be careful when you self-disclose online; if you send an electronic message and then decide you should not have disclosed something contained in the message (which could inadvertently be passed to someone else), you cannot retrieve it.

Identity markers are expressions of the self online. Screen names and personal home pages show individuality and give people insight into their originators. However, sometimes strange names or disorganized home pages give an unintended impression.

People are now able to initiate, maintain, and terminate conversations and relationships through technological means. People use abbreviated language and graphic accents to efficiently communicate, although these are open to misinterpretation. People can communicate using blogs (online journals), but they should use discretion when blogging about private matters.

Whereas traditional dating is random, involving good timing and luck, online dating is an inexpensive process that is not as arbitrary because many people are using the same venues for the same purpose. In addition, the user has control over the information divulged, can find out how the other thinks and writes, what the potential date looks like, and his or her likes and dislikes before deciding whether to meet face to face. Some people engage in hyperdating, or developing an online relationship quickly. Others find lifelong friends, not romantic partners, in online venues. Still other online relationships don't develop into interpersonal relationships.

To ably communicate online, senders and receivers need certain skills. Senders should be succinct, write clearly to avoid misinterpretation, stay polite, and reflect on their messages before sending them. Receivers should check about the sender's intent, show empathy when possible, and read between the lines. Both senders and receivers should take responsibility for their words, build their dialogue, and recall the challenge that online communication poses.

Communication technology continues to redefine how people meet and relate to one another. As technology evolves, it expands our relational horizons in unimagined directions. Despite the advances made in communication technology, as technology changes, new challenges await those who utilize it.

Understanding Interpersonal Communication Online

Now that you've read Chapter 11, use your Understanding Interpersonal Communication CD-ROM for quick access to the electronic study resources that accompany this text. Your CD-ROM gives you access to the CNN video clip "France and Cyberspace" on page 324, the Ethics & Choice interactive activity on page 332, the Communication Assessment Test on page 338, InfoTrac College Edition, and the Understanding Interpersonal Communication website. When you get to the Understanding Interpersonal Communication home page, click on "Student Book Companion Site" in the Resource box at right to access the online study aids for this chapter, including a digital glossary, review quizzes, and the chapter activities.

Terms for Review

abbreviated language 336	electronic trial balloon 344	postcyberdisclosure panic (PCDP) 333
articon 337	flaming 327	
blog 337	global village 322	screen names 335
browser 325	hate speech 327	search engine 325
chat rooms 325	home page 335	spam 325
computer-mediated communication (CMC) 321	hyperdating 340	technological determinism 322
	hyperlink 325	
	identity marker 334	uniform resource locator (URL) 325
convergence 320	Internet 324	
cookies 325	personal home page 325	World Wide Web 325

Questions for Understanding

Comprehension Focus

1. Explain what convergence means and how it relates to interpersonal communication.
2. Discuss and differentiate among the characteristics of communication technology. Provide examples in your explanation.
3. Explore the implications of technological accessibility in the United States. Why is this topic particularly important in the twenty-first century?
4. Identify several dark and bright features of the Internet. Offer examples of each.
5. Describe each of the identify markers discussed in this chapter and provide examples of each in your response.

Application Focus

1. **CASE IN POINT**
   Review our opening vignette of Marjorie and Carrie. Discuss what type of communication technology bridges the gap between the two women. What are the strengths of using technology in the manner that Carrie proposes? What are

the shortcomings? Is letter writing a lost art, and if so, is that a good or a bad thing? Explain with examples.

2. Do you think that developing online relationships is just a fad? Discuss your response in the context of the information presented in the chapter.
3. What additional markers, besides the ones discussed in this chapter, can you think of that serve to communicate another's identity online?
4. Defend or criticize the following statement: "When discussing interpersonal communication, the effects of technology cut both ways." What does the statement mean? What additional or substituted words would you place in the statement? Use examples to defend your view.
5. Explore future avenues of how technology and interpersonal interactions might intersect. In other words, what would you predict on the horizon with respect to communication technology and relationships? Provide examples.

Interactive Activities and InfoTrac College Edition Exercises

Complete the Interactive Activities and InfoTrac College Edition Exercises for Chapter 11 online at the Understanding Interpersonal Communication website. Select the chapter resources for Chapter 11, then click on "Activities" or "InfoTrac College Edition." If requested, you can submit your answers to your instructor.

Interactive Activities

InfoTrac College Edition Exercises

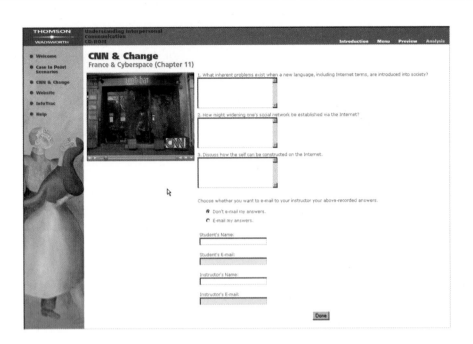

Glossary

A

abbreviated language   Shorthand used for efficient communication in online relationships.

abstract   Not able to be seen, smelled, tasted, touched, or heard.

account   An explanation for a transgression that may accompany an apology.

action-centered listening style   A listening style associated with listeners who want messages to be highly organized, concise, and error-free.

active conflict   The third stage of Filley's process model of conflict, in which both parties engage in interaction about their differences.

active listening   Suspending our own responses while listening so we can concentrate on what another person is saying.

affection and instrumentality dialectic   The tension between framing a friendship with someone as an end in itself (affection) or seeing it as a means to another end (instrumentality).

affinity seeking   Emphasizing the commonalities we think we share with another person.

aftermath   The last stage of Filley's process model of conflict, in which the residue of having engaged in a conflict and the feelings that both parties have about their interaction feed back into the context for future conflicts.

ambushing   Listening carefully to a message and then using the information later to attack the sender.

American Sign Language (ASL)   A visual rather than auditory form of communication that is composed of precise hand shapes and movements.

apology   A simple statement like "I am really sorry."

approaching   Providing nonverbal signals that indicate we'd like to initiate contact with another person, such as going up to a person or smiling in that person's direction.

articon   A graphic image used in an electronic message that can be downloaded from a website or compiled from keyboard characters. An articon may or may not be used to communicate emotion. *See also* emoticon.

attending and selecting   The first stage of the perception process, requiring us to use our visual, auditory, tactile, and olfactory senses to respond to stimuli in our interpersonal environment.

attribution theory   A theory that explains how we create explanations or attach meaning to another person's behavior or our own.

autonomy and connection dialectic   The tension between our desire to be independent or autonomous while simultaneously wanting to feel a connection with our partner.

avoiding stage   A stage in the coming apart section of Knapp's model of relationship development in which two partners stay away from each other because they feel that being together is unpleasant.

B

blind self   In the Johari Window, the pane that includes information others know about us that we are unaware of.

blog   An online journal that usually includes personal thoughts and feelings about a particular topic or individual.

bodily artifacts   Items we wear that are part of our physical appearance and that have the potential to communicate, such as clothing, religious symbols, military medals, body piercings, and tattoos.

body orientation   The extent to which we turn our legs, shoulders, and head toward (or away) from a communicator.

bonding stage   The final stage in the coming together part of Knapp's model of relationship development, in which partners make a public commitment to their relationship.

boundaries or openness   A systems principle referring to the fact that hierarchy is formed by creating boundaries around each separate system (e.g., a brother and sister, the family as a whole, and so forth). However, human systems are inherently open, which means that information passes through these boundaries. Therefore, some researchers call this principle "openness," and some call it "boundaries."

breadth   A dimension of self-disclosure that indicates how many topics we disclose about within a relationship.

browser   A program that determines how documents are displayed on our computers, enabling us to view websites.

C

calibration   The process of systems setting their parameters, checking on themselves, and self-correcting.

categorical imperative   An ethical system, based on the work of philosopher Immanuel Kant, in which individuals follow moral absolutes. The underlying tenet in this ethical system suggests that we should act as an example to others.

catharsis   A therapeutic release of tensions and negative emotion as a result of self-disclosing.

channel   A pathway through which a message is sent.

chat room   Live online dialogue with other people who share similar interests.

chronemics   The study of a person's use of time.

chunking   Placing pieces of information into manageable and retrievable sets.

circumscribing stage   A stage in the coming apart section of Knapp's model of relationship development in which two people's communication behaviors are restrained so that fewer topics are raised (for fear of conflict), more issues are out of bounds, and they interact less.

citing gestures   Gestures that acknowledge another's feedback in a conversation.

co-culture   A culture within a culture.

codability   The ease with which a language can express a thought.

code-switching   Shifting back and forth between languages in the same conversation.

coercive power   Power that derives from the ability to punish others.

collectivism   A cultural mindset that emphasizes the group and its norms, values, and beliefs over the self.

communicating emotionally   Communicating such that the emotion is not the content of the message but rather a property of it.

communication apprehension   A fear or an anxiety pertaining to the communication process. This fear or anxiety is the result of a legitimate life experience that usually negatively affects our communication with others.

communication competency   The ability to communicate with knowledge, skills, and thoughtfulness.

community   The common understandings among people who are committed to coexisting.

comparison level   A person's standard level for what types of costs and rewards should exist in a given relationship.

comparison level for alternatives   A comparison of the costs and rewards of a current relationship to the possibility of doing better in a different relationship.

computer-mediated communication (CMC)   The use of various technologies to facilitate communication with others.

computing   Disqualifying the emotional aspects of a conflict (the context) and focusing on the rational aspects.

concrete   Able to be seen, smelled, tasted, touched, or heard.

confirmation   A response that acknowledges and supports another.

connotative meaning   The meaning of a verbal symbol that is derived from our personal and subjective experience with that symbol.

content conflict   A conflict that revolves around an issue. *Also called* a substantive conflict.

content information   The verbal and nonverbal information contained in a message that indicates the topic of the message.

content-centered listening style   A listening style associated with listeners who focus on the facts and details of a message.

context   The environment in which a message is sent. *See also* physical context, cultural context, social-emotional context, and historical context.

convergence   The integration of various technologies, such as online radio, or cell phones with cameras.

conversational narcissism   Engaging in an extreme amount of self-focusing during a conversation, to the exclusion of another person.

cookies   Small data files that are left and stored on a computer by a browser to allow for online tracking of a user's activities.

corrective maintenance   Repairing a relationship when it runs into trouble.

costs   Those things in relational life that we judge as negative.

cultural context   The cultural environment in which communication occurs. In this type of context, messages are understood in relationship to the rules, roles, norms, and patterns of communication that are unique to particular cultures and co-cultures.

cultural empathy   The learned ability to accurately understand the experiences of people from diverse cultures and to convey that understanding responsively.

cultural relativity   The ability to avoid judging or condemning any practice in which any other culture engages.

culture   The shared, personal, and learned life experiences of a group of individuals who have a common set of values, norms, and traditions.

culture clash   A conflict over cultural expectations and experiences.

cyclic alternation   A strategy for dealing with dialectic tensions in a relationship that allows us to choose opposite poles of the dialectic at different times.

D

dark side of communication   Negative communication that may influence the communication process between and among people.

defensive listening   Viewing innocent comments as personal attacks or hostile criticisms.

delivery gestures   Gestures that signal shared understanding between communicators in a conversation.

denotative meaning   The literal, conventional meaning of a verbal symbol that most people in a culture have agreed is the meaning of that symbol.

depth   A dimension of self-disclosure indicating how much detail we provide about a specific topic.

descriptive disclosures   Self-revelations detailing feeling states (e.g., "I am really obsessed with John—I can't get him out of my mind"), past events (e.g., "I used to box professionally"), or current concerns (e.g., "I am concerned about our relationship—I am having trouble trusting you as I once did").

dialectics Contradictory tensions that result from competing, opposite desires in our interpersonal relationships.

dialogue enhancers Supporting statements, such as "I see" or "I'm listening," that indicate we are involved in a message.

differentiating stage The first stage in the coming apart section of Knapp's model of relationship development, in which two people begin to notice ways in which they differ.

direct and virtual use of power Communicating the potential use of a direct application of power.

direct application of power In a conflict situation, the use of any resource at our disposal to compel another to comply, regardless of that person's desires.

disconfirmation A response that fails to acknowledge and support another, leaving the person feeling ignored and disregarded.

disqualifying A strategy for coping with dialectic tensions in a relationship by exempting certain topics from discussion.

distracting Disqualifying the subject of a conflict by distracting both people in the conflict with behaviors such as laughing, crying, or changing the subject.

dualism A way of thinking that constructs polar opposite categories to encompass the totality of a thing. Dualism prompts us to think about things in an "either-or" fashion.

dyadic effect The tendency for us to return another's self-disclosure with one that matches it in level of intimacy.

E

electronic trial balloon An online overture that briefly responds to a sender's message in order to clarify the sender's intended message.

emoticon An icon that can be typed on a keyboard to express emotions; used to compensate for the lack of nonverbal cues in computer-mediated communication. *See also* articon.

emotion The critical internal structure that orients us to and engages us with what matters in our lives: our feelings about ourselves and others. Emotion encompasses both the internal feelings of one person (for instance, anxiety or happiness) as well as feelings that can be experienced only in a relationship (for instance, jealousy or competitiveness).

emotional communication Talking about an emotional experience.

emotional contagion The process of transferring emotions from one person to another.

emotional experience The feeling of emotion.

emotion work The effort or energy involved in maintaining emotional competence.

empathy The process of identifying with or attempting to experience the thoughts, beliefs, and actions of another.

empowerment Helping to actualize our own or another person's power.

encoding The process of putting thoughts and feelings into verbal symbols, nonverbal messages, or both.

equifinality The ability to achieve the same goals (or ends) by a variety of means.

equivocation A type of ambiguity that involves choosing our words carefully to give a listener a false impression without actually lying.

ethic of care An ethical system, based on the concepts of Carol Gilligan, that is concerned with the connections among people and the moral consequences of decisions.

ethics The perceived rightness or wrongness of an action or behavior, determined in large part by society.

ethnocentrism The process of judging another culture using the standards of our own culture.

evaluative disclosures Self-disclosures used to tell another how we judge other people.

experimenting stage A stage in the coming together part of Knapp's model of relationship development in which two people become acquainted by gathering information about each other.

expert or information power Power derived from the knowledge a person possesses.

external dialectics Tensions between oppositions that have to do with how relational partners negotiate the public aspects of their relationship.

external feedback The feedback we receive from other people.

F

face The image of the self we choose to present to others in our interpersonal encounters.

fact A piece of information that is verifiable by direct observation.

feedback A verbal or nonverbal response to a message. *See also* internal feedback and external feedback.

feeling rules The cultural norms used to create and react to emotional expressions.

feminine culture A culture that emphasizes characteristics stereotypically associated with feminine people, such as sexual equality, nurturance, quality of life, supportiveness, affection, and a compassion for the less fortunate.

field of experience The influence of a person's culture, past experiences, personal history, and heredity on the communication process.

flaming Exchanging malicious, hostile, or insulting comments over the Internet.

G

gap fillers   Listeners who think they can correctly guess the rest of the story a speaker is telling and don't need the speaker to continue.

gender   The learned behaviors a culture associates with being a male or female, known as masculinity or femininity.

gender role socialization   The process by which women and men learn the gender roles appropriate to their sex. This process affects the way the sexes perceive the world.

gender schema   A mental framework we use to process and categorize beliefs, ideas, and events as either masculine or feminine in order to understand and organize our world.

generic *he*   The use of the masculine pronoun *he* to function generically when the subject of the sentence is of unknown gender.

global village   The concept that all societies, regardless of their size, are connected in some way. The term also can be used to describe how communication technology ties the world into one political, economical, social, and cultural system.

golden mean   An ethical system, articulated by Aristotle, that proposes a person's moral virtue stands between two vices, with the middle, or the mean, being the foundation for a rational society.

grammar   The rules that dictate the structure of language.

H

halo effect   Matching like qualities with each other to create an overall perception of someone or something.

haptics   The study of how we communicate through touch.

hate speech   Extremely offensive language that is directed toward a particular group of people.

hearing   The physical process of letting in audible stimuli without focusing on the stimuli.

hidden power   A type of power in which one person in a relationship suppresses or avoids decisions in the interest of one of the parties. *Also called* unobtrusive power.

hidden self   In the Johari Window, the pane that includes the information about ourselves we are aware of but that we have chosen not to disclose.

hierarchy   A principle that states that all relationships are embedded within larger systems.

high-context culture   A culture in which there is a high degree of similarity among members and in which the meaning of a message is drawn primarily from its context, such as one's surroundings, rather than from words.

historical context   A type of context in which messages are understood in relationship to previously sent messages.

history   Information that may sound personal to another person but that is relatively easy for us to tell.

home page   The first page of a website.

hyperdating   The very rapid development of an online relationship.

hyperlink   An image or text on a web page that is linked to another web page or another part of the same web page.

I

ideal and real dialectic   The tension between an idealized vision of friendship and the real friends one has.

identity management   The communication behaviors we exhibit to influence how others perceive us.

identity marker   An electronic extension that communicates a person's identity, such as a screen name or a personal home page.

idiom   A word or a phrase that has an understood meaning within a culture but whose meaning is not derived by exact translation.

image conflict   A conflict with another about one's sense of oneself.

imagined conversation   A conversation with oneself in which one partner plays the parts of both partners in a mental rehearsal.

I-message   A message phrased to show we understand that our feelings belong to us and aren't caused by someone else.

implicit personality theory   The theory that we rely on a set of a few characteristics to draw inferences about others and use these inferences as the basis of our communication with them.

indexing   Avoiding generalizations by acknowledging the time frame in which we judge others and ourselves.

indirect application of power   Employing power without making its employment explicit.

individualism   A cultural mindset that emphasizes self-concept and personal achievement and that prefers competition over cooperation, the individual over the group, and the private over the public.

inference   A conclusion derived from a fact, but it does not reflect direct observation or experience.

in-group   A group to which a person feels he or she belongs.

initial awareness   The second stage of Filley's process model, in which either one or both parties in a conflict become aware that there is a problem.

initiating stage   The first stage in the coming together part of Knapp's model of relationship development, in which two people notice each other and indicate to each other that they are interested in making contact.

integrating stage   A stage in the coming together part of Knapp's model of relationship development in which two partners form a clear identity as a couple.

integration   A strategy for dealing with the dialectic tension in a relationship that allows us to synthesize the opposites. Integration can take three forms: neutralizing, disqualifying, and reframing.

intensifying stage   A stage in the coming together part of Knapp's model of relationship development in which the intimacy between the partners intensifies.

interaction   A necessary condition for conflict, given that conflicts are created and sustained through verbal and non-verbal communication.

interaction adaptation theory   A theory that suggests individuals simultaneously adapt their communication behavior to the communication behavior of others.

interactional model of communication   A characterization of communication as a two-way process in which a message is sent from sender to receiver and from receiver to sender. In the interactional view, one can be both a sender and a receiver, but not both simultaneously.

intercultural communication   Communication between and among individuals and groups from different cultural backgrounds.

interdependence   A necessary condition for conflict, given that people involved in conflict rely on each other, need each other, and are in a relationship with each other.

internal dialectics   Tensions resulting from oppositions inherent in relational partners' communication with each other.

internal feedback   The feedback we give ourselves when we assess our own communication.

Internet   An extended network of smaller computer networks interconnected with one another.

interpersonal communication   The process of message transaction between two people to create and sustain shared meaning.

interpersonal conflict   The interaction of interdependent people who perceive incompatible goals and interference from each other in achieving those goals.

interpreting   The third stage of the perception process, in which we assign meaning to what we perceive.

intimate distance   The distance that extends about eighteen inches around each of us that is normally reserved for people with whom we are close, such as close friends, romantic partners, and family members.

irreversibility   The fact that what we say to others cannot be "unsaid" or reversed.

J

Johari Window   A model used to understand the process of self-disclosure consisting of a square with four panels that provides a pictorial representation of how "known" we are to ourselves and others.

judgment and acceptance dialectic   Our desire to criticize a friend as opposed to accepting a friend for who he or she is.

K

kinesics   The study of a person's body movement and its effect on the communication process.

L

language   The ability to transmit thoughts from the mind of one individual to another through the process of encoding.

legitimate power   Power that is based on the position a person occupies.

lexical gaps   Experiences that are not named.

linear model of communication   A characterization of communication as a one-way process that transmits a message from a sender to a receiver.

linguistic determinism   A theory that argues that our language determines our ability to perceive and think about things. If we don't have a word for something in our language, this theory predicts we won't think about it or notice it.

linguistic relativity   A theory that states that language influences our thinking but doesn't determine it. Thus, if we don't have a word for something in our language, this theory predicts it will be difficult, but not impossible, to think about it or notice it.

listening   The dynamic, transactional process of receiving, recalling, rating, and responding to stimuli, messages, or both, from another.

listening gap   The time difference between our mental ability to interpret words and the speed at which they arrive at our brain.

listening style   A predominant and preferred approach to listening to the messages we hear.

long-term attraction   Judgment of a relationship that makes us want to continue a relationship after initiating it. This attraction sustains and maintains relationships.

low-context culture   A culture in which there is a high degree of difference among members and in which the meaning of a message must be explicitly related, usually in words.

M

man-linked words   Words that include the word *man* but that are supposed to operate generically to include women as well, such as *mankind*.

masculine culture   A culture that emphasizes characteristics stereotypically associated with masculine people, such as achievement, competitiveness, strength, and material success.

meaning   What the sender intends to convey with a message, and what the receiver extracts from a message.

message   Spoken, written, or unspoken information sent from a sender to a receiver.

message exchange   The transaction of verbal and nonverbal messages being sent simultaneously between two people.

message overload   The result when senders receive more messages than they can process.

metacommunication   Communication about communication.

meta-emotion Emotion felt about experiencing another emotion.

mindful Having the ability to engage our senses so that we are observant and aware of our surroundings.

mindless Being unaware of the stimuli around us.

mixed message The incompatibility that occurs when our nonverbal messages are not congruent with our verbal messages.

models of communication Visual, simplified representations of complex relationships in the communication process.

multitasking The simultaneous performance of two or more tasks.

muted groups People whose experiences are not well represented in verbal symbols and who have trouble articulating their thoughts and feelings verbally because their language doesn't give them an adequate vocabulary.

N

negative face Our desire that others refrain from imposing their will on us, respect our individuality and our uniqueness, and avoid interfering with our actions or beliefs.

negative feedback Feedback that causes a system to reject recalibration and stay the same.

negative halo Occurs when we group negative qualities (e.g., unintelligent, rude, and temperamental) together.

networking In relational development, finding out information about a person from a third party.

neutralizing A strategy for coping with dialectic tensions in a relationship that allows us to strike a compromise between the two opposing poles of a dialectic.

noise Anything that interferes with accurate transmission or reception of a message. *See also* physical noise, physiological noise, psychological noise, and semantic noise.

nonjudgmental feedback Feedback that describes another's behavior and then explains how that behavior made us feel.

nonverbal communication All behaviors other than spoken words that communicate messages and create shared meaning between people.

novelty and predictability dialectic Our simultaneous, opposing desires for excitement and stability in our relationships.

O

offering Putting ourselves in a good position for another to approach us in a social situation.

openness and protection dialectic Our desire for self-disclosures, which make us transparent to another, and our desire for withholding disclosures, which keeps us safe from another's disapproval.

open self In the Johari Window, the pane that includes all the information about us that we know and that we have shared with others through disclosures.

opinion A view, judgment, or appraisal based on our beliefs or values.

organizing The second stage of the perception process, in which we place what are often a number of confusing pieces of information into an understandable, accessible, and orderly arrangement.

out-group A group to which a person feels he or she does not belong.

outsourcing A practice in which a nation sends work and workers to a different country because doing so is cost-efficient.

owning Verbally taking responsibility for our own thoughts and feelings.

P

paralanguage The study of a person's voice. *Also called* vocalics.

paraphrasing Restating the essence of a sender's message in our own words.

parasocial relationship A one-way relational tie with a media personality or character that reminds us of a face-to-face interaction.

people-centered listening style A listening style associated with concern for other people's feelings or emotions.

perception The process of using our senses to understand and respond to stimuli. The perception process occurs in four stages: attending and selecting, organizing, interpreting, and retrieving.

personal distance Ranging from eighteen inches to four feet, the space most people use during conversations.

personal home page A website that provides personal information about a person, allowing online viewers an opportunity to better know that person.

personal issue An issue related to a relationship that can cause a content conflict.

personal space The distance we put between ourselves and others.

perspective-taking Acknowledging the viewpoints of those with whom we interact.

persuasive power Power derived from being seen as a good, logical communicator who can sway others to a certain point of view.

phatic communication Communication consisting of words and phrases that are used for interpersonal contact only and are not meant to be translated verbatim.

physical characteristics Aspects of physical appearance, such as body size, skin color, hair color and style, facial hair, and facial features.

physical context The tangible environment in which communication occurs.

physical environment   The setting in which our behavior takes place.

physical noise   Any stimuli outside of a sender or a receiver that interfere with the transmission or reception of a message. *Also called* external noise.

physiological noise   Biological influences on a sender or a receiver that interfere with the transmission or reception of a message.

placating   Being passive or ignoring our own needs in a conflict.

polarization   The tendency to use "either-or" language and speak of the world in extremes.

positive face   Our desire to be liked by significant others in our lives and have them confirm our beliefs, respect our abilities, and value what we value.

positive feedback   Feedback that causes a system to recalibrate and change.

positive halo   Occurs when we place positive qualities (e.g., warm, sensitive, and intelligent) together.

postcyberdisclosure panic (PCDP)   A situation in which we disclose personal information in an email message only to experience significant anxiety later because we begin to think about the number of people who could have access to that message.

pouncing   Responding in an aggressive manner without acknowledging the needs of another person in a conflict.

power   In interpersonal relationships, the ability to control the behavior of another.

power distance   How a culture perceives and distributes power.

preventative maintenance   Paying attention to our relationships even when they are not experiencing troubles.

prior conditions   The first stage of Filley's process model, consisting of the history between the two parties, the areas of disagreement they have discussed in the past, and so forth.

private information   Assessments, both good and bad, that we make about ourselves, including our personal values and our interests, fears, and concerns.

process   When used to describe interpersonal communication, an ongoing, unending, vibrant activity that always changes.

process of abstraction   The ability to move up and down the ladder of abstraction from specific to general and vice versa.

proxemics   The study of how people use, manipulate, and identify their personal space.

pseudolisten   To pretend to listen by nodding our heads, looking at the speaker, smiling at the appropriate times, or practicing other kinds of attention feigning.

psychological noise   Biases, prejudices, and feelings that interfere with the accurate transmission or reception of a message. *Also called* internal noise.

public and private dialectic   The tension between how much of a friendship is demonstrated in public and what parts are kept private.

public distance   Communication that occurs at a distance of twelve or more feet, allowing listeners to see a person while he or she is speaking.

public information   Personal facts, usually socially approved characteristics, we make part of our public image.

public issue   An issue outside a relationship that can cause a content conflict.

pursuit-withdrawal   In a conflict, a pattern consisting of one party pressing for a discussion about a conflictual topic while the other party withdraws.

R

rating   Evaluating or assessing a message.

recalibrate   Adjust a relationship to accommodate changing needs of the parties.

recalling   Understanding a message, storing it for future encounters, and remembering it later.

receiver   The intended target of a message.

receiving   The verbal and nonverbal acknowledgment of a message.

reciprocity   The tendency to respond in kind to another's self-disclosure.

referent   The thing a verbal symbol represents.

referent power   A type of power that derives from the charisma and attractiveness a person possesses.

reframe   To change something that has a negative connotation to something with a more positive connotation (e.g., a problem can become a concern, or a challenge can become an opportunity). This strategy can also be used to cope with dialectic tensions in a relationship.

reification   The tendency to respond to words or labels for things as though they were the things themselves.

relational conflict   A conflict that focuses on issues concerning the relationship between two people.

relational history   The prior relationship experiences two people share.

relational message   A message that defines a relationship and implicitly states that the sender has the power to define the relationship.

relational rules   Negotiable rules that indicate what two relational partners expect and allow when they talk to each other.

relational schema   A mental framework or memory structure that we rely on to understand experience and to guide our future behavior in relationships.

relational uniqueness   The ways in which the particular relationship of two relational partners stands apart from other relationships they experience.

relational uppers People who support and trust us as we improve our self-concept.

relationship A bond between two people that is reflected in their interaction patterns and their perceptions of those patterns.

relationship information The information contained in a message that indicates how the sender and the receiver feel about each other.

resolution The fourth stage of Filley's process model, in which both parties decide on a way to manage the conflict.

responding Providing observable feedback to a sender's message.

retrieving The fourth and final stage of the perception process, in which we recall information stored in our memories.

reward power Power that derives from the ability to reward others.

rewards Those parts of being in a relationship that we find pleasurable.

S

Sapir-Whorf hypothesis A theory that points to connections among culture, language, and thought. In its strong form, this theory is known as linguistic determinism, and in its weak form, it is known as linguistic relativity.

screen name A nickname we use to introduce ourselves online.

search engine A tool that enables users to locate content on the World Wide Web.

second-guess To question the assumptions underlying a message.

seeking gestures Gestures that request agreement or clarification from a sender during a conversation.

segmentation A strategy for dealing with dialectic tensions in a relationship that allows us to isolate separate arenas, such as work and home, for using each pole in the opposition.

selection A strategy for dealing with dialectic tensions in a relationship that allows us to choose one of the opposite poles of a dialectic and ignore our need for the other.

selective listening Responding to some parts of a message and rejecting others.

selective perception Directing our attention to certain stimuli while ignoring other stimuli.

selective retention Recalling information that agrees with our perceptions and selectively forgetting information that does not.

self-actualization The process of gaining information about ourselves in an effort to tap our full potential, our spontaneity, and our talents, and to cultivate our strengths and eliminate our shortcomings.

self-awareness Our understanding of who we are.

self-concept A relatively stable set of perceptions we hold of ourselves.

self-disclosure Evaluative and descriptive information about the self, shared intentionally, that another would have trouble finding out without being told.

self-esteem An evaluation of who we perceive ourselves to be.

self-fulfilling prophecy A prediction or expectation about our future behavior that is likely to come true because we believe it and thus act in ways that make it come true.

self-monitoring Actively thinking about and controlling our public behaviors and actions.

semantic noise Occurs when senders and receivers apply different meanings to the same message. Semantic noise may take the form of jargon, technical language, and other words and phrases that are familiar to the sender but that are not understood by the receiver.

sender The source of a message.

sex The biological make-up of an individual (male or female).

sexist language Language that is demeaning to one sex.

short-term attraction A judgment of relationship potential that propels us into initiating a relationship.

significant choice An ethical system, conceptualized by Thomas Nilsen, in which communication is ethical to the extent that it maximizes our ability to exercise free choice. In this system, information should be given to others in a noncoercive way so that people can make free and informed decisions.

small talk Conversational interactions that are relaxed, pleasant, uncritical, and casual.

social distance Ranging from four to twelve feet, the spatial zone usually reserved for professional or formal interpersonal encounters.

social-emotional context The relational and emotional environment in which communication occurs. In this type of context, messages are associated with the nature of a relationship.

social penetration model A model of self-disclosure and relational development that reflects shared information ranging from the most obvious to the most personal.

spam Unsolicited junk mail on the Internet.

stagnating stage A stage in the coming apart section of Knapp's model of relationship development in which circumscribing is extended so far that a couple no longer talks much except in the most routinized ways.

static evaluation The tendency to speak and respond to someone today the same way we did in the past, not recognizing that people and relationships change over time.

stereotyping Categorizing individuals according to a fixed impression, whether positive or negative, of an entire group to which they belong.

story Information we feel we are taking a risk telling another.

strategic ambiguity Leaving out cues in a message on purpose to encourage multiple interpretations by others.

subsystems Lower-level systems of relationship, such as a sibling relationship within a family.

suprasystems Higher-level systems of relationship, such as a neighborhood consisting of several families.

sustaining Behaving in a way that keeps an initial conversation going, such as asking questions.

symbolic interactionism The theory that our understanding of ourselves and of the world are shaped by our interactions with those around us.

symbols Arbitrary labels or representations (such as words) for feelings, concepts, objects, or events.

symmetrical escalation In a conflict, each party choosing to increase the intensity of the conflict.

symmetrical negotiation In a conflict, each party mirroring the other's negotiating behaviors.

symmetrical withdrawal In a conflict, neither partner being willing to confront the other.

T

taboo topic An issue that is out of bounds for discussion.

talkaholic A compulsive talker who hogs the conversational stage and monopolizes encounters.

technological determinism A theory that states that technology is irreversible, inevitable, and inescapable.

terminating stage The last stage in the coming apart section of Knapp's model of relationship development, in which a relationship is ending.

territoriality Our sense of ownership of space that remains fixed.

territorial markers Items or objects that humans use to mark their territories, such as a table in a coffee shop.

time-centered listening style A listening style associated with listeners who want messages to be presented succinctly.

topical intimacy The nature of a topic discussed in relation to the closeness of a relationship.

transactional model of communication A characterization of communication as the reciprocal sending and receiving of messages. In a transactional encounter, the sender and receiver do not simply send meaning from one to the other and then back again; rather, they build shared meaning through simultaneous sending and receiving.

turn gestures Gestures that indicate that another person can speak or that are used to request to speak in a conversation.

turn-taking In a conversation, nonverbal regulators that indicate who talks when and to whom.

U

uncertainty avoidance A cultural mindset that indicates how tolerant (or intolerant) a culture is of uncertainty and change.

uniform resource locator The address of a web page. *Also* referred to by its acronym, URL.

unknown self In the Johari Window, the pane that includes the information that neither we nor others are aware of about ourselves.

utilitarianism An ethical system, developed by John Stuart Mill, in which what is ethical is what will bring the greatest good for the greatest number of people. In this system, consequences of moral actions, especially maximizing satisfaction and happiness, are important.

V

valence An attribute of emotion that refers to whether the emotion reflects a positive or negative feeling.

value conflict A conflict in which the content is specifically about a question of right and wrong.

verbal symbols Words.

vocal characterizers Nonverbal behaviors such as crying, laughing, groaning, muttering, whispering, and whining.

vocalics *See* paralanguage.

vocal qualities Nonverbal behaviors that include pitch, rate, volume, inflection, tempo, and pronunciation, as well as the use of vocal segregates and silence.

vocal segregates The "ums" and "ers" used in conversation.

W

wholeness A principle that states that we can't fully understand a system by simply picking it apart and understanding each of its parts in isolation from one another.

withdrawal-pursuit In a conflict, a pattern in which one party withdraws, which prompts the other party to pursue.

worldview A unique personal frame for viewing life and life's events.

World Wide Web An extensive collection of Internet servers that gives users visual access to documents. *Also* referred to by its acronym, WWW.

References

Acor, A. A. (2001). Employer's perceptions of persons with body art and an experimental test regarding eyebrow piercing (Doctoral dissertation, Marquette University, 2001). *Dissertation Abstracts International: Second B: The Sciences and Engineering, 61,* 3885.

Afifi, W. A., & Guerrero, L. K. (2000). Motivations underlying topic avoidance in close relationships. In S. Petronio (Ed.), *Balancing the secrets of private disclosures* (pp. 165–179). Mahwah, NJ: Lawrence Erlbaum.

Alexander, J. E., & Tate, M. A. (1999). *Web wisdom: How to evaluate and create information quality on the web.* Mahwah, NJ: Lawrence Erlbaum.

Altman, I., & Taylor, D. (1973). *Social penetration: The development of interpersonal relationships.* New York: Holt, Rinehart & Winston.

American Cancer Society. (2001). *Talking with your doctor. Building a support network.* http://www.cancer.org/docroot/ESN/content/ESN_2_2X _Talking_with_your_doctor.asp?sitearea=ESN.

Andersen, J. (1996). *Communication theory: Epistemological foundations.* New York: Guilford.

Andersen, P. A. (1993). Cognitive schemata in personal relationships. In S. Duck (Ed.), *Individuals in relationships* (pp. 1–29). Newbury Park, CA: Sage.

Andersen, P. A. (2003). In different dimensions: Nonverbal communication and culture. In L. A. Samovar & R. E. Porter (Eds.), *Intercultural communication: A reader* (pp. 239–252). Belmont, CA: Wadsworth.

Anderson, R., & Ross, V. (2002). *Questions of communication: A practical introduction to theory.* New York: St. Martin's.

Are you suffering from data smog? (2003, August 21). *AskOxford.com.* http://www.askoxford.com/pressroom/ archive/odelaunch/?view=uk.

Asante, M. K. (1998). *The Afrocentric idea.* Philadelphia: Temple University Press.

Aune, K. S., & Aune, R. K. (1996). Cultural differences in the self-reported experience and expression of emotions in relationships. *Journal of Cross-Cultural Psychology, 27,* 67–81.

"Axis of evil" remark sparks damaging backlash. (2002, February 19). *USA Today,* p. 16A.

Axmaker, L. (2002–2004). Is there humor in your relationships? http://vanderbiltowc.wellsource.com/dh/Content .asp?ID=690.

Babrow, A. S., Hines, S. C., & Kasch, C. R. (2000). Managing uncertainty in illness explanation: An application of problematic integration theory. In B. Whaley (Ed.), *Explaining illness: Research, theory, and strategies* (pp. 41–68). Mahwah, NJ: Lawrence Erlbaum.

Ballard, D. I., & Seibold, D. R. (2000). Time orientation and temporal variation across work groups: Implications for group and organizational communication. *Western Journal of Communication, 64,* 218–242.

Barker, L., & Watson, K. (2001). *Listen up: At home, at work, in relationships: How to harness the power of effective listening.* New York: St. Martin's.

Barnes, S. B. (2001). *Online connections: Internet interpersonal relationships.* Cresskill, NJ: Hampton.

Barnes, S. B. (2003). *Computer-mediated communication: Human-to-human communication across the Internet.* Boston: Allyn and Bacon.

Barnlund, D. C. (1970). A transactional model of communication. In K. K. Sereno & C. D. Mortensen (Eds.), *Foundations of communication theory* (pp. 83–102). New York: Harper and Row.

Basso, K. H. (1990). *Western Apache language and culture: Essays in linguistic anthropology.* Tucson, AZ: University of Arizona.

Bate, B., & Bowker, J. (1997). *Communication and the sexes* (2nd ed.). Prospect Heights, IL: Waveland.

Bates, B., & Cleese, J. (2001). *The human face.* London: BBC.

Bateson, G. (1972). *Steps to an ecology of mind.* New York: Ballantine Books.

Bavelas, J. B. (1994). Gestures as part of speech: Methodological implications. *Research on Language and Social Interaction, 27,* 201–222.

Baxter, L. A. (1987). Self-disclosure and relationship disengagement. In V. J. Derlega & J. H. Berg (Eds.), *Self-disclosure: Theory, research, and therapy* (pp. 155–174). New York: Plenum Press.

Baxter, L. A. (1988). A dialectical perspective on communication strategies in relationship development. In S. Duck (Ed.), *A handbook of personal relationships* (pp. 257–273). New York: Wiley.

Baxter, L. A., & Braithwaite, D. O. (2002). Performing marriage: Marriage renewal rituals as cultural performance. *Southern Communication Journal, 67,* 94–109.

Baxter, L. A., & Montgomery, B. M. (1996). *Relating: Dialogues and dialectics.* New York: Guilford.

Baxter, L. A., & Wilmot, W. (1985). Taboo topics in close relationships. *Journal of Social and Personal Relationships, 2,* 253–269.

Bechar-Israeli, H. (1996). *From <Bonehead> to <CloNehEAd>: Nicknames, play and identity on the Internet relay chat.* http:// www.ascusc.org/jcmc/vol1/issue2/bechar.html.

Bell, R. A., & Daly, J. A. (1984). The affinity-seeking function of communication. *Communication Monographs, 51,* 91–115.

Bem, S. (1993). *The lenses of gender: Transforming the debate on sexual inequality.* New Haven, CT: Yale University.

Benjamin, B., & Werner, R. (2004). Touch in the Western world. *Massage Therapy Journal, 43,* 28–32.

Bentley, S. C. (2000). Listening in the 21st century. *International Journal of Listening, 14,* 129–142.

Berg, J. H., & Archer, R. L. (1980). Disclosure or concern: A second look at liking for the norm-breaker. *Journal of Personality, 48,* 245–257.

Berg, J. H., & Clark, M. S. (1986). Differences in social exchange between intimate and other relationships: Gradually evolving or quickly apparent? In V. J. Derlega & B. A. Winstead (Eds.), *Friendship and social interaction* (pp. 101–128). New York: Springer-Verlag.

Bergmann, J. R. (1993). *Discreet indiscretions: The social organization of gossip.* New York: Aldine de Gruyter.

Berkman, L. F., Leo-Summers, C., & Horowitz, R. I. (1992). Emotional support and survival after myocardial infarction: A prospective population-based study of the elderly. *Annals of Internal Medicine, 117,* 1003–1009.

Bernstein, F. A. (2004, March 7). On campus, rethinking biology 101. *New York Times,* pp. 9–1, 9–6.

Bharat, K., & Broder, A. (1998). *Measuring the web.* http://research.compaq.com/SRC/whatsnew/sem.html.

Blumer, H. (1969). *Symbolic interactionism: Perspective and method.* Englewood Cliffs, NJ: Prentice Hall.

Bochner, A. P. (1982). On the efficacy of openness in close relationships. In M. Burgoon (Ed.), *Communication yearbook 5* (pp. 109–124). New Brunswick, NJ: Transaction Books.

Bodine, A. (1990). Androcentrism in prescriptive grammar: Singular "they," sex-indefinite "he," and "he or she." In D. Cameron (Ed.), *The feminist critique of language* (pp. 166–186). London: Routledge.

Booth, R., & Yung, M. (1996). *Romancing the net.* Rocklin, CA: Prima Publishing.

Booth-Butterfield, M., & Booth-Butterfield, S. (1998). *Emotionality and affective orientation.* In J. C. McCroskey, J. A. Daly, M. M. Martin, & M. J. Beatty (Eds.), *Communication and personality: Trait perspectives* (pp. 171–190). Cresskill, NJ: Hampton.

Bostrom, R. N. (1990). *Listening behavior: Measurement and application.* New York: Guilford.

Bostrom, R. N., & Waldhart, E. S. (1988). Memory models in the measurement of listening. *Communication Education, 37,* 1–12.

Bradford, L. (1993). *A cross-cultural study of strategic embarrassment in adolescent socialization.* (Doctoral dissertation, Arizona State University, 1993). *Dissertation Abstracts International. A: The humanities and social sciences, 29,* 2003.

Bradford, L., & Petronio, S. (1998). Strategic embarrassment: The culprit of emotion. In P. A. Andersen & L. K.

Guerrero (Eds.), *The handbook of communication and emotion* (pp. 99–121). San Diego, CA: Academic Press.

British girls baffles teacher with SMS essay. (2003, March 2). *Yahoo News.* http://story.news.yahoo.com/news?tmpl= story2&u=/nm/20030303/wr_mn/odd_britain_texting_dc.

Brody, J. E. (2002, May 28). Why angry people can't control the short fuse. *New York Times,* D7.

Brownell, J. (2002). *Listening: Attitudes, principles, and skills* (2nd ed.). Boston: Allyn and Bacon.

Buber, M. (1970). *I and thou* (W. Kaufmann, Trans.). New York: Scribner.

Bugeja, M. (2004, July 30). Unshaken hands on the digital street. *Chronicle of Higher Education,* p. B5.

Burgoon, J. K., Buller, D. B., & Woodall, W. G. (1996). *Nonverbal communication: The unspoken dialogue.* New York: McGraw-Hill.

Burgoon, J. K., & Hale, J. L. (1987). Validation and measurement of the fundamental themes of relational communication. *Communication Monographs, 54,* 19–41.

Burgoon, J. K., & Hoobler, G. D. (2002). Nonverbal signals. In M. L. Knapp & J. A. Daly (Eds.), *Handbook of interpersonal communication* (pp. 240–299). Thousand Oaks, CA: Sage.

Burgoon, J. K., Stern, L. A., & Dillman, L. (1995). *Interpersonal adaptation: Dyadic interaction patterns.* New York: Cambridge University Press.

Burleson, B. B., & Planalp, S. (2000). Producing emotion(al) messages. *Communication Theory, 10,* 221–250.

Burleson, B. R. (2003). Emotional support skills. In J. O. Greene & B. R. Burleson (Eds.), *Handbook of communication and social interaction skills* (pp. 551–594). Mahwah, NJ: Lawrence Erlbaum.

Burrell, N. A., Buzzanell, P. M., & McMillan, J. J. (1992). Feminine tensions in conflict situations as revealed by metaphoric analyses. *Management Communication Quarterly, 6,* 115–149.

Buston, P. M., & Emlen, S. T. (2003). Cognitive processes underlying human mate choice: The relationship between self-perception and mate preference in Western society. *Proceedings of the National Academy of Sciences, 100,* 8805–8810.

Buysse, A., De Clercq, A., Verhofstadt, L., Heene, E., Roeyers, H., & Van Oost, P. (2000). Dealing with relational conflict: A picture in milliseconds. *Journal of Social and Personal Relationships, 17,* 574–597.

Buzzanell, P. M., & Burrell, N. A. (1997). Family and workplace conflict: Examining metaphorical conflict schemas and expressions across context and sex. *Human Communication Research, 24,* 109–146.

Buzzanell, P. M., Sterk, H., & Turner, L. H. (2004). Introduction: Challenging common sense. In P. M. Buzzanell, H. Sterk, & L. H. Turner (Eds.), *Gender in applied communication contexts* (pp. xiii-xxii). Thousand Oaks, CA: Sage.

Buzzanell, P. M., & Turner, L. H. (2003). Emotion work revealed by job loss discourse: Backgrounding-foregrounding of feelings, construction of normalcy, and (re)instituting of traditional masculinities. *Journal of Applied Communication Research, 31,* 27–57.

Calloway-Thomas, C., Cooper, P. J., & Blake, C. (1999). *Intercultural communication: Roots and routes.* Boston: Allyn and Bacon.

Canary, D. J., Cupach, W. R., & Serpe, R. T. (2001). A competence-based approach to examining interpersonal conflict: Test of a longitudinal model. *Communication Research, 28,* 79–104.

Canary, D. J., & Dindia, K. (Eds.). (1998). *Sex differences and similarities in communication.* Mahwah, NJ: Lawrence Erlbaum.

Canary, D. J., & Hause, K. S. (1993). Is there any reason to research sex differences in communication? *Communication Quarterly, 41,* 129–144.

Capaldi, N. (2004). *John Stuart Mill: A biography.* Cambridge, England: Cambridge University Press.

Carbaugh, D. (1999). "Just listen": "Listen" and landscape among the Blackfeet. *Western Journal of Communication, 63,* 250–270.

Career Solutions Training Group. (2000). *Quick skills: Listening.* Mason, OH: Thomson South-Western.

Carrasquillo, H. (1997). Puerto Rican families in America. In M. K. DeGenova (Ed.), *Families in cultural context: Strengths and challenges in diversity* (pp. 155–172). Mountain View, CA: Mayfield.

Cash, T. F., & Derlega, V. J. (1978). The matching hypothesis: Physical attractiveness among same-sexed friends. *Personality and Social Psychology Bulletin, 4,* 240–243.

Caughlin, J. P., & Vangelisti, A. L. (2000). An individual difference explanation of why married couples engage in the demand/withdraw pattern of conflict. *Journal of Social and Personal Relationships, 17,* 523–551.

Chang, H. N. (1999). Multiculturalism benefits society. In M. E. Williams (Ed.), *Culture wars: Opposing viewpoints* (pp. 140–147). San Diego, CA: Greenhaven.

Chen, G.-M. (1995). Differences in self-disclosure patterns among Americans versus Chinese: A comparative study. *Journal of Cross-Cultural Psychology, 26,* 84–91.

Chen, G.-M., & Starosta, W. J. (1998). *Foundations of intercultural communication.* Boston: Allyn and Bacon.

Chen, L. (2004). How we know what we know about Americans: Chinese sojourners account for their experiences. In A. Gonzalez, M. Houston, & V. Chen (Eds.), *Our voices: Essays in culture, ethnicity, and communication* (4th ed) (pp. 266–273). Los Angeles: Roxbury.

Chopra, R. (2001). Retrieving the father: Gender studies, "father love" and the discourse of mothering. *Women's Studies International Forum, 24,* 445–455.

ClickZ Stats staff. (2004, September 10). *Population explosion!* http://www.clickz.com/stats/sectors/geographics/article.php/151151.

Cline, R. J., & McKenzie, N. J. (1996). HIV/AIDS, women, and threads of discrimination: A tapestry of disenfranchisement. In E. B. Ray (Ed.), *Communication and disenfranchisement: Social health issues and implications* (pp. 365–386). Mahwah, NJ: Lawrence Erlbaum.

Coates, J., & Cameron, D. (Eds.). (1989). *Women and their speech communities.* New York: Longman.

Cole, S. W., Kemeny, M. E., Taylor, S. E., Visscher, B. R., & Fahey, J. L. (1996). Accelerated course of human immunodeficiency virus infection in gay men who conceal their homosexual identity. *Psychosomatic Medicine, 58,* 219–231.

Cooks, L. (2000). Family secrets and the lie of identity. In S. Petronio (Ed.), *Balancing the secrets of private disclosures* (pp. 197–211). Mahwah, NJ: Lawrence Erlbaum.

Coplin, W. (2004). *10 things employers want you to learn in college.* Berkeley, CA: Ten Speed Press.

Corballis, M. C. (2002). *From hand to mouth: The origins of language.* Princeton, NJ: Princeton University.

Coupland, N., & Nussbaum, J. F. (Eds.). (1993). *Discourse and lifespan identity.* Newbury Park, CA: Sage.

Coyne, J. C., Rohrbaugh, M. J., Shoham, V., Cranford, J. A., Nicklas, J. M., & Sonnega, J. (2001). Prognostic importance of marital quality for survival of congestive heart failure. *American Journal of Cardiology, 88,* 526–529.

Cramer, D. (1998). *Close relationships: The study of love and friendship.* London: Arnold.

Cupach, W. R., & Metts, S. M. (1994). *Facework.* Thousand Oaks, CA: Sage.

Cupach, W. R., & Spitzberg, B. H. (2004). *The dark side of relationship pursuit: From attraction to obsession and stalking.* Mahwah, NJ: Lawrence Erlbaum.

Cupach, W. R., & Spitzberg, W. R. (Eds.). (1994). *The dark side of interpersonal communication.* Mahwah, NJ: Lawrence Erlbaum.

Darling, A., & Dannels, D. P. (2003). Practicing engineers talk about the importance of talk: A report on the role of oral communication in the workplace. *Communication Education, 52,* 1–16.

Darrand, T. C., & Shupe, A. (1983). *Metaphors of social control.* New York: Edwin Mellen Press.

Davis, M. S. (1973). *Intimate relations.* New York: Free Press.

de Sousa, R. (1987). *The rationality of emotion.* Cambridge, MA: MIT Press.

Deetz, S. A. (1992). *Democracy in an age of corporate colonization: Developments in communication and the politics of everyday life.* Albany: SUNY Press.

Derlega, V. J., Metts, S., Petronio, S., & Margulis, S. T. (1993). *Self-disclosure.* Newbury Park, CA: Sage.

Derlega, V. J., Winstead, B. A., Wong, P. T. P., & Hunter, S. (1985). Gender effects in an initial encounter: A case where men exceed women in disclosure. *Journal of Social and Personal Relationships, 2,* 25–44.

Dickson, F. C., & Walker, K. L. (2001). The expression of emotion in later-life married men. *Qualitative Research Reports in Communication, 2,* 66–71.

Diggs, R. C., & Clark, K. D. (2002). It's a struggle but worth it: Identifying and managing identities in an interracial friendship. *Communication Quarterly, 50,* 368–390.

Dillard, J. P. (1990). Primary and secondary goals in interpersonal influence. In M. J. Cody & M. L. McLaughlin (Eds.), *The psychology of tactical communication* (pp. 70–90). Clevedon, England: Multilingual Matters.

Dindia, K. (1994). A multiphasic view of relationship maintenance strategies. In D. J. Canary & L. Stafford (Eds.), *Communication and relational maintenance* (pp. 91–110). San Diego, CA: Academic Press.

Dindia, K. (1998). "Going into and coming out of the closet": The dialectics of stigma disclosure. In B. M. Montgomery & L. A. Baxter (Eds.), *Dialectical approaches to studying personal relationships* (pp. 83–108). Mahwah, NJ: Lawrence Erlbaum.

Dindia, K. (2000). Sex differences in self-disclosure, reciprocity of self-disclosure, and self-disclosure and liking: Three meta-analyses reviewed. In S. Petronio (Ed.), *Balancing the secrets of private disclosures* (pp. 21–35). Mahwah, NJ: Lawrence Erlbaum.

Dindia, K. (2003). Definitions and perspectives on relational maintenance communication. In D. J. Canary & M. Dainton (Eds.), *Maintaining relationships through communication: Relational, contextual, and cultural variations* (pp. 1–28). Mahwah, NJ: Lawrence Erlbaum.

Dindia, K., & Allen, M. (1992). Sex-differences in self-disclosure: A meta-analysis. *Psychological Bulletin, 112,* 106–124.

Dindia, K., Fitzpatrick, M. A., & Kenny, D. A. (1997). Self-disclosure in spouse and stranger dyads: A social relations analysis. *Human Communication Research, 23,* 388–412.

Douglas, W. (1987). Affinity-testing in initial interaction. *Journal of Social and Personal Relationships, 4,* 3–16.

Do you know? (2002, February). *Allure,* p. 28.

Duck, S., & Wood, J. T. (1995). For better, for worse, for richer, for poorer: The rough and smooth of relationships. In S. Duck & J. T. Wood (Eds.), *Confronting relationship challenges* (pp. 1–21). Thousand Oaks, CA: Sage.

Dunbar, R. (1998). *Grooming, gossip, and the evolution of language.* Cambridge, MA: Harvard University Press.

Eisenberg, E. M. (1984). Ambiguity as strategy in organizational communication. *Communication Monographs, 51,* 227–242.

Emmers-Sommer, T. M. (2003). When partners falter: Repair after a transgression. In D. J. Canary & M. Dainton (Eds.), *Maintaining relationships through communication: Relational,* *contextual, and cultural variations* (pp. 185–205). Mahwah, NJ: Lawrence Erlbaum.

Englehardt, E. E. (2001). *Ethical issues in interpersonal communication.* Fort Worth, TX: Harcourt.

Erard, M. (2004, January 3). Just like, er, words, not, um, throwaways. *New York Times,* p. B7.

Ethnocentrism scale (n.d.). http://www.jamescmccroskey.com/measures/ethnocentrism_scale.htm.

Eugenides, J. (2002). *Middlesex.* New York: Farrar, Straus, and Giroux.

Fehr, B., & Russell, J. A. (1984). Concept of emotion viewed from a prototype perspective. *Journal of Experimental Psychology, 113,* 464–486.

Fels, A. (2002, May 21). Mending of hearts and minds. *New York Times,* p. D5.

Field, T. (1999). American adolescents touch each other less and are more aggressive toward their peers as compared with French adolescents. *Adolescence, 34,* 753–759.

Filley, A. C. (1975). *Interpersonal conflict resolution.* Glenview, IL: Scott, Foresman.

Finkenauer, C., & Hazam, H. (2000). Disclosure and secrecy in marriage: Do both contribute to marital satisfaction? *Journal of Social and Personal Relationships, 17,* 245–263.

Fleishman, J., Sherbourne, C., & Crystal, S. (2000). Coping, conflictual social interactions, social support, and mood among HIV-infected persons. *American Journal of Community Psychology, 28,* 421–453.

Floyd, K., & Morman, M. T. (2000). Reacting to the verbal expression of affection in same-sex interaction. *Southern Journal of Communication, 65,* 287–299.

Floyd, K., & Parks, M. (1995). Manifesting closeness in the interactions of peers: A look at siblings and friends. *Communication Reports, 8,* 69–76.

Folger, J. P., Poole, M. S., & Stutman, R. K. (2001). *Working through conflict: Strategies for relationships, groups, and organizations* (4th ed.). New York: Longman.

Forbes, G. B. (2001). College students with tattoos and piercings: Motives, family experiences, personality factors, and perception by others. *Psychological Reports, 89,* 774–786.

Forgas, J. P. (2002). How to make the right impression. In J. A. DeVito (Ed.), *The interpersonal communication reader* (pp. 28–33). Boston: Allyn and Bacon.

Foss, S. K. (1988). *Rhetorical criticism: Exploration and practice.* Prospect Heights, IL: Waveland.

French, J. R. P., Jr., & Raven, B. (1968). The bases of social power. In D. Cartwright & A. Zander (Eds.), *Group dynamics: Research and theory* (pp. 259–269). New York: Harper and Row.

Fulghum, R. (1989). *All I really need to know I learned in kindergarten.* New York: Ivy.

Galvin, K. (2004). International and transracial adoption: A communication research agenda. *Journal of Family Communication, 3,* 237–253.

Gao, G., & Ting-Toomey, S. (1998). *Communicating effectively with the Chinese.* Thousand Oaks, CA: Sage.

Gastil, J. (1990). Generic pronouns and sexist language: The oxymoronic character of masculine generics. *Sex Roles, 23,* 629–641.

Georgia considers banning "evolution." (2004, January 30). *CNN.com.* http://www.cnn.com/2004/EDUCATION/01/30/striking.evolution.ap/.

Gerth, H., & Mills, C. W. (1964). *Character and social structure: The psychology of social institutions.* New York: Harcourt, Brace & World.

Getz, M. A. (2002). *Improvement in physical health and social relationships among very elderly women in a rural county after participation in arthritis courses.* http://ruralwomenshealth.psu.edu/sposter_mgetz.html.

Gibb, J. (1961). Defensive communication. *Journal of Communication, 11,* 141–148.

Gibb, J. (1964). Climate for trust formation. In L. Bradford, J. Gibb, & K. Benne (Eds.), *T-group theory and laboratory method* (pp. 279–309). New York: Wiley.

Gibb, J. (1970). Sensitivity training as a medium for personal growth and improved interpersonal relationships. *Interpersonal Development, 1,* 6–31.

Gilligan, C. (1982). *In a different voice: Psychological theory and women's development.* Cambridge, MA: Harvard University.

Goffman, E. (1959). *The presentation of self in everyday life.* New York: Anchor.

Goldschmidt, W. (1990). *The human career: The self in the symbolic world.* Cambridge, England: Blackwell Publishers.

Goldsmith, D. J., & Fulfs, P. A. (1999). "You just don't have the evidence": An analysis of claims and evidence in Deborah Tannen's *You just don't understand.* In M. E. Roloff (Ed.), Communication yearbook 22 (pp. 1–49). Thousand Oaks, CA: Sage.

Goleman, D. (1995). *Emotional intelligence: Why it can matter more than IQ.* New York: Bantam Books.

Goleman, D. (n.d.). *Emotional intelligence test.* http://www.utne.com/interact/test_iq.html

Goode, E. (2002). Therapists redraw line of self-disclosure. *New York Times,* pp. D5, D7.

Gosselin, P., Kirouac, G., & Dore, F. Y. (1995). Components and recognition of facial expression in the communication of emotion by actors. *Journal of Personality and Social Psychology, 68,* 83–96.

Gottman, J. M. (2004, March 25). *Fresh Air* interview [radio show].

Gottman, J. M. (1994). *Why marriages succeed or fail.* New York: Simon and Schuster.

Gottman, J. M. (1999). *The marriage clinic: A scientifically-based marital therapy.* New York: W.W. Norton and Company.

Gottman, J. M., Katz, L. F., & Hooven, C. (1997). *Meta-emotion: How families communicate emotionally.* Mahwah, NJ: Lawrence Erlbaum.

Graham, E. E. (2003). Dialectic contradictions in postmarital relationships. *Journal of Family Communication, 4,* 193–214.

Graham, E. E. (1997). Turning points and commitments in post-divorce relations. *Communication Monographs, 64,* 350–368.

Grau, J., & Grau, C. (2003). New communication demands of the 21st century.

Gray, J. (1992). *Men are from Mars, women are from Venus: A practical guide to improving communication and getting what you want in your relationships.* New York: HarperCollins.

Grice, H. P. (1975). Logic and conversation. In P. Cole & J. L. Morgan (Eds.), *Syntax and semantics: Vol. 3. Speech acts* (pp. 41–58). New York: Seminar.

Griffin, C. L. (2004). *Invitation to public speaking.* Belmont, CA: Wadsworth.

Gudykunst, W. B., & Kim, Y. Y. (1997). *Communicating with strangers: An approach to intercultural communication.* New York: McGraw-Hill.

Gudykunst, W. B., Ting-Toomey, S., Sudweeks, S., & Stewart, L. P. (1995). *Building bridges: Interpersonal skills for a changing world.* Boston: Houghton Mifflin.

Gueguen, N., & De Gail, M. (2003). The effect of Smiling on helping behavior: smiling and good Samaritan behavior. *Communication Reports, 16,* 133–140.

Guerrero, L. K., & Afifi, W. A. (1995). What parents don't know: Topic avoidance in parent-child relationships. In T. J. Socha & G. H. Stamp (Eds.), *Parents, children, and communication: Frontiers of theory and research* (pp. 219–245). Mahwah, NJ: Lawrence Erlbaum.

Guerrero, L. K., Andersen, P. A., & Trost, M. R. (1998). Communication and emotion: Basic concepts and approaches. In P. A. Andersen & L. K. Guerrero (Eds.), *Handbook of communication and emotion: Research, theory, applications, and contexts* (pp. 3–27). San Diego, CA: Academic Press.

Guy, S. (2004, Feb 18). *"Digital divide' continues to split urban, rural dwellers.* http://www.suntimes.com.

Hall, B. J. (2005). *Among cultures: The challenge of communication.* Fort Worth, TX: Harcourt.

Hall, E. T. (1959). *The silent language.* New York: Doubleday.

Hall, E. T., & Hall, M. R. (1990). *Understanding cultural differences.* Yarmouth, ME: Intercultural Press.

Hall, J. A., Carter, J. D., & Horgan, T. G. (2000). Gender differences in nonverbal communication of emotion. In A. H. Fischer (Ed.), *Gender and emotion: Social psychological perspectives* (pp. 97–117). Cambridge, England: Cambridge University Press.

Hamacheck, D. E. (1992). *Encounters with the self.* Fort Worth, TX: Harcourt.

Hamid, P. N. (2000). Self-disclosure and occupational stress in Chinese professionals. *Psychological Reports, 87*, 1075–1082.

Hamilton, W.L. (2004, July 5). For Bantu refugees, hard-won American dreams. *New York Times*, pp. A1, A14.

Hammond, A. (2001, March/April). *Digitally empowered development*. www.digitaldividend.org/pdf/0201ar04.pdf.

Harris, T. M. (2004). "I know it was the blood": Defining the biracial self in a Euro-American society. In. A. Gonzalez, M. Houston, & V. Chen (Eds.), *Our voices: Essays in culture, ethnicity, and communication* (4th ed.) (pp. 203–209). Los Angeles: Roxbury.

Harvey, J. H., & Weber, A. L. (2002). *Odyssey of the heart: Close relationships in the 21st century* (2nd ed.). Mahwah, NJ: Lawrence Erlbaum.

Hashem, M. (2004). The power of Wastah in Lebanese speech. In A. Gonzalez, M. Houston, & V. Chen (Eds.), *Our voices: Essays in culture, ethnicity, and communication* (4th ed.) (pp. 169–173). Los Angeles, CA: Roxbury.

Hastings, S. O. (2000). "Egocasting" in the avoidance of disclosure: An intercultural perspective. In S. Petronio (Ed.), *Balancing the secrets of private disclosures* (pp. 235–248). Mahwah, NJ: Lawrence Erlbaum.

Hatfield, E. (1984). The dangers of intimacy. In V. J. Derlega (Ed.), *Communication, intimacy, and close relationships* (pp. 207–220). New York: Academic Press.

Hayakawa, S. I. (1990*). Language in thought and action*. San Diego, CA: Harcourt Brace.

Hayavadana, R. C. (1996). *Indian caste system*. Delhi, India: AES.

Hecht, M. L., Collier, M. J., & Ribeau, S. A. (1993). *African American communication: Ethnic identity and cultural interpretation*. Newbury Park, CA: Sage.

Heider, F. (1958). *The psychology of interpersonal relations*. New York: Wiley.

Hickson, M., Stacks, D. W., & Moore, N.-J. (2004). *Nonverbal communication: Studies and applications*. Los Angeles, Roxbury.

Hinde, R. A. (1995). A suggested structure for a science of relationships. *Personal Relationships, 2*, 1–15.

Hinsz, V. B. (1989). Facial resemblance in engaged and married couples. *Journal of Social and Personal Relationships, 6*, 223–229.

Hochschild, A. R. (1983). *The managed heart: Commercialization of human feeling*. Berkeley: University of California Press.

Hoffman, C. (2003, May 14). At Brandeis, unlikely partners in peace. *New York Times*, p. A22.

Hofstede, G. (1980). *Culture's consequences*. Beverly Hills, CA: Sage.

Hofstede, G. (1984). The cultural relativity of the quality of life concept. *Academy of Management Review, 9*, 389–398.

Hofstede, G. (1991). *Cultures and organizations: Software of the mind*. New York: McGraw-Hill.

Hofstede, G. (2001). *Culture's consequence: Comparing values, behaviors, institutions, and organizations across nations*. Thousand Oaks, CA: Sage.

Hoijer, H. (1994). The Sapir-Whorf hypothesis. In L. A. Samovar & R. E. Porter (Eds.), Intercultural communication: A reader. Belmont, CA: Wadsworth.

Holmberg, D., & MacKenzie, S. (2002). So far, so good: Scripts for romantic relationship development as predictors of relational well-being. *Journal of Social and Personal Relationships, 19*, 777–796.

Honeycutt, J. M. (2003). *Imagined interactions*. Cresskill, NJ: Hampton Press.

Honeycutt, J. M., Cantrill, J. G., Kelly, P., & Lambkin, D. (1998). How do I love thee? Let me consider my options: Cognition, verbal strategies, and the escalation of intimacy. *Human Communication Research, 25*, 39–63.

Horton, D., & Wohl, R. (1956). Mass communication and parasocial interaction: Observation on intimacy at a distance. *Psychiatry, 19*, 215–229.

Houston, M. (2004). When Black women talk with White women: Why dialogues are difficult. In A. Gonzalez, M. Houston, & V. Chen (Eds.), *Our voices: Essays in culture, ethnicity, and communication* (4th ed.) (pp. 133–139). Los Angeles: Roxbury.

Hunter, M. (2000, December). Getting in touch with your emotions. *Phoenix Newspaper*. http://www.phoenixrecovery.org/backissues/00december-article.html.

Huston, T. L., McHale, S. M., & Crouter, A. C. (1986). When the honeymoon's over: Changes in the marriage relationship over the first year. In R. Gilmour & S. Duck (Eds.), *The emerging science of personal relationships* (pp. 109–132). Hillsdale, NJ: Lawrence Erlbaum.

Ijams, K., & Miller, L. D. (2000). Perceptions of dream-disclosure: An exploratory study. *Communication Studies, 51*, 135–148.

Imhof, M. (2003). The social construction of the listener: Listening behavior across situations, perceived listener status, and cultures. *Communication Research Reports, 20*, 357–366.

Infante, D. A., & Rancer, A. S. (1982). A conceptualization and measure of argumentativeness. *Journal of Personality Assessment, 46*, 72–80.

International Telework Association and Council. (2004). *Advancing work from anywhere*. http://www.telecommute.org/resources.

In the news. (1999, October 1). *Commercial Appeal* [an E.W. Scripps newspaper], p. A-1.

Ishii-Kuntz, M. (1997). Japanese American families. In M. K. DeGenova (Ed.), *Families in cultural context: Strengths and challenges in diversity* (pp. 109–130). Mountain View, CA: Mayfield.

Ivy, D. K., & Backlund, P. (2000). *Exploring genderspeak* (2nd ed.). New York: McGraw-Hill.

Ivy, D. K., Bullis-Moore, L., Norvell, K., Backlund, P., & Javidi, M. (1995). The lawyer, the babysitter, and the student: Inclusive language usage and instruction. *Women and Language, 18,* 13–21.

Jackson, R. L. (2002). Cultural contracts theory: Toward an understanding of identity negotiation. *Communication Quarterly, 50,* 359–367.

Jamison, S. L. (2003, December 12). Clicking on the links to friendship. *New York Times,* p. C13.

Jandt, F. E. (2004). *An introduction to intercultural communication: Identities in a global community.* Thousand Oaks, CA: Sage.

Jensen, J. V. (1997). *Ethical issues in human communication* (5th ed.). Prospect Heights, IL: Waveland.

Johanneson, R. L. (2000). *Ethics in human communication* (5th ed.). Prospect Heights, IL: Waveland.

Johnson, A. J. (2002). Beliefs about arguing: A comparison of public issue and personal issue arguments. *Communication Reports, 15,* 99–111.

Johnson, F. L. (1996). Friendships among women: Closeness in dialogue. In J. T. Wood (Ed.), *Gendered relationships* (pp. 79–94). Mountain View, CA: Mayfield.

Johnson, F. L. (2000). *Speaking culturally: Language diversity in the United States.* Thousand Oaks, CA: Sage.

Johnson, M. P. (1995). Patriarchal terrorism and common couple violence: Two forms of violence against women. *Journal of Marriage and the Family, 57,* 283–294.

Johnston, M. K., Weaver, J. B., Watson, K. W., & Barker, L. B. (2000). Listening styles: Biological or psychological differences? *International Journal of Listening, 14,* 32–46.

Joinson, A. N. (2001). Knowing me, knowing you: Reciprocal self-disclosure in Internet-based surveys. *Cyberpsychology and Behaviour, 4,* 587–591.

Jones, D. (2004, January 9). Women trump the men in first episode. *USA Today,* p. 3B.

Jones, G. P., & Dembo, M. H. (1989). Age and sex role differences in intimate friendships during childhood and adolescence. *Merrill-Palmer Quarterly of Behavior and Development, 35,* 445–462.

Jones, S. E., & Yarbrough, A. E. (1985). A naturalistic study of the meanings of touch. *Communication Monographs, 52,* 19–56.

Jones, S. G. (1998). Introduction. In S. G. Jones (Ed.), *Cybersociety 2.0* (pp. xi–xvii). Thousand Oaks, CA: Sage.

Jourard, S. M. (1959). Healthy personality and self-disclosure. *Journal of Mental Hygiene, 43,* 499–507.

Jourard, S. M. (1971). *The transparent self* (2nd ed.). New York: Van Nostrand-Reinhold.

Kakutani, M. (2001, October 20). Fear: The new virus of a connected era. *New York Times,* p. 13.

Kirtley, M. D., & Honeycutt, J. (1996). Listening styles and their correspondence with second-guessing. *Communication Research Reports, 13,* 1–9.

Kitzinger, C. (2000). How to resist an idiom. *Research on Language and Social Interaction, 33,* 121–154.

Klinkenborg, V. (2004, February 27). Behind the rise of Google lies the rise in internet credibility. *New York Times,* p. A24.

Klopf, D. W. (1998). *Intercultural encounters: The fundamentals of intercultural communication.* Englewood, CO: Morton Publishing.

Knapp, M. L. (1978). *Social intercourse: From greeting to goodbye.* Boston: Allyn and Bacon.

Knapp, M. L., & Hall, J. A. (2002). *Nonverbal communication in human interaction.* Belmont, CA: Wadsworth.

Knapp, M. L., & Vangelisti, A. L. (2000). *Interpersonal communication and human relationships* (4th ed.). Boston: Allyn and Bacon.

Knapp, M. L., & Vangelisti, A. L. (2005). *Interpersonal communication and human relationships* (5th ed.). Boston: Allyn and Bacon.

Kornblum, J. (2003, February 10). Online dating: No longer in the "geeky" domain. *USA Today,* p. 6D.

Korzybski, A. (1958). *Science and sanity: An introduction to non-Aristotelian systems and general semantics* (4th ed.). Lakeville, CT: International Non-Aristotelian Library Publishing Company.

Kovecses, Z. (2000). *Metaphor and emotion: Language, culture, and body in human feeling.* Cambridge, England: Cambridge University Press.

Kowalski, R. M. (2001). The aversive side of social interaction revisited. In R. M. Kowalski (Ed.), *Behaving badly: Aversive behaviors in interpersonal relationships* (pp. 297–309). Washington, DC: American Psychological Association.

Kramarae, C. (1981). *Women and men speaking.* Rowley, MA: Newbury House.

Kuehn, M. (2001). *Kant: A biography.* New York: Cambridge University Press.

Lakey, S. G., & Canary, D. J. (2002). Actor goal achievement and sensitivity to partner as critical factors in understanding interpersonal communication competence and conflict strategies. *Communication Monographs, 69,* 217–235.

Lakoff, G., & Johnson, M. (1980). *Metaphors we live by.* Chicago: University of Chicago Press.

Lakoff, R. (1975). *Language and women's place.* New York: Harper and Row.

Langer, E. (1989). *Mindfulness.* Reading, MA: Addison-Wesley.

Larsen, E. (2004). Deeper understanding, deeper ties: Taking faith online. In P. N. Howard & S. Jones (Eds.), *Society online: The Internet in context* (pp. 43–56). Thousand Oaks, CA: Sage.

Lazarus, R. S. (1991). *Emotion and adaptation.* New York: Oxford University Press.

Leggitt, J. S., & Gibbs, R. W. (2000). Emotional reactions to verbal irony. *Discourse Processes, 29,* 1–24.

Lerner, H. (2001). *The dance of connection.* New York: Harper-Collins.

Levenson, R. W., & Gottman, J. M. (1985). Physiological and affective predictors of change in relationship satisfaction. *Journal of Personality and Social Psychology, 45,* 587–597.

Levinson, D. (1996–2004). It's only words. *Gay and Lesbian Issues.* http://www.rslevinson.com/gaylesissues/features/main/gl970822.htm.

Lewis, R. D. (1999). *When cultures collide: Managing successfully across cultures.* London: Nicholas Brealey.

Linguistic Society of America (1997, January). *LSA resolution on the Oakland "Ebonics" issue.* http://www.linguistlist.org/topics/ebonics/lsa-ebonics.html.

Lippert, T., & Prager, K. J. (2001). Daily experiences of intimacy: A study of couples. *Personal Relationships, 8,* 283–298.

Lippman, W. (1922). *Public opinion.* New York: Macmillan.

Littlejohn, S. W., & Domenici, K. (2001). *Engaging communication in conflict.* Thousand Oaks, CA: Sage.

Lloyd, S. A. (1987). Conflict in premarital relationships: Differential perceptions of males and females. *Family Relations, 36,* 290–294.

Loftus, E. F., & Palmer, J. C. (1974). Reconstruction of automobile destruction: An example of the interaction between language and memory. *Journal of Verbal Learning and Verbal Behavior, 13,* 585–589.

Luft, J. (1970). *Group process: An introduction to group dynamics.* Palo Alto, CA: Mayfield.

Lulofs, R. S., & Cahn, D. D. (2000). *Conflict: From theory to action* (2nd ed.). Boston: Allyn and Bacon.

Lustig, M. W., & Koester, J. (1999). *Intercultural competence: Interpersonal communication across cultures.* New York: Longman.

Lustig, M. W., & Koester, J. (2000). The nature of cultural identity. In M. W. Lustig & J. Koester (Eds.), *AmongUS: Essays on identity, belonging, and intercultural competence* (pp. 3–8). New York: Addison-Wesley.

Maccoby, E. (1998). *The two sexes: Crowing up apart, coming together.* Cambridge, MA: Harvard University Press.

Mackay, H. (2001). *Listening is the hardest of the "easy" tasks.* http://www.listen.org/pages/mackay.

Maltz, D. J., & Borker, R. A. (1982). A cultural approach to male-female miscommunication. In J. J. Gumpertz (Ed.), *Language and social identity* (pp. 196–216). Cambridge, England: Cambridge University Press.

Marano, H. E. (2004). The new sex scorecard. *Psychology Today.* http://cms.psychologytoday.com/articles.

Martin, J. N., & Nakayama, T. K. (2000). *Intercultural communication in contexts* (2nd ed.). New York: McGraw-Hill.

Martin, J.N., & Nakayama, T.K. (2004). *Intercultural communication in contexts* (3rd ed.). New York: McGraw-Hill.

Martinez, R. (2000, July 16). The next chapter: America's next great revolution in race relations is already underway. *New York Times Magazine,* pp. 11–12.

Martyna, W. (1978). What does "he" mean? Use of the generic masculine. *Journal of Communication, 28,* 131–138.

Marwell, G., & Schmitt, D. R. (1967). Dimensions of compliance-gaining behavior: An empirical analysis. *Sociometry, 30,* 350–364.

Marwell, G., & Schmitt, D. R. (1990). An introduction. In J. P. Dillard (Ed.), *Seeking compliance: The production of interpersonal influence messages* (pp. 3–5). Scottsdale, AZ: Gorsuch Scarisbrick.

Maslow, A. H. (1954/1970). *Motivation and personality.* New York: Harper and Row.

Maslow, A. H. (1968). *Toward a psychology of being.* New York: Van Nostrand Reinhold.

McCroskey, J. C., & Richmond, V. P. (1995). Correlates of compulsive communication: Quantitative and qualitative characteristics. *Communication Quarterly, 43,* 39–52.

McFedries, P. (2004). *Word spy: The word lover's guide to modern culture.* New York: Broadway Books.

McGeorge, C. (2001). Mars and Venus: Unequal planets. *Journal of Marital and Family Therapy, 27,* 55–68.

McGowan, W. (2001). *Coloring the news : How crusading for diversity has corrupted American journalism.* San Francisco: Encounter.

McIlwain, C. D. (2002). Death in Black and White: A study of family differences in the performance of death rituals. *Qualitative Research Reports in Communication, 3,* 1–6.

McLuhan, M. (1964). *Understanding media; The extensions of man.* New York: McGraw-Hill.

McLuhan, M., & McLuhan, E. (1988). *Laws of media: The new science.* Toronto, Canada: Toronto Press.

McQuail, D., & Windahl, S. (1993). *Communication models.* New York: Longman.

Mead, G. H. (1934). *Mind, self and society: From the standpoint of a social behaviorist.* Chicago: University of Chicago Press.

Medved, C. E., & Kirby, E. L. (in press). Family CEOs: A feminist analysis of corporate mothering discourses. *Management Communication Quarterly.*

Meer, J. (1985, September). The light touch. *Psychology Today,* 60–67.

Mehrabian, A. (1981). *Silent messages: Implicit communication of emotions and attitudes* (2nd ed.). Belmont, CA: Wadsworth.

Mehrabian, A., & Ferris, S. R. (1967). Inference of attitudes from nonverbal communication in two channels. *Journal of Consulting Psychology, 21,* 248–252.

Mental Health Net (n.d.). *Methods for Developing Skills.* http://mentalhelp.net/psyhelp/chap13.

Merriam-Webster Online Dictionary. (2004). http://www .m-w.com/cgi-bin/dictionary.

Messman, S. J., & Mikesell, R. L. (2000). Competition and interpersonal conflict in dating relationships. *Communication Reports, 13,* 21–34.

Metzger, D. (1995). *The lost cause of rhetoric: The relation of rhetoric and geometry in Aristotle and Lacan.* Carbondale, IL: Southern Illinois University.

Meyers, S. A., & Berscheid, E. (1997). The language of love: The difference a preposition makes. *Personality and Social Psychology Bulletin, 23,* 347–362.

Michigan State University Counseling Center (2003). *Improving communication skills: Suggestions for improving communication skills in relationships.* http://www.couns.msu.edu/ self-help/suggest.htm.

Miller, G. R., & Parks, M. R. (1982). Communication in dissolving relationships. In S. Duck (Ed.), *Personal relationships 4: Dissolving personal relationships* (pp. 127–154). New York: Academic Press.

Miller, J. B., Plant, E. A., & Hanke, E. (1993). Girls' and boys' views of body type. In C. Berryman-Fink, D. Ballard-Reisch, L. H. Newman (Eds.), *Communication and sex-role socialization* (pp. 49–58). New York: Garland.

Miller, G. R., & Steinberg, M. (1975). *Between people: A new analysis of interpersonal communication.* Chicago: Science Research Associates.

Mills, S. (2003). Caught between sexism, anti-sexism and "political correctness": Feminist women's negotiations with naming practices. *Discourse and Society, 14,* 87–110.

Miura, S. Y. (2000). The mediation of conflict in the traditional Hawaiian family: A collectivistic approach. *Qualitative Research Reports in Communication, 1,* 19–25.

Molloy, J. T. (1978). *Dress for success.* New York: Warner.

Molm, L. D. (2001). Theories of social exchange and exchange networks. In G. Ritzer & B. Smart (Eds.), *Handbook of social theory* (pp. 260–272). London: Sage.

Morrison, T., Conaway, W. A., & Borden, G. A. (1994). *Kiss, bow, or shake hands.* Holbrook, MA: Adams Media.

Morton, J. B., & Trehub, S. E. (2001). Children's understandings of emotions in speech. *Child Development, 72,* 834–843.

Moyers, B. (1993). *Healing and the mind.* New York: Doubleday.

Mulac, A., Bradac, J. J., & Gibbons, P. (2001). Empirical support for the gender-as-culture hypothesis: An intercultural analysis of male/female language differences. *Human Communication Research, 27,* 121–152.

Mulac, A., Incontro, C. R., & James, M. R. (1985). Comparison of the gender-linked language effect and sex role stereotypes. *Journal of Personality and Social Psychology, 49,* 1098–1109.

Murphy, D. E. (2002, May 26). Letting go: Beyond justice: The eternal struggle to forgive. *New York Times.*

Myers, S. A., & Bryant, L. E. (2002). Perceived understanding, interaction involvement, and college student outcomes. *Communication Research Reports, 19,* 146–155.

Nakayama, T. K., & Martin, J. N. (1999). Introduction: Whiteness as the communication of social identity. In T. K. Nakayama & J. N. Martin (Eds.), *Whiteness: The communication of social identity* (pp. vi-xiv). Thousand Oaks, CA: Sage.

National Association of Colleges and Employers (2002). *Do employers and colleges see eye to eye? College student development and assessment.* http://www.naceweb.com.

National Communication Association (n.d.) *How Americans communicate* [poll conducted by Roper Starch Worldwide in the summer of 1998]. http://www.natcom.org/research/ Poll/how_americans_communicate.htm.

National Council on Economic Education. (2000–2004). *A case study: United States international trade in goods and services—July 2002.* http://www.econedlink.org.

National Telecommunications and Information Administration (1999). *Falling through the net: Defining the digital divide.* http://www.ntia.doc.gov/ntiahome/fttn99/contents.html.

National Telecommunications and Information Administration (2002). *A nation online: How Americans are expanding their use of the Internet.* http://www.ntia.doc.gov/ntiahome/ dn/.

Neff, G., & Stark, D. (2004). Permanently beta: Responsive organization in the Internet era. In P. Howard & S. Jones (Eds.), *Society online: The Internet in context* (pp. 173–188). Thousand Oaks, CA: Sage.

Nettle, D., & Romaine, S. (2000). *Vanishing voices: The extinction of the world's languages.* Oxford, England: Oxford University Press.

Nichols, R. (1948). Factors in listening comprehension. *Speech Monographs, 15,* 154–163.

Nilsen, T. (1966). *Ethics of speech communication.* Indianapolis, IN: Bobbs-Merrill.

Noll, A. M. (1997). *Highway of dreams.* Mahwah, NJ: Lawrence Erlbaum.

Nunberg, G. (2003, May 29). *Fresh Air* interview [radio show].

Oatley, K., & Duncan, E. (1992). Incidents of emotion in daily life. In K. T. Strongman (Ed.), *International review of studies on emotion* (Vol. 2, pp. 249–293). Chichester, England: Wiley.

Oberg, A. C. (2003). New umbilical cords tie young adults to parents. *USA Today,* p. 11A.

Ogden, C. K., & Richards, I. A. (1923). *The meaning of meaning.* London: Kegan, Paul, Trench, Trubner.

Okimoto, J. D., & Stegall, P. J. (1987). *Boomerang kids: How to live with adult children who return home.* New York: Pocket.

Olson, L. N. (2002). Compliance gaining strategies of individuals experiencing "common couple violence." *Qualitative Research Reports in Communication, 3*, 7–14.

Olson, L. N. (2003). "From lace teddies to flannel PJ's": An analysis of males' experience and expressions of love. *Qualitative Research Reports in Communication, 4*, 38–44.

Omarzu, J. (2000). A disclosure decision model: Determining how and when individuals will self-disclose. *Personality and Social Psychology Review, 4*, 174–185.

Orbe, M. P. (1998). *Constructing co-cultural theory: An explication of culture, power, and communication.* Thousand Oaks, CA: Sage.

Orrego, V. O., Smith, S. W., Mitchell, M. M., Johnson, A. J., Yun, K. A., & Greenberg, B. (2000). Disclosure and privacy issues on television talk shows. In S. Petronio (Ed.), *Balancing the secrets of private disclosures* (pp. 249–259). Mahwah, NJ: Lawrence Erlbaum.

Ortony, A., Clore, G. L., & Foss, M. (1987). The referential structure of the affective lexicon. *Cognitive Science, 11*, 361–384.

Owen, W. F. (1989). Image metaphors of women and men in personal relationships. *Women's Studies in Communication, 12*, 37–57.

Pais, S. (1997). Asian Indian families in America. In M. K. DeGenova (Ed.), *Families in cultural context: Strengths and challenges in diversity* (pp. 173–190). Mountain View, CA: Mayfield.

Palmer, K. S. (2002, October 10). Cultures clash in workplaces. *USA Today*, p. 13A.

Pan, Y. (2000). *Politeness in Chinese face-to-face interaction.* Stamford, CT: Ablex.

Parks, M. R. (1982). Ideology in interpersonal communication: Off the couch and into the world. In M. Burgoon (Ed.), *Communication yearbook 6* (pp. 79–107). Newbury Park, CA: Sage.

Parks, M. R., & Floyd, K. (1996). Meanings for closeness and intimacy in friendship. *Journal of Social and Personal Relationships, 13*, 85–107.

Pearce, W. B., & Sharp, S. M. (1973). Self-disclosing communication. *Journal of Communication, 23*, 409–425.

Pearson, J. C. (1992). *Lasting love: What keeps couples together.* Dubuque, IA: Wm. C. Brown.

Pearson, J. C., West, R., & Turner, L. H. (1995). *Gender and communication.* Madison, WI: Brown and Benchmark.

Peel, K. (1997). *The family manager's everyday survival guide.* New York: Ballantine Books.

Pennebaker, J. W., Barger, S. D., & Tiebout, J. (1989). Trauma and health among Holocaust survivors. *Psychosomatic Medicine, 51*, 577–589.

Petronio, S. (1991). Communication boundary management: A theoretical model of managing disclosures of private information between marital couples. *Communication Theory, 1*, 311–335.

Petronio, S. (2000). Preface. In S. Petronio (Ed.), *Balancing the secrets of private disclosures* (pp. xiii–xvi). Mahwah, NJ: Lawrence Erlbaum.

Petronio, S. (2002). *Boundaries of privacy: Dialectics of disclosure.* Albany, NY: SUNY Press.

Pew Internet and American Life Project. (2004). *Internet use by region in the United States.* http://www.pewinternet.org/pdfs/PIP_Regional_Report_Aug_2003.pdf.6

Pfeiffer, R. S., & Forsberg, R. L. (2005). *Ethics on the job: Cases and strategies.* Belmont, CA: Wadsworth.

Pipher, M. (2003, March/April). In praise of hometowns: Staying home in the global village. *UU World, XVII*, 39–41.

Planalp, S. (1998). Communicating emotion in everyday life: Cues, channels, and processes. In P. A. Andersen & L. K. Guerrero (Eds.), *Handbook of communication and emotion: Research, theory, applications, and contexts* (pp. 30–48). San Diego, CA: Academic Press.

Planalp, S. (1999). *Communicating emotion: Social, moral, and cultural processes.* Cambridge, England: Cambridge University Press.

Planalp, S., DeFrancisco, V., & Rutherford, D. (1996). Varieties of cues to emotion in naturally occurring situations. *Cognition and Emotion, 10*, 137–153.

Planalp, S., & Fitness, J. (1999). Thinking/feeling about social and personal relationships. *Journal of Social and Personal Relationships, 16*, 731–750.

Plutchik, R. (1984). Emotions: A general psychoevolutionary theory. In K.R. Scherer & P. Ekman (Eds.), *Approaches to emotion* (pp. 197–219). Hillsdale, NJ: Lawrence Erlbaum.

Priest, P. J. (1995). *Public intimacies: Talk show participants and tell-all T.V.* Cresskill, NJ: Hampton Press.

Primitive Baptist Web Station (n.d.). *Common emoticons and acronyms.* http://www.pb.org/emotican.html.

Pullum, G. K. (1991). *The great Eskimo vocabulary hoax and other irreverent essays on the study of language.* Chicago: University of Chicago Press.

Purdy, M. (2004). *Listen up, move up.* http://www.featuredreports.monster.com.

Ravitch, D. (2003). *The language police: How pressure groups restrict what students learn.* New York: Alfred A. Knopf.

Rawlins, W. K. (1992). *Friendship matters: Communication, dialectics, and the life course.* New York: Aldine de Gruyter.

Reissman, C. (1990). *Divorce talk: Women and men make sense of personal relationships.* New Brunswick, NJ: Rutgers University Press.

Ribeau, S. A., Baldwin, J. R., & Hecht, M. L. (2000). An African American communication perspective. In L. A. Samovar & R. E. Porter (Eds.), *Intercultural communication: A reader* (9th ed.) (pp. 128–135). Belmont, CA: Wadsworth.

Richmond, V. P., & McCroskey, J.C. (1998). *Communication: Apprehension, avoidance, and effectiveness.* Needham Heights, MA: Allyn and Bacon.

Riggs, K. E. (2004). *Granny at work: Aging and technology on the job in America.* New York: Routledge.

Ritts, V., Patterson, M. L., & Tubbs, M. E. (1992). Expectations, impressions, and judgements of physically attractive students: A review. *Review of Educational Research, 64,* 413–426.

Roethlisberger, F. L., & Dickson, W. (1939). *Management and the worker.* New York: Wiley.

Roloff, M. E. (1981). *Interpersonal communication: The social exchange approach.* Beverly Hills, CA: Sage.

Roloff, M. E. (1987). Communication and conflict. In C. R. Berger & S. H. Chaffee (Eds.), *Handbook of communication science* (pp. 484–534). Newbury Park, CA: Sage.

Roloff, M. E., & Ifert, D. E. (2000). Conflict management through avoidance: Withholding complaints, suppressing arguments, and declaring topics taboo. In S. Petronio (Ed.), *Balancing the secrets of private disclosures* (pp. 151–163), Mahwah, NJ: Lawrence Erlbaum.

Rose, A., & Asher, S. (2000). Children's friendships. In C. Hendrick & S. Hendrick (Eds.), *Close relationships: A sourcebook* (pp. 47–57). Thousand Oaks, CA: Sage.

Rosenfeld, L. B. (2000). Overview of the ways privacy, secrecy, and disclosure are balanced in today's society. In S. Petronio (Ed.), *Balancing the secrets of private disclosures* (pp. 3–17). Mahwah, NJ: Lawrence Erlbaum.

Rosnow, R. L. (2001). Rumor and gossip in interpersonal interaction and beyond: A social exchange perspective. In R. M. Kowalski (Ed.), *Behaving badly: Aversive behaviors in interpersonal relationships* (pp. 203–232). Washington, DC: American Psychological Association.

Rourke, L., Anderson, T., Garrison, D. R., & Archer, W. (2001). Assessing social presence in asynchronous text-based computer conferencing. *Journal of Distance Education, 14,* 50–71.

Rubin, R. B., Palmgreen, P., & Sypher, H. E. (Eds.). (1994). *Communication research measures: A sourcebook.* New York: Guilford Press.

Rudawsky, D. J., Lundgren, D. C., & Grasha, A. F. (1999). Competitive and collaborative responses to negative feedback. *International Journal of Conflict Management, 10,* 172–190.

Russell, J. A. (1978). Evidence of convergent validity of the dimensions of affect. *Journal of Personality and Social Psychology, 36,* 1152–1168.

Russell, J. A. (1980). A circumplex model of affect. *Journal of Personality and Social Psychology, 39,* 1161–1178.

Russell, J. A. (1983). Pancultural aspects of the human conceptual organization of emotions. *Journal of Personality and Social Psychology, 45,* 1281–1288.

Sadka, D. (2004). *The Dewey color system.* New York: Three Rivers Press.

Samovar, L. A., & Porter, R. E. (2004). *Communication between cultures.* Belmont, CA: Wadsworth.

Sargent, S. L., Weaver, J. B., III, & Kiewitz, C. (1997). Correlates between communication apprehension and listening style preferences. *Communication Research Reports, 14,* 74–78.

Satir, V. (1972). *Peoplemaking.* Palo Alto, CA: Science & Behavior Books.

Schramm, W. L. (1954). *The process and effects of mass communication.* Urbana, IL: University of Illinois.

Seay, E. (2004, February 11). Lost city, lost languages. *Princeton Alumni Weekly,* pp. 17, 43.

Segrin, C. (1998). Interpersonal communication problems associated with depression and loneliness. In P. A. Andersen & L. K. Guerrero (Eds.), *Handbook of communication and emotion: Research, theory, applications, and contexts* (pp. 215–242). San Diego, CA: Academic Press.

Sentence completion (2004). *TakeSAT.com.* http://www.takesat.com/sentence.php.

Shaffer, D. R., & Ogden, J. K. (1986). On sex differences in self-disclosure during the acquaintance process: The role of anticipated future interaction. *Journal of Personality and Social Psychology, 51,* 92–101.

Shannon, C. E., & Weaver, W. (1949). *The mathematical theory of communication.* Urbana, IL: University of Illinois.

Shannon, C. E., & Weaver, W. (1999). *The mathematical theory of communication* (50th edition). Urbana, IL: University of Illinois.

Shaver, P. R., Schwartz, J., Kirson, D., & O'Connor, C. (1987). Emotion knowledge: Further explorations of a prototype approach. *Journal of Personality and Social Psychology, 17,* 69–79.

Shedletsky, L. J., & Aitken, J. E. (2004). *Human communication on the Internet.* Boston: Allyn and Bacon.

Shields, S. A. (2000). Thinking about gender, thinking about theory: Gender and emotional experience. In A. H. Fischer (Ed.), *Gender and emotion: Social psychological perspectives* (pp. 3–23). Cambridge, England: Cambridge University Press.

Shields, S. A., & Crowley, J. C. (1996). Appropriating questionnaires and rating scales for a feminist psychology: A multimethod approach to gender and emotion. In S. Wilkinson (Ed.), *Feminist social psychologies* (pp. 218–232). Philadelphia, PA: Open University Press.

Shimanoff, S. (1980). *Communication rules: Theory and research.* Beverly Hills, CA: Sage.

Shimanoff, S. B. (1985). Expressing emotions in words: Verbal patterns of interactions. *Journal of Communication, 35,* 16–31.

Shimanoff, S. B. (1987). Types of emotional disclosures and request compliance between spouses. *Communication Monographs, 54,* 85–100.

Shin, L. (2003, May 9). Ah, sweet mystery of e-mail. *New York Times,* p. D2.

Shlain, L. (1998). *The alphabet versus the goddess: The conflict between word and image.* New York: Penguin/Arkana.

Shuter, R., & Turner, L. H. (1997). African American and European American women in the workplace: Perceptions of conflict communication. *Management Communication Quarterly, 11,* 74–96.

Sillars, A. L., Roberts, L., Leonard, K. E., & Dun, T. (2000). Cognition during marital conflict: The relationship of thought and talk. *Journal of Social and Personal Relationships, 17,* 479–502.

Silva-Corvalán, C. (1994). *Language contact and change: Spanish in Los Angeles.* New York: Oxford University Press.

Silverstein, J., & Lasky, M. (2004). *Online dating for dummies.* Indianapolis, IN: Wiley.

Simpson, L. (2003). Get around resistance and win over the other side. *Harvard Management Communication Letter,* pp. 3–5.

Smitherman, G. (2000). *Black talk: Words and phrases from the hood to the amen corner.* Boston: Houghton Mifflin.

Snyder, M. (1979). Self-monitoring processes. In L. Berkowitz (Ed.), *Advances in experimental social psychology* (pp. 86–131). New York: Academic Press.

Southern Poverty Law Center. (2004). *About the center: Advocates for justice and equality.* http://www.splcenter.org/center/about.jsp 2004.

Spencer, T. (1994). Transforming relationships through ordinary talk. In S. Duck (Ed.), *Understanding relationship processes 4: Dynamics of relationships* (pp. 58–85). Thousand Oaks, CA: Sage.

Spiegel, D., & Kimerling, R. (2001). Group psychotherapy for women with breast cancer: Relationships among social support, emotional expression, and survival. In C. D. Ryff & B. H. Singer (Eds.), *Emotion, social relationships, and health* (pp. 97–123). Oxford, England: Oxford University Press.

Spitzberg, B. H., & Cupach, W. R. (1984). *Interpersonal communication competence.* Beverly Hills, CA: Sage.

Spitzberg, B. H., & Cupach, W. R. (1989). *Handbook of interpersonal communication research.* New York: Springer-Verlag.

Spitzberg, B. H., & Cupach, W. R. (Eds.) (1998). *The dark side of close relationships.* Mahwah, NJ: Lawrence Erlbaum.

Spooner, T., & Rainie, L. (2000). *African Americans and the Internet.* Washington, DC: The Pew Internet and American Life Project.

Stearns, P. N. (1994). *American cool: Constructing a twentieth-century emotional style.* New York: New York University Press.

Sternberg, R. J., & Whitney, C. (2002). How to think clearly about relationships. In J. A. DeVito (Ed.), *The interpersonal communication reader* (pp. 152–161). Boston: Allyn and Bacon.

St. John, W. (2001, April 21). Young, single and dating at hyperspeed. *New York Times,* pp. D1, D2.

St. John, W. (2002, August 24). Sorrow so sweet: A guilty pleasure in another's woe. *New York Times,* pp. B7, B9.

Stone, D., Patton, B., & Heen, S. (2002). How to understand another person's understanding. In J. A. DeVito (Ed.), *The interpersonal communication reader* (pp. 34–39). Boston: Allyn and Bacon.

Stringer, J. L., & Hopper, R. (1998). Generic *he* in conversation? *Quarterly Journal of Speech, 84,* 209–221.

Sullivan, A. (2002, May). *The blogging revolution.* http://wired.com/wired.archive.

Sullivan, P. A., & Turner, L. H. (1996). *From the margins to the center: Contemporary women and political communication.* Westport, CT: Praeger.

Support4Hope. (2004). *Support4Hope chats.* http://support4hope.com/testimonial.htm.

Sweeney, N. (2004, March 7). Cyber cool: Teens' witty screen names don't always seem so at college time. *Milwaukee Journal Sentinel,* pp. B1–B2.

Swidey, N. (2003, February 2). A nation of voyeurs. *Boston Globe Magazine,* pp. 10–13, 21–25.

Tamosaitis, N. (1995). *Net.sex.* Emeryville, CA: Ziff-Davis Press.

Tannen, D. (1990). *You just don't understand: Women and men in conversation.* New York: William Morrow.

Tannen, D. (1995). *Gender and discourse.* Oxford, England: Oxford University Press.

Tardy, C. H. (2000). Self-disclosure and health: Revisiting Sidney Jourard's hypothesis. In S. Petronio (Ed.), *Balancing the secrets of private disclosures* (pp. 111–122). Mahwah, NJ: Lawrence Erlbaum.

Tavris, C. (2001). Anger defused. In K. Scott & M. Warren (Eds.), *Perspectives on marriage: A reader* (pp. 243–253). New York: Oxford University Press.

Taylor, D. A., & Altman, I. (1987). Communication in interpersonal relationships: Social penetration processes. In M. E. Roloff & G. R. Miller (Eds.), *Interpersonal processes: New directions in communication research* (pp. 257–277). Newbury Park: Sage.

Tedeschi, B. (2002, February 4). E-commerce report. *New York Times,* p. C6.

Thibaut, J., & Kelley, H. (1959). *The social psychology of groups.* New York: Wiley.

Thomas, R. W., & Seibold, D. W. (1996). Communicating with alcoholics: A strategic influence approach to personal intervention. In E. B. Ray (Ed.), *Communication and disenfranchisement: Social health issues and implications* (pp. 405–432). Mahwah, NJ: Lawrence Erlbaum.

Thompson, T. L. (1996). Allowing dignity: Communication with the dying. In E. B. Ray (Ed.), *Communication and disenfranchisement: Social health issues and implications* (pp. 387–404). Mahwah, NJ: Lawrence Erlbaum.

Thurlow, C., Lengel, L., & Tomic, A. (2004). *Computer-mediated communication.* Thousand Oaks, CA: Sage.

Tidwell, L. C., & Walther, J. B. (2002). Computer-mediated communication effects on disclosure, impressions, and interpersonal evaluations: Getting to know one another a bit at a time. *Human Communication Research, 28,* 317–348.

Ting-Toomey, S. (1999). *Communicating across cultures.* New York: Guilford.

Ting-Toomey, S., & Chung, L. C. (2005). *Understanding intercultural communication.* Los Angeles, CA: Roxbury.

Ting-Toomey, S., & Oetzel, J. G. (2001). *Managing intercultural conflict effectively.* Thousand Oaks, CA: Sage.

Toppo, G. (2002, December 10). Teens grasp sign language. *USA Today,* p. 9D.

Treichler, P. A., & Kramarae, C. (1983). Women's talk in the ivory tower. *Communication Quarterly, 31,* 118–132.

Trenholm, S. (1986). *Human communication theory.* Englewood Cliffs, NJ: Prentice Hall.

Trenholm, S., & Jensen, A. (2003). *Interpersonal communication* (5th ed.). New York: Oxford University Press.

Turk, D. R., & Monahan, J. L. (1999). "Here I go again": an examination of repetitive behaviors during interpersonal conflicts. *Southern Communication Journal, 64,* 232–44.

Turkle, S. (1995). *Life on the screen: Identity in the age of the Internet.* New York: Simon and Schuster.

Turner, L. H., & Shuter, R. (2004). African American and European American women's visions of workplace conflict: A metaphorical analysis. *Howard Journal of Communications, 15,* 169–183.

Turner, L. H., & West, R. (2006). *Perspectives on family communication* (3rd ed.). New York: McGraw-Hill.

Turner, L. H., Dindia, K., & Pearson, J. C. (1995). An investigation of female/male verbal behaviors in same-sex and mixed-sex conversations. *Communication Reports, 8,* 86–96.

Turner, M. M., Mazur, M. A., Wendel, N., & Winslow, R. (2003). Relational ruin or social glue? The joint effect of relationship type and gossip valence on liking, trust, and expertise. *Communication Monographs, 70,* 129–141.

Tutu, D. (1999). *No future without forgiveness.* New York: Image/Doubleday.

Ullrich, P. M., & Lutgendorf, S. K. (2002). Journaling about stressful events: Effects of cognitive processing and emotional expression. *Annals of Behavioral Medicine, 24,* 244–250.

U.S. Census Bureau (2000). *Fact sheet.* http://www.factfinder.census/gov.

U.S. Census Bureau. (2004, July 1). [Map of United States diversity.] *USA Today,* "Nation" section, p. 7A.

VanGelder, L. (1990). The strange case of the electronic lover. In G. Gumpert & S. L. Fish (Eds.), *Talking to strangers: Mediated therapeutic communication* (pp. 128–142). Norwood, NJ: Ablex.

Vangelisti, A. L., Caughlin, J. P., & Timmerman, L. (2001). Criteria for revealing family secrets. *Communication Monographs, 68,* 1–27.

Vangelisti, A. L., Knapp, M., & Daly, J. (1990). Conversational narcissism. *Communication Monographs, 57,* 251–274.

Vangelisti, A. L., & Young, S. L. (2000). When words hurt: The effects of perceived intentionality on interpersonal relationships. *Journal of Social and Personal Relationships, 17,* 395–425.

Vedantam, S. (2002, September 9). Psychiatrists back new class of illness. *Milwaukee Journal Sentinel,* pp. 1G-2G.

Victor, D. A. (1992). *International business communication.* New York: HarperCollins.

Vittengl, J. R., & Holt, C. S. (2000). Getting acquainted: The relationship of self-disclosure and social attraction to positive affect. *Journal of Social and Personal Relationships, 17,* 53–66.

von Bertalanffy, L. (1968). *General system theory.* New York: George Braziller.

Wade, N. (2003, July 15). Early voices: The leap to language. *New York Times,* pp. D1, D4.

Waldner, L. K., & Magruder, B. (1999). Coming out to parents: Perceptions of family relations, perceived resources, and identity expression as predictors of identity disclosure for gay and lesbian adolescents. *Journal of Homosexuality, 37,* 83–100.

Walker, L. (1984). *The battered woman syndrome.* New York: Springer.

Walther, J. B. (1994). Anticipated ongoing interaction versus channel effects on relational communication in computer-mediated interaction. *Human Communication Research, 20,* 473–501.

Warren, E. (2004, January 6). Grandma? No, please call her Moogie. *Chicago Tribune,* pp. 5–1, 5–6.

Watson, K. W., & Barker, L. L. (1995). *Winning by listening around.* Tega Cay, SC: SPECTRA Incorporated.

Watson, K. W., Lazarus, C. J., & Thomas, T. (1999). First year medical students' listener preferences: A longitudinal study. *International Journal of Listening, 13,* 1–11.

Watzlawick, P., Beavin, J., & Jackson, D. D. (1967). *Pragmatics of human communication.* New York: Norton.

Weinraub, B. (2004, March, 22). Love fest for soap opera fans, in two languages. *New York Times,* pp. B1, B8.

Wendland, M. (2002, October 21). *Poll: Rich people, suburbanites likelier to use Net.* http://www.freepress.com/newslibrary.

White, G. L. (1980). Physical attractiveness and courtship progress. *Journal of Personality and Social Psychology, 39,* 660–668.

Whorf, B. (1956). *Language, thought, and reality.* Cambridge, MA: MIT Press.

Wilmot, W. W. (1995). *Relational communication.* New York: McGraw-Hill.

Winters, A. M., & Duck, S. (2001). You ****!: Swearing as an aversive and a relational activity. In R. M. Kowalski (Ed.), *Behaving badly: Aversive behaviors in interpersonal relationships* (pp. 59–77). Washington, DC: American Psychological Association.

Witmer, D. F. & Katzman, M. L. (1997). *On-line smiles: Does gender make a difference in the use of graphic accents?* http://www.ascusc.org/jcmc/vol2/issue4/witmer1.html.

Wolf, A. (2000). Emotional expression online: Gender differences in emoticon use. *Cyberpsychology and Behavior, 3,* 827–833.

Wolvin, A. D., & Coakley, C. G. (1996). *Listening.* Madison, WI: Brown and Benchmark.

Wolvin, A. D., & Coakley, C. G. (2000). Listening education in the 21st century. *International Journal of Listening, 14,* 143–152.

Wood, D. B. (2004, April 6). A not-so-mobile society. *Christian Science Monitor.* http://www.csmonitor.com/2004/0406/p01s03–ussc.html.

Wood, J. T. (1998). *But I thought you meant . . . misunderstandings in human communication.* Mountain View, CA: Mayfield.

Wood, J. T. (2000). *Gendered lives: Communication, gender and culture* (4th ed.). Belmont, CA: Wadsworth.

Wood, J. T. (2002). A critical essay on John Gray's Mars and Venus portrayals of men and women. *Southern Communication Journal, 67,* 201–210.

Wood, J. T. (2005). *Gendered lives: Communication, gender and culture (6th ed).* Belmont, CA: Wadsworth.

Yager, J. (2002). *When friendship hurts.* New York: Simon and Schuster.

Young, S. L., & Bippus, A. M. (2001). Does it make a difference if they hurt you in a funny way? Humorously and non-humorously phrased hurtful messages in personal relationships. *Communication Quarterly, 49,* 35–52.

Index

Photo Credits

Chapter 1. 15: © Gabe Palmer/Corbis; 19: © Karen Preuss/The Image Works; 21: © Jose Carillo/PhotoEdit

Chapter 2. 39: © Tim Mosenfelder/Corbis; 40: © Thompson/Anthro-Photo; 50: © Michael Newman/PhotoEdit; 57: © Brad Wrobleski/Masterfile

Chapter 3. 68: © J. Emilio Flores/Getty Images; 72: © Chuck Savage/Corbis; 72: © Setboun/Corbis; 75: © David H. Wells/The Image Works; 81: © Ethel Wolvovitz/The Image Works

Chapter 4. 92: © Annie Griffiths/Corbis; 99: © Reuters/Corbis; 106: © Michelle D. Bridwell/PhotoEdit; 112: © AP/Wide World Photos; 120: © Tony Freeman/PhotoEdit

Chapter 5. 128: © Bill Aron/PhotoEdit; 131: left, Jason Harris, right, Jason Harris 141: © Richard Lord Enterprises, Inc./The Image Works; 142: © Smiley N. Pool/Dallas Morning News/Corbis; 144: © Danny Lehman/Corbis

Chapter 6. 153: © Peter Turnley/Corbis; 156: © Mitch Wojnarowicz/The Image Works; 162: © Mike Blake/Reuters/Corbis; 168: © George Pickow/Hulton Archive/Getty Images; 173: Working Title/Havoc/The Kobal Collection/Todd Demmie

Chapter 7. 187: © Ryan McVay/The Image Bank/Getty Images; 189: © Tannen Maury/The Image Works; 195: © Bob Mahoney/The Image Works; 199: © Alan Schein Photography/Corbis; 202: © Richard Bickel/Corbis

Chapter 8. 214: © Royalty-Free/Corbis; 222: © Jason Harris; 230: © Image 100/Royalty-Free/Corbis; 232: AP/Wide World Photos; 235: © David Lees/Taxi/Getty Images

Chapter 9. 249: © Michael Newman/PhotoEdit; 251: © Image 100/Royalty-Free/Corbis; 257: © Mark Richards/PhotoEdit; 261: © Bonnie Kamin/PhotoEdit; 269: © Jason Harris

Chapter 10. 280: © Ariel Skelley/Corbis; 285: © Bill Aron/PhotoEdit; 296: © Image 100/Royalty-Free/Corbis; 304: © Arnaldo Magnani/Getty Images Entertainment; 305: © Lon C. Diehl/PhotoEdit

Chapter 11. 321: © Jon Feingersh/The Image Bank/Getty Images; 327: © Reuters/Corbis; 334: © Thomson Higher Education; 339: Copyright © 2003-2005 Ask Jeeves, Inc. All rights reserved; 345: © Ahmad Al-Rubaye/AFP/Getty Images